the
Unofficial
Guide® to
Walt Disney
World®
2000

Also available from Macmillan Travel:

Beyond Disney: The Unofficial Guide to Universal, Sea World, and the Best of Central Florida, by Amber Morris and Bob Sehlinger

Inside Disney: The Incredible Story of Walt Disney World and the Man Behind the Mouse, by Eve Zibart

Mini-Mickey: The Pocket-Sized Unofficial Guide to Walt Disney World, by Bob Sehlinger

The Unofficial Guide to Bed & Breakfasts in New England, by Lea Lane

The Unofficial Guide to Branson, Missouri, by Bob Sehlinger and Eve Zibart

The Unofficial Guide to California with Kids, by Collen Dunn Bates and Susan LaTempa

The Unofficial Guide to Chicago, by Joe Surkiewicz and Bob Sehlinger

The Unofficial Guide to Cruises, by Kay Showker with Bob Sehlinger

The Unofficial Guide to Disneyland, by Bob Sehlinger

The Unofficial Guide to Florida with Kids, by Pam Brandon

The Unofficial Guide to the Great Smoky and Blue Ridge Region, by Bob Sehlinger and Joe Surkiewicz

The Unofficial Guide to Las Vegas, by Bob Sehlinger

The Unofficial Guide to Miami and the Keys, by Bob Sehlinger and Joe Surkiewicz

The Unofficial Guide to New Orleans, by Eve Zibart with Bob Sehlinger

The Unofficial Guide to New York City, by Eve Zibart and Bob Sehlinger with Jim Leff

The Unofficial Guide to San Francisco, by Joe Surkiewicz and Bob Sehlinger with Richard Sterling

The Unofficial Guide to Skiing in the West, by Lito Tejada-Flores, Peter Shelton, Seth Masia, Ed Chauner, and Bob Sehlinger

The Unofficial Guide to Walt Disney World for Grown-Ups, by Eve Zibart

The Unofficial Guide to Walt Disney World with Kids, by Bob Sehlinger

The Unofficial Guide to Washington, D.C., by Bob Sehlinger and Joe Surkiewicz

the Unofficial Guide® to Walt Disney World® 2000

Bob Sehlinger

Macmillan • USA

For George, the comeback kid

Every effort has been made to ensure the accuracy of information throughout this book. Bear in mind, however, that prices, schedules, etc., are constantly changing. Readers should always verify information before making final plans.

Macmillan Travel
Macmillan General Reference USA, Inc.
1633 Broadway
New York, New York 10019-6785

Produced by Menasha Ridge Press

ISBN 0-02-863039-4

ISSN 1059-3578

Manufactured in the United States of America

10 9 8 7 6 5 4 3 2 1

Contents

14 The Water Theme Parks   658

15 Beyond the Parks   674

16 Nightlife in and out of Walt Disney World   688

List of Maps

Acknowledgments

Special thanks to our field research team who rendered a Herculean effort in what must have seemed like a fantasy version of Sartre's *No Exit* to the tune of "It's a Small World." We hope you all recover to tour another day.

Betsy Amster	Amber Morris
Lynne Bachleda	Madeline O'Bryan
Molly Burns	Taylor O'Bryan (the Human Probe)
Holly Cross	Tiffany Prewitt-McClain
Leslie Cummins	Rebecca Self
Shelley DeLuca	Grace Walton
Chris Mohney	Barbara Williams

Peals of laughter and much appreciation to nationally renowned cartoonists Tami Knight and William Nealy for their brilliant and insightful work.

Psychologists Dr. Karen Turnbow, Dr. Gayle Janzen, and Dr. Joan Burns provided much insight concerning the experiences of young children at Walt Disney World. "Hotel Women" Holly Cross and Tiffany Prewitt-McClain inspected many dozens of hotels. *Unofficial Guide to Cruises* author Kay Showker assisted with our coverage of the Disney Cruise Line.

Many thanks also to Holly Cross, Molly Burns, Chris Mohney, Georgia Goff, and Amy Hayworth for production and editorial work on this book. Caroline Carr, Steve Jones, and Amy Sloan earned our appreciation for their fine work and for keeping tight deadlines in providing the typography. Cartography was provided by Tim Krasnansky and Brian Taylor, and the index was prepared by Ann Cassar.

the Unofficial Guide® to Walt Disney World® 2000

Introduction

How Come "Unofficial"?

DECLARATION OF INDEPENDENCE

The author and researchers of this guide specifically and categorically declare that they are and always have been totally independent of the Walt Disney Company, Inc.; of Disneyland, Inc.; of Walt Disney World, Inc.; and of any and all other members of the Disney corporate family not listed.

The material in this guide originated with the author and researchers and has not been reviewed, edited, or in any way approved by the Walt Disney Company, Inc.; Disneyland, Inc.; or Walt Disney World, Inc.

This guidebook represents the first comprehensive *critical* appraisal of Walt Disney World. Its purpose is to provide the reader with the information necessary to tour Walt Disney World with the greatest efficiency and economy, and with the least hassle and standing in line. The authors believe in the wondrous variety, joy, and excitement of the Disney attractions. At the same time, we recognize that Walt Disney World is a business, with the same profit motivations as businesses the world over.

In this guide we represent and serve you, the consumer. If a restaurant serves bad food, or a gift item is overpriced, or a certain ride isn't worth the wait, we can say so, and in the process we hope to make your visit more fun, efficient, and economical.

THE IMPORTANCE OF BEING GOOFY

A Disney board of directors meeting. The hour is late; suit coats are draped over chairs and shirt sleeves are rolled up. Everyone is leaning forward and tense. A balding man with heavy jowls breaks the silence. "If this is true, we've got a major scandal on our hands. The tabloids will have a field day."

The men stir restlessly in their seats, nodding. The accountant, usually quiet, poses the question on everyone's mind, "Does Mickey know yet?"

"We don't think so, but he'll find out sooner or later. She'll slip up, you know . . . leave some little clues that'll make him wonder. He's not stupid."

"Well, they're *not* married . . . I guess she can go out with other guys if she wants."

"No, by heavens, George, she can't!," the chairman thunders. "She's a corporate symbol. She's got to think of the company."

"I'm afraid it's too late for that, boss. At this point, I think our only play is to protect Mickey and to try to keep the press from sniffing it out."

"This whole thing tears me up," the chairman hisses, red-faced now and pounding the table. "Why now? And why *him*? I can understand that Minnie might need a change, but Yosemite Sam? He's not even a Disney character!"

And so it goes. . . .

What really makes writing about Walt Disney World fun is that the Disney people take everything so seriously. Day to day, they debate momentous decisions with far-ranging consequences: Will Goofy look swishy in a silver cape? Have we gone too far with the Little Mermaid's cleavage? At a time when the nation is concerned about the drug problem, can we afford to have a dwarf named "Dopey"?

Unofficially, we think having a sense of humor is important. This guidebook has one, and it's probably necessary that you do, too—not to use this book but, more significantly, to have fun at Walt Disney World. Walt Disney World is to tourist destinations as New York is to cities: big, complex, and intimidating. A certain amount of levity is required simply to survive. Think of the *Unofficial Guide* as a private trainer to help get your sense of humor in shape. It will help you understand the importance of being Goofy.

HONEY, I BLEW UP THE BOOK!

The first edition of *The Unofficial Guide to Walt Disney World* was considerably less than 200 pages, a mere shadow of its present size. In the years since that edition, Disney World has grown tremendously, adding Disney-MGM Studios, Downtown Disney, the BoardWalk, Typhoon Lagoon, Blizzard Beach, several new attractions in Epcot and the Magic Kingdom, about 21,500 new hotel rooms and, in summer 1998, the Animal Kingdom, Walt Disney World's fourth theme park. The *Unofficial Guide* has grown to match this expansion (and the author has put on a little weight himself).

We have no idea where it all will end. In 30 years we may be selling an alphabetized, 26-volume edition, handsomely packaged in its own imitation-oak bookcase. In the meantime, we offer a qualified apology for the bulk of this edition. We know it may be too heavy to be carried comfort-

ably without the assistance of a handcart, llama, or Sherpa, but we defend the inclusion of all the information presented. Not every diner uses catsup, A-1 Sauce, and Tabasco, but it's nice to have all three on the table.

For Those Who Need Additional Assistance

As thorough as we try to make *The Unofficial Guide to Walt Disney World*, there is not sufficient space to share all the tips and information that may be important and useful to certain readers. Thus, we have developed five additional Disney World guides, each designed to work in conjunction with this book. All five guides provide specialized information tailored to specific Walt Disney World visitors. Although some tips from the big book (like arriving at the theme parks early) are echoed or elaborated in the other guides, most of the information is unique and was developed especially for our readers who require additional help. In addition to *The Unofficial Guide to Walt Disney World*, the following titles are available:

Mini-Mickey: The Pocket-Sized Unofficial Guide to Walt Disney World, by Bob Sehlinger; 320 pages; $10.95.

Inside Disney: The Incredible Story of Walt Disney World and the Man Behind the Mouse, by Eve Zibart; 225 pages; $11.95.

The Unofficial Guide to Walt Disney World with Kids, by Bob Sehlinger; 250 pages; $11.95.

The Unofficial Guide to Walt Disney World for Grown-Ups, by Eve Zibart; 192 pages; $11.95.

Beyond Disney: The Unofficial Guide to Universal, Sea World, and the Best of Central Florida, by Bob Sehlinger and Amber Morris; 250 pages; $12.95.

Mini-Mickey is a nifty, portable, *"Cliff Notes"* version of *The Unofficial Guide to Walt Disney World.* Updated annually, it distills information from this comprehensive guide to help short-stay or last-minute visitors decide quickly how to plan their limited hours at Disney World. *Inside Disney* is a behind-the-scenes unauthorized history of Walt Disney World, and it is loaded with all the amazing facts and great stories that we can't squeeze into this guide. *The Unofficial Guide to Walt Disney World for Grown-Ups* helps adults traveling without children make the most of their Disney vacation, while *The Unofficial Guide to Walt Disney World with Kids* presents a wealth of planning and touring tips for a succesful Disney family vacation. Finally, *Beyond Disney* is a complete consumer guide to the non-Disney attractions, restaurants, outdoor recreation, and nightlife in Orlando and central Florida. All of the guides are available from Macmillan Travel and at most bookstores.

The Death of Spontaneity

One of our all-time favorite letters came from a man in Chapel Hill, North Carolina:

> *Your book reads like the operations plan for an amphibious landing. . . . Go here, do this, proceed to Step 15. . . . You must think that everyone [who visits Walt Disney World] is a hyperactive, Type-A, theme-park-commando. Whatever happened to the satisfaction of self-discovery or the joy of spontaneity? Next you will be telling us when to empty our bladders.*

As it happens, *Unofficial Guide* researchers are a pretty existential crew. We are big on self-discovery if the activity is walking in the woods or watching birds. Some of us are able to improvise jazz, and others can whip up a mean pot of chili without a recipe. When it comes to Walt Disney World, however, we all agree that you either need a good plan or a frontal lobotomy. The operational definition of self-discovery and spontaneity at Walt Disney World is the "pleasure" of heat prostration and the "joy" of standing in line.

It's easy to spot the free spirits at Walt Disney World, particularly at opening time. While everybody else is stampeding to Space Mountain, they are standing in a cloud of dust, puzzling over the park map. Later, they are the people running around like chickens in a thunderstorm, trying to find an attraction with less than a 40-minute wait. Face it, Walt Disney World is not a very existential place. In many ways it's the quintessential system, the ultimate in mass-produced entertainment, the most planned and programmed environment anywhere. Spontaneity and self-discovery work about as well at Walt Disney World as they do on your tax return.

We aren't saying that you can't have a great time at Walt Disney World. What we *are* saying is that you need a plan. You don't have to be compulsive or inflexible; just think about what you want to do before you go. Don't delude yourself by rationalizing that the information in this guide is only for the pathological and the superorganized. Ask not for whom the tome tells, Bubba—it tells for thee.

Dance to the Music

When you dance, you hear the music and move in harmony with the rhythm. Like each day at Walt Disney World, a dance has a beginning and an end. However, your objective is not to get to the end, but rather to enjoy the dance while the music plays. You are totally in the moment and care nothing about where on the floor you stop when the dance is done.

As you begin to contemplate your Walt Disney World vacation, you may not have much patience for a philosophical discussion about dancing, but it's relevant. If you are like most travel guide readers, you are apt to plan and organize, to anticipate and control, and you like things to go smoothly. And, truth to tell, this leads us to suspect that you are a person who looks ahead and is outcome oriented. You may even feel a bit of pressure concerning your vacation. Vacations, after all, are special events, and expensive ones to boot. So you work hard to make the most of your vacation.

As discussed in the previous section, we believe that work, planning, and organization are important, and at Walt Disney World even essential. But if they become your focus, you won't be able to hear the music and enjoy the dance. Though much dancing these days resembles highly individualized *grand mal* seizures, there was a time when each dance involved specific steps that you committed to memory. At first you were tentative and awkward, but eventually the steps became second nature and you didn't have to think about them anymore.

Metaphorically, this is what we want for you and your companions as you embark on your Walt Disney World vacation. We want you to learn the steps ahead of time, so that when you're on vacation and the music plays, you will be able to hear it. And you will dance with effortless grace and ease.

How This Guide Was Researched and Written

While much has been written about Walt Disney World, very little has been comparative or evaluative. Many guides parrot Disney World's own promotional material. In preparing this guide, however, nothing was taken for granted. Each theme park was visited at different times throughout the year by trained observers. They conducted detailed evaluations and rated each theme park, with all its component rides, shows, exhibits, services, and concessions. Patrons were interviewed to determine what tourists of all age groups enjoyed most and least during their Disney World visit.

While our observers were independent and impartial, we don't claim special expertise or scientific backgrounds relative to the types of exhibits, performances, or attractions. Like you, we visit Walt Disney World as tourists, noting our satisfaction or dissatisfaction. We don't believe it's necessary to be an agronomist to know whether we enjoyed the agricultural exhibits in the Epcot Land pavilion. Disney offerings are marketed to the touring public, and it is as the public that we have experienced them.

In compiling this guide, we recognize that a tourist's age, gender, background, and interests will strongly influence his or her taste in Disney World offerings and will account for a preference of one ride or feature over another. Given this, we make no attempt to compare apples with oranges. How, indeed, could a meaningful comparison be made between the priceless historic artifacts in Epcot's Mexican pavilion and the wild roller coaster ride of the Magic Kingdom's Space Mountain? Instead, our objective is to provide the reader with sufficient description, critical evaluation, and pertinent data to make knowledgeable decisions according to individual tastes.

The essence of this guide, therefore, consists of individual critiques and descriptions of each feature of the Magic Kingdom, Epcot, Disney-MGM Studios, and the Animal Kingdom, along with detailed touring plans to help you avoid bottlenecks and crowds. Also included are in-depth descriptions for Typhoon Lagoon, Blizzard Beach, Pleasure Island, and the nearby Universal Florida theme parks.

A WORD TO OUR READERS ABOUT ANNUAL REVISIONS

Some of you who purchase each new edition of the *Unofficial Guide* have chastised us for retaining examples, comments, and descriptions from previous years' editions. This letter from a Grand Rapids, Michigan, reader is typical:

Your guidebook still has the same little example stories. When I got my [new] book I expected a true update and new stuff, not the same-old, same-old!

First, the *Unofficial Guide* is a reference work. Though we are flattered that some readers read the guide from cover to cover and that some of you find it entertaining, our objective is fairly straightforward: to provide information that will enable you to have the best possible Walt Disney World vacation.

Each year during our revision research, we check every theme park, water park, attraction, hotel, restaurant, nightspot, shop, and entertainment offering. While there are many changes (most attributable to Disney World's exponential growth), much remains the same from year to year. When we profile and critique an attraction, we try to provide the reader with the most insightful, relevant, and useful information, written in the clearest possible language. It is our opinion that if an attraction does not change, then it makes little sense to risk clarity and content for the sake of freshening up the prose. Walt Disney World guests who try the Mad Tea Party, the Haunted Mansion, or the *Country Bear Jamboree* today, for example, experience exactly the same presentation as guests who visited Disney World in 1997, 1990, or 1986. Moreover, according to our extensive patron surveys (several thousand each year), today's guests respond to these attractions in the same way as prior-year patrons.

The bottom line: we believe our readers are better served if we devote our time to that which is changing and new as opposed to that which remains the same. The success or failure of the *Unofficial Guide* is determined not by the style of the writing, but by the accuracy of the information and, ultimately, whether you have a positive experience at Walt Disney World. Every change to the guide we make (or don't make) is evaluated in this context.

LETTERS AND COMMENTS FROM READERS

Many of those who use *The Unofficial Guide to Walt Disney World* write us to make comments or share their own strategies for visiting Walt Disney World. We appreciate all such input, both positive and critical, and encourage our readers to continue writing. Readers' comments and observations are frequently incorporated into revised editions of the *Unofficial Guide* and have contributed immeasurably to its improvement. If you write us or return our reader survey form, you can rest assured that we won't release your name and address to any mailing list companies, direct mail advertisers, or other third party.

Reader Questionnaire and Restaurant Survey

At the back of this guide is a short questionnaire you can use to express opinions about your Walt Disney World visit. The questionnaire is designed to allow every member of your party, regardless of age, to tell us what they think. There is also a separate restaurant survey that you can use to describe your Disney World dining experiences. Clip the questionnaire and the restaurant survey on the dotted lines and mail them to:

> Reader Survey
> The *Unofficial Guide* Series
> P.O. Box 43673
> Birmingham, AL 35243

How to Write the Author

> Bob Sehlinger
> *The Unofficial Guide to Walt Disney World*
> P.O. Box 43673
> Birmingham, AL 35243

When you write, put your address on both your letter and envelope. Sometimes the two get separated. It is also a good idea to include your phone number. And remember, as travel writers, we're often out of the office for long periods of time, so forgive us if our response is slow.

Questions from Readers

Questions frequently asked the author by readers are answered in an appendix at the end of the *Unofficial Guide*.

Walt Disney World: An Overview

If you're choosing among tourist destinations of Florida, the question is not whether to visit Walt Disney World but how to see the best of the Disney offerings with some economy of time, effort, and finances.

Make no mistake, there is nothing on earth like Walt Disney World. Incredible in its scope, genius, beauty, and imagination, it's a joy and wonder for people of all ages. A fantasy, a dream, and a vision all rolled into one, it transcends simple entertainment, making us children and adventurers, freeing us to live the dreams of our past, present, and future.

We are critics, but it is the responsibility of critics to credit what is done well as surely as it is to point out what is done poorly. Disney attractions are special, a quantum leap beyond most man-made entertainment offerings.

WHAT WALT DISNEY WORLD ENCOMPASSES

Walt Disney World encompasses 43 square miles, an area twice as large as Manhattan island or roughly the size of Boston. Situated strategically in this vast expanse are the Magic Kingdom, Epcot, Disney-MGM Studios, and the Animal Kingdom theme parks; three swimming theme parks; two nighttime entertainment areas; a sports complex; several golf courses, hotels, and campgrounds; almost 100 restaurants; four large interconnected lakes; a shopping complex; three convention venues; a nature preserve; and a complete transportation system consisting of four-lane highways, elevated monorails, and a system of canals.

THE MAJOR THEME PARKS

The Magic Kingdom

When people think of Walt Disney World, most think of the Magic Kingdom. It's comprised of the collection of adventures, rides, and shows symbolizing the Disney cartoon characters, and Cinderella Castle. Although the Magic Kingdom is only one element of Disney World, it remains its heart. The Magic Kingdom is divided into seven subareas or "lands," six of which are arranged around a central hub. First encountered is Main Street, U.S.A., which connects the Magic Kingdom entrance with the central hub. Clockwise around the hub are Adventureland, Frontierland, Liberty Square, Fantasyland, and Tomorrowland. Mickey's Toontown Fair (originally named Mickey's Birthdayland), the first new land added to the Magic Kingdom since the park opened, is situated along the Walt Disney Railroad on three acres between Fantasyland and Tomorrowland. Access is through Fantasyland or Tomorrowland, or via the railroad. Main Street and the other six lands will be described in detail later. Three hotels (the Contemporary, Polynesian, and Grand Floridian Beach resorts) are close to the Magic Kingdom and are directly connected to it by monorail and boat. Two additional hotels, Shades of Green (formerly the Disney Inn) and Disney's Wilderness Lodge Resort, are nearby but aren't served by the monorail.

Epcot

Epcot opened in October 1982. Divided into two major areas, Future World and World Showcase, the park is twice as big as the Magic Kingdom and comparable in scope. Future World consists of futuristic pavilions relating to different themes concerning human creativity and technological advancement. World Showcase, arranged around a 41-acre lagoon, presents the architectural, social, and cultural heritages of almost a dozen nations, with each country represented by replicas of famous landmarks and local

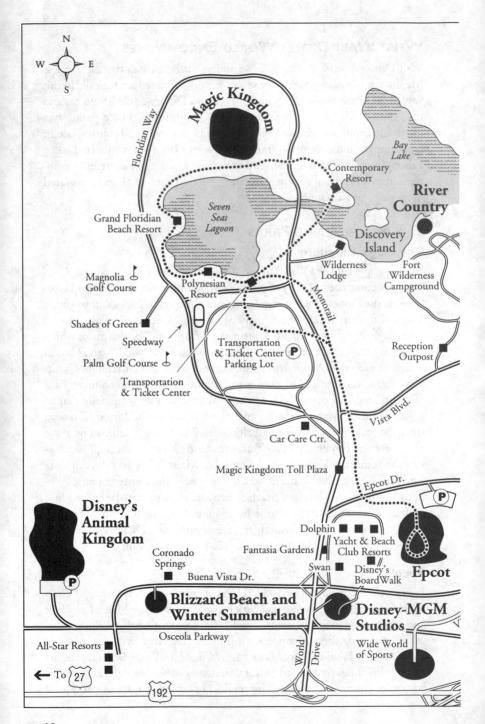

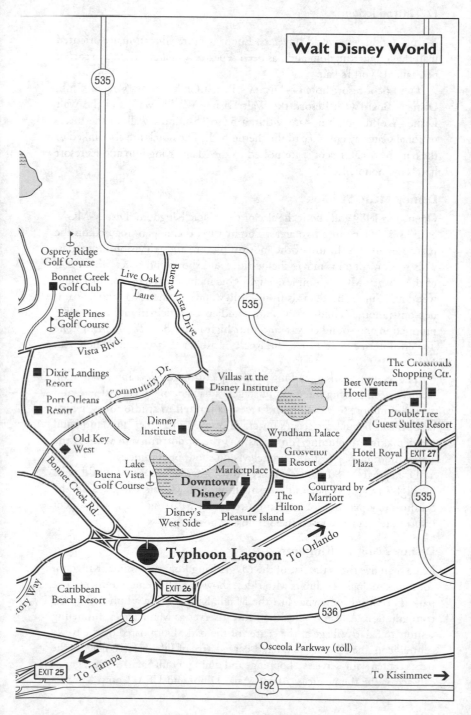

Walt Disney World

settings familiar to world travelers. Epcot is more educationally oriented than the Magic Kingdom and has been repeatedly characterized as a sort of permanent World's Fair.

The Epcot resort hotels—Disney's Beach Club, Disney's Yacht Club, Disney's BoardWalk Resort, the Walt Disney World Swan, and the Walt Disney World Dolphin—are within a 5- to 15-minute walk of the International Gateway entrance to the theme park. The hotels are also linked to the park by canal. Epcot is connected to the Magic Kingdom and its resort hotels by monorail.

Disney-MGM Studios

Opened in 1989 and about the size of the Magic Kingdom, Disney-MGM Studios is divided into two areas. The first is a theme park focused on the past, present, and future of the motion picture and television industries. This section contains movie-theme rides and shows and covers about half of the Disney-MGM complex. Highlights include a re-creation of Hollywood and Sunset Boulevards from Hollywood's Golden Age, movie stunt demonstrations, a children's play area, audience-participation shows on TV production and sound effects, and four high-tech rides: *The Twilight Zone* Tower of Terror, Star Tours, the Rock 'n' Roller Coaster, and The Great Movie Ride.

The second area is a working motion picture and television production facility encompassing three sound stages, a backlot of streets and sets, and creative support services. Public access is limited to studio tours, which take visitors behind the scenes for crash courses on Disney animation and moviemaking, including (on occasion) the opportunity to witness the actual shooting of a feature film, television show, or commercial.

Disney-MGM Studios is connected to other Walt Disney World areas by highway and canal, but not by monorail. Guests can park in the Studios' pay parking lot or commute by bus. Patrons staying in Epcot resort hotels can also reach the Studios by boat.

Disney's Animal Kingdom

More than five times the size of the Magic Kingdom, the Animal Kingdom combines zoological exhibits with rides, shows, and live entertainment. The park is arranged somewhat like the Magic Kingdom, in a hub-and-spoke configuration. A lush tropical rain forest serves as Main Street, funneling visitors to Safari Village at the center of the park. Dominated by the park's central icon, the 14-story-tall, hand-carved Tree of Life, Safari Village is the park's center, with services, shopping, and dining. From Safari Village, guests can access the theme areas: Africa, Asia, DinoLand USA, Camp Minnie-

Mickey, and Mythical Beasts (tentative name). Scheduled to open in phases, Safari Village, Africa, Camp Minnie-Mickey, and DinoLand U.S.A. came on-line in 1998, followed by Asia in 1999, with Mythical Beasts to be added over the next couple of years. Africa, the largest theme area at 100 acres, features free roaming herds in a re-creation of the Serengeti Plain. Guests tour in open-air safari vehicles.

Disney's Animal Kingdom has its own pay parking lot and is connected to other Disney World destinations by the Disney bus system. Although, for the moment, there are no hotels at the Animal Kingdom, the All-Star and Coronado Springs resorts are nearby.

THE WATER THEME PARKS

There are three major swimming theme parks in Walt Disney World: Typhoon Lagoon, River Country, and Blizzard Beach. Typhoon Lagoon is distinguished by a wave pool capable of making six-foot waves. River Country, a pioneer among water theme parks, is much smaller but very well done. Since Typhoon Lagoon opened in 1989, River Country has catered primarily to Disney World campground and resort hotel guests. Blizzard Beach is the newest Disney water park and features more slides than the other two parks combined. All three parks are beautifully landscaped, with great attention to atmosphere and aesthetics. Typhoon Lagoon and Blizzard Beach have their own adjacent parking lots. River Country can be reached on foot by campground guests or on Disney boat or bus by others.

DISCOVERY ISLAND

The park was closed to the public in 1999 and is now used only for private parties and Disney corporate events.

OTHE WALT DISNEY WORLD VENUES

Downtown Disney (Downtown Disney Marketplace, Pleasure Island, and Disney's West Side)

Downtown Disney is a large shopping, dining, and entertainment complex encompassing the Downtown Disney Marketplace on the east, the gated (admission-required) Pleasure Island nighttime entertainment venue in the middle, and Disney's West Side on the west. Downtown Disney Marketplace is home to the largest Disney character merchandise store in the world, upscale resort-wear and specialty shops, and several restaurants, including the tacky, but popular, Rainforest Cafe. Pleasure Island offers, in addition to the gated attractions described below, several upscale restaurants

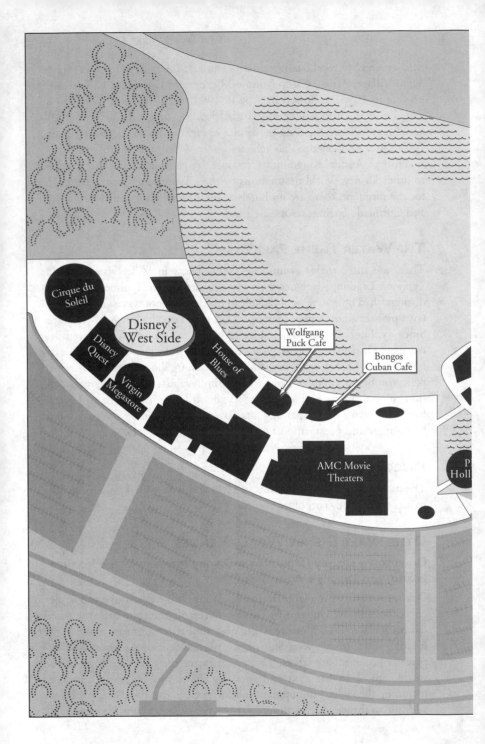

Cirque du Soleil

Disney's West Side

Disney Quest

Virgin Megastore

House of Blues

Wolfgang Puck Cafe

Bongos Cuban Cafe

AMC Movie Theaters

P Holl

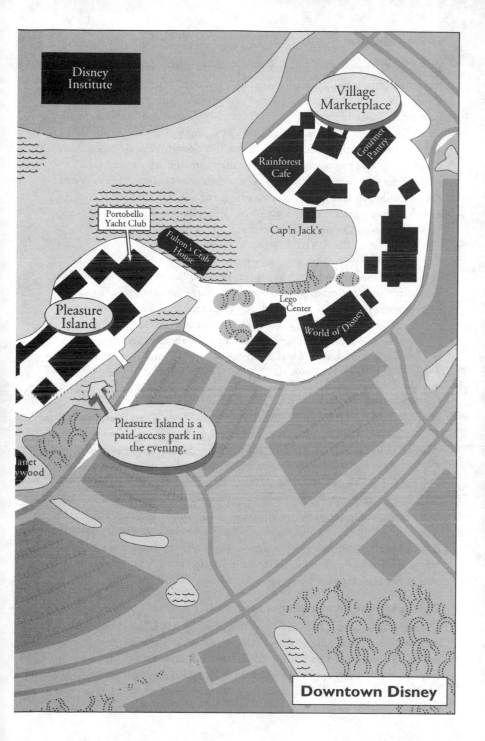

Disney
Institute

Village
Marketplace

Gourmet
Pantry

Rainforest
Cafe

Portobello
Yacht Club

Fulton's Crab
House

Cap'n Jack's

Lego
Center

Pleasure
Island

World of Disney

Pleasure Island is a
paid-access park in
the evening.

Planet
Hollywood

Downtown Disney

and shops. Disney's West Side, which opened in 1997, combines nightlife, shopping, dining, and entertainment. Dan Aykroyd's House of Blues serves Cajun/Creole dishes in its restaurant and electric blues in its music hall. Bongos, a Cuban nightclub and cafe created by Gloria and Emilio Estefan, offers Caribbean flavors and rhythms. Wolfgang Puck Cafe, sandwiched among pricey boutiques (including a three-level Virgin Records megastore), is the West Side's prestige eatery. In the entertainment department are a 24-screen cinema; a permanent showplace for the extraordinary, 70-person cast *Cirque du Soleil;* and DisneyQuest, a high-tech, interactive virtual reality and electronic games venue. Downtown Disney can be accessed via Disney buses from most Disney World locations.

Pleasure Island

Part of the Downtown Disney complex, Pleasure Island is a six-acre night-time entertainment center where one cover charge gets a visitor into any of eight nightclubs. The clubs have different themes and feature a variety of shows and activities. Music ranges from pop rock, to country and western, to jazz. For the more sedentary (or exhausted), there is an adjacent 24-screen movie complex, or for the hungry, several restaurants, including a much-hyped Planet Hollywood.

Disney's BoardWalk

Located near Epcot, Disney's BoardWalk is an idealized replication of an east coast turn-of-the-century waterfront resort. Open all day, the Board-Walk features upscale restaurants, shops and galleries, a brew pub, and an ESPN sports bar. In the evening, a nightclub with dueling pianos (New Orleans Pat O'Brien's–style) and a swanky dance club join the lineup. While there is no admission fee for the BoardWalk per se, individual clubs may levy a cover charge at night. In addition to the public facilities are a 378-room deluxe hotel and a 532-unit time-share development. The BoardWalk is within walking distance of the Epcot resorts and the International Gateway of the Epcot theme park. Boat transportation is available from Disney-MGM Studios, with buses serving other Disney World locations.

Disney's Wide World of Sports

Covering 200 acres, Disney's Wide World of Sports is a state-of-the-art competition and training facility consisting of a 7,500-seat ballpark, a field house, and venues for baseball, softball, tennis, track and field, beach volleyball, and 27 other sports. In addition to being the spring training home of the Atlanta Braves, the complex hosts a mind-boggling calendar of professional and amateur competitions. Although Walt Disney World guests are welcome at the complex as paid spectators, none of the facilities are available for use by guests unless they are participants in a scheduled competition.

The Disney Institute and Disney University

The Disney Institute offers life-enriching learning experiences to Walt Disney World resort guests, while Disney University conducts professional-development courses for private groups and corporations. Both programs share the campus located near the Downtown Disney Marketplace and are connected to other Disney World locations by Disney bus service.

DISNEY CRUISE LINE

In 1998, Disney launched (literally) its own cruise line with the 2,400-passenger *Disney Magic*. Its twin ship, the *Disney Wonder,* was launched in 1999. Cruises depart from Port Canaveral (about a 90-minute drive from Walt Disney World) and stop at Nassau in the Bahamas and at Castaway Cay, Disney's own private island. Three- or four-day cruises are available and can be packaged with a stay at Walt Disney World. Although the cruises are family oriented, extensive children's programs and elaborate childcare facilities allow parents plenty of opportunity for time away from the kids.

DISNEYSPEAK POCKET TRANSLATOR

Although it may come as a surprise to many, Walt Disney World has its own somewhat peculiar language. Here are some of terms you are likely to bump into:

DisneySpeak	English Definition
Adventure	Ride
Attraction	Ride or theater show
Attraction Host	Ride operator
Audience	Crowd
Backstage	Behind the scenes, out of view of customers
Bull Pen	Queuing area
Cast Member	Employee
Character	Disney cartoon character impersonated by an employee
Costume	Work attire or uniform

DisneySpeak	English Definition (continued)
Dark Ride	Indoor ride
Day-guest	Any customer not staying at a Disney resort
Face Character	A character that does not wear a head-covering costume (Snow White, Cinderella, Jasmine, etc.)
General Public	Same as day-guest
Greeter	Employee positioned at the entrance of an attraction
Guest	Customer
Hidden Mickeys	Frontal silhouette of Mickey's head worked subtly into the design of buildings, railings, vehicles, golf greens, attractions, and just about anything else
In Rehearsal	Operating though not officially open
Lead	Foreman or manager, the person in charge of an attraction
On Stage	In full view of customers
Preshow	Entertainment at an attraction prior to the feature presentation
Resort Guest	A customer staying at a Disney resort
Role	An employee's job
Security Host	Security guard
Soft Opening	Opening a park or attraction before its stated opening time
Transitional Experience	An element of the queuing area and/or preshow that provides a story line or information essential to understanding the attraction

What's a Queue?

Although it's not commonly used in the United States, "queue" is the universal English language word for a line (such as you wait in to cash a check at the bank or to board a ride in a theme park). In fact, there is an entire mathematical area of specialization within the field of operations research called Queuing Theory that studies and models how lines work. Because the *Unofficial Guide* draws heavily on this discipline, we use some of its terminology. In addition to the noun, the verb "to queue" means to get in line, and a "queuing area" is a waiting area that accommodates a line.

Readers Speak Out

Walt Disney World patrons, especially *Unofficial Guide* readers, express strong opinions about their Disney vacation experience. The following is a sampling from our readers and survey respondents.

In the complaint department, readers were extremely outspoken about the Animal Kingdom. Gripes about poor park layout and design, inadequate signage, and lack of shade were legion, eclipsing complaints about all other aspects of Walt Disney World. Following is a representative sample:

From a mother of two from Lumberton, North Carolina:

> *The Animal Kingdom was packed when we visited, and Disney's design didn't help. The central hub from Safari Village works but the "lands" do not connect like the Magic Kingdom so Safari Village remains in chaos all day!*

And from a Lakeland, Tennessee, mom:

> *The Animal Kingdom is poorly laid out. You have to walk past a gazillion shops/restaurants to get to attractions.*

A dad from West Lafayette, Indiana, had this to say:

> *I wonder who established the sign size for this park? If you lost your park map and needed to find a rest room, you were really in trouble! Even with the map, we had to look behind foliage or people to find the signs that indicated the presence of the rest rooms. I suppose the idea was that with the sweltering heat and subsequent dehydration, no one needed to use them.*

A woman from Kansasville, Wisconsin, agrees, writing:

> *It's very hard to find your way around the park; heavy foliage, narrow pathways, and especially the lack of signs all serve to make it very hard to get your bearings, even with the park map.*

This father of two was hot, and not just under the collar:

> *What Disney emulates best in this park is a realistic re-enactment of heat stroke that one might experience in Africa. The foliage is high enough to block any breeze, but not complete enough to provide any significant shade from the Florida sun. On the line into* It's Tough to Be a Bug, *this heating effect was increased by the dark walls lining both sides of the walk which absorbed the heat of the sun overhead. This resulted in quite a number of sauteed tourists.*

Along similar lines:

> *The lack of air-conditioning in the lines and most of the shops is fine for a realistic [simulation] of Africa, but it had a devastating effect upon the Cast Members. Most Cast Members, dripping in sweat wearing sweat-soaked clothing, looked as though they had been reduced to self-survival instincts instead of the service of Disney guests.*

The same reader had this advice:

> *Go before the temperature reaches 90 degrees. After our first withering experience, we went in the evening two hours before closing and were able to get around much better because all the other Disney guests that had visited the Animal Kingdom prior to us were now in local hospitals receiving intravenous fluids to rehydrate them.*

For the record, the Animal Kingdom generally received rave reviews for its theming and attractions, complaints about park layout, signs, and heat notwithstanding.

Second on the gripe list was crowd control at *Fantasmic!*, the nighttime water, laser, and fireworks spectacle at the Disney-MGM Studios. A Shelbyville, Kentucky, woman writes:

> *Fantasmic! is a great show, but the time and effort you invest to see it is mind-boggling. Crowds are huge and apparently managed for Disney's convenience with little regard for the guests.*

A mother of two from Tiffin, Ohio, concurs:

> *I was unnerved by the crowd in entering and exiting* [Fantasmic!] *There was only one way in/out. Avoid if you have any tendency toward claustrophobia.*

And from a Milledgeville, Georgia, reader:

> *When I read about the big* Fantasmic! *stadium I thought no sweat. But Disney figured a way to turn seeing the show into an ordeal.*

Gripes about the quality and cost of food at Disney World decreased last year but still ranked third on our complaint hit parade. Happily, we acknowledge that significant improvement has been made in food quality and variety. Still, most readers have a higher opinion of Disney food than we do. A Charleston, West Virginia, woman let us have it with both barrels, writing:

Get a life! It's crazy and unrealistic to be so snobbish about restaurants at a theme park. Considering the number of people Disney feeds each day, I think they do a darn good job. Also, you act so surprised that the food is expensive. Have you ever eaten at an airport? HELLO IN THERE? . . . Surprise, you're a captive! It's a theme park!

And from a Lafayette, Louisiana, reader:

Your opinion on food varies greatly from mine and my party's. I'm not sure what the solution to this is, but by the end of the trip we were all laughing about it. Perhaps you can put more emphasis on the readers' opinion as a whole.

In response, we display our readers' opinion about each restaurant right alongside that of our dining critic and encourage you to take both into consideration when selecting a restaurant. Likewise we encourage you to send us the dining survey form in the back of this guide so that we can include your opinions in our tabulation. In any event, we don't believe that being "captive," as the reader from Charleston puts it, gives Disney the license to serve mediocre food at inflated prices. Many readers, including this mother of three from Dallas, Texas, agree:

Stick to your guns on the food. It was uniformly bad and exorbitantly expensive. For example, a character breakfast at the Polynesian (all family-style, ho-hum fare) was $100 for a family of five. Eating was a downer three times a day in what would have otherwise been a fabulous vacation.

A reader from Albany, New York, weighed in with this:

We love good food and found your critiques fairly accurate.

Finally on the subject of food, an Erie, Pennsylvania, woman struck a practical note, writing:

Most of the food [at Walt Disney World] is OK. Certainly in our experience, more of it is good than bad. If you pay attention to what other visitors say and what's in the guidebooks, you can avoid the yucky places. It's true that you pay more than you should, but it's more convenient [to eat in Walt Disney World] than to run around trying to find cheaper restaurants somewhere else. When it comes to Disney World, who needs more running around?

Fourth on the hit parade of complaints are the crowd levels at the Magic Kingdom. This letter from a Sandy, Utah, man is typical:

Anybody who thinks there is an "Off-Season" any more at the Magic Kingdom seriously needs a reality check. We've tried all different times of the year and just about every day of the week. From our experience crowds come in two basic sizes, huge and huger.

Rude guests, including sometimes unruly teenage tour groups from Brazil, always rank high among reader complaints, and this year is no exception. For a couple of months each year (usually October and July) we are inundated at the *Unofficial Guide* with "Brazil mail:"

A man from Chicago writes:

The only time we can go on vacation is during the summer and all of the parks are full of teenage Brazilian tour groups. All of the groups are loud, obnoxious, and under-supervised. I understand that this brings money into the country and I also understand that this does not mean all teens from Brazil are necessarily bad people. But on several occasions it was so awful [that] I felt like standing up and singing "God Bless America!"

A young mom found jamming the aisle more effective than singing:

The Brazilians at all the Worlds were very rude and would jump in line at anytime. Me and my daughter used the technique of holding hands & then holding on to the bars on each side. We would NOT let them in front of us!

And an Australian father of two had this to say:

The most annoying part of our visit was being subjected to the boorish behaviour of the many groups of Brazilian teenagers. They seemed to think that they were the attraction, and in some areas their chanting and 'singing' made it impossible to hear information and introduction to attractions.

We also received a lot of mail from Brazilian readers responding to the torrent of criticism. These two letters are representative:

From a twenty-something woman:

I was choked when I read the comments about the Brazilian people. Not all teenagers or Brazilians (in general) are ill-behaved, noisy or cut in lines. We are not out-of-control or misbehaved animals like an American woman said.

And from a Brazilian couple:

> *I am 24 and my husband 28 and we go to WDW twice a year.
> I want to say that Americans should be more concerned about their
> comments because we spend a lot of money in your country. Some of
> our kids may be a little noisy, but they do not bring guns to the
> classroom and shoot teachers and friends. We do not have a killer
> instinct. We do have a party instinct.*

A mother from Providence, Rhode Island, points out that indecision can
be as maddening as outright discourtesy, especially when you're hungry:

> *It's amazing that I didn't go crazy waiting in those lines for 15
> minutes only to have the person in front of me waste more time
> trying to decide if she should get the Mickey bar or the strawberry
> bar. Tell these people to read the signs in the very long lines and
> make up their minds ahead of time.*

This just in: Walt Disney World has surrendered
unconditionally to Brazil.

A woman from Wilmington, Delaware, reports being the victim of numerous hit-and-runs:

> *Nothing prepared me for the countless rude and inconsiderate people that we would come in contact with on a daily basis. I can not even begin to guess how many times we were run over by strollers and wheelchairs! The straw that broke the camel's back was when we saw a man running to get in line for a ride . . . he had a cast on his foot that went to his knee! Please!*

A lady from Houston complains about character hogs:

> *One of the worst parts to deal with are the people with movie cameras who take about three minutes filming their child with Mickey, asking everyone else to move. A 35 mm camera takes about two seconds.*

And finally, a complaint that our readers make with regrettable frequency concerns able-bodied guests pretending to be disabled in order to receive preferential treatment. An outraged Stevens Point, Wisconsin, mother writes:

> *As the parent of a handicapped child, I was appalled to see the blatant misuse of wheelchairs. People who loaded them with purchases and hopped in as they came to a ride. One party came in with the father in the wheelchair. At the next ride, one of the kids was in the chair. At the next, the mother was in the chair! This practice is not only unfair to nonhandicapped people [waiting in line], but also is an affront to those who really need [a wheelchair].*

A woman from Crystal City, Virginia, agreed, stating:

> *Wheelchair abuse is out of control! We saw a woman hop out of her wheelchair and vigorously climb Swiss Family Treehouse!*

On the same topic, a woman from Rockford, Illinois, made a well-considered appeal for tolerance and understanding:

> *I read with interest readers' comments about apparently able-bodied people "abusing" wheelchairs at WDW. I am sure there are a few scoundrels, but the vast majority of people are honest. People with lupus or a number of other connective tissue diseases, people with heel spurs, hip or knee problems, heart or kidney disease, and people on chemotherapy can all look perfectly healthy—even though they would never be able to walk through WDW. Readers may ask why so many of these folks would go to Disney World. Where else*

can you vacation with your healthy, active spouse and young
children and still keep up with them? These are families who can't
go surfing or skiing or to water parks together.

And if readers find themselves resenting the fact that the
children of these people don't have to wait, they might consider that
these children do wait—51 weeks a year. They wait at doctors'
offices, they wait until the next round of chemo's over before they can
go to the zoo (if dad feels better), they wait till mom can walk better
before they can go to the mall, they wait until next year and maybe
dad will be able to coach soccer—they wait, and wait, and wait.

Have a heart, healthy people. Just because someone can walk a little bit or get on a ride without help or doesn't look as handicapped as your child, it doesn't mean they don't need special facilities. Limp a mile in my shoes (with the orthotics).

Complaints about the high volume levels of Disney sound systems hold down sixth place. The following letter from a Canton, Ohio, father is representative:

One thing that I don't think you emphasize enough is the sound level at the attractions. The Disney sound technicians must be recruited from rock concert tours. In almost every live show, movie, and animated attraction we went to my children had to literally hold their ears because of the volume (my wife and I also found it uncomfortable). I will definitely take some earplugs for the whole family the next time we go.

A Mobile, Alabama, mother of two agrees, reporting:

Our five-year-old kept his hands over his ears through much of the parks. The sounds in almost all of the rides are ear-splitting. It was truly awful. I think they really need to tone down the sound in all of the attractions.

Seventh place goes to an unprecedented rash of complaints about maintenance, cleanliness, and upkeep of Disney hotels, an area where gripes have previously been few. The following letter from an Avon, Ohio, woman is typical:

We were very disappointed with the room at the Caribbean Beach [Resort]. This is one of the older resorts and the room looked like it. When making reservations, ask as many questions as you can concerning the rooms and their condition.

We should point out that most hotels over five years old, both in and out of Walt Disney World refurbish between 10 and 20% of their guest rooms each year. This incremental approach minimizes disruption of normal business but also makes your room assignment a crapshoot. You might luck into a newly renovated room or alternatively be assigned a threadbare room. Disney resorts will not gaurantee specific rooms but will annotate your request for a recently refurbished room on your reservation record and will try to accommodate you when you arrive. Non-Disney hotels will often guarantee an updated room when you book.

Eighth and ninth on the complaint list relate to two things Disney does not offer, namely an 800 number and a good map of the property that can be obtained in advance of your trip. Regarding the latter, maps are available when you check into your Disney resort, but as of this writing, Disney will not part with them in advance by mail. Guests not staying at a Disney resort, as ever second-class citizens, are generally left in the lurch, though they can sometimes procure Walt Disney World maps from Guest Relations at the major theme parks.

Tenth is a laundry list of problems relating to the Walt Disney World transportation system. (For an in-depth discussion, see the chapter "How to Travel around the World" in Part 7.)

Finally, there is an apparently growing trend that relates to Disney's exponential growth and the resultant difficulty that Disney guest relations and information staff are having keeping up. Many complaints, like this one from a Miami, Ohio, woman, center on Disney attractions outside the theme parks:

> *Our concierge didn't have the foggiest notion what was going on at the Disney sports complex [Disney's Wide World of Sports]. He told us the [Atlanta] Braves were practicing (they weren't) and that there was a big soccer tournament going on (there wasn't). We spent about $40 for the privilege of seeing a bunch of empty stadiums and ball fields.*

A Dalton, Georgia, woman reported similar problems:

> *I must have made five different calls to make sure that Typhoon Lagoon would be open during our visit. Each time I was assured it would be. I made my last call three days before we left home and received the same assurances. When we arrived at Disney World and checked into Port Orleans, I found out that Typhoon Lagoon was closed and had been for three weeks!*

Readers also offer compliments, especially on the courtesy, friendliness, and helpfulness of most Disney cast members (employees). A woman from Yucaipa, California, described the attentiveness of cast members to her injured husband:

> *My husband cracked his head open on a mushroom in the Honey, I Shrunk the Kids! playground and the Disney-MGM people were terrific. Seeing us wandering about with blood streaming down my husband's head, one of the cast members took us straight to First Aid. There they dressed the wound, offered to take us to the emergency room in an ambulance (not necessary), gave my husband a place to rest where they could observe him, and finally called a car from the Grand Floridian to return him to the hotel.*

A waiter at Le Cellier Steakhouse at Epcot turned into a hero for this Crystal Lake, Illinois, couple:

> *Our waiter took our kids on a kitchen tour "to give us some time alone," and gave them make-your-own ice cream sundaes at no charge.*

And a Massachusetts couple, battle-weary from the crowds, related this story:

> *After coming out of the live production of Beauty and the Beast we must have looked a little shopworn. A Disney cast member came up to us and asked if we were OK and if we were enjoying ourselves. Her concern and reaching out stunned us. Here we were obviously a bit older than the majority of the other park-goers, probably looking somewhat frazzled by then (3:30 p.m.), but she treated us as if we were the most important of guests.*

Disabled guests and their families give Walt Disney World high marks for accessibility and general consideration for the needs of disabled patrons. An Arlington, Virginia, woman writes:

> *Before the trip, I thought of Disney as a sort of corporate monster that successfully accessed my pocketbook through my innocent and trusting children with its diabolical marketing expertise. I also considered a Disney vacation pretty ersatz compared to, say, a week in Provence. However, I must say that Disney is dynamite in its treatment of handicapped vacationers and this perspective has turned me into a fan. My mom has mobility problems that got a lot worse between the time my Dad made reservations and the time we arrived, and she was worried about getting around. Disney supplied a free wheelchair, and every bus had kneeling steps for wheelchair users. The disabled brochures for each park were incredibly informative about access for each attraction, and the hosts sprang into action when they saw us coming.*

Along similar lines, a Montgomery, New York, family appreciated the attention they received at the theme park first-aid stations:

> *First-aid stations were first rate! We battled a 24-hour stomach virus at the Magic Kingdom. My wife was visited by Donald and Belle!*

We get quite a bit of mail about maids at Disney World resort hotels. This letter from a St. Louis family is typical:

Each day when we returned to our room, we would find that the maid had arranged our kids' stuffed animals in a different and highly creative manner. For instance, the animals might be all lined up by the window with the snacks we left in the room in the animals' arms. Our kids loved it and looked forward to seeing the arrangement every day. I was impressed that Disney could even get the maids into the entertainment act—cast members, indeed!

A maid's mistake led to a happy ending for a Port Neches, Texas, family:

We were thoroughly impressed with the service at the All-Star Music Resort. We had bought our daughter a Cinderella doll and the maid accidentally threw away its shoes and stand. We placed a call to the front desk and they put us through to a manager. Although it was 10 at night they were at our door within ten minutes with a brand new doll!

Although some readers have noticed some slippage in the maintenance of the theme parks, cleanliness continues to impress most visitors. An

Austin, Texas, woman discovered that rest rooms are subject to a quick tidying up at any time:

> *I was in a stall in the rest room one day when I dropped my map. Before I could retrieve it, the hand of a cleaning woman appeared, grabbed the map and had it in the trash before I knew what was happening. As you know, everything there works this way.*

Many readers have applauded Disney's initiatives to make the World Showcase section of Epcot more lively and fun. This reader from New York is representative, writing:

> *We also like how Epcot, in general, is more kid-friendly than it was 11 years ago, and the KIDS' ZONES at each country are great. However, by the second day our son was only interested in running to the KIDS' ZONE immediately, getting his passport stamped, and dashing on to the next country (that's because he's O.C. just like his dad).*

Disney landscaping and the beauty of the property rank high for plaudits, as do safety and personal security in Walt Disney World in general. Also receiving praise are the quality of rooms and swimming facilities at Disney hotels as well as the quality of special Disney tours and educational programs.

In addition to praising and criticizing Disney, our readers not unexpectedly also have strong opinions about the *Unofficial Guide* and a number of other subjects. These opinions and comments, as well as questions to the author, can be found in the appendix at the end of this book.

Part One

Planning Before You
Leave Home

*Visiting Walt Disney World is a bit like childbirth—you never really
believe what people tell you, but once you have been through it
yourself you know exactly what they were saying!*

—Hilary Wolfe, a mother and *Unofficial Guide* reader
from Swansea, United Kingdom

Gathering Information

In addition to this guide, we recommend that you obtain:

**1. The Walt Disney Travel Company Walt Disney World Vacations
Brochure** This full-color booklet describes Walt Disney World in its
entirety, lists rates for all Disney resort hotels and campgrounds, and describes Disney World package vacations. It's available from most travel
agents or by calling the Walt Disney Travel Company at (800) 327-2996
or (407) 828-3232. Be prepared to hold; you may have a long wait.

2. The Disney Cruise Line Brochure This elaborate color brochure will
provide all the particulars on vacation packages that combine a cruise on
the Disney Cruise Line with a stay at Walt Disney World. The brochure is
available from travel agents, by calling the Walt Disney Travel Company at
(800) 327-2996, or at www.disneycruise.com.

3. Walt Disney World Guidebooks for Guests with Disabilities If members of your party are sight- and/or hearing-impaired, or partially or wholly
nonambulatory, these small guides (one for each theme park) will be very
helpful. For copies, call (407) 824-4321. Allow 15 business days for delivery.

4. Orlando MagiCard   If you're considering lodging outside of Walt Disney World or if you think you might patronize attractions and restaurants outside of Disney World, it's worthwhile to obtain an Orlando MagiCard, a Vacation Planner, and the Orlando Official Accommodations Guide (all free) from the Orlando/Orange County Convention and Visitors Bureau. The MagiCard makes you eligible for discounts at hotels, restaurants, and attractions outside Disney World. To order the accommodations guide, call (800) 255-5786. For additional information and materials, call (407) 363-5872. Phones are manned during weekday business hours. Allow four weeks for delivery. On the Internet, see www.go2orlando.com.

5. Florida Traveler Discount Guide   Another good source of discounts on lodging, restaurants, and attractions throughout the state is the Florida Traveler Discount Guide. Published by Exit Information Guide, the guide is free, but you will be charged $3 ($5 shipped to Canada) for handling. Call (352) 371-3948, 8 a.m. to 8 p.m. EST Monday–Friday. Similar guides to other states are available at the same number. It's sometimes difficult to get through on the phone, however.

6. Kissimmee–St. Cloud Tour & Travel Sales Guide   This full-color directory of hotels and attractions is one of the most complete available and is of particular interest to those who intend to book lodging outside of Disney World. In addition to hotels and motels, the directory lists rental houses, time shares, and condominiums. To receive a copy, call the Kissimmee–St. Cloud Convention and Visitors Bureau at (800) 327-9159 or check out www.floridakiss.com.

7. *The Eclectic Gourmet Guide to Orlando*   Researched and written by the same team that produces this *Unofficial Guide,* the *Eclectic Gourmet* is the best resource available for finding great restaurants outside Walt Disney World. The guide, which rates, ranks, and profiles more than 150 restaurants, is available for $11.95 plus shipping by calling (800) 247-9437.

REQUEST INFORMATION EARLY

Request information as far in advance as possible and allow four weeks for delivery. Make a checklist of information you have requested and follow up if you haven't received your materials within six weeks. Sometimes, as a Garland, Texas, man notes, persistence is the key:

> *Per your advice, I called WDW to get the "Florida Vacation Guide." They never sent it. Called back two more times and finally got it the week before we left. In fact, got two.*

DISNEY MAGAZINE

If you're really a Disneyholic, this magazine will supply full-color hype of all developments in the Walt Disney Company, including theme parks, movies, Disney art, collectibles, and merchandise. The quarterly publication also offers glimpses of Disney behind-the-scenes history. Though there's not much useful information, the Disney Magazine is usually a fun read. The magazine is free to Magic Kingdom Gold Card members or can be purchased separately for $17 for a two-year subscription. Write Disney Magazine, P.O. Box 37263, Boone, Iowa 50037-2263.

MOUSETALES

Mousetales is a quarterly newsletter of Disney data. Totally independent of Walt Disney World, *Mousetales* costs $13 a year. To subscribe, write *Mousetales*, P.O. Box 383, Columbus, OH 43216.

GATHERING INFORMATION ON THE WORLD WIDE WEB

In planning your Walt Disney World vacation, you will find all of your favorite characters on the World Wide Web. But, in addition to Mickey, Minnie, Donald, Pluto, and Goofy, you will also find Delta, American, Hertz, Hyatt, and Hilton.

The advent of the World Wide Web and its immense popularity have brought about a lot of changes in the way we seek out everyday information. In just a few short years we have gone from getting most of our travel information from printed books or magazines and our favorite travel agent to booking entire vacations online. But as wonderful as this sounds, there are pitfalls. It's no small task figuring out how to find the information you need and understanding the tricks that make navigating the Web easy. Finally, even as an accomplished Web user, you may be surprised to find that your most valuable travel resource is still your tried-and-true travel agent.

You may have heard that travel providers like to sell directly to consumers on the Web in order to avoid paying commissions to travel agents, and that the commission savings are passed along to the buyer. While there is some truth in this, discounts (on the Web or anywhere else) have much more to do with time perishability of travel products than with commissions. An empty seat on a jet, for example, cannot be sold once the plane has left the gate. As the point of perishability approaches, the travel provider (hotel, airline, cruise line, etc.) begins cutting deals to fill its rooms, cabins, and seats. Web sites provide a cheap, quick, and efficient way for travel sellers to make these deals known to the public. You should understand, however, that the same deals are usually also communicated to travel agents.

We like the Web as a method of window shopping for travel, for scouting deals, and for obtaining information. We do not believe that the Web is necessarily the best or cheapest way of purchasing travel or that it can be substituted for the services of a good travel agent. The people who get the most out of the Web are those who work in cooperation with their travel agent, using the Web as a tool to help their agent help them. This is because almost any deal you locate on the Web can be purchased through a travel agent, and the more business you give your travel agent, the harder your agent will work for you. It's all about relationships.

It is a bit convoluted to write about the interactive travel experience on paper without the benefit of the very medium we are discussing. We urge you to use your computer or to find a friend with a computer and a Web connection in order to get the most out of these guidelines. We guarantee that you will discover some wonderful things along the way, many things, in all likelihood, that even we haven't seen. Each person's experience on the Web is unique, and you'll find many compelling distractions along the way. But bring your patience to the Web, because it can take some getting used to and it is not perfect. Once you know your way around even slightly you will save a lot of time and, occasionally, some money. When you find resources that you like, bookmark them in your browser. The more you use them, the more efficient you will be.

Walt Disney World on the Web

Searching the World Wide Web for Disney information is like navigating an immense maze for a very small piece of cheese. To be sure, there is a lot of information available on the Web, but you may have to wade through list after list until you find the Internet addresses you want and need. Once you have the addresses you want, finding information can also be extremely time consuming.

Disney's official Web page offers much of the same information as the Walt Disney Travel Company's vacation guidebook, but the guidebook has better pictures. Though the Web page is supposedly updated daily, we found a number of errors, including an offer for a terminated program. You can, however, now purchase theme park admissions and make resort and dining reservations on the Internet. The Web page also offers on-line shopping, weather forecasts, and information on renovations and special events. Disney's official company Web address is **www.disney.com.** Universal Studios Florida also offers a home page at **www.usf.com.**

If you search for additional information, you will find that there are many individuals who maintain very elaborate Disney-related Web pages. One woman in California maintains a Web page through which you may access everything from official Disney pages to the "Arielholics Anonymous

Home Page." Individuals also maintain Disney chat groups, which can be sources of both information and misinformation, depending on who is chatting. Disneyphile techies from all over the world help to maintain lists. There are lists of hidden Mickeys, lists of attractions ranked and rated by Joe Blow from Kokomo, lists of characters, and more lists of lists. You could explore the Web for weeks on end for myriad information maintained by these people. While a lot of this information is fun and interesting, and some is useful, the best way to get specific, detailed information without too long a wait is to call Disney's main information phone number: (407) 824-4321. Alternatively, if you are looking for an evening's entertainment, try the Net.

Information about Walt Disney World is also available at the public library, travel agencies, and AAA, or by calling or writing any of the following:

Important Walt Disney World Addresses

Walt Disney World Info/Guest Letters/Letters to Mickey Mouse
P.O. Box 10040
Lake Buena Vista, FL 32830-0040

Walt Disney World Central Reservations
P.O. Box 10100
Lake Buena Vista, FL 32830-0100

Convention and Banquet Information
Walt Disney World Resort South
P.O. Box 10000
Lake Buena Vista, FL 32830-1000

Walt Disney World Educational Programs
P.O. Box 10000
Lake Buena Vista, FL 32830-1000

Merchandise Mail Order (Guest Service Mail Order)
P.O. Box 10070
Lake Buena Vista, FL 32830-0070

Walt Disney World Ticket Mail Order
P.O. Box 10100
Lake Buena Vista, FL 32830-0140

Important Walt Disney World Addresses (continued)

Compliments, Complaints, and Suggestions
Walt Disney World Guest Communications
P. O. Box 10040
Lake Buena Vista, Florida 32830-1000

IMPORTANT WALT DISNEY WORLD TELEPHONE NUMBERS

When you call the main information number, you will be offered a menu of options for recorded information on theme park operating hours, recreation areas, shopping, entertainment complexes, tickets and admissions, resort reservations, and directions by highway and from the airport. If you are using a rotary telephone, your call will be forwarded to a Disney information representative. If you are using a touchtone phone and have a question not covered by recorded information, press eight (8) at any time to speak to a Disney representative.

Important Phone Numbers	
General Information	(407) 824-4321
Accommodations/Reservations	(407) 934-7639
	or (407) 824-8000
All-Star Cafe	(407) 827-8326
All-Star Movie Resort	(407) 939-7000
All-Star Music Resort	(407) 939-6000
All-Star Sports Resort	(407) 939-5000
AMC Theaters Pleasure Island	(407) 298-4488
Beach Club Resort	(407) 934-8000
Blizzard Beach	(407) 560-3400
BoardWalk Resort	(407) 939-5100
Business Programs (corporate training)	(407) 824-4740
Caribbean Beach Resort	(407) 934-3400
Celebration Realty Office	(407) 566-4663
Centracare	(407) 238-3000
The Crossroads	(407) 934-2273
Disney Main Gate	(407) 397-7032
Kissimmee	(407) 390-1888

Important Phone Numbers (continued)	
Lake Buena Vista	(407) 239-7777
Cirque du Soleil	(407) 939-7600
Contemporary Resort	(407) 824-1000
Convention Information	(407) 828-3200
Coronado Springs Resort	(407) 939-1000
Dining Priority Seating	(407) 939-3463
Disney Institute Programs	(800) 827-4800
Disney Institute Resort	(407) 827-1100
DisneyQuest	(407) 828-4600
Disney's Wide World of Sports	(407) 363-6600
Disney University Professional Seminars	(407) 824-7997
Dixie Landings Resort	(407) 934-6000
Downtown Disney Guest Relations	(407) 828-3058
Downtown Disney Marketplace	(407) 828-3800
Fantasia Gardens Miniature Golf	(407) 560-8760
Fort Wilderness Campground	(407) 824-2900
Golf Reservations and Information	(407) WDW-GOLF
Grand Floridian Beach Resort and Spa	(407) 824-3000
Guided Tour Information	(407) 939-TOUR
Guided VIP Solo Tours	(407) 560-6233
House of Blues Tickets and Information	(407) 934-2583
Lost and Found for articles lost:	
Yesterday or before	
(All parks)	(407) 824-4245
Today at Magic Kingdom	(407) 824-4521
Today at Epcot	(407) 560-6236
Today at Disney-MGM	(407) 560-3720
Today at Animal Kingdom	(407) 938-2265
Mediclinic, Highway 192, Kissimmee	(407) 239-1195
Merchandise Mail Order	
and Merchandise Return	(407) 363-6200
Ocala Chamber of Commerce	(352) 629-8051
Ocala Disney AAA Travel Center	(352) 854-0770
Old Key West Resort	(407) 827-7700
Outdoor Recreation Reservations	
and Information	(407) WDW-PLAY
Pleasure Island Information	(407) 934-6374
Polynesian Resort	(407) 824-2000
Port Orleans Resort	(407) 934-5000

Important Phone Numbers (continued)	
Resort Dining and Recreational Information	(407) 939-3463
River Country Information	(407) 824-2760
Shades of Green U.S. Armed Forces Hotel	(407) 824-3400
Telecommunication for the Deaf	
Reservations	(407) 939-7670
WDW Information	(407) 939-8255
Tennis Reservations/Lessons	(407) 939-7529
Typhoon Lagoon Information	(407) 560-4141
Walt Disney Travel Company	(407) 828-3232
Walt Disney World Dolphin	(407) 934-4000
Walt Disney World Speedway	(407) 939-0130
Walt Disney World Swan	(407) 934-3000
Weather Information	(407) 827-4545
Wilderness Lodge Resort	(407) 824-3200
Winter Summerland Miniature Golf	(407) 560-3000
Wrecker Service	(407) 824-0976
Yacht Club Resort	(407) 934-7000

When to Go to Walt Disney World

Why do they call it tourist season if we can't shoot them?
— Palatka, Florida outdoorsman

WALT DISNEY WORLD AND THE MILLENNIUM

Walt Disney World plans to celebrate the millennium for 15 months (October 1999 through January 1, 2001). Disney's millennium plans will include special versions of IllumiNations at Epcot; Fantasmic! at Disney-MGM Studios; and parades, fireworks, and live entertainment at all the parks. Each park will herald a new attraction for the millennium. At Epcot it will be the new ride at the Imagination Institute pavilion along with the World's Fair–type Millenniun Village exhibit hall in the World Showcase. The Studios will unveil the new Rock 'n' Roller Coaster, and the Magic Kingdom will showcase its Winnie the Pooh ride in Fantasyland. The new rage at the Animal Kingdom is a stage show combining elements of a rock concert and the X-Games under the unlikely umbrella of a Tarzan theme (I promise I'm not making this up). Gratefully, there's no plan to disguise Cinderella Castle as a giant birthday cake (as was done for Walt Disney

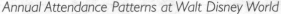

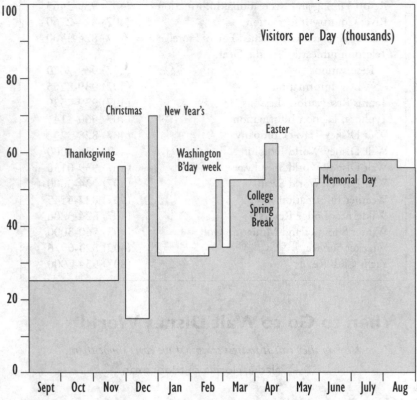

Annual Attendance Patterns at Walt Disney World

Visitors per Day (thousands)

Christmas   New Year's

Thanksgiving   Washington B'day week   Easter

College Spring Break   Memorial Day

(Attendance figures represent weekly averages)

World's 25th anniversary celebration) or costume the Tree of Life as a humongous candelabra.

Disney's millennium press and advertising blitz will be in full swing by the time you read this guide, and you can bet it will wrap its tentacles around any brain in America that's not comatose or on drugs. Linda Warren, senior vice president of marketing for Walt Disney attractions said, "The Walt Disney World Millennium Celebration represents our *most aggressive* campaign ever; no other event will be as heavily promoted as this one." Randy Garfield, president of Walt Disney Travel Company, told the travel industry "We'll be orchestrating a synchronized marketing campaign that's going to create very intense awareness." Just to make sure nobody missed the point, he added, "Travel agents who are not coordinating their plans with ours are, in effect, leaving money on the table." The point is that you can expect much larger than usual crowds throughout the 15-month celebration. We hammer you year after year about the wisdom of visiting Walt Disney World during the off season. If you haven't been listening, this might be the year to start.

SELECTING THE TIME OF YEAR FOR YOUR VISIT

Walt Disney World is busiest Christmas Day through New Year's Day. Thanksgiving weekend, the week of Washington's birthday, Martin Luther King holiday weekend, spring break for colleges, and the two weeks around Easter are also extremely busy. What does "busy" mean? As many as 92,000 people have toured the Magic Kingdom alone on a single day in these peak times! While this level of attendance isn't typical, it is possible, and only the ignorant or foolish challenge the Disney parks at their peak periods.

The least busy time is from after the Thanksgiving weekend until the week before Christmas. The next slowest times are November through the weekend preceding Thanksgiving, January 4 through the first week of February, and the week after Easter through early June. Late February, March, and early April are dicey. Crowds ebb and flow according to spring break schedules and the timing of Presidents' Day weekend. Though crowds have grown markedly in September and October as a result of special promotions aimed at locals and the international market, these months continue to be good for weekday touring at the Magic Kingdom, Disney-MGM Studios, and the Animal Kingdom, and for weekend visits to Epcot.

Many readers share their thoughts about the best time to visit Walt Disney World. These letters are representative:

From a Centerville, Ohio, family:

> *Catching on to the "off-season," we took the kids out of school and went to WDW in mid-May. So did a lot of other people. In fact, there were enough people there for me to think crowds must be increasing in the off-season as more people wise up about avoiding the masses. If I'm wrong, and this really was half the summer crowd, "high season" these days must be total and complete gridlock.*

Confirming the Ohio family's experience, a mom from West Plains, Missouri, writes:

> *We have visited WDW three times in the past eight years, each time in the second week of June. Each time the crowds were worse,*

and this time they were so big that we won't go at this time of year anymore.

Y2K Precautions

If you travel over the New Year's holiday at the change of the millennium or during the first couple of weeks of January 2000, take the following precautions:

1. If you drive, be aware that filling stations may be shut down by Y2K problems. Fill your tank on December 31. Also, check in advance with your car manufacturer to determine whether any problems are anticipated for your year and model. Finally, be aware that traffic signals, including railroad crossing warnings, could be impaired.

2. If you fly, get printed tickets as opposed to electronic tickets. Avoid flying on December 31 and January 1 and 2. Book direct flights. If you must make a connection, allocate twice the normal time between flights. Arrive at the airport an hour earlier than normal for check-in.

3. Credit card transactions may be affected, so carry more in cash and travelers checks.

4. If you intend to rent a car, obtain a record of your reservation on the rental car company's form or letterhead (as opposed to the letterhead of your travel agent). Make sure you have confirmation numbers and, if prepaid, proof of purchase.

5. Obtain a record of your hotel reservation on the hotel's letterhead (as opposed to the letterhead of your travel agent). Make sure you have confirmation numbers and, if prepaid, proof of purchase. It is highly probable that travelers affected by Y2K will remain at their hotel beyond their scheduled departure date. Try to arrange your travel so you don't check in to a hotel on December 31 or during the first week of January. If this cannot be avoided, book a guaranteed early check-in to provide a hedge against computer malfunctions and overbooking.

6. Carry medications, eyeglass and contact lens prescriptions, proof of auto and health insurance, and all travel documentation on your person. Do not put anything in checked baggage that you can't live without for a few days. Some medical devices have computer chips that could be impacted; check with the manufacturer before leaving home.

7. Reconfirm all reservations and flight itineraries 24 hours in advance. Check the airline's or airport's Web site or information number for last-minute cancellations and information about delays.

8. If you plan to take a Disney cruise over New Year's or the subsequent week, be aware that circumstances beyond Disney's control might impact your itinerary. Y2K bugs could possibly impair refueling and port operations, especially at Disney's two ports of call in the Bahamas.

The Downside of Off-Season Touring

Though we strongly recommend going to Walt Disney World in the fall or spring, there are trade-offs. The parks often open late and close early on fall and spring days. When they open as late as 10 a.m., everyone arrives about the same time, making it hard to beat the crowd. A late opening coupled with an early closing drastically reduces the hours available to tour. Even when crowds are small, it's difficult to see a big park like the Magic Kingdom or Epcot between 10 a.m. and 6 p.m. Early closing (before 8 p.m.) also usually means that evening parades or fireworks are eliminated. And, because these are slow times at Disney World, some rides and attractions may be closed for maintenance or renovation. Finally, central Florida temperatures fluctuate wildly during the late fall, winter, and early spring; daytime lows in the 40s and 50s are not uncommon.

Given the choice, however, we never would go to Walt Disney World in summer or during a holiday period. To us, small crowds, bargain prices, and stress-free touring are well worth risking a little cold weather or a couple of closed attractions. So much easier is touring in the fall and other "off" periods that our research team, at the risk of being blasphemous, would advise taking children out of school for a week at those times rather than battling the summer crowds.

Most readers who have tried Disney World at various times agree. A gentleman from Ottawa, Ontario, who toured in early December writes:

> *It was the most enjoyable trip [to Walt Disney World] I have ever had, and I can't imagine going [back] to Disney World when it is crowded. Even without the crowds, we were still very tired by afternoon. Fighting crowds certainly would have made a hellish trip. We will never go again at any other time.*

A father of two from Reynoldsburg, Ohio, offers this opinion:

> *Taking your kids out of school. Is it worth it? Yes! Excuse my editorial comment at this point, but it used to be true that missing a*

week of school would place your child so far behind it could take months for him/her to regain that lost week. Not so today. With advance preparations and informing the teachers months before our departure, this was no problem. With less than an hour of homework after dinner, our kids went back to school with assignments completed and no makeup work. But it was all those other hours with no lines and no heat that were the real payoff.

Dazed and Confused To present a complete picture, we must warn you that the difference between high and low seasons has blurred considerably in recent years. Even during off-season, crowd size can vary enormously. With Walt Disney World promotional hype in perpetual overdrive, huge crowds can materialize anytime, as these *Unofficial Guide* readers attest:

First, a mother from Bridgewater, New Jersey:

> *Although you mentioned the fact that school trips are [common] in Epcot during September and October, we were unprepared for the impact these groups had, especially since the kids are often unsupervised. From what I can see, the park can be enjoyed only on weekends during these months. Our visit was completely destroyed by unsupervised hordes of 10- to 12-year-olds.*

A New York woman related this:

> *We planned our trip for the off-season (October) because we thought it would be less crowded, but we were sadly mistaken. The crowds were still overwhelming (especially at Magic Kingdom!).*

A reader from Laureldale, Pennsylvania, agreed, writing:

> *Five years ago a trip to WDW in October was a pleasure. Now the crowds are getting larger. By midmorning at the M.K. lines for Splash Mountain were 50–60 minutes long.*

Ditto for a mother of two from Tallahassee, Florida:

> *Do not go in October; it was packed!*

A Huntsville, Alabama, mom agreed, writing:

> *I think you should really emphasize to people: DO NOT GO TO THE MAGIC KINGDOM ON A SATURDAY IN OCTOBER. Whatever you want to see there—it's not worth it.*

A Lima, Ohio, family encountered large crowds in early December:

> *Even though we went at the slowest time of year, it got very crowded by noon.*

And an Enid, Oklahoma, woman found mid-November too crowded:

> *Our stay was considered the "slow" time, but we found the crowds huge.*

A family from Staten Island, New York, found weekdays tranquil, but ran into a mess at the Magic Kingdom on Saturday:

> *Saturday (at MK) was rather horrifying. There were what seemed to be hordes of "day-trippers" (Scout troops, church groups, the Demolay Temple from Tampa, etc.). Even Tom Sawyer's Island was no idyllic oasis at 11:30 a.m. We left at about 1:30 p.m. for a swim and nap back at our motel and returned at 8 p.m. (the MK was open until midnight that night) to discover that the crowds had not thinned appreciably.*

Other readers visiting during slower periods, however, report light crowds and easy touring. A Sanford, Maine, family toured during the second week of December:

> *It was so slow that most of the backtracking was unnecessary. The most fun came from looking at the empty, roped-off queuing areas and saying, "I'm so glad we came at the time we did!" and not having to wait.*

And a West Seneca, New York, woman liked September:

> *The last week in September was dead. It was like we had the park to ourselves. We didn't wait longer than 15 minutes for a ride.*

Finally, a Massachusetts family had good luck in late August:

> *Overall, the week we were at WDW was not crowded. Often there were no lines except at the Magic Kingdom "Mountains." Except for the heat, late August is a good time to go—it's not crowded and the parks are still open late.*

In the final analysis, the only thing you can really count on is that, high or low season, Disney will be out beating the bushes to get people through the turnstiles. Plus, everything is relative. A busy day during off-season may catch you off guard if you had expected to have the parks to yourself. But believe us, the busiest off-season day is nothing compared to the masses you'll encounter during holidays and high season. Our advice, regardless of time of year, is to arrive at the park early and be prepared for big crowds. If attendance is light, you can kick back and forget the touring plans and our other crowd-beating strategies. On the other hand, if the place is jammed, you'll have a plan and be ready to go.

As a postscript, the likelihood of tangling with locals in September, October, and November can be significantly reduced by avoiding the Magic Kingdom and the Animal Kingdom on Saturday and Epcot on weekdays.

We Got Weather!   As if the crowds aren't enough, you must also consider the weather. September, October, and November are pleasant enough, but December and January can hit you with just about anything. And thunderstorms and pouring rain are not uncommon at any time of year.

A New Yorker who is accustomed to the vagaries of weather offers this bit of advice:

> *The weather when we were there was quirky. We were pepared and brought along umbrellas, ponchos, sweaters, etc. We learned quickly (the hard way) always to have these items with us, because the local weather forecasters were not to be trusted.*

From a Dalton, Massachusetts, mother of two:

> *We visited the Magic Kingdom on a day that included about five hours of torrential downpours. We were wet, but we were also cool and got to ride any ride we wanted multiple times. Your advice about praying for rain was very sound, but maybe we prayed too hard. A few light showers would have done as well.*

An Owings Mills, Maryland, family braved the cruel depths of the central Florida winter:

> *Believe it or not it is possible to have a good time in early January. Even with a high of 45 degrees, we were able to enjoy the Magic Kingdom one day since many attractions are indoors. Still, with young kids we braved Dumbo and other "wind chill" rides with hats and gloves. Best of all, the parks were almost empty before 11 a.m.*

SELECTING THE DAY OF THE WEEK FOR YOUR VISIT

Selecting the best day to visit a Walt Disney World theme park requires analyzing several variables. Entering into the equation are:

1. The time of year of your visit (holiday, summer, or off-season).
2. Attendance patterns for each day of the week at the respective parks.
3. Whether you are staying in a Walt Disney World hotel or campground (thereby making yourself eligible for early entry to the theme parks on specified days).
4. Habits of people traveling to Walt Disney World from outside of Florida.

A typical vacation scenario during summer would be for a family to arrive in the Orlando area on Sunday and to visit the Magic Kingdom and the Animal Kingdom on Monday and Tuesday; Epcot and Disney-MGM Studios on Wednesday and Thursday; and Typhoon Lagoon, Blizzard Beach, or a non-Disney area attraction on Friday. For those traveling by car, Friday often is reserved for heading home or to another Florida destination. If this were all we had to consider, we could recommend Fridays and Sundays as the best days all year to avoid crowds at the theme parks.

During the off-season, however, Disney initiates dozens of promotions to attract locals to Walt Disney World. Because these folks aren't on vacation, they tend to visit the theme parks on weekends. During fall, late winter, and spring, crowds might be larger on weekends than weekdays at the Magic Kingdom, the Animal Kingdom, and Disney-MGM Studios.

Crowds at Epcot, however, particularly during September and October, are almost always larger on weekdays. In addition to its promotions, Disney has a cooperative program with local schools that brings tens of thousands of children to Epcot for field trips in March, September, and October. Similarly, in late spring, high school students on "senior days" or prom nights fill the theme parks. Many of these programs are on weekdays.

The most significant shift in daily attendance patterns is the result of an early-entry program for guests staying at Walt Disney World resort hotels and campgrounds (but not for guests at Disney Village Hotel Plaza hotels). Initiated in 1993, the program originally applied only to the Magic Kingdom and operated on four days of the week. In 1994, the program was amended to include Epcot and Disney-MGM Studios. Each day of the week, Disney World lodging guests are invited to enter a designated theme park one hour before the general public.

During the early entry hour, Disney resort guests can enjoy attractions opened early for them. At the Magic Kingdom, for example, most attractions in Fantasyland and Tomorrowland are open to the early arrivals. At Epcot, Spaceship Earth, The Living Seas, The Land, Test Track, and Journey into Imagination open early, and at Disney-MGM Studios, early entrants can enjoy *The Twilight Zone* Tower of Terror, The Great Movie Ride, Star Tours, and *MuppetVision 4-D,* among others. Attractions open for early entry change from time to time. The Animal Kingdom does not participate in the early entry program.

Many guests who try early entry are surprised and disappointed that the entire park is not open. At each park, only specifically designated attractions are operational for early entry. The remainder of the park is shut down (and usually roped off) until the general public is admitted later. Take heart, morning zombies: there will be at least one counter-service restaurant open serving coffee and something to eat.

• WALT DISNEY WORLD WEATHER •

	Average Daily Low	Average Daily High	Average Daily Temperature	Average Daily Humidity %	Average Rainfall per Month (inches)	Number of Days of Rain per Month
January	49°	72°	61°	74	2.1	6
February	50°	73°	62°	71	2.8	7
March	55°	78°	67°	71	3.2	8
April	60°	84°	72°	69	2.2	6
May	66°	88°	77°	72	3.9	9
June	71°	91°	81°	77	7.4	14
July	73°	92°	82°	79	7.8	17
August	73°	92°	82°	80	6.3	16
September	73°	90°	81°	80	5.6	14
October	65°	84°	75°	77	2.8	9
November	57°	78°	68°	76	1.8	6
December	51°	73°	62°	76	1.9	6

Hurricane Season

How Early Entry Affects Attendance at the Theme Parks

Early entry strongly affects attendance at the theme parks, especially during busier times of year. Each day, vast numbers of Disney resort guests tour whichever theme park is designated for early entry. If the Magic Kingdom is tapped for early entry on Monday, for example, it will be more crowded that day, and Epcot, the Animal Kingdom, and Disney-MGM Studios will be less crowded. Accordingly, Epcot and Disney-MGM Studios will be more crowded when those parks are respectively slated for early entry.

During holiday periods and summer, when Disney hotels are full, early entry makes a tremendous difference in crowds at the designated park. The program funnels so many people into the early-entry park that it fills by about 10 a.m. and is practically gridlocked by noon. Whatever edge resort guests gain by taking advantage of early entry is completely offset by horrendous crowds later in the day. Our advice during busier times of year, regardless of where you're lodging, is to avoid any park scheduled for early entry.

An alternative strategy for Disney resort guests is to take advantage of early entry, but only until the designated park begins to get crowded. At that time, leave the early-entry park and go to another park. This plan works particularly well at the Magic Kingdom for families with young children who love the attractions in Fantasyland. If you use your early-entry privileges, be among the first early entrants.

A mother of three from Lee Summit, Missouri, writes:

> *Our first full day at WDW, we went to the Magic Kingdom. This was on a Monday, an early-entry day for resort guests. We were there at 7:30 and were able to walk onto all the rides in Fantasyland with no wait. At 8:45 we positioned ourselves at the Adventureland rope and ran towards Splash Mountain when the rope dropped. We were able to ride Splash Mountain with no wait (switching off), and then Big Thunder with about a 15-minute wait (switching off). We then went straight to the Jungle Cruise and the wait was already 30 minutes, so we skipped it. The park became incredibly crowded as the day progressed, and we were all exhausted from getting up so early to get there for early entry. We left the park around noon. After that day, I resolved to avoid early-entry days and instead be at a non-early-entry park about a half hour before official opening time. This worked much better for us.*

This note from a North Bend, Washington, dad emphasizes the importance of arriving at the beginning of the early-entry period:

> *We only used early entry once—to [Disney-] MGM. We got there 20 minutes after early entry opened and the wait for the Tower of Terror was already 1½ hours long. We skipped it!*

A lady from Ann Arbor, Michigan, who is clearly working overtime trying to figure all this stuff out, says:

> *We are starting to think that reverse-reverse psychology might work: Disney opens one park earlier for all their guests, so all the guests go to that park, but then, everyone buys your book in which you tell them not to go to that park because all Disney guests are there, so no one goes to that park, therefore we can go to that park because people think it's going to be packed and they avoid it. What do you think?*

Because Disney has changed the early-entry program numerous times in the past, we suggest you call Walt Disney Information at (407) 824-4321 before you leave home to verify the early-entry schedule during your stay.

And Now . . . Ta Da! Our Recommendations

1. Off-Season Touring   If you're a Disney resort or campground guest in the off-season or other less busy time, use your early-entry privileges. You'll get a jump on the general public and add an extra hour to what, in the off-season, is an already short touring day. If you're staying outside of Disney World and aren't eligible for early entry, avoid the park scheduled for early entry and visit one of the other theme parks instead.

A reader from Providence found early admission to be a great advantage during the off-season, writing:

> *During the off-season, the early admission was great. Only on Saturday did the crowd get so large that there were lines and bottlenecks. The mother behind me at Dumbo told me that they had waited three hours to ride Dumbo during their last visit to WDW. She took advantage of early admission to let her kid ride three times in a row with no waiting.*

2. E-Ticket Express   In 1999, Disney experimented with a program called the E-Ticket Express, where multiday pass holders could (for an extra $10) remain in the Magic Kingdom after official closing time and ride all the biggies with little or no waiting. Offered exclusively in the off-seasons, the E-Ticket Express program is described in detail on pages 453–454. Needless to say, the E-Ticket Express is the best thing since catsup on fries for folks who want to sleep in. Like most Disney programs, it is subject to termination at any time.

3. Least Crowded Days   From September through May (excluding holidays and spring break), Friday, Saturday, and Sunday are the most crowded days, while during summer the opposite is true (because locals stay home and out-of-state guests use Friday, Saturday, and Sunday for traveling).

Magic Kingdom At the Magic Kingdom, Sunday and Friday are least crowded in summer, and Tuesday and Wednesday are least crowded during the rest of the year.

Disney-MGM Studios At Disney-MGM Studios, Monday and Friday are best during summer. During off-season, try Monday and Tuesday.

Epcot Monday, Wednesday, and Thursday are least crowded from January through May, as well as in November and December. During summer, crowds are smaller on Saturday and Sunday. In September and October, when school groups inundate Epcot, visit on Saturday or Sunday.

Animal Kingdom High- or low-season, visit the Animal Kingdom on Thursday, Friday, or Sunday.

THE CRUELEST TIMES OF ALL: SUMMER AND HOLIDAYS

A reader from Columbus, Ohio, once observed, "the main thing I learned from your book is not to go during the summer or at holiday times. Once you know that you don't need a guidebook." While we might argue with the reader's conclusion, we certainly agree that avoiding summer and holidays is a strategy worth pursuing. That having been said, we also understand that many folks have no choice concerning the time of year they visit Walt Disney World. Much of this book, in fact, is dedicated to making sure those readers who visit during the busier times of year enjoy their Walt Disney World experience. Sure, off-season touring is preferable, but, armed with a little knowledge and some basic strategy, you can have a great time whenever you visit.

To put it in perspective, early summer (up to about June 15th) and late summer (after August 15th) are not nearly as crowded as the intervening period. And even the crowds of midsummer pale in comparison to the vast hordes that invade during holiday periods. If you visit in midsummer or during a holiday, the first thing you need to know is that the guest capacity of the theme parks is not infinite. In fact, once a park reaches capacity, its parking lot is closed, and only Disney resort guests arriving via the Disney transportation system are allowed to enter. If you are not a Disney resort guest, you may find yourself in a situation similar to this dad from Boise, Idaho:

This is the worst of it. The Magic Kingdom and the [Disney-] MGM Studios were so full they closed the parks. For three days we could not enter those parks, so we were forced to go to Epcot and use up two days of our four-day pass. We decided to pay for another night at our hotel to see if the crowds would let up, but no luck. All we could do was just drive around Orlando and sightsee.

The reader didn't tell us what time he arrived at the Magic Kingdom or the Studios, but we can pretty much assume he wasn't on hand for opening. If you roll out of bed early and get yourself to one of the parks not scheduled for early entry an hour or so prior to official opening time, you are practically certain to be admitted. Regardless of the time of year, if you aren't eligible for early entry, stay clear of the early-entry park.

The thought of teeming, jostling throngs jockeying for position in endless lines under the baking Fourth of July sun is enough to wilt the will and ears of the most ardent Mouseketeer. The Disney folks, however, feeling bad about those long, long lines and the nearly impossible touring conditions on packed holidays, compensate their patrons with a no-less-than-incredible array of first-rate live entertainment and happenings.

Shows, parades, concerts, and pageantry continue throughout the day. In the evening, particularly, so much is going on that you have to make some tough choices. Concerts, parades, light shows, laser shows, fireworks, and dance productions occur almost continually. No question about it, you can go to Walt Disney World on the Fourth of July (or on any other extended-hours, crowded day), never get on a ride, and still have a good time. Admittedly, it isn't the ideal situation for a first-timer who really wants to experience the attractions, but for anyone else it's a great party.

Disney provides colorful holiday decor for most holidays, as well as special parades and live entertainment for Christmas, New Year's, Easter, and Fourth of July, among others. Regarding Christmas, our advice is to visit in early December when you can enjoy the decorations and festivities without battling the crowds. A particularly well-known special event is Mickey's Very Merry Christmas Party, for which a separate admission ticket is required. A reader from Pineville, Louisiana, tried the Very Merry Christmas Party during the Christmas–New Year's week and found the guest list too large for her liking, writing:

Another thing I will not do again is buy tickets and go to the Very Merry Christmas Party. The event was sold out with 20,000 actually in attendance. We went in December to avoid crowds and were taken by surprise to find wall-to-wall people at the Very Merry Christmas Party. They had some great shows offered, but we could not get to them. The parade at 9 [p.m.] and fireworks at 10 [p.m.], then fighting our way back to the parking lot was all we could muster. We spent 30 minutes on arrival just getting a stroller. We did not ride anything, and there were some things that we had wanted to go back and ride. Mickey's Very Merry Christmas Party is not the time for rides!

Disney monitors the occupancy of hotels in the area in order to project attendance. On days when huge crowds are expected, Disney will often open the parks well in advance of the official opening time. This applies to all the parks, not just the one scheduled for early entry, and it is done to prevent parking toll booths, ticket windows, transportation systems, and entrance plazas from being overwhelmed. When Disney puts its early-opening plan into operation, the parks generally do not discriminate between Disney resort guests and day-guests (those not staying at Disney hotels). In other words, when really big crowds are expected, Disney will often open all of the parks early and admit any guest.

Unfortunately, Disney does not disclose in advance that it plans to open the parks early (except the park scheduled for early entry), nor will operators at Disney's main information phone number clue you in. You basically must guess based on the time of year whether implementation of the early-opening procedure is likely. Over major holidays, the probability of Disney opening the parks early is high. For nonholiday periods during the peak summer season, it's a lot iffier.

When we visit during the summer or holidays, we sometimes make a reconnaissance run to one of the Disney transportation system information windows (located at each of the parks and at the Transportation and Ticket Center [TTC]) and ask what time the parks actually opened that morning. Make it clear that you are not inquiring about the official opening time, but rather that you want to know exactly what time guests were admitted. If the parks opened early on the day in question, there is a great likelihood that the same conditions will prevail for the next couple of days.

If you visit on a nonholiday, midsummer day, arrive an hour to 70 minutes before the stated opening. If you visit during a major holiday period, arrive 90 minutes to 2 hours ahead of the official opening time. In either case, avoid the park that is scheduled for early entry. Hit your favorite rides early using one of our touring plans, and then return to your hotel for lunch, a swim, and perhaps a nap. Don't forget to have your hand stamped for re-entry when you exit. If you are interested in the special parades and shows, return to the park in the late afternoon or early evening. Work under the assumption that early morning will be the only time you can experience the attractions without long waits. Finally, do not wait until the last minute in the evening to leave the park. The exodus at closing is truly mind-boggling.

Epcot is usually the least crowded park during holiday periods, unless it's scheduled for early entry. Expect the other parks to be mobbed. To save time in the morning, purchase your admission in advance. Also, consider bringing your own stroller or wheelchair instead of renting one of Disney's. If you are touring Epcot or the Magic Kingdom and plan to spend the day, try exiting the park for lunch at one of the nearby resort hotels. Above all, bring your sense of humor and pay attention to the morale of your party. Bail out when it gets to be more work than fun.

Part Two

Making the Most of Your Time and Money

Allocating Money

Did Walt really intend for it to be so expensive that the average family couldn't afford it?

—Unofficial Guide reader and mother of one from Amarillo, Texas

How much you spend depends on how long you stay at Walt Disney World. But even if you only stop by for an afternoon, be prepared to drop a bundle. In Part 3 we'll show you how to save money on lodging, and in Part 9 you'll find lots of tips for economizing on meals. This section will give you some sense of what you can expect to pay for admissions, as well as which admission option will best meet your needs.

WALT DISNEY WORLD ADMISSION OPTIONS

Reviewers who complain that prices quoted in guidebooks are out of date should note that Walt Disney World ticket prices change about as often as the prime rate. Prices quoted below are those prevailing at press time. We expect an increase at the end of May 2000. Admission price increases historically have been in the 3–5% range.

There are basically ten Walt Disney World admission options (many with silly names), but several of them are endangered species:

Type of Pass	Adult Price w/ Tax	Child Price w/ Tax
1-Day/One-Park Only Pass	$47	$37
1-Day/One-Park Bounce-Back Pass	$36–42	$30–33

4-Day Park-Hopper Pass	$177	$142
5-Day Park-Hopper Pass	$210	$168
5-Day Park-Hopper Plus Pass	$243	$194
6-Day Park-Hopper Plus Pass	$275	$220
7-Day Park-Hopper Plus Pass	$306	$245
Unlimited Magic Pass	*Varies according to length of stay*	
Annual Passports*	$328–387	$275–334
Florida Resident/Seasonal	$169	$144

* More expensive Annual Passports include water parks, Pleasure Island, and Disney's Wide World of Sports.

The **1-Day/One-Park Only Ticket** is good for admission and unlimited use of "attractions and experiences" at the Magic Kingdom, Epcot, the Animal Kingdom, or Disney-MGM Studios, but does not provide same-day admission to more than one of the four.

The **1-Day/One-Park Bounce-Back Pass** was introduced in 1999 and is a good example of why Walt Disney World doesn't have an 800 number. It took a Disney information operator over 12 minutes to explain how the Bounce-Back works, and she had to consult her supervisor twice in the process. The pass is evidently intended for folks who drop in for a day and then decide to stay an extra day or two. Here's how it works (we think): If you purchase a 1-Day/One-Park Pass (see above) at the regular price, you are eligible to buy another 1-Day/One Park Bounce-Back Pass at a discounted rate, *as long as you buy it on the same day you bought the original pass.* But wait, there's more: If you purchase a 1-Day/One-Park Pass and a second, discounted 1-Day/One-Park Bounce-Back Pass, you are eligible to buy a third and fourth 1-Day/One-Park Bounce-Back Pass at an even greater discount. All passes must be bought on the same day.

If you buy four days of 1-Day/One-Park admissions on a given day, you will spend $47 for the first pass, $42 for the second, and $36 for the third and fourth, or $161 total (for adult passes; it's $130 for a child's passes). This is approximately $16 per adult and $12 per child less than you would pay for 4-Day Park-Hopper Passes (see below). For the savings you forfeit two features of the Park-Hopper Pass. First, you give up the right to visit more than one park in a single day, and second, Bounce-Back passes expire where Park-Hopper Passes are good forever. If you buy a 1-Day/One-Park Pass and then buy a 1-Day/One-Park Bounce-Back Pass, the Bounce-Back Pass expires four days from the date of purchase. If you buy two Bounce-Back passes, the first one expires in four days and the second one in six days. If you buy three, the third expires in eight days.

Though only Disney could dream up something like this, it's a pretty good deal for anyone who wants to visit the theme parks over a 3- or 4-day period and doesn't care about hopping from park to park on the same day.

The **4-Day** and **5-Day Park-Hopper Passes** provide same-day admission to the Magic Kingdom, the Animal Kingdom, Epcot, and Disney-MGM Studios. You can tour the Studios in the morning, have lunch at the Animal Kingdom and dinner at Epcot, and stop by the Magic Kingdom for the evening parades and fireworks. Unused days are good forever.

The **5-Day, 6-Day,** and **7-Day Park-Hopper Plus Passes** provide for unlimited use of the major theme parks as well as Pleasure Island, Blizzard Beach, Typhoon Lagoon, River Country, and the Wide World of Sports for the number of the days stated on the pass. Like the Park-Hopper Pass, Park-Hopper Plus Passes are good forever and do not have to be used during one stay or on consecutive days.

The 5-Day, 6-Day, and 7-Day Park-Hopper Plus Passes were introduced in the summer of 1999 and replace the All-in-One Passes. Regarding the water parks, Pleasure Island, and Wide World of Sports, the 5-Day Park-Hopper Plus allows two visits to the venues of your choice. The 6- and 7-Day Park-Hopper Plus Passes come with three and four visits respectively. Any admissions you don't use are good forever, including your visits to the minor parks of your choice (water parks, Pleasure Island, and the sports complex). This represents a change from the All-in-One passes, where admissions to minor parks expired one week after the pass was first used.

The **Unlimited Magic Pass,** for Walt Disney World lodging and camp ground guests, provides the same benefits as the Park-Hopper Plus Pass but can be purchased for any length of stay two days or longer. This program replaces the Length of Stay Passes and offers a comprehensive admission option (all major and minor parks) for stays shorter than four days. These passes are incredibly convenient: guests are issued a card that functions as a combination park pass and credit card. The card can be used at restaurants, shops, and other facilities throughout Walt Disney World, and purchases are charged to the guest's room. On the negative side, Unlimited Magic Passes are good only for the guest's stay.

Also, because the Unlimited Magic Pass is only available to Disney resort guests, Disney does not publish the price. This makes prices subject to manipulation and increases the difficulty of comparing various admission options.

The **Annual Passport** is good for unlimited use of the major theme parks for one year. An add-on is available to provide unlimited use of the minor theme parks. In addition to admission, Annual Pass holders get a number of perks, including complimentary parking and seasonal special offers such as room rate discounts at Disney resorts. This pass is not valid for special events.

The **Florida Resident's Passport.** In 1995, Walt Disney World expanded the admission options for Florida residents. Florida residents now can select from a menu of choices, including:

Florida Resident's Seasonal Passport. This pass (about $169 for adults) allows unlimited use of the major theme parks during specified (quieter) times of year.

Florida Resident's Epcot After 4 p.m. Passport. About $84 for adults, this pass allows Floridians to visit Epcot any day after 4 p.m.

Florida Resident's Annual Passport. These passports are available to residents at about 12% off the regular price.

While applicants must prove Florida residency to be eligible, it isn't necessary to have a Florida driver's license or to live in Florida year-round. A utility bill in your name for a Florida address will suffice.

WHICH ADMISSION SHOULD YOU BUY?

If you only have one day at Walt Disney World, select the park that most interests you and buy the 1-Day/One-Park Only Ticket. If you have two days and don't plan to return to Florida for a couple of years, buy two 1-Day tickets (or an Unlimited Magic Pass if you're a Disney lodging guest). If you think you might pass through the area again in the next year or two, spring for a 4-, 5-, 6-, or 7-day pass. Use two days of admission to see as much as you can, and save the remaining days for another trip.

If you plan to spend three or more days at Walt Disney World, buy a 4- or 5-day pass. If you live in Florida or plan to spend seven or more days in the major theme parks, the Annual Passport is a good buy. If you live in Florida and don't mind being restricted to visiting Disney World at designated off-peak times, the Florida Resident's Seasonal Pass should be considered.

If you visit Walt Disney World every year, here's how to save big bucks. Let's say you usually take your vacation during summer. This year, plan your Disney vacation for July and buy an Annual Passport. Next year, go in June. Because Annual Passports start on the date of purchase, those you buy this year will still be good for next year's vacation if you go a month earlier! If you spend four days each year at Disney World (eight days in the two consecutive years), you'll cut your daily admission to about $36 per adult per day. The longer your Disney vacation, of course, the more you save with the Annual Passport. If you visit the theme parks seven days each year, your admission will be less than $21 per day.

DISCOUNTS ON ADMISSION

At Disney World as at Wal-Mart, volume rules. If you buy a 5-day pass, you will pay less per day than if you buy a 1-day or 4-day pass. Admission discounts ranging between 3–5% are available to Magic Kingdom Gold Card holders, AAA members, and Disney time-share owners.

OLD PASSPORTS AND THE ANIMAL KINGDOM

Unused days on multiday passports sold before the Animal Kingdom opened in 1998 are good only for the other three parks. In other words, you can't use them for admission to the Animal Kingdom.

THE BLACK MARKET

Many readers ask if they can use remaining admissions on partially redeemed 4- and 5-day passes brought home by relatives. The facts are:

1. The pass is sold to the purchaser on a nontransferable basis. The pass states on the back, "To be valid this Pass must be used by the same person for all days."
2. On passes sold before February 1994, there is nothing on the pass that identifies the purchaser. On certain multiday, all-park passes sold after that date, the bearer's photograph and/or signature appear.
3. Admission attendants don't request a receipt or other proof of purchase for passes.

A corollary question concerns what to do with unused admissions on 4-, 5-, 6-, or 7-day passes that you purchase legally during your vacation. Our advice is to hang onto the passes. For starters, resale of unused multiday passes is a misdemeanor, and the guy offering you cash for your unused ticket may be a security officer. Second, because Disney raises admission prices almost every year, using an old pass during your next visit will save you money.

WHERE TO BUY YOUR ADMISSION AT WALT DISNEY WORLD

You can purchase passports at the major theme parks and at the resort hotels.

WHERE TO BUY YOUR ADMISSION IN ADVANCE

You can buy most multiday passes at a Disney Store before you leave home. The stores also can order 1-Day/One-Park Only tickets (allow three weeks for delivery). If you're driving to Disney World, buy your admission at the Ocala Disney AAA Travel Center at Exit 68 on I-75. If you fly, buy tickets at the airport Disney Store.

Tickets are also available by mail from the Walt Disney World Ticket Mail Order service (address on page 36) and via the Internet at www.disney.com.

WHERE NOT TO BUY YOUR ADMISSION IN ADVANCE

Because passes to Walt Disney World aren't discounted, offers of free or cut-rate tickets should trigger caution. Anyone offering free tickets to any attraction in the Orlando/Kissimmee area is probably selling real estate or time-share condominiums. You may receive a free ticket, but you will have to endure a lengthy site inspection and/or high-pressure sales pitch.

Many hotels outside of Walt Disney World maintain a desk or kiosk where independent brokers sell tickets to area attractions. These brokers are legitimate, but convenience is the only advantage to buying from them. Expect to pay regular Disney prices or a little more if you buy tickets from an independent broker.

HOW MUCH DOES IT COST PER DAY AT WALT DISNEY WORLD?

A typical day would cost $366.95, excluding lodging and transportation, for a family of four—Mom, Dad, 12-year-old Tim, and 8-year-old Sandy—driving their own car and staying outside of Disney World. They plan to be in the area for a week, so they buy 5-Day Park-Hopper Passes. Here's a breakdown:

How Much Does a Day Cost?	
Breakfast for four at Denny's with tax & tip	$25.50
Epcot parking fee	5.00
One day's admission on a 5-Day Park-Hopper Pass	
Dad: Adult 5-Day with tax = $210 divided by five (days)	42.00
Mom: Adult 5-Day with tax = $210 divided by five (days)	42.00
Tim: Adult 5-Day with tax = $210 divided by five (days)	42.00
Sandy: Child 5-Day with tax = $168 divided by five (days)	33.60
Morning break (soda or coffee)	7.00
Fast-food lunch (sandwich or burger, fries, soda), no tip	29.00
Afternoon break (soda and popcorn)	14.35
Dinner at Italy (no alcoholic beverages) with tax & tip	88.00
Souvenirs (Mickey T-shirts for Tim and Sandy) with tax*	38.50
One-Day Total	$366.95
(does not include lodging or transportation)	

*Cheer up, you won't have to buy souvenirs every day.

Allocating Time

During Disney World's first decade, a family with a week's vacation could enjoy the Magic Kingdom and River Country and still have several days for the beach or other area attractions. Since Epcot opened in 1982, however, Disney World has steadily been enlarging to monopolize the family's entire week. Today, with the addition of Blizzard Beach, Typhoon Lagoon, Disney-MGM Studios, the Animal Kingdom, and Downtown Disney, you should allocate six days for a whirlwind tour (or seven to ten days if you're old-fashioned and insist on a little relaxation during your vacation). If you don't have six or more days or think you might want to venture beyond the edge of "The World," be prepared to make some hard choices.

The theme parks and swimming attractions are huge and require a lot of walking and, sometimes, a lot of waiting in lines. Moving in typically large crowds all day is exhausting. The unrelenting Florida sun often zaps the most hardy traveler, making tempers short. In our many visits to Walt Disney World, we observed, particularly on hot summer days, a dramatic transition from happy, enthusiastic tourists upon arrival to plodding zombies later in the day. Visitors who began their day enjoying the Disney wonders lapsed into an exhausted, production-line mentality. ("We've got two more rides in Fantasyland, then we can go back to the hotel.")

We recommend you approach Walt Disney World the same way you would an eight-course Italian dinner: with plenty of time between courses. The best way not to have fun is to cram too much into too little time.

WHICH PARK TO SEE FIRST?

This question is less academic than it appears, especially if there are children or teenagers in your party. Children who see the Magic Kingdom first expect more of the same type of entertainment at the other parks. At Epcot, they're often disappointed by the educational orientation and more serious tone (many adults react the same way). Disney-MGM offers some pretty wild action, but the general presentation is educational and more adult. Though most children enjoy zoos, animals can't be programmed to entertain. Thus, children may not find the Animal Kingdom as exciting as the Magic Kingdom or Disney-MGM.

First-time visitors especially should see Epcot first; you will be able to enjoy it fully without having been preconditioned to think of Disney entertainment as solely fantasy or adventure. Parties with children definitely should see Epcot first. Children will be more likely to enjoy Epcot on its own merits if they see it first, and they will be more relaxed and patient in their touring.

See the Animal Kingdom second. Like Epcot, it has an educational thrust, but it provides a change of pace because it features live animals.

Next, see Disney-MGM Studios, which helps all ages make a fluid transition from the educational Epcot and Animal Kingdom to the fanciful Magic Kingdom. Also, because Disney-MGM Studios is smaller, you won't walk as much or stay as long.

Save the Magic Kingdom for last.

OPERATING HOURS

Disney can't be accused of being inflexible regarding operating hours at the parks. They run a dozen or more schedules each year, making it advisable to call (407) 824-4321 for the *exact* hours before you arrive. In the off-season, parks may be open for as few as ten hours (from 9 a.m. to 7 p.m.). By contrast, at busy times (particularly holidays), they may be open from 8 a.m. until 2 a.m. the next morning.

Usually hours approximate the following: from September through mid-March, excluding holiday periods, the Magic Kingdom is open from 9 a.m. to 7, 8, or 9 p.m. During the same period, Epcot is open from 9 a.m. to 9 p.m., and Disney-MGM Studios is open from 9 a.m. to 7 or 8 p.m. The Animal Kingdom is open from 7 or 8 a.m. until 7 or 8 p.m.

During summer, expect the Animal Kingdom to remain open until 8 p.m. Epcot and Disney-MGM Studios are normally open until 9 or 10 p.m., with the Magic Kingdom sometimes open as late as 1 a.m.

OFFICIAL OPENING VS. REAL OPENING

Operating hours you're quoted when you call are "official hours." The parks actually open earlier. Many visitors, relying on information disseminated by Disney Guest Relations, arrive at the official opening time and find the park packed with people. If the official hours are 9 a.m. to 9 p.m., for example, Main Street in the Magic Kingdom will open at 8 or 8:30 a.m. and the remainder of the park will open at 8:30 or 9 a.m. If the official opening for the Magic Kingdom is 8 a.m. and you're eligible for early entry, you will be able to enter the park at 6:30 a.m.

Disney publishes hours of operation well in advance but allows the flexibility to react daily to gate conditions. Disney traffic controllers survey local hotel reservations, estimate how many visitors to expect on a given day, and open the theme parks early to avoid bottlenecks at parking facilities and ticket windows and to absorb the crowds as they arrive.

If you don't have early-entry privileges, tour a park where early entry *isn't* in effect, arriving 30 minutes before the official opening time during the off-season. In mid-summer, arrive 70 minutes before official opening. If you visit on a major holiday, arrive 1 hour and 20 minutes before the official opening.

If you're a Disney resort guest and want to take advantage of early entry, arrive 1 hour and 40 minutes before the early-entry park is scheduled to open to the general public. Buses, boats, and monorails will initiate service to the early-entry park about two hours before it opens to the general public.

At day's end, rides and attractions shut down at approximately the official closing time. Main Street in the Magic Kingdom remains open 30 minutes to 1 hour after the rest of the park has closed.

THE VACATION THAT FIGHTS BACK

A vacation is what you make it, but visiting Walt Disney World requires levels of industry and stamina more often associated with running marathons. A mother from Middletown, New York, spells it out:

> *A vacation at WDW is not a vacation in the usual sense—sleeping late, total relaxation, leisurely meals, etc. It is a doing vacation that's frankly exhausting, but definitely worth doing. It's a magical place, where the visitor feels welcomed from the minute they arrive at their accommodations to the last second before boarding the shuttle bus back to the airport.*

A mother of two from Indianapolis, Indiana, adds:

> *My main thought throughout our time at WDW was, "It's so much work to have so much fun!" I can't imagine going without your touring plans in hand—I'm sure we'd have only seen half as much and we'd have become so angry with each other over trying to decide what to see next. Even with generally careful following of the one-day plans and arriving an hour early, we missed at least one "not to be missed" feature per [theme park], mostly due to brain death in the heat.*

The point is: At Walt Disney World, *less is more.* Take the World in small doses, with plenty of swimming, napping, reading, and relaxing in between. And here's some comforting news: Disney World *won't* be packed up and shipped to Tibet next year. If you don't see everything this trip, you can come back!

Hitting the Wall

As you plan your time at Walt Disney World, consider your physical limitations. It is extremely exhausting to rise at the crack of dawn and run around a theme park for 8–12 hours day after day. Sooner or later (usually sooner), you're going to hit the wall. Every Disney World vacation itinerary should include break days (when you don't go to a theme park) and sleeping-in days (when you take the morning off). Plan your break days and sleeping-in days to follow unusually long and arduous days, particularly after days at the Magic Kingdom and Epcot when you stay to see the evening parades or fireworks. Keep telling yourself over and over that you'll enjoy your vacation more if you are well rested.

A mom from LaGrange, Illinois, tried to sidestep our advice to stay rested, writing:

> *As I was planning, I was very sure we would not be taking a swim/nap break in the middle of the day. "No Way!" On the very first day of touring (at the Magic Kingdom) my seven-year-old said (at 9:30 a.m.—after only two hours at the park), "I'm hot—when can we go back to the hotel and swim?" Needless to say, we took that little break every day.*

If you neglect this all-important element of self-preservation and pacing, you'll be writing us letters like this one from a father of three from Unionville, Connecticut:

> *It's really difficult to follow your [touring plans] for more than one day in a row. The kids are just too exhausted to last through the fireworks and there isn't time to return to the hotel because of the crowdedness of the [parks].*

OPTIMUM TOURING SITUATION

We don't believe there is one ideal itinerary. Tastes, energy levels, and perspectives on what constitutes entertainment and relaxation vary. This understood, here are some considerations for developing your own ideal itinerary.

Optimum touring at Disney World requires a good itinerary, a minimum of six days on-site (excluding travel time), and a fair amount of money. It also requires a prodigious appetite for Disney entertainment. The essence of optimum touring is to see the attractions in a series of shorter, less exhausting visits during the cooler, less crowded times of day, with plenty of rest and relaxation between excursions.

Since optimum touring calls for leaving and returning to the theme parks on most days, it makes sense to stay in one of the Walt Disney World resort hotels. Also, if you stay in the World, you have early-entry privileges at designated parks and the option of advance reservations for the *Hoop-Dee-Doo Revue* and dinner shows performed at the hotels. Disney lodging guests also have freer use of the bus, boat, and monorail systems and have more choices for babysitting and children's programs. Sound good? It is, but be prepared to pay.

If you visit Walt Disney World during busy times (see page 41), you need to get up early to beat the crowds. Short lines and stress-free touring are incompatible with sleeping in. If you want to sleep late *and* enjoy your touring, visit Disney World when attendance is lighter.

THE CARDINAL RULES FOR SUCCESSFUL TOURING

Many visitors don't have six days to devote to Disney. Some are en route to other destinations or may wish to sample additional attractions of Orlando and central Florida. For these visitors, efficient touring is a must.

Even the most time-effective touring plan won't allow you to cover two or more major theme parks in one day. Plan to allocate at least an entire day to each park (an exception to this rule is when the parks close at different times, allowing you to tour one park until closing and then proceed to another park). If your schedule permits only one day of touring, concentrate on one theme park and save the others for another visit.

One-Day Touring

A comprehensive, one-day tour of the Magic Kingdom, the Animal Kingdom, Epcot, or Disney-MGM Studios is possible, but requires knowledge of the park, good planning, and plenty of energy and endurance. One-day touring doesn't leave much time for sit-down meals, prolonged browsing in shops, or lengthy breaks. One-day touring can be fun and rewarding, but allocating two days per park, especially for the Magic Kingdom and Epcot, is always preferable.

Successful touring of the Magic Kingdom, the Animal Kingdom, Epcot, or Disney-MGM Studios hinges on *three rules:*

I. Determine in Advance What You Really Want to See

What rides and attractions appeal most to you? Which additional rides and attractions would you like to experience if you have time left? What are you willing to forgo?

To help you set your touring priorities, we describe the theme parks and every attraction in detail in this book. In each description, we include the author's evaluation of the attraction and the opinions of Walt Disney World guests expressed as star ratings. Five stars is the best possible rating.

Finally, because attractions range from midway-type rides and horse-drawn trolleys to colossal, high-tech extravaganzas, we have developed a hierarchy of categories to pinpoint attractions' magnitude:

Super Headliners   The best attractions the theme park has to offer. Mind-boggling in size, scope, and imagination. Represents the cutting edge of modern attraction technology and design.

Headliners   Full blown, multimillion-dollar, full-scale, themed adventures and theater presentations. Modern in technology and design and employing a full range of special effects.

Major Attractions   Themed adventures on a more modest scale, but incorporating state-of-the-art technologies. Or, larger-scale attractions of older design.

Minor Attractions   Midway-type rides, small "dark" rides (cars on a track, zig-zagging through the dark), small theater presentations, transportation rides, and elaborate walk-through attractions.

Diversions   Exhibits, both passive and interactive. Includes playgrounds, video arcades, and street theater.

Though not every Walt Disney World attraction fits neatly into these descriptions, the categories provide a comparison of attraction size and scope. Remember that bigger and more elaborate doesn't always mean better. Peter Pan's Flight, a minor attraction in the Magic Kingdom, continues to be one of the park's most beloved rides. Likewise, for many young children, no attraction, regardless of size, surpasses Dumbo.

2. Arrive Early! Arrive Early! Arrive Early!

This is the single most important key to efficient touring and avoiding long lines. First thing in the morning, there are no lines and fewer people. The same four rides you can experience in one hour in early morning can take as long as three hours to see after 10:30 a.m. Have breakfast before you arrive so you won't waste prime touring time sitting in a restaurant.

The earlier a park opens, the greater your potential advantage. This is because most vacationers won't make the sacrifice to rise early and get to a theme park before it opens. Fewer people are willing to be on-hand for an 8 a.m. opening than for a 9 a.m. opening. On those rare occasions when a park opens at 10 a.m., almost everyone arrives at the same time, so it's almost impossible to get a jump on the crowd. If you're a Disney resort guest and have early-entry privileges, arrive as early as early entry allows (6:30 a.m. if the park opens to the public at 8 a.m., or 7:30 a.m. if the park opens to the public at 9 a.m.). If you are visiting during midsummer, arrive at non-early-entry parks 70 minutes before the official opening time. During holiday periods, arrive at non-early-entry parks 90 minutes to 2 hours before the official opening.

3. Avoid Bottlenecks

Helping you avoid bottlenecks is what this guide is about. Bottlenecks are caused by crowd concentrations and/or faulty crowd management. Avoiding bottlenecks involves being able to predict where, when, and why they occur. Concentrations of hungry people create bottlenecks at restaurants during lunch and dinner, concentrations of people moving toward the exit near closing time create bottlenecks in gift shops en route to the gate; concentrations of visitors at new and popular rides, and at rides slow to load and unload, create bottlenecks and long lines.

We provide touring plans for the Magic Kingdom, the Animal Kingdom, Epcot, Disney-MGM Studios, and Pleasure Island to help you avoid bottlenecks. In addition, we provide detailed information on all rides and performances, enabling you to estimate how long you may have to wait in line and allowing you to compare rides for their capacity to accommodate large crowds. Touring plans for the Magic Kingdom begin on page 449; Epcot, page 520; the Animal Kingdom, page 568; Disney-MGM Studios, page 604; and Pleasure Island, page 699. We have also included One-Day Touring Plans for the Universal Studios Florida park on page 631 and Universal's Islands of Adventure park on page 652.

In response to reader requests, we have added clip-out versions of the touring plans at the end of this book.

TOURING PLANS: WHAT THEY ARE
AND HOW THEY WORK

We followed your plans to the letter—which at times was troublesome to the dad in our party . . . somewhat akin to testing the strength of your marriage by wallpapering together!

—Unofficial Guide reader and mother of two from Milford, Connecticut

When we interviewed Walt Disney World visitors who toured the theme parks on slow days, they invariably waxed eloquent about the sheer delight of their experience. When we questioned visitors who toured on moderate or busy days, however, they talked at length about the jostling crowds and how much time they stood in line. What a shame, they said, that so much time and energy are spent fighting crowds in a place as special as Walt Disney World.

Given this complaint, our researchers descended on the World to determine whether a touring plan could be devised that would liberate visitors from the traffic flow and allow them to see any theme park in one day with minimal waiting in line. On some of the busiest days of the year, our team monitored traffic into and through the parks, noting how they filled and how patrons were distributed among the attractions. We also observed which rides and attractions were most popular and where bottlenecks were most likely to occur.

After many days of collecting data, we devised preliminary touring plans, which we tested during one of the busiest weeks of the year. Each day, our researchers would tour the park using one of the preliminary plans, noting how long it took to walk from place to place and how long the wait in line was for each attraction. Combining the information gained on trial runs, we devised a master plan that we retested and fine-tuned. This plan, with very little variance from day to day, allowed us to experience all major rides and attractions and most lesser ones in one day, with an average wait in line of less than five minutes at each.

From this master plan, we developed alternative plans that took into account the varying tastes and personal requirements of different Disney World patrons. Each plan operated with the same logic as the master plan but addressed the special needs and preferences of its intended users.

Finally, after all of the plans were tested by our staff, we selected (using convenience sampling) Walt Disney World visitors to test the plans. The only requisite for being chosen to test the plans was that the guests must be visiting a Disney park for the first time. A second group of patrons was chosen for a "control group." These were first-time visitors who would tour the park according to their own plans but who would make notes about what they did and how much time they spent in lines.

When the two groups were compared, the results were amazing. On days when major theme park attendance exceeded 48,000, visitors touring without our plans *averaged* 3⅔ hours' more waiting in line per day than the patrons touring with our plans, and they experienced 37% fewer rides and attractions.

General Overview of the Touring Plans

Our touring plans are step-by-step guides for seeing as much as possible with a minimum of standing in line. They're designed to help you avoid crowds and bottlenecks on days of moderate-to-heavy attendance. On days of lighter attendance (see "Selecting the Time of Year for Your Visit," page 41), the plans will still save time but won't be as critical to successful touring.

What You Can Realistically Expect from the Touring Plans

Though we present one-day touring plans for each of the theme parks, you should understand that the Magic Kingdom and Epcot have more attractions than you can see in one day, even if you never wait in line. If you must cram your visit into a single day, the one-day touring plans will allow you to see as much as is humanly possible. Under certain circumstances you may not complete the plan, and you definitely won't be able to see everything. For the Magic Kingdom and Epcot, the most comprehensive, efficient, and relaxing touring plans are the two-day plans. Although Disney-MGM Studios has grown considerably since its 1989 debut, you should have no problem seeing everything in one day. Likewise, the Animal Kingdom is a one-day outing.

Variables That Will Affect the Success of the Touring Plans

How quickly you move from one ride to another; when and how many refreshment and rest room breaks you take; when, where, and how you eat meals; and your ability (or lack thereof) to find your way around will all have an impact on the success of the plans. Smaller groups almost always move faster than larger groups, and parties of adults generally can cover more ground than families with young children. Switching off (see pages 190–192), among other things, prohibits families with little ones from moving expeditiously among attractions. Plus, some children simply cannot conform to the "early-to-rise" conditions of the touring plans.

A mom from Nutley, New Jersey, writes:

> *[Although] the touring plans all advise getting to parks at opening, we just couldn't burn the candle at both ends. Our kids (10, 7, and 4)*

would not go to sleep early and couldn't be up at dawn and still stay relatively sane. It worked well for us to let them sleep a little later, go out and bring breakfast back to the room while they slept, and still get a relatively early start by not spending time on eating breakfast out. We managed to avoid long lines with an occasional early morning, and hitting popular attractions during parades, mealtimes, and late evenings.

And a family from Centerville, Ohio, says:

The toughest thing about your tour plans was getting the rest of the family to stay with them, at least to some degree. Getting them to pass by attractions in order to hit something across the park was no easy task (sometimes impossible).

Finally, if you have young children in your party, be prepared for character encounters. The appearance of a Disney character is usually sufficient to stop a touring plan dead in its tracks. What's more, while some characters continue to stroll the parks, it is becoming more the rule to assemble characters in some specific venue (like the Hall of Fame at Mickey's Toontown Fair) where families must queue up for photos and autographs. Meeting characters, posing for photos, and collecting autographs can burn hours of touring time. If your kids are into character autograph collecting, you will need to anticipate these interruptions to the touring plan and negotiate some understanding with your children about when you will follow the plan and when you will collect autographs. Our advice is to either go with the flow or alternatively set aside a certain morning or afternoon for photos and autographs. Be aware, however, that queues for autographs, especially in Toontown at the Magic Kingdom and Camp Minnie-Mickey at the Animal Kingdom, are every bit as long as the queues for major attractions. The only time-efficient way to collect autographs is to line up at the character greeting areas first thing in the morning. Because this is also the best time to experience the more popular attractions, you may have some tough decisions to make.

While we realize that following the touring plans is not always easy, we nevertheless recommend continuous, expeditious touring until around noon. After that hour, breaks and diversions won't affect the plans significantly.

Some variables that can profoundly affect the touring plans are beyond your control. Chief among these are the manner and timing of bringing a particular ride to capacity. For example, Big Thunder Mountain Railroad, a roller coaster in the Magic Kingdom, has five trains. On a given morning it may begin operation with two of the five, then add the other three if and when needed. If the waiting line builds rapidly before operators decide to go to full capacity, you could have a long wait, even in early morning.

Another variable relates to the time you arrive for a theater performance. Usually, your wait will be the length of time from your arrival to the end of the presentation in progress. Thus, if *Country Bear Jamboree* is 15 minutes long and you arrive one minute after a show has begun, your wait for the next show will be 14 minutes. Conversely, if you arrive as the show is wrapping up, your wait will be only a minute or two.

What to Do If You Lose the Thread

Anything from a blister to a broken attraction can throw off a touring plan. If unforeseen events interrupt a touring plan:

1. Skip one step on the plan for every 20 minutes you're delayed. If you lose your billfold, for example, and spend an hour finding it, skip three steps and pick up from there.
2. Forget the touring plan and organize the remainder of your day using the *Optimum Touring Times* clip-out charts at the back of this guide. These charts summarize the best times to visit each attraction.

What to Expect When You Arrive at the Parks

Because each touring plan is based on being present when the theme park opens, you need to know a little about opening procedures. Disney transportation to the parks, as well as the respective theme park parking lots, open an hour and a half to two hours before official opening time. If a park is scheduled for early entry (also called Surprise Mornings), parking facilities and the transportation system will crank up 60 to 90 minutes in advance of the early entry admission time.

Each park has an entrance plaza just outside the turnstiles. Usually you will be held outside the turnstiles until 30 minutes before the official opening time. At 30 minutes prior to the official opening time you will generally be admitted through the turnstiles. What happens next depends on the season of the year and the anticipated crowds for that day.

1. **Low Season** slower times of year you will usually be confined in a small section of the park until the official opening time. At the Magic Kingdom you will be admitted to Main Street, U.S.A.; at the Animal Kingdom to The Oasis and sometimes to Safari Village; at Epcot to the fountain area around Spaceship Earth; and at Disney-MGM Studios to Hollywood Boulevard. If you proceed farther into a park, you will encounter a rope barrier manned by Disney cast members who will keep you from entering the remainder of the park. You will remain here until the "rope drop,"

when the rope barrier is removed and the park and all (or most) of its attractions are opened at the official opening time.

2. **High Season and Holidays**   During high season or when large crowds are expected, you will be admitted through the turnstiles 30 minutes prior to the official opening time, just as during slower times of year, only this time the entire park will be up and running and you will not encounter any rope barriers.

3. **Variations**   Sometimes, Disney will run a variation of the two opening procedures described above. In this situation you will be permitted through the turnstiles and will find that one or several specific attractions are open early for your enjoyment. At Epcot, Spaceship Earth and sometimes Test Track will be operating. At Animal Kingdom you may find Kilimanjaro Safaris and *It's Tough to Be a Bug!* up and running early. At Disney-MGM Studios look for Tower of Terror and/or Rock 'n' Roller Coaster. The Magic Kingdom almost never runs a variation. At the Magic Kingdom you'll encounter either number 1 or 2 as described above.

All parks except the Animal Kingdom participate in the Surprise Morning, early-entry program, where a specific park is designated each day for early entry. The early-entry privilege is available only to Walt Disney World resort and campground guests. On an early-entry morning, the designated park will permit you through the turnstiles 90 minutes before the official opening time. Thus, if the official opening time for the Magic Kingdom is 9 a.m. and it is the park slated for early entry, you will be admitted at 7:30 a.m. Once through the turnstiles, Disney cast members will direct you to the sections of the park and attractions that are open. All remaining areas will be roped off until 30 minutes prior to official opening when the rope is dropped and the "general public" (i.e., guests not staying in Disney resorts) is admitted.

A Word about the Rope Drop   Until recently, at all four parks, Disney cast members would dive for cover when the rope was dropped as thousands of adrenaline-charged guests stampeded to the parks' most popular attractions. This practice occasioned the legendary Space Mountain Morning Mini-Marathon and the Splash Mountain Rapid Rampage at the Magic Kingdom, the Tower of Terror Trot at Disney-MGM Studios, and the Safari Sprint at Animal Kingdom, among others. Each morning, a huge throng would crowd the rope barriers waiting for the signal to sprint to the entrance of their favorite ride. It was each person for himself—parents against offspring, brother against sister, coeds against truck drivers, nuns against beauticians. So there you were, a dental hygienist from Toledo thinking you'd like to ride Space Mountain and finding yourself embroiled in this ritual insanity. There was nothing to do except tie up your Reeboks and get ready to run.

Lest you think we're exaggerating, consider the words of those who have experienced it. From an Oakland, Tennessee, teen:

> *We waited for the half hour, made new friends and discussed the "Space Mountain Mini Marathon." I wasn't sure if I believed it or not, but when the announcement came over the loudspeaker and the rope dropped, we all took off. First walking fast, then jogging, then running. What seemed like thousands of people trucking it as fast as their legs could take them over what felt like miles even though no one was sure just how far it actually was because the adrenaline was pumping and no one was stopping to look at the scenery! Well, in that mess I lost my Mom. She quit, figuring she didn't want to ride anything bad enough to fall over with a heart attack. I made it. I don't know how, but I did it. I was also one of the first 25 or 30 people in line. I let some people go on in front of me because I was waiting for my Mom who never showed up. The Mini Marathon is seriously underrated. There are thousands more people involved in this than I ever imagined, and it covers what seems like the same distance as an actual marathon with people running much faster. Even though Space Mountain wasn't as great as I had hoped, I wasn't disappointed. I recommend that everyone young or old, no matter who they are, should be in the marathon and ride Space Mountain at least once. It is incredible, and no matter where you go in the world, you will never experience anything like the Space Mountain Mini Marathon.*

A family of four from Barre, Vermont, told us:

> *Running to Space Mountain when the [rope dropped] almost gave us a heart attack. Felt I was part of a wildebeest stampede out of* The Lion King *movie.*

Well, this scenario no longer exists—at least not in the crazed versions of years past. Recently, Disney has beefed up the number of cast members supervising the rope drop in order to suppress the mayhem. In some cases the rope is not even "dropped." Instead, it's walked back. In other words, Disney cast members lead you with the rope at a fast walk toward the attraction you're straining to reach, forcing you (and everyone else) to maintain their pace. Not until they come within close proximity of the attraction do the cast members step aside. A New Jersey mom described it thus:

> *You are no longer allowed to sprint to these [attractions] because*
> *of people being trampled. Now there is a phalanx of cast members*
> *lined up at the rope who instruct you in friendly but no uncertain*
> *terms that when the rope drops they will lead you to the rides at a*
> *fast walk. However, you are not allowed to pass them. (No one ever*
> *said what would happen if you did pass). To my surprise, everyone*
> *followed the rules and we were splish-splashing within 5 minutes*
> *after 9 a.m.*

A variation of the same tune was reported by a Kansasville, Wisconsin, mom:

> *No more Rapid Rampage/Space Mountain Mini Marathon! A*
> *"helper" was picked by a waiting cast member from the group of*
> *people waiting before the rope was dropped, and the cast member*
> *and "helper" escorted the crowd—we were given specific instructions*
> *to stay behind them—to Splash Mountain, picking up additional*
> *groups being escorted along the way. Safer, yes . . . but a LOT less*
> *fun! Having experienced the "Mini Marathon," I will miss it . . . it*
> *was one of the few uncontrolled things that happened at WDW,*
> *which is probably why it was squashed!*

You never know with Disney, though. The new rope drop procedure may be abandoned and the traditional insanity allowed to resume. Because Disney likes to control everything, however, we don't think so. And while we'll miss the passion of the early-morning races, we have to admit that the new practice is probably safer.

So, here's the straight poop. If Disney persists in walking the rope back, the only way you can gain an advantage over the rest of the crowd is to arrive early enough to be one of those up front close to the rope. Be alert, though, sometimes the Disney folks will step out of the way after about fifty yards or so. If this happens you can fire up the afterburners and speed the remaining distance to your destination.

Touring Plan Clip-Out Pocket Outlines

For your convenience, we have prepared outlines of all the touring plans in this guide. These pocket versions present the same itineraries as the detailed plans, but with vastly abbreviated directions. Select the plan appropriate for your party, then familiarize yourself with the detailed version. Once you understand how the plan works, clip the pocket version from the back of this guide and carry it with you as a quick reference at the theme park.

Will the Plans Continue to Work Once the Secret Is Out?

Yes! First, all of the plans require that a patron be there when the theme parks open. Many Walt Disney World patrons simply refuse to get up early while on vacation. Second, less than 1% of any day's attendance has been exposed to the plans, too little to affect results. Last, most groups tailor the plans, skipping rides or shows according to personal taste.

How Frequently Are the Touring Plans Revised?

Because Disney is always adding new attractions and changing operations, we revise the touring plans every year. Most complaints we receive about them come from readers who are using out-of-date editions of the *Unofficial Guide*. Be prepared, however, for surprises. Opening procedures and show times, for example, may change, and you never know when an attraction might break down.

A Word about Early Entry and the Touring Plans

If you're a Disney resort guest and use your early-entry privileges, complete your early-entry touring *before* the general public is admitted and position yourself to follow the touring plan. Usually at Epcot, Disney-MGM Studios, and sometimes at the Magic Kingdom, the general public is admitted a half hour before the published opening time. When the general public is admitted, the park will suddenly swarm. Be prepared, a mother from Wilmington, Delaware, advises:

> *The early-entry times went like clockwork. We were finishing up*
> *The Great Movie Ride when Disney-MGM opened [to the public],*
> *and [we] had to wait in line quite awhile for* Voyage of the Little
> Mermaid, *which sort of screwed up everything thereafter. Early-*
> *opening attractions should be finished up well before regular opening*
> *time so you can be at the plan's first stop as early as possible.*

In the Magic Kingdom, the attractions open during early entry are in Fantasyland and Tomorrowland. At Epcot, early-entry attractions are on the right side of the park's Future World section. At Disney-MGM Studios, they're dispersed. Practically, see any attractions on the touring plan that are open for early entry, crossing them off as you do. If you finish all early-entry attractions that are on the touring plan and still have time left before the general public is admitted, sample early-entry attractions not included in the plan. Stop touring about ten minutes before the public is admitted and position yourself for the first attraction on the touring plan that wasn't open for early entry. In the Magic Kingdom, for example, you usually can experience Peter Pan's Flight and It's a Small World in Fantasyland, as well as Space Mountain and *Alien Encounter* in Tomorrowland, during early entry. As official opening time approaches, go to the boundary between Fantasyland and Liberty Square and be ready to blitz to Splash Mountain and Big Thunder Mountain Railroad according to the touring plan when the rest of the park opens.

FASTPASS

In 1999, Disney tested a new system for moderating the waiting time for popular attractions. Called FASTPASS, it was originally tried at the Animal Kingdom and then subsequently expanded to cover attractions at other parks. If FASTPASS is offered during your visit, here's how it works.

Your handout park map, as well as signage at respective attractions, will tell you which attractions are included. Attractions operating FASTPASS will have a regular line and a FASTPASS line. A sign at the entrance will tell you how long the wait is in the regular line. If the wait is acceptable hop in line. If the wait seems too long, you can insert your park admission pass into a special FASTPASS turnstile and receive an appointment time (for sometime later in the day) to come back and ride. When you return at the appointed time, you will enter the FASTPASS line and proceed directly to the attraction's preshow or boarding area with no further wait. There is no extra charge to use FASTPASS, but you can get an appointment for only one attraction at a time. Interestingly, this procedure was pioneered by Universal Studios Hollywood many years ago and has been pretty much ignored by major theme parks ever since. It works well, however, and can really save a lot of time standing in line.

Because FASTPASS is still evolving and being tested, it was impossible to integrate it into our touring plans for this edition. Attractions continue to be added and deleted from the lineup, and questions concerning whether FASTPASS will operate during regular park hours or just during the busier times of day have yet to be settled. Pending issues aside, here's an example of how to use FASTPASS if it's running when you tour.

Let's say you have only one day to tour the Magic Kingdom. You arrive early and ride Space Mountain and experience Alien Encounter with only minimal waits. Then, following our touring plan, you head across the park to Splash Mountain and find a substantial line. If Splash Mountain is designated as a FASTPASS attraction, you could insert your admission pass into the turnstile and receive an appointment time to come back and ride, thus avoiding a long wait. Let me emphasize that this is only a hypothetical example and that FASTPASS attractions at the Magic Kingdom had not been designated when this guide went to press.

Tour Groups from Hell

We have discovered that tour groups of up to 200 people sometimes use our plans. A lady from Memphis writes:

> *When we arrived at The Land [pavilion at Epcot], a tour guide was holding your book and shouting into a bullhorn, "Step 7. Proceed to Journey into Imagination." With this, about 65 Japanese tourists in red T-shirts ran out the door.*

Unless your party is as large as that tour group, this development shouldn't alarm you. Because tour groups are big, they move slowly and have to stop periodically to collect stragglers. The tour guide also has to accommodate the unpredictability of five dozen or so bladders. In short, you should have no problem passing a group after the initial encounter.

"Bouncing Around"

Many readers object to crisscrossing a theme park as our touring plans sometimes require. A lady from Decatur, Georgia, said she "got dizzy from all the bouncing around" and that the "running back and forth reminded [her] of a scavenger hunt." We empathize, but here's the rub, park by park.

In the Magic Kingdom, the most popular attractions are positioned across the park from one another. This is no accident. It's good planning, a method of more equally distributing guests throughout the park. If you want to experience the most popular attractions in one day without long waits, you can arrive before the park fills and see those attractions first thing (requires crisscrossing the park), or you can enjoy the main attractions on one side of the park first thing in the morning then try the popular attractions on the other side during the hour or so before closing when crowds presumably have thinned. All other approaches will subject you to awesome waits at some attractions if you tour during busy times of year.

The best way to minimize "bouncing around" at the Magic Kingdom is to use the Magic Kingdom Two-Day Touring Plan, which spreads the more popular attractions over two mornings and works beautifully even when the park closes at 8 p.m. or earlier.

We have revised the Epcot touring plans to eliminate most of the "bouncing around" and have added special instructions to even further minimize walking.

Disney-MGM Studios is configured in a way that precludes an orderly approach to touring, or to a clockwise or counterclockwise rotation. Orderly touring is further confounded by live entertainment that prompts guests to intermittently interrupt their touring to head to whichever theater is about to crank up. At the Studios, therefore, you're stuck with "bouncing around" whether you use the touring plan or not. In our opinion, when it comes to Disney theme parks, it's best to have a plan.

The Animal Kingdom is arranged in a spoke-and-hub configuration like the Magic Kingdom, simplifying crisscrossing the park.

Touring Plans and the Obsessive-Compulsive Reader

We suggest you follow the touring plans religiously, especially in the mornings, if you're visiting Disney World during busy, more-crowded times. The consequence of touring spontaneity in peak season is hours of otherwise avoidable standing in line. During quieter times of year, there's no need to be compulsive about following the plans.

A mom in Atlanta, Georgia, suggests:

> *Emphasize perhaps not following [the touring plans] in off-season. There is no reason to crisscross the park when there are no lines.*

A father from Marlboro, New Jersey, writes:

> *The time we went in November, the longest line was about a five-minute wait. [At this time of year], your readers do not have to be so neurotic about running into the park and then to various attractions.*

A mother in Minneapolis expresses her opinion:

> *I feel you should let your readers know to stop along the way to various attractions to appreciate what else may be going on around them. We encountered many families using the* Unofficial Guide *[who] became too serious about getting from one place to the next, missing the fun in between.*

We realize the touring plans can contribute to some stress and fatigue. A mother from Stillwater, Maine, writes:

> *We were thankful for the touring plan and were able to get through the most popular rides early before the lines got long. One drawback was all the bouncing around we did backtracking through different parts of the Magic Kingdom in order to follow the touring plan. It was tiring and a bit hectic at times.*

What can we say? It's a lesser-of-two-evils situation. If you visit Walt Disney World at a busy time, you can either get up early and hustle around, or you can sleep in and see less, spending a lot of time in lines.

When using the touring plans, however, relax and always be prepared for surprises and possible setbacks. When your blood pressure rises and your Type-A brain does cartwheels, reflect on the advice of a woman from Trappe, Pennsylvania:

You cannot emphasize enough the dangers of using your touring plans that were printed in the back of the book, especially if the person using them has a compulsive personality. I have a compulsive personality. I planned for this trip for two years, researched it by use of guidebooks, computer programs, video tapes, and information received from WDW. I had a two-page itinerary for our one-week trip in addition to your touring plans of the theme parks. On night three of our trip, I ended up taking a non-scheduled trip to the emergency room of Sand Lake Hospital in Lake Buena Vista. When the doctor asked what seemed to be the problem, I responded with "I don't know, but I can't stop shaking, and I can't stay here very long because I have to get up in a couple hours to go to MGM according to my itinerary." Diagnosis: an anxiety attack caused by my excessive itinerary. He gave me a shot of something, and I slept through the first four attractions the next morning. This was our third trip to WDW (not including one trip to Disneyland); on all previous trips I used only the Steve Birnbaum book, and I suffered no ill effects. I am not saying your book was not good. It was excellent! However, it should come with a warning label for people with compulsive personalities.

Tour Plan Rejection

We have discovered you can't implant a touring plan in certain personalities without rapid and often vehement rejection. Some folks just do not respond well to the regimentation. If you bump into this problem with someone in your party, it's best to roll with the punches as this couple from Maryland did:

The rest of the group was not receptive to the use of the touring plans. I think they all thought I was being a little too regimented about planning this vacation. Rather than argue, I left the touring plans behind as we ventured off for the parks. You can guess the outcome. We took our camcorder with us and watched the movies when we returned home. About every five minutes or so there is a shot of us all gathered around a park map trying to decide what to do next.

Finally, as a Connecticut woman alleges, the touring plans are incompatible with some readers' bladders as well as their personalities:

I want to know if next year when you write those "day" schedules if you could schedule bathroom breaks in there too. You expect us to be at a certain ride at a certain time and with no stops in between. Like one of the letters in your book a guy writes, "You expect everyone to be theme park commandos." When I read that I thought, there is a man who really knows what a problem the schedules are if you are a laid-back, slow-moving, careful detail noticer. What were you thinking when you made these schedules?

A Clamor for Customized Touring Plans

We're inundated by letters urging us to create additional touring plans. These include a plan for ninth- and tenth-graders, a plan for rainy days, a senior's plan, a plan for folks who sleep late, a plan omitting rides that "bump, jerk, and clonk," a plan for gardening enthusiasts, and a plan for single women.

The touring plans in this book are intended to be flexible. Adapt them to your preferences. If you don't like rides that bump and jerk, skip them when they come up in a touring plan. If you want to sleep in and go to the park at noon, use the afternoon part of a plan. If you're a ninth-grader and want to ride Space Mountain three times in a row, do it. Will it decrease the touring plan's effectiveness? Sure, but the plan was created only to help you have fun. It's your day. Don't let the tail wag the dog.

Understanding Walt Disney World Attractions

Walt Disney World's primary appeal is in its rides and shows. Understanding how these are engineered to accommodate guests provides information that is not only interesting but invaluable to developing an efficient itinerary.

All attractions at Disney World, regardless of location, are affected by two overriding elements: capacity and popularity. Capacity is how many guests the attraction can serve at one time, in an hour, or in a day. Popularity shows how well visitors like an attraction. Capacity can be adjusted at some attractions. It's possible, for example, to add additional trams at the Disney-MGM Studios Backlot Tour or to put extra boats on the water at the Magic Kingdom's Jungle Cruise. Generally, however, capacity remains relatively fixed.

From a designer's perspective, the idea is to match capacity and popularity as closely as possible. A high-capacity ride that isn't very popular is a failure of sorts. Lots of money, space, and equipment have been poured into the attraction, yet there are empty seats. El Río del Tiempo, a ride in Epcot, comes closest to fitting this profile.

While it's extremely unusual for a new attraction not to measure up, it is fairly common for an older ride to lose its appeal. The Magic Kingdom's

Tropical Serenade (Enchanted Tiki Birds), for example, played to half-capacity audiences until its 1998 renovation.

In general, attractions are immensely popular when they're new. Some, like Space Mountain (Magic Kingdom), have sustained great appeal years beyond their debut, while others, like Epcot's The Living Seas and El Río del Tiempo, have declined in popularity after just a few years. Most attractions, however, work through the honeymoon and then settle down to handle the level of demand for which they were designed. When this happens, there are enough interested guests during peak hours to fill almost every seat, but not so many that prohibitively long lines develop.

Sometimes Disney correctly estimates an attraction's popularity but fouls the equation by mixing in a third variable such as location. Spaceship Earth, the ride inside the geosphere at Epcot, is a good example. Placing the ride squarely in the path of every person entering the park assures that it will be inundated during morning hours when the park is filling up. On the flip side, *The American Adventure,* at the extreme opposite end of Epcot, has a huge capacity but plays to a partially filled theater until about noon, when guests finally work their way into that part of the park.

If demand is high and capacity is low, large lines materialize. Dumbo the Flying Elephant in the Magic Kingdom has the smallest capacity of almost any Disney World attraction, yet it probably is the most popular ride among young children. The result of this mismatch is that children and parents often suffer long, long waits for a one-and-a-half-minute ride. Dumbo is a simple yet visually appealing midway ride. Its capacity (and that of many other attractions, including Space Mountain) is limited by the very characteristics that make it popular.

Capacity design is predicated on averages: the average number of people in the park, the normal distribution of traffic to specific areas within the park, and the average number of staff needed to operate the ride. On a holiday weekend, when all the averages are exceeded, all but a few attractions operate at maximum capacity, and even then they are overwhelmed by the huge crowds. On low-attendance autumn days, full capacity is often not even approximated and guests can walk onto most rides without any wait.

The Magic Kingdom offers the greatest variety in capacity and popularity, offering vastly differing rides and shows. Only the Magic Kingdom offers low-capacity midway rides and spook-house genre "dark" rides. Only the Magic Kingdom and the Disney-MGM Studios offer roller coasters. Technologically, the mix ranges from state-of-the art to antiquated. This diversity makes efficient touring of the Magic Kingdom much more challenging. If guests don't understand the capacity/popularity relationship and plan accordingly, they might spend most of the day waiting in line.

While Epcot, the Animal Kingdom, and Disney-MGM Studios have fewer rides and shows than the Magic Kingdom, almost all of their attractions are major features and rank on a par with the Magic Kingdom's Pirates of the Caribbean and The Haunted Mansion in scope, detail, imagination, and spectacle. All but one or two of the Epcot, Animal Kingdom, and Disney-MGM Studios rides are fast loading, and most have large capacities. Because Epcot, the Animal Kingdom, and Disney-MGM Studios attractions are on average well engineered and very efficient, lines may appear longer than those in the Magic Kingdom but usually move more quickly. There are no midway rides at Epcot, the Animal Kingdom, or Disney-MGM Studios and fewer attractions specifically intended for children.

In the Magic Kingdom, crowds are more a function of the popularity and engineering of individual attractions. At Epcot and the Animal Kingdom, traffic flow and crowding is much more affected by park layout. For touring efficiency, it's important to understand how Magic Kingdom rides and shows operate. At Epcot and the Animal Kingdom, this knowledge is decidedly less important.

Crowds at Disney-MGM Studios have been larger than anticipated since the park opened. Unexpectedly large attendance coupled with relatively few attractions has resulted in long lines and frustrated guests. Though Disney has added new attractions, a well-considered touring plan is essential. Likewise, the Animal Kingdom is currently operating with only five of its six planned theme areas open. Lack of capacity plus the allure of a new park translates into lengthy queues.

It's necessary to understand how rides and shows are designed and function to develop an efficient touring plan. We will examine both.

A WORD ABOUT DISNEY THRILL RIDES

Readers of all ages should attempt to be open-minded about the so-called Disney "thrill rides." In comparison with rides at other theme parks, the Disney thrill attractions are quite tame, with more emphasis on sights, atmosphere, and special effects than on the motion, speed, or feel of the ride itself. While we suggest you take Disney's preride warnings seriously, we can tell you that guests of all ages report enjoying rides such as Tower of Terror, Big Thunder Mountain, and Splash Mountain. The biggest, baddest thrill ride in Florida is the Montu inverted roller coaster at Busch Gardens.

A reader from Washington sums up the situation well:

Our boys and I are used to imagining typical amusement park rides when it comes to roller coasters. So, when we thought of Big Thunder Mountain and Space Mountain, what came to mind was gigantic hills, upside down loops, huge vertical drops, etc. I actually hate roller coasters, especially the unpleasant sensation of a long drop, and I have never taken a ride that loops you upside down.

In fact, the Disney [thrill rides] are all tame in comparison. There are never any long and steep hills (except Splash Mountain, and it is there for anyone to see, so you have informed consent going on the ride). I was able to build up courage to go on all of them, and the more I rode them, the more I enjoyed them—the less you tense up expecting a big long drop, the more you enjoy the special effects and even swinging around curves. Swinging around curves is really the primary motion challenge of Disney roller coasters.

Seniors who experience Disney thrill rides generally enjoy the smoother rides like Splash Mountain, Big Thunder Mountain, and Tower of Terror, and tend to dislike more jerky attractions. This letter from a Gig Harbor, Washington, woman is typical:

I am a senior woman of small stature and good health. I am writing my comments on Space Mountain, Splash Mountain, Big Thunder Mountain, and Star Tours. My experience [is that] all of the rides, with the exception of Star Tours, were wonderful rides. Star Tours is too jerky and fast, the music is too loud, and I found it to be unacceptable.

Not withstanding the reader's comment, we receive mostly positive comments from seniors concerning Star Tours. Body Wars, Test Track, and the Rock 'n' Roller Coaster, however, are different stories.

Disney, recognizing that it needs more attractions that appeal to the youth and young adult markets, is in the process of adding some roller coasters to its parks. The first coaster to go on-line was the Rock 'n' Roller Coaster, opened at the Disney-MGM Studios in 1999. It's by far Disney's wildest coaster ever in the United States (Space Mountain at Paris Disneyland is comparable). In addition to the coaster at the Studios, Disney is planning for one or more coasters at the Animal Kingdom.

CUTTING DOWN YOUR TIME IN LINE BY UNDERSTANDING THE RIDES

There are many types of rides at Walt Disney World. Some, like The Great Movie Ride at Disney-MGM Studios, are engineered to carry more than 3,000 people every hour. At the other extreme, such rides as Dumbo the

Flying Elephant can only accommodate around 400 people an hour. Most rides fall somewhere in between. Many factors figure into how long you will wait to experience a ride: its popularity; how it loads and unloads; how many persons can ride at one time; how many units (cars, rockets, boats, flying elephants, etc.) are in service at a time; and how many staff are available to operate the ride. Let's take each factor one by one.

1. How Popular Is the Ride?

Newer rides like the Rock 'n' Roller Coaster at Disney-MGM Studios, Kali River Rapids at the Animal Kingdom, and Test Track at Epcot attract a lot of people, as do such longtime favorites as the Jungle Cruise in the Magic Kingdom. If you know a ride is popular, you need to know how it operates in order to determine the best time to ride. But a ride need not be especially popular to form long lines; the lines can result from weak traffic engineering (i.e., it takes so long to load and unload that a line builds regardless). This is the case at the Mad Tea Party and Cinderella's Golden Carrousel in Fantasyland. Since mostly children and teens ride the Mad Tea Party, it serves only a small percentage of any day's attendance at the Magic Kingdom. Yet, because it takes so long to load and unload, long waiting lines form.

2. How Does the Ride Load and Unload?

Some rides never stop. They are like circular conveyor belts that go around and around. These are "continuous loaders." The Magic Kingdom's The Haunted Mansion and Epcot's Spaceship Earth are continuous loaders. The number of people that can be moved through in an hour depends on how many cars, "doom buggies," or whatever are on the conveyor. The Haunted Mansion and Spaceship Earth have lots of cars on the conveyor belt and consequently can each move more than 2,000 people an hour.

Other rides are "interval loaders." Cars are unloaded, loaded, and dispatched at set intervals (sometimes controlled manually, sometimes by computer). Space Mountain in Tomorrowland is an interval loader. It has two tracks (the ride has been duplicated in the same facility). Each track can run as many as 14 space capsules, released at 36-, 26-, or 21-second intervals. (The bigger the crowd, the shorter the interval.)

In one kind of interval loader (Space Mountain), empty cars (space capsules) are returned to where they line up for reloading. In a second type, one group of riders enters the vehicle while the previous group departs. These are "in-and-out" interval loaders. Splash Mountain is a good example of an in-and-out loader. As a boat docks, those who have just completed their ride exit to the left. At almost the same time, those waiting to ride enter the boat from the right. The reloaded boat is released to the dispatch point a few yards down the line where it is launched according to the interval being used.

Interval loaders of both types can be very efficient at moving people if (1) the dispatch (launch) interval is relatively short and (2) the ride can accommodate a large number of vehicles at one time. Since many boats can be floating through Pirates of the Caribbean at one time, and since the dispatch interval is short, almost 3,000 people an hour can see this attraction.

The least efficient rides, in terms of traffic engineering, are "cycle rides," also called "stop-and-go" rides. On cycle rides, those waiting to ride exchange places with those who have just ridden. Unlike in-and-out interval rides, cycle rides shut down during loading and unloading. While one boat is loading and unloading in It's a Small World (an interval loader), many other boats are advancing through the ride. But when Dumbo the Flying Elephant touches down, the whole ride is at a standstill until the next flight is launched. Likewise, with Cinderella's Golden Carrousel, all riders dismount and the Carrousel stands idle until the next group is ready to ride.

In cycle rides, the time the ride is in motion is "ride time." The time the ride idles while loading and unloading is "load time." Load time plus ride time equals "cycle time," or the time from the start of one run of the ride until the start of the next.

The only cycle rides in Disney World are in the Magic Kingdom.

3. How Many Persons Can Ride at One Time?

This figure expresses "per-ride capacity" or "system capacity." Either way, it's the number of people who can ride at one time. The greater the carrying capacity of a ride (all other things being equal), the more visitors it can accommodate in an hour. Some rides can add extra units (cars, boats, etc.) as crowds build to increase capacity, while others, like the Astro Orbiter in Tomorrowland, have a fixed capacity (it's impossible to add rockets).

4. How Many "Units" Are in Service at a Given Time?

"Unit" is our term for the vehicle in which you ride. At the Mad Tea Party the unit is a tea cup; at Peter Pan's Flight it's a pirate ship. On some rides (mostly cycle rides), the number of units operating at a given time is fixed. Thus, there are always 16 flying elephants on the Dumbo ride and 90 horses on Cinderella's Golden Carrousel. There is no way to increase the capacity of such rides by adding more units. On a busy day, therefore, the only way to carry more people each hour on a fixed-unit cycle ride is to shorten the loading time or decrease the actual time the ride is in motion. The bottom line on a busy day for a cycle ride is that you will wait longer and possibly be rewarded with a shorter ride. This is why we steer you away from cycle rides unless you're willing to ride them early in the morning or late at night. The following are cycle rides, all in the Magic Kingdom:

Fantasyland	Dumbo the Flying Elephant
	Cinderella's Golden Carrousel
	Mad Tea Party
Tomorrowland	Astro Orbiter

Many other rides throughout Walt Disney World can increase their capacity by adding units as crowds build. Big Thunder Mountain Railroad in Frontierland is a good example. If attendance is light, Big Thunder can start the day by running only one of its five mine trains from one of two available loading platforms. If lines build, the other loading platform is opened and more mine trains are placed into operation. At full capacity, the five trains can carry about 2,400 persons an hour. Likewise, Star Tours at Disney-MGM Studios can increase its capacity by using all of its simulators, and the Maelstrom boat ride at Epcot can add more Viking ships. Sometimes a long queue will disappear almost instantly when new units are brought on-line. When an interval loader places more units into operation, it usually shortens the dispatch intervals, allowing more units to be dispatched more often.

5. How Many Staff Are Available to Operate the Ride?

Allocating additional staff to a ride can allow more units to operate or additional loading or holding areas to open. In the Magic Kingdom, Pirates of the Caribbean and It's a Small World can run two separate waiting lines and loading zones. The Haunted Mansion has a one-and-a-half-minute preshow that is staged in a "stretch room." On busy days, a second stretch room can be activated, permitting a more continuous flow of visitors to the actual loading area.

Additional staff makes a world of difference to some cycle rides. Often, the Mad Tea Party has only one attendant. This person alone must clear visitors from the ride just completed, admit and seat visitors for the upcoming ride, check that each tea cup is properly secured, return to the control panel, issue instructions to the riders, and finally activate the ride (whew!). A second attendant divides these responsibilities and cuts loading time by 25 to 50%.

By knowing the way a ride loads, its approximate hourly capacity, and its relative popularity, we can anticipate which rides are likely to develop long lines and, more important, how long we will have to wait to ride at any given time of day.

CUTTING YOUR TIME IN LINE
BY UNDERSTANDING THE SHOWS

Many featured attractions at Walt Disney World are theater presentations. While they aren't as complex as rides from a traffic engineering standpoint, understanding their operation may save touring time.

Most theater attractions operate in three phases:

1. Guests are in the theater viewing the presentation.

2. Guests who have passed through the turnstile wait in a hold-ing area or lobby. These people will be admitted to the theater as soon as the show in progress concludes. Several attractions offer a preshow in their lobby to entertain guests until they're admitted to the main show. Examples include *Tropical Sere-nade (Enchanted Tiki Birds)* and *Alien Encounter* in the Magic Kingdom; The Living Seas and *Honey, I Shrunk the Audience* at Epcot; and *Sounds Dangerous* and *MuppetVision 4D* at Disney-MGM Studios.

3. A line waits outside. Guests in line will enter the lobby when there is room and will ultimately move into the theater.

Theater capacity, the presentation's popularity, and attendance level in the park determine how long lines will be at a theater attraction. Except for holidays and other days of heavy attendance, the longest wait for a show usually doesn't exceed the length of one complete performance.

Since almost all theater attractions run continuously, stopping only long enough for the previous audience to leave and the waiting audience to enter, a performance will be in progress when you arrive. *Impressions de France* in the French pavilion at Epcot is 18 minutes in duration; your longest wait under normal circumstances is about 18 minutes if you arrive just after the show has begun.

All theaters (except the Main Street Cinema in the Magic Kingdom and various amphitheater productions) are very strict about access. Unlike a movie theater at home, you can't enter during a performance. This being the case, you will always have at least a short wait.

Most theaters hold a lot of people. When a new audience is admitted, the outside line (if there is one) usually will disappear. Exceptions are *Country Bear Jamboree* and *The Legend of the Lion King* in the Magic Kingdom; *The Making of Me* in the Wonders of Life pavilion and *Honey, I Shrunk the Audience* in the Imagination pavilion at Epcot; and *Voyage of the Little Mermaid* and *MuppetVision 4D* at Disney-MGM Studios; and *It's Tough to Be a Bug!* and *Festival of the Lion King* at the Animal Kingdom. Because these shows are so popular (or have a small capacity, like *The Making of Me*), you may have to wait through two or more shows before you're admitted (unless you go early in the morning).

HOW TO DEAL WITH OBNOXIOUS PEOPLE

At every theater presentation at Walt Disney World, visitors in the preshow area elbow, nudge, and crowd one another in order to make sure they're admitted to the performance. It's unnecessary. If you are admitted through the turnstile into the preshow area, a seat has automatically been allocated for you in the theater. When it's time to enter the theater, don't rush. Relax and let other people jam the doorways. When the congestion eases, stroll in and take a seat.

Attendants at many theaters will instruct you to enter a row of seats and move completely to the far side, filling every seat. Invariably, some inconsiderate yahoo will plop down in the middle of the row, stopping traffic or forcing other visitors to climb over him. Take our word for it: There is no such thing as a bad seat. All Disney theaters are designed to provide a near-perfect view from every seat. Our recommendation is to follow instructions and move to the far end of the row.

Visitors are also asked not to use flash photography in the theaters (the theaters are too dark for the pictures to turn out, and the flash disturbs other viewers). This admonition is routinely ignored. Flashers are more difficult to deal with than row-blockers. Options: Threaten to turn the offender over to Disney security or, better, hold your hand over the lens (you have to be quick) when they raise their camera.

Part Three

Selecting Your Hotel

The Basic Considerations

Locating a suitable hotel or condo is critical to planning any Walt Disney World vacation. The basic question is whether to stay in the World. Luxury lodging can be found both in and out of Disney World. Budget lodging is another story. Room rates start at about $90 a night in the World and range to more than $500. Outside Disney World, rooms are as low as $35 a night at some independent motels.

Beyond affordability is the convenience issue. We've lodged both in and out of Walt Disney World, and there is special magic and peace of mind associated with staying inside Disney World. "I feel more a part of everything and less like a visitor," one guest writes.

There's no real hardship in staying outside Disney World and driving (or taking a hotel shuttle) to the theme parks. Meals can be less expensive, and rooming outside the World makes you more receptive toward other Orlando-area attractions and eating establishments. Universal Studios, Universal's Islands of Adventure, Kennedy Space Center, Sea World, and Cypress Gardens, among others, are well worth your attention.

Lodging prices are subject to change, but our researchers lodged in an excellent (though not plush) motel surrounded by beautiful orange groves for half the cost of staying in the least expensive Disney hotel. Our commute to the Magic Kingdom or Epcot parking lots was 17 minutes one way.

If you have young children, read Part 5: Walt Disney World with Kids (pages 163–211) before choosing lodging. Similarly, seniors, couples on a honeymoon or romantic holiday, and disabled guests should read the applicable sections of Part 6: Special Tips for Special People (pages 212–228) before choosing a hotel.

BENEFITS OF STAYING IN THE WORLD

Walt Disney World resort hotel and campground guests have privileges and amenities unavailable to those staying outside the World. Though some of these perks are only advertising gimmicks, others are real and potentially valuable. Here are the benefits and what they mean:

1. Convenience The commute to the theme parks is short via the Disney Transportation System. This is especially advantageous if you stay in one of the hotels connected by the monorail or boat service. If you have a car, however, there are dozens of hotels outside Disney World that are within 5 to 10 minutes of theme park parking lots.

2. Early Entry at the Theme Parks Walt Disney World lodging guests (excluding guests at the independent hotels of Disney Village Hotel Plaza) are invited to enter a designated theme park one hour earlier than the general public each day. Disney lodging guests are also offered specials on admission, including a passport good for the exact number of days of their visit and discount tickets to the water theme parks. These benefits are subject to change without notice. The early-entry program, however, is in its eighth year.

Early entry can be quite valuable during peak season when the parks are mobbed. If you're willing to get up before sunrise and arrive at the park as early as 6:30 a.m., you'll be rewarded with the least congested, most stress-free touring of your vacation. Early entry is also handy during off-season when the parks close early. Though crowds are manageable at these times, adding an extra hour and a half to an otherwise short touring day significantly increases the number of attractions you'll be able to see.

Disney has also been running a program that (for an extra $10) allows resort guests with certain multiday passes to remain in the park two to three hours after official closing time. For more on this program see pages 453–454.

3. Babysitting and Childcare Options A number of options for baby-sitting, childcare, and children's programs are offered to Disney hotel and campground guests. Each of the resort hotels connected by the monorail, as well as several other Disney hotels, offers "clubs," or themed childcare centers, where potty-trained children ages 3 to 12 can stay while the adults go out.

Though somewhat expensive, the clubs do a great job and are highly regarded by children and parents. On the negative side, they're open only in the evening and not all Disney hotels have them. If you're staying at a Disney hotel that doesn't have a childcare club, you're better off using one of the private in-room babysitting services such as Fairy Godmother or Kinder-Care (page 209). In-room babysitting is also available at hotels outside Disney World.

4. Guaranteed Theme Park Admissions   On days of unusually heavy attendance, Disney resort guests are guaranteed admission to the theme parks. In practice, no guest is ever turned away until a theme park's parking lot is full. When this happens, that park most certainly will be packed to the point of gridlock. Under such conditions, you would have to possess the common sense of an amoeba to exercise your guaranteed-admission privilege. The privilege, by the way, doesn't extend to the swimming parks, Blizzard Beach, Typhoon Lagoon, or River Country.

5. Children Sharing a Room with Their Parents   There is no extra charge per night for children younger than 18 sharing a room with their parents. Many hotels outside Disney World also observe this practice.

6. Free Parking   Disney resort guests with cars don't have to pay for parking in the theme park lots. This privilege saves about $5 per day.

7. Recreational Privileges   Disney resort guests get preferential treatment for tee times at the golf courses.

STAYING IN OR OUT OF THE WORLD: WEIGHING THE PROS AND CONS

1. Cost   If cost is a primary consideration, you'll lodge much less expensively outside of Disney World. Our hotel quality and cost ratings (pages 136–147) compare specific hotels both in and out of the World.

2. Ease of Access   Even if you stay in Disney World, you're dependent on some mode of transportation. It may be less stressful to use Disney transportation, but with the single exception of commuting to the Magic Kingdom, the fastest, most efficient, and most flexible way to get around is usually a car. If you're at Epcot, for example, and want to take the kids back to Disney's Grand Floridian Beach Resort for a nap, forget the monorail. You'll get back much faster in your own car.

A reader from Raynham, Massachusetts, who stayed at the Caribbean Beach Resort (and liked it very much) writes:

> *Even though the resort is on the Disney bus line, I recommend renting a car if it [fits] one's budget. The buses do not go directly to*

many destinations and often you have to switch at the
Transportation and Ticket Center. Getting a [bus] seat in the
morning is no problem [because] they allow standees. Getting a bus
back to the hotel after a hard day can mean a long wait in line.

It must be said that the Disney transportation system, particularly the bus system, is about as efficient as humanly possible. No matter where you're going, you rarely wait more than 15 to 20 minutes for a bus, monorail, or boat. Although it is only for the use and benefit of Disney guests, it nonetheless *is* public transportation and users must expect the inconveniences inherent in any transportation system: conveyances that arrive and depart on their schedule, not yours; the occasional need to transfer; multiple stops; time lost loading and unloading large numbers of passengers; and, generally, the challenge of understanding and using a large, complex transportation network.

If you plan to have a car, consider this: Walt Disney World is so large that some destinations within the World can be reached more quickly from off-property hotels than from Disney hotels. For example, guests at hotels and motels on US 192 (near the so-called Walt Disney World main entrance) are closer to Disney-MGM Studios, the Animal Kingdom, and Blizzard Beach water park than guests at many hotels inside Disney World.

3. Young Children   Although the hassle of commuting to most outside-World hotels is only slightly (if at all) greater than that of commuting to Disney hotels, a definite peace of mind results from staying in Walt Disney World. The salient point, regardless where you stay, is to make sure you get your young children back to the hotel for a nap each day.

4. Splitting Up   If you're in a party that probably will split up to tour (as frequently happens in families with children of widely varying ages), staying in the World offers more transportation options and, thus, more independence. Mom and Dad can take the car and return to the hotel for a relaxed dinner and early bedtime while the teens remain in the park for evening parades and fireworks.

5. Feeding the Army of the Potomac   If you have a large crew that chows down like cattle on a finishing lot, you may do better staying outside the World, where food is far less expensive.

6. Visiting Other Orlando-Area Attractions   If you plan to visit Sea World, Kennedy Space Center, Universal Studios, or other area attractions, it may be more convenient to stay outside the World.

How to Get Discounts on Lodging at Walt Disney World

There are so many guest rooms in and around Walt Disney World that competition is brisk, and everyone, including Disney, wheels and deals to keep them filled. This has led to a more flexible discount policy for Disney World hotels. Here are tips for getting price breaks:

1. Seasonal Savings   You can save from $15 to $50 per night on a Walt Disney World hotel room by scheduling your visit during the slower times of the year. Disney uses so many adjectives (regular, holiday, peak, value, etc.) to describe its seasonal calendar, however, that it's hard to keep up without a scorecard. To confuse matters more, the dates for each "season" vary from resort to resort. Our advice: if you're set on staying at a Disney resort, obtain a copy of the Walt Disney Travel Company Walt Disney World Vacations Brochure, described on page 32.

2. Ask about Specials   When you talk to Disney reservationists, inquire specifically about special deals. Ask, for example, "What special rates or discounts are available at Disney hotels during the time of our visit?" Being specific and assertive paid off for an Illinois reader:

> *I called Disney's reservations number and asked for availability and rates. . . . [Because] of the* Unofficial Guide *warning about Disney reservationists answering only the questions posed, I specifically asked, "Are there any special rates or discounts for that room during the month of October?" She replied, "Yes, we have that room available at a special price. . . ." [For] the price of one phone call, I saved $440.*

3. Ocala Disney AAA Travel Center   The Ocala Disney AAA Travel Center off I-75 in Ocala, Florida, routinely books Disney hotel rooms at discounts of up to 43%! The discounts are offered as an incentive to walk-in travelers who may not have considered lodging at a Disney property or even going to Disney World. The number of rooms available varies according to date and season, but you almost always can count on getting a good deal. Because the program is designed to snare uncommitted travelers, you must reserve your room in person at the center. If you call in advance and tell staffers you're on your way down, however, they usually will tell you what's available and at what discount. The phone number is (352) 854-0770. You can also arrange priority seating for dining. The center is open daily from 9 a.m. to 6 p.m.

4. Travel Agents   Once ineligible for commissions on Disney bookings, travel agents now are active players and particularly good sources of information on time-limited special programs and discounts.

5. Disney Shareholder Discounts   The discount program for Walt Disney Company shareholders has been effectively dismantled. Disney shareholders are currently offered only a modest discount on the purchase of a Magic Kingdom Club Gold Card, available to the public for about $65. For information, call (800) 49-DISNEY.

6. Magic Kingdom Club Gold Card   The Magic Kingdom Club is offered as a benefit by employers, credit unions, and organizations. Membership provides a 10–20% discount on Disney lodging and a 5% discount on theme park tickets, among other things. Almost all state and federal government employees are Magic Kingdom Club members (though many don't know it). Ask your personnel department if this benefit is provided. Persons not signed up through work can buy a two-year individual Magic Kingdom Club Gold Card for about $65. A seniors card is about $50. For information, call (714) 781-1550 or write:

Magic Kingdom Club Gold Card
P.O. Box 3850
Anaheim, CA 92803-9832

A dad from Bay Minette, Alabama, chastised us for not giving the Gold Card its due:

> *You didn't say much about the MK Club Gold Card. We went again in late September. It was really crowded. We bought the MK Club Gold Card and saved $300–400 on our rooms and tickets.*

Another pleased Gold Club card holder wrote, suggesting:

> *Contrive to emphasize the MK Gold Card. Between the vacation package and rental car, I estimate I saved about $600 to $700.*

7. Annual Passports   Walt Disney World Annual Passport holders are offered special discounts on rooms at various times. For details on passports, see page 57.

8. Organizations and Auto Clubs   Eager to sell rooms, Disney has developed time-limited programs with some auto clubs and other organizations. Recently, for example, AAA members were offered a 10–20% savings on Disney hotels, preferred parking at the theme parks, and discounts on Disney package vacations. Such deals come and go, but the market suggests there will be more in the next year. If you're a member of AARP, AAA, or any travel or auto club, ask whether the group has a program before shopping elsewhere.

9. Room Upgrades Sometimes, a room upgrade is as good as a discount. If you're visiting Disney World during a slower time, book the least expensive room your discounts will allow. Checking in, ask very politely about being upgraded to a "water-" or "pool-view" room. A fair percentage of the time, you'll get one at no additional charge.

10. Extra-Night Discounts During slower times, book your Disney hotel for half the period you intend to stay. Often, the hotel will offer extra nights at a discounted rate to get you to stay longer.

WALT DISNEY WORLD LODGING*

The Grand Floridian, Polynesian, Contemporary, Wilderness Lodge, and Shades of Green resorts are near the Magic Kingdom. The Walt Disney World Swan and Dolphin hotels, the Yacht and Beach Club Resorts, and Disney's BoardWalk Inn and Villas are near Epcot. The Villas at the Disney Institute (formerly the Disney Institute Resort) are on the far northeast side of Walt Disney World. The All-Star and Coronado Springs resorts occupy a similar position on the far southwest side. Centrally located are the Caribbean Beach Resort and, along Bonnet Creek, the Old Key West, Port Orleans, and Dixie Landings resorts.

Choosing a Walt Disney World Hotel

If you want to stay in Walt Disney World but don't know which hotel to choose, consider:

1. Cost First, look at your budget. Rooms start at about $75 a night at the All-Star resorts and top out near $650 at the Grand Floridian. Suites are more expensive.

The BoardWalk Villas, Old Key West Resort, and Villas at the Disney Institute offer condo-type accommodations with one-, two-, and three-bedroom units complete with kitchens, living rooms, VCRs, and washers and dryers. Prices range from about $295 per night for a one-bedroom townhouse at the Disney Institute to more than $1,150 per night for a three-bedroom villa at the BoardWalk Villas. Fully equipped cabins and house trailers at Fort

---

*Rates vary depending on room location (view) and/or season, and are subject to change.

Wilderness Campground cost $180–275 per night. A limited number of suites are available at the more expensive Disney resorts, but they don't have kitchens.

Also at Disney World are the seven hotels of the Disney Village Hotel Plaza. Although commodious, rooms in these hotels are sometimes more expensive than at hotels served by the monorail. We find few bargains at the Village Hotel Plaza and feel less of the excitement one has when staying inside the World. While the Village Hotel Plaza is technically part of Disney World, staying there is like visiting a colony rather than the mother country. Early entry and free parking at the theme parks aren't offered, and the hotels operate their own buses rather than use Disney transportation.

Not included in these rankings or in the following discussion is Shades of Green, formerly known as the Disney Inn. Shades of Green was purchased by the U.S. Department of Defense in 1994 for the exclusive use of active-duty and retired servicemen. Rates at Shades of Green, one of the nicest Disney World hotels, are based on the guest's rank: the higher the rank, the greater the cost. All rooms, however, regardless of rank, go for a fraction of what military personnel would pay at other Disney resorts. According to a serviceman from Fort Worth, Texas, Shades of Green is the way to go:

> *Shades of Green is the best-kept secret in Disney. It is actually a [military] resort in the Disney complex with all the benefits of being a Disney resort. It was a great deal, and military members usually look for the best deals. When my wife and I stayed there in May, we paid $58 a night. That is not per person. That was the total price. The price will vary according to your rank. The hotel was very nice. The rooms were huge. It had two double beds and a lot of room to spare. They also had VCRs in the rooms and a movie vending machine on the second floor. The rooms also had a coffee machine with packets of coffee, the drink of the military. Shades of Green is right across the street from the Polynesian Resort. It is about a 10–15 minute walk to the Ticket and Transportation Center. The hotel does have shuttle buses that take you to the TTC and that is about a 2-minute ride. Our overall stay at Shades of Green was wonderful. I would highly recommend this hotel to anyone who is eligible to use it.*

What It Costs to Stay in a Disney Resort Hotel	
Grand Floridian	$300–650
Swan (Westin)	$290–455
Dolphin (Sheraton)	$290–455
Polynesian Resort	$275–530
Beach Club Resort	$265–540
Yacht Club Resort	$265–540
BoardWalk Inn	$255–500
BoardWalk Villas	$255– 350 (studio)
Old Key West Resort	$230–300 (studio)
Contemporary Resort	$215–460
Villas at the Disney Institute	$205–275 (bungalow)
Wilderness Lodge	$180–390
Coronado Springs Resort	$120–185
Caribbean Beach Resort	$120–185
Dixie Landings Resort	$120–185
Port Orleans Resort	$120–185
All-Star resorts	$75–105

What It Costs to Stay in the Disney Village Hotel Plaza	
The Hilton Resort	$190–460
Wyndham Palace	$155–465
DoubleTree Guest Suites Resort	$140–270
Best Western Hotel	$125–300
Grosvenor Resort	$110–230
Hotel Royal Plaza	$110–215
Courtyard by Marriott	$90–180

2. Location   Once you have determined your budget, think about what you want to do at Walt Disney World. Will you go to all four theme parks, or will you concentrate on one or two?

If you intend to use your own car, the location of your Disney hotel isn't especially important unless you plan to spend most of your time at the Magic Kingdom. (Disney transportation is always more efficient than your car in this case because it bypasses the Transportation and Ticket Center and deposits you at the theme park entrance.) If you haven't decided whether you want a car for your Disney vacation, see "How to Travel around the World" (pages 235–251).

Most convenient to the Magic Kingdom are the three resorts linked by monorail: the Grand Floridian, Contemporary, and Polynesian. Commuting to the Magic Kingdom via monorail is quick and simple, allowing visitors to return to their hotel for a nap, swim, or meal.

The Contemporary Resort, in addition to being on the monorail, is only a 10–15–minute walk to the Magic Kingdom. Contemporary Resort guests reach Epcot by monorail but must transfer at the Transportation and Ticket Center. Buses connect the Contemporary to Disney-MGM Studios and the Animal Kingdom. No transfer is required, but the bus makes several stops before heading to either destination.

The Polynesian Resort is served by the Magic Kingdom monorail and is an easy walk from the Transportation and Ticket Center, Disney World's transportation hub. At the transportation center you can catch an express monorail to Epcot. This makes the Polynesian the only Disney resort with direct monorail access to both Epcot and the Magic Kingdom. To minimize your walk to the transportation center, book a room in the Pago Pago, Moorea, or Oahu guest buildings.

Most convenient to Epcot and Disney-MGM Studios are the Board-Walk Inn, BoardWalk Villas, Yacht and Beach Club Resorts, and Swan and Dolphin. Though all are within easy walking distance of Epcot's International Gateway, boat service is also available. Vessels also connect Epcot hotels to Disney-MGM Studios. Epcot hotels are best for guests planning to spend most of their time at Epcot and/or Disney MGM Studios.

If you plan to use Disney transportation and intend to visit all four major parks and one or more of the swimming theme parks, book a centrally located resort with good transportation connections. The Epcot resorts and the Polynesian, Caribbean Beach, Old Key West, Dixie Landings, and Port Orleans resorts fit the bill.

Though not centrally located, the All-Star and Coronado Springs resorts have very good bus service to all Disney World destinations and are closest to the new Animal Kingdom theme park. Wilderness Lodge and Fort Wilderness Campground have the most convoluted transportation service.

If you plan to golf, book the Villas at the Disney Institute or the Old Key West Resort. Both resorts are built around golf courses. Shades of Green, the armed forces recreation center, is adjacent to two golf courses. Located near but not on a golf course are the Grand Floridian, Polynesian, Dixie Landings, and Port Orleans resorts. For boating and water sports, try the Polynesian, Contemporary, or Grand Floridian resorts or Wilderness Lodge. The Lodge is also the best hotel for hikers, bikers, and joggers.

3. Room Quality   Few Walt Disney World guests spend much time in their hotel rooms, though they're among the best designed and most well appointed anywhere. Plus, they're meticulously maintained. Top of the line are the spacious and luxurious rooms of the Grand Floridian. Bringing up the rear are the small, garish rooms of the All-Star resorts. But even these are sparkling clean and livable.

Here's how the Disney hotels (along with the Swan and the Dolphin, which are Westin and Sheraton hotels, respectively) stack up for quality:

Hotel	Room Quality Rating
1. Grand Floridian Beach Resort	96
2. BoardWalk Villas (studio)	95
3. Old Key West Resort (studio)	94
4. BoardWalk Inn	93
5. Beach Club Resort	92
6. Yacht Club Resort	92
7. Polynesian Resort	90
8. Contemporary Resort	87
9. Coronado Springs Resort	86
10. Dolphin (Sheraton)	86
11. Swan (Westin)	86
12. Wilderness Lodge	86
13. Caribbean Beach Resort	84
14. Dixie Landings Resort	84
15. Port Orleans Resort	84
16. Villas at the Disney Institute	82
17. All-Star resorts	73

4. The Size of Your Group   Larger families and groups may be interested in how many persons can be accommodated in a Disney resort room, but only Lilliputians would be comfortable in a room filled to capacity. Groups requiring two or more guest rooms should consider condo/villa accommodations, either in or out of Walt Disney World. The most cost-efficient lodging in Walt Disney World for groups of five or six persons are the cabins or the wilderness homes at Fort Wilderness Campground. Both sleep six adults plus a child or toddler in a crib. If there are more than six in your party, you will need either two hotel rooms, a suite (see Wilderness Lodge below), or a condo.

Hotel	Maximum Number of Persons per Room
All-Star Resorts	4 persons plus child in crib
Beach Club Resort	5 persons plus child in crib

BoardWalk Inn	4 or 5 persons plus child in crib
BoardWalk Villas	8 persons plus child in crib
Caribbean Beach Resort	4 persons plus child in crib
Contemporary Resort	5 persons plus child in crib
Coronado Springs Resort	4 persons plus child in crib
Dixie Landings Resort	4 persons plus child in crib; 5 persons in room with child's trundle bed
Dolphin (Sheraton)	5 persons
Fort Wilderness Homes	6 persons plus child in crib
Grand Floridian Beach Resort	4 or 5 persons plus child in crib
Old Key West Resort	8 persons plus child in crib
Polynesian Resort	5 persons plus child in crib
Port Orleans Resort	4 persons plus child in crib
Swan (Westin)	4 persons
Villas at Disney Institute	8 persons plus child in crib
Wilderness Lodge	4 persons plus child in crib; junior suites with bunk beds accommodate 6 persons
Yacht Club Resort	5 persons plus child in crib

5. Theme All of the Disney hotels are themed. Each is designed to make you feel you're in a special place or period of history. Here are the themes at Disney resorts:

Hotel	Theme
All-Star Resorts	Sports, music, and movies
Beach Club Resorts	New England beach club of the 1870s
BoardWalk Inn	East coast boardwalk hotel of the early 1900s
BoardWalk Villas	East coast beach cottage of the early 1900s
Caribbean Beach Resort	Caribbean islands
Contemporary Resort	The future as perceived by past and present generations
Coronado Springs Resort	Northern Mexico and the American Southwest
Dixie Landings Resort	Life on the Mississippi in the antebellum South
Dolphin (Sheraton)	Modern Florida resort
Grand Floridian Beach Resort	Turn-of-the-century luxury hotel
Old Key West Resort	Key West

Polynesian Resort	Hawaii/South Sea islands
Port Orleans	Turn-of-the-century New Orleans and Mardi Gras
Swan (Westin)	Modern Florida resort
Villas at the Disney Institute	Combination rustic villas and country club atmosphere
Wilderness Lodge	National park grand lodge of the early 1900s in the American northwest
Yacht Club Resort	New England seashore hotel of the 1880s

Some resorts carry off their themes better than others, and some themes are more exciting. The Wilderness Lodge, for example, is extraordinary. The lobby opens eight stories to a timbered ceiling supported by giant columns of bundled logs. One look eases you into the Northwest-wilderness theme. Romantic and isolated, the lodge is a great choice for couples and seniors, and is heaven for children.

The Polynesian, likewise dramatic, conveys the feeling of the Pacific islands. It's great for romantics and families. Waterfront rooms in the Moorea building offer a perfect view of Cinderella Castle and the Magic Kingdom fireworks across Seven Seas Lagoon.

Grandeur, nostalgia, and privilege are central to the Grand Floridian and Yacht and Beach Club resorts and the BoardWalk Inn and Villas. Although modeled after eastern-seaboard hotels of different eras, the resorts are amazingly similar. Thematic distinctions are subtle and are lost on many guests.

The Port Orleans Resort lacks the mystery and sultriness of the New Orleans French Quarter, but it's hard to replicate the Big Easy in a sanitized Disney version. Dixie Landings, however, hits the mark with its antebellum Mississippi River theme, as does Old Key West Resort with its Florida Keys theme. The Caribbean Beach Resort's theme is much more effective at night, thanks to creative lighting. By day, the resort looks like a Miami condo development.

Coronado Springs Resort offers several styles of Mexican and Southwestern American architecture. Though the lake setting is lovely and the resort is attractive and inviting, the theme (with the exception of the main swimming area) isn't especially stimulating. Coronado Springs feels more like a Scottsdale, Arizona, country club than a Disney resort.

The All-Star resorts encompass 30 three-story, T-shaped hotels with almost 6,000 guest rooms. There are 15 themed areas: five celebrate sports (surfing, basketball, tennis, football, and baseball), five recall Hollywood movie themes, and five have musical motifs. The resort's design, with entrances shaped like giant dalmations, Coke cups, footballs, and the like, is pretty adolescent, sacrificing grace and beauty for energy and novelty. Guest rooms are small, with decor reminiscent of your teenage son's bedroom. Despite the theme, there are no sports, music, or movies at the All-Star Resorts.

Pretense aside, the Contemporary, Swan, and Dolphin are essentially themeless though architecturally interesting. The Contemporary is a 15-story, A-frame building with monorails running through the middle. Views from guest rooms in the Contemporary Tower are among the best at Disney World. The Swan and Dolphin resorts are massive yet whimsical. Designed by Michael Graves, they're excellent examples of "entertainment architecture." Unfortunately, a little too much whimsy and entertainment worked their way into the guest rooms, which are "busy," bordering on garish.

6. Dining The best resorts for quality and selection in dining are the Epcot resorts: Swan, Dolphin, Yacht, and Beach Club resorts, and Board-Walk Inn and Villas. Each has good restaurants and is within easy walking distance of the others and of the ten ethnic restaurants in the World Showcase section of Epcot. If you stay at an Epcot resort, you have 21 of Walt Disney World's finest restaurants within a 5- to 12-minute walk.

The only other place in Disney World where restaurants and hotels are similarly concentrated is at the Disney Village Hotel Plaza. In addition to restaurants in the hotels themselves, the Hilton, Courtyard by Marriott, Grosvenor Resort, and Wyndham Palace are within walking distance of restaurants at Downtown Disney.

Guests at the Contemporary, Polynesian, and Grand Floridian can eat in their hotel, or they can commute to restaurants in the Magic Kingdom (not recommended) or in other monorail-linked hotels. Riding the monorail to another hotel or to the Magic Kingdom takes about ten minutes each way, not counting the wait for the train.

All of the other Disney resorts are somewhat isolated. This means you're stuck dining at your hotel unless (1) you have a car and can go anywhere you like or (2) you eat your meals at the theme parks or Downtown Disney.

Here's the deal. Disney transportation works fine for commuting from hotels to the theme parks and Downtown Disney, but it's hopeless for getting from one hotel to another. If you're staying at Dixie Landings and want to dine at the Swan, forget it. It will take you up to an hour and a half each way by bus. You could take a bus to the Magic Kingdom and catch a train to one of the monorail-served hotels for dinner. That would take "only" 45 minutes each way.

Of the more isolated resorts, the Wilderness Lodge serves the best food and offers the most varied selection. Next in quality are the Villas at the Disney Institute. The Coronado Springs, Port Orleans, Dixie Landings, Old

Key West, and Caribbean Beach resorts each have a full-service restaurant of acceptable quality, a food court, and in-room pizza delivery. None of the isolated resorts, however, offer enough variety for the average person to be happy eating in his/her hotel every day. The All-Star resorts, Disney's most isolated hotel, have nearly 6,000 guest rooms but no full-service restaurant. There are three food courts, but you have to get to them before 11 p.m.

7. Amenities and Recreation   Disney resorts offer a staggering variety of amenities and recreational opportunities. All provide elaborate swimming pools, themed shops, restaurants or food courts, bar or lounge, and access to the five Disney golf courses. Predictably, the more you pay for your lodging, the more amenities and opportunities you have. The Grand Floridian, Yacht and Beach Club resorts, and Swan and Dolphin, for example, offer concierge floors.

For sunning and swimming, the Contemporary, Polynesian, Wilderness Lodge, and Grand Floridian offer both pools and white-sand beaches on Bay Lake or Seven Seas Lagoon. The Caribbean Beach Resort also provides both pools and beaches. Though lacking a beach, the Yacht and Beach Club, Port Orleans, Dixie Landings, and Coronado Springs resorts and the BoardWalk Inn and Villas have exceptionally creative pools.

Bay Lake and the Seven Seas Lagoon are the best venues for boating. Resorts fronting these lakes are the Contemporary, Polynesian, Wilderness Lodge, Grand Floridian, and Fort Wilderness Campground. Though situated on smaller bodies of water, the Caribbean Beach, Old Key West, Port Orleans, Dixie Landings, Coronado Springs, Villas at the Disney Institute, Yacht and Beach Club, and Swan and Dolphin resorts also rent watercraft.

For sports and fitness, the Villas at the Disney Institute are unrivaled. The only Disney resort with a golf course on-site, the Villas also boast one of the nation's largest and most high-tech fitness centers. In addition, swimming, aerobics, weight training, tennis, full-court basketball, and even a climbing wall are available. Other Disney resorts with good fitness and weight-training facilities include Old Key West, BoardWalk Inn and Villas, the Contemporary, Yacht and Beach Club, and Grand Floridian resorts. Tennis is also available at Fort Wilderness Campground and the Swan and Dolphin, Grand Floridian, Yacht and Beach Club, Old Key West, and Contemporary resorts.

While there are many places to bike or jog at Disney World (including golf-cart paths), the best biking and jogging is at the Fort Wilderness Campground and the adjacent Wilderness Lodge. Also good for biking and jogging is the area along Bonnet Creek extending from Dixie Landings through Port Orleans and the Old Key West resorts toward Downtown Disney. Epcot sports several less scenic trails.

Seven Disney resorts offer evening childcare programs on-site: the Grand Floridian, Yacht and Beach Club, Polynesian, Wilderness Lodge, and Board-Walk Inn and Villas. All others offer in-room babysitting.

In the table nearby, we've outlined the amenities and recreational opportunities at each of the Disney resorts. Note that each resort listed also offers restaurants or snack bars, lounges/bars, pools, children's activities, babysitting, and shopping.

8. Nightlife The boardwalk at BoardWalk Inn and Villas has an upscale dance club, a New Orleans Pat O'Brien's–type club with dueling pianos and sing-alongs, a brew pub, and a sports bar. Boardwalk clubs are within easy walking distance of all the Epcot resorts. Similarly, some of the Villas at the Disney Institute are within walking distance of the nightlife at Downtown Disney. Nightlife at other Disney resorts is limited to lounges that stay open late. The best are Mizner's Lounge at the Grand Floridian and the California Grill Lounge on the 15th floor of the Contemporary Resort. At the California Grill Lounge, you can relax with a drink and watch the fireworks at the nearby Magic Kingdom.

Camping at Walt Disney World

Fort Wilderness Campground is a spacious resort campground for tent and RV camping. Fully equipped, air-conditioned trailers also are available for rent, as are newer prefab log cabins. The log cabins offer essentially the same square footage as the trailers (known as "wilderness homes") but are newer, more aesthetically appealing, and have an elevated outdoor deck. Campsites, "preferred" or "regular," are arranged on loops branching from three thoroughfares. The only difference between a preferred and regular campsite is that preferred sites are closer to the campground amenities (swimming pools, restaurants, and shopping). All sites have a 110- and 220-volt outlet, picnic table, and grill. Most RV sites have sanitary hookups. RV sites are roomy by eastern-U.S. standards, but tent campers will probably feel a little cramped. On any day, about 90% of campers will be RVers.

When booking, tent campers should request a site on Loop 1500, Cottontail Curl, or on Loop 2000, Spanish Moss Lane. The better loops for RVers are Loops 200, 400, 500, and 1400. All loops have a comfort station with showers, toilets, phones, an ice machine, and a coin laundry.

Rental trailers and cabins offer a double bed and two bunk beds in the only bedroom, augmented by a Murphy bed (pulls down from the wall) in the living room. There is one rather small bathroom with shower and tub.

Aside from offering economy accommodations, Fort Wilderness Campground has a group camping area, evening entertainment, horseback riding,

Disney Resort Amenities and Recreation

	Suites	Concierge
Disney's All-Star Sports and Music Resorts		
Disney's BoardWalk Inn	•	•
Disney's BoardWalk Villas	•	
Disney's Caribbean Beach Resort		
Disney's Contemporary Resort	•	•
Disney's Coronado Springs Resort	•	
Disney's Dixie Landings Resort		
Disney's Fort Wilderness Homes		
Disney's Grand Floridian Beach Resort	•	•
Disney's Old Key West Resort	•	
Disney's Polynesian Resort	•	•
Disney's Port Orleans Resort		
Disney's Wilderness Lodge	•	
Disney's Yacht and Beach Club Resorts	•	•
Disney Institute Resort	•	
Shades of Green		•
Walt Disney World Dolphin		
Walt Disney World Swan		•

bike trails, jogging trails, swimming, and a petting farm. River Country water theme park is nearby. Access to the Magic Kingdom and Discovery Island is by boat from the Fort Wilderness landing on Bay Lake. Access to other destinations is by private car or shuttle bus.

If you rent a cabin or a wilderness home, particularly in the fall or spring, keep abreast of local weather conditions. These accommodations are essentially mobile homes, definitely not the place you want to be if the area is under a tornado warning.

Fort Wilderness Campground

| 784 campsites | boat/bus service | $35–74 per night |
| 408 wilderness homes and cabins (sleeps 4–6) | boat/bus service | $180–275 per night |

Number of Rooms	Room Service	Fitness Center	Water Sports	Marina	Beach	Tennis	Biking
5,760							
378	•	•		•		•	•
517	•	•		•		•	•
2,112			•	•	•		•
1,041	•	•	•	•	•	•	
1,967	•	•	•	•			•
2,048			•	•			•
408			•	•	•		•
900	•	•	•	•		•	
709		•	•	•		•	•
853	•		•	•	•		
1,008			•	•			•
728	•		•	•	•		
1,213	•	•	•	•	•	•	
584		•	•	•		•	•
287	•	•			•		
1,509	•	•	•	•	•	•	
758	•	•	•	•	•		•

WALT DISNEY WORLD HOTEL PROFILES

For those of you who have plowed though the foregoing and remain undecided, we provide profiles of each of the Walt Disney World resorts.

The Magic Kingdom Resorts

Disney's Grand Floridian Beach Resort   Walt Disney World's flagship resort is inspired by the grand Victorian seaside resorts of turn-of-the-century Florida. A complex of four- and five-story white frame buildings, the Grand Floridian integrates verandas, intricate laticework, dormers, and turrets beneath a red shingle roof to capture the most memorable elements of 19th-century ocean-resort architecture. A five-story domed lobby encircled by enameled balustrades and overhung by crystal chandaliers establishes the resort's tone of understated opulence. Covering 40 acres along the Seven Seas Lagoon, the resort offers lovely pools, white-sand beaches, and a multifaceted marina. The spa at the Grand Floridian is equaled only by that of the Disney Institute.

The 900 guest rooms, while luxurious with Victorian wood trim and soft-colored-print wall coverings, are warm-and inviting without being stuffy or overly feminine. Armoires, marble-topped sinks, and ceiling fans maintain the Victorian theme. The typical room is 440 square feet (dormer rooms are smaller), large by any standard, and furnished with two queen beds, a daybed, a reading chair, and a table with two side chairs. Many rooms have a balcony.

With a high ratio of staff to guests, service is outstanding. There are several full-service restaurants at the Grand Floridian, with a number of others a short monorail ride away. The resort is connected directly to the Magic Kingdom by monorail and to other Walt Disney World destinations by bus. Walking time to the monorail and bus loading areas from the most remote guest rooms is about seven to ten minutes.

Disney's Polynesian Resort   The tropics of the South Pacific are re-created at this deluxe Walt Disney World resort. The Polynesian is composed of 11 two- and three-story Hawaiian "longhouses" situated around the four-story "Great Ceremonial House." The buildings at the Polynesian feature natural wood tones, with exposed-beam roofs and tribal-inspired geometric inlays in the cornices. The Great Ceremonial House contains restaurants, shops, and a rain-forest atrium lobby. With a rocky waterfall and over 70 species of tropical plants, the lobby reinforces the lush, verdant image of the South Seas. Spread over many acres along the Seven Seas Lagoon, the resort has a white-sand beach with volleyball courts. The Polynesian's two landscaped pools look best at night when they are illuminated with bamboo torches.

Many of the 853 guest rooms at the Polynesian offer views of the Seven Seas Lagoon. Typical rooms measure 409 square feet. While the guest rooms are smaller than most of Disney's deluxe rooms, they are quite comfortable. The rooms are furnished with two queen-size beds, a daybed, an armoire, and a table and chairs. With batik-design bedspreads and curtains and bamboo furniture, guest rooms maintain the island theme and are visually interesting. Bathrooms are somewhat small, although well designed. Many rooms have balconies.

A problem unique to the Polynesian is the proximity of the Walt Disney World Speedway. A number of guests have written complaining about the noise of roaring racecars while they were trying to nap. Rooms with parking lot views are most likely to be affected.

Service at the Polynesian is excellent. There are two full-service restaurants with easy access to others in the Magic Kingdom area via monorail. The Polynesian has a monorail station on-site and is within easy walking distance of the Transportation and Ticket Center. Bus service is available to other Walt Disney World destinations. Walking time to the bus and monorail loading areas from the most remote rooms is 8–11 minutes.

Disney's Wilderness Lodge   This deluxe Walt Disney World resort is inspired by turn-of-the-century national park lodges. The Wilderness Lodge is the most impressively themed and meticulously detailed of the Disney resorts. Situated on Bay Lake, the Lodge features an eight-story central building flanked by two seven-story guest-room wings. The rustic building features exposed timber columns, log cabin–style facades, and dormer windows. The Lodge is surrounded by evergreen pine and pampas grass landscaping. An eight-story lobby boasts an 87-foot stone fireplace and two 55-foot Pacific Northwest totem poles. In addition to these centerpieces, details like timber pillars; giant teepee chandeliers; and stone, wood, and marble-inlaid floors maintain the resort's feeling of rustic luxury. Although the Wilderness Lodge is not situated on vast acreage, it does have a beach and a delightful pool. The pool, with its mountain hot spring atmosphere, is modeled after a stone quarry and offers a waterfall and a geyser.

The 728 guest rooms at the Wilderness Lodge are suited with darkly stained mission-style furniture, which is accented by the primary colors in the decor. The Native American–patterned bedspreads, animal-motif armoires, and faux-calfskin fixtures create a cozy feeling. At 340 square feet, average rooms at the Lodge are the smallest Walt Disney World "deluxe" rooms. Typical rooms have two queen-size beds, and some have one queen-size bed and bunk beds. All rooms have a table and chairs, and a vanity outside the bathroom. Most rooms have balconies.

Service at the Wilderness Lodge is rated as excellent. There are two full-service restaurants, with several more a boat ride away. The resort is connected to the Magic Kingdom by boat and to other Disney theme parks by bus. Walking time to the bus and boat loading areas from the most remote rooms is about five to eight minutes.

Disney's Contemporary Resort   This deluxe resort is the least themed of the Walt Disney World–owned properties. The Contemporary is unique in its A-frame design that permits the Magic Kingdom monorail to pass through the structure's cavernous atrium. The only real source of color in the atrium is a 90-foot mosaic depicting Native American children and nature scenes. The white cement A-frame tower is flanked by two three-story "garden" buildings. The landscaping at the Contemporary is a little bizarre, with trees and shrubs trimmed like overgrown poodles. Situated on Bay Lake, the Contemporary offers a marina and a white-sand beach. Its swimming pool, at 6,500 square feet, is the largest of all Walt Disney World resorts.

The rooms in the Contemporary's tower building enjoy fantastic views of either Bay Lake or the Magic Kingdom. At 436 square feet, the rooms are only slightly smaller than those at the Grand Floridian. All of the rooms are tasteful albeit somewhat dull, with simple lines and neutral colors. The Contemporary is a bit cold in our opinion, and the angular lines of the furnishings make the ambiance somewhat uninviting. Most rooms have two queen-size beds, a daybed, and a table and chair. All tower rooms have balconies.

The Contemporary has a new 6,500-square-foot pool with slides and waterfalls. The resort is home to two full-service restaurants (including the well-known California Grill), a buffet restaurant, and a counter-service restaurant. There are six shops at the Contemporary. This resort is within easy walking distance to the Magic Kingdom, and transportation via monorail is available to both the Magic Kingdom and Epcot. Other Walt Disney World destinations can be accessed by bus or boat. Walking time to transportation loading areas from the most remote rooms is six to nine minutes.

Shades of Green   This deluxe resort is owned and operated by the U.S. Armed Forces and is available only to U.S. military personnel (including the National Guard, reserves, and Department of Defense). Shades of Green consists of one three-story building nestled among three golf courses. Tastefully nondescript, Shades of Green is at the same time pure peace and quiet. There is no beach or lake at Shades of Green, but there are several pools, including one shaped like Mickey's head. Although Shades of Green is open only to the military, the surrounding golf courses are open to all Walt Disney World guests.

At 455 square feet, the 288 guest rooms at Shades of Green are larger than those at the Grand Floridian. The rooms are luxuriously decorated with an English-countryside theme, with light-oak furniture, dust ruffles, and soft colors. Most rooms have two queen-size beds, a daybed, and a table and four chairs, as well as a television in an armoire. All rooms have either a patio or balcony.

Even though Shades of Green is not operated by Disney, the service here is comparable to the deluxe Walt Disney World properties. The single restaurant at Shades of Green offers both buffet and menu service. Transportation to all theme parks is by bus, with a transfer required to almost all destinations. Walking time to the bus loading area from the most remote rooms is about five minutes.

Disney's Fort Wilderness Campground   Walt Disney World's Fort Wilderness consists of 700 wooded acres with 408 Wilderness Homes and Cabins, and 784 traditional campsites. The Wilderness Homes are small mobile homes situated on a series of one-way loops near Bay Lake. The beige and brown aluminum siding on the homes blends nicely with the cypress and pine around them. While the homes are only about 20 feet apart, the vegetation between them is dense enough to provide families with a sense of privacy. Disney's Fort Wilderness area is unique in its recreation offerings; canoeing, trail rides, a petting zoo, and a beach are all within walking distance from the homes. Additionally, the homes share two "swimmin' holes" (actually modern pools).

The wilderness theme is maintained inside the mobile homes, which feature mason-jar glassware, rough-hewn furniture, and reproductions of American landscape masterpieces. However, the Wilderness Homes are not luxurious. Each home has a picnic table, a grill, and a one-car driveway. Inside the 504-square-foot homes, there is one bedroom; one bathroom; and an open living, dining, and full-kitchen area. Most Wilderness Homes sleep six people, with a queen-size bed and a set of bunk beds crammed into the bedroom, and a Murphy bed that folds out of the living room wall. Surprisingly, given the spartan accommodations, daily maid service is provided. Finally, about a dozen specially equipped disabled units are available.

Disney is in the process of replacing the older Wilderness Homes with prefab log cabins. The cabins offer the same square footage as the Wilderness Home trailers but are newer, more appealing to the eye, and offer an elevated wood deck. Inside, the cabins provide the same space division as the trailers, with a slight reconfiguration of the living room and kitchen-dining area. Cabins go for about $30 more a night than the Wilderness Homes and are, in our opinion, worth it.

There are several restaurants at Fort Wilderness, the largest of which is inaccessible by car. The Wilderness Homes are connected to the theme parks by bus and boat. Walking time to the transportation loading areas from the most remote homes and campsites is about eight minutes.

The Epcot Resorts

Disney's Yacht and Beach Club Resorts   These five-story deluxe resorts are similarly themed and adjoin each other. Both resorts have clapboard facades with whitewashed-wood trim. The Yacht Club is painted a subdued gray, while the Beach Club is painted a brighter blue. The Yacht Club has a nautical theme with model ships and antique navigational instruments gracing the public areas. The Beach Club is appointed with beach scenes in foam green and white. Both resorts have themed lobbies, with a giant globe in the Yacht Club and sea horse fixtures in the Beach Club. The resorts face 25-acre Crescent Lake and share an elaborate swimming complex.

There are 630 guest rooms at the Yacht Club and 583 at the Beach Club. Most of the rooms are 381 square feet and contain two queen-size beds, a daybed, and a table and two chairs. Like the Grand Floridian, rooms here have a lot of drawer space. Rooms at the Yacht Club are decorated with navy blue and white, while rooms at the Beach Club offer a more muted, soft-green look. Some rooms have balconies.

As deluxe Walt Disney World resorts, the Yacht and Beach clubs provide excellent service. The resorts house nine restaurants and lounges and are within walking distance of Epcot and Disney's BoardWalk. Transportation to other destinations is by bus or boat. Walking time to the transportation loading areas from the most remote rooms is seven minutes.

Disney's BoardWalk Inn and BoardWalk Villas   Situated on Crescent Lake across from the Yacht and Beach Club resorts, the BoardWalk Inn is the newest of Walt Disney World's deluxe resorts. As viewed from Crescent Lake, the complex is a detailed replica of an early-20th-century Atlantic coast boardwalk. Varied facades of hotels, diners, and shops create a waterfront skyline that is both inviting and exciting. In reality, the BoardWalk Inn and Villas form a single integrated structure behind the varied facades. Restaurants and shops occupy the boardwalk level, while Inn and Villas accommodations rise up to six stories above. Painted bright red and yellow along with weathered pastel greens and blues, the BoardWalk resorts are the only Disney hotels that use neon signage as architectural detail. The Inn and Villas share a single, old-fashioned amusement park–themed swimming pool.

The 378 deluxe rooms of the BoardWalk Inn measure 422 square feet, and most contain two queen-size brass beds, a child's cherry daybed, a cherry table and two chairs, and ceiling fans. Decorating touches include blue and yellow gingham wallpaper and print curtains with a blue postcard pattern. Rooms at the BoardWalk have more closet space than other deluxe Disney rooms. Most rooms have balconies.

The 517 BoardWalk Villas are decorated with warmer tones and primary colors, with bright tiles in the kitchen and bathrooms. Villas range in size from 359 to 1,071 square feet (studio through three-bedroom), and sleep 4 to 12 people. Many villas have full kitchens, laundry rooms, and whirlpool bathtubs. The BoardWalk Villas tend to be more expensive than similar accommodations at other Disney resorts—you pay for the address.

As the newest deluxe Walt Disney World resort, the BoardWalk Inn and Villas are very well staffed and offer excellent service. Additionally, some of Disney World's finest restaurants and shops are located at the BoardWalk. The Inn and Villas are within walking distance of Epcot and are connected to other destinations by bus and boat. Walking time to transportation loading areas from the most remote rooms is five to six minutes.

The Walt Disney World Swan and Dolphin   Although these resorts are inside Walt Disney World and Disney handles their reservations, they are owned by Sheraton (Dolphin) and Westin (Swan). The resorts face each other and are situated on either side of an inlet of Crescent Lake. The Dolphin is a 27-story triangular turquoise building. On its roof are two 56-

foot-tall fish balanced with their tails in the air. The Swan has a 12-story main building flanked by two 7-story towers. Two 47-foot-tall swans adorn its roof, staring incredulously at the fish across the way. The Swan and Dolphin have been described as "bizarre" and stylistically disjointed. At the very least they are eclectic in their theming. Disney, for its part, claims that you will step into a "fantasy world." For our part, however, the experience is more akin to a drug-induced hallucination of art deco gone haywire. The giant swans look swanlike enough, but the fish on the Dolphin look like catfish from outer space. The mood at these properties could be described alternately as adventurous or confusing, depending on how much you value the work of a good interior decorator.

The lobby at the Dolphin is the more ornate, themed like a circus big top (after all, big tops and dolphins go together like peanut butter and jelly). At the other end of the spectrum, the lobby of the Swan is so small as to appear an afterthought. Both resorts feature artwork of wildly different styles and eras (from Matisse to Roy Lichtenstein). The resorts each have their own pool. The Dolphin's "Grotto" pool is shaped like a seashell and has a waterfall, while the Swan's pool is of a conventional rectangular configuration.

The rooms at the two properties are decorated similarly, with fine art prints and bold colors. However, the rooms at the Dolphin are slightly larger, with an extra vanity. The 1,509 guest rooms at the Walt Disney World Dolphin are 360 square feet, and the 758 rooms at the Swan are 340 square feet. Both are decorated in bright turquoise and peach. Most rooms have two queen-size beds, a desk, and a reading chair. The furniture is modern, with wood and metal marine-inspired accents. Some rooms at the Dolphin have balconies.

Since the Walt Disney World Swan and Dolphin are not run by Disney, the service at these resorts is less sugar-coated than service at other Disney resorts. The Swan and Dolphin collectively house more than a dozen restaurants and lounges, and more are within easy walking distance at Epcot and the BoardWalk. The resorts are connected to other destinations by bus and boat. Walking time from the most remote rooms to the transportation loading areas is seven to nine minutes.

Disney's Caribbean Beach Resort   The Caribbean Beach Resort is situated on 200 acres surrounding a 45-acre lake called Barefoot Bay. This mid-priced Disney resort, modeled after resorts of the Caribbean islands, is comprised of the registration area, called the "Custom House," and five two-story "villages" named after Caribbean islands. Each village has its own pool, laundry room, and beach. The Caribbean motif is maintained with red tile roofs, widow's walks, and wooden railed porches. The atmosphere at this resort is cheerful, with buildings painted blue, lime green, and sherbet orange. In addition to the five village pools, the main swimming pool at the Caribbean Beach is themed as an old Spanish fort, complete with slides and water cannons.

Most of the 2,112 guest rooms at the Caribbean Beach are 315 square feet and contain two double beds and a table and two chairs. Some of the rooms are decorated with bright tropical colors, while others are decorated with neutral beachy tones. All of the rooms are suited with the same light-oak furniture. Rooms do not have balconies. Some rooms at the Caribbean are in need of refurbishment. When you make your reservations, request a recently renovated room. Also, be aware that the Caribbean Beach Resort is not known for its check-in efficiency.

One of the most centrally located of the Disney resorts, transportation to all Walt Disney World destinations is by bus. Though the Caribbean Beach has one full-service restaurant and a food court, food service is woefully inadequate for the size of the resort. Because food service at the Caribbean is limited and because it is immensely time consuming to commute to other resorts by Disney bus, guests at the Caribbean Beach should seriously consider renting a car. Walking time to the bus loading area from the most remote rooms is seven to ten minutes.

The Bonnet Creek Resorts

Disney's Old Key West Resort   This is the first of the Disney Vacation Club properties. Although the resort is a time-share property, units not being used by owners are rented on a nightly basis. Old Key West is a large aggregation of two- to three-story buildings modeled after Caribbean residences and guest houses of the Florida Keys. Arranged subdivision-style around a golf course and along Bonnet Creek, the buildings are situated in small neighborhoodlike clusters. They feature pastel-colored facades, white trim, and shuttered windows. The registration area is housed in the Conch Flats Community Hall, along with a full-service restaurant, modest fitness center, marina, and sundries shop. There is a quiet pool in each cluster of accommodations and a larger pool at the Conch Flats Community Hall.

With studios at 376 square feet, one-bedroom villas at 942 square feet, and two-bedroom villas at 1,333 square feet, this resort offers some of the roomiest accommodations at Walt Disney World. Studios contain two queen-size beds, a table and two chairs, and an extra vanity outside the bathroom. One-bedroom villas contain a king-size bed in the master bedroom, a queen-size sleeper sofa in the living room, a laundry room, and a fully equipped kitchen. Two-bedroom villas include an additional bedroom with two queen-size beds. All of the villas have enough closet space to bring your whole wardrobe.

Each villa at the Old Key West has its own private balcony that opens onto a delightfully landscaped private courtyard. Finally, rooms and villas at the Old Key West are tastefully decorated, with wicker and upholstered furniture, and peach and light-green color schemes.

As a Disney Vacation Club resort, Old Key West's service is very personal. Transportation to other Walt Disney World destinations is by bus. Walking time to transportation loading areas from the most remote rooms is about six minutes.

Disney's Port Orleans Resort   This mid-priced resort is a sanitized Disney version of the New Orleans French Quarter. Comprised of seven three-story guest-room buildings situated next to Bonnet Creek, the resort gives you an idea of what New Orleans would look like if its buildings were painted every year and the garbage collectors never went on strike. There are very prim pink and blue guest buildings, with wrought-iron filigree, shuttered windows, and old-fashioned iron lampposts. In keeping with the Crescent City theme, Port Orleans is landscaped with magnolia trees and overgrown vines. The centrally located "Mint" houses the registration area and restaurants, and is a reproduction of a turn-of-the-century building where Mississippi Delta farmers sold their harvests. The registration desk features a vibrant Mardi Gras mural and old-fashioned bank teller windows. "Doubloon Lagoon," the only pool at the Port Orleans, surrounds a colorful fiberglass creation depicting Neptune riding a sea serpent.

The 1,008 guest rooms at the Port Orleans each measure 315 square feet. Most contain two double beds, a table and two chairs, and a vanity outside the bathroom. The gold and deep-green rooms feature hardwood furniture and valances over the curtains. None of the rooms at Port Orleans have private balconies.

With a moderate ratio of staff to guests, service at the Port Orleans is good. There is one full-service restaurant as well as a food court at the resort. Port Orleans is connected to other Walt Disney World destinations by bus. Walking time to the transportation loading areas from the most remote rooms is seven to ten minutes.

Disney's Dixie Landings Resort   This mid-priced Walt Disney World resort draws on the lifestyle and architecture of Mississippi River communities in antebellum Louisiana, though it conveniently ignores any reference to slavery. Spread along Bonnet Creek, which encircles "Old Man Island" (the resort's main swimming area), Dixie Landings is divided into two themed areas: the "mansion" area, which features plantation-style architecture, and the "bayou" area, with tin-roofed rustic (imitation) wooden buildings. The mansions are three stories tall, while the bayou guest houses are a story shorter. The theme is augmented by landscaped groves of azalea and juniper. Southern river life is also depicted at Dixie Landings' food court, which houses a working cotton press powered by a 32-foot waterwheel.

The 2,048 rooms at Dixie Landings each measure 315 square feet. Most provide two double beds, a table and two chairs, and two pedestal sinks outside the bathroom. Some rooms also contain a child's trundle bed. All rooms feature brass bathroom fixtures, hickory-branch bedposts, and quilted bedspreads. The rooms are decorated in tasteful neutrals and blues. None of the rooms have private balconies.

Dixie Landings has one full-service restaurant as well as a food court. The resort is served by the Disney bus system, connecting it to all Walt Disney World destinations. Walking time from the most remote rooms to the transportation loading areas is ten minutes.

The Villas at the Disney Institute

This resort offers a wide variety of accommodations stretching from Downtown Disney to Bonnet Creek. Tucked in clusters fronting the Buena Vista Golf Course and along several streams and canals, the various villas are some of the oldest and most geographically dispersed of all Disney lodging options. The grounds are landscaped with native Florida flora, and the forest surrounding the resort provides a quiet barrier between the Disney Institute and the rest of Walt Disney World. There are five small swimming pools at the Disney Institute as well as Walt Disney World's finest guest fitness center and spa.

Of the 584 units at the Disney Institute, there are five different types of accommodations available. There are 316 one-bedroom Bungalows, which measure 500 square feet and offer separate living rooms. These units contain two queen-size beds and a daybed, a wetbar with refrigerator and microwave, and a balcony or patio. They are decorated nicely, with turtle lamp fixtures and maps of the world on the print curtains.

There are 60 Treehouse Villas at the Disney Institute. These accommodations are smaller than they look. Each Treehouse has three bedrooms (each with one queen-size bed), two bathrooms, a small kitchen, and a living room with a sleeper sofa. They are decorated in natural tones, with rustic wooden furniture. Though somewhat dated, the Treehouse Villas are the most isolated and quietest of all the villas and offer guests the most serene setting at Walt Disney World. For some guests, including this woman from La Crescent, Minnesota, the Treehouse Villas are a tad more rustic than anticipated:

We reserved a Treehouse Villa and I tell you, "It ain't no villa." When we pulled up and had to park half a block away with woods and swamp, my worst nightmare came true! The rustic interior both in furniture and decor was not like any Disney [accommodation] we had ever had. Our children looked at us like, why the camping trip?

There are 128 one- and two-bedroom Town Houses. These Disney Institute accommodations offer a sleeper sofa in the living room, a queen-size bed in the master bedroom, and a full kitchen. The two-bedroom units offer two twin beds in the second bedroom. While the decor in these units is truly bland, many guests enjoy the walking proximity to Downtown Disney.

The fourth type of accommodation are the 64 Fairway Villas at the Disney Institute. These villas have cathedral ceilings, two bedrooms, a full kitchen, and a separate living room. They are furnished with two double beds in one bedroom, a queen-size bed in the other bedroom, and a sleeper sofa in the living room. These villas also feature modern furniture and large windows.

There are only four Grand Vista Homes at the Disney Institute. Visiting Saudi princes will want to check on the availability of these three-bedroom homes. Amenities include nightly turndown service and stocked refrigerators.

Though the Disney Institute staff caters to those who are participating in classes, our research team ranks housekeeping at the Villas as the poorest Disney has to offer. There is only one full-service restaurant at the Disney Institute, but there are plenty of restaurants nearby at Downtown Disney. Disney bus service to other World destinations is marginal compared to other resorts. If you stay at the Villas, we recommend that you rent a car. Walking time to the transportation loading areas from the most remote rooms is 8–11 minutes.

The Animal Kingdom Resort Area

Disney's Coronado Springs Resort The Coronado Springs Resort, located near the Animal Kingdom, is Disney's only mid-priced convention property. Inspired by northern Mexico and the American Southwest, the resort is divided into three separately themed areas. The two- and three-story Ranchos call to mind vast Southwestern cattle ranches, while the two- and three-story Cabanas are modeled after Mexican beach resorts. Finally, the multistoried Casitas embody elements of Spanish architecture found in Mexico's great cities. The lobby is part of the Casitas and features a mosaic ceiling and tiled floor. The vast resort surrounds a 15-acre lake, and there are three small pools as well as one large main swimming complex. The main pool is designed to look like ancient ruins and features a reproduction of an Aztec/Mayan steppe pyramid with a waterfall cascading down its side.

There are 1,967 guest rooms at the Coronado Springs. Most of the rooms measure 315 square feet and contain two double beds, a table and chairs, and a vanity outside the bathroom. They are decorated with the colors of the sunset and feature handpainted Mexican wall hangings. All rooms have coffeemakers. None of the rooms have their own balcony.

The Coronado Springs offers one full-service restaurant as well as the best food court at Walt Disney World. Unfortunately, however, there is not nearly enough food service for a resort this large and remote. If you book the Coronado Springs, we suggest that you rent a car to expand your dining options. The resort is connected to other Walt Disney World destinations by bus only. Walking time from the most remote rooms to the bus stop is eight to ten minutes.

As a convention hotel, the Coronado Springs is somewhat peculiar. Unlike most convention hotels, where everything is centrally located with the guest rooms in close proximity, guest rooms at the Coronado Springs are arrayed around a huge lake. If you are assigned one of the rooms on the opposite side of the lake from the meeting and convention area (and restaurants!) plan on a 11- to 15-minute hike every time you leave your room. If your organization books the Coronado Springs for a meeting, think about having your meals catered. The hotel's restaurants simply do not have the capacity during a large convention to accommodate the morning breakfast rush or to serve a quick lunch between meeting sessions.

Disney's All-Star Sports, All-Star Music, and All-Star Movie Resorts
Disney's version of a budget resort features three distinct themes executed in the same hyperbolistic style. Spread over a vast expanse, the resorts are comprised of almost 35 three-story motel-style guest-room buildings. Although the three resorts are neighbors, each has its own lobby, food court, and registration area. The All-Star Sports Resort features huge sports icons: bright football helmets, tennis rackets, and baseball bats, all taller than the buildings they adorn. Similarly, the All-Star Music Resort features 40-foot guitars, maracas, and saxophones, while the All-Star Movie Resort showcases giant popcorn boxes and icons from Disney films. Lobbies of all three resorts are loud (in both decibels and brightness) and cartoonish, with checkerboard walls and photographs of famous athletes, musicians, and film stars. There's even a photo of Mickey Mouse with Alice Cooper. (Does Mickey know that Alice is a man who wears sundresses and bites the heads off bats at rock concerts?) The swimming pool at the Music Resort is shaped like a giant guitar, and the pool at the Sports Resort features plastic replicas of the Disney characters shooting water pistols. At the All-Star Movie Resort, the pool is star shaped.

At 260 square feet, the guest rooms at each of the All-Star resorts are very small. They are so small that a family of four attempting to stay in one room might well redefine family values by the end of the week. Each room has two double beds, a separate vanity area, and a table and chairs. The bedspreads feature famous athletes, movie stars, and musicians, and the light fixtures are star-shaped. None of the rooms at the All-Stars have balconies.

If you are planning to save for years for your grand Disney vacation, save enough money for a bigger room. Also, the prevalence of young children running wild makes the All-Stars the noisiest of the Disney resorts, though the guest rooms are well soundproofed and quiet.

With a very low ratio of staff to guests, service is not the greatest at the All-Star resorts. Additionally, there are no full-service restaurants at the resorts. Because the All-Stars are the most remote of the Walt Disney World resorts, the bus ride to a full-service restaurant at another resort takes about 45 minutes each way. There is, however, a new McDonalds about a quarter of a mile away. Bus service to the theme parks and the water parks is pretty efficient. Walking time to the bus stop from the most remote guest rooms is about eight minutes.

HOW TO EVALUATE A WALT DISNEY WORLD TRAVEL PACKAGE

Hundreds of Walt Disney World package vacations are offered each year. Some are created by the Walt Disney Travel Company, others by airline touring companies, independent travel agents, and wholesalers. Almost all include lodging at or near Disney World and theme park admissions. Packages offered by airlines include air transportation.

Prices vary seasonally; mid-February to the end of April and holiday periods are the most expensive. Off-season, forget packages: there are plenty of empty rooms, and you can negotiate great discounts (especially at non-Disney properties). Similarly, airfares and rental cars are cheaper off-peak.

Almost all package ads are headlined "5 Days at Walt Disney World from $605" (or such). The key word is "from." The rock-bottom price includes the least desirable hotels. If you want better or more convenient digs, you'll have to pay more, often much more.

Packages offer a wide selection of hotels. Some, like the Disney resorts, are very dependable. Others run the gamut of quality. If you consider a non-Disney hotel, check its quality as reported in an independent rating such as those offered by the *Unofficial Guides, AAA Directories, Mobil Guides,* or *Frommer's America on Wheels.* Checking two or three independent sources is best. Also, before you book, ask how old the hotel is and when the guest rooms were last refurbished. Locate the hotel on a map to verify its proximity to Disney World. If you won't have a car, make sure the hotel has an adequate shuttle service.

Packages with non-Disney lodging are much less expensive. But guests at Disney-owned properties get free parking and early entry to designated theme parks. These privileges don't apply to guests at the seven independent hotels of the Disney Village Hotel Plaza (Wyndham Palace, Grosvenor

Resort, DoubleTree Guest Suites Resort, The Hilton Resort, Courtyard by Marriott, Hotel Royal Plaza, and Best Western Hotel).

Packages should be a win/win proposition for both buyer and seller. The buyer makes only one phone call and deals with one salesperson to set up the whole vacation (transportation, rental car, admissions, lodging, meals, and even golf and tennis). The seller, likewise, deals with the buyer only one time. Some packagers also buy airfares in bulk on contract, like a broker playing the commodities market. By buying a large number of airfares in advance, the packager saves significantly over posted fares. The practice is also applied to hotel rooms. Because selling packages is efficient and because the packager often can buy package components (airfare, lodging, etc.) in bulk at discount, savings in operating expenses realized by the seller are sometimes passed on to the buyer, making the package both convenient and an exceptional value.

In practice, however, the seller may realize all of the economies and pass on no savings to the buyer. In some instances, packages are loaded with extras that cost the packager almost nothing but run the retail price of the package sky high. Not surprisingly, the savings passed on to customers are still somewhere in Fantasyland.

Choose a package that includes features you're sure to use. Whether you use all of the features or not, you will pay for them. If price is more important than convenience, call around to see what the package would cost if you booked its components on your own. If the package price is less than the a la carte cost, the package is a good deal. If costs are about equal, the package probably is worth it for the convenience.

An Example   A popular package offered by the Walt Disney Travel Company is the *Disney Resort Magic* plan, which includes:

1. Three or more nights' accommodation at your choice of any Disney resort. Rates vary with choice of lodging; the Grand Floridian is the most expensive, and the All-Star Resorts are the least expensive.

2. Unlimited use of the Walt Disney World transportation system.

3. Admission and unlimited use of all Walt Disney World theme parks during your stay.

4. Admission and unlimited use of Pleasure Island nighttime entertainment complex; River Country, Typhoon Lagoon, and Blizzard Beach swimming parks; and unlimited admission to Disney's Wide World of Sports and DisneyQuest during your stay. (Admission becomes effective upon check-in and is valid until midnight of your check-out day.)

5. Free parking.

The *Disney Resort Magic* plan also includes a "flex feature," which consists of one of the following per person:

1. A round of golf at Disney's *Oak Trail Course* (a 9-hole walking course).

2. *Birnbaum's Walt Disney World, 1999; The Official Guide.*

3. Planet Hollywood or ESPN Club T-shirt.

4. One Official All-Star Cafe lunch or dinner with souvenir sports bottle.

5. One Mickey 'n You photo session.

6. Disney character breakfast.

7. One of a number of theme park tours, such as Gardens of the World Tour at Epcot or the mystery family tour at Magic Kingdom.

8. Admission to DisneyQuest (includes unlimited play for the day).

9. *Fantasmic!* cap with four collector pins.

10. Children's fishing excursion at select Walt Disney World resort hotels ages 6–12 only.

11. 90-minute tennis clinic available at select Walt Disney World resorts.

12. Animal Kingdom collector's box.

Loaded with benefits and amenities, this is one of Walt Disney World's most popular packages (price varies with hotel and room choice and length of stay). Depending on how you use it, you can come out a winner or a loser.

Our sample analysis is done for a couple from Baltimore, Maryland, on a six-night package, traveling in August and arriving in Orlando by air. The couple's choice of hotels is Old Key West Resort, connected to the theme parks by bus. Because check-in time at Old Key West is 3 p.m. or later, the couple plans to arrive at Walt Disney World in the late afternoon and begin touring the theme parks the next day. Their itinerary calls for additional touring on their check-out day prior to leaving for the airport. The package in 1999 cost $1,084 for each adult (two to a room), or $2,168 for the couple (tax included). Their round-trip airfare from Baltimore and transportation from and to the airport are in addition to the package price.

Six days' use of the transportation system is no big deal. Anyone who buys a regular five- or six-day admission can ride all day on the buses, boats, and monorails.

The package provides six days' admission to the major theme parks as well as River Country, Blizzard Beach, Typhoon Lagoon, DisneyQuest, and Pleasure Island. Since it takes at least five days to see the major theme parks, little time is left to visit Typhoon Lagoon, Blizzard Beach, River Country, DisneyQuest, and Pleasure Island.

Another problem with the six days' admission is that whatever you don't use, you lose. Admissions are good only for the days of the package, unlike the non-package Hopper Passes. Unused days on the Hopper and Hopper Plus are good forever. If you come back next month or three years from now, you'll be able to finish using your pass. Not so with the package admission.

The package's "flex features" can all be purchased a la carte. Birnbaum's *Official Guide to Walt Disney World* is available at bookstores, exclusive of the package. And the private photo session with Mickey may be more of a liability than an asset, as a Texas gentleman notes:

> *Included in our vacation package was a photograph session with Mickey at You & Me Kid, a shop in the Downtown Disney Marketplace (aka WDW Village). Two caveats emptor here: First, the procedure for the photo session was very poorly arranged and executed with molasses-like speed (much to the ire of a gaggle of bedraggled parents). Second, we suspect that the delay was at least partially intentional: the more hours you were detained at the Disney Village before your appointment with The Mouse, the more steadily your billfold could be emptied on the relentless parade of Disney merchandise. Indeed, since this shopping center was the only location given for this special photo-op, our hunch is that the whole affair is little more than a lure to draw families off the beaten path to a nice but très expensive Disney Marketplace.*

In the final analysis, the *Disney Resort Magic Plan* is best suited to vacationers who plan to be on the go from dawn until midnight and visit the theme parks every day. And, you may have concluded, it's set up in a way that makes it almost impossible not to waste many of its benefits.

Getting Down to Dollars and Cents   If you exclude the recreational extras, here's how the package compares with going it on your own:

Option A: *Disney Resort Magic Plan* for two people
in August, sharing a deluxe studio room at the
Old KeyWest Resort: $1,084 per person × 2 $2,168

Option B: Creating your own vacation with the same basic
features of the *Disney Resort Magic Plan*

The Old Key West Resort (same room as package)
for six nights with tax included for two adults $1,525

Two 6-Day Park-Hopper Plus Passes (unlimited admission to
four major parks and three visits to the minor parks) with tax $550

Birnbaum's *Official Guide to Walt Disney World* $14

Grand total for two people $2,089

Amount saved by arranging things yourself $79

Another Example   Most Delta Dream Vacations offer almost the same features as *Disney's Resort Magic Plan,* plus round-trip air transportation. If a couple from St. Louis buys a six-night Delta package for late August at the Old Key West Resort, they'll pay $2,833 for both people. If they book the same components themselves, the cost will be $2,112 *before* buying airline tickets.

If you subtract the a la carte costs of package components from the package price ($2,833 minus $2,112), the remainder ($721) is what the couple is being charged for airfare, in this case $360.50 per person ($721 divided by two). If they can fly round trip to Orlando from St. Louis for less than $360.50 a person, the package isn't such a great deal. If airfares from St. Louis equal or exceed $360.50 per person, the package makes sense.

If you buy a package from Disney, don't expect reservationists to offer suggestions or help you sort out your options. Generally, they won't volunteer information and will respond only to your specific questions, ducking queries that require an opinion. A reader from North Riverside, Illinois, complains:

> *I have received various pieces of literature from WDW, and it is very confusing to try and figure everything out. My wife made two telephone calls, and the representatives from WDW were very courteous. However, they only answered the questions posed and were not very eager to give advice on what might be most cost effective. [The] WDW reps would not say if we would be better off doing one thing over the other. I feel a person could spend eight hours on the telephone with WDW reps and not have any more input than you get from reading the literature.*

If you can't get the information you need from Disney, contact a good travel agent. Chances are the agent can help you sort out your options. A dad from Valley Stream, New York, used the Walt Disney Travel Company, travel wholesalers, and travel agents to comparison-shop successfully:

> *Nothing pays greater dividends than planning in advance. A year before our vacation we joined the Magic Kingdom Club. Some 8–9*

months before our vacation I secured a package price from the Magic Kingdom Club, which I was able to use to negotiate a lower package with my travel agent. Yes, the travel agent packages are negotiable (much to my own surprise). What I now realize is that travel agents get WDW packages from different wholesalers and may not be immediately inclined to give you a package offered through the lowest-priced wholesaler. The first quotes I received were from AAA and Liberty Travel but, unbeknownst to me, both packages were, in fact, purchased through Delta Airlines. It was only after I was able to obtain a lower land package price by booking directly through Disney (as a Magic Kingdom Club member) that I was assured by each agent that they could beat the price I was able to secure—and they did, saving me several hundred dollars. The air package was another reason to book through a travel agent. Our agent reserved seats for us on one airline only to call us three weeks later to tell us of discounts being offered through another airline. We acted quickly and bought the discounted tickets, saving another $200 on our air package.

Information Needed for Evaluation   For quick reference, contact Walt Disney World accommodations reservations at (407) 828-3232 or (407) 397-6515 and ask for a Walt Disney Travel Company Walt Disney World Vacations Brochure, which contains descriptions and room rates for all Disney properties. Ask also for a rate sheet listing admission options and prices for all major and minor parks. These in hand, you're ready to evaluate any vacation package. Remember that all packages are quoted on a per-person basis at two to a room (double occupancy), and there is an 11% combined sales and room tax. For about everything else you buy in Florida (except groceries and prescription medicine), a 6–7% sales tax applies.

SELECTING AND BOOKING A HOTEL OUTSIDE WALT DISNEY WORLD

Lodging costs outside Walt Disney World vary incredibly. If you shop around, you can find a clean motel with a pool within 20 minutes of the World for as low as $35 a night. You also can find luxurious, expensive hotels with all the extras. Because of hot competition, discounts abound, particularly for AAA and AARP members.

There are three primary out-of-the-World areas to consider:

1. International Drive Area   This area, about 15 to 20 minutes east of Walt Disney World, parallels I-4 on its southern side and offers a wide selection of both hotels and restaurants. Accommodations range from $35

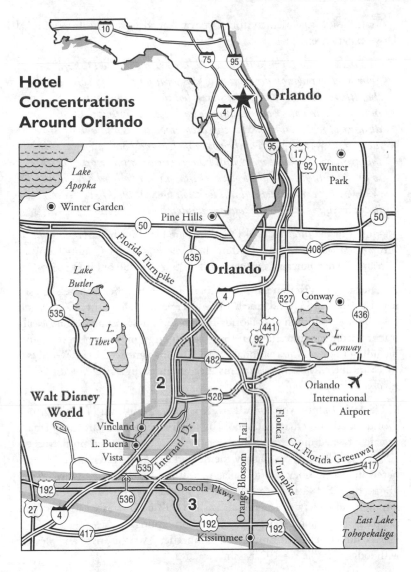

Hotel
Concentrations
Around Orlando

to $250 per night. The chief drawbacks of the International Drive area are its terribly congested roads, countless traffic signals, and inadequate access to westbound I-4. While the biggest bottleneck is the intersection with Sand Lake Road, the mile of International Drive between Kirkman Road and Sand Lake Road stays in near-continuous gridlock. It's common to lose 25 to 35 minutes trying to navigate this stretch.

Traffic aside, a gentleman from Ottawa, Canada, extols his International Drive experience:

International Drive is the place to stay when going to Disney. Your single paragraph description of this location failed to point out that [there are] several discount stores, boutiques, restaurants and mini-putts, and other entertainment facilities, all within walking distance of remarkably inexpensive accommodations and a short drive away from WDW. Many of the chain motels and hotels are located in this area, and the local merchants have created a mini-resort to cater to the tourists. It is the ideal place to unwind after a hard day visiting WDW. I have recommended this location for years and have never heard anything but raves about the wisdom of this advice.

Hotels in the International Drive area are listed in the *Orlando Official Accommodations Guide* published by the Orlando/Orange County Convention and Visitors Bureau. For a copy, call (800) 255-5786 or (407) 363-5872.

2. Lake Buena Vista and the I-4 Corridor   A number of hotels are situated along FL 535 and north of I-4 between Walt Disney World and I-4's intersection with the Florida Turnpike. These properties are easily reached from the interstate and are near a large number of restaurants, including those on International Drive. Driving time to Disney World is 5 to 15 minutes. Most hotels in this area are listed in the *Orlando Official Accommodations Guide.*

3. US 192   This is the highway to Kissimmee, southeast of Walt Disney World. In addition to a number of large, full-service hotels are many small, privately owned motels that are a good value. Several dozen properties on US 192 are closer to the Disney theme parks than are the more expensive hotels in Walt Disney World Village and the Disney Village Hotel Plaza. Traffic on US 192 is extremely heavy but usually moves smoothly. The number and variety of restaurants on US 192 has increased markedly in the past year, easing the area's primary shortcoming.

A senior citizen from Brookfield, Connecticut, was surprised and pleased with lodging in the US 192/Kissimmee area:

We were amazed to find that from our cheaper and superior accommodations in Kissimmee it took only 5 minutes longer to reach the park turnstiles than it did from the Disney accommodations. Kissimmee is the way to go, in our opinion.

Hotels on US 192 and in Kissimmee are listed in the *Kissimmee–St. Cloud Visitor's Guide,* available at (800) 327-9159 or on the Web at www.floridakiss.com.

Driving Time to the Theme Parks for Visitors Lodging outside Walt Disney World

For those staying outside Walt Disney World, we've calculated the approximate commuting time to the major theme parks' parking lots from several off-World lodging areas. Add a few minutes to our times to pay your parking fee and park. Once parked at the Transportation and Ticket Center (Magic Kingdom parking lot), it takes an average of 20 to 30 additional minutes to reach the Magic Kingdom. To reach Epcot from its parking lot, add 7 to 10 minutes. At Disney-MGM Studios and the Animal Kingdom, the lot-to-gate transit is 5 to 10 minutes. If you haven't purchased your theme park admission in advance, tack on another 10 to 20 minutes.

Driving Time to the Theme Parks				
Minutes From	**To Magic Kingdom Parking Lot**	**Epcot Parking Lot**	**Disney–MGM Studios Parking Lot**	**Animal Kingdom Parking Lot**
Downtown Orlando	35	31	33	37
North International Dr. and Universal Studios	24	21	22	26
Central International Dr.–Sand Lake Road	26	23	24	27
South International Dr. and Sea World	18	15	16	20
FL 535	12	9	10	13
FL 192, north of I-4	10–15	7–12	5–10	5–10
FL 192, south of I-4	10–18	7–15	5–13	5–12

GETTING A GOOD DEAL ON A ROOM OUTSIDE WALT DISNEY WORLD

Hotel development at Walt Disney World has sharpened the competition among lodgings throughout the Disney World/Orlando/Kissimmee area. Hotels outside Disney World, in particular, struggle to fill their guest rooms. Unable to compete with Disney resorts for convenience or perks, off-World hotels lure patrons with bargain rates. The extent of the bargain depends on the season, day of the week, and area events. In high season, during holiday periods, and when large conventions are held at the Orange County Convention Center, even the most modest lodging properties are sold out. Here are tips and strategies for getting a good deal on a room outside Disney World.

The following list may seem intimidating and may refer to travel-market players unfamiliar to you, but many tips we provide for getting a good deal at Disney World work equally well almost any other place you need a hotel. Once you understand these strategies, you'll routinely be able to obtain rooms at the best hotels for the lowest possible rates.

1. Orlando MagiCard   Orlando MagiCard is a discount program sponsored by the Orlando/Orange County Convention and Visitors Bureau. Cardholders are eligible for discounts of 20–50% at approximately 50 participating hotels. The MagiCard is also good for discounts at area attractions, including Sea World, Cypress Gardens, the Universal parks, several dinner theaters, Church Street Station, and Disney's Pleasure Island. Valid for up to six persons, the card isn't available for groups or conventions.

To obtain an Orlando MagiCard and a list of participating hotels and attractions, call (800) 255-5786 or (407) 363-5874. Anyone older than 18 years is eligible, and the card is free. If you miss getting a card before you leave home, you can get one at the Convention and Visitors Bureau at 8445 International Drive in Orlando. When you call for a MagiCard, also request the *Orlando Official Accommodations Guide* and the Orlando Vacation Planner.

2. Exit Information Guide   Exit Information Guide publishes a book of discount coupons for bargain rates at hotels statewide. The book is free in many restaurants and motels on main highways leading to Florida. Because most travelers make reservations before leaving home, picking up the coupon book en route doesn't help much. If you call and use a credit card, EIG will send the guide first class for $3 ($5 U.S. for Canadian delivery). Contact:

Exit Information Guide
4205 N.W. 6th Street
Gainesville, FL 32609
(352) 371-3948

3. Hotel Shopping on the Internet   To read the popular press, you'd think hotels were giving away rooms on the Internet. While they're not, of course, it is true that hotels are increasingly using the Internet to fill rooms during slow periods and to advertise time-limited specials. The Internet is one of many communications tools in the hotel's toolbox, and hotels use it along with more traditional practices, such as promoting specials through travel agents. If you enjoy cyber shopping, by all means have at it, but hotel shopping on the internet is not nearly as quick or convenient as handing the task to your travel agent. And, you'll be hard-pressed to find a deal that is not also available through your agent. When we bump into a great deal on the Web, we call our travel agent. Often our agent can beat the deal or improve on it (as in the case of an upgrade). Although a good travel agent working alone can achieve great things, the same agent working with a savvy, helpful client can work wonders.

4. Corporate Rates Many hotels offer corporate discounts of 5–20%. Usually, you don't need to work for a large company to obtain them. Simply call the hotel of your choice and ask for its corporate rates. Many hotels will guarantee the discounted rate when you make your reservation. Others may make the rate conditional on your providing some sort of *bona fides,* for instance a fax on your company's letterhead requesting the rate or a company credit card or business card when you check in. Generally, screening isn't rigorous.

5. Half-Price Programs Larger discounts on rooms (35–60%), in the Disney World area or anywhere else, are available through half-price hotel programs, often called travel clubs. Program operators contract with hotels to provide rooms at a deep discount, usually 50% off the rack rate, on a space-available basis. Generally, space available means you can reserve a room at the discount whenever the hotel expects occupancy will be less than 80%. To increase your chances for the discount, check the calendar to avoid high-season, big conventions, holidays, and special events.

Most half-price programs charge an annual membership or directory subscription fee of $25–125. Once enrolled, you're mailed a membership card and directory listing participating hotels. There are lots of restrictions and exceptions. Some hotels, for instance, "black out" (exclude) certain times. Others may offer the discount only on certain days of the week or may require you to stay a certain number of nights. Still others may offer a discount much smaller than 50%.

More established programs offer members up to 4,000 hotels in the United States. All of the programs have a heavy concentration of hotels in California and Florida. Offerings elsewhere in the United States vary considerably. The programs with the largest selection of hotels in the Disney World area are Encore, at (800) 638-0930, and Entertainment Publications, at (800) 285-5525.

One problem with half-price programs is that not all hotels offer a full 50% discount. Another is the base rate against which the discount is applied. Some hotels figure the discount on an exaggerated rack rate that virtually no one pays. A few participating hotels may deduct the discount from the rate for a "superior" or "upgraded" room, though the room assigned is the hotel's standard accommodation. The majority of participants base discounts on rates published in the *Hotel & Travel Index* (a quarterly reference journal used by travel agents) and work within the spirit of their agreement with the program operator. As a rule, if you travel several times a year, your savings will more than pay for your program membership.

A footnote to this information is that rooms through half-price programs aren't commissionable to travel agents. This means you usually must make your own inquiries and reservations. If you work frequently with your agent, however, he or she will probably do your legwork, lack of commission notwithstanding.

6. Wholesalers, Consolidators, and Reservation Services Wholesalers and consolidators buy rooms, or options on rooms (room blocks), from hotels at a low, negotiated rate. They then resell the rooms at a profit through travel agents and tour packagers, or directly to the public. Most wholesalers and consolidators make provisions for returning unsold rooms to participating hotels but are disinclined to do so. The wholesaler's or consolidator's relationship with any hotel is tied to volume. If unsold rooms are returned, the hotel might not make as many rooms available the next time. So wholesalers and consolidators often offer rooms at rates from 15 to 50% off rack rate, occasionally sacrificing profit to avoid returning the rooms unsold.

When wholesalers and consolidators deal directly with the public, they frequently represent themselves as "reservation services." When you call, ask for a rate for your chosen hotel or for the best deal in the area where you'd like to stay. Say if there's a maximum amount you're willing to pay. The service likely will find something for you, even if it has to shave off a dollar or two of profit. You may have to pay by credit card when you reserve a room. Other times, you pay when you check out. Here are two services that frequently offer substantial discounts:

Accommodations Express   (800) 444-7666
Hotel Reservations Network   (800) 964-6835

7. If You Make Your Own Reservation Always call the hotel in question, not the hotel chain's national 800 number. Often, reservationists at the 800 number are unaware of local specials. Always ask about specials before you inquire about corporate rates. Don't hesitate to bargain, but do it before you check in. If you're buying a hotel's weekend package, for example, and want to extend your stay, you can often obtain at least the corporate rate for the extra days.

8. Condominium Deals A large number of condo resorts, time shares, and all-suite properties in the Kissimmee/Orlando area rent to vacationers for a week or less. Look for bargains, especially during off-peak periods. Reservations and information can be obtained from:

Condolink	(800) 733-4445
Holiday Villas	(800) 251-1112
Hospitality Vacation Homes	(800) 969-7077
Kissimmee–St. Cloud Reservations	(800) 333-5477
Vistana Resort	(800) 877-8787
Ramada Suites by Sea World	(800) 633-1405
Holiday Inn Family Suites	(877) 387-KIDS

We frequently receive letters from readers extolling the virtues of renting a condo or vacation home. This endorsement by a family from Glenmont, New York, is typical:

> *I would recommend that you include the Vistana Resort in your hotel section. Such luxury for so little. On two past visits we stayed in Disney's Lake Buena Vista Hotel Village. To have two BR, two baths, kitchen, DR, LR, deck, and Jacuzzi for less money was heaven. The children could go to bed at 8:30, and we could stay up and have some privacy. The full kitchen saved $, too—especially at breakfast time. I highly recommend this for families. So close (five minutes to Epcot, ten to MK, seven to Sea World) and convenient.*

A majority of rental condos are listed with travel agents. Condo owners often pay an enhanced commission to agents who rent the units for reduced consumer rates.

Hotels and Motels: Rated and Ranked

In this section, we compare hotels in three main areas outside Walt Disney World (pages 126–129) with those inside the World.

In addition to Disney properties and the three lodging areas we rate, there are hotels at the intersection of US 27 and I-4, on US 441 (Orange Blossom Trail), and in downtown Orlando. All of these require more than 20 minutes' commuting time to Walt Disney World. We also haven't rated lodging south of Siesta Lago Road on US 192.

WHAT'S IN A ROOM?

Except for cleanliness, state of repair, and decor, travelers pay little attention to hotel rooms. There is, of course, a clear standard of quality and luxury that differentiates Motel 6 from Holiday Inn, Holiday Inn from Marriott, and so on. Many hotel guests, however, fail to appreciate that some rooms are better engineered than others. Making the room usable to its occupants is an art, a planning discipline that combines both form and function.

Decor and taste are important, certainly. No one wants to stay in a room that is dated, garish, or ugly. But beyond decor, how "livable" is the room? In Orlando, for example, we have seen some beautifully appointed rooms that simply aren't well designed for human habitation. The next time you stay in a hotel, note the details and design elements of your room. Even more than decor, these are the things that will make you feel comfortable and at home.

Room Star Ratings		
★★★★★	*Superior Rooms*	Tasteful and luxurious by any standard
★★★★	*Extremely Nice Rooms*	What you would expect at a Hyatt Regency or Marriott
★★★	*Nice Rooms*	Holiday Inn or comparable quality
★★	*Adequate Rooms*	Clean, comfortable, and functional without frills—like a Motel 6
★	*Super Budget*	

ROOM RATINGS

To evaluate properties for their quality, tastefulness, state of repair, cleanliness, and size of their *standard rooms,* we have grouped the hotels and motels into classifications denoted by stars. Star ratings in this guide apply to Orlando-area properties only and don't necessarily correspond to ratings awarded by Frommer, Mobil, AAA, or other travel critics. Because stars have little relevance when awarded in the absence of recognized standards of comparison, we have tied our ratings to expected levels of quality established by specific American hotel corporations.

Star ratings apply *only to room quality* and describe the property's standard accommodations. For most hotels and motels, a standard accommodation is a hotel room with either one king bed or two queen beds. In an all-suite property, the standard accommodation is either a one- or two-room suite. In addition to standard accommodations, many hotels offer luxury rooms and special suites, which aren't rated in this guide. Star ratings for rooms are assigned without regard to whether a property has restaurant(s), recreational facilities, entertainment, or other extras.

In addition to stars (which delineate broad categories), we use a numerical rating system. Our rating scale is 0 to 100, with 100 as the best possible rating and zero (0) as the worst. Numerical ratings are presented to show the difference we perceive between one property and another. Rooms at The Villas at the Disney Institute, Buena Vista Suites, and Courtyard by Marriott are all rated as three-and-a-half stars (★★★½). In the supplemental numerical ratings, The Villas are rated an 82, the Buena Vista Suites an 81, and the Courtyard a 76. This means that within the three-and-a-half-star category, The Villas at the Disney Institute and Buena Vista Suites are comparable, and both have slightly nicer rooms than the Courtyard.

The location column identifies the area around Walt Disney World where you will find a particular property. The designation "WDW" means that the property is inside Walt Disney World. A "1" means that the property is on or near International Drive. Properties on US 192 (a.k.a. Irlo Bronson Memorial Highway, Vine Street, and Space Coast Parkway) are indicated by a "3." All others are marked with "2" and for the most part are along the I-4 corridor, though some are in nearby locations that don't meet any other criteria.

Properties along US 192 also carry location designations with their names, such as the Holiday Inn Maingate East. The consensus in Orlando seems to be that the main entrance to Walt Disney World is the broad interstate-type road that runs off of US 192. This is called Maingate. Properties along US 192 call themselves Maingate East or West to differentiate their positions along the highway. So, driving southeast from Clermont or the Florida Turnpike, the properties before you reach the Maingate turnoff are called Maingate West, while the properties after you pass the Maingate turnoff are called Maingate East.

How the Hotels Compare

Cost estimates are based on the hotel's published rack rates for standard rooms. Each "$" represents $40. Thus a cost symbol of "$$$" means a room (or suite) at that hotel will be about $120 a night.

Here's a hit parade of the nicest rooms in town. We've focused strictly on room quality and excluded consideration of location, services, recreation, or amenities. In some instances, a one- or two-room suite is available for the same price or less than that of a hotel room.

If you have used an earlier edition of this guide, you'll notice that new properties have been added and many ratings and rankings have changed, some because of room renovation or improved maintenance and housekeeping. Failure to maintain guest rooms or lax housekeeping can bring down ratings.

Before you shop for a hotel, consider this letter we received from a man in Hot Springs, Arkansas:

> *We canceled our room reservations to follow the advice in your book [and reserved a hotel highly ranked by the* Unofficial Guide]. *We wanted inexpensive, but clean and cheerful. We got inexpensive, but [also] dirty, grim, and depressing. I really felt disappointed in your advice and the room. It was the pits. That was the one real piece of information I needed from your book! The room spoiled the holiday for me aside from our touring.*

This letter was as unsettling to us as the bad room was to our reader. Our integrity as travel journalists is based on the quality of the information we provide our readers. Even with the best of intentions and the most conscientious research, we can't inspect every room in every hotel. What we do, in statistical terms, is take a sample: we check several rooms selected at random in each hotel and base our ratings and rankings on those rooms. The inspections are conducted anonymously and without the knowledge of the property's management. Although unusual, it's certainly possible that the rooms we randomly inspect aren't representative of the majority of rooms. Another possibility is that the rooms we inspect in a hotel are representative, but by bad luck a reader is assigned an inferior room. When rechecking the hotel our reader disliked, we discovered our rating was correctly representative, but that he and his wife had unfortunately been assigned one of a small number of threadbare rooms scheduled for renovation.

The key to avoiding disappointment is to snoop in advance. Ask the hotel to send a photo of its standard guest room before you book, or at least get a copy of the hotel's promotional brochure. Be aware that some hotel chains use the same guest-room photo in promotional literature for *all* hotels in the chain and that the guest room in a specific property may not resemble the photo in the brochure. When your travel agent or you call, ask how old the property is and when the guest room you are being assigned was last renovated. If you arrive and are assigned a room inferior to that which you had been led to expect, demand to be moved.

How the Hotels Compare

Hotel	Location	Room Star Rating	Room Quality Rating	Cost ($=$40)	Phone (A/C 407)
WDW Grand Floridian Resort	WDW	★★★★★	96	$$$$$$+	934-7639
WDW Boardwalk Villas	WDW	★★★★½	95	$$$$$$+	934-7639
WDW Old Key West Resort	WDW	★★★★½	94	$$$$$$−	934-7639
Hotel Royal Plaza (tower rooms)	WDW	★★★★½	93	$$$$$$−	828-2828
Shades of Green	WDW	★★★★½	93	na	824-3400

How the Hotels Compare (continued)

Hotel	Location	Room Star Rating	Room Quality Rating	Cost ($=$40)	Phone (A/C 407)
WDW Boardwalk Inn	WDW	★★★★½	93	$$$$$$+	934-7639
Marriott Orlando World Center	2	★★★★½	92	$$$$+	239-4200
WDW Beach Club Resort	WDW	★★★★½	92	$$$$$$$−	934-7639
WDW Yacht Club Resort	WDW	★★★★½	92	$$$$$$$−	934-7639
Peabody Orlando	1	★★★★½	91	$$$$$$$+	352-4000
Hyatt Regency Grand Cypress	2	★★★★½	90	$$$$$	239-1234
WDW Polynesian Resort	WDW	★★★★½	90	$$$$$$$−	934-7639
Renaissance Orlando Resort	2	★★★★	89	$$$+	351-5555
Crowne Plaza Resort	3	★★★★	87	$$$	239-1222
Hawthorne Suites Orlando	1	★★★★	87	$$+	351-6600
WDW Contemporary Resort	WDW	★★★★	87	$$$$$+	934-7639
Wyndham Royal Safari	2	★★★★	87	$$$$	(800) 423-3297
Embassy Suites Orlando International	1	★★★★	86	$$$$$$	352-1400
WDW Coronado Springs Resort	WDW	★★★★	86	$$$$	934-7639
WDW Dolphin Resort	WDW	★★★★	86	$$$$$$−	934-7639
WDW Swan	WDW	★★★★	86	$$$$$$−	934-7639
WDW Wilderness Lodge	WDW	★★★★	86	$$$$$	934-7639
Embassy Suites Resort	2	★★★★	85	$$$$+	239-1144

How the Hotels Compare (continued)

Hotel	Location	Room Star Rating	Room Quality Rating	Cost ($=$40)	Phone (A/C 407)
The Castle Hotel (Doubletree)	1	★★★★	84	$$$$–	345-1511
Doubletree Orlando Suites & Villas	3	★★★★	84	$$$$	397-0555
Hilton Disney Village	WDW	★★★★	84	$$$$$$$+	827-4000
WDW Caribbean Beach Resort	WDW	★★★★	84	$$$$–	934-7639
WDW Dixie Landings Resort	WDW	★★★★	84	$$$$	934-7639
WDW Port Orleans Resort	WDW	★★★★	84	$$$$	934-7639
Embassy Suites Plaza International	1	★★★★	83	$$$$	345-8250
Sierra Suites Lake Buena Vista	2	★★★★	83	$$$$	239-4300
Sierra Suites Pointe Orlando	1	★★★★	83	$$$$	903-1500
Sunterra Resorts Cypress Pointe	3	★★★★	83	$$$	532-1000
Clarion Suites Resort World	3	★★★½	82	$$$$	396-8300
Doubletree Guest Suites	WDW	★★★½	82	$$$$$+	934-1000
Radisson Twin Towers Hotel	1	★★★½	82	$$$$–	(800) 327-2110
Sheraton Studio City Hotel	1	★★★½	82	$$$–	351-2100
WDW Villas at the Disney Institute (bungalows)	WDW	★★★½	82	$$$$$	934-7639
Wyndham Palace	WDW	★★★½	82	$$$$–	827-2727
Amerisuites Orlando Convention Center	1	★★★½	81	$$$	370-4720
Buena Vista Suites	3	★★★½	81	$$$+	239-8588

How the Hotels Compare (continued)

Hotel	Location	Room Star Rating	Room Quality Rating	Cost ($=$40)	Phone (A/C 407)
Clarion Plaza Hotel	1	★★★½	81	$$$$$	352-9700
Radisson Resort Parkway	3	★★★½	81	$$$$–	396-7000
Summerfield Suites	1	★★★½	81	$$$$$$+	352-2400
Caribe Royale Resort Suites	3	★★★½	80	$$$$	238-8000
Holiday Inn Sun Spree Resort	2	★★★½	80	$$+	239-4500
Homewood Suites Maingate	3	★★★½	80	$$$+	396-2229
Omni Rosen Hotel	1	★★★½	80	$$$$$+	354-9840
Radisson Inn Lake Buena Vista	2	★★★½	80	$$$$	239-8400
Residence Inn Lake Cecile	3	★★★½	80	$$$	396-2056
Residence Inn Orlando	1	★★★½	80	$$+	345-0117
Summerfield Suites Lake Buena Vista	2	★★★½	79	$$$$$$+	238-0777
WDW Fort Wilderness Resort	WDW	★★★½	79	$$$$$	934-7639
Country Inn & Suites (suites)	2	★★★½	78	$$	239-1115
Orlando Marriott	1	★★★½	77	$$+	351-2420
RUI Orlando	2	★★★½	77	$$$$	239-8500
Courtyard by Marriott	1	★★★½	76	$$$+	351-2244
Grosvenor Resort	WDW	★★★½	76	$$$	828-4444
Holiday Inn Hotel & Suites Maingate East (suites)	3	★★★½	76	$$+	396-4488
Radisson Barcelo Inn International	1	★★★½	76	$$$–	345-0505
Courtyard Disney Village	WDW	★★★½	75	$$$+	828-8888
Courtyard Maingate	3	★★★½	75	$$	396-4000

How the Hotels Compare (continued)

Hotel	Location	Room Star Rating	Room Quality Rating	Cost ($=$40)	Phone (A/C 407)
Holiday Inn Universal Studios	1	★★★	74	$$$+	351-3333
Hyatt Orlando	3	★★★	74	$$$	396-1234
Quality Suites International Drive	1	★★★	74	$$$	363-0332
Ramada Plaza and Inn Gateway (tower rooms)	3	★★★	74	$$+	396-4400
Sheraton World Resort	1	★★★	74	$$$$+	352-1100
Nikki Bird Resort	3	★★★	73	$$	396-7300
Quality Suites Maingate East	3	★★★	73	$$+	396-8040
Westgate Lakes	2	★★★	73	$$$$$$	352-8051
WDW All Star Resort	WDW	★★★	73	$$+	934-7639
Country Inn & Suites (rooms)	?	★★★	72	$$	239-1115
Days Suites Maingate East	3	★★★	72	$$+	396-7900
La Quinta Inn Int'l	1	★★★	72	$$	351-1660
Wellesley Inn	1	★★★	72	$$+	345-0026
Country Hearth Inn	1	★★★	71	$$+	352-0008
Holiday Inn Hotel & Suites Maingate East (rooms)	3	★★★	71	$$+	396-4488
Holiday Inn International Resort	1	★★★	71	$$$−	351-3500
Holiday Inn Express	1	★★★	70	$$+	351-4430
Travelodge Hotel Disney Village	WDW	★★★	70	$$$−	828-2424
Comfort Suites Orlando	2	★★★	69	$$+	351-5050
Travelodge Suites Eastgate	3	★★★	69	$+	396-7666
Hampton Inn International Drive	1	★★★	68	$$	345-1112

		Room Star Rating	Room Quality Rating	Cost ($=$40)	Phone (A/C 407)
Hotel	**Location**				
Hampton Inn Maingate	3	★★★	68	$$+	396-8484
Hampton Inn Universal Studios	1	★★★	68	$$	351-6716
Hotel Royal Plaza (garden rooms)	WDW	★★★	68	$$$$$$–	828-2828
Enclave Suites	1	★★★	67	$$$$–	351-1155
Four Points Hotel by Lakeside	3	★★★	67	$$+	396-2222
Ramada Resort Florida Center	1	★★★	67	$$$–	351-4600
Westgate Towers	3	★★★	67	$$$$$$	396-2500
Hampton Inn Sandlake	1	★★★	66	$$	363-7886
Red Roof Inn Kissimmee	3	★★★	66	$+	396-0065
Wilson World Maingate	3	★★★	66	$$+	396-6000
Club Hotel by Doubletree	2	★★★	65	$$+	239-4646
Courtyard by Marriott	2	★★★	65	$$$	239-6900
Holiday Inn Maingate West	3	★★★	65	$$	396-1100
MIC Lakefront Inn	1	★★★	65	$+	345-5340
Best Western Plaza International	1	★★½	64	$$+	345-8195
Days Inn Maingate East	3	★★½	64	$$+	396-7900
Days Inn Orlando Lakeside	1	★★½	64	$+	351-1900
Delta Orlando Resort	1	★★½	64	$$$+	351-3340
Floridian of Orlando	1	★★½	64	$$$–	351-5009
Howard Johnson Maingate West	3	★★½	64	$$	396-9300
Howard Johnson Resort Hotel	3	★★½	64	$$+	396-4343

How the Hotels Compare (continued)

Hotel	Location	Room Star Rating	Room Quality Rating	Cost ($=$40)	Phone (A/C 407)
Quality Inn Lake Cecile	3	★★½	64	$+	396-4455
Doubletree Resort & Conference Center	3	★★½	63	$$$$$+	396-1400
Howard Johnson South Int'l Drive	1	★★½	63	$$$–	351-5100
Days Inn	3	★★½	62	$+	(800) 544-5713
Days Inn Eastgate	3	★★½	62	$+	396-7700
Days Inn Lake Buena Vista	2	★★½	62	$$$$+	239-4441
Howard Johnson Express Inn and Suites (suites)	3	★★½	62	$+	396-4762
La Suite Inn & Suites	1	★★½	62	$$+	351-4410
Quality Inn Plaza	1	★★½	62	$+	345-8585
Ramada Inn Westgate	3	★★½	62	$$	(941) 424-2621
Ramada Resort Maingate	3	★★½	62	$$	396-4466
Days Inn Maingate West	3	★★½	61	$$–	396-1000
Days Inn Universal Studios	1	★★½	61	$$-	351-3800
Fairfield Inn International	1	★★½	61	$$$	363-1944
Ramada Plaza and Inn Gateway (garden rooms)	3	★★½	61	$$	396-4400
Clarion Suites Resort World (rooms)	3	★★½	60	$$$+	396-8300
Comfort Inn at Lake Buena Vista	2	★★½	60	$$+	239-7300
Gateway Inn (renovated rooms)	1	★★½	60	$$	351-2000
Larson's Lodge Maingate	3	★★½	60	$$–	396-6100
Las Palmas Hotel	1	★★½	60	$$$–	351-3900

How the Hotels Compare (continued)

Hotel	Location	Room Star Rating	Room Quality Rating	Cost ($=$40)	Phone (A/C 407)
Quality Inn Maingate West	3	★★½	60	$$–	396-1828
Ramada Eastgate Fountain Park	3	★★½	60	$$–	396-1111
Travelodge Maingate East	3	★★½	60	$$	396-4222
Best Western Eastgate	3	★★½	59	$+	396-0707
Econo Lodge Maingate Hawaiian	3	★★½	59	$+	396-2000
Howard Johnson Express Inn and Suites (rooms)	3	★★½	59	$+	396-4762
Magic Castle	3	★★½	59	$	396-2212
Quality Inn International	1	★★½	59	$	351-1600
Wynfield Inn Westwood	1	★★½	59	$$+	(800) 346-1551
Ramada Limited Universal Maingate	1	★★½	58	$$–	354-3996
Red Roof Inn Orlando	1	★★½	58	$$+	352-1507
Super 8 Maingate	3	★★½	58	$+	396-8883
Comfort Inn Maingate	3	★★½	57	$+	396-7500
Days Inn Sea World/ Convention Center	1	★★½	57	$$+	352-8700
Econo Lodge International	1	★★½	57	$+	(800) 327-0750
Howard Johnson Inn Maingate East	3	★★½	57	$$+	396-1748
Motel 6 Maingate East	3	★★½	57	$	396-6333
Economy Inns of America	3	★★½	56	$	396-4020

How the Hotels Compare (continued)

Hotel	Location	Room Star Rating	Room Quality Rating	Cost ($=$40)	Phone (A/C 407)
Kissimmee Super 8 Motel	3	★★½	56	$+	396-1144
Riande Continental Plaza	1	★★½	56	$+	352-8211
Super 8 Universal	1	★★½	56	$+	352-8383
Travelodge Suites	3	★★½	56	$$−	396-1780
Knights Inn Maingate	3	★★	55	$$+	396-4200
Rodeway Inn International	1	★★	55	$$−	351-4444
Golden Link Motel	3	★★	54	$	396-0555
Howard Johnson Lodge	1	★★	54	$$	351-2900
Wynfield Inn Maingate	3	★★	54	$$−	(800) 346-1551
Days Inn International Drive	1	★★	53	$$	351-1200
Park Inn International	3	★★	53	$	396-1376
Knights Inn Maingate East	3	★★	52	$+	396-8186
Motel 6 Maingate West	3	★★	52	$	396-6427
Sleep Inn Maingate	3	★★	52	$+	396-1600
Traveler's Inn	3	★★	52	$+	396-1668
Universal Inn	1	★★	52	$$+	351-4100
Central Motel	3	★★	51	$	396-2333
Gateway Inn	1	★★	51	$$	351-2000
Red Carpet Inn East	3	★★	50	$	396-1133
Motel 6 International Drive	1	★★	49	$	351-6500
Monte Carlo	3	★★	48	$−	396-4700
Sun Motel	3	★½	46	$	396-2673

THE TOP 30 BEST DEALS

Having listed the nicest rooms in town, let's take a look at the best combinations of quality and value in a room. As before, the rankings are made without consideration of location or the availability of restaurant(s), recreational facilities, entertainment, and/or amenities.

A reader recently wrote us to complain that he had booked one of our top-ranked rooms in terms of value and had been very disappointed in the room. We noticed that the room the reader occupied had a quality rating of ★★½. We would remind you that the list of top deals are intended to give you some sense of value received for dollars spent. A ★★½ room at $30 may have the same value as a ★★★★ room at $85, but that does not mean the rooms will be of comparable quality. Regardless of whether it's a good deal or not, a ★★½ room is still a ★★½ room.

Listed below are the top 30 room buys for the money, regardless of location or star classification, based on average rack rates. Note that a suite can sometimes cost less than a hotel room.

The Top 30 Best Deals					
Hotel	Location	Room Star Rating	Room Quality Rating	Cost $=$40	Phone (A/C 407)
1. Hawthorne Suites Orlando	1	★★★★	87	$$+	351-6600
2. Magic Castle	3	★★½	59	$	396-2212
3. Quality Inn International	1	★★½	59	$	351-1600
4. Travelodge Suites Eastgate	3	★★★	69	$+	396-7666
5. Country Inn & Suites (suites)	2	★★★½	78	$$	239-1115
6. Motel 6 Maingate East	3	★★½	57	$	396-6333
7. Courtyard Maingate	3	★★★½	75	$$	396-4000
8. MIC Lakefront Inn	1	★★½	65	$+	345-5340
9. Red Roof Inn Kissimmee	3	★★★	66	$+	396-0065
10. Holiday Inn Sun Spree Resort	2	★★★½	80	$$+	239-4500
11. Economy Inns of America	3	★★½	56	$	396-4020

The Top 30 Best Deals (continued)

Hotel	Location	Room Star Rating	Room Quality Rating	Cost $=$40	Phone (A/C 407)
12. Golden Link Motel	3	★★	54	$	396-0555
13. Orlando Marriott	1	★★★½	77	$$+	351-2420
14. Best Western Eastgate	3	★★½	59	$+	396-0707
15. Econo Lodge Maingate Hawaiian	3	★★½	59	$+	396-2000
16. Days Inn Orlando Lakeside	1	★★½	64	$+	351-1900
17. Crowne Plaza Resort	3	★★★★	87	$$$	239-1222
18. Quality Inn Lake Cecile	3	★★½	64	$+	396-4455
19. Monte Carlo	3	★★	48	$−	396-4700
20. Comfort Inn Maingate	3	★★½	57	$+	396-7500
21. Super 8 Maingate	3	★★½	58	$+	396-8883
22. Sunterra Resorts Cypress Pointe	3	★★★★	83	$$$	532-1000
23. Residence Inn Orlando	1	★★★½	80	$$+	345-0117
24. Howard Johnson Express Inn and Suites (suites)	3	★★½	62	$+	396-4762
25. Kissimmee Super 8 Motel	3	★★½	56	$+	396-1144
26. Riande Continental Plaza	1	★★½	56	$+	352-8211
27. Days Inn	3	★★½	62	$+	(800) 544-5713
28. Nikki Bird Resort	3	★★★	73	$$	396-7300
29. Country Inn & Suites (rooms)	2	★★★	72	$$	239-1115
30. Howard Johnson Express Inn and Suites (rooms)	3	★★½	59	$+	396-4762

Part Four

The Disney Cruise Line

The Mouse at Sea

In case you've been raising chinchillas on Venus, here's the news: The Walt Disney Company is now in the cruise business with two almost identical ships called the *Disney Wonder* and the *Disney Magic*. Cruises originate at Port Canaveral (about an hour's drive from the Orlando airport) and visit Nassau in the Bahamas and Castaway Cay, Disney's private island, on three- and four-day itineraries.

Cruises can be purchased separately or as part of weeklong packages that split the seven days between the cruise and three or four days at Walt Disney World. Included in the packages are your Disney World hotel, theme park admissions, transportation (called transfers) from Walt Disney World or the airport to the ship, and the cruise.

When Disney does something, it usually does it in a big, spare-no-expenses way. So, we were ready for the new Disney Cruise Line to make a huge splash in July 1998, when its first ship, *Disney Magic,* was launched. Owing to typical Disney determination to reinvent the wheel, however, the enterprise got off to a rocky start, with management predictably ignoring the lessons learned by every other cruise line since the beginning of time. After loads of bad press and thousands of livid customers, Disney finally adopted the conventional, proven, industry-standard method of operating and managing cruise ships. Now everything is fine.

What you will see is the result of three years of intensive planning. From the outset, Disney assembled a team of highly respected veterans of the cruise industry and dozens of the world's best-known ship designers and put them together with their own unrivaled team of creative talent. Together, they conceptualized and created the Disney ships, recognizing that every detail would be critical to the line's success.

Their task was to design a product that would have every adult on board feeling like the vacation was intended for them, and at the same time, give every kid the feeling that the vacation was likewise created just for them.

The first surprise is the appearance of the Disney ships. They are simultaneously classic and innovative. The exteriors are based on traditional lines, reminiscent of the great oceanliners of the past, but even in that respect, you'll find a Disney twist or two. Inside, they are up to the minute in technology and full of novel ideas for dining, entertainment, cabin design, and entertainment facilities. Even the cruise terminal built for Disney's exclusive use at Port Canaveral is an integral part of the overall strategy; namely, to make even embarkation and debarkation—revealed to be a negative aspect of cruising by Disney's market research—experiences that are now, if not exactly enjoyable, at least tolerable.

The major innovation is in dining. Each evening on board you dine in a different restaurant, each with a different motif, but your waiters and dining companions move with you. Overcoming another cruising negative—the hassle of tendering passengers—was also an important consideration for Disney in selecting its private Bahamian island that is included on all cruises; namely, finding one with deep water where facilities could be built for their ships to pull dockside.

Disney's plan has been to create a "seamless vacation package" combining a three- or four-day stay at Walt Disney World with a three- or four-day cruise. Disney Cruise Line passengers are met at the airport by Disney staff and transported to the terminal in easily identifiable Disney Cruise Line buses. During the hour-long ride from the airport to Port Canaveral, they watch a video preview of the cruise. To allow a smooth embarkation, Disney has taken the "seamless vacation" a step further. There are meant to be no lines to check in for your cruise. When your cruise is packaged with a stay at a Disney hotel, you check in once. The same key that unlocks your hotel room door opens the door to your cruise ship cabin.

The Disney Cruise Line targets first-time cruisers, counting on Disney's reputation for quality, service, and entertainment to dispel noncruisers' doubts about cruise vacations. At the same time, a great deal of time and effort has been spent to ensure that the ships are designed to appeal to adults—with or without children—as much as to accommodate children and families. Adults are catered to in myriad ways and presented with an extensive menu of adult-oriented activities. For example, the ships have an alternative restaurant, swimming pool, and nightclub for use by adults only, and entertainment choices range from family musicals to adults-only improv comedy. Meanwhile, from virtually sunrise to almost midnight, children are offered an equally varied selection of programs from which to choose. Because the programs for both adults and for children are offered on an à la carte basis, families can choose how much time to spend together or pursuing separate interests.

If you need a breather from the kids, you won't have much trouble escaping, even with hundreds of children on board. The children's programs are excellent—in fact, they are rated as the best in the cruise industry in the current edition of the *Unofficial Guide to Cruises,* by Kay Showker and Bob Sehlinger. Thus, it's no big surprise that many parents only see their kids at breakfast and dinner. Much more difficult to escape than children, however, is Disney's syrupy, wholesome, cuter-than-a-billion-Beanie-Babies brand of entertainment, which permeates every aspect of the cruise. Expressed differently, to enjoy a Disney cruise you'd better love Disney.

Disney Cruise Line Standard Features

Officers   European.

Staffs   Cabin, dining/European; Cruise/American.

Dining Facilities   Three themed family restaurants with "rotation" dining; alternative adults-only restaurant; indoor/outdoor cafe for breakfast, lunch, snacks, and buffet dinner for children; pool bar/grill for burgers, pizza, and sandwiches; ice cream bar.

Special Diets   On request; health-conscious cuisine program.

Room Service   24 hours.

Dress Code   Casual by day; casual and informal in the evenings.

Cabin Amenities   Direct-dial telephone with voicemail messaging; both tub and shower; TV; safe; hair dryer; mini-bar stocked for fee.

Electrical Outlets   110 AC.

Wheelchair Access   Yes.

Smoking   Smoking not allowed except in special areas.

Disney Suggested Tipping   Waiter: 3-night cruise, $10; 4-night, $14; assistant waiter, $6 and $8. Cabin steward: 3-night cruise, $10.50; 4-night, $14; 15% service charge added to bar bills.

Credit Cards   For cruise payment and on-board charges, all major credit cards.

The Ships

Disney Magic and *Disney Wonder* are modern cruise ships with long, sleek lines, twin smokestacks, and nautical styling that recalls a classic oceanliner but with instantly recognizable Disney signatures. The colors—black, white, red, and yellow—and the famous face-and-ears silhouette on the stacks are clearly those of Mickey Mouse. Look closely and you'll see that the figurehead is a 15-foot Goofy, swinging upside down from a boat-swain's chair, "painting" the stern.

The interior decor combines nautical themes with art deco inspiration, but Disney images are everywhere, from the more subtle use of Mickey's familiar profile in the wrought-iron balustrades to the bronze statue of Helmsman Mickey at the center of the three-deck Grand Atrium. Disney art is on every wall, stairwell, and corridor. Some are valuable prints of Disney animated cartoon characters. From the atrium lobby a grand staircase sweeps up to shops that feature Disney Cruise Line–themed clothing, collectibles, jewelry, and sundries, and another shop with classic Disney toys, T-shirts, and souvenirs. (The shops are always full of eager buyers; some people speculate that the cruise line will derive as much revenue here as other lines do from their casinos, which the Disney ships do not have.)

The ships' layout has two lower decks with cabins, three decks with dining rooms and show rooms, then three decks of cabins, and two sports and sun decks with separate pools and other facilities for children and families and for adults without kids. Signs with the names of lounges and facilities on each deck have arrows pointing the way, and all elevator banks are clearly marked—forward, aft, or amidship.

Our main complaint concerning the design of the ships is that all outdoor public areas are inwardly focused, that is, toward the pools as opposed to seaward, as if Disney wanted you to forget you are on a cruise liner. In fact, there is no public place on any deck where you can curl up in shady spot and watch the ocean (at least not without a wall of Plexiglas between you and it). If this quintessential cruise pleasure ranks high on your hit parade, your only option is to spring for a cabin with a private veranda. A second predictable, but nonetheless irritating, design characteristic is the extent to which the ship is childproofed. There's enough Plexiglas on the *Magic* to build a subdivision of transparent homes. On the pool deck (Deck 9) especially, it feels as if the ship is hermetically sealed.

CABINS

The Disney ships have spacious cabins and suites. About three-fourths are outside and almost half of those come with private verandas. The ships offer 12 cabin categories from standard to deluxe, deluxe with veranda, family suite, one- and two-bedroom suites, and royal suite. Categories are similar to those at Walt Disney World hotels. Passengers who choose to spend three or four days at a Disney resort are matched with a cabin in a comparable category.

The design of the cabins, particularly, reveals Disney's finely tuned sense of the needs of families and children and offers a cruise industry first: a split bathroom with bathtub/shower and sink in one room and toilet, sink, and vanity in another. This configuration, found in all but the standard inside cabin category, is designed so that any member of the family can use the bathroom without monopolizing it entirely. Every bathroom has both a tub and shower.

The decor uses wood paneling generously and has unusual features, such as bureaus designed to look like steamer trunks—a nod to tradition. The cabins also have a direct-dial telephone with voicemail messaging; TV; hair dryer; and mini-fridge. All cabins sleep at least three and many can accommodate up to six people. In some cabins, pull-down Murphy beds allow for additional daytime floor space. Storage space is generous with deep drawers and large closets.

On each ship the cabin inventory includes 186 inside cabins and 689 outside cabins; 385 suites with verandas, 82 family suites, 16 one-bedroom suites, two two-bedroom suites, two royal suites; 14 wheelchair-accessible accommodations. All cabins accommodate three people; inside cabins up to four; deluxe with verandas up to four; family and one-bedroom suites up to five.

Services and Amenities

Passengers are lavish with their praise of Disney cast members. They are among the most accommodating you will ever encounter in travel, and they try hard to smooth your way from boarding to departure. *Unofficial Guide* cruise writer Kay Showker related, "More than once when I stopped to get my bearings on the ship or Castaway Cay, a Disney cast member was there within seconds to help me."

You will be given a Disney Magic Passport, a convenient purse-sized booklet that covers just about everything you need to know for your cruise. Daily in your cabin, you will find "Your Personal Navigator." These information sheets list on-board entertainment and daily activities, broken down into options for teens, children, adults, and families as well as information on shore excursions.

DINING

Dining is Disney's most innovative area. The ships have three different family restaurants, plus an alternative restaurant for adults only. Each night passengers move to a different family restaurant, each with a different theme and different menu, taking their table companions and wait staff with them. In each of the restaurants, the tableware, linens, menu covers, and waiters' uniforms have been designed specifically to fit the theme.

Lumière's, named for the candlestick character from *Beauty and the Beast*, is an elegant venue with handsome, refined, art-deco design and featuring continental cuisine served against a mural depicting Disney's *Beauty and the Beast*. Along with Palo, the alternative reservations-only restaurant, Lumière's serves the best food on board. It is also the preferred venue for cruisers who appreciate a bit more formal service and setting at their evening meal. Children like Lumière's, though the meal is served at a slightly more leisurely pace than elsewhere.

Parrot Cay dishes up Caribbean-accented food in a colorful, fun, tropical setting that reminds most Disney veterans on the Enchanted Tiki Room. Parrot Cay is the most popular of the three for breakfast. Children particularly enjoy the decor and festivity, but the food, although adequate, is not up to the standard of the other restaurants.

Animator's Palate, however, a concept restaurant that reflects the creative genius of Disney animation, is the ships' dining pièce de résistance (or for some, the straw that broke the camel's back). Diners have the impression that they have entered into a sketch in black and white, as though it were the outlines of an artist's inspiration. Over the course of the meal, the black and white sketches on the walls are transformed through the use of fiber optics into a full-color extravaganza. The waiters change their costumes from black and white to color. The first course is a montage of appetizers served on a plate in the shape of an artist's palette. The dessert—a mousse in the shape of Mickey's famous silhouette—comes with a parade by the waiters with trays of colorful syrups (mango, chocolate, and strawberry), which diners use to decorate their dessert. All of this is accompanied, of course, by the trumpeting theme music of Disney films, punctuated by various fanfares.

Animator's Palate is arguably a dinner theater. The food is well prepared and nicely presented, but it is the ongoing show that dominates the meal. Conversation is often difficult, and the entertainment, though creative, is the ultimate in Disney cute (and totally inescapable). Children, predictably, love it, but for many adults it's a little overwhelming.

Palo, the casual Italian restaurant named for the pole that gondoliers use to navigate the canals of Venice, is the intimate, adults-only alternative restaurant, located high in the ship. Palo is the ship's showcase restaurant and has its own kitchen. The lovely semicircular room in contemporary design with art deco touches has a sophisticated ambience with soft lighting, Venetian glass, inlaid wood, and a back-lit bar. The menu features northern Italian cuisine. The food and presentation are excellent. More than two dozen wines are available by the glass for $5.50–25. There is a $5-per-person cover charge (but no signs in the restaurant, on the menu, or in the ship literature alert you to it). Service is slow, though it may just seem that way in comparison to the staccato dining pace of the other restaurants on board. Reservations are required, and you need to make them as soon as you board the ship—Palo gets booked up quickly for the entire cruise. (Apparently, Disney underestimated the demand for the alternative venue, and it's hard to see how the ship can solve the problem given the room's limited capacity.)

There are two seatings, at 6 and 8:30 p.m., for dinner at Lumière's, Animator's Palate, and Parrot Cay. If your children are 12 years old or younger and you plan to dine as a family, we recommend the early seating. If your kids are involved in programs where they dine with the other children, go with your own preference. All three restaurants offer special kid's meals if your picky eaters can't find something they like on the regular menu.

On a three-day cruise, your normal rotation will have you dine one night each at Lumière's, Animator's Palate, and Parrot Cay. If you sign up to dine at Palo (adults only), you will skip the regular restaurant designated for that night on your rotation. Thus, choose your Palo night carefully. Our vote for the most expendable restaurant on the rotation is Parrot Cay. In any event, if you miss Parrot Cay for dinner, you can still try it at lunch or breakfast. On a four-day cruise, one of the regular restaurants will pop up twice on your rotation. If you want to eat at all of the restaurants, including Palo, make your Palo reservation on the night that you are scheduled to repeat one of the basic three.

Shortly after boarding Disney gives you the opportunity to both make Palo reservations (taken in the restaurant) and/or change your restaurant rotation if you desire. In our opinion, one night each at Animator's Palate or Parrot Cay is enough. If your rotation calls for you to repeat a night in either, eliminate the repeat by booking Palo or substituting a second night at Lumière's.

If you're wondering what to do with your children while you dine at Palo, you have several options. You can make a late reservation for Palo, and then keep your children company (but not eat) while they dine at the regularly assigned restaurant. This only works, however if you normally eat at the first seating. Alternatively, you can place your children in a program where they will eat dinner with the other enrolled kids; or, you can take your children to Pluto's Dog House, poolside on Deck 9, for hot dogs and burgers; or, you can order them a room service dinner and arrange for a private sitter.

Buffet & Fast Food Other dining options include Topsiders, an indoor/outdoor cafe serving buffet breakfast and lunch as well as snacks; a pool bar and grill for hamburgers, hot dogs, and sandwiches; Pinocchio's Pizzeria; an ice cream and frozen yogurt bar; and 24-hour room service. Topsiders is the weak sister of the bunch: It's OK for breakfast, but long on bulk and short on flavor for lunch. The pizza, dogs, burgers, yogurt, and ice cream are good.

FACILITIES AND ENTERTAINMENT

Disney is keeping its promise that the ships' nightly entertainment, featuring quality, Disney-produced shows, is unlike any other cruise line. Walt Disney Theater, a 1,000-seat theater with an orchestra pit and superb sight lines and acoustics, stages a different musical production each night, with quality actors, singers, and dancers. These uniquely Disney family musicals are on the level of the theme parks' entertainment rather than Broadway and will probably appeal to children more than adults.

Disney Dreams has about every Disney character and song you've ever heard and is based on a light plot with Peter Pan visiting a girl who dreams of Disney's famous animated characters. It's pure schmaltz, but the audience gave the show a standing ovation. As for the kids at the late show, many in the room had dozed off to their own dreamland before the curtain fell.

Another night offers *Hercules, The MUSE-ical,* a musical comedy that is decidedly less smarmy than the other two shows. *Voyage of the Ghost Ship* is an original musical with a story line, great staging and special effects, and songs and dances that show the talented singers and dancers at their best.

On the night that the ships dock in Nassau, the Walt Disney Theater gives way to a Bahamian *Jump Up Junkanoo* party on the pool deck featuring a stage show followed by dancing.

In the smaller Buena Vista Theater with full-screen cinema and Dolby sound, passengers can watch first-run movies and classic Disney films. Show times vary, and showings are not continuous. Check Your Personal Navigator to see what's on.

Studio Sea, modeled after a television- or film-production set, is a family-oriented nightclub offering dance music, family-oriented cabaret acts, passenger game shows, and multimedia entertainment. The art deco Promenade Lounge offers a haven for reading and relaxation by day and cocktails and piano music by night. The ESPN Skybox, a sports bar, is in the ship's forward, decorative funnel and has a bar, a big screen TV for viewing ESPN-televised sporting events, and a small viewing area with stadium-type seating.

Beat Street is an adult-oriented evening entertainment district with shops and three themed nightclubs—Rockin' Bar D, with live bands playing rock and roll, Top 40, and country music; Off Beat, an improv comedy club showcasing live talent nightly; and Sessions, a casual, yet sophisticated place to relax and enjoy easy-listening music.

Disney ships have no casinos. Disney says their research showed that its target markets were not interested in gambling at sea. The ships also have no library, no enrichment programs for adults (although the line says it will be adding them), nor does it serve afternoon tea, which is a highlight on many other cruise lines.

CHILDREN'S PROGRAMS

Kids have more than 15,000 square feet of space with playrooms and other facilities. The children's programs consist of age-specific activities, including challenging interactive programs and play areas supervised by a squadron of trained youth counselors. There are separate programs for ages 3–5, 6–8, 9–10, 11–12, and for teens. The ships also offer a children's drop-off service in the evening as well as private babysitting services for $11 per hour for the first child and $1 for each additional child in the same family. Even at these prices, babysitters are booked up almost immediately after passengers board.

Oceaneer's Adventure is the name of the overall children's program. Oceaneer's Club (ages 3–8) is themed to resemble Captain Hook's pirate ship, with plenty of places to run, climb, and perform. Children under three years of age are welcome to use the facility, but must be supervised by a parent. The club is an absolute paradise for most kids. There are costumes for dress-up play, toys, games, crafts, a huge climb-and-crawl jungle gym, and mats for tumbling (or sleeping).

Oceaneer's Lab (ages 9–12) has more high-tech play such as video games, computers, and lab equipment. There is also a small area for listening to CDs. The lab is divided into sections specially designed for specific activities such as arts and crafts, science, computers, games, and music.

Children move about the ship with their counselors to locations appropriate for the various programs, so you need to pick up a "Children's Events Guide" to determine your child's whereabouts on the ship when he or she is participating in a supervised activity. One place the counselors do not take their charges, however, is to the pools. When your children swim, either on board or at Castaway Cay, you will be responsible for watching them.

You can register at the clubs immediately after boarding by completing a Participation Confirmation Form. In addition to providing basic information about each child (name, age, cabin number, medical conditions, and so on), you will sign an authorization to administer first aid and will choose a password that must be provided to the counselors whenever you check your child in or out. If you want to designate other adults who are authorized to check your kids in and out, you can list them on the form. Like you, however, they must always provide the correct password. If your child is between 9 and 12 years old you can, at your discretion, give your child permission to check him- or herself in and out. Kids get ID bracelets, and parents are given pagers that enable them to leave their kids to play at their leisure, but still stay in touch.

Once your children are registered, you can select programs and activities on an à la carte basis. Just make sure you show up about 15 minutes in advance so you can get your child checked in before the program starts. In a similar vein, parents are requested not to check a child out while a program is in progress. In addition to the programs, the counselors will also take your children to lunch or dinner at Topsiders. The same check-in and check-out procedure applies as for programs and activities. At Castaway Cay the children's programs move ashore. Parents must escort their children off the ship and check them in at the activity area on the island.

The children's programs get high marks from both parents and kids. Common Grounds (on Deck 9) is a separate area for teens themed after a trendy coffee bar (as in the TV show *Friends*) and has a game arcade, a selection of video movies, and a CD listening lounge. There are also organized programs for teens, such as nighttime volleyball games on the Sports deck, making a video about the cruise, and kayaking at Castaway Cay. The teen program particularly seems to be a big hit, as the teens enjoy having a large part of the upper deck to themselves in the evenings. Teen activities are supervised in a way that makes the participants feel unfettered and autonomous. Other than counselors, for example, no adults are allowed in the Common Grounds teen club.

SPORTS, FITNESS, AND BEAUTY

Of the three top-deck pools, one, with a Mickey Mouse motif and a water slide, is intended for families, another is set aside for team sports, and the third is exclusively for adults. At night the pool area can be transformed into a stage for deck parties and dancing.

The 8,500-square-foot ocean-view Vista Spa and salon, situated above the bridge, is outfitted with Cybex exercise equipment and has an aerobics room, thermal-bath area, saunas, and steam rooms. It is supervised by a qualified fitness director and offers exercise instruction. The spa, run by the British-based Steiner group, which operates the majority of cruise ship spas, offers an array of pricey beauty treatments along with a sales pitch on Steiner products. But despite the high prices (the same on all ships), the spa has proven to be more popular than Disney planners had anticipated and is generally booked up for the entire cruise within the first few hours after passengers board.

The Sports Deck has a paddle tennis court, Ping-Pong, basketball court, shuffleboard, and a batting and driving range. There is also a full promenade deck for walking and jogging, but it has no lounge chairs.

Ports of Call

NASSAU

Disney Magic docks in Nassau for 18 hours, which is plenty of time to explore the island, enjoy a sport, visit the newly expanded Atlantis resort on Paradise Island, and take in a show and casino. We think the Nassau port of call is the weakest element in the cruise itinerary, especially if you are looking for something you and your children can do together that everyone will really enjoy. The shore excursions offered are expensive and not particularly compelling, and the island has limited appeal for walking or self-guided tours. Most families walk around for an hour or so, checking out the shopping and the street scene, and then spend the rest of the day back on board.

Shore Excursions The ship offers 12 different excursions for Nassau that it claims were designed especially for the line. Actually, all but one are fairly standard tours offered by most cruise ships. Among the choices are the Historical Harbor Cruise ($20 for adults; $14.50 for children); the Blue Lagoon Beach Day ($25/$17.50); Crystal Cay Marine Park ($23/$16.50); the Island World Exuma Adventure ($150 per person); and deep-sea fishing ($700 for 1–7 people for a half-day). All children's prices apply to ages 3 through 9.

CASTAWAY CAY

Each Disney cruise includes a day at Castaway Cay, Disney's 1,000-acre private island. The natural environment and beauty of the island, which Disney was careful to preserve, prevails ashore. The island has miles of white sand beaches surrounded by clear, emerald water. A pier was built at Castaway Cay to allow easy and convenient access for passengers and to avoid tendering. A four-car open tram (like those used at the theme park parking lots) carries you from the ship to Scuttle's Cove, the family beach. The shuttle runs continuously every five minutes. En route, a recording narrates a mythical version of the island's history. If you prefer, you can walk the quarter-mile distance from the ship to the family beach or the one-third mile to the teen beach. A second tram takes you to Serenity Bay, the adult beach on the other side of the island. Strollers are readily available, as are floats that rent for the day and bikes, kayaks, and snorkel gear that rent by the hour or half-hour. The beaches have plenty of lounge chairs under pastel-colored umbrellas and some hammocks under the palms, but there's very little shade otherwise.

All around the island, you'll see Disney Imagineers' handiwork, creating what is, in essence, stage sets and props. All the buildings—shops, rest rooms, and pavilions—look weathered to give the impression that they have been there for years. There's a special area for kids with supervised activity, including a "dig" at a half-buried whale skeleton.

There is a protected lagoon for water sports. The lagoon has two snorkeling courses—one close to shore and the other farther out, requiring more endurance. The longer course takes about an hour and a half to swim. Along the way, you'll see a variety of fish, some of which you can identify by using a waterproof card that comes with the rental equipment. The other side of the card displays the two courses to help you navigate from one buoy to another. Lifeguards who keep watch on the snorkelers are posted all around the courses. The cruise line has also planted several shipwrecks in the water. On one wreck in about ten feet of water, snorkelers can see Mickey Mouse riding the bow of the ship. There's also a treasure chest, its contents guarded by several large fish. Snorkel equipment can be rented for a pricey $27 for adults and $19.50 for children. Nature trails and bike paths provide a day alternative to snorkeling.

Kids and families are anchored to the main beach area with its supervised children's activities. There's also an entertainment stage with live Bahamian music, and shops. Cookie's Bar-B-Cue serves a buffet lunch featuring burgers, pork ribs, hot dogs, baked beans, slaw, corn on the cob, fruit, and potato chips.

On the opposite side of the island (about a half-mile removed), adults have a long, peaceful sweep of sugary sand to themselves. There is a bar serving drinks and they can enjoy a massage in one of the private cabanas on the beach with shuttered doors that open to the sea.

Passengers must be back on the ship by 3:15 p.m., which makes for a short day. Most folks say they would have liked more time on the island.

Rates

Although Disney bundles its cruises with a stay at Walt Disney World, you can usually beat the package price by buying your vacation components à la carte. Disney cruise only brochure rates start at $800 per person (based on double occupancy) for a standard inside cabin on a three-day cruise and run to about $1,750 for a cabin with a veranda on a four-day cruise. Suites cost up to $3,000 for a four-day cruise. Seven-day packages that include a stay at Walt Disney World start at $1,300 and run to about $4,300 per person. Fares for children sharing a cabin with their parents run $179 to $529. Port charges are included in the price.

Our advice is to shop the non-Disney cruise discount agencies. Some agencies sell only cruises, but others can sell the entire Disney cruise/land package. So far, however, we haven't seen a package that we couldn't beat by purchasing the components individually ourselves.

Cruise Discount Agencies		
All Cruise Travel	(800) 227-8473	www.allcruise.com
Crown Travel	(800) 869-7447	www.crowncruise.com
Cruise Match	(800) 925-8572	www.cruisematch.com
Cruise Value Center	(800) 231-7447	www.cruisevalue.com
Mann Travel & Cruises	(800) 438-3709	www.travelcruises.com
The Travel Company	(800) 895-3771	www.travelco.com

As a courtesy, once you've shopped around and determined the lowest price available, give your regular travel agent the opportunity to match or beat it. In addition to discounts offered by cruise sellers like those listed above, additional savings ("early bird" discounts) can be had by booking well in advance. If for some reason you prefer to book directly with Disney, here's how to get in touch:

Disney Cruise Line
210 Celebration Place, Suite 400
Celebration, FL 34747-4600
(407) 939-3727; fax: (407) 939-3750
www.disneycruise.com

A Few Tips

1. If you opt for a week that includes the cruise and a stay at Walt Disney World, go to Disney World first. Taking the cruise at the end of your vacation will ensure that you arrive home relaxed and rested.

2. Board the ship as early as possible. Check your dining rotation, and arrange for changes if you desire. Make reservations for Palo as soon as the reservations desk at the restaurant opens, usually 2 p.m.

3. After firming up your dining arrangements, register your children at Oceaneer Club (ages 3–8) and/or Oceaneer Lab (ages 9–12). If you board before 1:30 p.m., register your kids first and then attend to your dining arrangements.

4. If you are interested in a message or other spa services, sign up between 2 and 4 p.m. at the spa.

5. Disney requests that gentlemen wear jackets (no ties required) in the evening at Palo and Lumiere's.

6. If you are staying at a Disney resort prior to your cruise, be sure to fill out and hand in your cruise forms at the hotel. By flashing your shoreside room key card at the cruise terminal, you can bypass lines and board the ship directly. If you are a "cruise only" passenger, you might encounter a wait at check-in.

7. Because most cabins have a mini-fridge, we recommend bringing your own snacks and beverages.

8. The Sessions piano bar is one of the most relaxing and beautiful lounges we have ever seen on a cruise ship. Make a before- or after-dinner drink at The Sessions part of your daily routine. It's on Deck 3, forward.

9. Don't miss the Offbeat comedy club, located on Deck 3, forward.

10. We checked out all of the children's programs and interviewed lots of families. Listed below are the programs your kids won't want to miss:

Ages 3–5
Off to Neverland
Clarabell Cow's Moo Juice Jumble
Do Si Do with Snow White
Legend of Chick Chjarnie

Ages 6–8
Animation Antics
So You Want to See a Pirate
Professor Goo's Magical Experiments
Eggsperiment
Dig At Monstro Point
Noodle Frenzy
Gasses in Action

Ages 9–10
Now a Word
Quackamation
Radio Waves
Dig at Monstro Point
Apprentices Workshop

Ages 11–12
Goofin' Around with Animation
Soundtracks
Dig at Monstro Point
Science Sorcery

Part Five

Walt Disney World with Kids

The Ecstasy and the Agony

So overwhelming is the Disney media and advertising presence that any child who watches TV or shops with Mom is likely to get revved up about going to Walt Disney World. Parents, if anything, are even more susceptible. Almost every parent has brightened with anticipation at the prospect of guiding their children through the wonders of this special place. But the reality of taking a young child (particularly in summer) is usually closer to the agony than the ecstasy.

A mother from Dayton, Ohio, describes taking her five-year-old to Disney World in July:

> I felt so happy and excited before we went. I guess it was all worth it, but when I look back I think I should have had my head examined. The first day we went to [the Magic Kingdom] and it was packed. By 11 in the morning we had walked so far and stood in so many lines that we were all exhausted. Kristy cried about going on anything that looked or even sounded scary and was frightened by all of the Disney characters (they are so big!) except Minnie and Snow White.
>
> We got hungry about the same time as everyone else, but the lines for food were too long and my husband said we would have to wait. By one in the afternoon we were just plugging along, not seeing anything we were really interested in, but picking rides because the lines were short, or because whatever it was was air-conditioned. We rode Small World three times in a row, and I'll never get that song out of my head (Ha!). At around 2:30 we finally got something to eat, but by then we were so hot and tired that it felt like we had worked in the yard all day. Kristy insisted on being carried, and we had 50 fights about not going on rides where the lines were too long. At the end, we were so P.O.'d

*and uncomfortable that we weren't having any fun. Mostly by this time
we were just trying to get our money's worth.*

Before you stiffen in denial, let me assure you that the Ohio family's
experience is fairly typical. Most young children are as picky about the
rides as they are about what they eat, and more than half of preschoolers
are intimidated by the friendly Disney characters. Few humans (of any age)
are mentally or physically equipped to march all day in a throng of 50,000
people in the hot Florida sun. And would you be surprised to learn that
almost 60% of preschoolers said the thing they liked best about their Disney World vacation was the hotel swimming pool?

Reality Testing—Whose Dream Is It?

Remember when you were little and you got that nifty electric train for
Christmas, the one Dad wouldn't let you play with? Did you ever wonder
who that train was really for? Ask yourself the same question about your
vacation to Walt Disney World. Whose dream are you trying to make
come true: yours or your child's?

Young children are adept at reading their parents' emotions. When you
ask, "Honey, how would you like to go to Disney World?" your child will
respond more to your smile and excitement and the idea of doing something with Mom and Dad than to any notion of what Disney World is all
about. The younger the child, the more this is true. For many preschoolers,
you could elicit the same enthusiasm by asking, "Honey, how would you
like to go to Cambodia on a dogsled?"

So, is your happy fantasy of introducing your child to Disney magic a
pipe dream? Not necessarily, but you have to be practical and open to reality testing. For example, would you increase the probability of a happy,
successful visit by waiting a couple of years? Is your child adventuresome
enough to sample the variety of Disney World? Will your child have sufficient endurance and patience to cope with long lines and large crowds?

RECOMMENDATIONS FOR MAKING
THE DREAM COME TRUE

When considering a Disney World vacation with young children, consider:

Age   Although the color and festivity of Disney World excite all children
and specific attractions delight toddlers and preschoolers, Disney entertainment is generally oriented to older children and adults. Children should be
a fairly mature seven years old to *appreciate* the Magic Kingdom and the
Animal Kingdom, and a year or two older to get much out of Epcot or
Disney-MGM Studios.

Not unexpectedly, our readers engage in a lively and ongoing debate over how old a child should be, or what the ideal age is, to go to Walt Disney World.

A Waldwick, New Jersey, mother reports:

> *My kids, not in the least shy or clingy, were very frightened of many attractions. I thought my six-year-old was the "perfect age" but quickly realized this was not the case. Disney makes even the most simple, child-friendly story into a major theatrical production, to the point where my kids couldn't associate their beloved movies to the attraction in front of them.*

And a mother of two from Cleveland, Ohio, offers this:

> *The best advice for parents with young kids is to remember who you are there for and if possible accommodate the kids' need to do things again and again. I think you underestimate Disney's appeal to young children. Since we've gotten home my four-year-old has said "I don't want to live in Cleveland. I want to live at Disney World" at least five times a day.*

Finally, a northern Alabama woman encourages parents to be more open-minded about taking toddlers to Walt Disney World:

> *Parents of toddlers, don't be afraid to bring your little ones! Ours absolutely loved it, and we have priceless photos and videos of our little ones and their grandparents together with Mickey and the gang. For all those people in your book who complained about our little sweethearts crying, sorry, but we found your character-hugging, cursing, ill-mannered, cutting-in-line, screaming-in-our-ears-on-the-roller-coasters teens and preteens much more obnoxious. Guess it's just what you're used to.*

Hmmm . . . don't you hate it when people won't tell what they *really* think?

Time of Year to Visit   Avoid the hot, crowded summer months, especially if you have preschoolers. Go in October, November (except Thanksgiving), early December, January, February, or May. If you have children of varied ages and they're good students, take the older ones out of school and visit during the cooler, less-congested off-season. Arrange special assignments relating to the educational aspects of Disney World. If your children can't afford to miss school, take your vacation as soon as the school year ends in late May or early June. Alternatively, try late August before school starts. Nothing, repeat, nothing will enhance your Walt Disney World vacation as much as avoiding summer and holiday periods.

Build Naps and Rest into Your Itinerary   The theme parks are huge; don't try to see everything in one day. Tour in early morning and return to your hotel around 11:30 a.m. for lunch, a swim, and a nap. Even during off-season when the crowds are smaller and the temperature more pleasant, the size of the major theme parks will exhaust most children under age eight by lunchtime. Return to the park in late afternoon or early evening and continue touring. A family from Texas underlines the importance of naps and rest:

> Despite not following any of your "tours," we did follow the theme of visiting a specific park in the morning, leaving midafternoon for either a nap back at the room or a trip to the Dixie Landings pool, and then returning to one of the parks in the evening. On the few occasions when we skipped your advice, I was muttering to myself by dinner. I can't tell you what I was muttering. . . .

When it comes to naps, this mom does not mince words:

> One last thing for parents of small kids—take the book's advice and get out of the park and take the nap, take the nap, TAKE THE NAP! Never in my life have I seen so many parents screaming at, ridiculing, or slapping their kids. (What a vacation!) WDW is overwhelming for kids and adults. Even though the rental strollers recline for sleeping, we noticed that most of the toddlers and preschoolers didn't give up and sleep until 5 p.m., several hours after the fun had worn off, and right about the time their parents wanted them to be awake and polite in a restaurant.

A mom from Rochester, New York, was equally adamant:

> [You] absolutely must rest during the day. Kids went from 8 a.m. to 9 p.m. in the Magic Kingdom. Kids did great that day, but we were all completely worthless the next day. Definitely must pace yourself. Don't ever try to do two full days of park sight-seeing in a row. Rest during the day. Go to a water park or sleep in every other day.

If you plan to return to your hotel in midday and would like your room made up, let housekeeping know.

Where to Stay   The time and hassle involved in commuting to and from the theme parks will be lessened if you can afford to stay in the World. But even if you lodge outside, it's imperative that you take young children out of the parks each day for a few hours of rest. Neglecting to relax is the best way we know to get the whole family in a snit and ruin the day (or the vacation).

If you have young children, you must plan ahead. Make sure your hotel is within 20 minutes of the theme parks. Naps and relief from the frenetic pace of the theme parks, even during off-season, are indispensable. It's true you can revive somewhat by retreating to a Disney hotel for lunch or by finding a quiet restaurant in the theme parks, but there's no substitute for returning to the familiarity and comfort of your own hotel. Regardless of what you have heard, children too large to sleep in a stroller won't relax unless you take them back to your hotel.

Thousands of new rooms have been built in and near Disney World, many of them affordable. With sufficient lead time, you should have no difficulty finding accommodations that meet your requirements.

If you are traveling with children age 12 and younger, we recommend the Polynesian, Grand Floridian, or Wilderness Lodge resorts (in that order) if they fit your budget. For less expensive rooms, try the Dixie Landings, Port Orleans, or Caribbean Beach resorts. Bargain accommodations are available at the All-Star resorts. Fully equipped trailers and pre-fab log cabins at Fort Wilderness Campground are also good economy lodging.

Outside of Walt Disney World, an Atlanta mom recommends the Castle Double Tree, commenting:

> *This is the perfect place to stay for a great value for kids. Your book glides over it, but it has on-site childcare for $1 an hour, pizza on the premises, a video arcade, a kid's dining room, and kitchens in the rooms, all for $75 a night. More for a kid's suite or breakfast. We'd definitely go back. The room was very spacious and quiet.*

Be in Touch with Your Feelings   When you or your children get tired and irritable, call time out and regroup. Trust your instincts. What would feel best? Another ride, an ice cream break, or going back to the room for a nap?

The way to protect your considerable investment in your Disney vacation is to stay happy and have a good time. You don't have to meet a quota for experiencing attractions. Do what you want.

Least Common Denominators   Somebody is going to run out of steam first, and when they do the whole family will be affected. Sometimes a snack break will revive the flagging member. Sometimes, however, as Marshall Dillon would say: Get out of Dodge. Pushing the tired or discontented beyond their capacity will spoil the day for them—and you. Accept that energy levels vary and be prepared to respond to members of your group who poop out. *Hint:* "We've driven a thousand miles to take you to Walt Disney World and now you're going to ruin everything!" is not an appropriate response.

Building Endurance　Though most children are active, their normal play usually doesn't condition them for the exertion required to tour a Disney theme park. We recommend starting a program of family walks four to six weeks before your trip to get in shape. A mother from Wesconsville, Pennsylvania, reports:

> *We had our six-year-old begin walking with us a bit every day one month before leaving—when we arrived [at Walt Disney World], her little legs could carry her and she had a lot of stamina.*

Setting Limits and Making Plans　Avoid arguments and disappointment by establishing guidelines for each day, and get everybody committed. Include:

1. Wake-up time and breakfast plans.
2. When to depart for the park.
3. What to take with you.
4. A policy for splitting the group or for staying together.
5. What to do if the group gets separated or someone is lost.
6. How long you intend to tour in the morning and what you want to see, including plans in the event an attraction is closed or too crowded.
7. A policy on what you can afford for snacks.
8. A time for returning to the hotel to rest.
9. When you will return to the park and how late you will stay.
10. Dinner plans.
11. A policy for buying souvenirs, including who pays: Mom and Dad or the kids.
12. Determination of bedtimes.

Be Flexible　Any day at Walt Disney World includes some surprises; be prepared to adjust your plan. Listen to your intuition.

About the *Unofficial Guide* Touring Plans　Parents who adopt one of our touring plans are often frustrated by interruptions and delays caused by their young children. Here's what to expect:

1. Character encounters can wreak havoc with the touring plans. Many young children will stop in their tracks whenever they see a Disney character. Attempting to haul your child away before he has satisfied his curiosity is likely to cause anything from whining to a full-scale revolt. Our advice is to either go with the flow or set aside a certain morning or afternoon for photos and autographs. Be aware, however, that queues for autographs, especially in Toontown at the Magic Kingdom and Camp Minnie-Mickey at the Animal Kingdom, are every bit as long as the queues for major attractions.

2. Our touring plans call for visiting attractions in a sequence, often skipping attractions along the way. Children don't like skipping anything! If something catches their eye, they want to see it that moment. Some children can be persuaded to skip attractions if parents explain their plans in advance. Other kids flip out at skipping something, particularly in Fantasyland. A mom from Charleston, South Carolina, writes:

> *We did not have too much trouble following the touring plans at [Disney-]MGM and at Epcot. The Magic Kingdom plan, on the other hand, turned out to be a train wreck. The main problem with the plan is that it starts in Fantasyland. When we were on Dumbo, my five-year-old saw eight dozen other things in Fantasyland she wanted to see. The long and the short is that after Dumbo, there was no getting her out of there.*

A mother of two from Burlington, Vermont, adds:

> *I found out that my kids were very curious about the castle because we had read* Cinderella *at home. Whenever I wanted to leave Fantasyland, I would just say, "Let's go to the castle and see if Cinderella is there." Once we got as far as the front door to the castle, it was no problem going out to the [central] hub and then to another land.*

3. Children have an instinct for finding rest rooms. We have seen adults with maps search interminably for a rest room. Young children, on the other hand, including those who can't read, will head for the nearest rest room with the certainty of a homing pigeon. You can be sure your children will ferret out (and want to use) every rest room in the theme park.

4. If you are using a stroller, you won't be able to take it into attractions or onto rides. This applies to rides such as the Walt Disney World Railroad that are included in the touring plans as in-park transportation.

5. You probably won't finish the touring plan. Varying hours of opera-

tion, crowd levels, the size of your group, the ages of your children, and your stamina will all affect how much of the plan you will complete. Unless you tailor your expectations to this reality, you're likely to experience the frustration expressed by this mother of two from Nazareth, Pennsylvania:

> *We do not understand how anyone could fit everything you have on your plans into the time allotted while attending to small children. We found that long lines, potty stops, diaper changes, stroller searches, and autograph breaks ate huge chunks of time. And we were there during the off-season.*

While our touring plans will allow you to make the most of your time at the theme parks, it's impossible to define what "most" will be. It differs from family to family. If you have two young children, you probably won't see as much as will two adults. If you have four children, you probably won't see as much as will a couple with only two children.

Overheating, Sunburn, and Dehydration   These are the most common problems of younger children at Disney World. Carry and use sunscreen. Be sure to put some on children in strollers, even if the stroller has a canopy. Some of the worst cases of sunburn we've seen were on the exposed foreheads and feet of toddlers and infants in strollers. Protect skin from overexposure. To avoid overheating, rest regularly in the shade or in an air-conditioned restaurant or show.

Don't count on keeping young children hydrated with soft drinks and stops at water fountains. Long lines may hamper buying refreshments, and fountains may not be handy. Further, excited children may not realize or tell you that they're thirsty or hot. We recommend renting a stroller for children age six and younger and carrying plastic bottles of water. Plastic squeeze bottles with caps are sold in all major parks for about $3.

Blisters and Sore Feet   Guests of all ages should wear comfortable, well-broken-in shoes and two pairs of thin socks (better than one pair of thick socks). If you or your children are susceptible to blisters, precut Moleskin bandages. They offer the best protection, stick great, and won't sweat off. When you feel a hot spot, stop, air out your foot, and place a Moleskin bandage over the area before a blister forms. Moleskin is available by name at all drug stores. Young children may not tell their parents about a developing blister until it's too late, so inspect the feet of preschoolers two or more times a day.

First Aid   Each major theme park has a first-aid center. In the Magic Kingdom, it's behind the refreshment corner to the left after you enter. At Epcot, it's on the World Showcase side of the Odyssey Center. At Disney-MGM, it's in the Guest Relations Building just inside the main entrance. At

Animal Kingdom, it's in Safari Village. If you or your children have a medical problem, go to a first-aid center. Disney first-aid centers are warmer and friendlier than most doctor's offices and are accustomed to treating everything from paper cuts to allergic reactions.

Children on Medication   Some parents of hyperactive children on medication discontinue or decrease the child's normal dosage at the end of the school year. If you have such a child, be aware that Disney World might overly stimulate him/her. Consult your physician before altering your child's medication regimen.

Walkie-Talkies   An increasing number of readers stay in touch while on vacation by using walkie-talkies. Here's what they have to say:
From a Cabot, Arkansas, family:

> *Borrow or get walkie-talkies! The vacation is expensive enough so get some walkie-talkies! Our youngest was too scared or too short for some rides, plus I was expecting, so we would sit outside or go to a snack area, but we were always in contact. My husband, Joe, could tell me how long the wait was, when he was about to come down Splash Mountain (for me to take a photo!), or where to meet.*

Concerning the walkie-talkies, a dad from Roanoke is on the same wavelength:

> *The single best purchase we made was Motorola TalkAbout walkie-talkies. They have a two mile range and are about the size of a deck of cards. We first started using them at the airport when I was checking the bags and she took the kids off to the gate. At the parks, the kids would invariably have diverse interests. With walkie-talkies, however, we could easily split up and simply communicate with each other when we wanted to meet back up. At least a half dozen times, exasperated parents asked where they could rent/buy the walkie-talkies.*

Sunglasses   If you want your younger children to wear sunglasses, put a strap or string on the frames so that the glasses will stay on during rides and can hang from the child's neck while indoors.

Things You Forgot or Things You Ran Out Of   Rain gear, diapers, diaper pins, formula, film, aspirin, topical sunburn treatments, and other sundries are sold at all the major theme parks and at Typhoon Lagoon, Blizzard Beach, River Country, and Downtown Disney. Rain gear is a bargain, but most other items are high. A good place to find diapers is at the Baby Centers—two diapers plus ointment are $3.50. Ask for goods you don't see displayed.

Infants and Toddlers at the Theme Parks The major theme parks have centralized facilities for infant and toddler care. Everything necessary for changing diapers, preparing formulas, and warming bottles and food is available. Baby supplies are for sale, and there are rockers and special chairs for nursing mothers. At the Magic Kingdom, the Baby Center is next to the Crystal Palace at the end of Main Street. At Epcot, Baby Services is near the Odyssey Center, right of the Test Track in Future World. At Disney-MGM Studios, Baby Care is in the Guest Relations Building left of the entrance. At the Animal Kingdom, Baby Changing/Nursing is in Safari Village in the center of the park. Dads in charge of little ones are welcome at the centers and can use most services offered. In addition, many men's rooms in the major theme parks have changing tables.

Infants and toddlers are allowed to experience any attraction that doesn't have minimum height or age restrictions. But as a Minneapolis mother reports, some attractions are better for babies than others:

> *Theater and boat rides are easier for babies (ours was almost one year old, not yet walking). Rides where there's a bar that comes down are doable, but harder. Peter Pan was our first encounter with this type, and we had barely gotten situated when I realized he might fall out of my grasp. The standing auditorium films are too intense; the noise level is deafening, and the images unescapable. You don't have a rating system for babies, and I don't expect to see one, but I thought you might want to know what a baby thought (based on his reactions). [At the Magic Kingdom:] Jungle Cruise—Didn't get into it. Pirates— Slept through it. Riverboat—While at Aunt Polly's, the horn made him cry. Aunt Polly's—Ate the chicken while watching the birds in relative quiet. Small World—Wide-eyed, took it all in. Peter Pan— Couldn't really sit on the seat. A bit dangerous. He didn't get into it. Carousel of Progress—Long talks; hard to keep him quiet; danced during song. The Timekeeper—Too loud. Dinosaur at beginning scared him. WDW RR—Liked the motion and scenery. Tiki Birds—Loved it. Danced, clapped, sang along. At Epcot: Honey, I Shrunk the Audience—We skipped due to recommendation of Disney worker that it got too loud and adults screamed throughout. Journey into Imagination—Loved it. Tried to catch things with his hands. Bounced up and down, chortled. The Land—Watchful, quiet during presentation. Food Rocks—Loved it, danced. El Río del Tiempo—Loved it.*

The same mom also advises:

> *We used a baby sling on our trip and thought it was great when standing in the lines—much better than a stroller, which you have to*

park before getting in line (and navigate through crowds). The food at WDW [includes] almost nothing a baby can eat. No fruits or vegetables. My baby was still nursing when we went to WDW. The only really great place I found to nurse in MK was a hidden bench in the shade in Adventureland in between the freezee stand (next to Tiki Birds) and the small shops. It is impractical to go to the baby station every time, so a nursing mom better be comfortable about nursing in very public situations.

Strollers   Strollers are available for a modest daily fee at all four major theme parks. If you rent a stroller at the Magic Kingdom and decide to go to Epcot, the Animal Kingdom, or Disney-MGM Studios, turn in your Magic Kingdom stroller and present your receipt at the next park. You'll be issued another stroller without additional charge.

Strollers at the Magic Kingdom, the Animal Kingdom, and Epcot are large, sturdy models with sun canopies. We have seen families load as many as three children at once in one of these. Strollers at Disney-MGM Studios are the light, collapsible type. Strollers can be obtained to the right of the entrance at the Magic Kingdom, to the left of the Entrance Plaza at Epcot, and at Oscar's Super Service just inside the entrance of Disney-MGM Studios. Stroller rentals at the Animal Kingdom are just inside the entrance and to the right. Rental at all parks is fast and efficient, and returning the stroller is a breeze. Even at Epcot, where as many as 900 strollers are turned in after the evening fireworks, there's almost no wait or hassle. If you don't mind forfeiting your dollar deposit, you can ditch your rental stroller anywhere in the park when you're ready to leave.

When you enter a show or board a ride, you must park your stroller, usually in an open, unprotected area. If it rains before you return, you'll need a cloth, towel, or diaper to dry it.

Strollers are a must for infants and toddlers, but we have observed many sharp parents renting strollers for somewhat older children (up to five or so years old). The stroller prevents parents from having to carry children when they sag and provides a convenient place to carry water and snacks.

If you go to your hotel for a break and intend to return to the park, leave your rental stroller by an attraction near the entrance, marking it with something personal like a bandanna. When you return after your break, your stroller will be waiting for you.

It's permissible to bring your own stroller from home. Remember, however, that only collapsible strollers are permitted on monorails and buses. Your stroller is unlikely to be stolen, but mark it with your name.

Also, be aware that rental strollers are too large for all infants and many toddlers. If you plan to rent a stroller for your infant or toddler, bring along some pillows, cushions, or rolled towels to buttress him in. A mother of two from Falls Church, Virginia, advocates taking your own stroller:

> I was glad I took my own stroller, because the rented strollers aren't appropriate for infants. (We had a five-year-old and a five-month-old in tow.) No one at the Magic Kingdom said anything about my using a bike lock to secure our brand-new Aprica stroller. However, at [Disney] MGM, an attendent came over and told us not to lock it anywhere, because it's a fire hazard! (Outside?) When I politely asked the attendant if she wanted to be responsible for my $300 stroller, she told me to go ahead and lock it but not tell anyone! I observed the attendants at Magic Kingdom and [Disney-]MGM constantly moving the strollers. This seems very confusing—no wonder people think their strollers are getting ripped off!

Stroller Discontent   We are receiving an increasing number of complaints about Disney's rental stroller. The following are representative:

A mother from Williamsville, New York, didn't think much of the rental strollers at the Magic Kingdom and Epcot:

> My biggest complaint about the parks, and I would find it hard to believe if no one has mentioned this to you yet, concerns those antiquated strollers used at MK and Epcot. Those things are metal and vinyl monstrosities. Needless to say, the metal pieces had the tendency to become hot and the vinyl was sticky. Also, these little vehicles had no brakes, which, at times, made them difficult to get in and out of safely. Aside from these safety issues, which are reason enough for Disney to spring for newer models, the strollers alone date the park much more than Tomorrowland ever did.

A Canton, Ohio, dad agreed, writing:

> The strollers at the parks leave a lot to be desired. The strollers at the Animal Kingdom are by far the best, with adequate room for small children and good maneuverability. The strollers at MGM Studios have adequate room but are difficult to maneuver. The strollers at Epcot and the Magic Kingdom are old, too small except for very young children, and not very easy to maneuver (my five-year-old daughter had to sit with her legs hanging out of the stroller because it was so small).

And a Virginia dad who was doing double duty chimed in with this advice:

> At every park except the Animal Kingdom (where all the strollers were

great), the double strollers were terrible—cumbersome and uncomfortable. Instead, rent two single strollers.

Stroller Wars   Sometimes strollers disappear while you're enjoying a ride or show. Disney cast members will often rearrange strollers parked outside an attraction. Sometimes this is done to "tidy up." At other times, strollers are moved to clear a walkway. Don't assume your stroller has been stolen because it isn't where you left it. It may be "neatly arranged" a few feet away.

Sometimes, however, strollers are taken by mistake or ripped off by people not wanting to spend time replacing one that's missing. Don't be alarmed if yours disappears. You won't have to buy the missing stroller, and you'll be issued a new one for your continued use. In the Magic Kingdom, replacements are available at Tinker Bell's Treasures in Fantasyland, at Merchant of Venus in Tomorrowland, and at the main rental facility near the park entrance. At Epcot, get replacements at the Entrance Plaza rental headquarters and at the International Gateway (in World Showcase between the United Kingdom and France). Strollers at Disney-MGM can be replaced at Oscar's Super Service and at Endor Vendors near Star Tours. In the Animal Kingdom, stroller replacements are available at Garden Gate Gifts and Mombasa Marketplace.

While replacing a stroller is no big deal, it's inconvenient. A family from Minnesota complained that their stroller had been taken six times in one day at Epcot and five times in a day at Disney-MGM Studios. Even with free replacements, larceny on this scale represents a lot of wasted time. Through our own experiments and readers' suggestions, we have developed techniques for hanging on to a rented stroller: Affix something personal (but expendable) to the handle. Evidently, most strollers are pirated by mistake (they all look alike) or because it's easier to swipe someone else's stroller than to replace one when it disappears. Since most stroller "theft" results from confusion or laziness, the average pram pincher will hesitate to haul off a stroller bearing another person's property. After trying several items, we concluded that a bright, inexpensive scarf or bandanna tied to the handle works well. A sock partially stuffed with rags or paper works even better (the weirder and more personal the object, the greater the deterrent). Best of all might be an Ann Arbor, Michigan, mother's strategy:

> *We used a variation on your stroller identification theme. We tied a clear plastic bag with a diaper in it on the stroller. Jon even poured a little root beer on the diaper for effect. Needless to say, no one took our stroller and it was easy to identify.*

Strollers As Lethal Weapons   A father of one from Purcellville, Virginia, wrote complaining about how inconsiderate some parents are:

> *The biggest problem is surviving the migrating herds of strollers. The drivers of these contraptions appear to believe they have the right-of-way in all situations and use the strollers as battering rams to enforce their perceived right. I know they will not be banned from the parks, but how about putting speed governors on these things?*

In fact, you would be amazed at how many people are injured by strollers pushed by parents who are driving aggressively, in a hurry, or in the ozone. Though you may desire to use your stroller as a battering ram or to wedge through crowds like Moses parting the seas, think twice. It's very un-Disney to steamroll other guests.

Lost Children

Although it's amazingly easy to lose a child (or two) in the theme parks, it usually isn't a serious problem. All Disney employees are schooled in handling the situation. If you lose a child in the Magic Kingdom, report it to a Disney employee, then check at the Baby Center and at City Hall, where lost-children "logs" are kept. At Epcot, report the loss, then check at Baby Services near the Odyssey Center. At Disney-MGM Studios, report the loss at the Guest Relations Building at the entrance end of Hollywood Boulevard. At Animal Kingdom, go to the Baby Center in Safari Village. Paging isn't used, but in an emergency an "all-points bulletin" can be issued throughout the park(s) via internal communications. If a Disney employee encounters a lost child, he or she will take the child immediately to the park's guest relations center or its baby-care center.

We suggest that children younger than eight be color-coded by dressing them in purple T-shirts or equally distinctive clothes. It's also smart to sew a label into each child's shirt that states his name, your name, and the name of your hotel. The same thing can be accomplished by writing the information on a strip of masking tape. Hotel security professionals suggest the information be printed in small letters and the tape be affixed to the outside of the child's shirt, five inches below the armpit. Also, special name tags can be obtained at the major theme parks.

How Kids Get Lost

Children get separated from their parents every day at Disney parks under remarkably similar (and predictable) circumstances:

1. Preoccupied Solo Parent   In this situation, the party's only adult is preoccupied with something like buying refreshments, loading the camera, or using the rest room. Junior is there one second and gone the next.

2. The Hidden Exit Sometimes parents wait on the sidelines while two or more young children experience a ride together. Parents expect the kids to exit in one place and, lo and behold, the youngsters pop out somewhere else. Exits from some attractions are distant from the entrances. Make sure you know exactly where your children will emerge before letting them ride by themselves.

3. After the Show At the end of many shows and rides, a Disney staffer will announce, "Check for personal belongings and take small children by the hand." When dozens, if not hundreds, of people leave an attraction simultaneously, it's easy for parents to lose contact with their children unless they have them directly in tow.

4. Rest Room Problems Mom tells six-year-old Tommy, "I'll be sitting on this bench when you come out of the rest room." Three possibilities: One, Tommy exits through a different door and becomes disoriented (Mom may not know there is another door). Two, Mom decides she also will use the rest room, and Tommy emerges to find her gone. Three, Mom pokes around in a shop while keeping an eye on the bench, but misses Tommy when he comes out.

If you can't be with your child in the rest room, make sure there's only one exit. The rest room on a passageway between Frontierland and Adventureland in the Magic Kingdom is the all-time worst for disorienting visitors. Children and adults alike have walked in from the Adventureland side and walked out on the Frontierland side (and vice versa). Adults realize quickly that something is wrong. Young children, however, sometimes fail to recognize the problem. Designate a meeting spot more distinctive than a bench, and be thorough in your instructions: "I'll meet you by this flagpole. If you get out first, stay right here." Have your child repeat the directions back to you.

5. Parades There are many parades and shows at which the audience stands. Children tend to jockey for a better view. By moving a little this way and that, the child quickly puts distance between you and him before either of you notices.

6. Mass Movements Be on guard when huge crowds disperse after fireworks or a parade, or at park closing. With 20,000 to 40,000 people at once in an area, it's very easy to get separated from a child or others in your party. Use extra caution after the evening parade and fireworks in the Magic Kingdom, *Fantasmic!* at the Disney-MGM Studios, and *IllumiNations* at

Epcot. Families should have specific plans for where to meet if they get separated.

7. Character Greetings   Activity and confusion are common when the Disney characters appear, and children can slip out of sight. See "Then Some Confusion Happened" (page 198).

8. Getting Lost at the Animal Kingdom   It's especially easy to lose a child at the Animal Kingdom, particularly in the Oasis entryway, on the Maharaja Jungle Trek, and on the Pangani Forest Exploration Trail. Mom and Dad will stop to observe an animal. Junior stays close for a minute or so, and then, losing patience, wanders to the other side of the exhibit or to a different exhibit.

Especially in the multipath Oasis, locating a lost child can be maddening, as a mother from Safety Harbor, Florida, describes:

> *Manny wandered off in the paths that lead to the jungle village while we were looking at a bird. It reminded me of losing somebody in the supermarket when you run back and forth looking down each aisle but can't find the person you're looking for because they are running around, too. I was nutso before we even got to the first ride.*

A mother from Flint, Michigan, came up with yet another way to lose a kid: abandonment.

> *From the minute we hit the park it was gripe, whine, pout, cry, beg, scream, pick, pester, and aggravate. When he went to the rest room for the ninth time before 11 a.m., I thought I'M OUTTA HERE . . . let the little snothead walk back to Flint. Unfortunately, I was brought up Catholic with lots of guilt so I didn't follow through.*

Disney, Kids, and Scary Stuff

Disney rides and shows are adventures. They focus on themes of all adventures: good and evil, death, beauty and the grotesque, fellowship and enmity. As you sample the attractions at Walt Disney World, you transcend the spinning and bouncing of midway rides to thought-provoking and emotionally powerful entertainment. All of the endings are happy, but the adventures' impacts, given Disney's gift for special effects, often intimidate and occasionally frighten young children.

There are rides with menacing witches, burning towns, and ghouls popping out of their graves, all done with a sense of humor, provided you're old enough to understand the joke. And bones. There are bones everywhere: human bones, cattle bones, dinosaur bones, even whole skeletons. There's a stack of skulls at the headhunter's camp on the Jungle Cruise, a platoon of skeletons sailing ghost ships in Pirates of the Caribbean, and a haunting assemblage of skulls and skeletons in The Haunted Mansion. Skulls, skeletons, and bones punctuate Snow White's Adventures, Peter Pan's Flight, and Big Thunder Mountain Railroad. In the Animal Kingdom, there's an entire children's playground comprised exclusively of giant bones and skeletons.

Monsters and special effects at Disney-MGM Studios are more real and sinister than those in the other theme parks. If your child has difficulty coping with the witch in Snow White's Adventures, think twice about exposing him to machine-gun battles, earthquakes, and the creature from *Alien* at the Studios.

One reader tells of taking his preschool children on Star Tours:

> *We took a four-year-old and a five-year-old, and they had the shit scared out of them at Star Tours. We did this first thing in the morning, and it took hours of Tom Sawyer Island and Small World to get back to normal.*
>
> *Our kids were the youngest by far in Star Tours. I assume that other adults had more sense or were not such avid readers of your book.*
>
> *Preschoolers should start with Dumbo and work up to the Jungle Cruise in late morning, after being revved up and before getting hungry, thirsty, or tired. Pirates of the Caribbean is out for preschoolers. You get the idea.*

Expect the inevitable overload Disney World gives children. Be sensitive, alert, and prepared for almost anything, even behavior that is out of character for your child at home. Most young children take Disney's macabre trappings in stride, and others are easily comforted by an arm around the shoulder or a squeeze of the hand. Parents who know that their children tend to become upset should take it slow and easy, sampling more benign adventures like the Jungle Cruise, gauging reactions, and discussing with the children how they felt about what they saw.

Sometimes young children will rise above their anxiety in an effort to please their parents or siblings. This doesn't necessarily indicate a mastery of fear, much less enjoyment. If children leave a ride in apparently good shape, ask if they would like to go on it again (not necessarily now, but sometime). The response usually will indicate how much they actually enjoyed the experience. There's a big difference between having a good time and mustering the courage to get through something.

Evaluating a child's capacity to handle the visual and tactile effects of Disney World requires patience, understanding, and experimentation. Each of us, after all, has our own demons. If a child balks at or is frightened by a ride, respond constructively. Let your children know that lots of people, adults and children, are scared by what they see and feel. Help them understand that it's okay if they get frightened and that their fear doesn't lessen your love or respect. Take pains not to compound the discomfort by making a child feel inadequate; try not to undermine self-esteem, impugn courage, or ridicule. Most of all, don't induce guilt by suggesting the child's trepidation might be ruining the family's fun. It is also sometimes necessary to restrain older siblings' taunting or teasing.

A visit to Walt Disney World is more than an outing or an adventure for a young child. It's a testing experience, a sort of controlled rite of passage. If you help your little one work through the challenges, the time can be immeasurably rewarding and a bonding experience for you both.

The Fright Factor

While each youngster is different, there are seven attraction elements that alone or combined could punch a child's buttons:

1. Name of the Attraction   Young children will naturally be apprehensive about something called "The Haunted Mansion" or "Tower of Terror."

2. Visual Impact of the Attraction from Outside   Splash Mountain and Big Thunder Mountain Railroad look scary enough to give adults second thoughts, and they terrify many young children.

3. Visual Impact of the Indoor Queuing Area   Pirates of the Caribbean's caves and dungeons and The Haunted Mansion's "stretch rooms" can frighten children even before they board the ride.

4. Intensity of the Attraction   Some attractions are overwhelming, inundating the senses with sights, sounds, movement, and even smell. Epcot's Honey, I Shrunk the Audience, for example, combines loud sounds, lasers, lights, and 3-D cinematography to create a total sensory experience. For some preschoolers, this is two or three senses too many.

5. Visual Impact of the Attraction Itself   Sights in various attractions range from falling boulders to lurking buzzards, from grazing dinosaurs to attacking white blood cells. What one child calmly absorbs may scare the bejabbers out of another the same age.

6. Dark   Many Disney World attractions operate indoors in the dark. For some children, this triggers fear. A child who is frightened on one dark ride (Snow White's Adventures, for example) may be unwilling to try other indoor rides.

7. The Tactile Experience of the Ride Itself   Some rides are wild enough to cause motion sickness, wrench backs, and discombobulate patrons of any age.

SMALL-CHILD FRIGHT-POTENTIAL CHART

Our "Fright-Potential Chart" is a quick reference to identify attractions to be wary of, and why. The chart represents a generalization, and all kids are different. It relates specifically to kids ages three to seven. On average, children at the younger end of the range are more likely to be frightened than children in their sixth or seventh year.

MAGIC KINGDOM

Main Street, U.S.A.

Walt Disney World Railroad: Not frightening in any respect.
Main Street Cinema: Not frightening in any respect.
Main Street Vehicles: Not frightening in any respect.

Adventureland

Swiss Family Treehouse: Not frightening in any respect.
Jungle Cruise: Moderately intense, some macabre sights. A good test attraction for little ones.
Tropical Serenade: A thunderstorm, loud volume level, and simulated explosions frighten some preschoolers.
Pirates of the Caribbean: Slightly intimidating queuing area; intense boat ride with gruesome (though humorously presented) sights and a short, unexpected slide down a flume.

Frontierland

Splash Mountain: Visually intimidating from outside, with moderately intense visual effects. The ride, culminating in a 52-foot plunge down a steep chute, is somewhat hair-raising for all ages. Switching off option provided (pages 190–192).
Big Thunder Mountain Railroad: Visually intimidating from outside, with moderately intense visual effects. The roller coaster is wild enough to frighten many adults, particularly seniors. Switching off provided (pages 190–192).
Tom Sawyer Island: Some very young children are intimidated by dark, walk-through tunnels that can be easily avoided.

Frontierland (continued)

Country Bear Jamboree: Not frightening in any respect.
Frontierland Shootin' Arcade: Not frightening in any respect.
Diamond Horseshoe Saloon Revue: Not frightening in any respect.

Liberty Square

The Hall of Presidents: Not frightening, but boring for young ones.
Liberty Belle Riverboat: Not frightening in any respect.
Mike Fink Keelboats: Not frightening in any respect.
The Haunted Mansion: Name raises anxiety, as do sounds and sights of waiting area. Intense attraction with humorously presented macabre sights. The ride itself is gentle.

Fantasyland

Mad Tea Party: Midway-type ride can induce motion sickness in all ages.
The Many Adventures of Winnie the Pooh: Not frightening in any respect.
Snow White's Adventures: Moderately intense spook-house-genre attraction with some grim characters. Absolutely terrifies many preschoolers.
Legend of the Lion King: Certain special effects frighten some young children.
Dumbo the Flying Elephant: A tame midway ride; a great favorite of most young children.
Cinderella's Golden Carrousel: Not frightening in any respect.
It's a Small World: Not frightening in any respect.
Peter Pan's Flight: Not frightening in any respect.
Skyway to Tomorrowland: Not frightening, except to people afraid of heights.

Mickey's Toontown Fair

All attractions except roller coaster: Not frightening in any respect.
The Barnstormer at Goofy's Wiseacres Farm (children's roller coaster): May frighten some preschoolers.

Tomorrowland

Alien Encounter: Extremely intense. Capable of frightening all ages. Not for young children. Switching off provided (pages 190–192).

Tomorrowland (continued)

The Timekeeper: Realistic cinematic technique may frighten some young children. Audience must stand.

Buzz Lightyear's Space Ranger Spin: Dark ride with cartoonlike aliens may frighten some preschoolers.

Tomorrowland Transit Authority: Not frightening in any respect.

Skyway to Fantasyland: Not frightening in any respect.

Space Mountain: Very intense roller coaster in the dark; the Magic Kingdom's wildest ride and a scary roller coaster by any standard. Switching off provided (pages 190–192).

Astro Orbiter: Visually intimidating from the waiting area. The ride is relatively tame. See safety warning on page 194.

Walt Disney's Carousel of Progress: Not frightening in any respect.

Tomorrowland Speedway: Noise of waiting area slightly intimidates preschoolers; otherwise, not frightening.

EPCOT

Future World

Spaceship Earth: Dark and imposing presentation intimidates a few preschoolers.

Innoventions East and West: Not frightening in any respect.

Universe of Energy: Dinosaur segment frightens some preschoolers; visually intense, with some intimidating effects.

Wonders of Life—Body Wars: Very intense, with frightening visual effects. Ride causes motion sickness in susceptible riders of all ages. Switching off provided (pages 190–192).

Wonders of Life—Cranium Command: Not frightening in any respect.

Wonders of Life—The Making of Me: Not frightening in any respect.

Test Track: Intense thrill ride may frighten any age. Switching off provided (pages 190–192).

Journey into Imagination—Honey, I Shrunk the Audience: Extremely intense visual effects and loudness frighten many young children.

The Land—Living with the Land: Not frightening in any respect.

The Land—Circle of Life Theater: Not frightening in any respect.

The Land—Food Rocks: Not frightening in any respect, but loud.

World Showcase

Mexico—El Río del Tiempo: Not frightening in any respect.

Norway—Maelstrom: Visually intense in parts. Ride ends with a plunge down a 20-foot flume. A few preschoolers are frightened.

China—Wonders of China: Not frightening in any respect, but audience must stand.

Germany: Not frightening in any respect.

Italy: Not frightening in any respect.

The American Adventure: Not frightening in any respect.

Japan: Not frightening in any respect.

Morocco: Not frightening in any respect.

France—Impressions de France: Not frightening in any respect.

United Kingdom: Not frightening in any respect.

Canada—O Canada!: Not frightening in any respect, but audience must stand.

DISNEY-MGM STUDIOS

The Twilight Zone Tower of Terror: Visually intimidating to young children; contains intense and realistic special effects. The plummeting elevator at the ride's end frightens many adults. Switching off provided (pages 190–192).

The Great Movie Ride: Intense in parts, with very realistic special effects and some visually intimidating sights. Frightens many preschoolers.

Doug Live!: Not frightening in any respect.

Sounds Dangerous: Noises in the dark frighten some preschoolers.

Indiana Jones Epic Stunt Spectacular!: An intense show with powerful special effects, including explosions. Presented in an educational context that young children generally handle well.

Rock 'n' Roller Coaster: The wildest coaster at Walt Disney World. May frighten guests of any age. Switching off provided (pages 190–192).

Star Tours: Extremely intense visually for all ages; the ride is one of Disney's wildest. Not as likely to cause motion sickness as Body Wars at Epcot. Switching off is provided (pages 190–192).

Disney-MGM Studios Backlot Tour: Sedate and nonintimidating except for "Catastrophe Canyon," where an earthquake and a flash flood are simulated. Prepare younger children for this part of the tour.

DISNEY-MGM STUDIOS (continued)

Backstage Walking Tours: Not frightening in any respect.

Jim Henson's MuppetVision 4D: Intense and loud, but not frightening.

"Honey, I Shrunk the Kids" Movie Set Adventure Playground: Everything is oversized, but nothing is scary.

Voyage of the Little Mermaid: Not frightening in any respect.

The Magic of Disney Animation: Not frightening in any respect.

ANIMAL KINGDOM

The Boneyard: Not frightening in any respect.

Conservation Station: Not frightening in any respect.

Countdown to Extinction: High-tech thrill ride rattles riders of all ages. Switching off provided (pages 190–192).

Cretaceous Trail: Not frightening in any respect.

Discovery River Boats: Not frightening in any respect.

Festival of the Lion King: A bit loud, but otherwise not frightening in any respect.

Flights of Wonder: Swooping birds alarm a few small children.

Pangani Forest Exploration Trail: Not frightening in any respect.

Grandmother Willow's Grove: Not frightening in any respect.

It's Tough to Be a Bug!: Very intense and loud with special effects that startle viewers of all ages and potentially terrify young children.

Kilimanjaro Safaris: A "collapsing" bridge and the proximity of real animals make a few young children anxious.

Maharaja Jungle Trek: Some children may balk at the bat exhibit.

The Oasis: Not frightening in any respect.

Kali River Rapids: Potentially frightening and certainly wet for guests of all ages. Switching off provided (pages 190–192).

Theater in the Wild: Not frightening in any respect, but loud.

Wildlife Express Train: Not frightening in any respect.

A Bit of Preparation

We receive many tips from parents telling how they prepared their young children for the Disney experience. A common strategy is to acquaint children with the characters and the stories behind the attractions by reading Disney books and watching Disney videos at home. A more direct approach is to rent Walt Disney World travel videos that show the actual attractions. Of the latter, a father from Arlington, Virginia, reports:

> My kids both loved The Haunted Mansion, with appropriate preparation. We rented a tape before going so they could see it, and then I told them it was all "Mickey Mouse Magic" and that Mickey was just "joking you," to put it in their terms, and that there weren't any real ghosts, and that Mickey wouldn't let anyone actually get hurt.

A mother from Teaneck, New Jersey, adds:

> I rented movies to make my five-year-old more comfortable with rides (Star Wars; Indiana Jones; Honey, I Shrunk the Kids). We thought we might go to Universal, so I rented King Kong, and it is now my kid's favorite. If kids are afraid of rides in dark (like ours), buy a light-up toy and let them take it on the ride.

A mother from Gloucester, Massachusetts, solved the fright problem on the spot:

> The 3-½-year-old liked It's a Small World, [but] was afraid of The Haunted Mansion. We just pulled his hat over his face and quietly talked to him while we enjoyed [the ride].

ATTRACTIONS THAT EAT ADULTS

You may spend so much energy worrying about Junior that you forget to take care of yourself. If the motion of a ride is potentially disturbing, persons of any age may be adversely affected. Several attractions are likely to cause motion sickness or other problems for older children and adults.

A WORD ABOUT HEIGHT REQUIREMENTS

A number of attractions require children to meet minimum height and age requirements, usually 44 inches tall to ride with an adult or 44 inches and seven years of age to ride alone. If you have children too short or too young to ride, you have several options, including switching off (described later in this chapter). Although the alternatives may resolve some practical and logistic issues, be forewarned that your smaller children may nonetheless be resentful of their older (or taller) siblings who qualify to ride. A mom from Virginia bumped into just such a situation, writing:

Attractions That Eat Adults	
Magic Kingdom:	Tomorrowland—Space Mountain
	Tomorrowland—Alien Encounter
	Fantasyland—Mad Tea Party
	Frontierland—Big Thunder Mountain Railroad
	Frontierland—Splash Mountain
Epcot:	Future World—Body Wars
	Future World—Test Track
Disney-MGM Studios:	Star Tours
	The Twilight Zone Tower of Terror
	Rock 'n' Roller Coaster
Animal Kingdom	Countdown to Extinction
	Kali River Rapids

You mention height requirements for rides but not the intense sibling jealousy this can generate. Frontierland was a real problem in that respect. Our very petite five-year-old, to her outrage, was stuck hanging around while our eight-year-old went on Splash Mountain and [Big] Thunder Mountain with Grandma and Grandad, and the nearby alternatives weren't helpful [too long a line for rafts to Tom Sawyer Island, etc.]. If we had thought ahead, we would have left the younger kid back in Mickey's Toontown with one of the grown-ups for another roller coaster ride or two and then met up later at a designated point. The best areas had a playground or other quick attractions for short people near the rides with height requirements, like the Boneyard near the dinosaur ride [Countdown to Extinction] at the Animal Kingdom.

The reader makes a valid point, though in practical terms splitting the group and meeting later can be more complicated than she might imagine. If you choose to split up, ask the Disney greeter at the entrance to the attraction(s) with height requirements how long the wait is. If you tack five minutes for riding onto the anticipated wait and add five or so minutes to exit and reach the meeting point, you'll have an approximate sense of how long the younger kids (and their supervising adult) will have to do other stuff. Our guess is that even with a long line for the rafts, the reader would have had more than sufficient time to take her daughter to Tom Sawyer Island while the sibs rode Splash Mountain and Big Thunder Mountain with the grandparents. For sure she had time to tour the Swiss Family Treehouse in adjacent Adventureland.

Waiting Line Strategies for Adults with Young Children

Children hold up better through the day if you minimize the time they spend in lines. Arriving early and using our touring plans immensely reduce waiting. Here are additional ways to reduce stress for children:

1. Line Games   Wise parents anticipate children's getting restless in line and plan activities to reduce the stress and boredom. In the morning, have waiting children discuss what they want to see and do during the day. Later, watch for and count Disney characters or play simple guessing games like "20 Questions." Lines move continuously; games requiring pen and paper are impractical. Waiting in the holding area of a theater attraction, however, is a different story. Here, tic-tac-toe, hangman, drawing, and coloring make the time fly by.

2. Last-Minute Entry   If an attraction can accommodate an unusually

Attractions You Can Usually Enter at the Last Minute	
Magic Kingdom	
Liberty Square	*The Hall of Presidents*
	Liberty Belle Riverboat
Tomorrowland	*The Timekeeper*
Epcot	
Future World	*The Circle of Life* (except during mealtimes)
	Food Rocks (except during mealtimes)
World Showcase	*Wonders of China*
	The American Adventure
	O Canada!
Disney-MGM Studios	*Doug Live!*
	Sounds Dangerous
Animal Kingdom	*Theater in the Wild*

large number of people at once, it's often unnecessary to stand in line. The Magic Kingdom's *Liberty Belle* Riverboat is a good example. The boat holds about 450 people, usually more than are waiting in line. Instead of standing uncomfortably in a crowd, grab a snack and sit in the shade until the boat arrives and loading is well under way. After the line is almost gone, join it.

At large-capacity theaters like that for Epcot's *The American Adventure,* ask the entrance greeter how long it will be until guests are admitted for the next show. If it's 15 minutes or more, take a rest room break or get a snack, returning a few minutes before the show starts. You aren't allowed to carry food or drink into the attraction, so make sure you have time to finish your snack before entering.

3. The Hail Mary Pass   Certain lines are configured to allow you and your smaller children to pass under the rail to join your partner just before actual boarding or entry. This technique allows children and one adult to rest, snack, cool off, or go potty while another adult or older sibling stands in line. Other guests are very understanding about this strategy when used for young children. You're likely to meet hostile opposition, however, if you try to pass older children or more than one adult under the rail.

Attractions Where You Can Usually Complete a Hail Mary Pass	
Magic Kingdom	
Adventureland	Swiss Family Treehouse
	Jungle Cruise
Frontierland	*Country Bear Jamboree*
Fantasyland	Mad Tea Party
	Snow White's Adventures
	Dumbo the Flying Elephant
	Cinderella's Golden Carrousel
	Peter Pan's Flight
Tomorrowland	Tomorrowland Speedway
Epcot	
Future World	Spaceship Earth
	Living with the Land
Disney-MGM Studios	*ABC Sound Studio*
	Indiana Jones Epic Stunt Spectacular!

Attractions Where Switching Off Is Common	
Magic Kingdom	
Tomorrowland	Space Mountain
	Alien Encounter
Frontierland	Splash Mountain
	Big Thunder Mountain Railroad
Epcot	
Future World	Body Wars
	Test Track
Disney-MGM Studios	Star Tours
	The Twilight Zone Tower of Terror
	Rock 'n' Roller Coaster
Animal Kingdom	
DinoLand U.S.A.	Countdown to Extinction
Asia	Kali River Rapids

4. Switching Off (a.k.a. The Baby Swap)   Several attractions have minimum height and/or age requirements, usually 3'8" tall to ride with an adult, or age 7 *and* 3'8" to ride alone. Some couples with children too small or too young forgo these attractions, while others take turns to ride. Missing some of Disney's best rides is an unnecessary sacrifice, and waiting in line twice for the same ride is a tremendous waste of time.

Instead, take advantage of the "switching off" option, also called "The Baby Swap." To switch off, there must be at least two adults. Everybody waits in line together, adults and children. When you reach an attendant (called a "greeter"), say you want to switch off. The greeter will allow everyone, including the young children, to enter the attraction. When you reach the loading area, one adult rides while the other stays with the kids. Then the riding adult disembarks and takes charge of the children while the other adult rides. A third adult in the party can ride twice, once with each of the switching off adults, so that the switching off adults don't have to experience the attraction alone.

Most rides with age and height minimums load and unload in the same area, facilitating switching off. An exception is Space Mountain, where the first adult at the conclusion of the ride must also inform the unloading

Switching Off

attendant that he or she is switching off. The attendant will admit the first adult to an internal stairway that goes back to the loading area.

Attractions at which switching off is practiced are oriented to more mature guests. Sometimes it takes a lot of courage for a child just to move through the queue holding Dad's hand. In the boarding area, many children suddenly fear abandonment as one parent leaves to experience the attraction. Unless your children are prepared for switching off, you might have an emotional crisis on your hands. A mom from Edison, New Jersey, advises:

> Once my son came to understand that the switch-off would not leave him abandoned, he did not seem to mind. I would recommend to your readers that they practice the switch-off on some dry runs at home, so that their child is not concerned that he will be left behind. At the very least, the procedure could be explained in advance so that the little ones know what to expect.

Finally, a mother from Ada, Michigan, who discovered that the procedure for switching off varies from attraction to attraction, offered this suggestion:

> Parents need to tell the very first attendant they come to that they would like to switch off. Each attraction has a different procedure for this. Tell every other attendant too because they forget quickly.

5. How to Ride Twice in a Row without Waiting   Many young children like to ride a favorite attraction two or more times in succession. Riding the second time often gives them a feeling of mastery and accomplishment. Unfortunately, even in early morning, repeat rides can be time consuming. If you ride Dumbo as soon as the Magic Kingdom opens, for instance, you will wait only a minute or two for your first ride. When you come back for your second, the wait will be about 12 minutes. If you want to ride a third time, count on 20 minutes or longer.

The best way to get your child on the ride twice (or more) without blowing your morning is to use the "Chuck Bubba Relay" (named in honor of a Kentucky reader):

a. Mom and little Bubba enter the waiting line.

b. Dad lets a specific number of people go in front of him (24 at Dumbo), then gets in line.

c. As soon as the ride stops, Mom exits with Bubba and passes him to Dad to ride the second time.

d. If everybody is really getting into this, Mom can hop in line again, no fewer than 24 people behind Dad.

The Chuck Bubba Relay won't work on every ride, because waiting areas are configured differently (i.e., it's impossible in some cases to exit the ride and make the pass). For those rides (all in Fantasyland) where the Bubba Relay works, here are the numbers of people to count off:

Mad Tea Party: 53
Snow White's Adventures: 52
Dumbo the Flying Elephant: 24
Cinderella's Golden Carrousel: 75
Peter Pan's Flight: 64

If you're the second adult in the relay, you'll reach a place in line where it's easiest to make the hand-off. This may be where those exiting the ride pass closest to those waiting to board. In any event, you'll know it when you see it. If you reach it and the first parent hasn't arrived with Bubba, let those behind you pass until Bubba shows up.

6. Last-Minute Cold Feet   If your young child gets cold feet just before boarding a ride where there is no age or height requirement, you usually can arrange with the loading attendant for a switch off. This is common at Pirates of the Caribbean, where children lose their courage while winding through the dungeon-like waiting area.

No law says you have to ride. If you reach the boarding area and someone is unhappy, tell an attendant you've changed your mind and you'll be shown the way out.

7. Elevator Shoes for the Short and the Brave   If you have a child who is begging to go on the rides with height requirements but who is a little too short, slip heel lifts into his Nikes before he reaches the measuring point. Be sure to leave the heel lifts in, because he may be measured again before boarding.

A Huntsville, Alabama, mom has worked out all the details on the heel lift problem:

> *Knowing my wild child three-year-old as I do, I was interested in your comment regarding shoe lifts. I don't know about other places, but in the big city of Huntspatch where we live, one has to have a prescription for lifts. Normal shoe repair places don't make them. I couldn't think of a material with which to fashion a homemade lift that would be comfortable enough to stand on while waiting in line. I ended up purchasing some of those painfully ugly two-inch chunky-heeled sandals at my local mart where they carried these hideous shoes in unbelievably tiny sizes ($12). Since they didn't look too comfortable, we popped them on her right before we entered the ride lines. None of the height checkers ever asked her to remove them and she clip clopped onto Splash*

Mountain, Big Thunder Railroad (Dat BIG Choo-Choo), Star Wars, and The Tower of Terror—twice! However, the same child became so terrified at the Tiki Bird show that we were forced to leave—go figure! For adventuresome boys, I would suggest purchasing some of those equally hideous giant-heeled cowboy boots.

Along similar lines, a Long Pond, Pennsylvania, mom had this to offer:

Tower of Terror, Star Tours, and Body Wars are 40" requirements. Being persistent with a 39-1/2" child, we tried these several times. She got on Tower of Terror two of three times, Body Wars one of one time, and Star Tours one of two tries. She wore elevator shoes and a bun hairstyle to increase height.

8. Throw Yourself on the Grenade, Mildred!   For conscientious parents determined to sacrifice themselves on behalf of their children, we provide a Magic Kingdom One-Day Touring Plan called the "Dumbo-or-Die-in-a-Day Touring Plan, for Parents with Small Children." This plan (page 464) will ensure that you run yourself ragged. Designed to help you forfeit everything of your personal interest for the sake of your children's pleasure, the plan guarantees to send you home battered and exhausted, with extraordinary stories of devotion and perseverance. By the way, the plan really works. Anyone under age eight will love it.

9. Catch-22 at Tomorrowland Speedway   Though Tomorrowland Speedway is a great treat for young children, they're required to be 4'4" tall in order to drive. Few children age six and younger measure up, so the ride is essentially withheld from the very age group that would most enjoy it. To resolve this Catch-22, go on the ride with your small child. The attendants will assume that you will drive. After getting into the car, shift your child over behind the steering wheel. From your position, you will still be able to control the foot pedals. Your child will feel like she is really driving, and because the car travels on a self-guiding track, there's no way she can make a mistake while steering.

10. Astro Orbiter—A Safety Warning   Parents often board the rocket before lifting their child aboard. Because the attendant can't see small children beside the vehicle from his control station, the ride may start before a child is safely in the cockpit. If you take a small child on this ride, put the child in the rocket, then get in.

The Disney Characters

The large and friendly costumed versions of Mickey, Minnie, Donald, Goofy, and others—known as "Disney characters"—provide a link between Disney animated films and the theme parks. To people emotionally invested, the characters in Disney films are as real as next-door neighbors, never mind that they're drawings on plastic. In recent years, theme park personifications of the characters also have become real to us. It's not just a person in a mouse costume they see; it is Mickey himself. Similarly, meeting Goofy or Snow White in Fantasyland is an encounter with a celebrity, a memory to be treasured.

While there are hundreds of Disney animated film characters, only about 250 have been brought to life in costume. Of these, a relatively small number (less than a fifth) are "greeters" (characters who mix with patrons). The remaining characters perform in shows or parades. Originally confined to the Magic Kingdom, characters are now found in all the major theme parks and Disney hotels.

Character Watching   Character watching has become a pastime. Families once were content to meet a character occasionally. They now pursue them relentlessly, armed with autograph books and cameras. Because some characters are only rarely seen, character watching has become character collecting. (To cash in on character collecting, Disney sells autograph books throughout the World.) Mickey, Minnie, and Goofy are a snap to bag; they seem to be everywhere. But Daisy Duck seldom comes out. Other characters appear regularly, but only in a location consistent with their starring role. Cinderella, predictably, reigns at Cinderella Castle in Fantasyland, while Brer Fox and Brer Bear frolic in Frontierland near Splash Mountain.

A dad from Brooklyn thinks the character autograph–hunting craze has gotten out of hand, complaining:

> Whoever started the practice of collecting autographs from the characters should be subjected to Chinese water torture! We went to WDW eleven years ago, with an eight-year-old and an eleven-year-old. We would bump into characters, take pictures, and that was it. After a while, our children noticed that some of the other children were getting autographs. We managed to avoid joining in during our first day at the Magic Kingdom and our first day at Epcot, but by day three our children were collecting autographs. However, it did not get too out of hand, since it was limited to accidental character meeting.
>
> This year when we took our youngest child (who is now eight), he had already seen his siblings' collection, and was determined to outdo them. However, rather than random meetings, the characters are now available practically all day long at different locations, according to a printed schedule, which our son was old enough to read. We spent more time standing in line for autographs than we did for the most popular rides!

A family from Birmingham, Alabama, found some benefit in their children's relentless pursuit of characters, writing:

> We had no idea we would be caught up in this madness, but after my daughters grabbed your guidebook to get Pocahontas to sign it (we had no blank paper), we quickly bought a Disney autograph book and gave in. It was actually the highlight of their trip, and my son even got into the act by helping get places in line for his sisters. They LOVED looking for characters (I think it has all been planned by Kodak to sell film). The possibility of seeing a new character revived my seven-year-old's energy on many occasions. It was an amazing totally unexpected part of our visit.

Preparing Your Children to Meet the Characters Almost all characters are quite large, and several, like Brer Bear, are huge! Small children don't expect this, and preschoolers especially can be intimidated.

Discuss the characters with your children before you go. On first encounter, don't thrust your child at the character. Allow the little one to deal with this big thing from whatever distance feels safe. If two adults are present, one should stay near the youngster while the other approaches the character and demonstrates that it's safe and friendly. Some kids warm to the characters immediately; some never do. Most take a little time and several encounters.

There are two kinds of characters: those whose costume includes a face-covering headpiece (animal characters and such humanlike characters as Captain Hook) and "face characters," those who resemble the characters so no mask or headpiece is necessary. Face characters include Mary Poppins, Ariel, Jasmine, Aladdin, Cinderella, Belle, Snow White, Esmarelda, and Prince Charming.

Only face characters speak. Headpiece characters don't make noises of any kind. Because cast members couldn't possibly imitate the distinctive cinema voice of the character, Disney has determined it's more effective to keep them silent. Lack of speech notwithstanding, headpiece characters are very warm and responsive, and communicate very effectively with gestures. Tell children in advance that headpiece characters don't talk.

Some character costumes are cumbersome and give cast members very poor visibility. (Eye holes frequently are in the mouth of the costume or even on the neck or chest.) This means characters are somewhat clumsy

and have limited sight. Children who approach the character from the back or side may not be noticed, even if the child touches the character. It's possible in this situation for the character to accidently step on the child or knock him down. It's best for a child to approach a character from the front, but occasionally not even this works. Duck characters (Donald, Daisy, Uncle Scrooge), for example, have to peer around their bills. If a character appears to be ignoring your child, pick up your child and hold her in front of the character until the character responds.

It's okay for your child to touch, pat, or hug the character. Understanding the unpredictability of children, the character will keep his feet very still, particularly refraining from moving backward or sideways. Most characters will sign autographs or pose for pictures. If your child collects autographs, it's a good idea to carry a pen the width of a magic marker. Costumes make it exceedingly difficult for characters to wield a pen, so the bigger the better.

The Big Hurt   Many children expect to meet Mickey the minute they enter the park and are disappointed when he isn't around. If your children can't enjoy things until they see Mickey, ask a cast member where to find him. If the cast member doesn't know, he or she can find out quickly. Cast members have a number they can call to learn exactly where the characters are at any time.

"Then Some Confusion Happened"   Young children sometimes become lost at character encounters. Usually, there's a lot of activity around a character, with both adults and children touching it or posing for pictures. Most commonly, Mom and Dad stay in the crowd while Junior approaches to meet the character. In the excitement and with people milling and the character moving around, Junior heads off in the wrong direction to look for Mom and Dad. In the words of a Salt Lake City mom: "Milo was shaking hands with Dopey one minute, then some confusion happened and [Milo] was gone."

Families with several young children and parents who are busy with cameras can lose a youngster in a heartbeat. Our recommendation for parents with preschoolers is to stay with the kids when they meet characters, stepping back only to take a quick picture.

MEETING CHARACTERS FOR FREE

You can *see* Disney characters in live shows at all the theme parks and in parades at the Magic Kingdom and Disney-MGM Studios. Consult your daily entertainment schedule for times. If you want to *meet* the characters, get autographs, and take photos, consult the *Disney Character Greeting Location Guide* printed on the inside of each handout park map.

At the Magic Kingdom   Characters are encountered more frequently here than anywhere else in Walt Disney World. There almost always will be a character next to City Hall on Main Street and usually one or more in Town Square or near the railroad station. If it's rainy, look for characters on the veranda of Tony's Town Square Restaurant. Characters appear in all the lands but are more plentiful in Fantasyland and Mickey's Toontown Fair. At Mickey's Toontown Fair, you can meet Mickey privately in his "Judge's Tent." Characters actually work shifts at the Toontown Hall of Fame next to Mickey's Country House. Here, you can line up to meet three different assortments of characters. Each assortment has its own greeting area and, of course, its own line. One group, variously labeled Mickey's Pals, Toon Pals, Famous Friends, or some such, will include Minnie, Pluto, Goofy, Donald, and sometimes Chip 'n' Dale, Daisy, and Uncle Scrooge. The other two assortments vary and are more ambiguously defined. The 100 Acre Wood Friends are mostly Winnie the Pooh characters, while Fairy Tale Friends include Snow White, assorted dwarfs, Sleeping Beauty, the Beast, Belle, Cinderella, Prince Charming, etc. Sometimes, however, it's Villains (Captain Hook, Cruella DeVil, Jabar, et al.), and Princesses (Sleeping Beauty, Mary Poppins, yadda, yadda, yadda). Cinderella regularly greets diners at Cinderella's Royal Table in the castle. Also look for characters in the central hub and by Splash Mountain in Frontierland.

Characters are featured in afternoon and evening parades and also play a major role in Castle Forecourt shows (at the entrance to the castle on the moat side) and at the Galaxy Palace Theater in Tomorrowland. Find performance times for shows and parades in the park's daily entertainment schedule. Sometimes characters stay to greet the audience after shows.

At Epcot   At first Disney didn't think characters would be appropriate for the more serious, educational style of Epcot. Later, in response to criticism that Epcot lacked warmth and humor, characters were imported. To integrate them thematically, new and often bizarre costumes were created. Goofy roams Future World in a metallic silver cape reminiscent of Buck Rogers. Mickey greets guests at the American Adventure dressed like Ben Franklin.

It's unclear whether there are fewer characters at Epcot or if it just seems that way because the place is so big. In any event, don't expect to encounter either the number or variety of characters at Epcot that you would in the Magic Kingdom. Two Epcot original characters, Dreamfinder and Figment, are found at the Journey into Imagination pavilion in Future World, and assorted characters appear at the Showcase Plaza each morning. Characters are also occasionally found at the American Adventure pavilion and at the United Kingdom in World Showcase. Characters aren't featured in parades at Epcot, but character shows are performed daily at the American Gardens Theater in World Showcase. Check the park's daily entertainment schedule.

Characters may be rarer at Epcot, but they're often easier to meet. A father from Effingham, Illinois, writes:

> *Trying to get autographs and pictures with Disney characters in the Magic Kingdom was a nightmare. Every character we saw was mobbed by kids and adults. Our kids had no chance. But at Epcot and Disney-MGM, things were much better. We got autographs, pictures, and more involvement. Our kids danced with several characters and received a lot of personal attention.*

At Disney-MGM Studios   Characters are likely to turn up anywhere at the Studios but are most frequently found in front of the Animation Building, along Mickey Avenue (leading to the soundstages), and at the end of New York Street on the backlot. Mickey and his "friends" pose for keepsake photos (about $10 each) on Hollywood Boulevard and Sunset Boulevard. Characters are also prominent in shows, with *Voyage of the Little Mermaid* running almost continuously and an abbreviated version of *Beauty and the Beast* performed several times daily at the Theater of the Stars. Check the daily entertainment schedule for show times.

At the Animal Kingdom   Camp Minnie-Mickey in the Animal Kingdom is a special location designed specifically for meeting characters. There are four designated character greeting "trails" where you can meet Mickey, Minnie, and various characters from *The Jungle Book* and *The Lion King*. Also at Camp Minnie-Mickey are two stage shows featuring characters from *The Lion King* and *Pocahontas*.

Responding to requests, each theme park has added a lot of information about characters to its handout map. The reverse side lists where and when certain characters will be available and provides information on character dining. As mentioned earlier, a handout devoted exclusively to character watching, the *Disney Character Greeting Location Guide,* is now commonly available at all of the theme parks except the Animal Kingdom.

Disney has taken several initiatives intended to satisfy guests' inexhaustible desire to meet the characters. Most important, Disney assigned Mickey and a number of other characters to all-day duty in Mickey's Toontown Fair in the Magic Kingdom and Camp Minnie-Mickey in the Animal Kingdom. While making the characters more available has taken the guesswork out of finding them, it has robbed encounters of much of their spontaneity. Instead of chancing on a character, it's much more common now to wait in line to meet the character. Speaking of which, be aware that lines for face characters move m-u-c-h more slowly than do lines for nonspeaking characters. Because face characters are allowed to talk, they often engage children in lengthy conversations, much to the dismay of families still in the queue.

CHARACTER DINING

Fraternizing with characters has become so popular that Disney offers character breakfasts, brunches, and dinners where families can dine in the presence of Mickey, Minnie, Goofy, and other costumed versions of animated celebrities. Besides grabbing customers from Denny's and Hardee's, character meals provide a familiar, controlled setting in which young children can warm gradually to characters. Though we mention only the featured character(s) in the following descriptions, all meals are attended by several characters. Adult prices apply to persons age 12 or older, children's prices to ages 3 to 11. Little ones under age three eat free. For additional information on character dining, call (407) 939-3463 (WDW-DINE).

Because character dining is very popular, we recommend that you arrange priority seating as far in advance as possible. Make priority seating for dining up to 60 days before arrival by calling (407) 939-3463. If you forget to arrange priority seating in advance and all resort and theme park character meals are sold out, try to book a character meal at the Swan or Dolphin. Because the Swan and Dolphin aren't Disney-owned hotels, their character meals aren't booked through Disney central reservations. Consequently, the Swan and Dolphin often will have seating available when all other character meals are booked.

Priority seating is not a reservation, only a commitment to seat you ahead of walk-in patrons at the scheduled date and time. A reserved table won't await you, but you will be seated ahead of patrons who failed to call ahead. Even with priority seating, expect to wait at least 10–30 minutes to be seated.

Character Dining: What to Expect

Character meals are bustling affairs, held in hotels' or theme parks' largest full-service restaurants. Character breakfasts offer a fixed menu served family-style or a buffet. The typical family-style breakfast includes scrambled eggs; bacon, sausage, and ham; hash browns; waffles or French toast; biscuits, rolls, or pastries; and fruit. The meal is served in large skillets or platters at your table. If you run out of something, you can order seconds (or thirds) at no additional charge. Buffets offer much the same fare, but you have to fetch it yourself.

Character dinners range from a set menu served family-style to buffets or ordering off the menu. The character dinner at the Liberty Tree Tavern in the Magic Kingdom, for example, is served family-style and consists of turkey, ham, marinated flank steak, salad, mashed potatoes, green vegetables, and, for kids, macaroni and cheese. Dessert is extra. Character dinner buffets, such as those at 1900 Park Fare at the Grand Floridian and Chef Mickey's at the Contemporary Resort, offer separate adults' and children's serving lines. Typically, the children's buffet includes hamburgers, hot dogs, pizza, fish sticks, fried chicken nuggets, macaroni and cheese, and peanut butter and jelly sandwiches. Selections at the adult buffet usually include prime rib or other carved meat, baked or broiled Florida seafood, pasta, chicken, an ethnic dish or two, vegetables, potatoes, and salad.

At both breakfasts and dinners, characters circulate around the room while you eat. During your meal, each of the three to five characters present will visit your table, arriving one at a time to cuddle the kids (and sometimes the adults), pose for photos, and sign autographs. Keep autograph books (with pens) and loaded cameras handy. For the best photos, adults should sit across the table from their children. Always seat the children where characters can reach them most easily. If a table is against a wall, for example, adults should sit with their backs to the wall and children on the aisle.

At some of the larger restaurants, including 'Ohana at the Polynesian Resort and Chef Mickey's at the Contemporary, character meals involve impromptu parades of characters and children around the room, group singing, napkin waving, and other organized mayhem.

Disney people don't rush you to leave after you have eaten. You can get seconds on coffee or juice and stay as long as you wish to enjoy the characters. Remember, however, that there are lots of eager children and adults waiting not so patiently to be admitted.

When to Go

Though a number of character breakfasts are offered around Walt Disney World, attending them usually prevents you from arriving at the theme parks in time for opening. Because early morning is best for touring the parks and you don't want to burn daylight lingering over breakfast, we suggest:

1. Substitute a character breakfast for lunch. Have juice or coffee and roll or banana from room service or from your cooler first thing in the morning to tide you over. Then tour the theme park for an hour or two before breaking off around 10:15 a.m. to go to the character breakfast of your choice. Make a big brunch of your character breakfast and skip lunch. You should be fueled until dinner.

"Casting? This is George at the character breakfast. There's been a mistake. We were supposed to get the Assorted Character Package with one Mickey, one Goofy, one Donald, one Pluto . . ."

2. Go on your arrival or departure day. The day you arrive and check in is usually good for a character dinner. Settle in at your hotel, swim, then dine with the characters. This strategy has the added benefit of exposing your children to the characters before chance encounters at the parks. Some children, moreover, won't settle down to enjoy the parks until they have seen Mickey. Departure days also are good for a character meal. Schedule a character breakfast on your check-out day before you head for the airport or begin your drive home.

3. Go on a rest day. If you plan to stay five or more days, you probably will take a day or a half-day from touring to rest or do something else. These are perfect days for a character meal.

4. Go for dinner or lunch instead of breakfast. A character dinner or lunch in the afternoon or evening won't conflict with your touring schedule.

We receive a lot of mail from readers commenting on character meals. Here's some of what they had to say:

From a Philadelphia, Tennessee, mom:

> *The very best meal of the trip was the character breakfast at Cinderella's Royal Table [at the Magic Kingdom]. The smartest thing I did, the very best result of early planning, was making that reservation 60 days before our trip, It's certainly worth the cost when you factor in the atmosphere, the view, the food, the excellent coffee, and, best of all, the stuffed French toast.*

A Cincinnatti mother of two also likes Cinderella's Royal Table:

> *Cinderella's Royal Table has really improved its food as has the Coral Reef. Both waiters mentioned a new chef.*

A Frankenmuth, Michigan, family gives two thumbs up to the Crystal Palace, also at the Magic Kingdom:

> *We ate just about every character breakfast, lunch, and dinner. Our favorite, surprising even ourselves, was the Crystal Palace. The food was on the same level as the others, but the Crystal Palace was so much more quiet and relaxing. Even though it was a buffet, the waiter was extremely attentive. Having Pooh, Rabbit, Piglet, and Eeyore didn't hurt either.*

A Lexington, Kentucky, dad made this recommendation:

> *Garden Grill at Epcot for a character lunch: This was also good food (a pan of roast beef, chicken, stir-fry, and mashed potatoes) with a "country" Mickey and Minnie and Chip and Dale. Very highly recommended. Don't eat much breakfast!*

An Arlington, Virginia, family thinks character dinners make more sense than character breakfasts:

> *For character dining, we recommend the dinners instead of the breakfasts. The character dinner we went to was much less of an assembly line than the character breakfasts, and the kids got a lot more attention from Minnie, Goofy, and the Chipmunks. Plus, you don't lose that valuable morning attraction time.*

We agree, as long as you are still in a Disney mood. Sometimes after a long, hot day at the theme park, the last thing you want are more mice and chipmunks at dinner.

Character Breakfasts

If your kids are picky eaters or simply don't like eggs, choose a buffet breakfast. Priority seating is recommended for all character breakfasts. Call

(407) 939-3463 for breakfasts at Disney resorts or in theme parks. For non-Disney hotels, call the hotel directly.

Here are character breakfasts, by location:

Disney-MGM: Hollywood & Vine Cafeteria of the Stars This buffet, daily from 8:30 to 11:15 a.m., features Minnie, Chip 'n' Dale, Goofy, and Pluto. Cost is $15 for adults and $8 for children ages 3 to 11. The price of the character meal is in addition to your admission to the park. Priority seating is highly recommended.

Epcot: The Garden Grill Restaurant This breakfast is served daily from park opening to 11:10 a.m. The menu is fixed, but seconds are available. Cost is $15 for adults and $9 for children ages 3 to 11. Characters include Mickey, Pluto, and Chip 'n' Dale. The price of the character meal is in addition to your admission to the park.

Magic Kingdom: Cinderella's Royal Table in Cinderella Castle Served daily from 8 to 10 a.m., the breakfast features Cinderella and Snow White, plus visiting character friends. The menu is fixed. Cost is $15 for adults and $8 for children ages 3 to 11. The price of the character meal is in addition to your admission to the park. Call early; priority seating is required, and the breakfast is booked year-round. In fact, we recommend that you call 60 days prior to your desired reservation to ensure a table. No walk-ins are accepted.

Magic Kingdom: The Crystal Palace A Winnie the Pooh buffet breakfast is served daily from 8 to 10:45 a.m., hosted by Pooh, Tigger, and Eeyore. Cost is $15 for adults and $8 for children ages 3 to 11. Priority seating is recommended.

Disney's Beach Club Resort: Cape May Cafe This buffet breakfast is served daily from 7:30 to 11 a.m. The Characters in Charge are Goofy and Minnie, assisted by Chip 'n' Dale. Cost is $15 for adults and $9 for children ages 3 to 11. Softer background music and broader food choices make this a good location for adults who want a taste of characters or for parents who are maxed out on the World's frantic pace.

Wilderness Lodge: Artist Point Winnie the Pooh, Tigger, and Eeyore hold court at this breakfast served daily from 7:30 to 11:30 a.m. Cost is $15 for adults and $9 for children ages 3 to 11. The menu is all-you-can-eat, with family-style service. This breakfast is one of the quieter of the species.

Contemporary Resort: Chef Mickey's Mickey, Minnie, Goofy, and Chip 'n' Dale host this buffet daily from 7 to 11:30 a.m. Cost is $15 for adults and $8 for children ages 3 to 11. *Note:* Chef Mickey's was moved from the Downtown Disney Marketplace to the Contemporary Resort in 1995.

Polynesian Resort: 'Ohana   This tropical-theme breakfast is named Minnie's Menehune (difficult to pronounce at any time, but especially first thing in the morning). It's served daily from 7:30 to 11 a.m. Cost is $15 for adults and $9 for children ages 3 to 11. Minnie reigns, in a grass skirt no less, assisted by Goofy and Chip 'n' Dale. Service is family-style.

Grand Floridian Beach Resort: 1900 Park Fare   Mary Poppins, Minnie, Pluto, and Alice and the Mad Hatter host this buffet breakfast daily from 7:30 to 11:30 a.m. Cost is $16 for adults and $10 for children ages 3 to 11. Maddening calliope music plays throughout the meal.

Walt Disney World Swan: Garden Grove Cafe   Held only on Saturdays from 6:30 to 11 a.m., the Garden Grove character breakfast offers a choice of buffet or menu selection. Pluto and Goofy usually are the characters present. Cost is about $17 for adults and $11 for children ages 3 to 11. Priority seating is not accepted. For details, call (407) 934-3000 or (407) 934-1618.

Old Key West Resort: Olivia's Cafe   Winnie the Pooh, Tigger, and Eeyore host this breakfast on Sundays, Mondays, and Wednesdays from 7:30 to 11 a.m. Cost is $14 for adults and $9 for children ages 3 to 11.

Character Brunches and Lunches

Walt Disney World Dolphin: Coral Cafe   This buffet brunch is served only on Sundays from 7:30 to 11 a.m. Hosts are Chip 'n' Dale, Pluto, and Goofy. Cost is $17 for adults and $11 for children ages 3 to 12. For priority seating, call (407) 934 4000.

Disney-MGM: Hollywood & Vine Cafeteria of the Stars   A buffet, featuring Minnie, Chip 'n' Dale, Goofy, and Pluto, is served daily from 11:30 a.m. until 3:30 p.m. Cost is $16 for adults and $9 for children ages 3 to 11. The price of the character meal is in addition to your admission to the park. Priority seating is highly recommended.

Epcot: The Garden Grill Restaurant   This lunch is held daily from 11:30 a.m. to 4:30 p.m. The menu includes several selections, and seconds are available. Cost is $17 for adults and $10 for children ages 3 to 11. Characters include Mickey, Pluto, and Chip 'n' Dale.

Magic Kingdom: The Crystal Palace   A Winnie the Pooh buffet lunch is served daily from 11:30 a.m. to 2:45 p.m. Hosts are Pooh, Tigger, and Eeyore. Cost is $16 for adults and $8 for children ages 3 to 11. Priority seating is recommended.

Character Dinners

Magic Kingdom: The Crystal Palace Winnie the Pooh, Tigger, and Eeyore host this buffet served from 4 p.m. until park closing. Cost is $20 for adults and $10 for children ages 3 to 11. Priority seating is recommended.

Magic Kingdom: Liberty Tree Tavern A fixed menu is served family-style from 4 p.m. until park closing. Characters on-hand are Minnie, Goofy, Pluto, and Chip 'n' Dale. Cost is $20 for adults and $10 for children. Priority seating is recommended.

Walt Disney World Swan: Gullivers Held daily except for Tuesdays and Saturdays from 6 to 10 p.m., the dinner features Timon and Rafiki from *The Lion King* on Monday and Friday, Pooh and Tigger on Thursday, and Goofy and Pluto on Sunday and Wednesday. Diners order from the regular dinner menu. The entree range is $18.50–29.95; kids can eat for $6. An early-bird special is offered 5:30–7 p.m. Reservations are accepted for dinner only.

Grand Floridian Beach Resort: 1900 Park Fare Mickey and Minnie host a buffet daily from 5:15 to 9 p.m. Cost is $22 for adults and $13 for children ages 3 to 11. Be prepared for nonstop calliope music.

Polynesian Resort: Mickey's Tropical Luau This is a dinner show featuring Pacific-island dancing and Disney characters. Staged outdoors daily at 4:30 p.m., rain or shine, the show is fun (1) if you are hungry that early and (2) if you go during a cooler month of the year. Regardless of when you go, be prepared for lackluster food. Cost is $40 for adults and $20 for children ages 3 to 11. If you're planning ahead, we recommend that you try to book this dinner two years in advance. Cancellations must be made 48 hours before your reservation.

Contemporary Resort: Chef Mickey's This buffet is daily from 5 to 9:30 p.m. Chef Mickey appears, along with Goofy, Chip 'n' Dale, Pluto, and Minnie. Cost is $20 for adults and $9 for children ages 3 to 11.

Epcot: The Garden Grill Mickey, Pluto, and Chip 'n' Dale host dinner daily from 4:30 p.m. until park closing. The menu includes several selections, served family-style, with all-you-can-eat portions. The cost is $18 for adults and $10 for children ages 3 to 11.

Character Campfire

A campfire and sing-along are held nightly at 7 or 8 p.m. (depending on the season) near the Meadow Trading Post and Bike Barn at Fort Wilderness Campground. Chip 'n' Dale lead the songs, and a full-length Disney film is shown afterward. The program is free and open to resort guests. For a schedule, call (407) 824-2788.

Babysitting

Childcare Centers   Childcare isn't available within the theme parks, but each Magic Kingdom resort connected by the monorail and each Epcot resort (BoardWalk Inn and Villas, Yacht and Beach Club resorts) has a childcare center for potty-trained children older than three. Services vary, but children generally can be left between 4 p.m. and midnight. Milk and cookies and blankets and pillows are provided at all childcare centers. Play is supervised but not organized, and toys, videos, and games are plentiful. Guests at any Disney resort or campground may use the childcare services.

Childcare Clubs *			
Hotel	*Name of Program*	*Ages*	*Phone*
Wyndham Palace	All about Kids	All	(407) 812-9300
BoardWalk Inn & Villas	Harbor Club	4–12	(407) 939-5100
Contemporary Resort	Mouseketeer Clubhouse	4–12	(407) 824-1000 ext. 3700
Grand Floridian Beach Resort	Mouseketeer Club	4–12	(407) 824-2985
The Hilton	Vacation Station	4–12	(407) 827-4000
Polynesian Resort	Neverland Club	4–12	(407) 824-2000 ext. 2184
Wilderness Lodge Resort	Cub's Den	4–12	(407) 824-1083
Yacht and Beach Club resorts	Sandcastle Club	4–12	(407) 934-7000 ext. 3750

*Childcare clubs operate afternoons and evenings. All require reservations.

The most elaborate of the childcare centers (variously called "clubs" or "camps") is Neverland Club at the Polynesian Resort. This and the one at the Wilderness Lodge are the only centers that include a buffet dinner at the club, though at the other locations you can arrange for room service to provide your children's meals. A Disney character (usually Goofy) even visits the children each night at the Neverland Club. The rates for children ages 4–12 are $8 per hour for the first child and $6 per hour for each additional child.

We get a lot of mail praising the Neverland Club. A dad from Snohomish, Washington, writes:

> *The boys loved it! They got a good choice of food to eat in buffet style. It was educational—someone from Discovery Island brought some animals in—and it was fun. There was something for every age—appropriate toys, games, and a game room with free video games. The boys also had a Polaroid picture taken with Goofy, and the boys' smiles showed how good a time they were having. The supervisors seemed very pleasant and caring. As you might expect, it was all very professional and well done, and the beepers they had us carry made us feel extra secure.*

A Houston dad adds:

> *There were some outstanding surprises during our visit. One was the babysitting club at the Polynesian Hotel, the Neverland Club. I can tell you that our children enjoyed the Neverland Club as much as anything at WDW. It is somewhat expensive, but that includes dinner, free video games, Disney movies, group games and activities, and a visit by an expert from Discovery Island with several birds and animals. A woman registering her child told my wife that her daughter had stayed at the Neverland Club on a visit two years ago and considered it her favorite attraction at WDW!*

If you're staying in a Disney resort that doesn't offer a childcare club and you *don't* have a car, you're better off using in-room babysitting. Trying to take your child to a club in another hotel via Disney bus requires a 50- to 90-minute trip each way. By the time you have deposited your little one, it will almost be time to pick him up again. Be aware that the childcare clubs shut down at or before midnight. If you intend to make a late night of it, in-room babysitting is your best bet.

Kinder-Care Learning Centers also operate childcare facilities at Disney World. Originally developed for use by Disney employees, the centers now also take guests' children on a space-available basis. Kinder-Care provides basically the same services as a hotel club, except that the daytime *Learning While Playing Development Program* is more structured and educational. Kinder-Care is open Monday–Friday, 6 a.m.–9 p.m., and Saturday and Sunday, 6 a.m.–6 p.m. Accepted are children ages 1 (provided they're walking and can eat table food) through 12. For reservations, call (407) 827-5437 or (407) 824-3290.

In-Room Babysitting   For those staying in the World, in-room babysitting is offered by Kinder-Care (phone (407) 827-5444) and the Fairy Godmothers (no kidding) service described below. Base rates for Kinder-Care are $12 an hour.

All about Kids (phone (407) 812-9300) offers in-room service to all Buena Vista–area hotels. Sitters range in age from college students to grandparents and are licensed, bonded, and insured. Base rates are $9 an hour (add $1 an hour for each additional child), with a four-hour minimum and a $6 travel fee. For jobs that start after 9 p.m., add $2 an hour. They will even take your child to the theme parks if you pay the sitter's admission.

Outside of Walt Disney World, childcare services and in-room sitting can be arranged through most larger hotels and motels or by calling the Fairy Godmothers. Godmothers are on-call 24 hours a day (you never get an answering machine) and offer the most flexible and diversified service in town. They will come to any hotel at any hour. If you pay, they will take your children to the theme parks. No child is too young or too old, and Godmothers also care for the elderly and pets. All sitters are female nonsmokers. Base rates are $9 an hour for up to three children (in the same family), with a four-hour minimum and a $5 travel fee. For additional children in the same family, add $1 per child per hour. Godmothers will also tend a group of four or fewer children from different families for $6 an hour per family. For each additional child in excess of four, add $1 per child per hour to the base rate. Wishing won't get you a Godmother; you have to call (407) 277-3724 or (407) 275-7326.

WALT DISNEY WORLD LEARNING PROGRAMS FOR CHILDREN

Disney's educational programs are developed in coordination with leading educators and produced through the Disney Institute. Walt Disney World offers five programs for children ages 7–10 and six programs for children ages 11–15. Most programs last 3½ hours and are offered twice each week. Each course is $69 per child. Two courses taken on the same day cost $99 with lunch available for an additional charge. If the class visits a Disney theme park, admission is included. Due to small class sizes, you should make reservations six weeks in advance by calling (407) WDW-TOUR.

Disney is constantly tinkering with the learning programs. Some change and others are terminated to make room for new programs. Though the focus and presentation may vary, there are always programs available on art (including animation and architecture), performing arts (singing, dancing, acting, theatrical make-up, and backstage skills), and nature and ecology. Following are the specific courses that were offered when we went to press:

Programs for Children Ages 7–10

Broadway Bound   Hands-on introduction to stage show skills at the Magic Kingdom and Disney-MGM Studios.

Face Magic   Course on theatrical make-up (you won't recognize your child when you pick him up).

Art Surround   Kids tour theme parks to see how Disney artists translate concept into reality. Includes hands-on project.

Kidventure   Excursion into the Florida wetlands by boat for wildlife identification and hands-on animal encounters.

Swamp Stomp   Exploration of a Florida cypress swamp followed by a trip to Epcot to learn about the "Circle of Life."

Programs for Children Ages 11–15

Art Magic   Introduction to animation.

Showbiz Magic   Behind-the-scenes look at what goes into a theater attraction, including lighting, sound, Audio-Animatronics, and special effects.

Funny Papers   Participants learn to create a storyboard and draw Disney characters.

Stealing the Show   Kids go through the Walt Disney World talent process from audition to putting it all together for a live show.

Rock Climbing for Youth   Introduction to rock climbing on an artificial climbing wall.

Island Explorers   Wildlife identification and specimen-collecting field trip into a marsh. Microscope, journals, and field-sketching techniques are covered.

Part Six

Special Tips for Special People

Walt Disney World for Singles

Walt Disney World is great for singles. It is safe, clean, and low-pressured. If you're looking for a place to relax without being hit on, Disney World is perfect. Bars, lounges, and nightclubs are the most laid-back and friendly you're likely to find anywhere. In many, you can hang out and not even be asked to buy a drink. Parking lots are well lighted and constantly patrolled. For women alone, safety and comfort are unsurpassed.

With the opening of the BoardWalk and Downtown Disney in 1997, nightlife options increased exponentially. Virtually every type of entertainment performed fully clothed is available at an amazingly reasonable price at a Disney nightspot. If you drink more than you should and are a Disney resort guest, Disney buses will return you safely to your hotel.

If, however, you're looking to meet someone new and exciting, there are better places than Walt Disney World. Most singles at Disney World work there. Even at the Pleasure Island entertainment complex you need to check your dancing partner's wristband to determine whether he or she is old enough to buy a drink.

Far fewer single men vacation at Disney World than do single women. There are men, both single for real and single for the moment, attending meetings and conventions at the resorts, but their schedules rarely permit development of anything meaningful. Filling the void are local single (and married) men who understand that single women on vacation may be vulnerable. Avoid these guys.

The easiest and safest way to meet anyone at Disney World is at the theme parks, including the water theme parks. (Most local cruisers aren't going to shell out the price of admission and hang around the park all day.) Parks give guests something to talk about, and there's no easier place to strike up a conversation than waiting in line for an attraction. A more organized way to meet people is to take a tour for adults or join a program at the Disney Institute (pages 677–679).

Walt Disney World for Couples

So many couples marry or honeymoon at Walt Disney World that a department has been formed to take care of their needs. *Disney's Fairy Tale Weddings & Honeymoons* department offers a range of wedding venues and services, plus honeymoon packages.

Weddings

It takes big bucks to marry at Disney World. Disney's Intimate Wedding (six or fewer guests) includes four nights' lodging for the wedding couple, admission to the parks, a wedding officiant, and one dinner at a Disney "fine-dining" establishment—for $3,400! This price includes a musician, flower bouquet, limousine ride, and a wedding coordinator, as well. For even more, you can arrive at your wedding in Cinderella's glass coach, have Goofy as best man and Minnie as maid of honor, and drive away after the ceremony in a limo chauffeured by Mickey. If you don't have many friends, you can rent additional Disney characters by the half hour to attend your wedding. Volume discounts are available; characters cost $450 for one, $650 for two, $850 for three, and so on. If character prices sound steep, be comforted that they don't eat or drink. If you invite more than six guests to your wedding, you must purchase Disney's customized wedding package, which starts at $7,500.

Indoor and outdoor sites are available for weddings at theme parks as well as the Grand Floridian, Yacht Club, Beach Club, BoardWalk Inn and Villas, Contemporary, Wilderness Lodge, Polynesian, and Disney Village

resorts. You can have a nautical wedding aboard the *Kingdom Queen* stern-wheeler on Bay Lake or the riverboat at the Walt Disney World Village. Wedding sites for the nocturnal are available at Pleasure Island nightclubs. Disney operates its Fairy Tale Wedding pavilion on a private island near the Grand Floridian. The glass-enclosed pavilion is nondenominational and accommodates 250 guests as well as smaller, more intimate nuptials.

One of the more improbable services available is bachelor parties (obtain information at (407) 828-3400). What goes on at a Disney bachelor party? Stag cartoons or a private showing of *The Making of Me?* Get down!

If you wish to marry at Walt Disney World, you can get a marriage license ($89) at any county courthouse in Florida. Cash, traveler's checks, or money orders are accepted. There's no waiting period; your license is issued when you apply. The ceremony must occur within 60 days. Blood tests aren't required, but you must present identification (driver's license, passport, or birth certificate). If you were divorced within the year, you must produce a copy of your divorce decree. Call the wedding coordinator at (407) 828-3400 for more information.

Honeymoons

Honeymoon packages are adaptations of the regular Walt Disney Travel Company vacations. No special rooms or honeymoon suites are included unless you upgrade. In fact, the only honeymoon features are room service (in one package) and a photo session and keepsake album (in two others).

If you're interested in a Disney wedding or honeymoon, contact:

Disney's Fairy Tale Weddings & Honeymoons
P.O. Box 10020
Lake Buena Vista, FL 32830-0020
(800) 370-6009
www.disneyworld.com

Romantic Getaways

Walt Disney World is a favorite getaway for honeymooners and other couples. You don't have to buy a honeymoon package to enjoy a romantic interlude, but not all Disney hotels are equally romantic. Some are too family oriented; others swarm with convention-goers. We recommend these Disney lodgings for romantics:

1. Polynesian Resort
2. Wilderness Lodge Resort
3. Grand Floridian Beach Resort
4. BoardWalk Inn & Villas
5. Yacht and Beach Club resorts
6. Contemporary Resort (tower rooms)

All of these properties are expensive. There are also secluded villas in the Villas at the Disney Institute. Possibly the most romantic Disney accommodation is the Moorea building at the Polynesian Resort. Couples at the Moorea with a waterfront-view room can watch the Magic Kingdom fireworks across the Seven Seas Lagoon. Tower rooms at the Contemporary, especially those on the southwest side, also provide great views.

Quiet, Romantic Places to Eat

Quiet, romantic restaurants with good food are rare in the theme parks. Only the Coral Reef, the terrace at the Rose & Crown, and the San Angel Inn at Epcot satisfy both requirements. Waterfront dining is available at Portobello Yacht Club and Fulton's Crab House at Pleasure Island, Narcoossee's at the Grand Floridian, and Cap'n Jack's Oyster Bar at the Disney Village Marketplace.

The California Grill atop the Contemporary Resort has the best view at Walt Disney World. If window tables aren't available, ask to be served in the adjoining lounge. Victoria & Albert's at the Grand Floridian is the World's showcase gourmet restaurant; expect to pay big bucks. Other good choices for couples include the Yachtsman Steakhouse at the Yacht Club, Kimonos at the Swan and Dolphin resorts, 'Ohana at the Polynesian, and Spoodles and The Flying Fish Cafe at the BoardWalk.

Eating later in the evening and choosing among the restaurants we've mentioned will improve your chances for quiet, intimate dining, but children—well-behaved or otherwise—are everywhere at Walt Disney World, and you won't escape them. Honeymooners from Slidell, Louisiana, write:

> We made dinner reservations at some of the nicer Disney restaurants. When we made reservations, we made sure they were past the dinner hours and we tried to stress that we were on our honeymoon. [In] every restaurant we went to, we were seated next to large families. The kids were usually tired and cranky. After a whole day in the parks, the kids were not excited about sitting through a long meal. It's very difficult to enjoy a romantic dinner when there are small children crawling around under your table. We looked around the restaurant and always noticed lots of nonchildren couples. Our suggestion is this: Seat couples without children together and families with kids elsewhere. If Disney is such a popular honeymoon destination, then some attempt should be made to keep romantic restaurants romantic.

A couple from Woodbridge, Virginia, adds:

> We found it very difficult to find a quiet restaurant for dinner anywhere. We tried a restaurant which you recommended as quiet and

pleasant. We even waited until 8:30 p.m. to eat and we were still sur-rounded by out-of-control children. The waiters were even singing the Barney the Dinosaur theme song. The food was very good, but after a long day in the park, our nerves were shot.

For complete information about Disney restaurants, as well as recommendations for off-World dining, see Part 9: Dining in and around Walt Disney World (pages 268–381).

Romantic Stuff to Do

Couples, like everyone else, have their own agenda at Disney World. Nonetheless, here are romantic diversions you might not have on your list:

1. *Visit a lounge.* Atop the Contemporary Resort is a nice but pricey lounge. It's great for watching a sunset or viewing nighttime fireworks over the nearby Magic Kingdom. If you want to go for the view and not drink, access an outside promenade through a set of glass doors at the end of the lounge. Also wonderful is Mizner's Lounge on the Alcazar level of the Grand Floridian. It overlooks the hotel grounds and pools and the Seven Seas Lagoon. Each evening a six-piece dance band plays '20s and '30s music on the adjacent landing.

2. *View the Floating Electrical Pageant.* One of Disney's most romantic entertainments, the pageant consists of a train of barges, each with a spectacular light display depicting sea creatures. The show starts after dark to music by Handel played on synthesizers. You see only the lights. The best places to watch are from the piers at the Polynesian, Wilderness Lodge, the Grand Floridian, or Fort Wilderness.

3. *Ride a boat.* Small launches shuttle guests to and from the Grand Floridian, Polynesian, Magic Kingdom, Wilderness Lodge, and Fort Wilderness Campground well into the night. On a summer night, take a tranquil cruise around Bay Lake and the Seven Seas Lagoon. Disney vessels also cruise the canal connecting Disney-MGM Studios and Epcot, stopping at the Swan and Dolphin, Disney's BoardWalk, and the Yacht and Beach Club resorts.

   During daytime at the Fort Wilderness dock, you can rent boats for exploring Bay Lake and the Seven Seas Lagoon. The adjacent Fort Wilderness Campground is honeycombed with footpaths that are lovely for early-morning or early-evening walks.

   If you enjoy hiking and boating, visit Juniper Springs Recreation Area in the Ocala National Forest. About an hour and a half north of Disney World, the forest is extraordinarily beautiful. Trails are well marked, and canoes are available for rent (shuttle included). Paddling down Juniper Springs is like floating through a natural version of the Jungle Cruise. For Juniper Springs information, call (352) 625 2808.

4. *Have a picnic.* During more temperate months, picnic on the beaches of Bay Lake and the Seven Seas Lagoon. Room service at Disney resorts will prepare a carry-along lunch to order. Drinks, including wine and beer, are less expensive at hotel convenience shops. Fort Wilderness Campground also is good for picnics.

5. *Dine and dance on the BoardWalk.* Disney's BoardWalk offers several nice restaurants and an upscale dance club featuring music from the '20s to the '90s. Even if you don't dine or dance, the BoardWalk is romantic and picturesque for strolling.

6. *Go bicycling.* Rent a bike at Wilderness Lodge and explore the paths and roads of nearby Fort Wilderness Campground. Maps are available at the bike-rental shed.

Things to Bring

Once ensconced in your Disney World hideaway, it can be inconvenient to go out for something you've forgotten. Many couples write us to list things they wish they'd remembered to bring. Here are items most often mentioned:

1. Wine (Wine is sold by the bottle at Disney World, but the selection is pretty dismal. The best nearby selection of beer, wine, and champagne is at the Goodings Supermarket in the Crossroads Shopping Center on FL 535, across from the entrance to Disney Village Hotel Plaza.)
2. Corkscrew (Wine glasses are available from room service.)
3. Liquor, aperitifs, and cordials
4. Mixers for fancy drinks such as margaritas, olives for martinis, lemons, and limes
5. Portable tape or disc player and your favorite music
6. Bicycles
7. Picnic basket and blanket or tablecloth
8. Candles and holders
9. Cooler
10. Special snacks such as caviar, chocolates, cheeses (with knife), and fruit

Walt Disney World for Expectant Mothers

It is said that a good shepherd will lay down his life for his sheep. Heaven knows we have tried to be good shepherds for you. We have spun around in teacups and been jostled in simulators until we turned green. We have baked in the sun, flapped in the wind, and come close to drowning in the rain, all while researching this guide. But for expectant mothers we have failed. Try as he might, the author has never become pregnant, and as a consequence, the *Unofficial Guide* has never included good, first-hand information for mothers-to-be. Then, in our darkest hour, to the rescue came Debbie Grubbs, a reader from Colorado in her fifth month of pregnancy. Fearless and undaunted, Debbie waddled all over Walt Disney World, compiling observations and tips for expectant moms. The following is what she had to say.

I was very disappointed to find no information specifically directed to pregnant women, particularly concerning which attractions at the theme parks you can and cannot ride. Generally speaking, there is more that you can do at Walt Disney World than that you can't do. Therefore, I will outline only those rides that are prohibited to pregnant women and the reasons why. There were several rides that I just knew I could ride even though they were restricted, so I sent my husband and friends to ride first and they reported why they thought I could or could not ride.

Magic Kingdom: Splash Mountain *is restricted obviously due to the drop, or so I thought. It turns out that the seat configuration in the "logs" has more to do with it than the drop. The seats are made so that your knees are higher than your rear, causing compression on the abdomen (when it is this large). This is potentially harmful to the baby. As always, better safe than sorry. I really hated to miss this one.*

Big Thunder Mountain Railroad *is restricted for obvious reasons as well. It's just not a good idea to ride roller coasters when you are pregnant.*

Mad Tea Party *may be okay if you don't spin the cups. We didn't ride this one because I was advised by my doctor not to ride things with centrifugal [or centripetal] force. Dumbo and the Astro Orbiter (Tomorrowland) are okay, but the Mad Tea Party is too fast if you spin the cups.*

Space Mountain *is restricted. It's one of my favorite rides, but a roller coaster nonetheless.*

Tomorrowland Speedway *is not recommended due to the amount of rear-ending that always occurs due to overzealous younger drivers.*

Epcot Center: Body Wars *and* **Test Track** *are restricted, as are all simulator rides. They are too rough and jerky, much like a roller coaster.*

Disney-MGM Studios: Tower of Terror *is restricted for the drop alone, and Star Tours is restricted because it is a simulator. Although not as rough as Body Wars, Star Tours is still a no-no. The new Rock 'n' Roller Coaster is clearly off limits.*

There might be some question about the **Backlot Tour** *due to Catastrophe Canyon, where there is a simulated earthquake. It is very tame compared to Earthquake! at Universal Studios and posed no hazard to me. I rode with no problems.*

Animal Kingdom: Countdown to Extinction *is very jerky and should be avoided.*

Kali River Rapids *is a toss-up—the ride is somewhat bouncy and very wet.*

Water Theme Parks: *All of the slides are off-limits to pregnant women. You can, however, do Shark Reef at Typhoon Lagoon with an extra-large wetsuit vest. The wave pools and floating creeks are great for getting the weight off your feet.*

MORE TIPS

In addition to Debbie's tips, here are a few of our own:

1. Go over your Walt Disney World vacation plans with your obstetrician well in advance of your trip.
2. Be prepared for a lot of walking at Walt Disney World. Get in shape by walking at home, building up endurance and distance gradually.
3. While on vacation, get as much rest as you need, even if you have to sacrifice some time at the theme parks. Try to work in an afternoon nap each day.
4. Make sure you eat properly. Drink plenty of water throughout the day, especially if you visit Walt Disney World during the warmer seasons of the year.
5. Use in-park transportation whenever available to cut down on walking.
6. Stay in Walt Disney World if possible. This will make it much easier to separate from your group and return to your hotel for rest.

Walt Disney World for Seniors

Seniors' problems and concerns are common to Disney visitors of all ages. Seniors do, however, often get into predicaments caused by touring with people younger than they are. Run ragged and pressured by grandchildren to endure a frantic pace, many seniors concentrate on surviving Disney World rather than enjoying it. The parks have as much to offer older visitors as they do children, and seniors must either set the pace or dispatch the young folks to tour on their own.

An older reader in Alabaster, Alabama, writes:

> *The main thing I want to say is that being a senior is not for wussies. At Disney World particularly, it requires courage and pluck. Things that used to be easy take a lot of effort, and sometimes your brain has to wait for your body to catch up. Half the time, your grandchildren treat you like a crumbling ruin and then turn around and trick you into getting on a roller coaster in the dark. What you need to tell seniors is that they have to be alert and not trust anyone. Not their children or even the Disney people, and especially not their grandchildren. When your grandchildren want you to go on a ride, don't follow along blindly like a lamb to the slaughter. Make sure you know what the ride is all about. Stand your ground and do not waffle. He who hesitates is launched!*

Most seniors we interview enjoy Disney World much more when they tour with folks their own age. If, however, you're considering going to Disney World with your grandchildren, we recommend an orientation visit without them first. If you know first-hand what to expect, it's much easier to establish limits, maintain control, and set a comfortable pace when you visit with the youngsters.

If you're determined to take the grandkids, read carefully those sections of this book that discuss family touring. (*Hint:* The Dumbo-or-Die-in-a-Day Touring Plan has been known to bring grown-ups of any age to their knees.)

Because seniors are a varied and willing lot, there aren't any attractions we would suggest they avoid. For seniors, as with other Disney visitors, personal taste is more important than age. We hate to see mature visitors pass an exceptional attraction like Splash Mountain because younger visitors call it a "thrill ride." Splash Mountain is a full-blown adventure that gets its appeal more from music and visual effects than from the thrill of the ride. Because you must choose among those attractions that might interest you, we provide facts to help you make informed decisions.

We know it's easy to get caught up in the spectacle and wonder of Disney World, so much so that you follow a crowd onto something you hadn't fully considered. Here, then, are some of the attractions to know before you enter.

Magic Kingdom

Space Mountain   If you thought the roller coaster at Coney Island was a thrill, this won't be far behind, with dips and pops that pull you through curves and over humps. This ride vibrates a lot. Put your glasses in your fanny pack; we can't guarantee they'll stay in your pocket.

Big Thunder Mountain Railroad   Although sedate compared with Space Mountain, this ride is very jarring. Cars jerk back and forth along the track, though there are few drops. It's the side-to-side shaking that gets to most people.

Splash Mountain   This ride combines the whimsy of Disney with the thrill of a log flume. There's one big drop near the end and some splash (engineered by spray guns and a water cannon, not the drop itself). The enchanting Brer Rabbit story is worth getting wet for.

Swiss Family Treehouse   This isn't a thrill ride, but it does involve lots of stair climbing and a very unsteady pontoon bridge.

Mad Tea Party   An adaptation of a carnival ride, big tea cups spin until riders are nauseated. If you approach this instrument of the devil while it's sitting still, your cunning grandchildren may try to pass it off as an *al fresco* dining patio.

Epcot

Body Wars   This ride jolts more than Star Tours (at Disney-MGM Studios) and is more likely to cause motion sickness than the Mad Hatter's tea cups. It's like a graphic anatomy lesson combined with the trauma of being chauffeured by a teenager driving his first stick shift.

Test Track   The newest thrill ride in Future World, this attraction simulates test driving a car. One of the fastest rides in the Disney repertoire, Test Track whizzes you around hairpin turns, over rough road, down straightaways, and up and down steep inclines.

Disney-MGM Studios

Star Tours   Using the plot and characters from *Star Wars,* this flight-simulation ride is a Disney masterpiece. If you're extremely prone to motion sickness, this ride will affect you. Otherwise, it might be the highlight of your Walt Disney World vacation.

The Twilight Zone **Tower of Terror**   Though most of the thrills are visual, the Tower of Terror features a gut-gripping simulation of an elevator in free fall after its cable has broken.

Rock 'n' Roller Coaster   This is Disney's wildest coaster. If you thought Space Mountain was rough, stay away from this one.

Animal Kingdom

Countdown to Extinction   Fortunately, the name applies to dinosaurs, not those who ride it. The show consists primarily of visual effects, but the ride is pretty jerky.

Kali River Rapids   This ride simulates a whitewater raft trip. It's not all that rough, but it's very wet.

Getting Around

Many seniors like to walk, but a seven-hour visit to one of the theme parks normally includes four to eight miles on foot. If you aren't up for that much hiking, let a more athletic member of your party push you in a rented wheelchair. The theme parks also offer fun-to-drive electric carts (convenience vehicles). Don't let your pride get in the way of having a good time. Sure you could march ten miles if you had to, but *you don't have to!*

Your wheelchair-rental deposit slip is good for a replacement wheelchair in any park during the same day. You can rent a chair at the Magic Kingdom in the morning, return it, go to Epcot, present your deposit slip, and get another chair at no additional charge.

Timing Your Visit

Retirees should make the most of their flexible schedules and go to Disney World in fall or spring (excluding holiday weeks), when the weather is the nicest and the crowds are the thinnest. Crowds are also sparse from the end of January through the beginning of February, but the weather is unpredictable. If you visit Disney World in winter, bring coats and sweaters, plus warm-weather clothing. Be prepared for anything from near-freezing rain to afternoons in the 80s.

The Price of Admission

Only Florida residents get senior discounts on Disney World admission (page 58). For additional information, see our section on admission options (pages 55–58).

Lodging

If you can afford it, stay in Walt Disney World. If you're concerned about the quality of your accommodations or the availability of transportation, staying inside the Disney complex will ease your mind. The rooms are some of the nicest in the Orlando/Kissimmee area and are always clean and well maintained. Plus, transportation is always available to any destination in Disney World at no additional cost.

Disney hotels reserve rooms closer to restaurants and transportation for guests of any age who can't tolerate much walking. They also provide golf carts to pick up from and deliver guests to their rooms. Cart service can vary dramatically depending on the time of day and the number of guests requesting service. At check-in time (around 3 p.m.), for example, the wait for a ride can be as long as 40 minutes.

There are many quality hotels in the area, but we recommend seniors stay in Walt Disney World because:

1. The quality of the properties is consistently above average.
2. Transportation companies that operate buses for "outside" hotels run only every hour or so. Disney buses run continuously. Staying in Disney World guarantees you can get transportation whenever you need it.
3. You may be eligible for discounts on shows and early entrance to the parks.
4. Boarding pets overnight at the kennels is available only to Disney resort guests.
5. You get free parking in the major theme parks' lots.
6. You get preferential tee times on resort golf courses.

All Disney hotels are large and spread out. While it's easy to avoid most stairs, it is often a long hike to your room from the parking lot, bus stops, or public areas. Seniors intending to spend more time at Epcot and Disney-MGM Studios than at the Magic Kingdom or the Animal Kingdom should consider the Yacht and Beach Club resorts, Swan and Dolphin, or BoardWalk Inn.

The Contemporary Resort is a good choice for seniors who want to be on the monorail system, as are the Grand Floridian and Polynesian resorts, though both sprawl over many acres, necessitating a lot of walking. For a restful, rustic feeling, choose the Wilderness Lodge. If you want a kitchen and all the comforts of home, book Old Key West Resort or BoardWalk Villas.

RVers will find pleasant surroundings at Disney's Fort Wilderness Campground. There are also several KOA campgrounds within 20 minutes of Walt Disney World. None, however, offer the wilderness setting or amenities that Disney does, but they cost less.

Transportation

Roads in Walt Disney World can be daunting. Armed with a moderate sense of direction and an above-average sense of humor, however, even the most timid driver can learn to get around in the World. If you're easily intimidated, book a hotel on the monorail and stay off the road.

If you drive, parking isn't a problem. Lots are served by trams that link the parking area and the theme park's front gate. For guests with mobility problems, parking spaces for the disabled are available adjacent to each park's entrance. The attendant at the pay booth will give you a special ticket for your dashboard and will direct you to the reserved spaces. Though Disney requires that you be recognized officially as handicapped to use this parking, temporarily disabled or injured persons also are permitted access.

Senior Dining

Eat breakfast at your hotel restaurant or save money by having juice and rolls in your room. Although you aren't allowed to bring food into the parks, fruit, fruit juice, and soft drinks are sold throughout Disney World. Make your lunch priority seating for before noon to avoid the lunch crowds. Follow with an early dinner and be out of the restaurants, rested and ready for evening touring and fireworks, long before the main crowd begins to think about dinner.

We recommend seniors fit dining and rest times into the day. Remember Dad on the Dumbo-or-Die-in-a-Day Touring Plan? He'll be gobbling fast foods as he hauls his toddlers around the park at breakneck speed. Reserve a window table for your early lunch and wave to him as he races by. Plan lunch as your break in the day. Sit back, relax, and enjoy. Then return to your hotel for a nap.

Have a Plan

From planning the time to visit to observing our first rule of touring ("Arrive early! Arrive early! Arrive early!"), seniors generally are the perfect *Unofficial Guide* patrons. Those who can get by on less sleep enjoy the stress-free pleasure of touring the parks in early morning. Late sleepers should visit Disney World during less crowded, off-peak times.

It's imperative to follow our maxim, "Have a plan or get a frontal lobotomy." Select a touring plan. Before you go the park, read the ride and show descriptions and pick what you want to see or skip so that you'll be able to efficiently follow the plan. Arrive at the park's gates at least a half hour before official opening. Move as fast as you can early in the day so that you'll be able to slow down after an hour or so, knowing the most strenuous part of the plan and potential bottlenecks are behind you.

Seniors who ask us whether the touring plans work for folks who want to take things a little slower should take heart:

> *My mother (age 77) and myself (age 47) visited Disney for the first time. We followed your "Type A" schedule and really enjoyed the challenge of it. We were standing in line for Star Tours and the friendly attendant was advising us on the popular attractions to see. He suggested Tower of Terror, Indiana Jones, Voyage of the Little Mermaid, and Muppet Vision 4D. We said we had already seen them all. He said, "It's only 10 o'clock in the morning and you have seen all of those already?" We said, "Yes," and held up your guidebook.*

Every senior should take at least one behind-the-scenes tour, most of which are at Epcot. They offer an in-depth look at the operations of Walt Disney World. Especially worthwhile are Hidden Treasures and Gardens of the World. If you don't have time for these lengthy tours, the shorter Greenhouse Tour at Epcot's The Land pavilion is a "must-see." Backstage Magic visits behind-the-scenes locations at several theme parks, while Keys to the Kingdom provides a glimpse of the history and hidden operations of the Magic Kingdom. Ranging in duration from one to seven hours and in price from $5 to $160 per person, all of the tours require a lot of walking and standing.

Finally, include quiet time in your itinerary. We recommend Disney patrons of all ages return to their hotel during the hot, crowded part of the day for lunch, a nap, and even a swim.

When You Need to Contact the Outside World

Pay telephones are located throughout Walt Disney World. Amplified handsets are available for the hearing-impaired in all four major theme parks. Handset locations are marked on each park's map, provided free when you enter. A Telecommunication Device for the Deaf (TDD) is available at Guest Relations in all theme parks.

Telephones that guests in wheelchairs can reach are scattered throughout all parks except the Magic Kingdom, where they're under the Walt Disney World Railroad Station.

Walt Disney World for Disabled Guests

VISITORS WITH SPECIAL NEEDS

Wholly or Partially Nonambulatory Guests may rent wheelchairs. Most rides, shows, attractions, rest rooms, and restaurants in the World accommodate the nonambulatory disabled. For specific inquiries, call (407) 824-4321. If you're in a theme park and need assistance, go to Guest Relations.

A limited number of electric carts (motorized convenience vehicles) are available for rent. Easy and fun to drive, they give nonambulatory guests a tremendous degree of freedom and mobility. For some reason, vehicles at the Magic Kingdom are much faster than those at other parks.

Close-in parking is available for disabled visitors at all Disney lots. Request directions when you pay your parking fee. All monorails and most rides, shows, rest rooms, and restaurants accommodate wheelchairs.

An information booklet for disabled guests is available at wheelchair rental locations throughout the World. Theme park maps issued to each guest on admission are symbol-coded to show nonambulatory guests which attractions accommodate wheelchairs.

Even if an attraction doesn't accommodate wheelchairs, nonambulatory guests still may ride if they can transfer from their wheelchair to the ride's vehicle. Disney staff, however, aren't trained or permitted to assist in transfers. Guests must be able to board the ride unassisted or have a member of their party assist them. Either way, members of the nonambulatory guest's party will be permitted to go along on the ride.

Because waiting areas of most attractions won't accommodate wheelchairs, nonambulatory guests and their party should request boarding instructions from a Disney attendant as soon as they arrive at an attraction. Almost always, the entire group will be allowed to board without a lengthy wait.

A woman from New Orleans who traveled with a nonambulatory friend writes:

> *The most recent trip is what I really wanted to tell you about. I went with a very dear friend of mine who is a paraplegic, confined to a wheelchair. It was his first trip to WDW, and I knew that it was a handicap-friendly place, but we were still a little apprehensive about how much we would be able to do. The official pamphlet distributed by the WDW staff is helpful, but it implies limitations, such as stating that one must be able to navigate (i.e., walk) the catwalks of Space Mountain in case of emergency. After reading this, Brian and I thought that we would end up walking around the MK looking at the rides, not riding them. The reality is, nonambulatory visitors are*

able to do much more—one only has to ask the cast members what is really allowed. Of course, I'm sure the WDW publication is written to cover liability purposes; also, Brian is a very active person who is able to transfer from his wheelchair without too much difficulty, so we were able to ride almost everything we wanted! We both had a terrific time. The only ride that it seems we should have been able to ride but couldn't was Pirates of the Caribbean, and [this was] only because the railings at the loading site are just a few inches too close together for a wheelchair to pass through. Anyway, my point is that it may be encouraging to disabled readers of the Unofficial Guide *to know that there are options available; of course, with the caveat that it depends on the individual's mobility. I would recommend to anyone to not avoid a ride—ask first.*

Visitors with Dietary Restrictions can be assisted at Guest Relations in the theme parks. For Walt Disney World restaurants outside the theme parks, call the restaurant a day in advance for assistance.

Sight- and/or Hearing-Impaired Guests aren't forgotten. Guest Relations at the theme parks provide complimentary tape cassettes and portable tape players to assist sight-impaired guests ($25 refundable deposit required). At the same locations, TDDs are available for hearing-impaired guests. In addition to TDDs, many pay phones in the major parks are equipped with amplifying headsets. See your Disney map for locations.

In addition, braille guide maps are available from Guest Relations at all theme parks. And some rides provide closed captioning, while many theater attractions provide reflective captioning. If you give a seven-day notice, Walt Disney World will provide an interpretor for the live theater shows. To reserve an interpretor, call (407) 824-4321 (voice) or (407) 939-8255 (TTY).

Visitors from Other Countries

Foreign visitors are warmly welcomed at Walt Disney World and represent a large percentage of its guests. Most Magic Kingdom and Animal Kingdom attractions are straightforward and easily understood by visitors with limited English. Many attractions at Epcot and Disney-MGM Studios, however, depend heavily on narration. A Scandinavian visitor urges us:

You should write something about how interesting the attractions are to people who don't have English as their mother tongue. We are Norwegians, we all know English fairly well, but we still had problems understanding significant parts of some attractions because the Disney people talk too fast.

That goes especially for Body Wars, which we all thought was boring, but also for the Jungle Cruise and the Backstage Tour.

European guests frequently contrast the Magic Kingdom with Disneyland Paris. This comment from an English gentleman is typical:

The Magic Kingdom was a great disappointment. We all felt it was too crowded whatever the time of day. For European visitors, we recommend they visit Disneyland Paris instead of Magic Kingdom. It is much prettier and far better laid out. Their rides are also better.

The size of the portions in restaurants at Walt Disney World astounds many visitors from abroad, including this man from Surrey, England:

Please warn your readers who are not American about the very big helpings at all of the restaurants. We usually found that a starter alone or a main course shared between two was sufficient (even though at home we consider ourselves to be big eaters). We rarely made it to the dessert menu.

Incidentally, many Walt Disney World restaurants have menus available in French, German, Japanese, and Spanish.

Foreign language assistance is available throughout the World. Call (407) 824-4321 or stop by Guest Relations in the parks. There are also park maps available in German, Spanish, Japanese, Portuguese, and French.

The parks' unabashedly patriotic atmosphere is expressed in flag raisings, attractions that chronicle U.S. history, and entire themed areas inspired by events in America's past (Frontierland and Liberty Square in the Magic Kingdom, for example). While most patriotic fanfare is festive and enjoyable to anyone, *The Hall of Presidents* in the Magic Kingdom and *The American Adventure* at Epcot may be an overdose for some foreign visitors.

Foreign currency of most countries can be exchanged for dollars at the Guest Relations windows of the Ticket and Transportation Center and at the Guest Relations window in the ticketing areas of the theme parks. The amount these locations can exchange is limited. For large transactions, use the American Express office just outside the main entrance to Epcot or the Sun Trust Bank to the left of City Hall in the Magic Kingdom. Also, Goodings Supermarket on FL 535 (phone (407) 827-1200) operates a foreign currency exchange booth from 7 a.m. to 11 p.m.

Part Seven

Arriving and Getting Around

Getting There

DIRECTIONS

Motorists can reach any Walt Disney World destination via World Drive off US 192, or via Epcot Drive off I-4 (see map, pages 236–237).

Warning! I-4, connecting Daytona and Tampa, generally runs east to west but takes a north/south slant through the Orlando/Kissimmee area. This directional change complicates getting oriented in and around Disney World. Logic suggests that highways branching off I-4 should run north and south, but most run east/west here. Until you're somewhat familiar with the area, have a good map at your side.

From I-10 Take I-10 east across Florida to I-75 southbound. Exit I-75 onto the Florida Turnpike. Exit at Clermont and take US 27 south. Turn onto US 192 and follow the signs to Walt Disney World.

From I-75 Southbound Follow I-75 south to the Florida Turnpike. Exit at Clermont and take US 27 south. Turn onto US 192 and follow the signs to Walt Disney World.

From I-95 Southbound Follow I-95 south to I-4. Go west on I-4, passing through Orlando. Take Exit 26, marked Epcot/Disney Village, and follow the signs to your Disney destination.

From Daytona or Orlando Go west on I-4 through Orlando. Take Exit 26, marked Epcot/Disney Village, and follow the signs.

From the Orlando International Airport   Leaving the airport, go southwest on the Central Florida Greenway (FL 417), a toll road. FL 417 will intersect FL 536. FL 536 will cross over I-4 and become Epcot Drive. From here, follow the signs to your destination. An alternate route is to take FL 528 (Beeline Highway toll road) west for approximately 12 miles to the intersection with I-4. Go west on I-4 to Exit 26, marked Epcot/Disney Village, and follow the signs.

From Miami, Fort Lauderdale, and Southeastern Florida   Head north on the Florida Turnpike to I-4 westbound. Take Exit 26, marked Epcot/ Disney Village, and follow the signs.

From Tampa and Southwestern Florida   Take I-75 northbound to I-4. Go east on I-4, take Exit 25 onto US 192 westbound, and then follow the signs.

Walt Disney World Exits Off I-4

Going east to west (in the direction of Orlando to Tampa), three I-4 exits serve Walt Disney World.

Exit 27 (marked FL 535/Lake Buena Vista) primarily serves the Disney Village Hotel Plaza and Downtown Disney, including the Disney Village Marketplace, Pleasure Island, and Disney's West Side. This exit puts you on roads with lots of traffic signals. Avoid it unless you're headed to one of the above destinations.

Exit 26 (marked Epcot/Disney Village) delivers you to a four-lane expressway right into the heart of Disney World. It's the fastest and most convenient way for westbound travelers to access almost all Disney World destinations except the new Animal Kingdom and Disney's Wide World of Sports.

Exit 25 (marked US 192/Magic Kingdom) is the best route for eastbound travelers to all Disney World destinations. For westbound travelers, it's the best exit for accessing the Animal Kingdom and Disney's Wide World of Sports.

GETTING TO WALT DISNEY WORLD FROM THE AIRPORT

If you arrive in Orlando by plane, there are three basic options for getting to Walt Disney World:

1. Taxi   Taxis carry four to eight passengers (depending on the type of vehicle). Rates vary according to distance. If your hotel is in Walt Disney World, your fare will be about $32, not including tip. For the US 192 "Main Gate" area, your fare will be about $40. If you go to International Drive or downtown Orlando, expect to pay about $27.

2. Shuttle Service Two shuttle services, Mears Motor Transportation Service (phone (407) 423-5566) and Transtar (phone (407) 856-7777), operate from Orlando International Airport. Although these are the shuttle services that will provide your transportation if "airport transfers" are included in your vacation package, you do not have to be on a package to avail yourself of their services. In practice, both companies collect passengers until they fill a van, or sometimes in the case of Mears, a bus. Once the vehicle is full or close to full, it's dispatched. Mears and Transtar charge the same *per-person* rates (children under age four ride free). Both one-way and round-trip service are available.

From the Airport to:	One-Way	Round Trip
International Drive	$12	$21
Downtown Orlando	$12	$21
Walt Disney World/Lake Buena Vista	$14	$25
US 192 "Main Gate" Area	$14	$25

You might have to sit a spell at the airport waiting for a vehicle to fill to capacity and be dispatched. Once underway, your shuttle will probably make several stops to disembark other passengers before it reaches your hotel. We get a lot of reader mail discussing the shuttle services, and it would be fair to say that nobody accuses them of being overly expeditious. Transtar has an edge over Mears because they do not use any buses. Obviously, it takes less time to collect enough passengers to fill a van compared to a bus, as well as less time to deliver and unload those passengers at their destination hotels. On the return trip from your hotel to the airport, you're most likely to be transported in a van irrespective of which company you use (unless you are part of a large tour group, in which case Mears might send a bus). In our experience, because the shuttle services pick folks up at different hotels, they ask you to be ready for pick-up much earlier than you would ordinarily depart if you were taking a cab or returning a rental car.

3. Rental Cars Rental cars are readily available for both short- and long-term rentals. Most rental car companies allow you to drop a rental car at certain hotels or one of their subsidiary locations in the Walt Disney World general area if you do not want the car for your entire stay. Likewise, you can pick up a car at any time during your stay at the same hotels and locations without trekking back to the airport.

Dollars and Sense Which option is the best deal depends on the number of people in your party and the value you attach to your time. If you're traveling solo or only have two in your party, and you're pretty sure you won't need a rental car, the shuttle service is your least expensive bet. A cab for two people makes sense if you want to get there faster than the shuttle service can arrange. The cab will cost about $36 including tip. Splitting the fare equally this is $18 for each of you. The same shuttle service will cost $14 each, a savings of $4. It's up to you to decide whether the timeliness and convenience of the cab is worth the extra four bucks. A one-day car rental will cost you anywhere from $34–70 once all taxes and extras are figured in, plus you'll have to go to the trouble of completing the paperwork, retrieving the vehicle, and presumably filling the tank before you turn it in. If there are more than two of you, a cab becomes a more economical option than the shuttle. Likewise with the rental car, though the cab will still get you there faster.

Renting a Car

Readers planning to stay in the World frequently ask if they will need a car. If your plans don't include restaurants, attractions, or other destinations outside of Disney World, the answer is a very qualified no. You won't require a car, but, after considering the thoughts of this reader from Snohomish, Washington, you might want one:

> We rented a car and were glad we did. It gave us more options, though we used the [Disney] bus transportation quite extensively. With a car we could drive to the grocery store to restock our snack supply. It also came in handy for our night out. I shudder at how long it might have taken us to get from the Caribbean Beach to the Polynesian to leave our kids [at the childcare facility], then to Pleasure Island, then back to the Polynesian [to get the kids], and then back to the Caribbean Beach. At $8 an hour [for childcare] you don't want to waste time! It was also nice to drive to Typhoon Lagoon with a car full of clothes, lunches, and other paraphernalia. It was also easier to drive to the other hotels for special meals. And, of course, if you plan to travel out of the World during your stay, a car is a must.

A dad from Avon Lake, Ohio, adds:

> It was unbelievable how often we used our rental car. Although we stayed at the Grand Floridian, we found the monorail convenient only for the Magic Kingdom. Of the six nights we stayed, we used our car five days.

For a woman from Derry, New Hampshire:

> A rental car was essential. Considering the price of airport transfers, it doesn't cost much more and the hassle it saves is monumental.

For a grandmother from Allentown, Pennsylvania, however, the rental car was a waste of money:

> *The Disney bus was great, as a matter of fact, excellent! We never waited longer than 10 or 15 minutes, and we traveled everywhere, including resort to resort (the bus driver was very helpful here). I read in your guide that the bus service wasn't that great—we have no complaints. I'm only sorry I rented a car during our stay—it was a waste of money—believe me, I recommend the bus service.*

A family from Lynn Haven, Florida, disagrees:

> *The transportation system (buses specifically) was a mess. Nothing like the efficient system they had when we visited four years ago. What has happened? It took us one hour and 45 minutes to get from the BoardWalk to Fort Wilderness by bus. Bus transportation was very bad the whole time. Boat transportation was just fine.*

A family from Portland, Maine, did just that:

> *We stayed outside of WDW and tried to commute on the bus furnished by our hotel. After two days we gave up and rented a car.*

Renting a Car at Orlando International Airport

The airport has two terminals—A and B. Each airline serving Orlando is assigned to one of the two. Each terminal has three levels and an adjacent parking garage. Level Three is where you'll find the airline ticket counters. On Level Two you'll find the baggage claim, and Level One is where the car rental counters are located, or, if your rental company is located off-site, where you'll catch a courtesy vehicle to its headquarters.

Orlando is the largest rental car market in the world. At last count there were 22 rental car companies competing for your business. Five companies—Avis, Budget, Dollar, I&M, and National—have rental counters on Level One of both terminals. Alamo, Enterprise, Hertz, Thrifty, and thirteen other companies have locations near the airport and provide courtesy shuttles that pick you up outside both terminals on Level One. Most shuttles run continuously, so you don't have to call to arrange a pick-up. We prefer using one of the five companies located in the airport because (1) you can complete your paperwork while you wait for your checked luggage to arrive at baggage claim and (2) it's a short walk to the adjacent garage to pick up your car (i.e., you don't have to catch a courtesy shuttle).

If you rent from one of the on-site companies, you'll return your car to the garage adjacent to whichever terminal your airline is assigned. If you accidentally return your car to the wrong garage, you'll have to haul all your luggage on foot from one side of the airport to the other in order to reach your airline's terminal for check-in.

How the Orlando Rental Car Companies Stack Up

Unofficial Guide readers provide us with a lot of information about the quality of the car and service they receive from Orlando car rental companies. In general, most folks are looking for:

1. Quick, courteous, and efficient processing on pick-up.
2. A nice, well-maintained, late-model automobile.
3. A car that is clean and odor-free.
4. Quick, courteous, and efficient processing on return.
5. If applicable, an efficient shuttle service between the rental agency and the airport.

Most of our readers rent cars from Alamo, Avis, Budget, Dollar, Hertz, or National. On a scale of 0 (worst) to 100 (best), the following table shows how they rate the Orlando operations of each company, based on the five items listed above.

If you would like to participate in our rental car survey, send us your completed *Unofficial Guide* Reader Survey form from the back of this book.

Company	Pick-Up Efficiency	Condition of the Car	Cleanliness of the Car	Return Efficiency	Shuttle Efficiency
Alamo	65	83	87	85	82
Avis	78	92	94	87	—
Budget	77	92	95	90	—
Dollar	82	89	90	88	—
Hertz	78	92	93	91	90
National	80	92	94	91	—

If you rent a car, a 6–7% sales tax, a $2.03-per-day state surcharge, and a 40 cents-per-day vehicle license recovery fee will be heaped onto your rental fee. If you rent from an agency with airport facilities or shuttles, an additional 9% airport tax will be charged.

Remember that you can wait and rent a car at your hotel on the day you actually need it.

Getting Oriented

A GOOD MAP IS HARD TO FIND

Readers frequently complain about signs and maps provided by Disney. While it's easy to find the major theme parks, it can be quite an odyssey to locate other Walt Disney World destinations. Many Disney-supplied maps are stylistic and hard to read, while others provide incomplete information. Worse, the maps (produced by different Disney divisions) don't always agree. A good map—the Walt Disney World Property Map—is available from Guest Relations at any Disney theme park or hotel.

FINDING YOUR WAY AROUND

Walt Disney World is like any big city. It's easy to get lost there. Signs for the theme parks are excellent, but finding a restaurant or hotel is often confusing, even for Disney World veterans. The easiest way to orient yourself is to think in terms of five major areas, or clusters:

1. The first major cluster encompasses all the hotels and theme parks around the Seven Seas Lagoon. This includes the Magic Kingdom, hotels connected by the monorail, the Shades of Green resort, and two golf courses.

2. The second cluster includes developments on and around Bay Lake: Wilderness Lodge, Fort Wilderness Campground, River Country, and two golf courses.

3. Cluster three contains Epcot, Disney-MGM Studios, Disney's BoardWalk, Disney's Wide World of Sports, the so-called Epcot resort hotels, and the Caribbean Beach Resort.

4. The fourth cluster encompasses Walt Disney World Village; the Disney Institute; Downtown Disney (including the Disney Village Marketplace, Pleasure Island, and Disney's West Side); Typhoon Lagoon; a golf course; Disney Village Hotel Plaza, and the Port Orleans, Dixie Landings, and Old Key West resorts.

5. The fifth and newest cluster contains the Animal Kingdom, Blizzard Beach, and the Disney All-Star and Coronado Springs resorts.

How to Travel around the World (or the Real Mr. Toad's Wild Ride)

Trying to commute around Walt Disney World can be frustrating. A Magic Kingdom street vendor, telling me how to get to Epcot, proposed, "You can take the ferry or the monorail to the Transportation and Ticket Center. Then you can get another monorail, or you can catch the bus, or you can take a tram out to your car and drive over there yourself." What he didn't say was that it would be easier to ride a mule than to take any conceivable combination from this transportation smorgasbord.

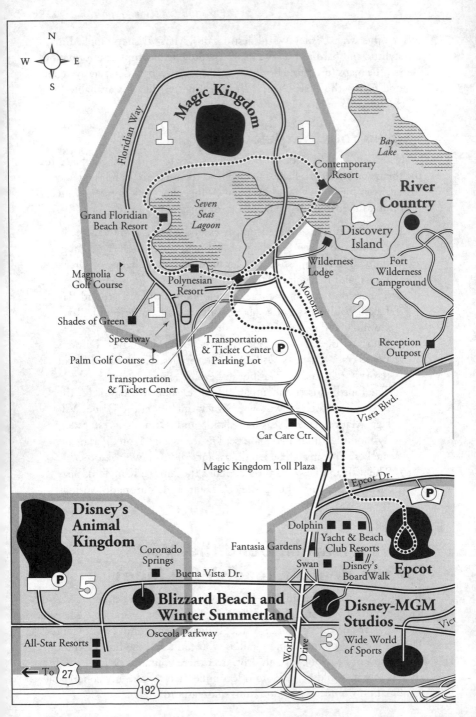

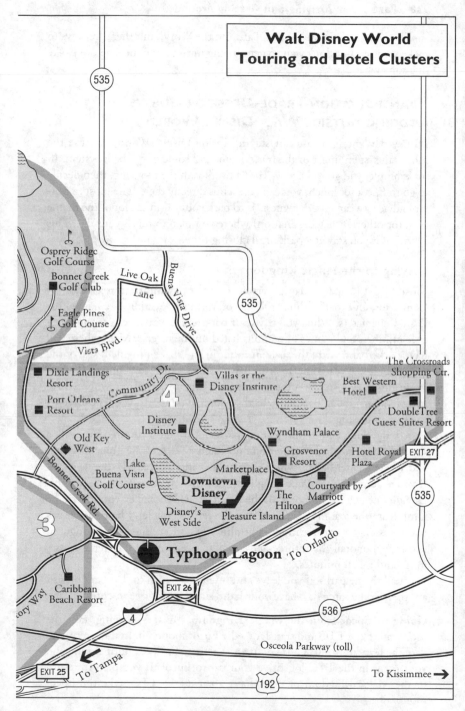

Walt Disney World Touring and Hotel Clusters

535

Osprey Ridge Golf Course
Bonnet Creek Golf Club
Live Oak Lane
Buena Vista Drive
535
Eagle Pines Golf Course
Vista Blvd.

The Crossroads Shopping Ctr.

Dixie Landings Resort
Community Dr.
4
Villas at the Disney Institute
Best Western Hotel
Port Orleans Resort
DoubleTree Guest Suites Resort
Disney Institute
Wyndham Palace
EXIT 27
Old Key West
Grosvenor Resort
Hotel Royal Plaza
Lake Buena Vista Golf Course
Marketplace
Downtown Disney
Courtyard by Marriott
535
Bonnet Creek Rd.
Disney's West Side
Pleasure Island
The Hilton
3
Typhoon Lagoon
To Orlando

Caribbean Beach Resort
EXIT 26
ory Way
4
536

EXIT 25
To Tampa
Osceola Parkway (toll)
To Kissimmee

192

237

There's no simple way to travel around the World, but there are ways to make it easier. Just don't wait to get moving until ten minutes before you're due somewhere.

TRANSPORTATION TRADE-OFFS FOR GUESTS: LODGING OUTSIDE WALT DISNEY WORLD

Disney day-guests (those not staying inside Disney World) can use the monorail system, most of the bus system, and some of the boat system. If, for example, you go to Disney-MGM Studios in the morning, then decide to go to Epcot for lunch, you can take a bus directly there. The most important advice we can give day-guests is to park your car in the lot of the theme park (or other Disney destination) where you plan to finish your day. This is critical if you stay at a park until closing time.

Driving to the Magic Kingdom

Most Magic Kingdom day-guests park in the Transportation and Ticket Center lot, an expanse about the size of Vermont. Sections are named for Disney characters. When you pay your parking fee, you'll get a receipt with aisle numbers and names of sections listed on the reverse. Mark where you have parked and write the aisle number in the space provided. Carry the receipt in a safe place and refer to it when you return to your car. (Failure to do this may result in a long search for your car at a time when you're tuckered out.) If you have a disabled person in your party, you'll be directed to close-in parking.

After parking and marking your space's location on your receipt, walk a short distance to a loading station and catch a tram to the Transportation and Ticket Center (TTC) where you can buy admission to the theme parks. If you're going to the Magic Kingdom, ride the ferryboat across Seven Seas Lagoon or catch the monorail. If the line for the monorail extends down the ramp from the loading platform, take the ferry. (One ferry holds almost as many passengers as three monorail trains.) The trip to the Magic Kingdom takes the monorail about three-and-a-half to five minutes. The ferry crosses in six-and-a-half minutes.

At all theme parks, if you leave and intend to return to that park or visit another on the same day, have your hand stamped for free re-entry.

Going to Epcot from the Magic Kingdom   In the morning, take the monorail to the TTC and transfer to the Epcot monorail. In the afternoon, take the ferry to the TTC. If you plan to remain at Epcot until closing and your car is in the TTC lot, drive your car to Epcot. If you plan to return to the Magic Kingdom or don't have a car at the TTC, take the Epcot monorail.

Going to Disney-MGM Studios from the Magic Kingdom If you plan to end your day at the Studios, drive. If you intend to return to the Magic Kingdom, take the bus. Incidentally, the loading area for the bus to the Studios is immediately to the left as you leave the Magic Kingdom. You don't have to return to the TTC.

Going to the Animal Kingdom from the Magic Kingdom If you intend to finish your day at the Animal Kingdom, drive. If you plan to return to the Magic Kingdom, take the bus.

Leaving the Magic Kingdom at the End of the Day If you need to return to the TTC, try the ferry first. If it's mobbed (usually happens only at closing), take the "express" (doesn't stop at hotels) or "local" monorail, whichever has the shortest line.

Sometimes when you reach the TTC, a throng is waiting to board the parking lot trams. Rather than join the crowd, walk to the nearest section in the lot (Chip 'n' Dale) and wait there. When the tram stops and people disembark, board and ride to where your car is parked.

Driving to Epcot

Park at the TTC (Magic Kingdom) lot and commute via monorail, or park in Epcot's lot. Parking at Epcot's lot is best unless you plan to visit the Magic Kingdom later and conclude your day there. Arrangements at Epcot's lot are much like those at the Magic Kingdom: trams shuttle among the parking areas and patrons get a receipt on which to mark their parking place for later reference. At Epcot, sections of the lot are named for pavilions in the park's Future World area. Close-in parking for the disabled is available. The big difference between Magic Kingdom and Epcot parking is that access to the park is direct from the tram at Epcot, whereas to reach the Magic Kingdom you must transfer from the tram to the ferry or monorail at the TTC.

Going to the Magic Kingdom from Epcot Take the monorail to the TTC, then transfer to the Magic Kingdom express monorail. If you don't plan to return to Epcot and your car is in Epcot's lot, drive to the TTC and take the ferry or monorail as crowd conditions allow.

Going to Disney-MGM Studios from Epcot You have three choices. If you plan to finish the day at the Studios, drive. If you plan to return to Epcot, exit the park through the main entrance and catch a bus to the Studios or exit through the International Gateway (in World Showcase) and catch a boat. This last option is definitely best if you're returning to Epcot for dinner at one of World Showcase's ethnic restaurants.

Going to the Animal Kingdom from Epcot If you plan to return to

Epcot, take the bus. If you intend to finish your day at the Animal Kingdom, drive.

Driving to Disney-MGM Studios

Disney-MGM Studios has its own pay lot. As at other lots, trams transport you to the park entrance and close-in parking is available for the disabled.

Going to the Magic Kingdom from Disney-MGM Studios   Regardless of where you intend to conclude the day, it is probably easier to take the bus to the Magic Kingdom. Because the bus unloads at the park's entrance rather than the TTC, you bypass the hassle of reparking, taking the tram to the TTC, and catching the monorail or ferry. It's the same story when you return to the Studios.

Going to Epcot from Disney-MGM Studios   Drive to Epcot if you don't intend to return to the Studios. If you plan to return, take a bus or a boat to Epcot. Take the bus if you want to begin your Epcot visit at the main entrance (Future World). If you're headed for World Showcase, take the boat.

Going to the Animal Kingdom from Disney-MGM Studios   If you plan to return to the Studios, take the bus. If you intend to end your day at the Animal Kingdom, drive.

Driving to the Animal Kingdom

The Animal Kingdom has its own pay parking lot. Trams shuttle you to the entrance.

Going to the Other Theme Parks from the Animal Kingdom   Isolated on the west side of Walt Disney World, the Animal Kingdom is accessible only by road. Because it generally closes earlier than the other parks, it's best to commute in your own car. The exception is when you intend to return to the Animal Kingdom from the Magic Kingdom. In this case only, use the bus.

Moving Your Car from Lot to Lot on the Same Day

Once you have paid to park in any major theme park lot, hang on to your receipt. If you visit another park later in the same day, you'll be admitted to that park's lot without additional charge when you show your receipt. Disney lodging guests park free in any theme park lot.

Taking a Shuttle Bus from Your Out-of-the-World Hotel

Many independent hotels and motels near Walt Disney World provide trams and buses. They're fairly carefree, depositing you near theme park entrances and saving you parking fees. The rub is that they might not get you there as early as you desire (a critical point if you take our touring advice) or be available when you wish to return to your lodging. Also, some shuttles go directly to Disney World, while others stop at additional area lodgings. Each service is a bit different; check the particulars before you make reservations.

Warning: Most hotel shuttles don't add vehicles at park opening or closing times. In the mornings, you may not get a seat. At closing or during a hard rain, expect a mass exodus from the park. More people will be waiting for the shuttle than the bus will hold, and some will be left behind. Most (not all) shuttles return for stranded guests, but the guests may wait 20 minutes to over an hour for a ride.

If you're depending on shuttles, leave the park at least 45 minutes before closing. If you stay until closing and lack the energy to hassle with the shuttle, take a cab. Cab stands are near the Bus Information buildings at the Animal Kingdom, Epcot, Disney-MGM Studios, and the Transportation and Ticket Center. If no cabs are on-hand, staff at Bus Information will call one for you. If you're leaving the Magic Kingdom at closing, it's easier to take the monorail to a hotel and catch a cab there (rather than the TTC taxi stand).

TRANSPORTATION TRADE-OFFS FOR GUESTS AT WALT DISNEY WORLD RESORTS AND CAMPGROUND

The most hotly debated topic among Disney resort guests is whether it's more efficient to use a car or Disney transportation to get around the World. These reader comments are representative:

A couple from Woodbridge, Illinois, writes:

> *This time down we rented a car. It really came in handy and turned out to be a good idea. We still took the buses to the major parks, because you just can't beat their system for that, dropping you off right by the gate with only a short walk and no trams, ferries, or monorail required. But the car was great for the water parks, the Marketplace, and going to other hotels for dinner or just to look around. The last two times, we commented [on] how hard and inconvenient it was to get to another hotel by bus. It easily took an hour vs. a five-minute drive by car. You can get around without a car, but it really was nice to have one.*

A man from New Orleans gives us his opinion:

> *We found a car to be an absolute necessity. It added at least two hours each day to our schedule. The monorail system was a bit confusing and slow, not to mention very crowded. The bus stops were not particularly convenient to our room, and there were always*

people waiting. On the other hand, with a car, parking was very easy, traffic was minimal, and once we had our basic orientation, it was easy to get around Disney World.

A dad from Bethel, Connecticut, states:

I have to disagree with your opinion about transportation. Though it may be faster to get from place to place with your own car, we were here to enjoy ourselves. The idea of not having to get behind a wheel for a week was part of the fun of this vacation. With a little patience you could get anywhere you wanted. Why do we have to be in such a hurry? I think Disney's transportation system is fabulous, comfortable, clean, and efficient. It allowed us the freedom of going off in different directions.

A family from Madison, New Jersey, tells us their story:

The second day, we had a problem. We had taken the monorail from the Magic Kingdom to the Contemporary hotel to eat dinner at the cafe, and after dinner we were unsure how to get back to the All-Star resorts. This was about 7 p.m. We asked two different hotel employees and were told to take the bus to the Disney Marketplace and then get another bus to the hotel. After we got on the bus and were on our way, it became obvious this could not have been the best way. It took 40 minutes to get to the Marketplace, then a 20-minute wait for the bus, and another 40 minutes back to the All-Star resorts. The whole time, my husband and I held sleeping children in our arms.

A father of two in Hillsboro, Oregon, writes:

We originally thought that being in a monorail hotel would be convenient. It turned out that it still takes nearly an hour to go to places other than the Magic Kingdom or the TTC. After one day of waiting for the Disney Transportation System, we decided to rent a car. The importance of having your own car in order to reduce the travel times cannot be said enough.

THE DISNEY TRANSPORTATION SYSTEM

The Disney transportation system is large, diversified, and generally efficient, but it sometimes is overwhelmed during peak periods, particularly at park opening and closing times. If you could be assured of getting on a bus, boat, or monorail at these critical times, we would advise you to leave your car at home. However, the reality is that when huge crowds want to go somewhere at the same time, delays are unavoidable. In addition, some destinations are served directly, while many others require one or more transfers. Finally, it's sometimes difficult to figure how the buses, boats, and monorails interconnect.

In the most basic terms, the Disney Transportation system is a "hub and spoke" system. Hubs include the Transportation and Ticket Center, Downtown Disney, and all four major theme parks (from two hours before official opening time to two to three hours after closing). Although there are some exceptions, there is direct service from Disney resorts to the major theme parks and to Downtown Disney, and from park to park. If you want to go from resort to resort or most anywhere else, you will have to transfer at one of the hubs.

If a hotel offers boat or monorail service, its bus service will be limited, meaning you'll have to transfer at a hub for many Disney World destinations. If you're staying at a Magic Kingdom resort served by monorail (Polynesian, Contemporary, Grand Floridian), you'll be able to commute efficiently to the Magic Kingdom via monorail. If, however, you want to visit Epcot, you must take the monorail to the TTC and transfer to the Epcot monorail. (Guests at the Polynesian can eliminate the transfer by walking five to ten minutes to the TTC and catching the direct monorail to Epcot.)

If you're staying at an Epcot resort (Swan, Dolphin, Yacht and Beach Club resorts, BoardWalk Inn and Villas) you can walk or commute via boat to the International Gateway (back door) entrance of Epcot. Although direct buses link Epcot resorts to the Magic Kingdom and the Animal Kingdom, there's no direct bus to Epcot's main entrance or to Disney-MGM Studios. To reach the Studios from Epcot resorts, you must take a boat.

The Villas of the Disney Institute and the Caribbean Beach, Dixie Landings, Port Orleans, Coronado Springs, Old Key West, and All-Star resorts offer direct buses to all the theme parks. The rub is that guests sometimes must walk a long way to bus stops or endure more than a half-dozen additional pick-ups before actually heading for the park(s). Commuting in the morning from these resorts is generally no sweat, though you may have to ride standing up. Returning in the evening, however, can be a different story.

The hotels of the Disney Village Hotel Plaza terminated their guest-transportation contract with Disney Transportation Operations, so they provide service with another carrier. The substitute, which we feel doesn't measure up, constitutes a real problem for guests at these hotels. Before booking a hotel in the Plaza, check the nature and frequency of shuttles.

Fort Wilderness guests must use the campground's own buses to reach boat landings or the Pioneer Hall bus stop. From these points, respectively, guests can travel directly by boat to the Magic Kingdom or by bus to Disney-MGM Studios, or to other destinations via transfer at the TTC. With the exception of commuting to the Magic Kingdom, the best way for Fort Wilderness guests to commute in Disney World is to drive their own car.

USING THE WALT DISNEY WORLD TRANSPORTATION SYSTEM VS. DRIVING YOUR OWN CAR

To enable you to assess your transportation options, we have developed a chart comparing the approximate commuting times from Disney resorts to various Walt Disney World destinations, using Disney transportation or your own car.

Disney Transportation   Times on the chart in the Disney Transportation System (DTS) columns represent a range. For example, if you want to go from the Caribbean Beach Resort to Epcot, the chart indicates a range of 12–45 minutes. The first number (12) is how long your commute will take if everything goes perfectly (your bus is at the stop when you walk up, departs for your destination as soon as you board, and isn't delayed by traffic jams or other problems en route). If you're staying at a resort where the bus makes numerous stops within the complex, the first number assumes that you board at the last embarkation point before the bus heads for its final destination. The second number (45) represents a worst-case scenario. (The bus is pulling away as you arrive at the stop, and you must wait 20 minutes for the next one. When you finally board, the bus makes six more stops in the Caribbean complex before heading for Epcot. Once en route, the bus hits every red light.)

On busier days, buses run every 20 minutes all day. On slower days, some buses (at the Disney Institute and Old Key West, among others) run only once every 45 minutes between noon and 6 p.m. Our worst-case scenario assumes that buses run every 20 minutes. If they're running only every 45 minutes, you must add 25 minutes to the second number to calculate the commute. If buses run from the Caribbean complex to Epcot every 45 minutes, for example, it could take as long as 1 hour and 10 minutes (45 minutes + 25 minutes) to complete the commute. Be sure to ask at your hotel how frequently buses will run during your stay. If your bus makes intermediate stops after leaving your resort, the time spent making the stops is figured into both the best and worst times, because the stops are unavoidable in either case.

Driving Your Own Car   The "Your Car" column on the chart indicates the best-case/worst-case situation for driving. To make these times directly comparable to Disney system times, we have added the time it takes to get from your parked car to the park's entrance. While Disney buses and monorails deposit guests at the front door, those who drive must sometimes take a tram from their car to the gate, or walk. At the Magic Kingdom, you must take a tram from the parking lot to the TTC, then catch a monorail or ferry to the park's entrance.

WALT DISNEY WORLD TRANSPORTATION SYSTEM FOR TEENAGERS

If you're staying at Walt Disney World and have teens in your party, familiarize yourself with the Disney bus system. Safe, clean, and operating until 1 a.m. on most nights, buses are a great way for teens to get around the World.

WALT DISNEY WORLD BUS SERVICE

Buses in Disney World have an illuminated panel above the front windshield that flashes the bus's destination. Also, theme parks have designated waiting areas for each Disney World destination. To catch the bus to the Caribbean Beach Resort from Disney-MGM Studios, for example, go to the bus stop and wait in the area marked "To the Caribbean Beach Resort." At the resorts, go to any bus stop and wait for the bus with your destination displayed on the illuminated panel. Directions to Disney World destinations are available when you check in or at your hotel's guest relations desk. The clerk at guest relations can also answer your questions about the Disney Transportation System.

Service from the resorts to the major theme parks is fairly direct. You may have to endure intermediate stops, but you won't have to transfer. More problematic, and sometimes requiring transfers, is service to the swimming theme parks and other Disney World hotels.

A dad from Palo Alto, California, describes trying to return to the Disney Inn (now Shades of Green) after dinner at the Beach Club:

> *It took 1½ hours to get back to the Disney Inn by bus, a 10-minute drive by car. Crowds? Breakdowns? Hurricanes? Nope, just waits, connections, and extra stops.*

The fastest way to commute from resort to resort by bus is to take a bus from your resort to one of the major theme parks and from there transfer to your resort destination. This only works, of course, when the major theme parks are open (actually from two hours before opening until two to three hours after closing). If you are attempting to commute to another resort for a late dinner during the off-season when the major parks close early, you will have to transfer at Downtown Disney or at the Transportation and Ticket Center.

Door-to-Door Commuting Times to and from the Disney Resorts and Parks: In Your Car versus the Disney Transportation System†

Time (in minutes) from	To Magic Kingdom		To Epcot		To MGM Studios	
	Your Car	Disney System	Your Car	Disney System	Your Car	Disney System
All-Star Resorts	26–47	11–31	13–23	8–28	11–20	7–27
Animal Kingdom	25–48	23–47	14–17	16–36	14–17	10–34
Beach Club	25–46	14–34	11–21	5–28*	9–18	16–36
Blizzard Beach	25–46	17–37	13–23	29–62	13–22	30–50
BoardWalk Inn and Villas	25–46	11–31	11–21	5–28*	9–18	16–36
Caribbean Beach	26–47	13–40	13–23	12–45	10–19	6–33
Contemporary	NA	12–23	16–26	13–29	18–27	22–42
Coronado Springs	26–47	11–31	13–23	8–28	11–20	7–27
Disney-MGM Studios	25–46	14–34	14–24	10–34		
Disney Institute	27–48	15–45	13–23	10–37	15–24	8–35
Dixie Landings	27–48	11–36	15–25	9–33	15–24	9–34
Dolphin	24–45	18–38	10–20	10–35*	10–19	12–32
Downtown Disney	27–49	24–58	14–25	21–57	12–22	30–69
Epcot	25–46	16–35			14–23	8–30
Fort Wilderness	26–47	13–33	13–23	14–60	14–23	17–50
Grand Floridian	NA	4–7	13–23	20–42	15–24	9–29
Magic Kingdom			12–39	13–42	13–29	14–34
Old Key West	25–46	12–40	13–23	7–35	13–22	9–36
Polynesian	NA	7–13	12–22	23–48	14–23	12–32
Port Orleans	26–47	19–39	14–24	15–35	14–23	17–37
Swan	24–45	21–41	10–20	10–35*	10–19	12–32
Typhoon Lagoon	26–47	18–51	13–23	29–62	10–19	38–75
Village Hotel Plaza	30–51	20–74	16–26	12–50	15–24	9–49
Wilderness Lodge	NA	11–41	15–25	12–42	17–26	18–48
Yacht Club	25–46	11–31	11–21	5–28*	9–18	16–36

† Driving time vs. time on the Disney Transportation System (DTS). Driving times include time in your car, stops to pay tolls, time to park, and transfers to Disney trams and monorails where applicable.

* This hotel is within walking distance of Epcot Center; time given includes boat ride from International Gateway, if necessary.

To Animal Kingdom		To Typhoon Lagoon		To Downtown Disney		To Blizzard Beach	
Your Car	*Disney System*	*Your Car*	*Disney System*	*Your Car*	*Disney System*	*Your Car*	*Disney System*
9–12	8–25	10–13	9–29	11–14	15–40	4–7	17–38
		15–19	43–57	17–21	33–53	7–13	7–30
15–18	14–33	7–10	22–42	8–11	13–35	10–13	21–41
7–13	8–40	11–14	33–76	12–15	44–77		
15–18	12–30	7–10	24–44	8–11	15–37	10–13	21–41
15–18	15–46	4–7	7–39	5–8	9–43	10–13	23–54
18–21	28–48	15–18	17–40	15–17	28–51	13–16	36–56
9–12	8–31	10–13	9–29	11–14	15–40	4–7	17–37
14–17	10–34	6–9	30–73	7–10	41–74	9–12	30–50
19–22	23–45	7–10	13–37	4–7	5–30	14–17	21–48
18–21	14–43	8–11	9–35	9–12	15–40	13–16	22–49
14–17	20–35	8–11	27–47	9–12	18–40	9–12	8–31
17–21	33–53	4–7	5–28			12–16	30–50
14–17	26–48	10–13	22–43	11–14	30–54	9–12	23–45
22–25	23–56	8–11	18–51	9–12	27–60	17–20	31–56
16–19	16–36	13–16	24–53	14–17	37–64	11–14	24–44
15–18	17–37	15–31	17–53	17–36	30–64	10–13	22–55
17–20	18–43	6–9	9–35	7–10	9–36	12–15	23–49
15–18	18–38	12–15	27–59	13–16	40–70	10–13	27–46
17–20	25–43	7–10	16–36	8–11	24–44	12–15	37–57
14–17	23–38	8–11	30–50	9–12	20–42	9–12	10–32
15–19	43–57			4–7	5–28	11–14	40–57
19–22	30–53	7–10	5–7	4–7	NA	14–17	30–50
18–21	23–51	15–18	23–46	16–19	27–67	13–16	31–54
15–18	16–36	7–10	24–44	8–11	15–37	10–13	21–41

Buses begin service to the theme parks at about 7 a.m. on days when the parks' official opening time is 9 a.m. Generally, buses run every 20 minutes. Buses to Disney-MGM Studios, Epcot, or the Animal Kingdom deliver you to the park entrance. Until one hour before the park opens (before 8 a.m. in this example), buses to the Magic Kingdom deliver you to the TTC, where you transfer to the monorail or ferry to complete your commute. Buses take you directly to the Magic Kingdom on early-entry mornings and starting one hour before the park's stated opening on other days.

To be on-hand for the real opening time (when official opening is 9 a.m.), catch direct buses to Epcot, the Animal Kingdom, and Disney-MGM Studios between 7:30 and 8 a.m. Catch direct buses to the Magic Kingdom between 8 and 8:15 a.m. If you must transfer to reach your park, leave 15 to 20 minutes earlier. On days when official opening is 7 or 8 a.m., move up your departure time accordingly.

If you're commuting to a theme park on an early-entry morning, count on the park's opening an hour to an hour and a half before the official opening time for the general public. Buses to the designated early-entry park

Next let's do Port Orleans to Blizzard Beach.

begin running about two hours before the stated opening time. On an early-entry day when the Magic Kingdom's official opening for the public is 8 a.m., for example, Disney lodging guests can catch a bus to the park as early as 6 a.m. and enter by 6:30 a.m.

For your return bus trip in the evening, leave the park 40 minutes to 1 hour before closing to avoid the rush. If you're caught in the mass exodus, you may be inconvenienced, but you won't be stranded. Buses, boats, and monorails continue to operate for two hours after the parks close.

Not All Hubs Are Created Equal

As mentioned earlier, all major theme parks, Downtown Disney, and the Transportation and Ticket Center (TTC) serve as hubs on the Disney bus system. If your route requires you to transfer at a hub, make your transfer at the closest theme park or the TTC, *except at theme park closing time.* Avoid using Downtown Disney as a transfer point. Because each bus makes three stops within the Downtown Disney complex, it takes 16–25 minutes just to get out of Downtown Disney!

Bus Transportation to the Water Parks

Evidently Disney assumes you will spend the entire day at the water park because direct service from and to the resorts is scheduled only in the early morning and late afternoon. At other times during the day, you must transfer at the TTC.

DISNEY VILLAGE HOTEL PLAZA BUS SERVICE

Although located in Walt Disney World, the hotels of the Disney Village Hotel Plaza provide their own bus service, a service that many, including a family from Prospect, Connecticut, find inferior:

> *We were disappointed in the shuttle bus for the Village hotels. They do not run often enough, and there is no schedule. [The b]us at the parks picks up in [the] middle of busy parking lots. Treats you as second class [compared] to Disney resort guests. Take a cab instead of waiting late at night to get back to [your] hotel. Costs only $9.*

WALT DISNEY WORLD MONORAIL SERVICE

Picture the monorail system as three loops. Loop A is an express route that runs counterclockwise connecting the Magic Kingdom with the Transportation and Ticket Center (TTC). Loop B runs clockwise alongside Loop A, making all stops, with service to (in this order) the TTC, Polynesian Resort, Grand Floridian Beach Resort, Magic Kingdom, and Contemporary Resort.

The long Loop C dips southeast like a tail, connecting the TTC with Epcot. The hub for all three loops is the TTC (where you usually park to visit the Magic Kingdom).

The monorail system serving Magic Kingdom resorts usually starts two hours before the official opening time on early-entry days, and an hour and a half before official opening on other days. If you're staying at a Magic Kingdom resort and wish to be among the first in the Magic Kingdom on a non-early-entry morning when official opening is 9 a.m., board the monorail at the times indicated below. On an early-entry morning (when official opening is 9 a.m.), leave 45–60 minutes earlier. If official opening is 8 a.m., bounce everything up yet another hour.

From the Contemporary Resort	7:45–8 a.m.
From the Polynesian Resort	7:50–8:05 a.m.
From the Grand Floridian Beach Resort	8–8:10 a.m.

What's that? You don't have the circadian rhythms of a farmer? Get with the program, Bubba! This is a *Disney* vacation. Haul your buns out of bed and go have fun!

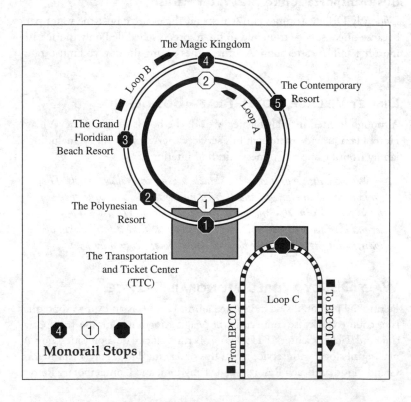

If you're a day-guest (no early-entry privileges), you'll be allowed on the monorail at the TTC between 8:15 and 8:30 a.m. on a day when official opening is 9 a.m. If you want to board earlier, walk from the TTC to the Polynesian Resort and board there.

The monorail loop connecting Epcot and the TTC begins operating at 7:30 a.m. on days when Epcot's official opening is 9 a.m. To be at Epcot when the park opens, catch the Epcot monorail at the TTC by 8:05 a.m.

While your multiday pass suggests you can flit at will among parks, actually getting there is more complex. For example, you can't go directly from the Magic Kingdom to Epcot. You must catch the express monorail (Loop A) to the TTC and transfer to the Loop C monorail to Epcot. If lines to board either monorail are short, you can usually reach Epcot in 25–35 minutes. But should you want to go to Epcot for dinner (as many do) and you're departing the Magic Kingdom in late afternoon, you may have to wait 30 minutes or more to board the Loop A monorail. Adding this delay bumps up your commute to 45–55 minutes.

Monorails usually run for two hours after closing to ensure that everyone is served. If a train is too crowded or you need transportation after the monorails have stopped running, catch a bus.

It's great fun to ride in the front cab of the monorail with the conductor. All you have to do is ask, according to a mom from Richmond, Virginia:

> *Speaking of the monorail—don't hesitate to ask about sitting up front—even if you aren't the first ones there. People are somewhat timid about asking, and the monorail attendants won't ever suggest it, so ask! We got to ride up front three times during our stay.*

Part Eight

Bare Necessities

Credit Cards and Money

CREDIT CARDS

- MasterCard, VISA, and American Express cards are accepted for theme park admission.

- Walt Disney World shops, full-service and counter-service restaurants, and resort hotels will accept only MasterCard, VISA, and American Express.

FINANCIAL MATTERS

Cash Bank service at Epcot, the Animal Kingdom, and Disney-MGM Studios is limited to an automatic teller machine. Branches of Sun Bank are across the street from Downtown Disney Marketplace and at 1675 Buena Vista Drive. Both branches will:

- *Provide cash advances* on MasterCard and VISA (no minimum; maximum equals the patron's credit limit).

- *Cash personal checks* of $200 or less drawn on Sun Bank upon presentation of a driver's license and major credit card.

- *Cash and sell traveler's checks.* The bank cashes the first check up to $100 without charge but levies a $2 service fee for each additional check.

- *Facilitate wiring of money* from the visitor's bank to Sun Bank.

- *Exchange foreign currency* for dollars.

Most VISA and MasterCard cards are accepted at automatic teller machines at Walt Disney World. To use an American Express card, however, you must sign an agreement with American Express before your trip. If your credit card doesn't work in the automatic teller machines, a teller will be able to process your transaction at any Sun Bank full-service location.

A LICENSE TO PRINT MONEY

One of Disney's more sublime ploys for separating you from your money is the printing and issuing of Disney Dollars. Available throughout Disney World in denominations of $5 (Goofy Greenbacks), $10 (Minnie Money or Simba Sawbucks), and $20 (Mickey Moolah), the colorful cash can be used for purchases at Walt Disney World, Disneyland, and Disney Stores nationwide. Disney Dollars can also be exchanged one for one with U.S. currency. Disney money is sometimes included as a perk (for which you're charged dollar for dollar) in Walt Disney Travel Company packages.

While the idea of Disney Dollars seems fun and innocent, it's one of Disney's better moneymakers. Some guests take the money home as souvenirs. Others forget to spend or exchange it before they leave the World, then fail to go to a Disney Store or to exchange the money by mail. Usually the funny money ends up forgotten in a drawer—exactly as Disney hoped.

A Michigan family, however, found a way to make their Disney Dollars useful:

> *Your criticism of Disney Dollars is valid if people are dumb enough not to cash them in or use them in their local Disney store. We used them. Since we had planned on going to Disney a year ahead of time, we asked people giving our children money for birthdays, Christmas, Tooth Fairy, etc., to give Disney Dollars instead. This forced both of our children (ages five and seven) to save the money for the trip instead of spending it beforehand.*

THE P.T. BARNUM MEMORIAL WALKWAY

Oh my stars and garters, Mildred, you won't believe what they're doing now! For only $110, you can buy a 10-inch hexagonal brick with your name on it. If you want to go all out, you can purchase a granite brick for $225. Of course, you aren't allowed to take your brick home. Disney is going to use it to build a walkway around a big lake down at Walt Disney World. (They need that walkway really bad in case the monorails and the ferry boats all break down at the same time.) Here's the really good news: It will cost us and our friends who buy bricks only about $9.6 million to build the whole dadgum thing, and we can visit our brick anytime we want . . . if we can find it. Maybe when they get our little sidewalk finished, they'll build another one from Walt Disney World out to Disneyland in California. Those interstate highways are about worn out, you know.

Problems and Unusual Situations

ATTRACTIONS CLOSED FOR REPAIRS

Check in advance with Disney World to see what rides and attractions may be closed for maintenance or repair during your visit. If you're interested in a specific attraction, the call could save you a lot of disappointment. A mother from Dover, Massachusetts, laments:

> We were disappointed to find Space Mountain, Swiss Family Treehouse, and the Liberty Belle Riverboat closed for repairs. We felt that a large chunk of the Magic Kingdom was not working, yet the tickets were still full price and expensive!

A woman from Pasadena, California, adds:

> Rides can close without warning. I had called in advance and knew that River Country [and] Horizons would be closed. Our hotel even gave us a list of closed attractions. So, imagine our surprise when we get to the Magic Kingdom and find that Space Mountain is closed with no prior warning. Needless to say, we were disappointed.

CAR TROUBLE

Security or tow truck patrols will help you if you lock the keys in your parked car or return to find the battery dead. For more serious problems, the closest repair center is Maingate Exxon, US 192 west of I-4, (407) 396-2721. Disney security will help you contact the service station. Arrangements can be made to take you to your Disney World destination or the nearest phone.

LOST AND FOUND

If you lose (or find) something in the Magic Kingdom, go to City Hall. At Epcot, Lost and Found is in the Entrance Plaza. At Disney-MGM Studios, it's at Hollywood Boulevard Guest Relations, and at the Animal Kingdom, it's at Guest Relations at the main entrance. If you discover your loss after you have left the park(s), call (407) 824-4245 (for all parks). See page 38 for the number to call in each park if you're still at the park(s) and discover something is missing.

"No, no, really, it's okay. It's just not what I expected."

MEDICAL MATTERS

Relief for a Headache   Aspirin and other sundries are sold at the Emporium on Main Street in the Magic Kingdom (they're kept behind the counter; you must ask), at most retail shops in Epcot's Future World and World Showcase, and in Disney-MGM Studios and the Animal Kingdom.

If You Need a Doctor   Main Street Physicians provides 24-hour service. Doctors are available for house calls to all area hotels and campgrounds (Disney and non-Disney). House calls are $160 per visit. If your problem doesn't require a house call, visit the clinic on a walk-in basis (no appointments taken) at 2901 Parkway Boulevard, Suite 3-A, in Kissimmee. Minimum charge for a physician consultation at the clinic is $80. The clinic is open daily from 8 a.m. to 8 p.m., and its main phone is (407) 396-1195.

Center Care walk-in clinic operates two locations that are across the street from one another. The first is at 12500 S. Apopka-Vineland Road and is open on weekdays from 8 a.m. to midnight and on weekends from 8 a.m. to 8 p.m. The second location is at 12139 S. Apopka-Vineland Road and is open on weekdays from 9 a.m. to 9 p.m. and on weekends from 10 a.m. to 10 p.m. They operate a total of five locations in the Disney area. Call (407) 239-7777 for fees and information. Center Care also operates an "in-room," 24-hour physician (house call) service and runs a shuttle that will pick you up free of charge. Phone (407) 238-2000.

Prescription Medicine　The closest pharmacy is Walgreen's Lake Buena Vista (phone (407) 238-0600). Turner Drugs (phone (407) 828-8125) charges $5 to deliver a filled prescription to your hotel's front desk. The service is available to Disney resort guests and guests at non-Disney hotels in the Turner Drugs area, and the fee is charged to your hotel account.

SERGEANT BLISTERBLASTER'S GUIDE TO HAPPY FEET AT WALT DISNEY WORLD

1. On Your Feet!　Get up, Easy-Boy rider: when you go to Disney World, you'll have to walk a lot farther than to the refrigerator. You can log from 5 to 12 miles a day no problem at the Disney parks, so now's the time to get them dogs in shape. Start with some short walks around the neighborhood and increase your distance gradually until you can do 6 miles on weekends without CPR.

2. Attention!　During your pre-Disney training program, pay attention when those puppies growl. They will give you a lot of information about your feet and the appropriateness and fit of your shoes. Listen up! No walking in flip-flops, loafers, or sandals. Wear well-constructed, broken-in running or hiking shoes. If you feel a "hot spot," that means a blister is developing. The most common sites for blisters are the heels, the toes, and the balls of your feet. If you note a tendency to develop a hot spot in the same place everytime you walk, cover it prophylactically with Moleskin (available in drugstores without prescription) before you set out. No, sofa bunny, I did not tell you to wear condoms on your feet! *Prophylactically* means to anticipate the problem and treat it in advance. One more thing: keep your toenails cut short and straight across.

3. Sock It Up, Trainee!　Good socks are as important as good shoes. When you walk, your feet sweat like a mule in a peat bog, and moisture increases friction. To minimize friction, wear two pairs of socks. The pair next to your feet should ideally be polypropylene thin socks or sock liners. The outer sock can be either a natural fiber like cotton or wool, or a synthetic fiber. To further combat moisture, dust your dogs with some antifungal talcum powder.

4. Who Do You Think You Are, John Wayne?　Don't be a hero. The time to take care of a foot problem is the minute you notice it. Carry a small foot emergency kit for your platoon. The kit should contain gauze, Betadyne antibiotic ointment, Moleskin or Spenco second skin, scissors, a sewing needle or some such to drain blisters, as well as matches to sterilize the needle. An extra pair of dry socks and some talc is optional.

5. Bite the Bullet! If you develop a hot spot, cover it ASAP with Moleskin or Spenco second skin. Cut the covering large enough to cover the skin surrounding the hot spot. If you develop a blister, air out and dry your foot. Next, drain the fluid but do not remove the top skin. Clean the area with your Betadyne, place a gauze square over the blister, and cover the whole shooting match with Moleskin. If you do not have Moleskin or Spenco second skin, do not try to cover the hot spot or blister with Band-Aids. Band-Aids slip and wad up.

6. Take Care of Your Platoon. If you have a couple of young green troops in your outfit, they might not sound off when a hot spot comes on. Stop several times a day and check their feet. If you forgot your emergency foot kit and a problem arises, don't be reluctant to call the Disney medics. They have all the stuff you need to keep your command in action.

Okay troops, prepare to move out. Hit the dusty trail and *move* those feet: left, right, left. When you get back old Sarge will teach you how to avoid VD at Walt Disney World.

RAIN

Weather bad? Go to the parks anyway. Crowds are lighter, and most attractions and waiting areas are under cover. Showers, especially during warmer months, are short.

Rain gear is one of the few bargains at the parks. It isn't always displayed in shops; you have to ask for it. Ponchos are available for about $5; umbrellas go for about $11. [Ponchos sold at Walt Disney World are all yellow. Picking out somebody in your party on a rainy day is like trying to identify a certain, individual bumblebee in a swarm.]

El Niño precipitated (no pun intended) dozens of reader suggestions for dealing with soggy days. Nobody, however, had their act together as well as this mom from Memphis, Tennessee. Here are her tips:

> *1. Rain gear should include poncho* and *umbrella. Umbrellas make the rain much more bearable. When rain isn't beating down on your ponchoed head, it's easier to ignore.*
> *2. Buy blue ponchos at Walgreens. We could keep track of each other much easier because we had blue ponchos instead of yellow ones.*
> *3. ScotchGuard your shoes. The difference is unbelievable.*

SUN, HEAT, AND HUMIDITY

Florida's sun, heat, and humidity can be brutal from late April through mid-October. A woman from Durham, North Carolina, advises:

> *Be prepared for the heat. I am a 24-year-old former aerobics instructor and felt dizzy after a long day in the Magic Kingdom. Carry clear water bottles, as they are the only beverages allowed on rides.*

A lady from Ardsley, New York, writes:

> *I would advise that people carry umbrellas for shelter against the sun. I was the only one with an umbrella, and every time I used it, I would hear people around me say, "She's smart. She brought an umbrella." This came in handy during the wait for the live show [at Disney-MGM Studios]. The show is absolutely the best event in all three parks (and I should know, because I'm a singer and musician), but the wait is absolutely the worst. They line you up on this open piece of pavement for at least 30 minutes. There is absolutely no shade or breeze, and the cement has been baking in the sun all day. If you bring umbrellas and lots of water to throw on the kids, you might make it until show time.*

ST. LOUIS ENCEPHALITIS

Although contraction occurs very rarely, St. Louis Encephalitis is an ongoing concern for Florida's health officials. The disease is transmitted to humans by mosquito bites, and is often more severe in children and the elderly. In spite of regular warnings by state and county agencies, many people (including Disney cast members) are still unsure how much of a threat the mosquito-borne infection poses. A reader from New York City wrote:

> *Something very important to keep in mind: our resort's pools were closed by 6 p.m. every night. Why? Mosquitoes. We heard from a cast member that there was an encephalitis scare, so pools were closed early to protect guests from possible exposure. Alternately, we heard it was encephalitis season—implying that this wasn't an isolated scare, but an annual event. We couldn't substantiate this, but either way, you should inform your readers, even if it's not annual. People should know to bring bug spray, and they should plan on possibly not having any late night swims.*

Since mosquitoes flourish during periods of summer rain, it can be said that Florida undergoes an annual "encephalitis season." However, encephalitis is not a common disease in Florida, and most summers see no cases reported. Rather, health officials advise taking precautions during periods of warmth and moisture. Precautions include:

- Avoid outdoor activities between dusk and dawn, when mosquitoes are most active.
- If you must be outside at night, wear long pants and long-sleeved shirts, as well as insect repellent on exposed skin.
- Avoid water, and especially standing water, at night.

There is no vaccine for St. Louis Encephalitis since it occurs in humans so rarely. The good news is that, due to conscientious preventive measures on the part of Florida locals as well as tourists, only a handful of cases were reported last year.

HOW TO LODGE A COMPLAINT WITH DISNEY OR ALL CORPSES MUST CARRY A PHOTO ID

Lodging a complaint about a leaky faucet or not having enough clean towels is pretty straightforward, and you will usually find the Disney folks extremely responsive. However, a gripe that is larger, more global, or beyond an on-site manager's ability to resolve is likely to founder in the labyrinth of Disney bureaucracy.

One of our all-time favorite examples of wandering in Disney corporate limbo came from a middle-aged British reader. He writes:

> *When we visited Disney we bought Premium Annual Passes. Things may have changed since then, but one thing that struck us as odd was that the normal tickets were plastic and durable, much like credit cards, [and] allowed easy entry using the turnstiles at the park entrances. However, the annual passes were made of thin card, were very flimsy, [and] could not be used at the normal turnstiles. On the very first day of their use, [you] had to place your two first fingers into a small slot on a special entry gate where your [fingerprints] were read and recorded. On subsequent entries your fingers would be recognized and you would gain entry. There were some hiccups with this system but usually you got in after a couple of tries.*
>
> *When we came to the entrance gate [of Typhoon Lagoon] there were none of the special finger-reading machines. We were therefore directed to a side gate [where] a lady official scrutinized our cards and asked to see some other means of ID. We were going swimming, so obviously we did not bring our passports but had our resort [ID] cards as well as several credit cards each. However, none of these contained our photos, so*

the lady was not very happy. After quite a bit of wrangling they allowed us in, but it annoyed me that having spent a total of about $1,100 for our Premium Annual Passes, they were proving to be far from user-friendly.

On return to our room I decided I would have a word with someone in the Disney hierarchy who would appreciate the inconvenience we had suffered and do something about it. I spent an interesting 20 minutes or so on the telephone trying to find someone who was at all interested. For a start, Disney [does] not have a central complaints (the word does not exist) department or a customer service division. Or if they had [one], they were not going to connect me to it under the circumstances. First of all, I was put through to the resort's front desk. Of course, they knew nothing about annual passes, finger tests, or water parks. Next, I was connected to Typhoon Lagoon. As they were the target of my complaint, this too seemed a bit pointless. Eventually I was passed on to someone in WDW's central administration who was willing to listen.

I spent the next few minutes relating my experience and difficulties in gaining entrance to Typhoon Lagoon, just because their turnstiles did not have the proper equipment to deal with holders of annual passes. I pointed out that I had been asked for my passport but that I did not normally carry such a document when going swimming. He missed the point totally and suggested that perhaps I should carry my driver's license with me. I explained that U.K. driving licenses do not contain a photograph of the holder, and as such it would not meet their stringent requirements for identification. He then advised me that one should always take one's driving license with one everywhere and asked if I would carry it if I were [on] holiday in Europe. I hastened to point out that we were holidaying in the USA and not in Europe and in any case I was not driving. Why, therefore, should I need to carry a driving license? "To identify yourself," he replied.

In what circumstances, I asked, apart from going swimming would I need to identify myself? He replied, "Supposing you were shot!!!!!" I asked him if I were likely to be shot in Walt Disney World, to which there was no answer. For a moment I had this brief vision of myself lying in the middle of Main Street U.S.A. riddled with bullets and bleeding profusely. As I lay there I was feebly waving my passport (or driving license—with or without passport) and gasping, "BUT I'M BRITISH, AND IN POSSESSION OF A VALID PREMIUM ANNUAL PASS!"

*It seemed purposeless pursuing this line of argument. I later tele-
phoned another department in the Disney empire and asked to speak
personally to a vice-president whose name I had gleaned from a questionnaire on customer satisfaction (handed to me at Typhoon Lagoon).
Naturally the person in question was not available, and, after speaking
to a couple of others (who I suspect were not real people at all but
Audio-Animatronic figures designed to ward off the likes of me), I
decided to gracefully admit defeat and just get on with my holiday. The
moral is not to complain but to take it lying down like a man!*

Like most companies, Disney would rather hear from you when the
message is good. Concerning complaints, they prefer to receive the complaint in writing, but by the time you get home and draft a letter, it's often
too late to correct the problem. And though Disney would have you
believe that it's a touchy-feely outfit, it's not generally the kind of company
that will "make things right for you" after the fact. You may get a letter
thanking you for writing and expressing generalized regret without
acknowledging responsibility (as in "We're sorry you *felt* inconvenienced,"
as if the perception arose from your imagination), but it's not likely they
will offer or commit to do anything remedial. That having been said, if you
want to lodge a complaint once you've returned home, write:

Walt Disney World Guest Communications
P.O. Box 10000
Lake Buena Vista, Florida 32830-1000

If you're at Walt Disney World and really need to get an issue settled,
keep your resort general manager in the middle of the fray and hold his feet
to the fire until he hooks you up with the right person to address your
grievance.

VISITING MORE THAN ONE PARK IN A SINGLE DAY

If you have a pass that allows you to visit the Magic Kingdom, the Animal
Kingdom, Epcot, and Disney-MGM Studios in the same day, it will be vali-
dated with the date when you enter your first park. If you decide to go later
to another park, you must have your hand stamped for re-entry before you
leave. If you start the day at the Magic Kingdom, for example, then go to
Epcot for dinner, you must get a re-entry stamp when you leave the Magic
Kingdom. At Epcot, you'll have to present your passport and show your
hand stamp. The stamp is visible only under ultraviolet light and usually
won't come off if you wash your hands or swim.

Services and Shopping

SHOPPING

The *Unofficial Guide* aims to help you see as much as possible, not buy as much as possible. But we acknowledge that for many, a vacation is an extended shopping spree. If you're among these shoppers, you'll love exploring the stores at Walt Disney World. You'll notice that our touring plans keep you on-track to see attractions, dissuading you somewhat from shopping. Because Disney doesn't need our help to keep your wallet flapping, we offer minimal coverage of shopping at Walt Disney World. However, to give you a notion of what it means to an enthusiast, we share this letter from a Los Angeles couple:

> We would like to point out that, although your book discourages it, the shopping is a divine experience at WDW for those who like to shop. One does not shop in WDW for bargains (that's what flea markets, garage sales, and Target are for), but Disney buyers obtain a large selection of above-average to excellent quality merchandise, much of it not available anywhere else (not even a Disney Store or catalog), and arrange it attractively and imaginatively (at the exit of almost every attraction). They are marketing geniuses! Not even the largest shops have all the merchandise they have to offer, hence, a shopper can make little discoveries in almost every shop—even the smallest hotel gift shops. That, coupled with congenial, helpful Disney staff, and services like complimentary hotel delivery, make shopping its own attraction at WDW.

An Avon, Ohio, woman suggests "planning a shopping day":

> Plan out what you want to buy, and if need be, start hopping from park to park using the [Disney] bus system. If time does not permit this, I suggest that when you see something you like, BUY IT RIGHT THEN (reader's emphasis). Don't say, "We will come back," or "We will find it in another shop," because you won't! Then you will regret it. And don't think that they have all this stuff at your local Disney store, because they don't.

And a woman from, Suffolk, Virginia, offers this:

> Let readers know if they are into shopping to allot at least six hours for Disney Marketplace and West Side.

Cameras and Film

Camera Centers at the major theme parks sell disposable cameras for about $10 ($19 with flash). Film is sold throughout the World. Developing is available at most Disney hotel gift shops and at Camera Centers. For two-hour developing, look for the photo express sign in the theme parks. Drop your film in the container and pick up your pictures at the Camera Center as you leave the park. If you use the express service and intend to stay in the park until closing, pick up your pictures earlier in the evening to avoid the end-of-day rush. The Magic Kingdom Camera Center almost always develops film within the advertised two hours. Camera Centers at the other parks frequently run late.

Photo tips and recommendations for settings and exposures are detailed in the respective maps provided free when you enter the theme parks.

Shopping for Walt Disney World Resort Guests

Disney resort guests who make purchases in a theme park shop can have their merchandise sent directly to their guest rooms.

Disney Souvenirs

Disney souvenirs can be found in any Walt Disney World structure large enough to hold a cash register. Still, readers often ask where to find the greatest variety and best deals.

Disney opened its first character superstore in 1996 at Downtown Disney Marketplace. Called World of Disney, the 50,000-square-foot facility offers the largest selection of Disney merchandise in the world (that's *the* world, Edith, not just Walt Disney World!). It's decidedly less crowded and frenetic than shops in the theme parks, and Downtown Disney Marketplace is accessible by Disney bus or boat. Magic Kingdom Club members get a 10% discount on most merchandise at Downtown Disney Marketplace. For sale are stuffed toys of Disney characters, Disney books and records, character hats, and other items which are difficult, if not impossible, to find outside Disney shops.

Disney T-shirts, the most popular souvenir, are available areawide. Shirts sold at Disney World are expensive ($19–40) but are high-quality, 100% cotton. Those sold outside the World are usually of lesser quality, 50% cotton/ 50% polyester, and sell for $7–18. Many of the same designs of Mickey, Minnie, and Goofy can be found both inside and outside Disney World. The only difference is that shirts sold in Disney shops will say "Walt Disney World" or perhaps "Epcot" or "Disney-MGM Studios" next to the imprint of the character. Shirts sold outside the World usually will say "Florida."

Theme Park Shops with the Best Variety of Disney Stuff	
Magic Kingdom	
Main Street	Emporium
	(largest selection at Magic Kingdom)
Tomorrowland	Mickey's Star Traders
Epcot	
Future World	Gateway Gifts
	Centorium
	(largest selection at Epcot)
World Showcase	Disney Traders
	(left side of Showcase Plaza)
Disney-MGM Studios	
Hollywood Boulevard	Mickey's of Hollywood
Sunset Boulevard	Once Upon a Time
Studio Courtyard	Animation Gallery
Animal Kingdom	
Safari Village	Village Merchantile
	Disney Outfitters

The only retailer selling discounted items from Walt Disney World is the Character Warehouse (phone (407) 345-5285) in Mall Two of the Belz Factory Outlet World at the north end of International Drive. Prices are good, but the selection is generally limited to close-outs and remainders. Don't expect to find the same merchandise that you saw in the parks. The store is open Monday through Saturday from 10 a.m. to 9 p.m. and on Sunday from 10 a.m. to 6 p.m.

A Kentucky family had a hard time getting to the Belz Outlet, warning:

> *Avoid International Drive between the BeeLine Expressway and Oak Ridge Road. After crawling for what seemed like an hour, we reached the Belz Outlet Stores. We were grinding our teeth at the congestion. Take Interstate 4 directly to the Oak Ridge Road exit. Much faster. PS: Belz Outlet Stores had some great buys on Disney stuff. Worth the trip.*

Bargain World (phone (407) 345-8772), with locations at 6454 International Drive (next to Shell World), 8102 International Drive, and 8520 International Drive, offers a good selection of the 50% cotton/50% polyester shirts, as well as Disney beach towels and other Disney character merchandise.

SERVICES

Messages
Messages left at City Hall in the Magic Kingdom, the Guest Relations lobby at Epcot, Hollywood Boulevard Guest Relations at Disney-MGM Studios, or Guest Relations at the Animal Kingdom can be retrieved at any of the four.

Pet Care
Pets aren't allowed in the major or minor theme parks. But never leave an animal in a hot car while you tour; the pet will die. Kennels and holding facilities are provided for temporary care of your pets. They're located adjacent to the Transportation and Ticket Center, left of the Epcot entrance plaza, left of the Disney-MGM Studios entrance plaza, at the outer entrance of the Animal Kingdom, and at Fort Wilderness Campground. If

you insist, kennel staff will accept about any type of animal (except natural wildlife pets), though owners of exotic and/or potentially vicious pets must place their charge in its assigned cage. Small pets (mice, hamsters, birds, snakes, turtles, alligators, etc.) must stay in their own escape-proof carrier.

Here are several additional details you may need to know:

- When traveling with your pet in Florida, bring proof of vaccination and immunization, including bordatella for dogs.
- It is against the law in Florida to leave a pet in a closed vehicle.
- Advance reservations for animals aren't accepted.
- Kennels open one hour before the park opens and close 30 minutes to one hour after the park closes. The kennels, however, are staffed 24 hours a day.
- Disney resort guests may board a pet overnight for $9 per pet, per night. Other patrons are charged $11 per pet, per night. Day care of pets for all guests costs $6 per day. The kennels aren't really set up for multiday boarding. You must exercise your own pet.
- Guests leaving exotic pets should supply their food.
- Pets are allowed at a limited number of sites at Fort Wilderness Campground.

For more information on pet care, call (407) 824-6568.

Religious Services

On Sundays at the Polynesian Resort, mass for Catholics is celebrated at 8 and 10:15 a.m., and nondenominational Protestant services are held at 9 a.m. For a schedule of services at churches and temples in the Walt Disney World area, inquire at your hotel's front desk.

Excuse Me, But Where Can I Find . . .

Someplace to Put All These Packages?   Lockers are available on the ground floor of the Main Street railroad station in the Magic Kingdom, to the right of Spaceship Earth in Epcot, and on the east and west ends of the TTC. At Disney-MGM Studios, lockers are to the right of the entrance on Hollywood Boulevard at Oscar's Super Service. At the Animal Kingdom, lockers are inside the main entrance to the left. Lockers are $3 a day plus a $2 deposit.

Package Pick-up is available at each major theme park. Ask the sales-person to send your purchases to Package Pick-up. When you leave the park, they'll be waiting for you. Epcot has two exits, thus two Package Pick-ups, so specify whether you want your purchases sent to the main entrance or to the International Gateway.

If you're a Disney resort guest, have the salesperson send your purchases from the theme parks directly to your guest room.

A Mixed Drink or a Beer?   Alcoholic beverages aren't sold in the Magic Kingdom; you must leave the park and go to a resort hotel to get one. Everywhere else in Disney World, wine, beer, and mixed drinks are readily available.

Some Chewing Gum?   Sorry, it isn't sold in any theme park. B.Y.O.

A Grocery Store?   Goodings Supermarket in the Crossroads Shopping Center (across FL 535 from the entrance to Walt Disney World) is a large, designer grocery with everything from sushi to fresh-baked doughnuts. If you're looking for gourmet foods, a good wine selection, or something exotic it's your best bet. If you just want to stock up on staples, however, you'll find the prices higher than the Tower of Terror, and just about as frightening. For more down-to-earth prices try Publix Supermarket on the corner of FL 535 and Vineland Road. There are also supermarkets on US 192, on the opposite side of Walt Disney World.

Suntan Lotion?   Suntan lotion and other sundries are sold at the Emporium on Main Street in the Magic Kingdom (they're kept behind the counter; you must ask) and in Epcot at many Future World and World Showcase shops. At Disney-MGM Studios and the Animal Kingdom, suntan lotion is sold at almost all shops.

A Smoke?   Cigarettes are sold throughout the Magic Kingdom, the Animal Kingdom, Epcot, and Disney-MGM Studios. But, smoking is prohibited on all attractions, in all attraction waiting areas, and in all shops.

Feminine Hygiene Products?   They're in women's rest rooms throughout Walt Disney World.

Part Nine

Dining in and around Walt Disney World

Dining outside Walt Disney World

Unofficial Guide researchers love good food and invest a fair amount of time scouting new places to eat. And, because food at Walt Disney World is so expensive, we (like you) have an economic incentive for finding palatable meals outside the World. Unfortunately, the area surrounding Disney World is not exactly a culinary nirvana. If you thrive on fast food and the fare at chain restaurants (Denny's, T.G.I. Fridays, Olive Garden, Chi Chi's, etc.), you'll be as happy as an alligator on a chicken farm. If, however, you'd like a superlative dining experience, you'll find the pickings outside the World about the same as those inside, only less expensive.

Some ethnic cuisines aren't represented in Walt Disney World restaurants. If you want Indian, Thai, Greek, or Caribbean, you'll have to forage in surrounding communities. Among specialty restaurants in and out of the World, location and price will determine your choice. There are, for example, decent Italian restaurants in Disney World and adjoining tourist areas. Which one you select depends on how much you want to spend and how convenient the place is. Our recommendations on specialty and ethnic fare served in and out of the World are summarized in the nearby table.

Better restaurants outside Walt Disney World cater primarily to adults and aren't as well equipped to deal with children. If, however, you're looking to escape children or want to eat in peace and quiet, you're more likely to find such an environment outside the World.

In or out of the World for Ethnic Cuisine?	
Cuisine/Specialty	Recommendations
American	Good selections both in and out of the World.
Barbecue	Better out of the World.
Buffets	This is a toss-up. Disney buffets are expensive but offer excellent quality and extensive selections. Off-World buffets aren't as upscale, but they are a better value.
Chinese	Eat out of the World.
French	Toss-up. Reasonably good but expensive both in and out of the World.
German	Passable, but not great, in or out of the World.
Italian	Tie on quality; better value out of the World.
Japanese	Teppanyaki Dining Room at Epcot is tops for teppan (table grill) dining. For sushi and sashimi, go off-World, or try Kimonos at the Swan Resort.
Mexican	We have not been able to find an off-World Mexican restaurant better than San Angel Inn Restaurante at Epcot.
Middle Eastern	More choice and better value out of the World.
Seafood	Toss-up.
Steak & Prime Rib	Though you can get a good piece of meat at many Walt Disney World restaurants, the edge goes to off-World restaurants for both quality and value.

TAKE OUT EXPRESS

If you're staying in a hotel *outside* Disney World, Take Out Express (phone (407) 352-1170) will deliver a meal from your choice among 20 restaurants, including T.G.I. Fridays, Ming Court, Passage to India, Siam Orchid, Bella Roma, Chili's, Ocean Grille, Houlihans, Italianni's, and Sizzler. The delivery charge is $4–5 per restaurant (depending on your distance from the restaurant), with a minimum $15 order. Tips aren't included. Cash, traveler's checks, MasterCard, Visa, and American Express are accepted. Hours are 4:30–11 p.m.

Where to Eat outside Walt Disney World

Now that you know how specialty and ethnic sites compare, here are our recommendations for dining outside Walt Disney World:

American

Cafe Tu Tu Tango: 8625 International Drive, Orlando; inexpensive to moderate; (407) 248-2222
Mediterranean-style tapas in an artist's garret setting.

Chatham's Place: 7575 Dr. Phillips Boulevard, Orlando; moderate to expensive; (407) 345-2992
New American cuisine: the dining room is small and unappealing, but the food and service are some of the best in Orlando.

Manuel's on the 28th: 390 North Orange Avenue, Orlando; expensive; (407) 246-6580
Creative American overlooking downtown Orlando from the 28th floor of the Barnett Bank building.

Pebbles: 12551 FL 535, Crossroads Shopping Center, Lake Buena Vista; moderate to expensive; (407) 827-1111
A casual homegrown chain featuring a Florida version of California cuisine.

Sam Snead's Tavern: 2461 South Hiawassee Road, Orlando; inexpensive to moderate; (407) 295-9999
A golfer's version of the Hard Rock Cafe.

Wild Jack's: 7364 International Drive, Orlando; moderate; (407) 352-4407
Cowboy cuisine in a Rodeo Drive setting.

Barbecue

Bubbalou's Bodacious B-B-Q: 5818 Conroy Road, Orlando (near Universal Studios Florida); inexpensive; (407) 295-1212
Tender smoky barbecue with a tomato-based "killer" sauce.

Beef

Butcher Shop Steakhouse: 8445 International Drive, Mercado Mediterranean Village, Orlando; moderate; (407) 363-9727
High-quality beef you can cook at the open pit.

Charlie's Steak House: 6107 South Orange Blossom Trail, Orlando; moderate; (407) 851-7130
There are other locations for this small chain, including one just south of the I-4 interchange on US 192.

Beef (continued)

Del Frisco's: 729 Lee Road, Orlando (quarter-mile west of I-4);
 expensive; (407) 645-4443
A little pricey, but if you're in the mood for a really great steak, it's
worth it.

Vito's Chop House: 8633 International Drive, Orlando; (407) 354-2467
Surprisingly upscale meat house with a taste of Tuscany.

Caribbean

Bahama Breeze: 8849 International Drive, Orlando; moderate; (407)
 248-2499
A creative—and tasty—version of Caribbean cuisine from the owners
of the Olive Garden and Red Lobster chains.

Chinese

Ming Court: 9188 International Drive, Orlando; expensive; (407)
 351-9988
Ask to see the dim sum menu.

Cuban

Numero Uno: 2499 South Orange Avenue, Orlando; inexpensive;
 (407) 841-3840
No trip to Florida is complete without a sampling of Cuban food.

Rolando's: 870 Semoran Boulevard, Casselberry; inexpensive; (407)
 767-9677
Some of the best Cuban in the area, served by some of the friendliest
people.

French

La Grille: 8445 International Drive, Orlando; moderate to expensive;
 (407)345-0883
Fine French in the middle of International Drive's most touristy area.

Le Coq au Vin: 4800 South Orange Avenue, Orlando; moderate; (407)
 851-6980
A perennial local favorite featuring country French in a not-too-stuffy
atmosphere. Reservations are required.

Le Provence: 50 East Pine Street, Orlando; moderate; (407) 843-1320
A more upscale French restaurant, small, intimate, and pricey—but good.

German/Eastern European

Cafe Europa: Church Street Market, 54 W. Church Street, Orlando; inexpensive to moderate; (407) 872-3388
The only Eastern European in town; good cabbage rolls.

Old Munich: 5731 South Orange Blossom Trail, Orlando; moderate; (407) 438-8997
Nothing special, but if you've just *got* to have some sauerbraten . . .

Indian

Kohinoor: Ethan Allen Plaza, 249 W. State Road 436, Altamonte Springs; moderate; (407) 788-6004
Try the lamb korma.

Passage to India: 5532 International Drive, Orlando; moderate; (407) 351-3456
A lot of locals brave International Drive just to dine here.

Shamiana: 7040 International Drive, Orlando; inexpensive; (407) 354-1160
Also serves Pakistani cuisine.

Italian

Capriccio: 9801 International Drive, Orlando; moderate to expensive; (407) 345-4450
The Peabody Orlando's casually upscale Italian restaurant serves a good Sunday brunch.

Tarantino's: 917 North Bermuda Avenue, Kissimmee; inexpensive to moderate; (407) 870-2622
An unassuming mom-and-popper owned by some New York transplants.

Japanese/Sushi

Hanamizuki: 8255 International Drive, Orlando; moderate to expensive; (407) 363-7200
Usually filled with Japanese visitors; can be expensive, but very authentic.

Ichiban: 19 South Orange Avenue, Orlando (near Church Street Station); moderate; (407) 423-2688
Sit on the floor or at a table; good sushi and tempura.

Mexican

Amigos: 6036 South Orange Blossom Trail, Orlando; inexpensive;
(407) 857-3144
Tex-Mex with the emphasis on the Tex.

Don Pablo's: 8717 International Drive, Orlando; inexpensive; (407)
354-1345
A pretty good chain that uses fresh ingredients. Can be a bit noisy.

Middle Eastern

Aladdin's Cafe: 1015 East Semoran Boulevard, Casselberry; moderate;
(407) 331-0488
Call for belly dancer's schedule.

Seafood

Sea Catch Market: 1455 Semoran Boulevard, Casselberry; inexpensive;
(407) 679-5999
Don't be fooled by the unassuming exterior (or interior, for that
matter)—you won't find better fish for the price anywhere.

Straub's Boatyard: 743 Lee Road, Orlando; moderate; (407) 628-0067
From the owners of Straub's Fine Seafood, which also serves fine
seafood.

Thai

Royal Thai: 1202 North Semoran Boulevard, Orlando; inexpensive to
moderate; (407) 275-0776
If you really like hot Thai food, you'll love this place; have the lemon
fish.

Siam Orchid: 7575 Universal Boulevard, Orlando; moderate to
expensive; (407) 351-0821
Fancier than most Thai places, and a bit pricier, but the best Thai in
the tourist areas.

ONE MAN'S TREASURE

A man from Richland, Washington, urges:

> *I think that you should in future editions promote the Crossroads of Buena Vista [Shopping Center] a little stronger. There are plenty of non-WDW restaurants at non-WDW prices. The Crossroads is nothing less than a small city that can service all of your needs.*

Crossroads Shopping Center is on FL 535 directly across from the entrance to Walt Disney World Village and Disney Village Hotel Plaza. As the reader suggests, it offers about everything you need. Fast food is sold at McDonald's, Burger King, and Taco Bell. Up a notch are T.G.I. Fridays, Perkins, Jungle Jim's, Pizzeria Uno, and Red Lobster. For a really nice meal, pick Pebbles, featuring fresh Florida seafood. When you finish eating, shop for sportswear, swimwear, and athletic shoes.

Dining in Walt Disney World

This section aims to help you find good food without going broke or tripping over one of Disney World's many culinary landmines. More than 100 restaurants operate in Walt Disney World, including more than five dozen full-service restaurants, 23 of which are inside the theme parks. Collectively, Disney restaurants offer exceptional variety, serving everything from Cajun to French, from Moroccan to Texas barbecue. Most restaurants are expensive, and many serve less than distinguished fare, but the culinary scene at Disney World is generally improving. You can find good deals if you know where to look, and there are ethnic delights rarely found outside of America's largest cities.

Disney Dining 2000

Disney has been busy reinventing the way it operates its restaurants, both in the resort hotels and in the theme parks. Gone are the days of a team of chefs managing several restaurants. Now, each Disney restaurant has its own chef and manager and is run like an independent, proprietary restaurant. Time will tell if these changes translate into better food and service.

All over Walt Disney World, the theme dining rage continues unabated. At Disney's Wide World of Sports is the Official All-Star Cafe, serving hearty American fare. There are two Rainforest Cafes, one at Downtown Disney Marketplace and one at the Animal Kingdom. At Pleasure Island, a Wild Horse Saloon features barbecue with line dancing on the side to help you work off the calories. Next door at Disney's West Side, there's a Planet

Hollywood with attitude and a House of Blues serving Cajun and Creole dishes with sides of R&B, jazz, and country. Other theme eateries on the West Side include Gloria and Emilio Estefan's Bongos for Cuban fare and Wolfgang Puck's Cafe for California Cuisine.

In addition to theme dining, you'll find two McDonald's at Walt Disney World, one at Downtown Disney Marketplace and one just outside the entrance to the All-Star Resorts.

At Epcot, Chefs de France has incorporated the other two smaller restaurants in the France pavilion—Au Petit Café and Bistro de Paris—into one large Chefs de France. Biergarten at Germany has been renovated, and an outdoor cafe is on tap for Italy. Disney is also concentrating on upgrading counter-service eateries. Watch for more new items, including fast-service, made-to-order pizzas.

WALT DISNEY WORLD RESTAURANT CATEGORIES

In general, food and beverage offerings at Walt Disney World are defined by service, price, and convenience:

Full Service Restaurants Full service restaurants are in all Disney resorts except the All-Star, and in all major theme parks, Downtown Disney Marketplace, Pleasure Island, and Disney's West Side. Disney operates the restaurants in the theme parks and its hotels. Contractors or franchisees operate the restaurants in hotels of the Disney Village Hotel Plaza, the Swan and Dolphin resorts, Pleasure Island, Disney's West Side, and some in Downtown Disney Marketplace. Priority seating (explained below), arranged in advance, is recommended for all full-service restaurants except those in Disney Village Hotel Plaza. The restaurants accept VISA, MasterCard, and American Express.

Buffets There has been an explosion of buffets at Disney World during recent years. Many have Disney characters in attendance, and most have a separate children's menu featuring hot dogs, burgers, chicken nuggets, pizza, macaroni and cheese, and spaghetti and meatballs. In addition to the buffets, several restaurants serve a family-style, all-you-can-eat, fixed-price meal. Priority seating arrangements are required for character buffets and recommended for all other buffets and family-style restaurants. Most major credit cards are accepted.

The table below lists buffets (where you can belly up for bulk loading) at Walt Disney World.

Walt Disney World Buffets

Location	Restaurant	Cuisine	Children's Selections	Disney Characters Present
Magic Kingdom	Crystal Palace	American	Yes	Yes
Epcot	Biergarten	German	No	No
Epcot	Restaurant Akershus	Scandinavian	No	No
Disney-MGM Studios	Hollywood and Vine	American	Yes	Yes
Contemporary Resort	Chef Mickey's	American	Yes	Yes
Beach Club Resort	Cape May Cafe	Clambake	Yes	No
Grand Floridian	1900 Park Fare	American	Yes	Yes
Fort Wilderness Campground	Trail's End	American	Yes	No

If you want to eat a lot but don't feel like standing in yet another line, consider one of the all-you-can-eat "family-style" restaurants. These feature platters of food that are brought to your table in courses by a server. You can sample everything on the menu and eat as much as you like. You can even go back to a favorite appetizer after you finish the main course. Food tends to be a little better than you'll find on a buffet line.

Family-style all-you-can-eat service is available at the Liberty Tree Tavern in the Magic Kingdom (character dining), The Garden Grill Restaurant in the Land pavilion in Epcot (character dining), 'Ohana in the Polynesian Resort (character dining), and Whispering Canyon Cafe in the Wilderness Lodge.

Cafeterias and Food Courts   Cafeterias, in all the major theme parks, offer a middle ground between full-service and counter-service dining. Food courts, featuring a collection of counter-service eateries under one roof, are found at the theme parks as well as at the moderate (Coronado Springs, Caribbean Beach, Dixie Landings, Port Orleans) and budget (All-Star) Disney resorts. No priority seating is required or available at cafeterias or food courts. VISA, MasterCard, and American Express are accepted.

Counter Service   Counter-service fast food is available in all theme parks and at Downtown Disney Marketplace, Pleasure Island, Disney's Board-

Walk, and Disney's West Side. The food compares in quality with McDonald's, Captain D's, or Taco Bell, but is more expensive, though often served in larger portions. VISA, MasterCard, and American Express are accepted.

Vendor Food Vendors abound at the theme parks, Downtown Disney Marketplace, Pleasure Island, Disney's West Side, and Disney's BoardWalk. Offerings include popcorn, ice cream bars, churros (Mexican pastry), soft drinks, bottled water, and (in theme parks) fresh fruit. Prices include tax, and payment must be in cash.

Hard Choices

Dining choices will definitely impact your Walt Disney World experience. If you're short on time and you want to see the theme parks, avoid full-service restaurants. Ditto if you're short on funds. If you want to try a Disney full-service restaurant, arrange priority seating in advance. That won't reserve you a table, but it will minimize your wait.

Integrating Meals into the *Unofficial Guide* Touring Plans

Arrive before the park of your choice opens. Tour expeditiously, using your chosen plan (taking as few breaks as possible), until about 11–11:30 a.m. Once the park becomes crowded around midday, meals and other breaks won't affect the plan's efficiency. If you intend to stay in the park for evening parades, fireworks, or other events, eat dinner early enough to be finished in time for the festivities.

Character Dining

A number of restaurants, primarily those serving all-you-can-eat buffets and family-style meals, offer character dining. At character meals, you pay a fixed price and dine in the presence of three to five Disney characters that circulate throughout the restaurant, hugging children (and sometimes adults), posing for photos, and signing autographs. Character breakfasts, lunches, and dinners are served at restaurants in and out of the theme parks. For an extensive discussion of character dining, see Walt Disney World with Kids (pages 201–208).

FAST FOOD IN THE THEME PARKS

Because most meals during a Disney World vacation are consumed on the run while touring, we'll tackle counter-service and vendor foods first. Plentiful in all theme parks are hot dogs, hamburgers, chicken breast sandwiches, green salads, and pizza. They're augmented by special items that relate to the park's theme or the part of the park you're touring. In Germany at Epcot, for example, counter-service bratwurst and beer are sold. In Frontierland in the Magic Kingdom, vendors sell smoked turkey legs. Counter-service prices are fairly consistent from park to park. Expect to pay the same for your coffee and hot dog at the Animal Kingdom as at Disney-MGM Studios.

The Cost of Counter-Service Food

To help you develop your dining budget, here are prices of common counter-service items. Sales tax isn't included.

Food

Barbecue Chicken Sandwich	$5.95
Barbecue Pork, Beef, or Turkey	$6.75
Brownie	$1.50
Cake or Pie	$2.25
Cheeseburger	$4.65–6.85 (double)
Chicken Breast Sandwich (grilled)	$4.55–6.50
Children's Meals	$3–4
Chips	$1.25
Cookies	$1.45
Deli Sandwich	$4.90–6.50
Fish Basket (fried)	$5.15
French Fries	$1.55
Fried Chicken Nuggets	$5.25
Fruit (whole piece)	$1
Fruit Cup/Fruit Salad	$2.10–4.85
Ham & Cheese, Turkey, or Tuna Sub	$4.65–4.90
Hot Dogs	$3.10–4.75
Ice Cream Bars	$2–2.60
Nachos with Cheese	$2.60
Pasta Salad	$1.35–5.85
Pizza (per slice)	$3.50–5.35
Pizza (individual)	$7–8.50
Popcorn	$1.90
Salad (entree)	$5.10–6.95
Salad (side)	$1.75–3.90
Smoked Turkey Leg	$4.50
Soup/Chili	$2.45–3.50
Taco	$4.45 for two tacos
Taco Salad	$4.85–6.40

The Cost of Counter-Service Food (continued)		
Drinks	**Small**	**Large**
Beer (not available in the Magic Kingdom)	$3.75	$4.25
Bottled Water	NA	$2
Cappuccino/Espresso	$2.95	
Coffee	$1.25	$1.45
Fruit Juice	$1.30–1.55	NA
Lemonade	$1.55	$2
Milk	$1	NA
Soft Drinks (Coke, etc.)	$1.75	$2.25
Tea	$1.45	NA

HEALTHFUL FOOD IN WALT DISNEY WORLD

One of the most commendable developments in food service at Walt Disney World has been the introduction of more healthful foods and snacks. Diabetics, vegetarians, weight-watchers, those requiring kosher meals, and guests on restricted diets should have no trouble finding *something* to eat. Ditto for anyone seeking wholesome, nutritious food. Healthful food is available at most fast-food counters and even from vendors. All major theme parks, for example, have fruit stands.

A Nashville, Tennessee, mom was delighted to see the changes, writing:

I was very happy to see vegetarian items on almost every menu. What a difference from a couple of years ago.

CUTTING YOUR DINING TIME AT THE THEME PARKS

Even if you confine your meals to vendor and counter-service fast food, you lose a lot of time getting food in the theme parks. At Walt Disney World, everything begins with a line and ends with a cash register. When it comes to fast food, "fast" may apply to the time you spend eating it, not the time invested in obtaining it.

A New York reader agrees, writing:

In terms of lunch, we found the lines, staff, and general service incredibly slow, unappetizing, and annoying. How is it that ski resorts throughout the country feed hordes of people at precisely the same time and offer an extensive array of quality food with a broad selection, prompt service, and quick check out? Perhaps WDW should visit Vail or Steamboat and learn a thing or two.

Here are suggestions for minimizing the time you spend hunting and gathering food:

1. Eat breakfast before arriving. Don't waste touring time eating breakfast at the parks. Besides, restaurants outside the World offer some outstanding breakfast specials. Some hotels furnish small refrigerators in their guest rooms or rent them. If you can get by on cold cereal, rolls, fruit, and juice, having a fridge in your room will save a ton of time. If you can't get a fridge, bring a cooler.

2. After a good breakfast, buy snacks from vendors in the parks as you tour, or stuff some snacks in a fanny pack. This is very important if you're on a tight schedule and can't spend a lot of time waiting in line for food.

3. All theme park restaurants are busiest between 11:30 a.m. and 2:15 p.m. for lunch and 6 and 9 p.m. for dinner. For shorter lines and faster service, avoid eating during these hours.

4. Many counter-service restaurants sell cold sandwiches. Buy a cold lunch (except for drinks) before 11 a.m. and carry it until you're ready to eat. Ditto for dinner. We met a family that routinely does this, with Mom bringing small plastic bags in which to pack the food. Drinks are purchased at the appropriate time from any convenient vendor.

5. Most fast-food eateries have more than one service window. Regardless of time of day, check the lines at all windows before queuing. Sometimes a window that's manned but out of the way will have a much shorter line or none at all. Note, however, that some windows may offer only some items. For example, some windows may serve only soup and salad, while others serve sandwiches.

6. If you're short on time and the park closes early, stay until closing and eat dinner outside Disney World before returning to your hotel. If the park stays open late, eat dinner about 4 or 4:30 p.m. at the restaurant of your choice. You should miss the last wave of lunchers and sneak in just ahead of the dinner crowd.

BEYOND COUNTER SERVICE: TIPS FOR SAVING MONEY ON FOOD

Though buying food from counter-service restaurants and vendors will save time and money (compared to full-service dining), additional strategies can bolster your budget and maintain your waistline:

1. Go to Disney World during a period of fasting and abstinence. You can save a fortune and save your soul at the same time!

2. Wear clothes that are slightly too small and make you feel like dieting (no spandex allowed!).

3. Whenever you're feeling hungry, ride the Mad Tea Party, Body Wars, or other attractions that induce motion sickness.

4. Leave your cash and credit cards at your hotel. Buy food only with money your children fish out of fountains and wishing wells.

Cost-conscious readers also have volunteered ideas for stretching food dollars. A family from Lee's Summit, Missouri, tells us:

> *Last year we requested a small refrigerator for our room and were given one for no charge. This year we were charged $5 a day for use of the fridge, but it was definitely worth it for us to be able to eat breakfast in the room to save time and money.*

A Missouri mom writes:

> *I have shared our very successful meal plan with many families. We stayed six nights and arrived at WDW after some days on the beach south of Sarasota. We shopped there and arrived with our*

steel Coleman cooler well stocked with milk and sandwich fixings. I froze a block of ice in a milk bottle, and we replenished it daily with ice from the resort ice machine. I also froze small packages of deli-type meats for later in the week. We ate cereal, milk, and fruit each morning, with boxed juices. I also had a hot pot to boil water for instant coffee, oatmeal, and soup.

Each child had a belt bag of his own, which he filled from a special box of "goodies" each day. I made a great mystery of filling that box in the weeks before the trip. Some things were actual food, like packages of crackers and cheese, packets of peanuts and raisins. Some were worthless junk, like candy and gum. They grazed from their belt bags at will throughout the day, with no interference from Mom and Dad. Each also had a small, rectangular plastic water bottle that could hang in the belt. We filled these at water fountains before getting into lines and were the envy of many.

We left the park before noon, ate sandwiches, chips, and soda in the room, and napped. We purchased our evening meal in the park, at a counter-service eatery. We budgeted for both morning and evening snacks from a vendor but often did not need them. It made the occasional treat all the more special. Our cooler had been pretty much emptied by the end of the week, but the block of ice was still there.

Note: Disney has a rule against bringing your own food and drink into the park. We interviewed one woman who ignored the rule and brought a huge picnic for her family of five packed in a large diaper/baby paraphernalia bag. She stowed the bag in a locker under the Main Street Station and retrieved it when the family was hungry. A Pennsylvania family adds:

Despite the warning against bringing food into the park, we packed a double picnic lunch in a backpack and a small shoulder bag. Even with a small discount, it cost $195 for the seven of us to tour the park for a day, and I felt that spending another $150 or so on two meals was not in the cards. We froze juice boxes to keep the meat sandwiches cool (it worked fine) and had an extra round of juice boxes and peanut butter sandwiches for a late-afternoon snack. We took raisins and a pack of fig bars for sweets, but didn't carry any other cookies or candy to avoid a "sugar-low" during the day. Fruit would have been nice, but it would have been squashed.

SUGGESTIONS FOR EATING AT THE THEME PARKS

Below are suggestions for dining at each of the major theme parks. If you are interested in trying a theme park full-service restaurant, be aware that

the restaurants continue to serve after the park's official closing time. For example, we showed up at The Hollywood Brown Derby just as Disney-MGM Studios closed at 8 p.m. We were seated almost immediately and enjoyed a leisurely dinner while the crowds cleared out. Incidentally, don't worry if you are depending on Disney transportation: buses, boats, and monorails run two to three hours after the parks close.

At the Magic Kingdom

Food at the Magic Kingdom has improved noticeably over the past several years. The Crystal Palace at the end of Main Street offers an excellent, albeit pricey, buffet, chaperoned by Disney characters, while the Liberty Tree Tavern in Liberty Square features hearty family-style dining, also with Disney characters in attendance. Even King Stefan's Restaurant, forever the butt of jokes and the poster child for everything wrong about dining at Walt Disney World, has experienced a renaissance. Reincarnated as Cinderella's Royal Table, this full-service restaurant on the second floor of the castle now delivers palatable meals in one of the World's most unique settings.

Fast food at the Magic Kingdom is, well, fast food. It's more expensive, of course, than what you would pay at McDonald's, but what do you expect? It's like dining at an airport—you're a captive audience. On the positive side, portions are large, sometimes large enough for children to share. Overall, the variety of fast food offerings provides a lot of choice, though the number of selections at any specific eatery remains quite limited. Check our mini-profiles of the park's counter-service restaurants before you queue up.

Here are dining recommendations for your day at the Magic Kingdom:

1. Take the monorail to one of the hotels for lunch. The trip over and back takes very little time, and because most guests have left the hotels for the parks, the resorts' restaurants are often uncrowded. The food is better than in the Magic Kingdom; the service is faster; the atmosphere is more relaxed; and beer, wine, and mixed drinks are available. Decent dinner buffets are served at Chef Mickey's at the Contemporary and at 1900 Park Fare at the Grand Floridian. Both feature characters; don't expect quiet dining. Commuting to the buffets is a snap by monorail. A more adult option is the family-style skillet dinner served at Whispering Canyon Cafe in the Wilderness Lodge. Lunch also is available. To reach Wilderness Lodge, take the boat from the Magic Kingdom docks.

2. If you choose to eat in the Magic Kingdom during the midday rush (11:30 a.m. to 2:15 p.m.) or the evening rush (5 to 8 p.m.), try El Pirata y el Perico in Adventureland, around the corner from Frontierland's Pecos Bill Cafe; or Aunt Polly's Dockside Inn (closes at dusk) on Tom Sawyer Island. These counter-service eateries offer passable food and usually aren't crowded. Another option is *The Diamond Horseshoe Saloon Revue,* which serves sandwiches between shows. All theme park counter-service restaurants are profiled later in this section.

3. Full-service restaurants that accept priority seating for lunch and/or dinner fill quickly. To obtain priority seating in advance, call (407) 939-3463 or hotfoot to your chosen restaurant as soon as you enter the park. Priority seating is explained and all Magic Kingdom full-service restaurants are profiled later in this section.

4. Of the park's three full-service restaurants, Liberty Tree Tavern in Liberty Square is the best. Tony's Town Square Restaurant on Main Street has a new menu and seems to be on an uptick. King Stefan's Banquet Hall in Cinderella Castle has been changed to Cinderella's Royal Table. In addition to the name change, the food has improved.

   Because children love Cinderella and everyone's curious about the inside of the castle, you need to make priority seating arrangements before you leave home if you want to eat at Cinderella's Royal Table. If you forget, and it's really, really important to eat there, hustle to the door of the restaurant as soon as you arrive at the park. Finally, if all else fails, you can see the inside of the castle (but not eat there) by just breezing in and trooping up the stairs for a quick look.

5. Arguably the best food in the park can be had at Crystal Palace character buffets. Though not inexpensive, the buffet offers an excellent selection, including a carving station and a groaning board of children's favorites.

6. A good rule at any full-service restaurant in the park is to keep it simple. Order sandwiches or basic dishes (roast turkey and mashed potatoes, for example) that are difficult to ruin.

At Epcot

From the beginning, dining has been an integral component of Epcot's basic entertainment product. The importance of dining is reflected both in the number of restaurants and their ability to serve consistently interesting and well-prepared meals. This is in stark contrast, say, to the Magic Kingdom, where, until recently, food service was seemingly a perfunctory afterthought, with quality and selection a distant runner-up to logistical efficiency.

For the most part, Epcot's restaurants have always served decent food, though the World Showcase restaurants have occasionally been timid about delivering an honest representation of the host nation's cuisine. While these eateries have struggled with authenticity and have sometimes shied away

Full-Service Restaurants in Epcot	
Future World Full-Service Restaurants	
Coral Reef	The Living Seas
The Garden Grill Restaurant	The Land
World Showcase Full-Service Restaurants	
Biergarten	Germany
Le Cellier Steakhouse	Canada
Chefs de France	France
L'Originale Alfredo di Roma Ristorante	Italy
Restaurant Akershus	Norway
Restaurant Marrakesh	Morocco
Tempura Kiku	Japan
Teppanyaki Dining Room	Japan
Nine Dragons Restaurant	China
Rose & Crown Dining Room	United Kingdom
San Angel Inn Restaurante	Mexico

from challenging the meat-and-potatoes palate of the average tourist, they are bolder now, encouraged by America's exponentially expanding appreciation of ethnic dining. True, the less adventuresome can still find sanitized and homogenized meals, but the same kitchens will serve up the real thing for anyone with a spark of curiosity and daring. You can, for example, enjoy mole (pronounced mow-lay, and not related to the tunneling yard pest) in Mexico, sushi in Japan, pickled fish in Norway, and bastila in Morocco.

Speaking of mole in Mexico, a Merrick, New York, reader offered this (and sounded disappointed):

> *They don't serve mole in Mexico. They serve a "chicken mole" dish, which means chicken in a spicy mix. It's chicken not mole. Thought you'd want to correct this.*

Our researchers find no logical correlation among price, quality, and popularity of World Showcase restaurants. We, for example, found L'Originale Alfredo di Roma Ristorante (Italy) sometimes disappointing despite the fact that it's almost always one of the first restaurants to fill its seatings.

Many Epcot restaurants are overpriced, most conspicuously Nine Dragons Restaurant (China) and the Coral Reef (The Living Seas). Representing relatively good value through the combination of ambiance and well-prepared food are Chefs de France (France), Restaurant Akershus (Norway), Biergarten (Germany), and Restaurant Marrakesh (Morocco). The Biergarten and the Marrakesh also have entertainment.

If cost is an issue, make lunch your main meal. Entrees are similar to those on the dinner menu, but prices are significantly lower.

Epcot has 13 full-service restaurants: 2 in Future World and 11 in World Showcase. With a couple of exceptions, these are among the best restaurants at Disney World, in or out of the theme parks. Profiles of Epcot full-service restaurants are presented at the end of this section.

While eating at Epcot can be a consummate hassle, an afternoon without priority seating for dinner in World Showcase is like not having a date on the day of the prom. Each pavilion has a beautifully seductive ethnic restaurant, offering the gastronomic delights of the world. To tour these exotic settings and not partake is almost beyond the limits of willpower. And although the fare in some World Showcase restaurants isn't always compelling, the overall experience is exhilarating. If you fail to dine in World Showcase, you'll miss one of Epcot's more delightful features.

If you follow one of our touring plans, you'll be near the United States (The American Adventure) pavilion at noon. We suggest, therefore, a lunch priority seating for 12:30 or 1 p.m. at nearby Germany or a lighter meal at Tempura Kiku in Japan. For dinner, we recommend priority seating at the

San Angel Inn in Mexico or Akershus in Norway. If you plan to eat dinner at the Coral Reef in Future World, wait until afterward to see the attraction.

If you want to sample the ethnic foods of World Showcase without eating in restaurants requiring priority seating, we recommend these counter-service specialties:

Norway	Kringla Bakeri og Kafé, for pastries, open-face sandwiches, and Ringnes beer (our favorite)
Germany	Sommerfest, for bratwurst and Beck's beer
Japan	Matsu No Ma Lounge, for sushi and sashimi
Japan	Yakitori House, for yakitori (meat or vegetables on skewers)
France	Boulangerie Pâtisserie, for French pastries
United Kingdom	Rose & Crown Pub, for Guinness, Harp, and Bass beers and ales

Epcot counter-service restaurants are profiled at the end of this section.

At Disney-MGM Studios

Dining at Disney-MGM Studios is more interesting than in the Magic Kingdom and less ethnic than at Epcot. Disney-MGM has four restaurants where priority seating is recommended: The Hollywood Brown Derby, 50's Prime Time Cafe, Sci-Fi Dine-In Theater Restaurant, and Mama Melrose's Ristorante Italiano. The upscale Brown Derby is by far the best restaurant at the Studios. For simple Italian food, including pizza, Mama Melrose's is fine. Just don't expect anything fancy (except the prices). At the Sci-Fi Dine-In, you eat in little cars at a simulated drive-in movie of the '50s. Though you won't find a more entertaining restaurant in Walt Disney World, the food is quite disappointing. Ditto for the 50's Prime Time Cafe, where you sit in Mom's kitchen of the '50s and scarf down pot roast while watching clips of vintage TV sitcoms. Like the Sci-Fi, the 50's Prime Time Cafe is fun, but the food is expensive and lackluster. The best way to experience either restaurant is to stop in for dessert or a drink between 2:30 and 4:30 p.m.

We receive considerable mail from readers recounting their Disney-MGM dining experiences. A man from Sumter, South Carolina, writes:

> *We had lunch at the Sci-Fi Dine-In. In the guide you gave it a terrible review, but I have always felt you guys are too hard on the Disney restaurants, so we went ahead and ate there. Well, on this one you were right on target! While the atmosphere was fun, and the clips were a hoot, the food was lousy . . . and expensive!*

A Menchanicsville, Virginia, family agreed:

> *You tried to warn us about the Sci-Fi Dine-In, but my four-year old was dying to eat there. The food was even worse than you said—and the cost! $9.50 for a hot dog and fries.*

From a Maryland reader:

> *Prime Time Cafe was a fun experience, but again, the food quality was, at best, mediocre. If my mom really did cook that way, I would have many times run away from home. Our poor reaction to the food quality pushed us quickly into the car and out of WDW. I never thought I would get down on my knees and kiss the sidewalk outside of a Perkins Pancake House.*

But a West Newton, Massachusetts, family loved the Prime Time:

> *50's Prime Time Cafe: We know you guys didn't rate it very well, but we decided to go against your recommendation and give it a shot. We're so glad we did! For the five of us (ages 16–20), this dining experience was a blast. Our waiter (and big brother for the meal), "Leroy," came and sat at our table and helped us set our places so we wouldn't get in trouble with "Mom." When one member of our party cursed "Mom" arrived to punish him, making him clear the table onto her tray, which he did shamefully. Overall, the experience was a total kick, which we talked about for the rest of the trip.*

Finally:

> *The Brown Derby was a special treat. Sitting in one of the wall booths enveloped by the wood paneling [and listening to] the piano player [in period costume] was a real experience . . . I think you should mention the Cobb salad. The lettuce was pulverized—not what I expected. I am used to having a salad with lettuce I could recognize. I would not order it again. The oyster-Brie soup, on the other hand, was fabulous! I asked for the recipe, and they very generously brought me a preprinted copy.*

Disney-MGM Studios' full-service restaurants are profiled at the end of this section.

If you arrive at Disney-MGM Studios without previously arranging priority seating for meals, do so at the the priority seating kiosk at the corner of Hollywood and Sunset boulevards or at the restaurants.

If you have no priority seating and become hungry during meal times, try the deli sandwiches at the Studio Catering Company or burgers at Rosie's.

Both are sometimes overlooked by the teeming hordes. On the park's opposite side, try Toy Story Pizza Planet.

Disney-MGM Studios counter-service restaurants are profiled at the end of this section.

At the Animal Kingdom

Because touring the Animal Kingdom takes less than a day, crowds are heaviest from 9:30 a.m. until about 3:30 p.m. Expect a mob at lunch and thinner crowds at dinner. We recommend you tour early after a good breakfast, then eat a very late lunch or graze on vendor food. If you tour later in the day, eat lunch before you arrive, then enjoy dinner in or out of the theme park.

The Animal Kingdom mostly offers counter-service fast food. Although grilled meats are available, don't expect a broad choice of exotic dishes. Most Animal Kingdom eateries serve up traditional Disney theme park fare: hot dogs, hamburgers, deli sandwiches, and the like. Even so, we found Animal Kingdom fast food to be a cut above the average Disney fare. Flame Tree Barbeque in Safari Village and Tusker House Restaurant in Harambe Village are our picks of the litter, both in terms of food quality and atmosphere. For a quiet refuge away from the crowds, you can't beat Flame Tree Barbeque's waterfront dining pavilions.

The only full-service restaurant is a Rainforest Cafe, with entrances both inside and outside the theme park (you don't have to purchase theme park admission, in other words, to eat at the restaurant). Consistent with the practice of the Rainforest Cafe at the Downtown Disney Marketplace, the Animal Kingdom branch will not accept reservations or priority seatings. Whether you arrive from inside or outside the park, you will be given a time to report for seating. If you arrive from inside the park, you can continue touring the park while waiting for your seating time.

READERS' COMMENTS ABOUT WALT DISNEY WORLD DINING

Eating is a popular topic among *Unofficial Guide* readers. In addition to participating in our annual restaurant survey, many readers share their thoughts. The following comments are representative.

This reader preferred restaurants managed by Disney to those operated by third parties, writing:

> *After a poor experience at the San Angel Inn, perhaps you could identify those restaurants not actually run by Disney in future editions of your guide. I would certainly steer clear of them.*

Interestingly, we received this request the same week:

In your next edition, please indicate which restaurants are managed by Disney so we can avoid them.

A couple from Delaware discovered a good buffet for adults at the Buena Vista Palace:

Also, one restaurant we would recommend, especially to those without kids and who are watching their money, is the Laughing Kookoobera in the Buena Vista Palace. They have great happy-hour prices and on Wednesday and Friday have a full shrimp and roast beef buffet. A great idea for those looking to save some money!

A mom from Williamsville, New York, also offers a positive report:

We sought out something better and found the lunch buffet at The Crystal Palace restaurant. For $14.95 (adult) we ate a late lunch (1:30 p.m.)—we were thankful for the many hot and cold choices, as well as salad, fresh fruit, fajitas, and dessert. I would definitely recommend this route over the hot dogs and fries fare. We were so full

Theme dining comes to Walt Disney World

that we did not eat again for the rest of the day—not even our 12-year-old who (until that point) had been requesting a meal every 2–3 hours!

A woman from Winchester, Virginia, shares this:

> *On another subject—the food. It was horrible. [Counter-]service restaurants did such a poor job on the $7 fast food entrees that we didn't want to risk spending $22 for entrees in the full-service restaurants. You are on target with your recommendation for Norway's Kringla Bakeri og Kafé. It was the only decent meal we had there. At MK the burger from Pecos Bill's was so cold that I couldn't be sure if it had been sitting for 30 minutes or 3 hours. I had already spent 30 minutes packed shoulder to shoulder waiting to get lunch so I took my chances. And even though we were there during the height of the tomato-picking season, the tomato for my burger was pink. At Epcot, the seagulls at the Cantina de San Angel are so aggressive that one landed on our table during dinner and snatched my daughter's churro right out of her basket.*

A family from Marlborough, Connecticut, however, found Disney food palatable, writing:

> *I was apprehensive about the food, [but] our experiences were very good overall at both the full-service and counter-service restaurants. Face it, you don't go to Disney for the dinner bargains.*

A Greenwood, Indiana, family agrees:

> *The food was certainly expensive, but contrary to many of the views expressed in the* Unofficial Guide, *we all thought the quality was excellent. Everything we had, from chicken strips and hot dogs in the parks to dinner at the Coral Reef, tasted great and seemed very fresh.*

A dad from Couderport, Pennsylvania, chides us:

> *You are tough on all Disney dining. . . . Everyone has to eat while there, so it benefits no one to be this critical. Lighten up a little bit and make your dining recommendations in the same spirit as the rest of the book.*

A family from Youngsville, Louisiana, got a leg up on other guests:

> *The best thing we ate were the smoked turkey legs at Magic Kingdom.*

A mom from Aberdeen, South Dakota, writes:

> *When we want great food we'll be on a different vacation. Who wants to waste fun time with the kids at a sit-down restaurant when you know the food will be mediocre anyway.*

A woman from Verona, Wisconsin, offers this:

> We think the character meals are under-rated in all guide books.
> These meals are in pleasant settings and provide an easy, efficient way
> for little kids to interact with characters while providing adults with an
> opportunity to relax. For value and good food, we especially like the
> breakfasts. Yes, they're a little pricey, but you get more than food.
> Probably our favorite is at The Garden Grill at The Land at Epcot.
> This year they even gave us souvenir hats.

A mother of one from Louisville, Kentucky, also likes the Garden Grill:

> We ate at the Garden Grill, which was one of the highlights of our
> trip! The food was excellent! The scenery was fun (due to the rotation
> of the restaurant), and my son was able to visit with Mickey, Minnie,
> and Chip 'n' Dale. You can check in at the restaurant and then ride
> rides or watch the beautiful hot air balloons and water fountain until
> it is time to eat. Families with young children should not miss this!

A mother of three from Jamaica, New York, waited 2 hours and 40 minutes for a table at the Rainforest Cafe and still had a good time:

> The Rainforest Cafe was an absolute delight. Our six-year-old sat
> right next to a gorilla that ranted every few minutes; our ten-month-
> old loved the huge fish tanks; and they loved the food. Our wait for a
> table was two hours, so we went back to the hotel and returned two
> hours later. We still had to wait 40 minutes, but it was worth it. The
> gorilla room had more of a jungle feel than the elephant room.

A Rehoboth Beach, Delaware, family suffered the same wait but was not
quite as accepting:

> We should have listened to you about the Rainforest Café . . . two
> words: GOD AWFUL! We waited 45 minutes for a table, then 40
> minutes for sandwiches that were not up to WDW standards. Then the
> nasty waiter questioned a 15% gratuity after poor service.

An Atlanta family reported:

> We had no problems making reservations way ahead of time or a
> day ahead even though we stayed outside the park.

On the topic of saving money, a woman from Seattle offered the following:

> First, for those wanting to save a few bucks (or in some cases several
> bucks) we would definitely suggest eating outside of WDW for as many
> meals as possible. To keep down our costs, we would eat a large

breakfast before leaving the hotel, have a fast-food lunch in the park, a
snack later to hold us over, and then eat a good dinner outside the park.
There are several good restaurants in the area that have excellent food
at reasonable prices, notably Cafe Tu Tu Tango and Ming [Court],
both on International Drive. We also obtained the "Entertainment
Book" for Orlando, which offers 50% off meals all over town.

Our readers have searched high and low for the best burgers at Walt
Disney World—not the counter-service, mass-produced variety, but the
hand-patted, cooked-to-order version. In a dead heat, the winners are
Beaches and Cream at the Yacht Club Resort and the Concourse Steakhouse at the Contemporary Resort. Here's a sample of what our readers
have to say, starting with a family from Tinley Park, Illinois:

We would highly recommend Beaches and Cream soda shop at the
Yacht Club. But even at this slow time of year, there was always a wait
for a table. It was without a doubt the best fast food we had in the
world. The burgers and ice cream creations were very good.

And from an Austin, Texas, dad:

If you're tired of food from under a heat lamp, take the monorail to
the Contemporary and have a cheeseburger at the Concourse
Steakhouse. I haven't had a hamburger that good in a restaurant since I
was a kid.

A mother from Knoxville, Tennessee, loved Cinderella's Royal Table,
commenting:

I love eating at [Cinderella's Royal Table]—we had dinner and breakfast
there. It is one spot in Fantasyland where you are not jostled, hurried, and
fighting for your life. We have three daughters, and Cinderella's Royal Table
is "princess paradise." We met the Fairy Godmother.

Finally, a Pennsylvania reader thinks he understands why Disney thrill
rides are so tame:

Mickey wouldn't want anyone to get sick on his rides. He wants you
to have a good enough appetite for the over-priced food, [but] I think
he wants you dizzy so the prices are a little blurry.

Counter-Service Restaurant Mini-Profiles

To help you find palatable fast-service food that suits your taste, we have
developed mini-profiles of Walt Disney World theme park counter-service
restaurants. The restaurants are listed alphabetically by theme park.

Counter-service restaurants profiled below are rated for quality and portion size (self-explanatory), as well as for value. The value rating ranges from A to F as follows:

A   =   Exceptional value, a real bargain
B   =   Good value
C   =   Fair value, you get exactly what you pay for
D   =   Somewhat overpriced
F   =   Extremely overpriced

THE MAGIC KINGDOM

Author's Favorite Counter-Service Restaurants

Aunt Polly's Dockside Inn—Frontierland
Columbia Harbour House—Liberty Square
The Diamond Horseshoe Saloon Revue—Frontierland
El Pirata y el Perico—Adventureland
The Plaza Pavilion—Tomorrowland

Aunt Polly's Dockside Inn   Frontierland, on Tom Sawyer Island

Portion: Medium
Selection: Turkey and ham sandwiches;
child's plate with chicken or peanut

QUALITY	VALUE
Good	B

butter and jelly sandwich (includes cookie and a child's beverage); and cookies, ice cream cones and floats, and apple pie.
Comments: Scenic and off the beaten path. One of our great favorites for lunch. Closes at dusk.

Casey's Corner   Main Street

Portion: Medium
Selection: Half-pound hot dogs and fries;
chips; peanuts; and brownies.

QUALITY	VALUE
Good	C

Comments: Restricted menu translates into snappy service.

Columbia Harbour House   Liberty Square

Portion: Medium

Selection: Fried fish and chicken; ham
and cheese, veggie, and tuna salad
sandwiches; child's plate with bologna

QUALITY	VALUE
Good	C

and cheese sandwich, cookie, and child's beverage; New England clam
chowder (in bread bowl) and vegetable chili; cole slaw; chips; fries;
seafood pasta salad; garden salad with chicken; and apple pie.

Comments: Tables usually available upstairs. Quickest service within
spitting distance of Fantasyland.

Cosmic Ray's Starlight Cafe   Tomorrowland

Portion: Large

Selection: Burgers (including vegetarian);
deli sandwiches; cheese steak subs;

QUALITY	VALUE
Fair	B

grilled chicken sandwiches; child's plate with corn dog-nuggets;
vegetable and cream of chicken soups; chef and chicken Caesar salads;
fries; ice cream bars; and sugar-free cheesecake.

Comments: Big place. Tables usually available. Out-of-this-world
entertainment on stage.

The Diamond Horseshoe Saloon Revue   Liberty Square

Portion: Medium to large

Selection: Ham and cheese, smoked
turkey, and roast beef sandwiches;

QUALITY	VALUE
Fair to Good	C

chicken Caesar and chef salads; child's plates with peanut butter and
jelly sandwich, chips, and a child's beverage; chips; dill pickles; ice cream
cones and floats; and hot fudge sundaes.

Comments: Combine lunch with a show. First come, first served.

El Pirata y el Perico   Adventureland

Portion: Medium

Selection: Tacos; nachos; taco salads;
quarter-pound hot dogs with chili,

QUALITY	VALUE
Good	C

cheese, and/or kraut; chili; child's plate with hot dog, cookie, and child's

beverage; and ice cream bars and churros.
Comments: Often overlooked. A good bet for lunch.

The Lunching Pad   Tomorrowland

Portion: Medium
Selection: Smoked turkey legs; Disney
    character cookies; and frozen sodas and
    juices.

QUALITY	VALUE
Good	C

Comments: Smack in the middle of Tomorrowland, The Lunching Pad is
good for a quick snack or for waiting for people on nearby rides.

Pecos Bill's Cafe   Frontierland

Portion: Medium
Selection: Double cheeseburgers; hot
    dogs; chicken wraps; chicken salad; fries

QUALITY	VALUE
Good	B

and chili cheese fries; root beer floats; brownies.
Comments: Enlarged with a new fixin's station to garnish your burger or
dog.

The Pinocchio Village Haus   Fantasyland

Portion: Medium
Selection: Burgers; double cheeseburger
    combo meal; hot dogs; chicken club
    wrap; garden salad (with or without

QUALITY	VALUE
Fair	C

chicken); child's plate with peanut butter and jelly sandwich, chips, and
a child's beverage; fruit cup; and cupcakes.
Comments: Almost always crowded. Try Columbia Harbour House on
the border with Liberty Square.

The Plaza Pavilion   Tomorrowland

Portion: Medium to large
Selection: Six-inch pizzas; pizza combo
    meal with small salad and beverage;

QUALITY	VALUE
Good	B

bread sticks; salads; deli sandwiches; chicken strips; child's plate with peanut butter and jelly sandwiches, chips, and a child's beverage; and ice cream bars.

Comments: Our pick of the Tomorrowland eateries. Try the Italian deli sandwich.

EPCOT
Author's Favorite Counter-Service Restaurants
Kringla Bakeri og Kafé Pasta Piazza Ristorante Pure and Simple Sommerfest Yakitori House

Boulangerie Pâtisserie   World Showcase, France

Portion: Small to medium

Selection: Coffee, croissants, and pastries; cheese plate; ham and cheese croissant; quiche Lorraine; and French wine and beer.

QUALITY	VALUE
Good	B

Comments: Okay for a light meal, better for a snack. No tables.

Cantina de San Angel   World Showcase, Mexico

Portion: Medium

Selection: Chips and salsa; beef and chicken hard and soft tacos; burritos; ensalada Mexicana; child's plate with burrito, chips, churro, and child's beverage; churros and flan with caramel sauce; and frozen margaritas.

QUALITY	VALUE
Fair	D

Comments: Most meals are served with refried beans and salsa. Tables are outdoors.

Electric Umbrella Restaurant   Future World, Innoventions, Plaza East

Portion: Medium

Selection: Burgers; chicken tenders with fries; chicken sandwiches; vegetable

QUALITY	VALUE
Good	B

wraps with grapes; child's plates with hot dogs or chicken tenders; hot dogs; chicken Caesar salad; fruit plate; chocolate chip cookies, chocolate cream pie, and apple pie; and Budweiser and Bud Light.

Comments: All items are served with french fries.

Kringla Bakeri og Kafé   World Showcase, Norway

Portion: Small to medium

Selection: Pastries; open-faced sandwiches (roast beef, smoked turkey, and smoked

QUALITY	VALUE
Good to Excellent	D

salmon); Norwegian cheese platter; sweet pretzels with raisins and almonds; cinnamon rolls; waffles; and Ringnes beer on tap.

Comments: Good, but pricey.

Liberty Inn   World Showcase, The American Adventure

Portion: Medium

Selection: Burgers and french fries; hot dogs; veggie wrap; chicken strips; grilled chicken sandwiches; salads; child's hot

QUALITY	VALUE
Fair	C

dog plate; fruit plate; ice cream cups and drumsticks, apple pie, chocolate chip cookies, and root beer floats; and Budweiser and Bud Light.

Comments: The only place in World Showcase for American fast food. Ample seating.

Lotus Blossom Café   World Showcase, China

Portion: Medium

Selection: Stir-fried beef, chicken, and vegetable dishes; sweet-and-sour chicken; fried-wonton basket; egg rolls; fried rice;

QUALITY	VALUE
Fair	D

egg drop soup with chicken; ginger ice cream, fruit cup with lychee, and fortune cookies; child's plate with sweet-and-sour chicken or eggroll and pork fried rice (includes beverage); and Chinese beer and wine.

Comments: Marginal Chinese at fancy prices.

Pasta Piazza Ristorante

Future World, Innoventions, Plaza West

Portion: Medium

Selection: Eggplant parmigiana; chicken parmigiana with pasta and bread sticks; Italian and meatball parmigiana subs;

QUALITY	VALUE
Good	B

personal pizza; sausage pasta; child's pasta; garden salad; bread sticks; cannoli; cake, fruit cup, and brownies; and Budweiser and Bud Light.

Comments: Healthy-choice items are available. Good people-watching.

Pure and Simple

Future World, Wonders of Life

Portion: Medium

Selection: Tuna salad pitas with chips; deli sandwiches; vegetable pizza; seasonal soups; salads; chicken-veggie

QUALITY	VALUE
Good to Excellent	B

wrap; baked potato with veggie chili; child's plate with healthy hot dog and fruit or chips; fruit cups; smoothies (natural fruit-blend drinks and papaya juice); yogurt sundaes, low-fat cheesecake and mousse, and root beer floats.

Comments: A good spot for those seeking low-fat, heart-healthy meals.

Refreshment Port

Between the World Showcase and Future World

Portion: Medium

Selection: Chicken Caesar BLT and grilled veggie wraps; hot dogs; chili; nachos; cookies, candy bars, and frozen yogurt.

QUALITY	VALUE
Good	B

Comments: A convenient place for a snack.

Rose & Crown Pub

World Showcase, United Kingdom

Portion: Medium

Selection: Cornish pasties; sausage rolls; shortbread; fruit and cheese; and

QUALITY	VALUE
Fair to Good	C

Guinness, Harp, and Bass beers and ales, as well as other spirits.

Comments: The attraction here is the pub atmosphere and the draft beer.

Sommerfest

World Showcase, Germany

Portion: Medium

Selection: Bratwurst and frankfurters with kraut; goulash; soft pretzels; apple strudel; sandwiches; and German wine and beer (Beck's).

QUALITY	VALUE
Good	B

Comments: Tucked in the entrance to the Biergarten restaurant, Sommerfest is hard to find from the street. Very limited seating.

Sunshine Season Food Fair

Future World, The Land

Portion: Medium

Selection: Potatoes stuffed with beef and chili, cheese and bacon, and sour cream

QUALITY	VALUE
Good to Excellent	B

and chives; soups and salads; barbecued chicken and ribs, and smoked sandwiches with corn on the cob, baked beans, cole slaw, and corn muffins; deli sandwiches such as Italian subs, ham, and turkey; pastas such as lasagna, tortellini, and chicken alfredo; veggie wrap; fruit and yogurt cups; brownies and cookies; ice cream and freshly baked goods; and wine by the glass, beer, and nonalcoholic beer.

Comments: This is a food court with eight different counters. Most of the counters offer adult and child combo meals, and several feature heart-healthy options. Most counters serve beverages, so you don't have to queue up twice. Very crowded at mealtimes. Tables difficult to find.

Yakitori House

World Showcase, Japan

Portion: Small to medium

Selection: Shogun combo meal with beef and chicken teriyaki and rice (adult and child versions); shrimp, chicken, and

QUALITY	VALUE
Excellent	B

beef skewers with rice; beef curry; shrimp tempura and beef udon; seafood salads; miso soup; ginger, green tea, and red bean ice cream; and Kirin beer, sake, and plum wine.

Comments: A great place for a light meal. Limited seating.

DISNEY-MGM STUDIOS

Author's Favorite Counter-Service Restaurants

ABC Commissary
Rosie's All American Cafe
Sunset Ranch
Toy Story Pizza Planet

ABC Commissary   Backlot

Portion: Medium to large
Selection: Red beans and rice; chicken
   nuggets; chicken sandwich combo;
   vegetable soup; roast beef sandwiches;

QUALITY	VALUE
Good	C

grilled cheese sandwiches; chicken wraps; quesadilla club; tomato salad;
child's chicken nugget plate; chef and pasta salads; fries; and milkshakes.
Comments: Indoors, centrally located, air-conditioned, and usually not
too crowded.

Backlot Express   Backlot

Portion: Medium to large
Selection: Burgers and french fries;
   chicken sandwiches with fruit or fries;

QUALITY	VALUE
Fair	C

chicken nuggets; chili; hot dog combos; chicken Caesar salad; tuna subs;
and churros, cookies, and brownies.
Comments: Frequently overlooked.

Catalina Eddie's   Sunset Boulevard

Portion: Medium to large
Selection: Cheese, pepperoni, and
   vegetable pizzas; side salads; and cookies
   and brownies.

QUALITY	VALUE
Good	B

Comments: Seldom crowded.

Min and Bill's Dockside Diner

Echo Lake

Portion: Medium
Selection: Shakes and beverages.
Comments: Limited outdoor seating.

QUALITY	VALUE
Fair	C

Rosie's All American Cafe

Sunset Boulevard

Portion: Large
Selection: All manner of hot dogs and
  sausages; barbecue beef sandwiches;
  cheeseburgers and veggie burgers; soup;

QUALITY	VALUE
Good	B

nachos; chili; side salads; turkey or ham subs; brownies; and cookies.
Comments: Best hot dog stand at Walt Disney World. We like it.

Starring Rolls Bakery

Sunset Boulevard

Portion: Small to medium
Selection: Pastries, pies, cookies,
  doughnuts, bagels, and rolls.

QUALITY	VALUE
Fair to Good	C

Comments: Open for breakfast on early-entry mornings.

Studio Catering Co.

Backlot

Portion: Medium
Selection: Stacked sandwiches (roast beef
  with Swiss, Italian, club, and turkey with

QUALITY	VALUE
Fair	C

cheddar); pretzels; popcorn; ice cream cones, sundaes, and ice cream bars.
Comments: Ice cream has separate service lines. Good place for a break
  while your kids enjoy the *Honey, I Shrunk the Kids* playground.

Sunset Ranch Turkey Legs

Sunset Boulevard

Portion: Medium
Selection: Smoked turkey legs, hot dogs,
  baked potatoes, pretzels, and beer.

QUALITY	VALUE
Good	B

Comments: This vendor stall serves up
  some of the tastiest fast food in the park. Often overlooked.

Toy Story Pizza Planet   Backlot

Portion: Medium
Selection: Cheese, pepperoni, and sausage
   pizzas; salads.
Comments: The place for pizza at the
   Studios. Gets good marks from readers.

QUALITY	VALUE
Good	B

THE ANIMAL KINGDOM

Author's Favorite Counter-Service Restaurants

Flame Tree Barbecue
Tusker House Restaurant

Dino Diner   Dinoland U.S.A.

Portion: Medium
Selection: Smoked turkey legs; fresh fruit;
   breakfast breads in the morning.
Comments: Often overlooked. Good for a quick snack.

QUALITY	VALUE
Good	C

Flame Tree Barbecue   Safari Village

Portion: Large
Selection: Smoked beef brisket, pork
   shoulder, and chicken breast; barbecue
   ribs; combination barbecue platters;
bread bowl salad with turkey; and child's plate with peanut butter and
jelly sandwich, chips, and cookie. Side items include baked beans, chili,
steak fries, and apple pie.
Comments: Queues very long at lunch time, but seating is ample and well
   shaded. One of our favorites for lunch.

QUALITY	VALUE
Good	C

Mr. Kamel's Burger Grill   Asia

Portion: Medium
Selection: Cheeseburgers.
Comments: Not a very good reason to
   walk to Asia.

QUALITY	VALUE
Fair	D

Pizzafari   Safari Village

Portion: Medium

Selection: Personal pizzas with cheese

QUALITY	VALUE
Good	C

only, pepperoni, or sausage, ham, pepperoni, peppers, and onions; mesquite chicken Caesar salad; Italian deli sandwiches; hot vegetable sandwich with chips; chocolate mousse cake, carrot cake, and frozen lemonade.

Comments: A favorite with children. Hectic at peak mealtimes, but the pizza is good.

Restaurantosaurus   Dinoland U.S.A.

Portion: Medium

Selection: Cheeseburgers and hot dogs;

QUALITY	VALUE
Fair to Good	D

McDonald's Chicken McNuggets and Happy Meals; mesquite-grilled chicken salad and vegetarian platter; fries, brownies, and cookies.

Comments: Picky children might enjoy Restaurantosaurus. Others will do better at another eatery.

Tamu Tamu   Africa

Portion: Large

Selection: Various flavors of yogurt or ice

QUALITY	VALUE
Good	C

cream, available in cones or as sundaes; ice cream floats; and coffee.

Comments: Seating is behind building and could easily be overlooked.

Tusker House Restaurant   Africa

Portion: Large

Selection: Half rotisserie chicken; fried

QUALITY	VALUE
Good	C

chicken dinner; beef stew in bread bowl; smoked turkey on focaccia; grilled chicken salad; roasted vegetable sandwich with tabouli; child's plate with macaroni and cheese; garlic mashed potatoes and fresh vegetables; cinnamon rolls and cookies.

Comments: Excellent selections for health-conscious diners. Salads are refreshing. Separate line for bakery items.

Full-Service Restaurants of Walt Disney World

More than five dozen full-service restaurants operate in Walt Disney World, with quality and variety of food improving every year. Unfortunately, the restaurants are generally overpriced, and Disney imposes on dining its genius for complication and regimentation. What elsewhere would be a simple dinner out is at Disney World a maze of busy phone numbers, pseudo-reservations, and waiting.

In the theme parks, variables affecting your odds of getting into a particular restaurant include its popularity and capacity, and the size of the crowd the day you visit. Each restaurant has lunch and dinner seatings. Lunch is 11 a.m. to 4 p.m. Dinner is served from 4 p.m. until one hour before the park closes.

PRIORITY SEATING

Disney ceaselessly tinkers with its restaurant reservations policy. Since 1997, reservations have been replaced with "Priority Seating." When you call, your name and essential information are taken as if you were making a reservation. The Disney representative then says you have priority seating for the restaurant on the date and time you requested and usually explains that priority seating means you will be seated ahead of walk-ins, i.e., those without priority seating.

From Disney's perspective, if restaurants don't have to hold reserved tables, they can run closer to capacity. Priority seating didn't work very well for the first year or so, but now guests are getting used to the process and things are going smoother, as our readers report:

According to this reader, priority seating posed no inconvenience:

> *You and your readers complained about priority seating for Disney restaurants. We used it twice and had no problem and saw no one else with a problem—and the parks were jammed and the restaurants busy. Both times, we were seated within five minutes of the appointed time. Disney can't control how long parties will stay at their tables after finishing their meals or reduce no-shows without charging a deposit, so I thought the priority seating system was fair to all. The reservations policy is now carefully explained by operators and signs at restaurants. Maybe priority seating was a problem at first that they've fixed by better predicting guest behavior.*

A Raleigh, North Carolina, dad chastised us for our jaundiced view of priority seating:

Your section on priority seating was misleading. You had me con-
vinced that we would waste our time. We had priority seating for lunch
at Coral Seas on Saturday. We arrived 15 minutes early and were
seated right away. We arrived 30 minutes early for lunch at Crystal
Palace on Sunday (Father's Day) to find the porch filled with customers
waiting to be seated. The kids and I sat down on the porch, my wife
checked us in, and within five minutes, we were on our way into the
dining room.

And a Roanoke, Virginia, family offers this advice:

As early as possible (months before your visit if you think about it),
make priority dining reservations for every meal, every day. Had we not
had reservations, we would have waited 60–90 minutes for every meal,
even though we were there during the "slow" time of the year. Even if
you later have to change the reservations, make them.

From an Upminster, England, man:

Whilst this system of table booking has attracted a lot of adverse
comment, we found that in most cases it worked for us. When we pre-
sented ourselves at whatever restaurant we had booked, we were seated
almost at once, or after a relatively short wait.

The same reader went on to say that being seated was sometimes an easier task than booking the priority seating in the first place:

The day we arrived at Dixie Landings just happened to be my
birthday. I had read somewhere that if you ate [at a Disney restaurant]
on your birthday you would be provided with a complimentary birth-
day cake. On our room phone, there was a button marked
"Boatwrights" [the full-service restaurant at the Dixie Landings],
which I pressed to make my [priority seating]. I had imagined that this
button would connect me directly with the restaurant, but after a
recorded message told me all about the cuisine and background of the
restaurant, I was answered by someone in a central dining reservation
office somewhere in WDW (but not at Boatwright's). Before asking
details of when I wanted to eat, I was asked where I wanted to eat. But
I had already pressed the Boatwright's button! I was then asked my sur-
name, my room number, my home address in the UK, my post code,
and my home telephone number. I was then given an explanation of
the priority seating system and was supplied with a reference number (I
never did find out what I was supposed to do with that!). All this just
to book a table!

Of course, there's an epilogue, though it has absolutely nothing to do with priority seating:

> *Anyway, I explained to the person taking my booking that it was my birthday and that I understood that I would automatically receive a birthday cake with my meal. He did not seem to have heard of this and [after consulting someone else] told me a cake was out of the question as they needed two day's notice.*
>
> *In due course, we presented ourselves at the restaurant and were made very welcome and showed to our table immediately. I just happened to mention to [our waitress] my disappointment over the birthday cake. Imagine my surprise when she appeared with a plate bearing a quite substantial birthday cake complete with lighted candle. It was a very nice sponge cake with butter icing and quite delicious. However, it did not end there. One of the waiters announced to the whole restaurant that it was my birthday and led them all in a rousing chorus of "Zipadee Doo-Dah" with special birthday lyrics, followed by a round of applause and a table visit by the manageress to offer her personal congratulations.*

Go Early, Go Late, or Be Prepared to Wait

Call (407) 939-3463 before you leave home and arrange priority seating at the restaurants of your choice. If you want to eat at a full-service restaurant during peak hours, you're much better off with a priority seating than with nothing. With priority seating, your wait almost always will be less than 30 minutes during peak hours, and often less than 15 minutes. If you just walk in, especially during busier seasons, expect to wait 40 to 75 minutes.

If you haven't arranged priority seating before you leave home:

1. If you're driving, make priority seating arrangements at Ocala Disney AAA Travel Center off I-75 in Ocala, Florida.

2. If you're lodging outside Walt Disney World or at a hotel in the Disney Village Hotel Plaza, call (407) 939-3463 for advance priority seating.

   Note: With no formal announcement, Disney dining representatives began accepting advance priority seatings from guests *not* staying in Disney hotels and campgrounds. Should this continue, it will help redress long-standing discrimination against day-guests. If the new practice is abandoned, guests lodging out of the World will have to make priority seating arrangements at the theme park on the day of the meal.

3. If you're a Disney resort guest, you'll find a button on your phone that will dial WDW-DINE directly.

4. In the theme parks, same-day priority seating can be arranged in the morning at the door of the restaurant. While the restaurants don't begin food service until 11 a.m., their front desks are staffed from park opening.

   At Epcot, arrive at the entrance, admission pass in hand, 45 minutes before the park opens. Upon admission, go quickly to the priority seating service at Guest Relations (left of the geosphere). Lunch and dinner priority seating can be made at the same time. Be ready with alternatives for both restaurants and seatings in case your first choices aren't available.

   If you don't arrive early at Epcot, you may have a long wait at Guest Relations, with no guarantee that any priority seatings will be available. On many days, World Showcase restaurants and the Coral Reef (in Future World) book solid for preferred seating within an hour to an hour and a half of the park's opening. Even if you get a seating, you'll have burned your most productive, crowd-free touring time in the process.

   At Disney-MGM Studios, a priority seating desk is operated on the corner of Hollywood and Sunset boulevards.

   Magic Kingdom restaurants have no central priority seating service. If you want same-day priority seating, go immediately to the restaurant's door after entering the park, or at a public phone dial *88 and then WDW-DINE (toll free).

   At the Animal Kingdom there is only one full-service restaurant, the Rainforest Cafe. No priority seatings are accepted.

5. If you're spontaneous and prefer to keep your schedule flexible, most full-service restaurants will take you with a minimal wait as a walk-in between 2:30 and 4:30 p.m.

BOOKING WALT DISNEY WORLD CHARACTER MEALS AND DINNER SHOWS

Priority seating is required for most character meals. Exceptions are the Crystal Palace and Liberty Tree Inn at the Magic Kingdom, which can accommodate walk-ins. Make arrangements from home as far in advance as possible. Call (407) 939-3463. Dinner shows continue to book actual reservations. Book your dinner show when you reserve your hotel room.

DRESS

Dress is informal at all theme park restaurants. While theme park attire (shorts, T-shirts, sneakers, etc.) is tolerated at hotel restaurants, you probably would feel more comfortable if you dressed up a bit. The only restaurant requesting jackets for men and dressy clothes for women is Victoria & Albert's at the Grand Floridian.

A FEW CAVEATS

Before you commence eating your way through Walt Disney World, you need to know:

1. However creative and enticing the menu descriptions, avoid fancy food, especially at full-service restaurants in the Magic Kingdom and Disney-MGM Studios. Order dishes the kitchen is unlikely to botch. An exception to this caveat is the Brown Derby Restaurant at the Studios.

2. Don't order baked, broiled, poached, or grilled seafood unless the restaurant specializes in seafood or rates at least ★★★★ on our restaurant profile.

3. Theme park restaurants rush their customers in order to make room for the next group of diners. Dining at high speed may appeal to a family with young, restless children, but for people wanting to relax, it's more like *Beat the Clock* than fine dining.

   If you want to linger over your expensive meal, *do not* order your entire dinner at once. Order drinks. Study the menu while you sip, then order appetizers. Tell the waiter you need more time to decide among entrees. Order your main course only after appetizers have been served. Dawdle over coffee and dessert.

4. If you're dining in a theme park and cost is an issue, make lunch your main meal. Entrees are similar to those on the dinner menu, but prices are significantly lower.

FULL-SERVICE DINING FOR FAMILIES WITH YOUNG CHILDREN

Disney restaurants offer an excellent (though expensive) opportunity to introduce young children to the variety and excitement of ethnic food. No matter how formal a restaurant appears, the staff is accustomed to wiggling, impatient, and often boisterous children. Chefs de France at Epcot, for example, may be the nation's only French restaurant where most patrons wear shorts and T-shirts and at least two dozen young diners are attired in basic black . . . mouse ears. Bottom line: Young children are the rule, not the exception, at Disney restaurants.

Almost all Disney restaurants offer children's menus, and all have booster seats and highchairs. They understand how tough it may be for children to sit for an extended period, and waiters will supply little ones with crackers and rolls and serve your dinner much faster than in comparable restaurants elsewhere. Letters from readers suggest that being served too quickly (not having enough time to relax) is much more common than having a long wait.

Good Walt Disney World Theme Park Restaurants for Children

In Epcot, preschoolers most enjoy the Biergarten in Germany, San Angel Inn Restaurante in Mexico, and Coral Reef in The Living Seas pavilion in Future World. The Biergarten combines a rollicking and noisy atmosphere with good basic food, including roast chicken. A German oompah band entertains. Children often have the opportunity to participate in Bavarian dancing. San Angel Inn is in the Mexican village marketplace. From the table, children can watch boats on El Río del Tiempo drift beneath a smoking volcano. With a choice of chips, tacos, and other familiar items, picky children usually have no difficulty finding something to eat. The Coral Reef, with tables beside windows looking into The Living Seas aquarium, offers a satisfying mealtime diversion for all ages. If your kids don't eat fish, Coral Reef also serves chicken.

The Biergarten and San Angel Inn offer reasonable value, plus good food. The Coral Reef is overpriced, though the food is palatable.

Cinderella's Royal Table in Cinderella Castle is the big draw in the Magic Kingdom. Interestingly, other Magic Kingdom full-service restaurants hold little appeal for children. For the best combination of food and entertainment, book a character meal at the Liberty Tree Tavern or The Crystal Palace.

At Disney-MGM Studios, all ages enjoy the atmosphere and entertainment at the Sci-Fi Dine-In Theater Restaurant and the 50's Prime Time Cafe. Unfortunately, the Sci-Fi's food is close to dismal and the Prime Time's is uneven. Eat only dessert at these restaurants.

The only full-service restaurant at the Animal Kingdom is the Rainforest Cafe, which is a great favorite of children.

DINING DISNEY STYLE (FORMERLY THE FOOD 'N FUN PLAN)

The current dining plan operates pretty much the same way as the previous iteration, only without any recreational privileges. Disney resort guests can sign up for the Dining Disney Style meal plan for the course of their stay. Cost is determined by the number of people in your party and the number of nights you stay. It's all or nothing: everyone in your group must participate for your entire length of stay. The dining plan works as follows:

For each night of your stay, you pay $55 per adult and $16 per child (ages three to nine), and Disney adds a "Bonus Credit" of $5 per adult and $2 per child. Your cost plus the Disney credit equals the amount you have in your "Food Account" to spend on meals at selected Disney restaurants during your stay.

For example, two adults and two children are staying five nights. They pay $550 for the adults (two adults × five days × $55 per adult) and $160 for the children (two children × five days × $16 per child). Their charge for participating in the dining plan is $710 ($550 + $160). Their Bonus Credits total $50 for the adults (two adults × five days × $5 Bonus Credit per adult per day) and $20 for the children (two children × five days × $2 Bonus Credit per child per day), or $70 in Bonus Credits. Add that $70 to the $710 they paid, and that's $780 in the Food Account.

Each guest signing up for the dining plan (including children) is issued a Resort Identification Card that identifies him/her as a participant. The card, when activated, also can be used as a credit card at Disney shops. If you don't want certain members of your party to have charge privileges, say so when you register for the plan.

Once guests are registered, they can commence eating their way across Walt Disney World. They can order whatever they want — appetizers, lobster, wine. When the check comes, they present their I.D. card. The meal's cost will be deducted from the balance in their food account. If, using the above example, the family begins with $780 in its account and eats a meal costing $100, including tax and gratuities, $100 will be subtracted from the account, leaving a balance of $680.

If you exceed your balance, you "will be notified immediately and given the option to pay the unpaid balance by cash or credit card or to charge it directly to your room account."

The dining plan can be used at most full-service restaurants in Disney World and at counter-service restaurants in the theme parks. Also covered are drinks in Disney World lounges and nightclubs; dinner shows, including the *Hoop-Dee-Doo Revue* and the Polynesian's luau; room service; and Disney pizza delivery at your resort, where available.

Excluded are restaurants at the Disney Village Hotel Plaza, Swan and Dolphin resorts, and Shades of Green resort. Also not covered are items from guest room mini-bars and from vendor carts.

It doesn't take a CPA to figure the plan's bottom line. From Disney's perspective, the dining plan accomplishes two things. It gets you to spend all of your food dollars at Disney restaurants. And, because you must eat all of your meals at Disney restaurants in order to get your money's worth, you will never leave Walt Disney World. Checkmate.

The plan's psychological side is less obvious. Some participants order more lavishly than they would if they were paying for one meal at a time, and they exceed their balance before their stay ends (necessitating further expenditures). Others, particularly families, draw down their account crumb by crumb, fearing they'll exceed their balance before it's time to go home. And, as it says in the fine print, "any funds remaining in the food account at the end of your stay are non-refundable." Gotcha.

With the dining plan, Disney is essentially paying you some amount in Bonus Credits to eat exclusively in Disney restaurants. By making you pay $55 per adult per day, they are trading up most guests (getting them to spend more on meals than they ordinarily would). Whether it's a good deal boils down to your alcohol consumption.

The average Disney World visitor spends most of his time in the theme parks or the water parks and eats only one full-service restaurant meal a day. Time is as valuable as money to the guest, and most meals are consumed at counter-service eateries. Even if you eat a big breakfast at your hotel and a hefty fast-food lunch at the park, your total for both meals will average about $21. Though the plan allows you to feast one day and fast the next (gobble your food account any way you want), you will have to eat an average of $39 worth each evening ($55 per day + the $5 bonus less the $21 for breakfast and lunch). That's a lot of food to put away, even at the more expensive restaurants. If, however, you throw drinks and wine into the equation, spending $39 per adult per night is no challenge at all.

If you consume a few dollars in alcoholic beverages each day, you can come out okay on the dining plan. But you must be comfortable with spending $55 a day on food and eating all your meals at Disney restaurants. If you don't drink much, you may have trouble getting your money's worth. Such a family from Dublin, Ohio, reports:

> We opted for the [dining] card with our package. We paid approximately $750 up front several weeks in advance. Our total for the week was $601 and we did every special show without skimping. The Food card was a rip-off. We recommend using American Express with 10% Disney discount for food buying.

A family from Sioux Falls, South Dakota, related their experience with the Deluxe Magic Plan, a vacation package that offers much the same benefits as the dining plan:

We used the Deluxe Magic Plan and loved [the] convenience of not being concerned by the cost of meals, recreation, etc. However, I added up our receipts when I got home, and we didn't spend what we paid for the package—it would be extremely hard to make that package save you $$!! We ate like crazy! Used boats, bikes, and Disney Institute—still didn't pay. And especially for first timers, I wouldn't recommend it because we spent a lot of time sitting in restaurants instead of touring the parks.

Finally, if you participate in the plan and lose your Resort Identification Card, report it immediately to the front desk of your Disney hotel. The lost card will be deactivated and replaced.

WALT DISNEY WORLD FULL-SERVICE RESTAURANT PROFILES*

To help you in your dining choices, we have developed profiles of full-service restaurants at Disney World. Each profile allows you to quickly check the restaurant's cuisine, location, star rating, cost range, quality rating, and value rating. *Profiles are listed alphabetically by restaurant and follow the listing by cuisine nearby.*

Star Rating   The star rating represents the entire dining experience: style, service, and ambiance, in addition to taste, presentation, and quality of food. Five stars is the highest rating and indicates that the restaurant offers the best of everything. Four-star restaurants are above average, and three-star restaurants offer good, though not necessarily memorable meals. Two-star restaurants serve mediocre fare, and one-star restaurants are below average. Our star ratings don't correspond to ratings awarded by AAA, Mobil, Zagat, or other restaurant reviewers.

Cost   The next rating tells how much a complete meal will cost. We include a main dish with vegetable or side dish, and a choice of soup or salad. Appetizers, desserts, drinks, and tips aren't included. We've rated the cost as inexpensive, moderate, or expensive.

Inexpensive	=	$12 or less per person
Moderate	=	$13–23 per person
Expensive	=	More than $23 per person

Quality Rating   If you want the best food available and cost isn't an issue, look no further than the quality rating. It's based on a scale of 0 to 100, with 100 as the best possible rating and zero (0) as the worst. The quality rating

*For additional information on Disney character dining, see pages 201–208

is based solely on preparation, presentation, taste, freshness of ingredients, and creativity of the food served. There is no consideration of price, service, or atmosphere—just the food.

Value Rating If you're looking for both quality and a good deal, check the value rating. Each ranges from A to F, as follows:

A   =   Exceptional value, a real bargain
B   =   Good value
C   =   Fair value, you get exactly what you pay for
D   =   Somewhat overpriced
F   =   Extremely overpriced

Payment We've listed the types of payment accepted at each restaurant using the following codes:

VISA   VISA
AMEX   American Express
MC   MasterCard
D   Discover
CB   Carte Blanche
DC   Diners Club

Readers' Restaurant Survey Responses For each Disney World restaurant profiled, we include the results of last year's readers' survey responses. Results are expressed as a percentage of responding readers who liked the restaurant well enough to eat there again (Thumbs Up), as opposed to the percentage of responding readers who had a bad experience and wouldn't go back (Thumbs Down). (Readers tend to be less critical than our *Unofficial Guide* restaurant reviewers.) If you would like to participate in the 2000 Walt Disney World Restaurant Survey, complete and return the restaurant survey form on the last page of this book.

Walt Disney World Restaurants by Cuisine					
Type of Restaurant	Location	Overall Rating	Price	Quality Rating	Value Rating
American					
California Grill	Contemporary	★★★★½	Expensive	96	C
Artist Point	Wilderness Lodge	★★★½	Moderate	87	C
Planet Hollywood	Pleasure Island	★★★½	Moderate	86	C

Walt Disney World Restaurants by Cuisine (continued)

Type of Restaurant	Location	Overall Rating	Price	Quality Rating	Value Rating
The Hollywood Brown Derby	Disney-MGM	★★★	Expensive	84	C
Kona Cafe	Polynesian	★★★	Moderate	84	B
Seasons Dining Room	Disney Institute	★★★	Moderate	84	C
Wild Horse Saloon	Pleasure Island	★★★	Moderate	84	C
Baskervilles	Grosvenor Resort	★★★	Moderate	82	C
Olivia's Cafe	Old Key West	★★★	Moderate	81	C
Yacht Club Galley	Yacht Club	★★★	Moderate	81	C
House of Blues	West Side	★★★	Moderate	80	C
Wolfgang Puck Cafe	West Side	★★★	Expensive	78	C
The Garden Grill Restaurant	Epcot	★★½	Moderate	79	C
Whispering Canyon Cafe	Wilderness Lodge	★★½	Moderate	79	B
Hollywood & Vine	Disney-MGM	★★½	Inexpensive	74	C
Liberty Tree Tavern	Magic Kingdom	★★½	Moderate	74	C
Boatwright's Dining Hall	Dixie Landings	★★½	Moderate	73	D
Cinderella's Royal Table	Magic Kingdom	★★½	Moderate	73	D
Rainforest Cafe	Downtown Disney/ Animal Kingdom	★★½	Moderate	73	D
ESPN Club	BoardWalk	★★	Moderate	73	C
Official All-Star Cafe	Disney's Wide World of Sports	★★	Moderate	72	C
Big River Grille & Brewing Works	BoardWalk	★★	Moderate	71	D
50's Prime Time Cafe	Disney-MGM	★★	Moderate	69	D
Grand Floridian Cafe	Grand Floridian	★★	Moderate	68	D
Pleasure Island Jazz Company	Pleasure Island	★★	Moderate	68	C
Coral Cafe	Dolphin	★★	Moderate	67	D
Gulliver's Grill at Garden Grove	Swan	★★	Expensive	67	D

Walt Disney World Restaurants by Cuisine (continued)

Type of Restaurant	Location	Overall Rating	Price	Quality Rating	Value Rating
Sci-Fi Dine-In Theater Restaurant	Disney-MGM	★★	Moderate	67	D
Buffet					
Cape May Cafe	Beach Club	★★★½	Moderate	89	B
Restaurant Akershus	Epcot	★★★½	Moderate	89	B
The Crystal Palace	Magic Kingdom	★★½	Moderate	79	C
1900 Park Fare	Grand Floridian	★★½	Moderate	79	C
Biergarten	Epcot	★★½	Moderate	75	C
Hollywood & Vine	Disney–MGM	★★½	Inexpensive	74	C
Chef Mickey's	Contemporary	★★	Moderate	67	C
Trail's End	Fort Wilderness	★★	Moderate	66	C
Chinese					
Nine Dragons Restaurant	Epcot	★★½	Expensive	74	F
Cuban					
Bongos Cuban Cafe	West Side	★★	Moderate	74	D
English					
Rose & Crown Dining Room	Epcot	★★★	Moderate	81	D
French					
Chefs de France	Epcot	★★★★	Moderate	90	C
Bistro de Paris	Epcot	★★★	Expensive	81	D
German					
Biergarten	Epcot	★★½	Moderate	75	C
Gourmet					
Victoria & Albert's	Grand Floridian	★★★★½	Expensive	96	D
Arthur's 27	Wyndham Palace	★★★★	Expensive	90	C
Italian					
Portobello Yacht Club	Pleasure Island	★★★½	Expensive	88	D

Walt Disney World Restaurants by Cuisine (continued)

Type of Restaurant	Location	Overall Rating	Price	Quality Rating	Value Rating
Palio	Swan	★★★	Expensive	81	C
Tony's Town Square Restaurant	Magic Kingdom	★★½	Moderate	78	D
Mama Melrose's Ristorante Italiano	Disney-MGM	★★½	Moderate	74	D
L'Originale Alfredo di Roma Ristorante	Epcot	★★½	Expensive	74	D
Japanese					
Kimonos	Swan	★★★★	Moderate	90	C
Teppanyaki Dining Room	Epcot	★★★½	Expensive	85	C
Tempura Kiku	Epcot	★★★	Moderate	83	C
Benihana— The Japanese Steakhouse	Hilton	★★½	Moderate	75	C
Mediterranean					
Citricos	Grand Floridian	★★★★	Expensive	91	C
Spoodles	BoardWalk	★★★½	Moderate	87	C
Mexican					
San Angel Inn Restaurante	Epcot	★★★	Expensive	84	D
Juan & Only's Bar and Jail	Dolphin	★★★	Moderate	80	B
Maya Grill	Coronado	★★	Expensive	66	D
Moroccan					
Restaurant Marrakesh	Epcot	★★★	Moderate	81	C
Norwegian					
Restaurant Akershus	Epcot	★★★½	Moderate	89	B
Polynesian					
'Ohana	Polynesian	★★★	Moderate	79	C

Walt Disney World Restaurants by Cuisine (continued)

Type of Restaurant	Location	Overall Rating	Price	Quality Rating	Value Rating
Seafood					
Flying Fish Cafe	BoardWalk	★★★★	Expensive	94	C
Fulton's Crab House	Pleasure Island	★★★½	Expensive	89	D
Narcoossee's	Grand Floridian	★★★½	Expensive	88	D
Artist Point	Wilderness Lodge	★★★½	Moderate	87	C
Cap'n Jack's Oyster Bar	Downtown Disney Marketplace	★★★	Moderate	84	D
Harry's Safari Bar and Grill	Dolphin	★★★	Expensive	81	D
Bonfamille's Cafe	Port Orleans	★★★	Moderate	80	C
Coral Reef	Epcot	★★½	Expensive	79	D
Captain's Tavern	Caribbean Beach	★★	Moderate	67	C
Finn's Grill	Hilton	★	Moderate	55	D
Steak					
Harry's Safari Bar and Grill	Dolphin	★★★	Expensive	81	D
Yachtsman Steakhouse	Yacht Club	★★★	Expensive	80	D
Concourse Steakhouse	Contemporary	★★½	Moderate	72	D
Le Cellier Steakhouse	Epcot	★★	Moderate	67	C
The Outback	Wyndham Palace	★★	Expensive	67	D

ARTHUR'S 27 ★★★★

Gourmet	Expensive	QUALITY
		87

Wyndham Palace, Disney Village	READERS' SURVEY RESPONSES:	VALUE
Hotel Plaza; (407) 827-2727	71% 👍 29% 👎	C

Customers: Hotel guests and locals
Reservations: Necessary
When to go: Sunset or during fire-
works at any of the three parks
Entree range: $25–60
Payment: VISA, MC, AMEX, DC
Service rating: ★★

Friendliness rating: ★★
Parking: Complimentary valet park-
ing
Bar: Full service
Wine selection: Excellent
Dress: Jackets preferred, tie optional
Disabled access: Yes

Dinner: Every day, 6–10 p.m.

Setting & atmosphere: From its perch on the 27th floor of the Wyndham Palace, Arthur's gives a breathtaking view of the glittering lights of the Downtown Disney Marketplace and the twirling searchlights of Pleasure Island. Diners sit at large booths, all set apart from each other with their own windows.

House specialties: Florida Gulf shrimp; herb-crusted tuna; medallions of veal; breast of duckling.

Other recommendations: Loin of lamb; salmon in strudel leaves; chilled breast of chicken Alexandra.

Entertainment & amenities: Live entertainment in lounge.

Summary & comments: The best values at this overpriced restaurant are the four-, five-, and six-course table d'hôte offerings for $54, $60, and $65. If you're not looking for a lot of food, you'll pay too much for what you get. Still, it is one of the most impressive views in the area, but only if you are facing the Disney side. Otherwise, you'll be looking at the taillights on Interstate 4 and you'll know what all the locals know: Florida is flat.

Honors & awards: DiRoNa winner.

ARTIST POINT   ★★★½

Seafood	Moderate	QUALITY
		87

Disney's Wilderness Lodge;	READERS' SURVEY RESPONSES:	VALUE
(407) 824-3200	84% 👍 16% 👎	C

Customers: Hotel guests, some locals
Priority seatings: Recommended for
  dinner and character breakfasts
When to go: Anytime
Entree range: $17–25
Payment: VISA, MC, AMEX
Service rating: ★★★★
Friendliness rating: ★★★★★

Parking: Hotel lot
Bar: Full service
Wine selection: Features selections
  from wineries in America's North-
  west
Dress: Casual
Disabled access: Yes

Breakfast: Every day, 7:30–11:30 a.m.
Dinner: Every day, 5:30–10 p.m.

Setting & atmosphere: Two-story-high paintings depicting the land-scapes of the Pacific Northwest dominate the interior walls of this casually appointed restaurant. Tall windows offer guests a view of the lake or a waterfall that flows off high rocks and past wildflowers. Huge cast-iron chandeliers hold 12 lanterns with milk-glass panes. Tables are uncovered, and each has a bust of an animal native to the Northwest engraved in it.

House specialties: Maple-glazed salmon fillet; grilled tuna loin steak; grilled halibut chop.

Other recommendations: Porterhouse steak; roasted duck chop; smoked prime rib; omelets; duck hash with egg.

Summary & comments: Unlike the other large hotels, the Wilderness Lodge's top-of-the-line restaurant is not an elegant gourmet room. Still, the beauty of the artwork and the room itself make dining here a pleasure. Breakfast is especially nice, as the landscaping can be fully appreciated in the sunlight.

BASKERVILLES ★★

American	Moderate	QUALITY
		71

Grosvenor Resort, Disney Village	READERS' SURVEY RESPONSES:	VALUE
Hotel Plaza; (407) 828-4444	59% 👍 41% 👎	C

Customers: Hotel guests
Reservations: Accepted
When to go: Anytime
Entree range: $8–25
Payment: VISA, MC, AMEX, DC, D
Service rating: ★★★

Friendliness rating: ★★
Parking: Hotel lot
Bar: Full service
Wine selection: Good
Dress: Casual
Disabled access: Yes

Breakfast: Every day, 7–11:30 a.m.
Lunch: Monday–Friday, 11:30 a.m.–1 p.m.
Dinner: Every day, 5–10 p.m.

Setting & atmosphere: This is a half-hearted attempt to create an English drawing room atmosphere. Unfortunately, it looks way too much like a cafeteria in a college dormitory.

House specialties: Prime rib; specialty buffets.

Other recommendations: Grilled grouper; stir-fried vegetables; Sherlock's breakfast.

Entertainment & amenities: Murder-mystery Saturdays where guests solve the crime (priority seatings required).

Summary & comments: Elementary fare. If you're having trouble being entertained, try the murder-mystery dinner—it might make the food a little more exciting. Otherwise, the only reason to dine here is if you're just too tired to leave the hotel or you can't get a priority seating anywhere else. Or if you really have your heart set on an average piece of prime rib.

BENIHANA—THE JAPANESE STEAKHOUSE ★★½

Japanese	Moderate	QUALITY
		75

The Hilton, Disney Village	READERS' SURVEY RESPONSES:	VALUE
Hotel Plaza; (407) 827-4865	50% 👍 50% 👎	C

Customers: Hotel guests and some
locals
Reservations: Recommended
When to go: Anytime

Entree range: $13–29
Payment: VISA, MC, AMEX, DC,
JCB, B
Service rating: ★★★★

(Benihana—The Japanese Steakhouse)

Friendliness rating: ★★★★
Parking: Hotel lot
Bar: Full service

Wine selection: Good
Dress: Casual
Disabled access: Yes

Dinner: Every day, 5:30–10:30 p.m.

Setting & atmosphere: Large tables with built-in grills are crammed into small rooms decorated with rice-paper panels and Japanese lanterns. Lighting is low and focused on the stage—the chef's grill.

House specialties: Teppanyaki service at large tables (where the chef cooks dinner in front of you). Specialties include New York steak; lobster tail; hibachi vegetables.

Other recommendations: Japanese onion soup.

Entertainment & amenities: Dinner is the show at this teppanyaki-service restaurant where the chef does a lot of noisy chopping and grilling.

Summary & comments: If you're looking for a nice, quiet dinner, be aware that diners sit at tables of eight and private conversation is almost impossible.

BIERGARTEN ★★½

German	Moderate	QUALITY
		75

Germany, World Showcase, Epcot; (407) 939-3463	READERS' SURVEY RESPONSES:		VALUE
	91% 👍	9% 👎	C

Customers: Theme park guests
Priority seatings: Recommended
When to go: After 6 p.m.
Entree range: $10.95, lunch; $15.75, dinner
Payment: VISA, MC, AMEX
Service rating: ★★★

Friendliness rating: ★★★
Parking: Epcot lot
Bar: Full service
Wine selection: German
Dress: Casual
Disabled access: Yes

Lunch: Every day, 11:30 a.m.–3:45 p.m.
Dinner: Every day, 4–8:30 p.m.

Setting & atmosphere: Now that Le Cellier has been renovated, Biergarten is the least appealing restaurant at Epcot. Although executives have been promising a makeover for at least three years, it looks as though it may

(Biergarten)

finally happen. As it stands, guests enter the restaurant through the kitchen, and instead of a traditional buffet line diners make all-you-can-eat selections from the windows of various village merchants and food shops. Guests sit at long tables in a tiered dining area that surrounds a sort of town square of a German village, with the exteriors of shops and houses as the backdrop for the bandstand and dance floor. An oompah-pah band plays on the stage and encourages diners to join them in sing-alongs and dancing. You may even find yourself swept up in a German version of a conga line.

House specialties: Even though it is all-you-can-eat, the pickings at the current buffet are rather meager. There is German potato salad; lentil salad; smallish sausages and wieners; spaetzle with gravy; and hot dogs in sauerkraut. There is also rotisserie chicken, which looks and tastes like the rotisserie chicken you would get at any other country in World Showcase—or in the world, for that matter. The buffet is set up on wooden barrels, and the food is served from vats, which is about as appealing as it sounds.

Other recommendations: Bratwurst; beer.

Entertainment & amenities: Oompah-pah band and German dancers perform after 12:30 p.m.

Summary & comments: This is not the greatest food at Epcot, and even the service, which for a serve-yourself buffet is already minimal, doesn't meet usual Disney standards. Go if you can't get enough of polka music. Be aware that you may find yourself seated with other guests.

BIG RIVER GRILLE & BREWING WORKS ★★

American	Moderate	QUALITY 71
Disney's BoardWalk; (407) 560-0253	READERS' SURVEY RESPONSES: 82% 👍 18% 👎	VALUE D

Customers: Tourists
Priority seatings: Not accepted
When to go: Anytime
Entree range: $6.95–18
Payment: VISA, MC, AMEX
Service rating: ★★
Friendliness rating: ★★★

Parking: BoardWalk lot. Note: Valet parking is free before 5 p.m., $6 after (for nonresort guests only).
Bar: Full service
Wine selection: Minimal
Dress: Casual
Disabled access: Good

(Big River Grille & Brewing Works)

Lunch & dinner: Every day, 11:30 a.m.–11:30 p.m.

Setting & atmosphere: Industrial cubist murals of factories, machinist-metal and wood chairs and tables, and a midnight-blue neon river that flows along the ceiling of the restaurant set a working-class atmosphere. The place is small—it seems like the huge copper brewing tanks take up more room than what is allotted to the diners.

House specialties: Breast of chicken sautéed with shiitake mushrooms; pan-seared salmon fillet with citrus salsa; peppercorn pork loin with gorgonzola; babyback ribs.

Summary & comments: Big River is out-sourced to a Tennessee company and is the first brewpub at Walt Disney World. The Brewing Works brews four regular beers and one or two specialty ales. If you're a beer drinker and like trying something new, you should like this. If you're a beer drinker and have a craving for your favorite brew, you're out of luck—the hand-crafted beers are the only beers sold here. The food is okay, though nothing special. It's another good late-night choice. There is outside seating and service, weather permitting.

BISTRO DE PARIS ★★★

French	Expensive		QUALITY
			81

France, World Showcase, Epcot; (407) 939-3463	READERS' SURVEY RESPONSES:		VALUE
	87% 👍	13% 👎	D

Customers: Theme park guests
Priority seatings: Recommended
When to go: Late dinner
Entree range: $24–32
Payment: AMEX, MC, VISA
Service rating: ★★★
Friendliness rating: ★★★★
Parking: Epcot lot or BoardWalk lot

and enter through back gate
Bar: Full service
Wine selection: Good but pricey; several by the glass
Dress: Casual
Disabled access: Elevator to second level

Dinner: Every day, 6–8:45 p.m.

Setting & atmosphere: Although the space was supposed to be completely renovated, it's pretty much the same as it has always been with, perhaps, a new coat of paint. That paint is yellow and is a bright contrast

(Bistro de Paris)

against the oxblood color of the leather banquettes. The bistro is on the second level of the France pavilion. A few windows look out over the World Showcase lagoon (good for watching *IllumiNations* if you can snag one of those tables), but otherwise there isn't a whole lot to look at here.

House specialties: Lobster fricassee in Sauterne wine with pink peppercorn sauce; baked red snapper with potato crust; double-cut veal chop with roasted garlic cloves; free-range capon with creamy port sauce.

Summary & comments: The France pavilion used to hold three separate restaurants, which were supposed to be combined into one when the main restaurant—Chefs de France downstairs—was redone last year. But Disney's culinary officials decided to keep Bistro de Paris separate. The menu is different, and the Bistro has its own kitchen upstairs. The food can be good, but the real focus of the staff here seems to be the restaurant downstairs.

BOATWRIGHT'S DINING HALL ★★½

American/Cajun	Moderate	QUALITY
		73

Disney's Dixie Landings Resort; (407) 934-6000	READERS' SURVEY RESPONSES:		VALUE
	78% 👍	22% 👎	D

Customers: Hotel guests
Priority seatings: Recommended for dinner
When to go: Early evening
Entree range: $9.95–17.95
Payment: VISA, MC, AMEX
Service rating: ★★

Friendliness rating: ★★★★
Parking: Hotel lot
Bar: Full service
Wine selection: Fair; the beer selection is better.
Dress: Casual
Disabled access: Good

Breakfast: Every day, 7–11:30 a.m.
Dinner: Every day, 5–10 p.m.

Setting & atmosphere: Diners sit in a large, noisy room under the skeleton of a riverboat under construction that looks sort of like the carcass of a mastodon. Tables are set with a boatwright's tool kit that contains condiments instead of tools. The real tools—the two-handed saws, hatchets, chisels, and a few that are too foreign to identify—hang along the walls.

House specialties: Cajun étouffée; seafood jambalaya; steak; prime rib.

Other recommendations: Pirogue of pasta and seafood (*pirogue* means

(Boatwright's Dining Hall)

boat); bayou bouillabaisse with shrimp, mussels, crawfish, catfish fillets, blue crab, and chunks of new potatoes; grilled catfish served with a Cajun butter sauce.

Summary & comments: Servers can get a little caught up in the theme, a working riverboat-building operation, and forget the basics of good service. Long waits gain no apologies. Fans of true Cajun food may be disappointed with this version, which has been toned down to please the masses. There is, however, a fine selection of regional beers, including Dixie Beer, Blackened Voodoo Lager, and Abita Beer. You'll have a chance to decide which is your favorite while you're waiting for your table.

BONFAMILLE'S CAFE ★★★

Seafood	Moderate	QUALITY
		80

Disney's Port Orleans Resort; (407) 934-5000	READERS' SURVEY RESPONSES:		VALUE
	83% 👍	17% 👎	C

Customers: Hotel guests	Friendliness rating: ★★★★
Priority seatings: Accepted	Parking: Hotel lot
When to go: Anytime	Bar: Full service
Entree range: $5.95–23.95	Wine selection: Fair
Payment: VISA, MC, AMEX	Dress: Casual
Service rating: ★★★★	Disabled access: Yes

Breakfast: Every day, 7–11:30 a.m.
Dinner: Every day, 5–10 p.m.

Setting & atmosphere: A casual setting that recalls New Orleans' French Quarter, only cleaner. Paddle fans and exposed bricks set the mood for this family-oriented restaurant.

House specialties: Limited Creole recipes featuring shrimp, oysters, and crawfish; jambalaya, chicken, and andouille sausage Creole in tomato sauce with onions and green peppers; blackened sea scallops.

Other recommendations: T-bone steak maître d'; roast prime rib of beef; center-cut pork chops; seafood kebab.

Summary & comments: The Creole creations aren't very authentic, and most of the food is pretty tame. Even the andouille sausage, which should have some fire in it, just tastes like Polish sausage. The bayou crawfish pasta appetizer, though, is pretty tasty and at $4.95 is a real bargain. It is also

(Bonfamille's Cafe)

available as an entree for $10.95, but the appetizer portion, along with a soup or salad, is plenty. The name Bonfamille means "good family," and the prices are fair enough for a family to eat pretty well. Don't expect anything out of the ordinary.

BONGOS CUBAN CAFE		★★

Cuban	Moderate	QUALITY
		74

Downtown Disney West Side; (407) 828-0999	READERS' SURVEY RESPONSES:		VALUE
	76% 👍	24% 👎	D

Customers: Gloria Estefan fans; Disney guests
Reservations: Accepted Monday–Thursday for parties of 15 or more
When to go: Anytime
Entree range: $8.95–25.95
Payment: VISA, MC, AMEX, DC, D

Service rating: ★★★
Friendliness rating: ★★★
Parking: Downtown Disney lot; valet parking available
Bar: Full service
Wine selection: Moderate
Dress: Casual
Disabled access: Elevator to second level

Lunch & dinner: Every day, 11 a.m.–midnight

Setting & atmosphere: This multilevel restaurant features an open, airy environment with a tropical theme built around a three-story pineapple. Other tropical touches include a banana leaf roof, banana leaf ceiling fans, and palm tree–shaped columns. You'll expect Carmen Miranda to dance through the door any minute. Hand-painted murals and mosaics lend an artistic air. A wrap-around, open porch provides a pleasant atmosphere for outdoor dining.

House specialties: Arroz con pollo (chicken with rice); camerones al ajillo (shrimp in garlic sauce); ropa vieja (shredded beef in tomato sauce); churrasco (grilled skirt steak).

Entertainment & amenities: Latin music.

Summary & comments: Miami resident and Latin singer Gloria Estefan and her husband-producer, Emilio, created this large restaurant that marries salsa music with Cuban cuisine, the adopted cuisine of Florida. There are any number of mom-and-pop Cuban restaurants in the area (not that the Estefans aren't mom-and-pop) that do a better and more consistent job with this wonderful cuisine. If you've never had Cuban food, try it somewhere else. Come here to have a drink with an umbrella in it and listen to music. Expect an upbeat but noisy dining experience.

CALIFORNIA GRILL ★★★★½

American	Expensive	QUALITY
		96

Disney's Contemporary Resort; (407) 939-3463	READERS' SURVEY RESPONSES:		VALUE
	83% 👍	17% 👎	C

Customers: Locals and hotel guests
Priority seatings: Recommended
When to go: During evening fireworks
Entree range: $16.75–28.75
Payment: AMEX, MC, VISA
Service rating: ★★★★

Friendliness rating: ★★★★
Parking: Complimentary valet
Bar: Full service
Wine selection: California wines
Dress: Casual
Disabled access: Yes

Dinner: Every day, 5:30–10 p.m.
Lounge: Every day, noon to midnight

Setting & atmosphere: From the 15th floor of the Contemporary Resort, California Grill commands one of the most impressive panoramas in central Florida. The dining room is inspired by Wolfgang Puck's Spago restaurant and the Rainbow Room in New York. A show kitchen where the chefs prepare all the food is the centerpiece of the dining room.

House specialties: The catchphrase for the menu is "market inspired," which means the menu changes regularly to take advantage of the freshest produce and available meats and fish. The menu is creative, with Pacific Rim accents. The pork tenderloin is quickly becoming a house favorite and is likely to be kept on most menu rotations.

Other recommendations: Spicy rock shrimp and lemongrass soup, similar to the Thai tom ka gai; goat-cheese ravioli; California designer pizzas; pan-seared tuna; chocolate quake dessert.

Entertainment & amenities: The lights are dimmed during the Magic Kingdom fireworks, and the accompanying music is piped in. You can also step outside onto the 15th floor deck for a closer look. Other entertainment includes watching the chefs; instead of begging for a window seat, sit at the counter. The chefs love to slip samples to the people sitting there.

Summary & comments: This restaurant was designed to be adult oriented and medium priced. It is operated under a recent policy that allows the chef and manager to run the restaurant as if it were their own. The result is a classy, well-operated restaurant that is attracting even Disney-reluctant locals. It is considered one of the best restaurants in central Florida.

CAPE MAY CAFE   ★★★½

Buffet	Moderate	QUALITY
		89

Disney's Beach Club Resort;	READERS' SURVEY RESPONSES:	VALUE
(407) 934-3358	86% 👍 14% 👎	C

Customers: Theme park and hotel guests
Priority seatings: Accepted and recommended
When to go: Anytime
Entree range: Breakfast: $14.95 adults, $8.50 children; dinner: $19.95 adults, $9.50 children

Payment: VISA, MC, AMEX
Service rating: ★★★★
Friendliness rating: ★★★★
Parking: Hotel lot
Bar: Full service
Wine selection: Limited
Dress: Casual
Disabled access: Yes

Breakfast: Every day, 7:30–11 a.m.
Dinner: Every day, 5:30–9:30 p.m.

Setting & atmosphere: The natural-finish wood furniture and padded booths are in a clean, nautical New England style—bright, airy, and informal.

House specialties: The buffet features peel-and-eat shrimp, tasty (albeit chewy) clams; mussels; baked fish; barbecued ribs; corn-on-the-cob; Caesar salad; and a good dessert bar.

Other recommendations: Lobster can be ordered as a supplement to the buffet.

Summary & comments: This buffet consistently serves some of the best food available at Walt Disney World. While the restaurant is large and tables turn over rapidly, priority seatings are recommended. Because the Cape May is within easy walking distance of the World Showcase entrance to Epcot, it is a perfect and affordable place to dine before *IllumiNations*.

CAP'N JACK'S OYSTER BAR ★★★

Seafood	Moderate	QUALITY
		84

Downtown Disney Marketplace; (407) 828-3971	READERS' SURVEY RESPONSES:		VALUE
	65% 👍	35% 👎	D

Customers: Tourists	Friendliness rating: ★★★★
Priority seatings: Not accepted	Parking: Marketplace lot
When to go: Anytime	Bar: Full service
Entree range: $14.95–33.95	Wine selection: Not a specialty
Payment: VISA, MC, AMEX	Dress: Casual
Service rating: ★★★★	Disabled access: Yes

Lunch & dinner: Every day, 11:30 a.m.–10:30 p.m.

Setting & atmosphere: An upscale pierhouse on the edge of the Buena Vista Lagoon.

House specialties: Cap'n Jack's has a limited menu, but what it does it does well. New England clam chowder; spicy conch chowder with tomatoes, carrots, and onions; crabcakes made with lump crabmeat and onions; peel-and-eat shrimp; and steamed and baked oysters and clams. You can also get a fresh-fish dinner—usually mahimahi, tuna, or grouper—at a fair price and a stuffed Maine lobster that is more than twice the cost of anything else on the menu, but stick with the oyster-bar items.

Entertainment & amenities: The lagoonside setting offers views of amateur boaters, and sunsets are pretty here.

Summary & comments: Most entrees are under $10—only the stuffed lobster climbs higher. But this is really a place for some shrimp or steamed clams and cold beer.

CAPTAIN'S TAVERN ★★

Seafood	Moderate	QUALITY
		67

Disney's Caribbean Beach Resort; (407) 939-3463	READERS' SURVEY RESPONSES:		VALUE
	69% 👍	31% 👎	C

Customers: Resort guests	Friendliness rating: ★★★
Priority seatings: Recommended	Parking: Resort lot
When to go: Anytime	Bar: Full service
Entree range: $11.95–15.95	Wine selection: Fair
Payment: VISA, AMEX, DC	Dress: Casual
Service rating: ★★★	Disabled access: Yes

(Captain's Tavern)

Dinner: Every day, 5–10 p.m.

Setting & atmosphere: A dark area across from the resort's food court outlets. It is nautical to the nth degree, with lots of dark woods, slatted blinds, and ship's wheel chandeliers. This is a restaurant that was never supposed to be, and to prove it there is no kitchen. The food court was supposed to meet all the resort's culinary needs, but management discovered that people wanted to be waited on after a long day in the parks. So the food court's eating area was converted to a restaurant, and servers schlep the trays across the hall from the food court's kitchens.

House specialties: Lightly blackened scallops with fresh herbs and Parmesan cheese; paella (chicken, shrimp, mussels, and sausage in rice); lightly breaded and baked chicken with a salsa of fruit and vegetables. Captain Morgan's rib eye, flavored with brown sugar; tropical pork chop; fresh catch of the day prepared with island spices and lime zest.

Summary & comments: The restaurant that wasn't supposed to be should probably cease to be. The limitations of the kitchen—or lack of a proper kitchen—show in the quality of the food. A cheddar soup served out of a dining room–based pot is a perfect example of what is wrong here. Guests who are too tired to wait in line at the food court should take a nap and then drive to another area restaurant. Guests not staying at the Caribbean Beach Resort may be hassled by the guards at the front gate (they don't believe anyone not staying at the resort would want to come in just to eat).

LE CELLIER STEAKHOUSE ★★

Steak	Moderate	QUALITY
		67

Canada, World Showcase, Epcot; (407) 939-3463	READERS' SURVEY RESPONSES:		VALUE
	86% 👍	14% 👎	C

Customers: Theme park guests	Parking: Epcot lot
Priority seatings: Recommended	Bar: Beer and wine only
When to go: Before 6 p.m.	Wine selection: Canadian wines are
Entree range: $11.50–21.95	featured
Payment: VISA, MC, AMEX	Dress: Casual
Service rating: ★★★	Disabled access: Yes
Friendliness rating: ★★★★	

Lunch: Every day, from noon–3 p.m.
Dinner: Everyday, from 4:30 p.m. until park closes

(Le Cellier Steakhouse)

Setting & atmosphere: Long chided as the worst dining room on Walt Disney World property, this dank space was given a makeover last year and is now, well, still the worst dining space on property. But it's not quite as depressing as it used to be. The space is more like a wine cellar now than the dungeon it was previously. Wine racks are easily visible with the bright chandeliers and wall sconces with fat candle lamps. There are no windows to the World here, but many guests say they like the sensory deprivation this basement provides.

House specialties: Meat.

Other recommendations: Roast turkey breast; Canadian cheddar cheese soup (a lot like Wisconsin cheese soup); smoked beef brisket; chicken and meatball stew.

Summary & comments: A steakhouse had been absent from the theme parks until the folks from Canada decided to try their hand. Previously a cafeteria-style restaurant, Le Cellier is now full-service with a modest menu of steaks and prime rib. When you really get down to it, steaks are the only Canadian food anyway, the penne pasta Vancouver notwithstanding. While the cuisine change is a vast improvement, this is still one of the least impressive restaurants in World Showcase.

CHEF MICKEY'S			★★
American/Buffet	Moderate	QUALITY	
		67	
Disney's Contemporary Resort;	READERS' SURVEY RESPONSES:		VALUE
(407) 939-3463	90% 👍	10% 👎	C

Customers: Theme park guests
Priority seatings: Recommended
When to go: Early evening
Entree range: Breakfast: $14.95
   adults, $7.95 children; dinner:
   $19.95 adults, $8.95 children
Payment: VISA, MC, AMEX

Service rating: ★★★
Friendliness rating: ★★★★
Parking: Resort valet or lot
Bar: Full service
Wine selection: Good
Dress: Casual
Disabled access: Yes

Breakfast: Every day, 7–11:30 a.m.
Dinner: Every day, 5–9:30 p.m.

Setting & atmosphere: A futuristic buffet that resembles Disney's idea of how the Jetsons would dine—colorful seatbacks and padded booths,

(Chef Mickey's)

geometric grids, flowing curves, and a buffet line that circles the center of the room. It is a noisy and bustling place, especially when Goofy, Minnie, and Mickey step out of the kitchen to say hello and dance with the diners.

House specialties: Breakfast: Cooked-to-order pancakes; French toast; biscuits and gravy. **Dinner:** Peel-and-eat shrimp; oven-roasted prime rib.

Other recommendations: Fresh greens and mixed salads; pasta selections; mashed potatoes and gravy.

Entertainment & amenities: Character visits.

Summary & comments: Mickey moved his pots and pans from his Village location to make room for the new Rainforest Cafe. In the process he changed the concept from a full-service restaurant to an all-you-can-eat buffet—something Disney is emphasizing currently. The "state-of-the-art" buffet does not use chafing dishes but places the food in casseroles and platters on special heated countertops. However, that doesn't make much difference in the quality. You've still got buffet food, chafing dishes or not, and it just isn't the same as something cooked fresh.

CHEFS DE FRANCE ★★★★

French	Moderate		QUALITY
			90

France, World Showcase, Epcot	READERS' SURVEY RESPONSES:		VALUE
(407) 939-3463	87% 👍	13% 👎	C

Customers: Theme park guests
Priority seatings: Recommended
When to go: Anytime
Entree range: $8.95–15.75, lunch;
$16.75–24.95, dinner
Payment: VISA, MC, AMEX
Service rating: ★★★★

Friendliness rating: ★★★★
Parking: Epcot lot
Bar: Full service
Wine selection: Very good
Dress: Casual
Disabled access: Yes

Lunch: Every day, noon–3 p.m.
Dinner: Every day, 5 p.m. until park closes

Setting & atmosphere: The smell of buttery croissants is as much a part of the decor here as the carefully placed copies of *Le Monde* and the huge mottled mirrors. White tablecloths and padded banquettes accentuate the classic bistro decor of the main dining room. Another room sits off to the

(Chefs de France)

side, this one a more casual sunroom with a better view of what's going on outside, but you're there for the illusion—insist on a seat in the main room. A recent renovation has enclosed the former sidewalk cafe and included that space in the main room. It is brighter than before to reflect a more authentic bistro atmosphere. The second level (the former Bistro de Paris) remains unchanged. Downstairs is a better place to sit.

House specialties: Chefs de France features some of the dishes served at the real restaurants of the three chefs for whom this restaurant is named: Paul Bocuse, Roger Verge, and Gaston LeNotre. You may sample Verge's brochette of prawns from Moulin de Mougins, LeNotre's fillet of orange roughy in a hazlenut butter from Pre Catelan, or Bocuse's beef braised in burgundy wine from his Lyon restaurant.

Other recommendations: Grilled snapper on artichoke and fennel, estouffade de boeuf, pot-au-feu.

Summary & comments: Here is your chance to eat in a restaurant supervised by three of France's best chefs. Paul Bocuse, Roger Verge, and Gaston LeNotre take turns visiting from France and supervising the staff in the preparation of their creations, so you just might get a chance to meet a culinary legend. But don't expect them to actually prepare your meal. And don't think what you're served here is even close to what you'd get at one of their hometown restaurants. In the past, most of the food coming out of the kitchen was cooked elsewhere in Disney's commissary and warmed here. The recent renovation installed an impressive kitchen (perhaps the best cooking facility of any Disney restaurant) that allows more à la minute preparations from executive chef Bruno Vrignon. Many of the same entrees are available at lunchtime for a reduced price (and smaller portion).

CINDERELLA'S ROYAL TABLE		★★½

American	Moderate	QUALITY
		73

Cinderella Castle, Fantasyland,	READERS' SURVEY RESPONSES:	VALUE
Magic Kingdom; (407) 939-3463	74% 👍 26% 👎	D

Customers: Theme park guests
Priority seatings: Required
When to go: Early
Entree range: $10.95–16.95 (adults, lunch); $4.75 (children, lunch and dinner); $20.95–27.50 (adults, dinner)
Payment: VISA, MC, AMEX
Service rating: ★★★
Friendliness rating: ★★★

(Cinderella's Royal Table)

Parking: Magic Kingdom lot
Bar: None
Wine selection: None

Dress: Casual
Disabled access: Limited

Lunch: Every day, 11:30 a.m.–2:45 p.m.

Dinner: Every day, 4 p.m. until park closes

Setting & atmosphere: A medieval banquet hall, appointed with the requisite banners and Round Table–like regalia, located on the second floor of Cinderella Castle. Windows look out over the park.

House specialties: Prime rib; steak; seafood.

Other recommendations: Caesar salad; beef barley soup; grilled swordfish with smoked pepper butter and sautéed beans; sea scallops, shrimp, fish, and vegetables sautéed in white wine and tossed with pasta.

Entertainment & amenities: Cinderella makes appearances.

Summary & comments: Formerly known as King Stefan's Banquet Hall and long the butt of jokes and unkind remarks from Disney workers and locals, Cinderella's has come a long way in improving the quality of the food. Preparations are more exact, and presentation is pleasing. The grilled swordfish is as good as any you'll find at other Disney seafood restaurants. This is the fanciest full service restaurant in the Magic Kingdom—and the priciest. With the name change Disney officials no longer have to try to explain why Sleeping Beauty's father King Stefan had a restaurant in Cinderella's castle.

CITRICOS ★★★★

Mediterranean	Expensive	QUALITY
		91

Disney's Grand Floridian Resort;	READERS' SURVEY RESPONSES:		VALUE
(407) 824-2496	63% 👍	37% 👎	C

Customers: Hotel guests and locals
Priority seatings: Required
When to go: Anytime
Entree range: $19–36
Payment: VISA, MC, AMEX
Service rating: ★★★★
Friendliness rating: ★★★★

Parking: Valet; self-parking is deceptively far away.
Bar: Full service
Wine selection: Very good
Dress: Casually dressy
Disabled access: Good

(Citricos)

Dinner: Every day, 5:30–10 p.m.; lounge open until 11 p.m.

Setting & atmosphere: This is another interior design by Martin Dorf, who also did the stylish California Grill and Flying Fish Cafe. Like those upscale restaurants, Citricos features a show kitchen. Autumnal colors in the carpeting are complemented by lemon, lime, and orange wall tiles (the restaurant name is Spanish for citrus). White tablecloths and napkins embroidered with the restaurant's name add an elegant touch.

House specialties: Originally the menu was to feature a plethora of citrus-based items, but the new chef, Roland Muller, wisely saw that as a one-note clunker. You may still find a citrus soufflé for dessert (and it's worth looking for), but the main fare features such nonlemons as braised veal shank with orzo, lamb rack with lobster ratatouille, and roasted sea bass in potato crust.

Other recommendations: Grilled foie gras; oyster and bay scallop risotto; grilled tiger shrimp with sweet potato puree.

Summary & comments: Citricos isn't quite as good as California Grill and Flying Fish Cafe, which it tries to emulate in feel and substance, but it's quite good in its own right. Although it doesn't quite live up to its original mission statement—to provide a Florida dining experience by using native citrus—it does a good job with the Mediterranean fare. If you really want something citrusy, order one of the citrus-infused martinis.

CONCOURSE STEAKHOUSE		★★½
Steak	Moderate	QUALITY 72
Disney's Contemporary Resort; (407) 939-3463	READERS' SURVEY RESPONSES: 80% 👍 20% 👎	VALUE D

Customers: Hotel guests	**Friendliness rating:** ★★★
Priority seatings: Recommended	**Parking:** Hotel lot
When to go: Anytime	**Bar:** Full service
Entree range: $6.50–27.95	**Wine selection:** Limited
Payment: VISA, MC, AMEX	**Dress:** Casual
Service rating: ★★★	**Disabled access:** Yes

Breakfast: Every day, 7:30–11 a.m.

Lunch: Every day, noon–2:30 p.m.

(Concourse Steakhouse)

Dinner: Every day, 5:30–10 p.m.

Setting & atmosphere: The decor is a cross between art deco and *2001: A Space Odyssey*. Large booths sit in the "open air" of the Contemporary's Concourse, with the monorails gliding by overhead on either side.

House specialties: Although the name says steaks, sandwiches, burgers, pizzas, and pasta dishes are also available.

Other recommendations: Besides red meat, roasted double breast of chicken; grilled chicken kebabs; grilled shrimp tossed with pasta, garlic, and fresh herbs; roasted salmon coated with maple syrup and black peppercorns; and Caesar salad are also offered.

Summary & comments: After a poor start over a year ago, the Concourse Steakhouse has done some fine-tuning in service and food preparation. There is still a big gap between quality and value and better restaurants are a short monorail ride away, but this steakhouse is acceptable in a pinch. If there is a wait you will be given a beeper, which reaches as far as the gift shop but not much farther.

CORAL CAFE ★★

American	Moderate		QUALITY 67
Walt Disney World Dolphin; (407) 934-4000	**READERS' SURVEY RESPONSES:** 61% 👍 39% 👎		VALUE D

Customers: Hotel guests who can't get into any other restaurants
Priority seatings: Not accepted
When to go: Anytime
Entree range: $10.95–20.95
Payment: VISA, MC, AMEX, D
Service rating: ★★

Friendliness rating: ★★
Parking: Hotel lot
Bar: Full service
Wine selection: Modest
Dress: Casual
Disabled access: Good

Lunch: Every day, 11 a.m.–3 p.m.
Dinner: Every day, 5–11 p.m.

Setting & atmosphere: The public relations people would like you to think you're dining in an atmosphere akin to a coral reef, but you're actually in a spot that looks like it never should have been a restaurant. It almost looks like someone said, "Hey, we could put some tables in here and sell food," which would be fine if the food were better.

(Coral Cafe)

House specialties: Either an all-you-can-stand buffet or an à la carte menu that changes seasonally. The fare looks interesting enough, with such things as duck in plum sauce or chicken with rigatoni. The kitchen just can't seem to pull it off.

Summary & comments: Ever since the hotel's star restaurant, Sum Chows, closed, the Dolphin has been lacking a main dining room. This doesn't even come close to filling that space. In fact, this restaurant would be a lot better as an open space for people to sit and plan where they can go for a real meal.

CORAL REEF		★★½

Seafood	Expensive	QUALITY
		79

The Living Seas, Future World, Epcot; (407) 939-3463	READERS' SURVEY RESPONSES:		VALUE
	77% 👍	23% 👎	D

Customers: Theme park guests
Priority seatings: Recommended
When to go: Lunch
Entree range: $12.95–18.95 lunch; $16.50–35.50 dinner
Payment: AMEX, MC, VISA
Service rating: ★★★

Friendliness rating: ★★★
Parking: Epcot lot
Bar: Full service
Wine selection: Good
Dress: Casual
Disabled access: Good

Lunch: Every day, 11:30 a.m.–3 p.m.
Dinner: Every day, 4:30 p.m. until park closes

Setting & atmosphere: Coral Reef has always offered one of the best views anywhere—below the water level of the humongous saltwater tank in The Living Seas pavilion. Sharks, rays, and even humans swim by, and every table has a great view. Even with the main focus of the room outside the room, Disney renovated the place in 1998. Seating still features tiers that afford perfect views, but now special lighting fixtures throw ripple patterns on the ceiling that make diners feel as though they're under water.

House specialties: Wood-fired grouper with spicy bean-and-herbed rice; whole roasted snapper with fennel; prosciutto-wrapped halibut; charred salmon.

Summary & comments: With the new dining room came a new chef and a new menu. Unfortunately this once fine restaurant is now sub par. The portions are small, the preparation is spotty, and the prices are perfectly

(Coral Reef)

ridiculous. You can get a better view of the aquarium from inside the pavilion, but if you really must have the experience of dining under the sea, go for lunch. The prices are a tad more reasonable.

THE CRYSTAL PALACE		★★½

American/Buffet	Moderate	QUALITY 79

Main Street, U.S.A., Magic Kingdom; (407) 939-3463	READERS' SURVEY RESPONSES: 90% 👍 10% 👎	VALUE C

Customers: Magic Kingdom guests
Priority seatings: Recommended
When to go: Anytime
Entree range: Adults: $14.95 breakfast, $15.50 lunch, $19.95 dinner; children: $7.95 breakfast and lunch, $9.95 dinner
Payment: VISA, MC, AMEX

Service rating: ★★
Friendliness rating: ★★★
Parking: Magic Kingdom lot
Bar: None
Wine selection: None
Dress: Casual
Disabled access: Yes

Breakfast: Every day, 7:30–10:30 a.m. (opens later on non–early-entry days)
Lunch: Every day, 11:30 a.m.–2:45 p.m.
Dinner: Every day, 4 p.m. until park closes; last seating is at 7:15 p.m.

Setting & atmosphere: A turn-of-the-century glass pavilion awash with sunlight and decorated with plenty of summer greenery. Seating is comfortable (a pleasant respite), and buffet lines are open and accessible. There is a low buffet area for kids to help themselves.

House specialties: Waffles and pancakes layered with fresh fruit; muesli; jambalaya; fried chicken with hoisin sauce; grilled vegetable platter; penne pasta tossed with romaine lettuce, grilled chicken, and Parmesan cheese; paella; leg of lamb carving station; grilled mahimahi, salmon, catfish, or marlin, served with caramelized onion relish.

Entertainment & amenities: Winnie the Pooh characters dance about and pose with the kids.

Summary & comments: Disney continues its latest emphasis on "new-age buffets" with this latest conversion. The Crystal Palace was a counter-service restaurant but now offers an all-you-can-eat buffet similar to the one found at Chef Mickey's in the Contemporary Resort. This state-of-the-art buffet boasts no steam tables. All the foods are presented in casserole dishes and

(The Crystal Palace)

pans that sit on special heated countertops. The steam may be missing, but this is still mass feeding and the quality is reflected. Still, with such limited dining in the Magic Kingdom, one more restaurant—and one less counter-service eatery—is a step in the right direction.

ESPN CLUB   ★★

American/Sandwiches	Moderate	QUALITY
		73

Disney's BoardWalk; (407) 939-5100	READERS' SURVEY RESPONSES:	VALUE
	73% 👍 27% 👎	C

Customers: Tourists
Priority seatings: Not accepted
When to go: Anytime
Entree range: $7–15.95
Payment: VISA, MC, AMEX, Disney Card
Service rating: ★★
Friendliness rating: ★★★

Parking: BoardWalk lot; valet parking is free before 5 p.m., $5 after
Bar: Full service
Wine selection: Minimal
Dress: Casual—helmets not required
Disabled access: Good

Open: Sunday–Thursday, 11:30 a.m.–1 a.m.; Friday and Saturday, 11:30 a.m.–2 a.m.

Setting & atmosphere: This is a sports bar to the nth degree, with basketball court flooring, sports memorabilia, and more television monitors than a network affiliate. The bar area has satellite sports-trivia video games. A large octagonal room with a wall of TV monitors serves as the main dining room and is nonsmoking. Smoking is permitted in the bar.

House specialties: Red wings (Buffalo-style wings); half-pound burger with cheddar or Swiss cheese; fresh fin tuna salad sandwich; penne pasta with grilled vegetables; marinated grilled chicken breast on a roll.

Entertainment & amenities: Live sports-trivia contests and televised sports.

Summary & comments: Disney is new to the sports bar concept, and it shows here. The first year was a little slow, but things have started to pick up. Service is a little more brusque than at other property restaurants. Portions are large, and the quality is in-line with the price. This is a good choice for late-night dining or when you have to choose between going out for a bite and staying in the room to catch "the big game."

50'S PRIME TIME CAFE ★★

American	Moderate	QUALITY
		69

Disney-MGM Studios; (407) 939-3463	READERS' SURVEY RESPONSES:		VALUE
	71% 👍	29% 👎	D

Customers: Theme park guests
Priority seatings: Suggested
When to go: Anytime
Entree range: $8.50–17, lunch;
$11.95–21, dinner
Payment: VISA, MC, AMEX
Service rating: ★★★★

Friendliness rating: ★★★★
Parking: Disney-MGM lot
Bar: Full service
Wine selection: Limited
Dress: Casual
Disabled access: Yes

Lunch: Every day, 11 a.m.–3:55 p.m.; opens at 10:30 a.m. on Sunday and Wednesday
Dinner: Every day, 4 p.m. until park closes

Setting & atmosphere: A meal at the 50's Prime Time Cafe is like eating a meal in your own kitchen, '50s-style. Pastel formica, gooseneck lamps, and black-and-white televisions that run vintage sitcoms are the rule.

House specialties: Meatloaf, pot roast, chicken, and other homey fare are featured. We get a lot of mail from readers who like the 50's Prime Time Cafe. Most say the food is good, the portions large, and that it is easy to find something the kids like. We, unfortunately, cannot concur in that opinion. By our evaluation the food is bland, more resembling the meals served in an elementary school cafeteria than in someone's home.

Entertainment & amenities: '50s sitcom clips on television.

Summary & comments: While we enjoy the ambiance of the 50's Prime Time Cafe and particularly like watching the old sitcoms, we cannot recommend having a meal there. Our suggestion for making the scene is to get late-afternoon or evening priority seatings and order only dessert.

FINN'S GRILL   ★

Seafood	Moderate	QUALITY
		55

The Hilton, Disney Village Hotel Plaza; (407) 827-4000	READERS' SURVEY RESPONSES:	VALUE
	69% 👍 31% 👎	D

Customers: Unsuspecting hotel guests

Reservations: Not necessary

When to go: Anytime

Entree range: $14.95–29.95

Payment: VISA, MC, AMEX, DC, D

Service rating: ★

Friendliness rating: ★★

Parking: Valet or hotel lot

Bar: Full service

Wine selection: Fair

Dress: Casual

Disabled access: Yes

Dinner: Sunday–Friday, 5:30–11 p.m.; Saturday, 5:30–10 p.m.

Setting & atmosphere: Walls are painted with the bright colors of the sea and are decorated with stylized fish fins, sort of abstract abalone. The oyster bar area is decorated with crab and lobster traps. Staff members wear silly fish hats that seem to denote some staffing hierarchy. The menu is fraught with puns on the word Finn, such as finn-omenal, finn-icky, and finn-tastic.

House specialties: Fresh fish, including snapper, salmon, and swordfish depending on availability, prepared blackened or grilled. Other items include shrimp scampi served with herb butter over yellow rice; Finn's gumbo, with shrimp, crabmeat, chicken, and sausage; and a number of pasta dishes.

Other recommendations: Alaskan king crab legs; steamed Maine lobster; fresh oysters; stone crab claws; shrimp.

Summary & comments: Someone spent an awful lot of time coming up with pleasing decor and a nice collection of dishes that accompany some of Florida's finest seafood. Unfortunately the rest of the time was spent on clever puns, leaving no time to train the staff on even the most rudimentary service skills. Most of the food is acceptable, but service this poor at a hotel this large is not. It might not be bad for a bucket of steamers and a few cold beers.

FLYING FISH CAFE ★★★★

		QUALITY
Seafood	Expensive	94

Disney's BoardWalk; (407) 939-3463	READERS' SURVEY RESPONSES:	VALUE
	90% 👍 10% 👎	C

Customers: Tourists and locals
Priority seatings: Recommended
When to go: Anytime
Entree range: $18–26
Payment: VISA, MC, AMEX
Service rating: ★★★★
Friendliness rating: ★★★★

Parking: BoardWalk lot; valet parking is free before 5 p.m., $5 after
Bar: Full service
Wine selection: Excellent but pricey
Dress: Casual dressy
Disabled access: Good

Dinner: Sunday–Thursday, 5:30–10 p.m.; Friday and Saturday, 5:30–10:30 p.m.

Setting & atmosphere: A whimsical remembrance of a circa-1920 Coney Island roller coaster served as the inspiration for the decor and the name. Actually the coaster was called The Flying Turns, and one of the cars on the ride was dubbed The Flying Fish. Booth backs resemble the climbs and swoops of a coaster. On the far wall is a Ferris wheel, and overhead fish fly on a parachute ride. Diners may choose to sit at the fishscale-covered counter that overlooks the open kitchen. Children are given a list of "flaws" in the decor to spot, such as the one fish flying backward on the parachute ride. If the decor is reminiscent of California Grill it's because they were both designed by Martin Dorf.

House specialties: The creative menu changes weekly. Some samplings of dishes include seared yellowfin tuna with spiced coriander crust and roasted eggplant; grilled Atlantic salmon with sun-dried tomatoes, baby-artichoke risotto, and calamata; and potato-wrapped yellowtail snapper with leek fondue and a cabernet sauvignon reduction (this one is something of a signature dish and is usually available). For dessert, the warm chocolate lava cake with a liquid chocolate center and citrus ice cream is incredibly indulgent—a must.

Summary & comments: The design, style, cuisine, and quality are all reminiscent of California Grill at the Contemporary Resort. However, you're more likely to find children here than at C.G. because of the BoardWalk location. Still, the fine food will be more appreciated by adults—and the high cost more respected. If you can't get a table, check on seating availablity at the counter. The service is just as good there, and the show in the kitchen is entertaining.

FULTON'S CRAB HOUSE ★★★½

Seafood	Expensive	QUALITY
		89

Empress Lilly, Pleasure Island; (407) 934-2628	READERS' SURVEY RESPONSES:	VALUE
	75% 👍 25% 👎	D

Customers: Locals, Disney guests
Priority seatings: Accepted
When to go: Early evening
Entree range: $16.95–43.95
Payment: VISA, MC, AMEX
Service rating: ★★★
Friendliness rating: ★★★

Parking: Pleasure Island lot
Bar: Full service
Wine selection: Good; mostly American wines
Dress: Casual
Disabled access: Yes

Lunch: Every day, 11:30 a.m.–4 p.m.
Dinner: Every day, 5–11 p.m.

Setting & atmosphere: Fulton's has taken over the entire three decks of the Empress Lilly, which underwent extensive remodeling that removed the rear paddle wheel and the smokestacks (they didn't really work anyway). The third deck is used mainly for banquets. There is a large lounge on the first deck, where you will spend a good deal of time waiting for your table. Separate dining areas include the Market Room, which is a tribute to New York's Fulton Fish Market (for which the restaurant is named); the Constellation Room, a semicircular room with a starlit night sky; and the Industry Room, which is a tribute to the commercial fishing industry.

House specialties: Stone crab; fresh fish flown in daily (the airbills are on display inside the front door); blue crab fingers; fresh oyster selection; Fulton's seafood chowder; cioppino with crab, shrimp, scallops, and fish in a tomato broth; Alaskan king crab; Alaskan Dungeness crab; calamari steak.

Other recommendations: Tuna filet mignon; crab cake and oyster combination; Crab House clam bake; mixed grill of fresh fish.

Summary & comments: The Levy Restaurants of Chicago operates Fulton's along with Portobello Yacht Club, also at Pleasure Island. Fulton's is an immense restaurant with over 700 seats, but service is geared toward the individual diner. There is no fresher fish available in central Florida (and much of it is flown in from waters around the country). Levy executive chef Ron Pollack is a seafood specialist and takes great pride in presenting the best. The menu is printed daily to reflect the fish that are available. Waits can be long—over an hour even on weekday nights. Have an appetizer in the lounge or on the outside deck while you wait for a table.

THE GARDEN GRILL RESTAURANT ★★½

American	Moderate	QUALITY
		79

The Land, Future World, Epcot; (407) 939-3463	READERS' SURVEY RESPONSES:	VALUE
	81% 👍 19% 👎	C

Customers: Theme park guests
Priority seatings: Recommended
When to go: Anytime
Entree range: $16.95–19.95 (adults);
$8.25–9.95 (children)
Payment: VISA, MC, AMEX
Service rating: ★★★

Friendliness rating: ★★★★
Parking: Epcot lot
Bar: Full service
Wine selection: Fair
Dress: Casual
Disabled access: Yes

Breakfast: Sunday, Monday, Wednesday, Thursday, and Saturday, 8:45–11:10 a.m.; Tuesday and Friday, 7:45–11:10 a.m.

Lunch & dinner: Every day, 11:30 a.m. until park closing

Setting & atmosphere: The Garden Grill is a revolving restaurant, but unlike the ones found at the top of high-rise hotels in large cities, this one is found at ground level and it doesn't even have windows. Instead the booths rotate past the various scenes of the Living with the Land boat ride. Although diners can't see the boats, they can see a rain forest and a prairie, among other things. When you're not looking at the scenes of the rain forest, you'll see brightly painted murals of sunflower fields.

House specialties: The restaurant recently switched from an a la carte menu to an all-you-can-eat concept of rotisserie chicken and farm-raised fish, which are brought to the table on large platters and served "family-style." Accompaniments include salad, bread, grilled vegetables, and potatoes.

Entertainment & amenities: The view.

Summary & comments: You can bet the vegetables are fresh—many of them are grown in the Epcot experimental farms seen on the pavilion's boat ride. And the lettuce is hydroponically grown.

GRAND FLORIDIAN CAFE   ★★

American	Moderate	QUALITY
		68

Disney's Grand Floridian Beach Resort; (407) 824-2496	READERS' SURVEY RESPONSES: 84% 👍 16% 👎	VALUE D

Customers: Hotel guests
Priority seatings: Not required
When to go: Breakfast or late evening
Entree range: $7.95–24.95
Payment: VISA, MC, AMEX
Service rating: ★★

Friendliness rating: ★★★
Parking: Valet; self-parking is deceptively far away
Bar: Full service
Wine selection: Very good
Dress: Casual
Disabled access: Yes

Breakfast: Every day, 7–11 a.m.
Lunch & dinner: Every day, 11:45 a.m.–11 p.m.

Setting & atmosphere: The large dining room, with high ceilings and decorative windows, looks out on the hotel's pool and center courtyard.

House specialties: Breakfast includes eggs prepared just about every way known to mankind, including omelets, frittatas, and huevos rancheros. Dinnertime appetizers are fairly pedestrian, including fried mozzarella cheese and chicken wings. Entrees have a Southern accent with items such as fried chicken (battered and deep-fried) served with mashed potatoes and gravy (of course); roast prime rib of beef with garlic and pan drippings; deep-fried cornmeal-battered catfish; and seafood "waterzooi" stew with fresh fish, scallops, shrimp, and rice.

Other recommendations: If fried Southern cooking and beef with pan drippings aren't on your diet this decade, G.F.C. offers a good selection of nutritional, lighter meals, including a fruit plate; vegetable lasagna; turkey burgers; and a smoked fish platter.

Summary & comments: The impersonal service detracts from the overall quality. Try it for breakfast or for a burger after the parks close.

GULLIVER'S GRILL AT GARDEN GROVE ★★

American	Expensive	QUALITY
		67

Walt Disney World Swan;
(407) 934-3000

READERS' SURVEY RESPONSES:		VALUE
64% 👍	36% 👎	D

Customers: Hotel guests
Reservations: Recommended
When to go: Lunch
Entree range: $7.95–19.95
Payment: VISA, MC, AMEX,
 DC, D
Service rating: ★★

Friendliness rating: ★★
Parking: Hotel lot
Bar: Full service
Wine selection: Good
Dress: Casual
Disabled access: Yes

Dinner: Every day, 6–10 p.m.

Setting & atmosphere: A large greenhouselike rotunda with tall palm trees and parrot figures attached to street lamps. Faux-stone tabletops are set with peach placemats and napkins.

House specialties: Lunch sandwiches include an Italian sub, chicken salad, French dip, and grilled salmon BLT. Evening appetizers are uninspired. Entrees include steaks, such as New York strip, filet mignon with béarnaise sauce, and 18-ounce porterhouse. Prime rib, swordfish, salmon, and snapper are also available. Dinners include Caesar salad tossed tableside, Italian bread with herb butter and rice, steak fries, or baked potato. Vegetables are extra.

Entertainment & amenities: Character breakfasts Wednesdays and Saturdays.

Summary & comments: The name has changed because the folks at the hotel believe you can't have a successful restaurant without a gimmick—food apparently doesn't matter. The menu includes a legend of the Gulliver in question (not Jonathan Swift's fictional character but an even more fictionalized "direct descendant" named Peter Miles Gulliver). The names of the dishes are listed in the language of Brobdingnag, the Land of the Giants. The only item on the dinner menu under $21 is the marinated chicken breast with mushrooms, or kluknkro de sokin & sromes. Oh, please.

HARRY'S SAFARI BAR AND GRILL   ★ ★ ★

Steak/Seafood	Expensive		QUALITY
			81

Walt Disney World Dolphin;	READERS' SURVEY RESPONSES:		VALUE
(407) 934-4000	69% 👍	31% 👎	D

Customers: Hotel guests
Priority seatings: Recommended
When to go: Early dinner
Entree range: $6.95–19.95
Payment: VISA, MC, AMEX,
　DC, D
Service rating: ★ ★

Friendliness rating: ★
Parking: Hotel lot
Bar: Full service
Wine selection: Good
Dress: Casual
Disabled access: Yes

Dinner: Five days a week, 6–11 p.m. (off days change weekly!)

Setting & atmosphere: A jungle atmosphere with huge stuffed animals sitting around on the floor. Waiters will often plop a hairy gorilla into an empty seat to fill up a table.

House specialties: The food here is extraordinarily expensive, and the quality doesn't warrant the high price. Appetizers include crab cakes; tiger shrimp; spring rolls stuffed with a mixture of alligator and kangaroo meat; and escargots. Entrees feature broiled South American lobster tail and filet mignon; roast duck; and prime rib.

Other recommendations: Mahimahi, salmon, tuna, or swordfish prepared to request: plank-roasted; pan-grilled with pistachios, pecans, and citrus; or jerk-blackened.

Summary & comments: The staff spends more time making the stuffed animals comfortable than making the guests comfortable. The food, though good, is terribly expensive. The prices are given in U.S. dollars and English pounds, ostensibly to fit in with Harry's "legend" (you can't have a restaurant here without a legend), which claims Harry grew up in Great Britain before heading to Africa to become an explorer.

HOLLYWOOD & VINE ★★½

American	Inexpensive	QUALITY
		74

Disney-MGM Studios, (407) 939-3463	READERS' SURVEY RESPONSES:	VALUE
	82% 👍 18% 👎	C

Customers: Theme park guests
Priority seatings: Recommended
When to go: Lunch
Entree range: $7.95–15.95
Payment: AMEX, MC, VISA
Service rating: ★★★

Friendliness rating: ★★★★
Parking: Disney-MGM lot
Bar: Full service
Wine selection: Limited
Dress: Casual
Disabled access: Yes

Breakfast: Monday–Tuesday and Thursday–Saturday, 8:10–11:30 a.m.; Sunday and Wednesday, 7:30–11:30 a.m.
Lunch: Every day, 11:30 a.m.–3:30 p.m.

Setting & atmosphere: Large art deco–style cafeteria with tile floors and lots of chrome. The walls are decorated with huge murals that resemble old postcards with vintage scenes of old Hollywood and other California landmarks.

House specialties: Breakfast: eggs; frittatas; oven-roasted potatoes; smoked salmon; fresh fruit; specialty breads. Lunch: roasted pork loin; smoked seafood; fried rice; mashed potatoes; salads and fresh fruit.

Summary & comments: If you feel the need to stuff yourself, try this all-you-can-eat buffet for breakfast or lunch. Be prepared for lots of noise—with all the glass, tile, and chrome, the noise echoes for days.

THE HOLLYWOOD BROWN DERBY ★★★

American	Expensive	QUALITY
		84

Disney-MGM Studios; (407) 939-3463	READERS' SURVEY RESPONSES:	VALUE
	85% 👍 15% 👎	C

Customers: Theme park guests
Priority seatings: Recommended
When to go: Early evening
Entree range: $11.95–19.75, lunch;
  $19.75–$24.95, dinner
Payment: VISA, MC, AMEX
Service rating: ★★★★

Friendliness rating: ★★★★
Parking: Disney-MGM lot
Bar: Full service
Wine selection: Very good
Dress: Casual
Disabled access: Yes

Lunch: Every day, 11:30 a.m.–3:45 p.m.
Dinner: Every day, 4 p.m. until park closes

(The Hollywood Brown Derby)

Setting & atmosphere: A replica of the original Brown Derby restaurant (not the one shaped like a derby) in California, including duplicates of the celebrity caricatures that cover the paneled walls. An elegant sunken dining room with curved booths, tables draped with yards of white linen, and romantic shaded candles. Tall palm trees in huge pots stand in the center of the room and reach for the high ceiling. Waiters wear white jackets and are better dressed than most of the park guests.

House specialties: Cobb salad (a Brown Derby creation named for Bob Cobb, not Lee J.); baked grouper (battered and topped with meunière butter and served over pasta).

Other recommendations: Fettucine Derby (pasta with parmesan sauce with a choice of shrimp or chicken); grilled steaks; mixed grill.

Summary & comments: The decor is so perfect you'll feel as though you're in 1930s Hollywood. In fact, it is so elegant that it is a shame it is located in a theme park full of T-shirted guests. Everyone should really dress in white ties and long chiffon gowns and do their best Fred Astaire and Ginger Rogers impersonations. Don't expect to see any real stars dining in the next booth, however. There is outdoor dining available, but it is much better to sit inside here.

HOUSE OF BLUES ★★★

Regional American	Moderate	QUALITY
		80

Downtown Disney West Side; (407) 939-2623	READERS' SURVEY RESPONSES:	VALUE
	82% 👍 18% 👎	C

Customers: Blues lovers
Priority seatings: Accepted for lunch weekdays 11 a.m.–4 p.m.
When to go: Early evening; Sunday gospel brunch
Entree range: $8.50–23.95
Payment: VISA, MC, AMEX
Service rating: ★★★

Friendliness rating: ★★
Parking: Downtown Disney lot; valet $6
Bar: Full service
Wine selection: Modest
Dress: Casual
Disabled access: Good

Brunch: 3 seatings on Sunday, 10:45 a.m., 1 p.m., and 3:30 p.m.
Lunch & dinner: Every day, 11 a.m.–2 a.m.

Setting & atmosphere: You'd think it was a ramshackle hut in the bayous

(House of Blues)

of Louisiana if the place weren't bigger than all of Louisiana. Nearly every available inch of wall space displays some type of folk art, which has a voodoo sort of feel to it. The restaurant area is separate from the performance hall, where blues and rock groups perform. There is often a live band in the restaurant as well. Outdoor dining is available overlooking the lagoon. When recorded music is featured, monitors throughout the restaurant give a detailed description of the artist and the selection.

House specialties: The menu features a selection of New Orleans favorites, including étouffée, jambalaya, and po'boy sandwiches with shrimp or catfish.

Other recommendations: Cajun meatloaf; fried chicken.

Summary & comments: What Hard Rock Cafe is to rock music House of Blues is to rhythm and blues. For a themed restaurant, H.O.B. does an impressively good job with the food. If you're planning on taking in one of the acts at the performance space next door, you're better off going there first so you can assure yourself of a good seat and then eating afterwards.

JUAN & ONLY'S BAR AND JAIL ★★★

Tex-Mex	Moderate		QUALITY
			80
Walt Disney World Dolphin; (407) 934-4000	READERS' SURVEY RESPONSES:		VALUE
	70% 👍	30% 👎	B

Customers: Hotel guests
Reservations: Recommended
When to go: Anytime
Entree range: $6.95–17
Payment: VISA, MC, AMEX, DC, D
Service rating: ★★

Friendliness rating: ★★★
Parking: Valet $8, or self-park in hotel lot
Bar: Full service
Wine selection: Fair
Dress: Casual
Disabled access: Yes

Dinner: Every day, 6–11 p.m.

Setting & atmosphere: An upscale jail setting with iron bars and the usual stereotypical bric-a-brac that decorates most Tex-Mex restaurants. However, the designer wisely decided not to trash the interior, much of which is left over from the previous Italian tenant.

House specialties: Fajitas; chile rellenos; grilled chicken Yucatan; tortilla soup.

Other recommendations: Juan & Only's sampler, including poblano chile stuffed with chicken, beef taco, and cheese enchilada.

(Juan & Only's Bar and Jail)

Summary & comments: This restaurant tries a little too hard to theme itself. The menu contains a lengthy description of Juan and his sidekick Only. Still, the food is good, and if you like it hot and spicy, you won't be disappointed.

KIMONOS			★★★★
			QUALITY
Japanese	Moderate		90
	READERS' SURVEY RESPONSES:		VALUE
Walt Disney World Swan;	75% 👍	25% 👎	C
(407) 934-1621			

Customers: Hotel guests, locals
Reservations: Accepted for parties over 10
When to go: Anytime
Entree range: Sushi and rolls à la carte, $3.75–5
Payment: VISA, MC, AMEX, DC, JCB, D

Service rating: ★★★★
Friendliness rating: ★★★★
Parking: Hotel lot
Bar: Full service
Wine selection: Very good
Dress: Casual
Disabled access: Yes

Dinner: Every day, 5:30 p.m.–1 a.m.; bar opens at 5 p.m.

Setting & atmosphere: The decor consists of black lacquered tabletops and counters, tall pillars rising to bamboo rafters with rice-paper lanterns, and elegant kimonos that hang outstretched on the walls and between the dining sections. The chefs will greet you with a friendly welcome, and you'll be offered a hot towel to clean your hands. Even if you're not in the mood for sushi, this is a delightful place to just sit and sip sake.

House specialties: Although sushi and sashimi are the focus, Kimonos also serves a number of hot appetizers, including tempura-battered shrimp, fish, and vegetables; skewered chicken yakitori; beef teriyaki and gyoza; and steamed dumplings stuffed with a pork mixture. The crispy soft-shell crab is wonderful.

Summary & comments: The skill of the sushi artists is as much a joy to watch as is eating the wonderfully fresh creations. There are no full entrees here, just good sushi and appetizers. The Walt Disney World Swan is host to many Japanese tourists, and you'll find many of them here on any given night. Enough said.

KONA CAFE ★★★

New American/Carribean	Moderate	QUALITY
		84

Polynesian Resort; (407) 939-3463	READERS' SURVEY RESPONSES:	VALUE
	70% 👍 30% 👎	B

Customers: Mostly hotel guests; some locals
Priority seatings: Accepted
When to go: Anytime
Entree range: $13.95–18.95
Payment: AMEX, MC, VISA
Service rating: ★★★

Friendliness rating: ★★★★
Parking: Polynesian lot; valet available
Bar: Full service
Wine selection: Moderate
Dress: Casual
Disabled access: Good

Breakfast: Every day, 7–11 a.m.
Lunch: Every day, noon–2:45 p.m.
Dinner: Every day, 5–10 p.m.

Setting & atmosphere: The postmodern decor might remind some regular Disney guests of the dining rooms at California Grill. Arched railings and grillwork cover the ceiling. Instead of a regular "on stage" kitchen, the stuff here put the pastry chef out front so you can watch all those lovely calories being loaded onto your plate.

House specialties: Ginger-carrot soup; Asian noodle soup; Kona crab cakes; chargrilled seafood served with pan-fried noodles and baby bok choy; Ko ko puffs (miniature cream puffs) and Kilauea torte.

Other recommendations: Estate-grown Kona coffee served in a French press pot.

Summary & comments: Kona Cafe replaced the Coral Isle Cafe in the Polynesian Resort. But the results of the renovation, both in the design of the restaurant and in the execution of the creative menu, are on a higher plane than your average java joint. It hardly seems necessary to mention chef John Guillemette and pastry chef Isaac Tamada because they will certainly be moved to higher profile positions in fancier restaurants very soon. But they've laid the groundwork for a pleasant dining surprise.

LIBERTY TREE TAVERN   ★★½

American	Moderate	QUALITY
		74

Liberty Square, Magic Kingdom; (407) 939-3463	READERS' SURVEY RESPONSES:		VALUE
	88% 👍	12% 👎	C

Customers: Theme park guests
Priority seatings: Suggested
When to go: Anytime
Entree range: Lunch: $9.75–14.25 (adults), $4.75–5.50 (children); dinner: $19.95 (adults), $9.95 (children)
Payment: VISA, MC, AMEX

Service rating: ★★★★
Friendliness rating: ★★★★
Parking: Magic Kingdom lot
Bar: None
Wine selection: None
Dress: Casual
Disabled access: Yes

Lunch: Every day, 11:30 a.m.–3 p.m.
Dinner: Every day, 4 p.m. until park closes

Setting & atmosphere: Low, exposed-beam ceilings in rooms framed by pastel gray chair rails. Colonial-period wall art, much with a nautical theme, accents simple dark wood tables and chairs with woven seats.

House specialties: Prime rib; roast turkey; chicken breast with Virginia ham. Family-style character dining.

Other recommendations: Sandwiches and salads are good here.

Summary & comments: Though the Liberty Tree is the best of the Magic Kingdom's full-service restaurants, it is often overlooked at lunch. A good plan is to make a priority seating at the Liberty Tree for about an hour or so before parade time. After you eat, you can walk right out and watch the parade.

MAMA MELROSE'S RISTORANTE ITALIANO   ★★½

Italian	Moderate	QUALITY
		74

Disney-MGM Studios; (407) 939-3463	READERS' SURVEY RESPONSES:		VALUE
	81% 👍	19% 👎	D

Customers: Theme park guests
Priority seatings: Suggested
When to go: Anytime
Entree range: $8.25–14.75, lunch; $11.25–21.50, dinner
Payment: VISA, MC, AMEX
Service rating: ★★★★

Friendliness rating: ★★★★
Parking: Disney-MGM lot
Bar: Full service
Wine selection: Limited
Dress: Casual
Disabled access: Yes

(Mama Melrose's Ristorante Italiano)

Lunch: Every day, 11:30 a.m.–3:50 p.m.

Dinner: Every day, 4 p.m. until park closes

Setting & atmosphere: Mama Melrose's looks like a big-city neighborhood restaurant of the '30s, with bare wooden floors, red-and-white checkered tablecloths, red vinyl booths, and grapevines hanging from the rafters. By far the most relaxing restaurant at Disney-MGM Studios, Mama Melrose's sports a worn, ethnic look that is as comfortable as an old sweatshirt.

House specialties: Pasta and seafood combos are excellent, as are salads and some of the designer pizzas. Bread is served in the traditional style with olive oil.

Other recommendations: Veal parmesan served with pasta; vegetable lasagna; chicken marsala.

Summary & comments: Because of its out-of-the-way location, you can sometimes just walk into Mama Melrose's, especially in the evening.

MAYA GRILL		★★

Mexican	Expensive	QUALITY
		66

Coronado Springs Resort;	READERS' SURVEY RESPONSES:		VALUE
(407) 939-3463	93% 👍	7% 👎	D

Customers: Hotel guests	Friendliness rating: ★★★
Priority seatings: Recommended	Parking: Hotel lot; no valet
When to go: Anytime	Bar: Full service
Entree range: $17–26	Wine selection: Fair
Payment: VISA, MC, AMEX	Dress: Casual
Service rating: ★★★	Disabled access: Good

Breakfast: Every day, 7–11 a.m.

Dinner: Every day, 5–10 p.m.

Setting & atmosphere: The dining room is meant to evoke the ancient world of the Maya with, according to the menu, "a harmony of fire, sun and water." The fire is fake and in the form of "flames" made of fabric that is fan-blown at the top of two large columns. Diners sit around the base of a Mayan pyramid with flecks of gold in it. The kitchen is open to view, but so is the barren and starkly lit walkway outside, which detracts a bit from the atmosphere.

(Maya Grill)

House specialties: Another attempt to create a new cuisine, this time it's nuevo Latino, for a fusion of New and Old World flavors. This is meant to take Latino foods and marry them with the flavors of the Caribbean, Mexico, and South America. Huachinango features snapper in a pumpkin seed crust. Ropa vieja, braised flank steak, is served on a fresh corn tamale.

Summary & comments: Disney's latest hotel was meant to be for those on a budget, but this restaurant certainly doesn't follow that credo. The prices are way too high here for the quality of the food, which, by the way, is offered by the same company that operates San Angel Inn at the Mexico pavilion in Epcot (the same people run the food court at Coronado Springs as well). The fusion cuisine sometimes works and sometimes falls flatter than a tortilla. Overall the quality doesn't come close to matching the prices, so you're better off eating somewhere else.

NARCOOSSEE'S   ★★★½

Seafood	Expensive	QUALITY
		88

Disney's Grand Floridian Beach Resort;	READERS' SURVEY RESPONSES:		VALUE
(407) 939-3463	82% 👍	18% 👎	D

Customers: Hotel guests, locals
Priority seatings: Recommended
When to go: Early evening
Entree range: $18.95–41.95
Payment: VISA, MC, AMEX
Service rating: ★★★★
Friendliness rating: ★★★★

Parking: Valet; self-parking is deceptively far away.
Bar: Full service
Wine selection: Good
Dress: Casual
Disabled access: Yes

Dinner: Every day, 5–10 p.m.; lounge open, 3–11 p.m.

Setting & atmosphere: Part of the Grand Floridian Beach Resort complex, Narcoossee's is a free-standing octagonal building at the edge of Seven Seas Lagoon. It offers a great view of the Magic Kingdom and the boats that dock nearby to pick guests up and drop them off after a day at the park. The lack of carpeting and tablecloths, and the high noise level, belie the fine-dining aspect.

House specialties: After a short experiment in a creative fusion cuisine (don't worry, no one in the kitchen knew what that was either), Anette Grecchi was hired to revamp the menu. She came up with a list of entrees that make use of local produce and seafood yet still manage to be creative.

(Narcoossee's)

Appetizers include duo of mushroom soup, shredded duck confit salad, and brick-baked focaccia with duck pastrami. Entrees include pan-seared fillet of black grouper with spelt pilaf; crab with potato cakes; and grilled shrimp with saffron couscous.

Other recommendations: Grilled filet mignon with mashed red skin potatoes; charred chicken breast with Dijon mustard mayonnaise.

Summary & comments: Narcoossee's is back on track in offering some of the best food on the property. Still, prices are extremely high for this atmosphere, which often features children running about delighting in the reverberating acoustics. This is a good choice for a lunchtime escape from the Magic Kingdom with a short ride by boat or Monorail. Prices are more reasonable at lunch.

NINE DRAGONS RESTAURANT ★★½

| Chinese | Expensive | QUALITY |
| | | 74 |

| China, World Showcase, Epcot, | READERS' SURVEY RESPONSES. | VALUE |
| (407) 939-3463 | 52% 👍 48% 👎 | F |

Customers: Theme park guests
Priority seatings: Suggested
When to go: Anytime
Entree range: $8.95–19, lunch;
    $10.95–24.75, dinner
Payment: VISA, MC, AMEX
Service rating: ★★★

Friendliness rating: ★★★★
Parking: Epcot lot
Bar: Full service
Wine selection: Limited
Dress: Casual
Disabled access: Yes

Lunch: Every day, noon–4:30 p.m.
Dinner: Every day, 4:45 p.m. until park closes

Setting & atmosphere: The Nine Dragons is a stunning restaurant, formal, elegant, and bright. Its decor reflects Asian artistry and sophistication, with combinations of bright lacquered colors and natural wood hues—what every Chinese eatery across America seeks to emulate. There are inlaid ceilings, large and elaborate wood sculptures, and a lush, red, floral-patterned carpet.

House specialties: The Nine Dragons' fare, unfortunately, does not live up to its decor. The limited menu features the same tired sweet-and-sour

(Nine Dragons Restaurant)

pork, beef with broccoli, and moo goo gai pan that you can buy for one-third the price at your own neighborhood Chinese restaurant.

Summary & comments: This should be one of the best Chinese restaurants in the United States, but it's not. The lack of a creative menu, along with assembly-line preparation and service, makes Nine Dragons a lost opportunity at best, and an overpriced tourist trap at worst.

OFFICIAL ALL-STAR CAFE   ★★

American	Moderate	QUALITY
		72

Disney's Wide World of Sports; (407) 827-8326	READERS' SURVEY RESPONSES:		VALUE
	74% 👍	26% 👎	C

Customers: People attending sports events at the Disney stadium; others who are lost
Reservations: Not accepted
When to go: Before 6 p.m. or after 10 p.m.
Entree range: $8–16
Payment: VISA, MC, AMEX

Service rating: ★★
Friendliness rating: ★★
Parking: Free lot, but during events parking may be up to a mile away
Bar: Full service
Wine selection: Minimal
Dress: Casual
Disabled access: Yes

Lunch & dinner: Every day, 11 a.m.–midnight

Setting & atmosphere: A sports bar theme done up to the max, with big- and small-screen televisions, sports memorabilia, and booths shaped like catchers' mitts. The large room is designed to give the feel of sitting beneath the bleachers of a stadium.

House specialties: Pizza; pasta dishes; sandwiches.

Summary & comments: Another mega-chain in the making from Orlando resident and Planet Hollywood chief Robert Earl. If you're familiar with Planet Hollywood, you pretty much have an idea of what the food is like. The decor is similar, too, if you just substitute sports stuff for movie stuff. But what is different here is that the quality of the food is not as good as that of Planet Hollywood. Official All-Star Cafe is part of Disney's Wide World of Sports complex and is located next to the stadium. There is nothing else around for miles, so this isn't the kind of place you just wander into to check out. You really have to want to come here. If you want to go to see the sports

(Official All-Star Cafe)

memorabilia (Tara Lipinski's tutu?), that's one thing. If you want to have some good food, that's quite another. Be warned: If there is a game at the stadium, you may be diverted to park nearly a mile away from the restaurant. That's something to consider when the food really isn't worth crossing the street for.

'OHANA		★★★
Polynesian	Moderate	QUALITY 79
Disney's Polynesian Resort; (407) 939-3463	READERS' SURVEY RESPONSES: 80% 👍 20% 👎	VALUE C

Customers: Resort guests
Priority seatings: Recommended
When to go: Anytime
Entree range: $20.95 (adults); $9.95 (children)
Payment: VISA, MC, AMEX
Service rating: ★★★

Friendliness rating: ★★★★
Parking: Hotel lot
Bar: Full service
Wine selection: Limited
Dress: Casual
Disabled access: Yes

Dinner: Every day, 5–10 p.m.

Setting & atmosphere: This restaurant replaces the Papeete Bay Verandah. A large open pit is the centerpiece of the room. Here the grilled foods are prepared with a flare—literally. From time to time the chef will pour some liquid on the fire, causing huge flames to shoot up. This is usually in response to something one of the strolling entertainers has said, evoking a sign from the fire gods. At any given moment there may be a hula-hoop contest or a coconut race where the children in the dining room are invited to push coconuts around the dining room with broomsticks.

House specialties: Skewer service is the specialty here. There is no menu. As soon as you are seated, your server will begin to deliver food. First a couple of sausages, which are portioned off from long skewers right onto the diner's plate. These are followed by smoked turkey, beef, and chicken. These are accompanied by assorted salads, placed on a lazy Susan in the center of the table, along with pot sticker dumplings and teriyaki noodles.

Entertainment & amenities: Strolling singers; games.

Summary & comments: 'Ohana, which means family, is a fun place. The food is good but not superior. The method of service and the fact that it

('Ohana)

just keeps coming make it all taste a little better. Insist on being seated in the main dining room, where the fire pit is located. There are tables around the back, but you can't see what's going on from back there.

OLIVIA'S CAFE ★★★

American	Moderate	QUALITY
		81

Old Key West Resort; (407) 939-3463	READERS' SURVEY RESPONSES:		VALUE
	77% 👍	23% 👎	C

Customers: Resort guests
Priority seatings: Recommended
When to go: Lunch
Entree range: $6.25–18.95
Payment: VISA, MC, AMEX
Service rating: ★★★★

Friendliness rating: ★★★★
Parking: Hotel lot
Bar: Full service
Wine selection: Limited
Dress: Casual
Disabled access: Yes

Breakfast: Every day, 7:30–11 a.m.
Lunch: Every day, noon–5 p.m.
Dinner: Every day, 5–10 p.m.

Setting & atmosphere: This is Disney's idea of Key West, with lots of pastels and rough wood siding on the walls, mosaic tile floors, potted palms and tropical trees in the center of the room, and plenty of nautical gewgaws, including vintage photos of Key West and its inhabitants of long ago. (Key West is nothing like this.) There is some outside seating, which looks out over the waterway. Tile, wood siding, and no tablecloths add up to a very noisy dining room.

House specialties: Appetizers include conch chowder; blue lump crab-cakes; and guacamole and chips. Entrees feature prime rib; breaded and deep-fried Gulf shrimp; fresh fish grilled with fresh spices; and fried chicken with mashed potatoes and gravy. Many of the dishes are accompanied by what is referred to as real Cuban-style black beans and rice, but these beans would look pretty Americanized to anyone from Havana.

Other recommendations: Fried chicken; country-fried steak.

Summary & comments: Though perhaps not Key West, the charming atmosphere and low-key pace make the food taste even better than it already is. Not wonderful, just nice. The servers are upbeat and move with alarming speed, though food tends to come out of the kitchen at a more Key Westerly pace (slowly).

L'ORIGINALE ALFREDO DI ROMA RISTORANTE ★★½

Italian	Expensive	QUALITY
		74

Italy, World Showcase, Epcot;	READERS' SURVEY RESPONSES:	VALUE
(407) 939-3463	74% 👍 26% 👎	D

Customers: Theme park guests
Priority seatings: Required
When to go: Midafternoon
Entree range: Lunch, $7.75–17.95; dinner, $9.95–25.75
Payment: VISA, MC, AMEX
Service rating: ★★★★

Friendliness rating: ★★★★
Parking: Epcot lot
Bar: Beer and wine only
Wine selection: All Italian
Dress: Casual
Disabled access: Yes

Lunch: Every day, noon–4:15 p.m.
Dinner: Every day, 4:30 p.m. until park closes

Setting & atmosphere: The elegant—some would say garish—Roman decor features huge murals of an Italian piazza along the wall behind the upholstered banquettes. Dark woods and latticework on the high ceilings add to a sumptuous atmosphere. It is, however, a noisy dining room, one that is nearly always filled. This is yet another location for the so-called famous restaurant of the inventor of fettucine Alfredo, the favorite dining spot of Mary Pickford and Douglas Fairbanks.

House specialties: Fettucine Alfredo (what else?); pasta e fagioli; linguine al pesto; vitello alla Milanese.

Other recommendations: Pollo alla Milanese; pollo alla parmigiana; roasted lamb chop.

Entertainment & amenities: Strolling opera singers at dinner.

Summary & comments: Although the word "original" appears in the name, the food is a little worn and old. (So what did Mary Pickford and Douglas Fairbanks know about restaurants?) Most of the entrees are heavy and will have you plodding the rest of the way through the park.

THE OUTBACK   ★★

Steak	Expensive	QUALITY
		67

Wyndham Palace,	READERS' SURVEY RESPONSES:	VALUE
Disney Village Hotel Plaza;	54% 👍 46% 👎	D
(407) 827-2727		

Customers: Tourists, locals
Reservations: Recommended
When to go: Very early dinner
Entree range: $12.95–35
Payment: VISA, MC, AMEX;
  DC, D
Service rating: ★

Friendliness rating: ★
Parking: Complimentary valet parking at the rear of the hotel
Bar: Full service
Wine selection: Excellent
Dress: Casual
Disabled access: Yes

Dinner: Every day, 5:30–10:45 p.m.

Setting & atmosphere: A large, open room with a two-story ceiling and a cascading waterfall. Servers are in Australian bush outfits. That and the menu printed on a boomerang are supposed to make it an Australian restaurant, though the bulk of the menu is what you'd find in just about any American restaurant.

House specialties: There aren't many places where you can get kangaroo steak and rattlesnake salad, but you can here if you really want it. Otherwise, there is filet mignon with béarnaise sauce; rack of spring lamb; grilled tuna; and prime rib.

Other recommendations: Six-pound live Maine lobster.

Summary & comments: For some reason that no one bothers to explain, dinner rolls are delivered to the table at the end of long poles. Staff members tend to treat guests as though they'll never be back. The food isn't good enough to put up with rude service. *Note:* This is not part of the Outback Steakhouse national chain.

PALIO ★★★

Italian	Expensive	QUALITY
		81

Walt Disney World Swan;	READERS' SURVEY RESPONSES:	VALUE
(407) 934-3000	79% 👍 | 21% 👎	C

Customers: Hotel guests
Reservations: Recommended
When to go: Anytime
Entree range: $18–24
Payment: VISA, MC, AMEX, DC,
  JCB, D
Service rating: ★★★

Friendliness rating: ★★★
Parking: Hotel lot
Bar: Full service
Wine selection: Very good
Dress: Casual
Disabled access: Yes

Dinner: Every day, 6–10 p.m.

Setting & atmosphere: The name means banner, and they're hanging all over this upscale Italian trattoria and are even draped over the tables. It is a pretty place and bustles with excitement and the sounds of happy diners. Like just about everything else in the hotel, designer Michael Graves had a hand in the decor and design of the restaurant, and it shows. It is a beautiful place.

House specialties: Veal alla limone, a scallopine served with lemon butter and linguine; saltimbocca alla Romana, veal medallions topped with prosciutto and sage, served with risotto; osso buco alla Milanese, veal shank braised in white wine and vegetable stock, served with saffron risotto.

Other recommendations: Veal picante alla marsala; sautéed chicken breast with tomato; red snapper with sautéed fennel.

Summary & comments: The food isn't bad, and the experience is satisfying overall, but there are more exciting dining options available. The roasted-garlic spread served with the hot bread is nice. Fill up on that and then order one of the reasonably priced pizzas.

PLANET HOLLYWOOD   ★★★½

American	Moderate	QUALITY
		86

Pleasure Island; (407) 827-7827	READERS' SURVEY RESPONSES:		VALUE
	73% 👍	27% 👎	C

Customers: Tourists, locals
Priority seatings: Accepted lunch and
   late-night only
When to go: Late lunch
Entree range: $8.95–18.95
Payment: VISA, MC, AMEX,
   DC, D

Service rating: ★★★★
Friendliness rating: ★★
Parking: Pleasure Island lot
Bar: Full service
Wine selection: Limited
Dress: Casual
Disabled access: Yes

Lunch & dinner: Every day, 11 a.m.–1 a.m.

Setting & atmosphere: A large planet-shaped structure "floating" in the lagoon next to Pleasure Island. Planet Hollywood's decor is something of a movie museum, with memorabilia from famous movies. These items are easy to come by since Sylvester Stallone, Arnold Schwarzenegger, Bruce Willis, and other actors are partners in the restaurant. Orlando is world headquarters for the chain, and the hometown restaurant is really a special structure. Still, the artifacts leave something to be desired. New York's Planet has Judy Garland's ruby slippers; Orlando's has the gilded potty seat from *The Last Emperor.*

House specialties: The menu is all over the place, with pasta dishes, fajitas, burgers, dinner salads, and pizzas. The burgers are huge (the bleu cheese burger is wonderful). Desserts are incredible, especially the white-chocolate bread pudding.

Other recommendations: Chicken fajitas; linguini and sausage; grilled swordfish.

Summary & comments: Because of its star power, Planet Hollywood attracts a lot of people. But even with the never-ending stream of guests, the kitchen doesn't slack off. The food is good and well thought out. And while $7.50 may seem like a lot of money for a burger, you'll get a thick, juicy patty, cooked the way you want it, with fries. And to give you an idea of the restaurant's attention to details, the potatoes for the fries are stored on the premises until the proper amount of sweetness from aging is achieved.

PLEASURE ISLAND JAZZ COMPANY ★★

Regional American	Moderate	QUALITY
		68

Pleasure Island; (407) 934-7781	READERS' SURVEY RESPONSES:	VALUE
	42% 👍 | 58% 👎	C

Customers: Tourists, locals
Priority seatings: Not accepted
When to go: Early evening to get a good seat for that night's jazz performance
Entree range: $4.25–8.75
Payment: VISA, MC, AMEX

Service rating: ★★
Friendliness rating: ★★
Parking: Pleasure Island lot
Bar: Full service
Wine selection: Moderate
Dress: Casual
Disabled access: Good

Dinner: Every day, 7 p.m.–2 a.m.

Setting & atmosphere: A large nightclub with tables set up in front of a performance space where jazz musicians play nightly. This is the sort of place where you don't go just to have the food and not stay for the show. However, you'll find plenty of people who come for the music with no intention of having anything to eat.

House specialties: Red beans and rice; spicy Cajun chicken stack; Oriental grilled salmon.

Summary & comments: Although the jazz club has been serving full dinners for a couple of years, it has remained something of a secret, which is surprising since this is one of the few Downtown Disney eating spots that is not operated by an outside concern. The food is simple, and the service tends to be a bit brusque. But the jazz experience is definitely enhanced when you have a bowl of red beans and rice in front of you.

PORTOBELLO YACHT CLUB ★★★½

Italian	Expensive	QUALITY
		88

Pleasure Island; (407) 934-8888	READERS' SURVEY RESPONSES:	VALUE
	80% 👍 | 20% 👎	D

Customers: Tourists, locals
Priority seatings: Recommended
When to go: Anytime
Entree range: $14.95–29.95
Payment: VISA, MC, AMEX
Service rating: ★★★★
Friendliness rating: ★★★★

Parking: Pleasure Island lot
Bar: Full service
Wine selection: Very good; heavy on Italian selections
Dress: Casual
Disabled access: Yes

(Portobello Yacht Club)

Lunch: Every day, 11 a.m.–4 p.m.
Dinner: Every day, 4 p.m.–midnight

Setting & atmosphere: This restaurant sports an upscale nautical theme with lots of polished brass, dark woods, and canvas window coverings. There is a patio overlooking the lagoon for those days with low humidity.

House specialties: Northern Italian cuisine; breaded veal ribeye; charcoal-grilled shrimp on a rosemary skewer; boneless half chicken marinated in olive oil, garlic, and fresh rosemary.

Other recommendations: Crispy thin-crust pizza appetizers, including a vegetarian pizza with eggplant, zucchini, and mushrooms and a four-cheese pizza with sun-dried tomatoes. The butterfly pasta with fresh asparagus and snow peas is a good inexpensive selection.

Summary & comments: Tends to be overpriced, but one can make a meal of a pizza and pasta selection for under $20. Ask for the patio if it's a cool evening.

RAINFOREST CAFE		★★½
American	Moderate	**QUALITY** 73
Downtown Disney Marketplace; (407) 827-8500	READERS' SURVEY RESPONSES: 76% 👍 24% 👎	**VALUE** D
Animal Kingdom; (407) 938-9100		

Customers: Tourists and locals
Priority seatings: Accepted
When to go: Late afternoon, after lunch crunch and before dinner hour
Entree range: $8–18
Payment: VISA, MC, AMEX, DC, JCB, D

Service rating: ★★
Friendliness rating: ★★★
Parking: Marketplace lot
Bar: Full bar
Wine selection: Limited
Dress: Casual
Disabled access: Good

Open: *Downtown Disney Marketplace:* Sunday–Thursday, 10:30 a.m.–11 p.m.; Friday and Saturday, 10:30 a.m.–midnight; *Animal Kingdom:* every day, 7:30 a.m.–8 p.m.

Setting & atmosphere: The Downtown Disney version of the national chain sits beneath a giant volcano that can be seen (and heard) erupting all over the Marketplace. The smoke coming from the volcano is nonpolluting,

(Rainforest Cafe)

in accordance with the restaurant's conservation theme. Inside is a huge dining room designed to look like a jungle (imagine all the silk plants in the world tacked to the ceiling), complete with Animatronic elephants, bats, and monkeys (not the most realistic Animatronics you've seen). There is occasional thunder and even some rainfall. Large aquariums connected with glass "swimways" serve as one of several waiting areas. Next to the dining room is a 5,000-square-foot retail shop. The Animal Kingdom version, featuring a huge waterfall, is easier on the eye externally. Once inside, however, you'll find the same food, decor, and retail space as at the Marketplace.

House specialties: "Pieces of ate" eggroll with chicken, red peppers, corn, and black beans wrapped inside wonton skins; seafood Galapagos with fish, zucchini, and shrimp (but no tortoise) served over pasta; Rainforest pita quesadilla with chicken.

Entertainment & amenities: After the wait you endure, a chair and some sustenance is all the entertainment you'll need.

Summary & comments: Let us say up front that while we are not impressed by the Rainforest Cafes, a lot of our readers rave about them. The slogan for Rainforest Cafe is "a wild place to shop and eat." The shopping experience must be the attraction, because it certainly isn't the food. Preparations are spotty; spicing is uneven; and the quality is not as high as at other area theme restaurants such as Planet Hollywood and Hard Rock Cafe. Waits can be horrendous. You must first queue up and wait to approach "the rock," where you will be given a passport with your name and approximate waiting time. This could easily be more than an hour. You are expected to shop in the retail space during this time. When your name is called you will be told to report to "the elephant" (seriously), only to be instructed to go wait at another podium. Even cattle in the world's diminishing rain forests aren't moved around this much. By all means visit the gift shop, but dine somewhere else.

RESTAURANT AKERSHUS ★★★½

Norwegian/Buffet	Moderate		QUALITY
			89

Norway, World Showcase, Epcot; (407) 939-3463	READERS' SURVEY RESPONSES:		VALUE
	88% 👍	12% 👎	B

Customers: Theme park guests
Priority seatings: Required
When to go: Anytime

Entree range: Lunch: $11.95 adults, $5.25 kids; dinner: $18.50 adults, $7.95 kids

(Restaurant Akershus)

Payment: VISA, MC, AMEX
Service rating: ★★★
Friendliness rating: ★★★★
Parking: Epcot lot

Bar: Full service
Wine selection: Good
Dress: Casual
Disabled access: Yes

Lunch: Every day, 11:30 a.m.–4 p.m.
Dinner: Every day, 4:15 p.m. until park closes

Setting & atmosphere: Modeled on a 14th-century fortress, Akershus entertains its guests in a great banquet hall under high A-framed ceilings and massive iron chandeliers. Stone arches divide the dining rooms. A red carpet alternates with patterned hardwood floors.

House specialties: A bountiful hot and cold buffet features salmon; herring; various Norwegian salads and cheeses; hearty stews; and a variety of hot fish and meats. Be sure to try the mashed rutabagas.

Other recommendations: Cold Ringnes beer on tap.

Summary & comments: Akershus offers a unique introduction to delightful Scandinavian cuisines. The dishes may not be familiar, but the quality is superb, and the overall experience is a real adventure in dining. Akershus's popularity grows every year as word of its quality spreads. We think it's one of the better restaurants at Walt Disney World.

RESTAURANT MARRAKESH			★★★
Moroccan	Moderate		QUALITY
			81
Morocco, World Showcase, Epcot; (407) 939-3463	READERS' SURVEY RESPONSES:		VALUE
	86% 👍	14% 👎	C

Customers: Theme park guests
Priority seatings: Required
When to go: Anytime
Entree range: $9.95–14.95, lunch; $12.95–24.95, dinner
Payment: VISA, MC, AMEX
Service rating: ★★★

Friendliness rating: ★★★★
Parking: Epcot lot
Bar: Full service
Wine selection: Limited
Dress: Casual
Disabled access: Yes

Lunch: Every day, 11:30 a.m.–3:45 p.m.
Dinner: Every day, 4 p.m. until park closes

Setting & atmosphere: One of the more exotic World Showcase restaurants, Marrakesh re-creates a Moroccan palace with gleaming tile mosaics,

(Restaurant Marrakesh)

high inlaid-wood ceilings with open beams and brass chandeliers, and red Bukhara carpets.

House specialties: Start with bastila (a minced chicken pie sprinkled with confectionary sugar), followed by cornish hen, tangine chicken, or roast lamb. Split an order of couscous. Beef and lamb kebabs are also available.

Other recommendations: If you are hungry, curious, or both, go for one of the combination platters for two persons.

Entertainment & amenities: Moroccan band and belly dancing.

Summary & comments: Interesting fare that is almost impossible to find except in the largest U.S. cities. Unlike diners at most Moroccan restaurants, those at Marrakesh sit at tables (instead of on the floor) and eat with utensils rather than with their hands. Because Moroccan food is unfamiliar to most visitors, Marrakesh sometimes has tables available for walk-ins.

ROSE & CROWN DINING ROOM ★★★

English	Moderate	QUALITY
		81

United Kingdom, World Showcase, Epcot; (407) 939-3463	READERS' SURVEY RESPONSES:		VALUE
	84% 👍	16% 👎	C

Customers: Theme park guests
Priority seatings: Recommended
When to go: Anytime
Entree range: $9.25–11.50, lunch; $10.75–20.75, dinner
Payment: VISA, MC, AMEX
Service rating: ★★★★

Friendliness rating: ★★★★
Parking: Epcot lot
Wine selection: Limited
Bar: Full bar with Bass ale and Guinness and Harp beers on tap
Dress: Casual
Disabled access: Yes

Lunch: Every day, 11:30 a.m.–4:30 p.m.
Dinner: Every day, 4:30 p.m. until park closes

Setting & atmosphere: The Rose & Crown is both a pub and dining establishment. The traditional English pub has a large cozy bar with rich wood appointments and trim, beamed ceilings, and a hardwood floor. The adjoining English country dining room is rustic and simple. Meals are served outdoors overlooking the World Showcase Lagoon when the weather is nice.

House specialties: Hearty but simple food; try fish and chips or the Welsh chicken and leek pie, washed down with Bass ale.

(Rose & Crown Dining Room)

Other recommendations: Steak and kidney pie; cottage pie; sautéed Irish chicken; grilled lamb chop.

Summary & comments: You do not need priority seatings to stop and refresh yourself on a hot (or cold) afternoon at the friendly bar. The waitresses and barmaids are saucy in the best English tradition and add immeasurably to the experience. Unfortunately, the number of selections on the menu has been cut significantly since our last visit. The Rose & Crown is usually more popular at lunch than at dinner. It is about the fifth Epcot restaurant to book its seatings, owing more to its small size than its popularity.

SAN ANGEL INN RESTAURANTE   ★★★

Mexican	Expensive		QUALITY
			84
Mexico, World Showcase, Epcot; (407) 939-3463	READERS' SURVEY RESPONSES:		VALUE
	78% 👍	22% 👎	D

Customers: Theme park guests	Friendliness rating: ★★★★
Priority seatings: Recommended	Parking: Epcot lot
When to go: Anytime	Bar: Full service
Entree range: $8.95–14.95, lunch; $12.50–23.25, dinner	Wine selection: Limited
Payment: VISA, MC, AMEX	Dress: Casual
Service rating: ★★★★	Disabled access: Yes

Lunch: Every day, 11:30 a.m.–4 p.m.
Dinner: Every day, 4:30 p.m. until park closes

Setting & atmosphere: The San Angel Inn is inside the great Aztec pyramid of the Mexican pavilion. A romantically crafted open-air cantina, the restaurant overlooks both El Río del Tiempo (The River of Time) and the bustling plaza of a small Mexican village.

House specialties: In addition to enchiladas, tacos, quesadillas, and other routine Mexican fare, San Angel Inn features (at dinner only) mole poblano (chicken with an exotic sauce made from several kinds of peppers and unsweetened Mexican chocolate) and some interesting regional fish preparations.

Other recommendations: Blackened mahimahi or poached red snapper.

Entertainment & amenities: Mariachi or marimba bands in the adjacent courtyard.

(San Angel Inn Restaurante)

Summary & comments: The San Angel Inn serves good, sometimes excellent, Mexican food at prices much higher than you would find at most Mexican restaurants. The shrimp grilled with pepper sauce, for example, is five medium-sized shrimp for the outrageous sum of $22 ($4.50 per shrimp!). The menu goes beyond normal Mexican selections, offering special and regional dishes that are difficult to find in the United States. If you go, we recommend you skip the tacos and try one of these more unique dishes.

SCI-FI DINE-IN THEATER RESTAURANT ★★

American	Moderate	QUALITY
		67

Disney-MGM Studios; (407) 939-3463	READERS' SURVEY RESPONSES:		VALUE
	67% 👍	33% 🗩	D

Customers: Theme park guests
Priority seatings: Required
When to go: Anytime
Entree range: $7.95–13.25, lunch;
  $10.25–22.95, dinner
Payment: VISA, MC, AMEX
Service rating: ★★★★★

Friendliness rating: ★★★★★
Parking: Disney-MGM lot
Bar: Full service
Wine selection: Limited
Dress: Casual
Disabled access: Yes

Lunch: Sunday and Wednesday, 10:30 a.m.–4 p.m.; Monday–Tuesday and Thursday–Saturday, 11 a.m.–4 p.m.
Dinner: Every day, 4 p.m. until park closes

Setting & atmosphere: You sit in little cars in a large building where it is always night and watch vintage film clips on a drive-in movie screen as you eat.

House specialties: The fare consists of sandwiches; burgers; salads; and shakes, as well as fancier stuff. While we think the food quality is way out of line with the cost, you can have an adequate meal at the Sci-Fi if you stick with simple fare.

Entertainment & amenities: Cartoons and clips of vintage horror and sci-fi movies are shown, such as *The Attack of the Fifty-foot Woman, Robot Monster,* and *Son of the Blob.* Also shown are lurid previews, proclaiming, "See a sultry beauty in the clutches of a half-crazed monster!"

Summary & comments: We recommend making a late-afternoon or late-evening priority seating and ordering only dessert. In other words, think of the Sci-Fi as an attraction (which it is) as opposed to a good dining opportunity (which it is not). If you want to try the Sci-Fi Dine-In and do not have priority seatings, try walking in at 11 a.m. or around 3 p.m.

SEASONS DINING ROOM ★★★

American/Eclectic	Moderate	QUALITY
		84

Disney Institute; (407) 939-3463	READERS' SURVEY RESPONSES:		VALUE
	63% 👍	37% 👎	C

Customers: Institute guests
Priority seatings: Recommended
When to go: Anytime
Entree range: $13.95–23.95
Payment: VISA, MC, AMEX
Service rating: ★★★★

Friendliness rating: ★★★★
Parking: Institute lot
Bar: Full service
Wine selection: Fair
Dress: Casual
Disabled access: Yes

Breakfast: Every day, 7–11:30 a.m.
Lunch: Every day, 11:30 a.m.–2:30 p.m.
Dinner: Every day, 5:30–10 p.m.

Setting & atmosphere: A huge, cavernous room probably meant to resemble an old dormitory dining hall but which looks more like a barn. Tables include a lazy Susan decorated to reflect the theme being featured that day.

House specialties: Seasons was so-named to reflect its ever-changing menu, which is based on availability of seasonal produce. There is a different menu each night of the week, and often the dinners are themed. Samples might include: Polynesia night with steamed dumpling salad, grilled turkey with pineapple-soy glaze, pan-seared mahimahi, and exotic fruit soup; New Orleans night with blackened pea and andouille sausage salad, blackened red snapper, and crawfish risotto; Mediterranean night with melon and prosciutto salad, broiled cod over sautéed spinach, and tiramisu; and Northwest night with dried-cherry and wild-rice cakes, roast loin of venison, grilled free-range chicken breast, and fruit cobbler.

Summary & comments: Diners can choose to order a la carte from the menu *or* to opt for fixed-price dinners served family-style, which means each course is brought to the table on platters for your party to dole out for themselves. The food is well executed for the most part, with an emphasis on healthful preparations. If you're really hungry, Seasons represents a good value. If you're lucky enough to dine on Northwest night, be sure to save plenty of room for the fruit cobbler (if they run out of it, it's because the staff has eaten it all).

SPOODLES ★★★½

			QUALITY
Mediterranean		Moderate	87

	READERS' SURVEY RESPONSES:	VALUE
Disney's BoardWalk; (407) 939-3163	69% 👍 31% 👎	C

Customers: Tourists and locals
Priority seatings: Recommended
When to go: Anytime
Entree range: Tapas, $4–9; entrees,
$10–22
Payment: VISA, MC, AMEX
Service rating: ★★★★
Friendliness rating: ★★★★

Parking: BoardWalk lot; valet park-
ing is free before 5 p.m., $5 after
Bar: Full service
Wine selection: Good selection of
Mediterranean countries
Dress: Casual
Disabled access: Good

Breakfast: Every day, 7:30–11 a.m.
Lunch: Every day, noon–2 p.m.
Dinner: Every day, 5–9:50 p.m.

Setting & atmosphere: The dining room is designed like a farmhouse you might find in the Mediterranean countryside—a really big farmhouse. Light fixtures of various sizes and styles (no two are alike), Fiestaware plates and cups stacked on the wooden tables along with a container of flatware, and posters of Mediterranean countries reinforce the family-style atmosphere. The open kitchen adds to the noise, which is already extensive because of the size of the room and the sound of people enjoying themselves and passing around plates of tapas.

House specialties: This is a true Mediterranean restaurant and not just an Italian trattoria that passes itself off as one. Any country with a shoreline on the Mediterranean is represented here, and the result is a plethora of exotic dishes with even more exotic spices. There are full entrees available, but the best way to experience Spoodles is to order an array of tapas, small appetizer-sized portions of entrees, and share them with everyone at the table.

Summary & comments: If you only order beef and a baked potato when you dine out, this is not the place for you (though there is a beef and potato selection on the menu if you get out-voted). This is for the adventurous who really wanted to go to Europe for vacation but wound up in Florida instead. The flavors are fresh and vibrant, and most everything is expertly prepared. Don't be intimidated by ingredients you don't recognize—the staff is very helpful and will gladly tell you what zhoug is.

TEMPURA KIKU   ★★★

Japanese	Moderate	QUALITY
		83

Japan, World Showcase, Epcot; (407) 939-3463	READERS' SURVEY RESPONSES:	VALUE
	81% 👍 19% 👎	C

Customers: Theme park guests   Friendliness rating: ★★★
Priority seatings: Not accepted   Parking: Epcot lot
When to go: Lunch   Bar: Full service
Entree range: $9.50–16.75, lunch;   Wine selection: Limited
  $15–22, dinner   Dress: Casual
Payment: VISA, MC, AMEX   Disabled access: Yes
Service rating: ★★★★

Lunch: Every day, noon–3:45 p.m.
Dinner: Every day, 4:30 p.m. until park closes

Setting & atmosphere: Tempura Kiku is a small (25-person) tempura bar where most patrons sit around the outside of a square counter. The setting is intimate, almost cramped, and very communal.

House specialties: Tempura-battered deep-fried foods featuring chicken, shrimp, and vegetables. The menu tells the story of tempura, which apparently came about when some Portuguese sailors were shipwrecked on a Japanese shore. The Catholic Portuguese did not eat meat on the holy days, which came four times a year and were called quattuor tempora. On these days the sailors ate fried shrimp. The Japanese adapted the word tempura to mean fried shrimp, and the rest of the world adapted it to mean all kinds of fried food.

Other recommendations: Kabuki beef; sushi; sashimi.

Summary & comments: Not the most appealing restaurant at Epcot, but the tempura is arguably the best in the Japan pavilion. The sushi and sashimi are not heavily marketed, but you can bet the sanitation—important in any restaurant but crucial where sushi is served—is impeccable.

TEPPANYAKI DINING ROOMS ★★★½

Japanese	Expensive	QUALITY
		85

Japan, World Showcase, Epcot; (407) 939-3463	READERS' SURVEY RESPONSES:		VALUE
	88% 👍	12% 👎	C

Customers: Theme park guests
Priority seatings: Required
When to go: Anytime
Entree range: $9.50–19.95, lunch;
  $14.95–30.25, dinner
Payment: VISA, MC, AMEX
Service rating: ★★★★

Friendliness rating: ★★★★
Parking: Epcot lot
Bar: Full service
Wine selection: Limited
Dress: Casual
Disabled access: Yes, via elevator

Lunch: Every day, noon–3:45 p.m.
Dinner: Every day, 4:30 p.m. until park closes

Setting & atmosphere: The decor is upscale Japanese, only roomier, with light wood-beam ceilings, grass-cloth walls, and lacquered-finish oak chairs. Overall very clean and spare.

House specialties: Chicken, shrimp, beef, scallops, and oriental vegetables stir-fried on a teppan grill by a knife-juggling chef. Teppanyaki is a fancy version of the Benihana restaurant chain.

Entertainment & amenities: Watching the teppan chefs.

Summary & comments: While this restaurant offers some of the best teppan dining you will find in the United States, it has missed a wonderful opportunity to introduce the diversity and beauty of authentic Japanese cuisine to the American public. Be aware that diners at the teppan tables (large tables with a grill in the middle) are seated with other parties. Finally, if you would like to try more traditional Japanese fare, consider Tempura Kiku, a small restaurant in the same building.

TONY'S TOWN SQUARE RESTAURANT ★★½

Italian	Moderate	QUALITY
		78

Main Street, U.S.A., Magic Kingdom; (407) 939-3463	READERS' SURVEY RESPONSES:		VALUE
	74% 👍	26% 👎	D

Customers: Theme park guests
Priority seatings: Recommended
When to go: Late lunch or early
  dinner

Entree range: $9.25–22.75, lunch;
  $16.25–22.75, dinner
Payment: VISA, MC, AMEX
Service rating: ★★★

(Tony's Town Square Restaurant)

Friendliness rating: ★★★★
Parking: Magic Kingdom lot
Bar: None

Wine selection: None
Dress: Casual
Disabled access: Yes

Breakfast: Every day, 8:30–10:45 a.m.
Lunch: Every day, noon–2:45 p.m.
Dinner: Every day, 4 p.m. until park closes

Setting & atmosphere: Decorated like a New York Italian eatery, with tile floors, tablecloths, dark woods, and lots of plants. The walls are filled with memorabilia from *Lady and the Tramp*. It is a bright and open place, but it somehow always has a trampled and unkempt appearance.

House specialties: Designer pizza; penne with Italian sausage; turkey with wild mushrooms and fettuccini.

Other recommendations: Fettuccini with prosciutto (lunch only).

Summary & comments: It's perhaps the most pleasant place to dine in the Magic Kingdom and now offers a more interesting menu. The pace can be hectic, but the atmosphere is light and airy and the pictures and other knickknacks from *Lady and the Tramp* are a lot of fun. Go ahead, share a plate of overpriced spaghetti with someone you love.

VICTORIA & ALBERT'S   ★★★★½

Gourmet	Expensive	QUALITY
		96

Disney's Grand Floridian Beach Resort; (407) 939-7707	READERS' SURVEY RESPONSES:		VALUE
	86% 👍	14% 👎	D

Customers: Hotel guests, locals
Priority seatings: Mandatory; must confirm by noon the day of your seating; call at least 120 days in advance to ensure a table
When to go: Anytime
Entree range: Fixed price: $80 per person or up to $145 with wine pairings

Payment: VISA, MC, AMEX
Service rating: ★★★★
Friendliness rating: ★★★
Parking: Valet parking; self-parking is deceptively far away.
Wine selection: Excellent
Dress: Jacket required
Disabled access: Yes

Dinner: Two seatings nightly at 5:45–6:30 p.m. and 9–9:45 p.m.

(Victoria & Albert's)

Setting & atmosphere: Victoria & Albert's is a small, intimate room under a domed ceiling. It is elegantly appointed, with large floral displays, fine china, crystal, and silver.

House specialties: The menu changes daily but always features selections of fresh game, poultry, fish, and beef.

Entertainment & amenities: A harpist or violinist entertains from the foyer. Guests receive souvenir menus personalized with gold lettering.

Summary & comments: Except for one bit of kitsch—instead of waiters, each table is attended by a maid and butler named Victoria and Albert—this is Disney's most elegant restaurant. It also features some of the finest culinary talent in the southeastern United States. Victoria & Albert's dining room is entirely nonsmoking.

For a special treat, book the chef's table. This will put you in the kitchen, where the executive chef will prepare a special meal for you and your guests, as few as one or as many as eight. There is only one seating each evening, and dinner may take as long as four hours. The cost is at least $115 per person ($160 with wine), but for those who truly love fine food, it's a bargain.

Honors & awards: AAA 4-Diamond Award.

WHISPERING CANYON CAFE		★★½

		QUALITY
American	Moderate	79

Disney's Wilderness Lodge;	READERS' SURVEY RESPONSES:		VALUE
(407) 939-3463	79% 👍	21% 👎	B

Customers: Hotel guests
Priority seatings: Accepted
When to go: Anytime
Entree range: Breakfast: $9.25 adult, $5.95 children; lunch: $12.95 adult, $6.95 children; dinner: $19.95 adult, $7.95 children
Payment: VISA, MC, AMEX

Service rating: ★★
Friendliness rating: ★★★
Parking: Hotel lot
Bar: Full service
Wine selection: Limited
Dress: Casual
Disabled access: Yes

Breakfast: Every day, 7:30–11 a.m.
Lunch: Every day, noon–3 p.m.
Dinner: Every day, 5–10 p.m.

(Whispering Canyon Cafe)

Setting & atmosphere: Located just off the hotel's atrium lobby, the restaurant looks out on the lobby on one side and a mountain prairie, created by the Disney landscapers, on the other. Tables have a barrel-top lazy Susan where the food is placed; diners dish out their own helpings from the platters.

House specialties: Barbecue-and-apple-glazed rotisserie chicken; maple-garlic pork spareribs.

Other recommendations: Smoked barbecue beef brisket; smoked barbecue veal ribs.

Summary & comments: The food is served "family-style," meaning it is brought to the table on platters or in crocks and you dish out however much you'd like. The food is pretty good, and if you're looking to stuff yourself silly, this is the place to be.

WILD HORSE SALOON		★★★

American/barbecue	Moderate	QUALITY
		84

Downtown Disney, Pleasure Island; (407) 827-9453	READERS' SURVEY RESPONSES:	VALUE
	80% 👍 20% 👎	C

Customers: Tourists, country music fans	Service rating: ★★★
	Friendliness rating: ★★★
Priority seatings: On nonconcert nights only	Parking: Downtown Disney lot
	Bar: Full service
When to go: Early evening	Wine selection: Not a strong suit
Entree range: $13.95–23.95	Dress: Cowboy boots and Stetsons
Payment: AMEX, MC, VISA, D	Disabled access: Good

Lunch: Every day, 11:30 a.m.–4 p.m.
Dinner: Every day, 5–10:30 p.m.

Setting & atmosphere: A huge barn of a building with a stage and dance floor downstairs and a balcony dining area upstairs. There are silhouettes of galloping horses, and the carpeting looks like it's covered with hay. Barstool seating is available at the railing of the balcony, which gives the best view of the dance floor. Dining tables have obstructed views.

House specialties: Bourbon-mustard pork chops; Wild Horse sirloin; barbecue-dusted grilled salmon.

(Wild Horse Saloon)

Entertainment & amenities: Live music and country-western dancing.

Summary & comments: This restaurant replaces Fireworks Factory and is owned and operated by the Levy Restaurants group, which also runs Fulton's Crab House and Portobello Yacht Club. The food is a little better than you might expect from a theme restaurant, and the menu is more ambitious than it needs to be. The real focus here is the music, which can be quite loud at times. If you eat too much, you can work it off on the dance floor.

WOLFGANG PUCK CAFE		★ ★ ★
Creative Californian	Expensive	**QUALITY**
		78
Downtown Disney West Side; (407) 938-9653	**READERS' SURVEY RESPONSES:**	**VALUE**
	71% 👍 29% 👎	C

Customers: Tourists and locals	Parking: Downtown Disney lot; valet evenings, $6
Priority seatings: Upstairs only	
When to go: Early evening	Bar: Full service
Entree range: Cafe, $11.95–14.95; upstairs, $24–34	Wine selection: Very good
	Dress: Casual in the Cafe; collared shirt for men upstairs
Payment: VISA, MC, AMEX	
Service rating: ★★★★	Disabled access: Good
Friendliness rating: ★★★★	

Dinner: Sunday–Thursday, 6–10 p.m.; Friday and Saturday, 6–11 p.m.; bar open until midnight

Setting & atmosphere: This is actually two restaurants in one—four if you count the attached Wolfgang Puck Express (and there's no reason to count it for anything) and the sushi bar that does a freeform flow into the restaurant's lounge area. The downstairs is the actual Cafe, with several open kitchen areas, colorful tile (one designer has called it a tile factory outlet store), and plenty of pictures of Wolfgang Puck hanging around the place. The upstairs is a more formal dining room, but in name only. Both spaces are inordinately loud and conversation is difficult. Throughout the restaurant are TV monitors trained on various culinary stations. One supposes this is so diners can watch their food being prepared (they certainly can't talk to one another), but unless you have excellent vision—and we're talking something along the lines of Superman—you probably won't be able to see anything. The images are like the surveillance cameras in convenience stores.

House specialties: Wolfgang Puck became famous with his Spago restaurant in California and is the father of the gourmet pizza. His "signature pizza" features smoked salmon, red onion, dill cream, and chives (none of his pizzas has traditional red sauce). You'll also find smoked sturgeon, roasted lamb chops, Maine lobster with linguine, and blackened catfish. The sushi is quite good. The upstairs dining room has fresh pastas, fish soup, free-range chicken, and Sonoma lamb chops. The Wiener schnitzel, however, is one of the best items on the menu.

Summary & comments: Puck, one of the original celebrity chefs, is a master at self-promotion. His cafe, which is really just a chain restaurant, is very much a shrine to his image. But many of the items on the menu are very good, and W.P.C. is one of the better dining options in Downtown Disney. To get out without sticker shock at the end of the meal, go with one of the pizzas and Puck's popular Chinois salad. If you're looking for a quiet, relaxing meal, however, this isn't the place for you.

YACHT CLUB GALLEY		★★★

American	Moderate	QUALITY
		81

Disney's Yacht Club Resort; (407) 939-3463	READERS' SURVEY RESPONSES:		VALUE
	87% 👍	13% 👎	C

Customers: Hotel guests
Priority seatings: Not necessary
When to go: Breakfast or lunch
Entree range: $10.95–26.95
Payment: VISA, MC, AMEX
Service rating: ★★★★

Friendliness rating: ★★★★
Parking: Hotel lot
Bar: Full service
Wine selection: Good
Dress: Casual
Disabled access: Yes

Breakfast: Every day, 7–11 a.m.
Lunch: Every day, 11:30 a.m.–2:30 p.m.
Dinner: Every day, 5–10 p.m.

Setting & atmosphere: The Yacht Club Galley features a bright nautical theme with colorful pastels, blue-striped wallpaper, and tablecloths. A moving seascape mural is the focal point of the large and somewhat noisy dining room.

House specialties: Daily fresh-fish specials; barbecued pork ribs; seafood stir-fry with shrimp, scallops, and fish. Breakfast features a buffet or an a la carte menu, with such selections as "eggs stockade": eggs with grilled sirloin steak.

Other recommendations: Roast prime rib with burgundy horseradish sauce; breaded clam strips.

Entertainment & amenities: Strolling band in the evening.

Summary & comments: Stop here for breakfast or lunch; it's a short walk from Epcot and a good escape if you just need to get out of the park and relax for a while.

YACHTSMAN STEAKHOUSE ★★★

Steak	Expensive	QUALITY
		80

Disney's Yacht Club Resort; (407) 939-3463	READERS' SURVEY RESPONSES:		VALUE
	96% 👍	4% 👎	D

Customers: Hotel guests, locals
Priority seatings: Required
When to go: Anytime
Entree range: $17–59
Payment: VISA, MC, AMEX
Service rating: ★★★

Friendliness rating: ★★★★
Parking: Hotel lot
Bar: Full service
Wine selection: Very good
Dress: Casual
Disabled access: Yes

Dinner: Every day, 5:30–10 p.m.

Setting & atmosphere: This restaurant is decorated in a country style—lots of knotty pine and chintz tablecloths. A refrigerated display case with big slabs of beef in various stages of the aging process allows you to get acquainted with your steak before you're seated. You can watch it being cooked at the show kitchen, if you wish, and the staff encourages you to ask questions about your meal's preparation. (How about "Is it ready yet?")

House specialties: All steaks are cut and trimmed on the premises daily. The Yacht Club porterhouse, Kansas City strip, and prime rib of beef au jus are just some of the cuts. The mixed grill includes filet, lamb chops, and chicken breast served with three sauces. All entrees include baked potato and bread-board assortment. Béarnaise and bordelaise sauces are available to complement your meat selection.

Other recommendations: Australian lobster stuffed with crabmeat; full rack of lamb; grilled pork chops.

Entertainment & amenities: Strolling musicians (the same ones who stroll through the Yacht Club Galley).

Summary & comments: For die-hard meat lovers who don't mind paying a lot for a good steak. The chintz tablecloths keep it from being a male domain, but women should be offended by the "yachtress" cut of meat. Besides a good wine list, the Yachtsman also has an impressive beer list.

Part Ten

The Magic Kingdom

ARRIVING

On specified days each week, the Magic Kingdom opens an hour early to Walt Disney World hotel and campground guests (excluding guests at the independent hotels of Disney Village Hotel Plaza). If you aren't a Disney resort guest, avoid the Magic Kingdom on early-entry days.

If you stay at a Disney hotel or campground and want to tour the park on a morning when early entry is in effect, arrive 1 hour and 40 minutes before the official opening time. If official opening is 9 a.m., for example, arrive at the park about 7:20 a.m. via Disney Transportation. Do not drive your own car. When you're admitted at 7:30 a.m., you'll be able to enjoy all attractions in Fantasyland except *Legend of the Lion King* and all Tomorrowland attractions except *The Timekeeper* and *Walt Disney's Carousel of Progress*. Sometimes, Space Mountain opens a half hour later than other Tomorrowland attractions (at 8 a.m. in this example).

One year during our research, the official opening time was 8 a.m. Testing the system, we were waiting at the bus stop at Dixie Landings Resort a little after 6 a.m. Sure enough, the bus rolled up a few minutes later, full of sleepy parents and excited children. We were admitted to the Magic Kingdom at 6:30 a.m., about a half hour before sunrise. Though Main Street was lighted, Disney cast members (employees) kept us moving past the closed shops to Fantasyland. There, dads huddled over coffee while moms and children soared aloft on Dumbo to greet the rising sun.

During summer and holiday periods, increased crowds (resulting from Disney resort guests exercising their early-entry option) create nearly unmanageable congestion by around 10 a.m. If you're eligible for early entry, tour one of the other parks where early entry is not in effect or take advantage of early entry for an hour or two first thing in the morning at the Magic Kingdom, then head to another park for the remainder of the day.

Because Disney is always changing things, call Walt Disney World Information at (407) 824-4321 before you leave home to verify the early-entry days during your stay. Visitors ineligible for early entry should not attempt to sneak in with early-entry guests. All Disney hotel and campground guests, including children, are issued dated identification cards upon check-in at their hotel and must present them with valid admission passes in order to enter a park early.

GETTING ORIENTED

If you drive, the Magic Kingdom / Transportation and Ticket Center (TTC) parking lot opens about two hours before the park's official opening. After paying a fee, you are directed to a parking space, then transported by tram to the TTC, where you catch either a monorail or ferry to the park's entrance.

If you're staying at the Contemporary, Polynesian, or Grand Floridian resorts, you can commute directly to the Magic Kingdom by monorail (guests at the Contemporary can walk there more quickly). If you stay at Wilderness Lodge or Fort Wilderness Campground, you will take a boat. Guests at other Disney resorts can reach the park by bus. All Disney lodging guests, whether they arrive by bus, monorail, or boat, are deposited at the park's entrance, bypassing the TTC.

At the Magic Kingdom, stroller and wheelchair rentals are to the right of the train station and lockers are on the station's ground floor. On your left as you enter Main Street is City Hall, the center for information, lost and found, guided tours, and entertainment schedules.

If you don't already have a handout guidemap of the park, get one at City Hall. The guidemap lists all attractions, shops, and eating places; provides helpful information about first aid, baby care, and assistance for the disabled; and gives tips for good photos. It also lists times for the day's special events, live entertainment, Disney character parades, concerts, and other activities. The *Disney Character Greeting Location Guide*, telling when and where to find Disney characters, is also included in the handout map.

Main Street ends at a central hub from which branch the entrances to five other sections of the Magic Kingdom: Adventureland, Frontierland, Liberty Square, Fantasyland, and Tomorrowland. Mickey's Toontown Fair is wedged like a dimple between the cheeks of Fantasyland and Tomorrowland and doesn't connect to the central hub.

Cinderella Castle is the entrance to Fantasyland and the Magic Kingdom's visual center. If you start in Adventureland and go clockwise around the Magic Kingdom, the castle spires will always be roughly on your right; if you start in Tomorrowland and go counterclockwise through

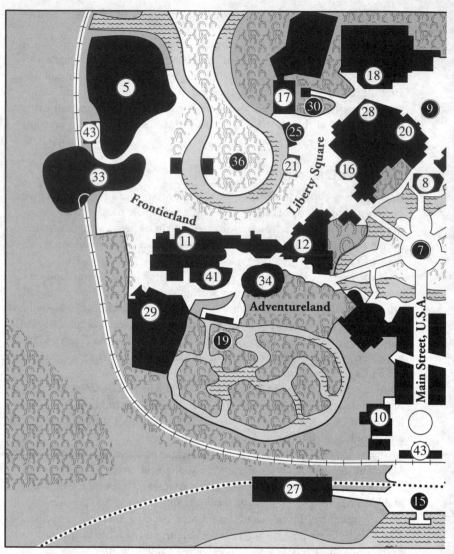

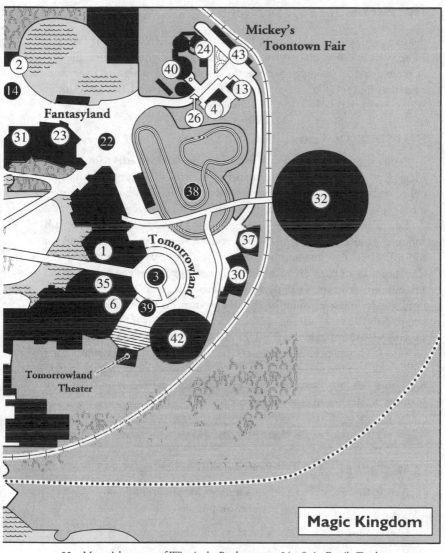

Mickey's Toontown Fair

Fantasyland

Tomorrowland

Tomorrowland Theater

Magic Kingdom

23. Many Adventures of Winnie the Pooh
24. Mickey's House
25. Mike Fink Keelboats
26. Minnie's House
27. Monorail Station
28. Peter Pan's Flight
29. Pirates of the Caribbean
30. Skyway
31. Snow White's Adventures
32. Space Mountain
33. Splash Mountain

34. Swiss Family Treehouse
35. *The Timekeeper*
36. Tom Sawyer Island
37. Tomorrowland Arcade
38. Tomorrowland Speedway
39. Tomorrowland Transit Authority
40. Toontown Hall of Fame
41. *Tropical Serenade*
    (Enchanted Tiki Birds)
42. *Walt Disney's Carousel of Progress*
43. WDW Railroad Station

the park, the spires will always be roughly on your left. Cinderella Castle is an excellent meeting place if your group decides to split up during the day or is separated accidentally. Because the castle is large, designate a very specific meeting spot, like the entrance to Cinderella's Royal Table restaurant at the rear of the castle.

STARTING THE TOUR

Everyone soon finds their favorite and not-so-favorite attractions in the Magic Kingdom. Be open-minded and adventuresome. Our personal experience and research indicate that each visitor differs on which attraction is most enjoyable. Don't dismiss a ride or show until *after* you have tried it.

Take advantage of what Disney does best: the fantasy adventures of Splash Mountain and The Haunted Mansion and the Audio-Animatronics (talking robots) attractions, including *The Hall of Presidents* and Pirates of the Caribbean. Don't burn daylight browsing the shops unless you plan to spend a minimum of two and a half days at the Magic Kingdom, and even then wait until midday or later. Minimize the time you spend on midway-type rides; you probably have something similar near your hometown. (Don't, however, mistake Space Mountain and Big Thunder Mountain Railroad as amusement park rides. They may be roller coasters, but they're pure Disney genius.) Eat a good breakfast early, and avoid lines at eateries by snacking during the day on food from vendors. Fare at most Magic Kingdom eateries is on a par with Hardee's or McDonald's (nothing special).

Not to Be Missed at the Magic Kingdom	
Adventureland	Pirates of the Caribbean
Frontierland	Big Thunder Mountain Railroad
	Splash Mountain
Liberty Square	The Haunted Mansion
Tomorrowland	Space Mountain
	The Timekeeper
Special events	Evening Parade

Main Street, U.S.A.

You begin and end your Magic Kingdom visit on Main Street, which opens a half hour before, and closes a half hour to an hour after, the rest of the park. The Walt Disney World Railroad stops at the Main Street Station; board here for a grand tour of the park or a ride to Frontierland or Mickey's Toontown Fair.

Main Street is a sanitized Disney re-creation of a turn-of-the-century, small-town American street. Its buildings are real, not elaborate props. Attention to detail is exceptional: all interiors, furnishings, and fixtures are true to the period. Along the street are shops and eating places, City Hall, a fire station, and an old-time cinema. Horse-drawn trolleys, double-decker buses, fire engines, and horseless carriages transport visitors along Main Street to the central hub.

Main Street Services	
Most park services are centered on Main Street, including:	
Wheelchair & Stroller Rental	Right of the main entrance before passing under the railroad station
Banking Services	Automated tellers (ATMs) are underneath the Main Street railroad station
Storage Lockers	Ground floor of the railroad station at the end of Main Street; all lockers are cleaned out each night.
Lost & Found	City Hall at the railroad station end of Main Street
Live Entertainment & Parade Info	City Hall at the railroad station end of Main Street
Lost Persons	City Hall
Walt Disney World & Local Attraction Information	City Hall
First Aid	Next to The Crystal Palace, left around the central hub (toward Adventureland)
Baby Center/ Baby-Care Needs	Next to The Crystal Palace, left around the central hub (toward Adventureland)

Walt Disney World Railroad

What It Is: Scenic railroad ride around perimeter of the Magic Kingdom, and transportation to Frontierland and Mickey's Toontown Fair

Scope & Scale: Minor attraction

When to Go: Anytime

Special Comments: Main Street is usually the least congested station.

Author's Rating: Plenty to see; ★★½ [Critical ratings are based on a scale of zero to five stars. Five stars is the best possible rating.]

Appeal by Age Group:

Pre-school	Grade School	Teens	Young Adults	Over 30	Senior Citizens
★★★★	★★★	★★	★★½	★★★	★★★

Duration of Ride: About 19 minutes for a complete circuit

Average Wait in Line per 100 People ahead of You: 8 minutes

Assumes: 2 or more trains operating

Loading Speed: Fast

Description and Comments   A transportation ride blending an unusual variety of sights and experiences with an energy-saving way to get around the park. The train provides a glimpse of all lands except Adventureland.

A Princeton, New Jersey, dad disputes our comment that there's "plenty to see" on the Walt Disney World Railroad:

> *I'm not sure why you say there is "plenty to see." We get a great view of lots of trees, a brief glimpse of the queue for Splash Mountain and a scene inside it, an even briefer glimpse of Fantasyland, and a view of Toontown Fair, and that's about it. Yeah, it's kind of fun to ride an old steam engine, and our two-year-old sure likes trains, but I found the sights kind of boring.*

Touring Tips   Save the train ride until after you have seen the featured attractions, or use it when you need transportation. On busy days, lines form at the Frontierland Station, but rarely at the Main Street and Mickey's Toontown Fair Stations. Strollers aren't allowed on the train. Wheel-chair access is available only at the Frontierland and Mickey's Toontown Fair stations.

Although you cannot take your rental stroller on the train, you can obtain a replacement stroller at your Walt Disney World Railroad destination. Just take your personal belongings, your stroller name card, and your rental receipt with you on the train.

Transportation Rides

Description and Comments   Trolleys, buses, etc., which add color to Main Street.

Touring Tips   Will save you a walk to the central hub. Not worth waiting in line.

Main Street Eateries and Shops

Description and Comments   Some of the Magic Kingdom's better food and specialty/souvenir shopping in a nostalgic, happy setting. The Emporium offers the park's best selection of Disney trademark souvenirs.

Touring Tips   If seeing the park attractions is your goal, save Main Street until day's end. If shopping is your objective, avoid the noon hour, parade times, and near closing time, when stores are most crowded. Remember, Main Street opens a half hour earlier and closes a half hour to an hour later than the rest of the park.

The Crystal Palace, at the central hub end of Main Street (toward Adventureland), offers a character buffet and is often overlooked by lunch-hour (but not dinner-hour) crowds. If you're nearby at noon, try it.

Adventureland

Adventureland is the first land to the left of Main Street. It combines an African safari theme with an old New Orleans/Caribbean atmosphere.

Swiss Family Treehouse

What It Is: Outdoor walk-through treehouse
Scope & Scale: Minor attraction
When to Go: Before 11:30 a.m. and after 5 p.m.
Special Comments: Requires climbing a lot of stairs
Author's Rating: A visual delight; ★★★
Appeal by Age Group:

Pre-school	Grade School	Teens	Young Adults	Over 30	Senior Citizens
★★★	★★★½	★★★	★★★	★★★	★★★

Duration of Tour: 10–15 minutes
Average Wait in Line per 100 People ahead of You: 7 minutes
Assumes: Normal staffing
Loading Speed: Doesn't apply

Description and Comments   An immense replica of the shipwrecked family's treehouse home will turn your children into arboreal architects. It's the castle of all treehouses, with its multiple stories, clever jerry-rigging, and mechanical wizardry.

Touring Tips   A self-guided walk-through tour involves a lot of stairs up and down, but no ropes, ladders, or anything fancy. People who stop for extra-long looks or to rest sometimes create bottlenecks that slow crowd flow. Visit in late afternoon or early evening if you're on a one-day tour, or in the morning of your second day.

Jungle Cruise

What It Is: Outdoor safari-themed boat ride adventure

Scope & Scale: Major attraction

When to Go: Before 10 a.m. or two hours before closing

Author's Rating: A long-enduring Disney masterpiece; ★★★

Appeal by Age Group:

Pre-school	Grade School	Teens	Young Adults	Over 30	Senior Citizens
★★★½	★★★½	★★½	★★★	★★★	★★★

Duration of Ride: 8–9 minutes

Average Wait in Line per 100 People ahead of You: 3½ minutes

Assumes: 10 boats operating

Loading Speed: Moderate

Description and Comments   An outdoor cruise through jungle waterways. Passengers encounter animatronic elephants, lions, hostile natives, and a menacing hippo. Boatman's spiel adds to the fun. Once one of the most grand and elaborate attractions at the Magic Kingdom, the Jungle Cruise's technology now seems dated and worn. Since the advent of the Animal Kingdom, the attraction's appeal has diminished, but in it's defense, you can always depend on the Jungle Cruise's robotic critters being present as you motor past.

An Albany, New York, woman agrees that the Jungle Cruise is past its prime:

> *Jungle Cruise needs updating! My husband gave it a five on the "cheese factor" scale.*

Touring Tips   Among the park's oldest attractions and one that occupies a good third of Adventureland. A convoluted queuing area makes it very difficult to estimate the length of the wait for the Jungle Cruise. A mother from the Bronx, New York, complains:

> *The line for this ride is extremely deceiving. We got in line towards the early evening; it was long but we really wanted to take this ride. Every time the winding line brought us near the loading dock and we thought we were going to get on, we'd discover a whole new section of winding lanes to go through. It was extremely frustrating. We must have waited a good 20–30 minutes before the two of us finally gave up and got out.*

Pirates of the Caribbean

What It Is: Indoor pirate-themed adventure boat ride

Scope & Scale: Headliner

When to Go: Before noon or after 5 p.m.

Special Comments: Frightens some young children

Author's Rating: Disney Audio-Animatronics at its best; not to be missed;
★★★★★

Appeal by Age Group:

Pre-school	Grade School	Teens	Young Adults	Over 30	Senior Citizens
★★★	★★★★★	★★★★	★★★★	★★★★½	★★★★½

Duration of Ride: About 7½ minutes

Average Wait in Line per 100 People ahead of You: 1½ minutes

Assumes: Both waiting lines operating

Loading Speed: Fast

Description and Comments An indoor cruise through a series of sets depicting a pirate raid on an island settlement, from bombardment of the fortress to debauchery after the victory. Regarding debauchery, Pirates of the Caribbean is one of several Disney attractions that has been administered a strong dose of political correctness. See if you can spot the changes.

Touring Tips Undoubtedly one of the park's most elaborate and imaginative attractions. Engineered to move large crowds in a hurry, Pirates is a good attraction to see during later afternoon. It has two waiting lines, both covered.

Tropical Serenade (Enchanted Tiki Birds)

What It Is: Audio-Animatronic Pacific island musical theater show

Scope & Scale: Minor attraction

When to Go: Before 11 a.m. and after 3:30 p.m.

Special Comments: Frightens some preschoolers

Author's Rating: Very, very unusual; ★★★½

Appeal by Age Group:

Pre-school	Grade School	Teens	Young Adults	Over 30	Senior Citizens
★★★★	★★★½	★★★	★★★	★★★	★★★

Duration of Presentation: 15½ minutes

Preshow Entertainment: Talking birds

Probable Waiting Time: 15 minutes

Description and Comments   Upgraded in 1998, this theater presentation now features two of Disney's most beloved bird characters, Iago from *Aladdin,* and Zazu from *The Lion King.* A new song, "Friend Like Me," and a revamped plotline add some much needed zip, but the production remains (pardon the pun) a featherweight in the Disney galaxy of attractions. Even so, the *Tiki Birds* are a great favorite of the eight-and-under set. Although readers like the *Enchanted Tiki Birds* show, they caution that the new version is more frightening to younger children than was the old. The remarks of this Provo, Utah, mom are typical:

> *I want to address the new* Tiki Bird *show. It was a refreshing change from the other show and is definitely more interesting. Although there is a new element with the Tiki gods that may frighten small children because of loud noises.*

Concerning the scary parts, a mother of three from Coleman, Michigan, was somewhat more outspoken:

> *The* Tiki Bird *show was very scary, with a thunder and lightening storm and a loud volcano goddess with glowing red eyes. Can't Disney do anything without scaring young children? It's a bird show!*

A New Jersey dad concurred, commenting:

> Enchanted Tiki Birds *are now REALLY intense—far more intense than I remember fondly from previous visits. Tiki Gods storming and smoking, the whole room plunged into utter darkness, and thunder and lightening that quite literally shakes the benches you're sitting on—our child (2½) was terrified. Definitely not recommended for very young children; it seems the attraction is aimed at older children now.*

Touring Tips   One of the more bizarre Magic Kingdom entertainments.

Usually not too crowded. We go in the late afternoon when we especially appreciate sitting briefly in an air-conditioned theater.

Adventureland Eateries and Shops

Description and Comments   Restaurants tend to be less crowded during lunch than other Magic Kingdom eateries.

Touring Tips   El Pirata y el Perico, featuring Mexican fast food and hot dogs, is often overlooked.

Frontierland

Frontierland adjoins Adventureland as you move clockwise around the Magic Kingdom. The focus is on the Old West, with stockade-type structures and pioneer trappings.

Splash Mountain

What It Is: Indoor / outdoor water-flume adventure ride

Scope & Scale: Super headliner

When to Go: As soon as the park opens, during afternoon or evening parades, or just before closing

Special Comments: Children must be 40" tall to ride; those younger than 7 must ride with an adult. Switching off option provided (pages 190–192).

Author's Rating: A wet winner; not to be missed; ★★★★★

Appeal by Age Group:

Pre-school	Grade School	Teens	Young Adults	Over 30	Senior Citizens
†	★★★★★	★★★★★	★★★★★	★★★★★	★★★½

† Many preschoolers are too short to meet the height requirement, and others are visually intimidated when they see the ride from the waiting line. Among preschoolers who actually ride, most give the attraction high marks (3–5 stars).

Duration of Ride: About 10 minutes

Average Wait in Line per 100 People ahead of You: 3½ minutes

Assumes: Operating at full capacity

Loading Speed: Moderate

Description and Comments   Amusement park flume ride, Disney-style. Bigger than life and more imaginative than anyone thought possible. Combines steep chutes with excellent special effects. Covers over half a

WARNING!

For Bouffants, Rug Wearers, and Elvis Impersonators

This Ride Will Muss Your 'Do'

mile, splashing through swamps, caves, and backwood bayous before climaxing in a five-story plunge and Brer Rabbit's triumphant return home. More than 100 Audio-Animatronic characters, including Brer Rabbit, Brer Bear, and Brer Fox, regale riders with songs including "Zip-a-Dee-Doo-Dah."

Touring Tips   This happy, exciting, adventuresome ride vies with Space Mountain in Tomorrowland as the park's most popular attraction. Crowds build fast in the morning, and waits of more than two hours can be expected once the park fills. Get in line first thing, certainly no later than 45 minutes after the park opens. Long lines will persist all day.

As occurs with Space Mountain, when the park opens, hundreds are poised to dash to Splash Mountain. The best strategy is to go to the end of Main Street and turn left to The Crystal Palace restaurant. In front of the restaurant is a bridge that provides a shortcut to Adventureland. Stake out a position at the barrier rope. When the park opens and the rope drops, move as fast as you comfortably can and cross the bridge to Adventureland.

Here's another shortcut: Just past the first group of buildings on your right, roughly across from the Swiss Family Treehouse, is a small passageway containing rest rooms and phones. Easy to overlook, it connects Adventureland to Frontierland. Go through the passageway into Frontierland and take a hard left. As you emerge along the waterfront, Splash Mountain is straight ahead. If you miss the passageway, don't fool around looking for it. Continue straight through Adventureland to Splash Mountain.

Less exhausting in the morning is to reach Splash Mountain via the Walt Disney World Railroad. Board at Main Street Station and wait for the park to open. The train will pull out of the station at the same time the rope drops at the central hub end of Main Street. Ride to Frontierland Station (the first stop) and disembark. As you come down the stairs at the station, the entrance to Splash Mountain will be on your right. Because of the time required to unload at the station, train passengers will arrive at Splash Mountain about the same time as the lead element from the central hub.

A Suffolk, Virginia, mom contends that there are more important considerations than beating the crowds:

> *The only recommendation I do have for the Magic Kingdom plan is to definitely wait to do Splash Mountain at the end of the day. We were seated in the front of the ride and needless to say we were soaked to the bone. If we had ridden the ride [first thing in the morning] according to your plan, I personally would have been miserable for the rest of the day. Parents, Beware! It says you will get wet, not drowned.*

At Splash Mountain, if you ride in the front seat, you almost certainly will get wet. Riders elsewhere get splashed, but usually not doused. Since you don't know which seat you'll be assigned, go prepared. On a cool day, carry a plastic garbage bag. Tear holes in the bottom and sides to make a water-resistant (not waterproof) sack dress. Be sure to tuck the bag under your bottom. Leave your camera with a nonriding member of your group or wrap it in plastic.

The scariest part of this adventure ride is the steep chute you see when standing in line, but the drop looks worse than it is. Despite reassurances, however, many children wig out after watching it. A mom from Grand Rapids, Michigan, recalls her kids' rather unique reaction:

> *We discovered after the fact that our children thought they would go underwater after the five-story drop and tried to hold their breath throughout the ride in preparation. They were really too preoccupied to enjoy the clever Brer Rabbit story.*

Another reader thought he was in the clear after his kids took *Alien Encounter* in stride, writing:

> *I'm sure you're going to think our sense of humor is really warped and a sign of the imminent collapse of our civilization, but my ten-year-old son and I found* Alien Encounter *funnier than it was scary, and very well done overall. Just to show, though, that it's often hard to predict what will push somebody's buttons the wrong way, at Splash Mountain the drop in the dark and the big final drop terrified both my kids (ages 10 and 13!). And they handled flume rides at other parks without a problem. It will probably be years before they get on a flume ride anywhere again.*

Big Thunder Mountain Railroad

What It Is: Tame, western-mining-themed roller coaster

Scope & Scale: Headliner

When to Go: Before 10 a.m. or in the hour before closing

Special Comments: Children must be 40" tall to ride. Those younger than

age 7 must ride with an adult. Switching off option provided (pages 190–192).

Author's Rating: Great effects; relatively tame ride; not to be missed; ★★★★

Appeal by Age Group:

Pre-school	Grade School	Teens	Young Adults	Over 30	Senior Citizens
★★★	★★★★	★★★★	★★★★	★★★★	★★★

Duration of Ride: Almost 3½ minutes

Average Wait in Line per 100 People ahead of You: 2½ minutes

Assumes: 5 trains operating

Loading Speed: Moderate to fast

Description and Comments   Roller coaster through and around a Disney "mountain." The idea is that you're on a runaway mine train during the Gold Rush. This roller coaster is about 5 on a "scary scale" of 10. First-rate examples of Disney creativity are showcased: realistic mining town, falling rocks, and an earthquake, all humorously animated.

Touring Tips   A superb Disney experience, but not too wild a roller coaster. Emphasis is much more on the sights than on the thrill of the ride.

Nearby Splash Mountain affects the traffic flow to Big Thunder Mountain Railroad. Adventuresome guests ride Splash Mountain first, then go next door to ride Big Thunder. This means large crowds in Frontierland all day and long waits for Big Thunder Mountain. The best way to experience the Magic Kingdom's "mountains" is to ride Space Mountain when the park opens, Splash Mountain immediately afterward, then Big Thunder Mountain.

Guests experience Disney attractions differently. Consider this letter from a lady in Brookline, Massachusetts:

> *Being in the senior citizens' category and having limited time, my friend and I confined our activities to those attractions rated as four or five stars for seniors. Because of your recommendation and because you*

listed it as "not to be missed," we waited for one hour to board the Big Thunder Mountain Railroad, [which you] rated a "5" on a scary scale of "10." After living through three-and-a-half minutes of pure terror, I will rate that attraction a "15" on a scary scale of "10." We were so busy holding on and screaming and even praying for our safety that we did not see any falling rocks, a mining town, or an earthquake. In our opinion, the Big Thunder Mountain Railroad should not be recommended for seniors or preschool children.

Another woman from New England writes:

My husband, who is 41, found Big Thunder Mountain too intense for his enjoyment, and feels that anyone who does not like roller coasters would not enjoy this ride.

However, a reader from West Newton, Massachusetts, dubbed Big Thunder Mountain "a roller coaster for people who don't like roller coasters."

Country Bear Jamboree

What It Is: Audio-Animatronic country hoedown theater show

Scope & Scale: Major attraction

When to Go: Before 11:30 a.m., before a parade, or during the two hours before closing

Special Comments: Shows change at Christmas and during summer

Author's Rating: A Disney classic; ★★★

Appeal by Age Group:

Pre-school	Grade School	Teens	Young Adults	Over 30	Senior Citizens
★★★½	★★★	★★½	★★★	★★★	★★★

Duration of Presentation: 15 minutes

Preshow Entertainment: None

Probable Waiting Time: This attraction is very popular but has a comparatively small capacity. Waiting time between noon and 5:30 p.m. on a busy day will average 30–50 minutes.

Description and Comments A charming cast of Audio-Animatronic (robotic) bears sing and stomp their way through a western-style hoedown. Although one of the Magic Kingdom's most humorous and upbeat shows, *Country Bear Jamboree* hasn't been revised for many moons, disappointing some repeat visitors.

One reader thinks the *Jamboree* is way past its prime, writing:

Country Bear Jamboree—*"A Disney classic ★★★"*—*You cannot be serious!! Although I must admit my ten-year-old daughter enjoyed it and got very angry about all the jokes we made about it for the remainder of the holiday!*

A Sandy Hook, Connecticut, mom agrees, commenting:

I know they consider it a classic, and kids always seem to love it, but could they PLEASE update it after half a century?

But, a dad from Cape Coral defends the show:

Don't sell the Country Bear Jamboree *short. It may be boring to repeat visitors, but the look on our three-year-old son's face as he saw the show was priceless. In addition, he was astounded when he left the theater and found the mounted heads on the wall of the restaurant still singing away. It was the best thing we saw for him that day.*

Touring Tips The *Jamboree* is extremely popular and draws large crowds, even early in the day.

Tom Sawyer Island and Fort Sam Clemens

What It Is: Outdoor walk-through exhibit/rustic playground

Scope & Scale: Minor attraction

When to Go: Midmorning through late afternoon

Special Comments: Closes at dusk

Author's Rating: The place for rambunctious kids; ★★★

Appeal by Age Group:

Pre-school	Grade School	Teens	Young Adults	Over 30	Senior Citizens
★★★★★	★★★★★	★★	★★	★★	★★

Description and Comments Tom Sawyer Island is a getaway within the park. It has hills to climb, a cave and windmill to explore, a tipsy barrel bridge to cross, and paths to follow. It's a delight for adults and a godsend for children who have been in tow and closely supervised all day. They love the freedom to explore and the excitement of firing air guns from the walls of Fort Sam Clemens. There even is a "secret" escape tunnel.

Touring Tips Tom Sawyer Island isn't one of the Magic Kingdom's more celebrated attractions, but it's one of the park's better conceived ones. Attention to detail is excellent, and kids revel in its frontier atmosphere. It's a must for families with children ages 5 through 15. If your group is adults, visit on your second day or stop by on your first day after you've seen the attractions you most wanted to see.

Although children could spend a whole day on the island, plan on at least 20 minutes. Access is by raft from Frontierland; two operate simultaneously and the trip is pretty efficient, though you may have to stand in line to board both coming and going. Despite its limited menu, Aunt Polly's Dockside Inn on Tom Sawyer Island is our favorite place for lunch in the Magic Kingdom.

For a mother from Duncan, South Carolina, Tom Sawyer Island is as much a refuge as an attraction:

> *I do have one tip for parents. In the afternoon when the crowds were at their peak, the weather [at] its hottest, and the kids started lagging behind, our organization began to suffer. We then retreated over to Tom Sawyer Island, which proved to be a true haven. My husband and I found a secluded bench and regrouped while sipping iced tea and eating delicious soft ice cream. Meanwhile, the kids were able to run freely in the shade. Afterward, we were ready to tackle the park again, refreshed and with direction once more. (Admittedly, I got this tip from another guidebook.)*

According to a dad from Hampton, Connecticut, Tom Sawyer Island was a hit with three generations of his family:

> *Tom Sawyer Island was grandfather's favorite [attraction]—he fell asleep in the rocking chair on Aunt Polly's Landing while the kids explored the islands and mom and dad rested with cool drinks*

And a Chesterfield, Missouri, dad liked the low-tech simplicity of the attraction:

> *Tom Sawyer Island was a huge hit with our kids (seven and five). Despite the lack of robots, lasers, or soundtracks, it was pure and simple Disney magic.*

The Diamond Horseshoe Saloon Revue

What It Is: Live western song and dance show

Scope & Scale: Minor attraction

When to Go: Check the daily entertainment schedule

Special Comments: No Disney characters appear in this show

Author's Rating: Fast-paced and funny; ★★★

Appeal by Age Group:

Pre-school	Grade School	Teens	Young Adults	Over 30	Senior Citizens
★★	★★★	★★	★★★½	★★★½	★★★½

Duration of Show: About 40 minutes

Average Wait in Line per 100 People ahead of You: No wait

Description and Comments   The *Diamond Horseshoe Saloon Revue* is a PG-rated version of a cattle-town saloon show, with comedy, song, and sometimes dancing. Audience members are conscripted to join the cast.

Disney World Problem 204: Too Short to Ride

Touring Tips The *Revue* was reservations-only until 1995, when it was reworked. Now, just walk in, have a seat, and wait for the show to begin. Times are listed in the entertainment column of the official guidemap. Sit in the balcony if you want to avoid being part of the show. Sandwiches, chips, cookies, and soft drinks are available at the bar. *The Diamond Horseshoe* is often overlooked by lunch crowds, especially between shows. We like to catch the *Revue* over lunch or after the afternoon parade.

Frontierland Shootin' Arcade

What It Is: Electronic shooting gallery

Scope & Scale: Diversion

When to Go: Whenever convenient

Special Comments: Costs 25¢ per play

Author's Rating: Very nifty shooting gallery; ★½

Appeal by Age Group:

Pre- school	Grade School	Teens	Young Adults	Over 30	Senior Citizens
★★★	★★★	★★★	★★	★★	★★

Description and Comments Very elaborate. One of few attractions not included in Magic Kingdom admission.

Touring Tips Not a place to blow your time if you're on a tight schedule. If time allows, go on your second day. The fun is entirely in the target practice—no prizes can be won.

Walt Disney World Railroad

Description and Comments Stops in Frontierland on its circle tour of the park. See the description under Main Street for additional details regarding sights along the route.

Touring Tips Pleasant, feet-saving link to Main Street and Mickey's Toontown Fair, but the Frontierland Station is usually more congested than those stations. You cannot take your rental stroller on the train. If you don't want to make a round trip to pick up your stroller, take your personal belongings, your stroller name card, and your rental receipt with you on the train. You'll be issued a replacement stroller at your Walt Disney World Railroad destination.

Frontierland Eateries and Shops

Description and Comments Coonskin caps and western-theme shopping. Fast-food eateries usually are very crowded between 11:30 a.m. and 2 p.m.

An exception is Aunt Polly's Dockside Inn on Tom Sawyer Island. Under cover but outdoors, Aunt Polly's is a great place to escape the jostling crowds on a busy day. Sit on the veranda and watch riverboats float past on the waterway below. Fare is limited to ham and Swiss cheese, turkey, and peanut butter and jelly sandwiches. Prices are reasonable, and food is good.

Touring Tips   Don't waste time shopping unless that's what you came for or you have a very relaxed schedule. If the wait to board the raft to Tom Sawyer Island isn't prohibitive, lunch at Aunt Polly's Dockside Inn. Another time-saver is to eat at the *Diamond Horseshoe* just after a show has concluded.

Liberty Square

Liberty Square re-creates Colonial America at the time of the American Revolution. The architecture is Federal or Colonial. A real, 130-year-old live oak (dubbed the "Liberty Tree") lends dignity and grace to the setting.

The Hall of Presidents

What It Is: Audio-Animatronic historical theater presentation

Scope & Scale: Major attraction

When to Go: Anytime

Author's Rating: Impressive and moving; ★★★

Appeal by Age Group:

Pre-school	Grade School	Teens	Young Adults	Over 30	Senior Citizens
★	★★½	★★★	★★★½	★★★★	★★★★

Duration of Presentation: Almost 23 minutes

Preshow Entertainment: None

Probable Waiting Time: Lines for this attraction look awesome but are usually swallowed up as the theater exchanges audiences. Your wait will probably be the remaining time of the show that's in progress when you arrive. Even during the busiest times of day, waits rarely exceed 40 minutes.

Description and Comments   A 23-minute, strongly inspirational and patri-otic program highlighting milestones in American history. The performance climaxes with a roll call of presidents from Washington through the present, with a few words of encouragement from Presidents Lincoln and Clinton. A very moving show, coupled with one of Disney's best and most ambitious Audio-Animatronic (robotic) efforts. The narration is by Maya Angelou.

Our high opinion notwithstanding, we receive a lot of mail from readers who get more than entertainment from *The Hall of Presidents*. A lady in St. Louis writes:

> *We always go to* The Hall of Presidents *when my husband gets cranky so he can take a nice nap.*

A young mother in Marion, Ohio, adds:

> The Hall of Presidents *is a great place to breast feed.*

Touring Tips   Detail and costumes are masterful. If your children fidget during the show, notice the presidents do, too. This attraction is one of the park's most popular, particularly among older visitors, and draws large crowds from 11 a.m. through about 5 p.m. Don't be put off by long lines. The theater holds more than 700 people, thus swallowing large lines at a single gulp when visitors are admitted. One show is always in progress while the lobby is being filled for the next show. At less busy times, you probably will be admitted directly to the lobby without waiting in line. When the lobby fills, those remaining in line are held outside until those in the lobby move into the theater for the next show, at which time another 700 people are admitted into the lobby.

Liberty Belle Riverboat

What It Is: Outdoor scenic boat ride

Scope & Scale: Major attraction

When to Go: Anytime

Author's Rating: Slow, relaxing, and scenic; ★★½

Appeal by Age Group:

Pre-school	Grade School	Teens	Young Adults	Over 30	Senior Citizens
★★★½	★★★	★★½	★★★	★★★	★★★

Duration of Ride: About 16 minutes

Average Wait to Board: 10–14 minutes

Assumes: Normal operation

Description and Comments   Large-capacity paddle-wheel riverboat navigates the waters around Tom Sawyer Island and Fort Sam Clemens. A beautiful craft, the riverboat provides a lofty perspective of Frontierland and Liberty Square.

Touring Tips   One of two boat rides that survey the same real estate. Since the Mike Fink Keelboats are slower loading, we prefer the riverboat. If you don't want to ride, see the same sights by hiking around Tom Sawyer Island.

The Haunted Mansion

What It Is: Haunted-house dark ride

Scope & Scale: Major attraction

When to Go: Before 11:30 a.m. or after 8 p.m.

Special Comments: Frightens some very young children

Author's Rating: Some of Walt Disney World's best special effects; not to be missed; ★★★★

Appeal by Age Group:

Pre-school	Grade School	Teens	Young Adults	Over 30	Senior Citizens
(Varies)	★★★★★	★★★★	★★★★	★★★★	★★★★

Duration of Ride: 7-minute ride plus a 1½-minute preshow

Average Wait in Line per 100 People ahead of You: 2½ minutes

Assumes: Both "stretch rooms" operating

Loading Speed: Fast

Description and Comments More fun than scary, with some of the Magic Kingdom's best special effects, the Haunted Mansion is a masterpiece of detail. "Doom Buggies" on a conveyor belt transport you throughout the house from parlor to attic, and then through a graveyard. Disney claims there's a storyline, but it's so thin and unemphasized you won't notice. Some children become overly anxious about what they think they'll see. Almost nobody is scared by the actual sights.

The Haunted Mansion is one of veteran *Unofficial Guide* writer Eve Zibart's favorite attractions. She warns:

> *Don't let the childishness of the old-fashioned Haunted Mansion put you off: This is one of the best attractions in the Magic Kingdom. It's jam packed with visual puns, special effects, hidden Mickeys, and really lovely Victorian-spooky sets. It's not scary, except in the sweetest of ways, but it will remind you of the days before ghost stories gave way to slasher flicks.*

Touring Tips This attraction would be more at home in Fantasyland, but no matter. It's Disney at its best. Lines here ebb and flow more than those at most other Magic Kingdom high spots because the mansion is near *The Hall of Presidents* and the *Liberty Belle* Riverboat. These two attractions disgorge 700 and 450 people respectively when each show or ride ends, and many of these folks head straight for the mansion. If you can't go before 11:30 a.m. or after 8 p.m., try to slip in between crowds.

Mike Fink Keelboats

What It Is: Outdoor scenic boat ride

Scope & Scale: Minor attraction

When to Go: Before 11:30 a.m. or after 5 p.m.

Special Comments: Don't ride if the lines are long; closes at dusk

Author's Rating: ★★

Appeal by Age Group:

Pre-school	Grade School	Teens	Young Adults	Over 30	Senior Citizens
★★★	★★★	★★½	★★½	★★½	★★½

Duration of Ride: 9½ minutes

Average Wait in Line per 100 People ahead of You: 15 minutes

Assumes: 2 boats operating

Loading Speed: Slow

Description and Comments   Small river keelboats circle Tom Sawyer Island and Fort Sam Clemens. The keelboat's top deck is exposed to the elements.

Touring Tips   The boats cruise the same circle traveled by the *Liberty Belle* Riverboat. Because keelboats load slowly, we prefer the riverboat. If you don't want to ride, see the same sights by hiking around Tom Sawyer Island.

Liberty Square Eateries and Shops

Description and Comments   American crafts and souvenirs in shops. The one full-service restaurant, Liberty Tree Tavern, is often overlooked by lunch crowds.

Touring Tips   Liberty Tree Tavern offers character lunches and dinners with a fixed menu served family-style. Characters aside, the food is rivaled only by the Crystal Palace buffet as the Magic Kingdom's best. Priority seating is required, but it usually isn't hard to come by. Call ahead at (407) 939-3463 or check at the door of the restaurant.

Fantasyland

Fantasyland is the heart of the Magic Kingdom, a truly enchanting place spread gracefully like a miniature Alpine village beneath the steepled towers of Cinderella Castle.

It's a Small World

What It Is: World brotherhood–themed indoor boat ride
Scope & Scale: Major attraction
When to Go: Anytime
Author's Rating: Exponentially "cute"; ★★★
Appeal by Age Group:

Pre-school	Grade School	Teens	Young Adults	Over 30	Senior Citizens
★★★½	★★★	★★½	★★½	★★½	★★★

Duration of Ride: Approximately 11 minutes
Average Wait in Line per 100 People ahead of You: 1¾ minutes
Assumes: Busy conditions with 30 or more boats operating
Loading Speed: Fast

Description and Comments   Happy, upbeat, indoor attraction with a catchy tune that will replay in your head for weeks. Small boats carry visitors on a tour around the world, with singing and dancing dolls showcasing the dress and culture of each nation. One of Disney's oldest entertainment offerings, It's a Small World first unleashed it's brain-flogging song and adorable ethnic dolls on the real world at the 1964 New York World's Fair. Though it bludgeons you with sappy redundancy, almost everyone enjoys It's a Small World (at least the first time). It stands, however, along with the *Enchanted Tiki Birds,* in the "What Kind of Dope Were They Smoking When They Thought This Up?" category.

A woman from Holbrook, New York, apparently underwhelmed, suggests that "Small World" would be much better "if each person got three to four softballs on the way in!" (We continue to hear from "the Softball Lady." She's still pitching.)

A couple from the Carolinas added this:

> It's a Small World and Snow White's Adventures simply don't stack up among the newer, flashier shows and attractions. While they certainly pack a lot of nostalgic value, this is offset by their blandness and dated feel.

Touring Tips   Cool off here during the heat of the day. It's a Small World loads fast with two waiting lines and usually is a good bet between 11 a.m. and 5 p.m. If you wear a hearing aid, turn it off.

Skyway to Tomorrowland

What It Is: Scenic transportation to Tomorrowland

Scope & Scale: Minor attraction

When to Go: Before noon or during special events

Special Comments: If there's a line, it probably will be quicker to walk

Author's Rating: Nice view; ★★★

Appeal by Age Group:

Pre-school	Grade School	Teens	Young Adults	Over 30	Senior Citizens
★★★★	★★★★	★★★	★★★	★★★	★★★

Duration of Ride: About 5 minutes one way

Average Wait in Line per 100 People ahead of You: 10 minutes

Assumes: 45 or more cars operating

Loading Speed: Moderate to slow

Description and Comments Part of the Magic Kingdom internal transportation system, the Skyway is a chair lift that carries guests high above the park to Tomorrowland. The view is great, and sometimes the Skyway can save a little shoe leather. Usually, however, you can reach Tomorrowland much faster afoot.

Touring Tips We take this scenic trip in the morning, during the afternoon character parade or evening parade, or just before closing. This ride opens later and closes earlier than other rides in Fantasyland. In other words, ride before crowds build, when they're otherwise occupied, or when they're declining. These times also provide the most dramatic and beautiful vistas. Parents can't take strollers on the Skyway.

Peter Pan's Flight

What It Is: Indoor track ride

Scope & Scale: Minor attraction

When to Go: Before 10 a.m. or after 6 p.m.

Author's Rating: Happy, mellow, and well done; ★★★★

Appeal by Age Group:

Pre-school	Grade School	Teens	Young Adults	Over 30	Senior Citizens
★★★½	★★★½	★★★½	★★★½	★★★½	★★★½

Duration of Ride: A little over 3 minutes

Average Wait in Line per 100 People ahead of You: 5½ minutes

Assumes: Normal operation

Loading Speed: Moderate to slow

Description and Comments   Though not considered a major attraction, Peter Pan's Flight is superbly designed and absolutely delightful, with a happy theme uniting some favorite Disney characters, beautiful effects, and charming music. An indoor attraction, Peter Pan's Flight offers a relaxing ride in a "flying pirate ship" over old London and thence to Never-Never Land. Unlike Snow White's Adventures, there's nothing here that will jump out at you or frighten young children.

Touring Tips   Because Peter Pan's Flight is very popular, count on long lines all day. Ride before 10 a.m., during a parade, or just before the park closes.

Legend of the Lion King

What It Is: Live mixed-media and puppet theater show
Scope & Scale: Major attraction
When to Go: Before 11 a.m. and during parades
Author's Rating: Uplifting and fun; ★★★
Appeal by Age Group:

Pre-school	Grade School	Teens	Young Adults	Over 30	Senior Citizens
★★★	★★★½	★★★	★★★	★★★	★★★

Duration of Presentation: About 16 minutes
Preshow Entertainment: 7-minute preshow
Probable Waiting Time: 12 minutes (before 10:30 a.m.)

Description and Comments   In production and script, the attraction is a close cousin to *Voyage of the Little Mermaid* at Disney-MGM Studios. The story is poignant and engaging, with some dark moments before it ends on a happy, triumphant note. Imaginative puppetry, animation, and special effects create an effective collage.

A Durham, North Carolina, couple had high praise for the *Lion King* show, writing:

> *We were mesmerized by the* Legend of the Lion King *and the* Voyage of the Little Mermaid *[at Disney-MGM Studios] shows. These represent a level of sophistication in execution and in spectacle that are several orders of magnitude superior to the standard amusement park show (more akin to a good off-Broadway production).*

However, a Connecticut woman found the production lacking:

> *Regarding* [The Festival of the] Lion King—*I cannot understand the interest in Disney's "live" performances where there is more lip sync-*

ing than singing. If I want to hear the soundtrack, I'll play my CDs or watch the videos.

Touring Tips Popularity of *Legend of the Lion King* has grown as guests have become more familiar with its characters and their story. See this show in early morning or during live events. The audience must stand for the preshow in the waiting area. If you have small children, maneuver them to the front of the room so that they can see. The theater holds about 500 persons, thus most of the line outside disappears each time guests are admitted. Even so, after 10 a.m., budget a 30- to 40-minute wait.

Cinderella's Golden Carrousel

What It Is: Merry-go-round
Scope & Scale: Minor attraction
When to Go: Before 11 a.m. or after 8 p.m.
Special Comments: Adults enjoy the beauty and nostalgia of this ride
Author's Rating: A beautiful children's ride; ★★★
Appeal by Age Group:

Pre- school	Grade School	Teens	Young Adults	Over 30	Senior Citizens
★★★★	★★½	—	—	—	—

Duration of Ride: About 2 minutes
Average Wait in Line per 100 People ahead of You: 5 minutes
Assumes: Normal staffing
Loading Speed: Slow

Description and Comments One of the most elaborate and beautiful merry-go-rounds you'll ever see, especially when the lights are on.

A shy and retiring nine-year-old girl from Rockaway, New Jersey, thinks our rating of the carrousel for grade schoolers should be higher:

> *I am nine year old and I want to complain. I went on Cinderella's Golden Carrousel four times and I loved it! Raise those stars right now!! Also kids who don't like things jumping out at them should not go on* Honey, I Shrunk the Audience *[at Epcot].*

Touring Tips Unless young children in your party insist on riding, appreciate this attraction from the sidelines. While lovely to look at, the Carrousel loads and unloads very slowly.

The Many Adventures of Winnie the Pooh

What It Is: Indoor track ride

Scope & Scale: Minor attraction

When to Go: Before 10 a.m. or in the 2 hours before closing

Author's Rating: Fantasyland's newest attraction: ★★★½

Appeal by Age Group:

Pre-school	Grade School	Teens	Young Adults	Over 30	Senior Citizens
★★★½	★★★½	★★★	★★★	★★★	★★★

Duration of Ride: About 4 minutes

Average Wait in Line per 100 People ahead of You: 4 minutes

Assumes: Normal operation

Loading Speed: Moderate

Description and Comments   Opened in the summer of 1999, this newest addition to Fantasyland replaced the alternately praised and maligned Mr. Toad's Wild Ride. Pooh is sunny, upbeat, and fun—more in the image of

After 30 years, Mr. Toad croaks...

Peter Pan's Flight or Splash Mountain. You ride a Hunny Pot (sic) through the pages of a huge picture book into the Hundred Acre Wood where you encounter Pooh, Piglet, Eeyore, Owl, Rabbit, Tigger, Kanga, and Roo as they contend with a blustery day. There's even a dream sequence with Heffalumps and Woozles.

Touring Tips We're happy to welcome Pooh into the Fantasyland attraction mix. Disney guests, especially younger ones, love Pooh and his friends and have lobbied for a Winnie the Pooh–themed attraction for many years. Because it's new, expect larger-than-average crowds for a while. Try to ride before 10 a.m., during a parade, or in the hours prior to closing.

Snow White's Adventures

What It Is: Indoor track ride

Scope & Scale: Minor attraction

When to Go: Before 11 a.m. and after 6 p.m.

Special Comments: Terrifying to many young children

Author's Rating: Worth seeing if the wait isn't long; ★★½

Appeal by Age Group:

Pre-school	Grade School	Teens	Young Adults	Over 30	Senior Citizens
★	★★½	★★	★★½	★★½	★★½

Duration of Ride: Almost 2½ minutes

Average Wait in Line per 100 People ahead of You: 6¼ minutes

Assumes: Normal operation

Loading Speed: Moderate to slow

Description and Comments Mine cars travel through a spook house showing Snow White as she narrowly escapes harm at the hands of the wicked witch. Action and effects are not as good as Peter Pan's Flight or Winnie the Pooh.

Touring Tips We get more mail about this ride than any other Disney attraction. It terrifies many children age 6 and younger. Though a 1995 upgrade gave Snow White a larger role, the witch (who is relentless and ubiquitous) continues to be the focal character. Many readers tell us their children have refused to ride any attraction that operates in the dark after having experienced Snow White's Adventures.

A mother from Knoxville, Tennessee, writes:

> *The outside looks cute and fluffy, but inside, the evil witch just keeps coming at you. My five-year-old, who rode Space Mountain three times and took The Great Movie Ride's monster from* Alien *right in stride,*

was near panic when our car stopped unexpectedly twice during Snow White. [After Snow White] my six-year-old niece spent a lot of time asking "if a witch will jump out at you" before other rides. So I suggest that you explain a little more what this ride is about. It's tough on preschoolers who are expecting forest animals and dwarfs.

A mom from Long Island, New York, adds:

My daughter screamed the whole time and was shot for the day. Grampa kept asking, "Where in the hell is Snow White?"

Experience Snow White if lines aren't too long, or on a second day at the park.

20,000 Leagues Under the Sea

This submarine ride based on the Disney film of the same name became the subject of a prolonged corporate argument. Closed five years ago for refurbishment, the attraction never reopened. For almost two years, while Disney bigwigs debated 20,000 Leagues' fate, the submarines sat in the water and deteriorated. Finally in 1997, with no decision having been made, the subs were hauled from the lagoon. For now, the former attraction's loading area is being used for character greetings, and there's a rumor that a thrill ride will be built on the site.

Ariel's Grotto

What It Is: Interactive fountain and character greeting area

Scope & Scale: Minor attraction

When to Go: Before 10 a.m. and after 9 p.m.

Author's Rating: One of the most elaborate of the character-greeting venues; ★★★

Appeal by Age Group:

Pre-school	Grade School	Teens	Young Adults	Over 30	Senior Citizens
★★★★★	★★★★	★★	★	★	★

Average Wait in Line per 100 People ahead of You: 30 minutes

Description and Comments On the submarine-lagoon side of Dumbo, Ariel's Grotto consists of a small children's play area with an interactive fountain and a rock grotto where Ariel, the Little Mermaid, poses for photos and signs autographs. If "interactive fountain" is new to you, it means an opportunity for your children to get ten times wetter than a trout. Can you say "hy-po-ther-mi-a"?

Touring Tips The Grotto is small, and the wait to meet Ariel is usually long. Because kids in line are fresh from the fountain, it's very difficult for adults to remain dry. A mother from Hagerstown, Maryland, said the experience was "like being packed in a pen with wet cocker spaniels."

If your children spot the Grotto before you do, there's no turning back. Except before 10 a.m., count on a long queue and a 20–40 minute wait to see Ariel. Then there's the fountain. Allow your children to disrobe to the legal limit. (Don't bother with umbrellas or ponchos, because water squirts up from below.) When you're finished meeting Ariel, you will have to navigate an armada of variously aged males plowing upstream through the exit to admire the Little Mermaid's cleavage.

Dumbo the Flying Elephant

What It Is: Disneyfied midway ride

Scope & Scale: Minor attraction

When to Go: Before 10 a.m. and after 9 p.m.

Author's Rating: An attractive children's ride; ★★★

Appeal by Age Group:

Pre-school	Grade School	Teens	Young Adults	Over 30	Senior Citizens
★★★★★	★★★★	★½	★½	★½	★½

Duration of Ride: 1½ minutes

Average Wait in Line per 100 People ahead of You: 20 minutes

Assumes: Normal staffing

Loading Speed: Slow

Description and Comments A tame, happy children's ride based on the lovable flying elephant, Dumbo. Despite being little different from rides at state fairs and amusement parks, Dumbo is the favorite Magic Kingdom attraction of many younger children.

A lot of readers take us to task for lumping Dumbo with carnival rides. A reader from Armdale, Nova Scotia, writes:

> *I think you have acquired a jaded attitude. I know [Dumbo] is not for everybody, but when we took our oldest child (then just four), the sign at the end of the line said there would be a 90-minute wait. He knew and he didn't care, and he and I stood in the hot afternoon sun for 90 blissful minutes waiting for his 90-second flight. Anything that a four-year-old would wait for that long and that patiently must be pretty special.*

Touring Tips If Dumbo is critical to your child's happiness, make it your first stop, preferably within 15 minutes of park opening. Also, consider this advice from an Arlington, Virginia, mom:

> *Grown-ups, beware! Dumbo is really a tight fit with one adult and two kids. My kids threw me out of their Dumbo and I had to sit in a Dumbo all by myself! Pretty embarrassing, and my husband got lots of pictures.*

Mad Tea Party

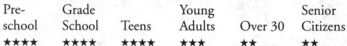

Motion Sickness

WARNING!

What It Is: Midway-type spinning ride

Scope & Scale: Minor attraction

When to Go: Before 11 a.m. and after 5 p.m.

Special Comments: You can make the tea cups spin faster by turning the wheel in the center of the cup

Author's Rating: Fun, but not worth the wait; ★★

Appeal by Age Group:

Pre-school	Grade School	Teens	Young Adults	Over 30	Senior Citizens
★★★★	★★★★	★★★★	★★★	★★	★★

Duration of Ride: 1½ minutes

Average Wait in Line per 100 People ahead of You: 7½ minutes

Assumes: Normal staffing

Loading Speed: Slow

Description and Comments   Riders whirl feverishly in big tea cups. Alice in Wonderland's Mad Hatter provides the theme. A version of this ride, without Disney characters, can be found at every local carnival. Teenagers like to lure adults onto the tea cups, then turn the wheel in the middle, making the cup spin faster, until the adults are plastered against the side of the cup and on the verge of throwing up. Unless your life's ambition is to be the test subject in a human centrifuge, don't even consider getting on this ride with anyone younger than 21.

Touring Tips   This ride, well done but not unique, is notoriously slow loading. Skip it on a busy schedule—if the kids will let you. Ride the morning of your second day if your schedule is more relaxed.

Fantasyland Eateries and Shops

Description and Comments   Many of the Magic Kingdom visitors we surveyed wanted to know, "What is in the castle?" or "Can we go up into the castle?" The answer is: You can't see it all, but you can inspect a fair-sized chunk if you eat at Cinderella's Royal Table in the castle.

However, you don't have to eat at Cinderella's Royal Table to see Cinderella. A mother from Stone Mountain, Georgia, reports:

> *Cinderella greets diners in the waiting area of Cinderella's Royal Table at Cinderella Castle. You can meet her there without eating at the restaurant. Just enter the area through the left door by the hostess stand. The hostess at the door can tell you when Cinderella is scheduled to appear.*

Touring Tips   Priority seating is required at Cinderella's Royal Table. Call (407) 939-3463 before you leave home, preferably 60 days in advance to ensure a table. We don't recommend eating at Cinderella's Royal Table if you're on a tight schedule or are sensitive about paying fancy prices for average food. If you plan to spend two days in the Magic Kingdom and are curious about the castle, try Cinderella's your second day. If there are young children in your party, ask when Cinderella will be present before making your priority seating.

Another Fantasyland lunch option is The Pinocchio Village Haus, which regrettably no longer serves bratwurst.

Fantasyland offers abundant specialty and souvenir shopping, but don't waste time in the shops unless you have a relaxed schedule or shopping is a priority.

Mickey's Toontown Fair

Mickey's Toontown Fair is the first new "land" to be added to the Magic Kingdom since its opening and the only land that doesn't connect to the central hub. Attractions include an opportunity to meet Mickey Mouse, Mickey's house, Minnie Mouse's house, and a child-sized roller coaster.

Mickey's Toontown Fair is sandwiched between Fantasyland and Tomorrowland, like an afterthought, on about three acres formerly part of the Tomorrowland Speedway. It's the smallest of the lands and more like an attraction than a section of the park. Though you can wander in on a somewhat obscure path from Fantasyland or on a totally obscure path from Tomorrowland, Mickey's Toontown Fair generally receives guests arriving by the Walt Disney World Railroad.

Opened in 1988 and reworked in 1996 with a county fair theme, Mickey's Toontown Fair now serves as the Magic Kingdom's character-greeting headquarters. The Fair provides a place where Disney characters are available to guests on a continuing and reliable schedule. Mickey, in the role of the Fair's chief judge, meets guests for photos and autographs in the Judge's Tent. Other characters appear in the Toontown Hall of Fame. Characters are available throughout the day except during parades.

In general, Mickey's Toontown Fair doesn't handle crowds very well. If your children are into collecting character autographs and want to enjoy the various Toontown attractions without extraordinary waits, we recommend touring first thing in the morning. If you only have one day to visit the Magic Kingdom and hitting the children-oriented attractions is a priority, head first to Fantasyland and ride Dumbo, Pooh, and Peter Pan, then split for Toontown. In Toontown, ride Goofy's Barnstormer first and then tour Mickey's and Minnie's houses. Go next to the Toontown Hall of Fame for character pics and autographs. For adults without children, Toontown is visually interesting but otherwise expendable.

Mickey's Country House & Judge's Tent

What It Is: Walk-through tour of Mickey's house and meeting with Mickey

Scope & Scale: Minor attraction

When to Go: Before 11:30 a.m. and after 4:30 p.m.

Author's Rating: Well done; ★★★

Appeal by Age Group:

Pre-school	Grade School	Teens	Young Adults	Over 30	Senior Citizens
★★★½	★★★	★★½	★★½	★★½	★★½

Duration of Tour: 15–30 minutes (depending on the crowd)

Average Wait in Line per 100 People ahead of You: 20 minutes

Assumes: Normal staffing

Touring Speed: Slow

Description and Comments   Mickey's Country House is the starting point of a self-guided tour through the famous mouse's house, into his backyard, and past Pluto's doghouse. If you want to tour Mickey's house, but skip meeting Mickey, you'll find an exit just before entering his tent.

Touring Tips   Discerning observers will see immediately that Mickey's Country House is a cleverly devised queuing area for delivering guests to Mickey's Judge's Tent for the Mouse Encounter. It also heightens anticipation by revealing the corporate symbol on a more personal level. Mickey's Country House is well conceived and contains a lot of Disney memorabilia. Children touch *everything* as they proceed through the house, hoping to find some artifact not welded into the set. (An especially tenacious child actually ripped a couple of books from a bookcase.)

Meeting Mickey and touring his house are best done during the first two hours the park is open, or in the evening. If meeting Mickey is your child's priority, take the railroad from Main Street to Mickey's Toontown Fair as soon as you enter the park. Some children are so obsessed with seeing Mickey that they can't enjoy anything else until they have him in the rearview mirror.

Minnie's Country House

What It Is: Walk-through exhibit

Scope & Scale: Minor attraction

When to Go: Before 11:30 a.m. and after 4:30 p.m.

Author's Rating: Great detail; ★★

Appeal by Age Group:

Pre-school	Grade School	Teens	Young Adults	Over 30	Senior Citizens
★★★	★★★	★★½	★★½	★★½	★★½

Duration of Tour: About 10 minutes

Average Wait in Line per 100 People ahead of You: 12 minutes

Touring Speed: Slow

Description and Comments Minnie's Country House offers a self-guided tour through the rooms and backyard of Mickey's main squeeze. Similar to Mickey's Country House, only predictably more feminine, Minnie's also showcases fun Disney memorabilia. Among highlights of the short tour are the fanciful appliances in Minnie's kitchen.

Touring Tips The main difference between Mickey's and Minnie's houses is that Mickey is home to receive guests. Minnie was never home during our visits. We did, however, bump into her on the street and in the Toontown Hall of Fame. Minnie's Country House is one of the more accessible attractions in the Fair, but we nonetheless recommend touring early or late in the day.

Toontown Hall of Fame

What It Is: Character-greeting venue

Scope & Scale: Minor attraction

When to Go: Before 10:30 a.m. and after 5:30 p.m.

Author's Rating: You want characters? We got 'em! ★★

Appeal by Age Group:

Pre-school	Grade School	Teens	Young Adults	Over 30	Senior Citizens
★★★★	★★★★	★★	★★	★★	★★

Duration of Greeting: About 7–10 minutes

Average Wait in Line per 100 People ahead of You: 35 minutes

Touring Speed: Slow

Description and Comments   The Toontown Hall of Fame is at the end of a small plaza between Mickey's and Minnie's houses. Just inside to the right are entrances to three queuing areas. Signs over each suggest, somewhat ambiguously, which characters you will meet. Character assortments in each greeting area change, as do the names of the assortments themselves. Thus, on a given day you will find three of the following groupings available: Famous Friends (also called Toon Pals and sometimes Minnie's Famous Pals) include Minnie, Goofy, Donald, Pluto, and sometimes Uncle Scrooge, Chip 'n' Dale, Roger Rabbit, and Daisy. The 100 Acre Wood Pals are mostly Winnie the Pooh characters but may include any character that

fits the forest theme. Fairy Tale Friends are Snow White, various dwarfs, Belle, the Beast, Sleeping Beauty, Prince Charming, etc. Other categories we have seen include Mickey's Pals, Disney Princesses, and Disney Villains.

Each category of characters occupies a greeting room where 15–20 guests are admitted at a time. They're allowed to stay 7–10 minutes, long enough for a photo, autograph, and hug with each character.

Touring Tips If your children want to visit each category, you'll have to queue up three times. Each line is long and slow-moving, and during busier hours you can lose a lot of time here. While Famous Friends (aka Toon Pals and Minnie's Famous Pals) are slightly more popular than the other categories, the longest wait is usually to see the Fairy Tale Friends. The reason is that most Fairy Tale Friends are "face characters," actresses who strongly resemble the character they portray and don't wear any head-covering costume. Face characters are allowed to speak and thus engage children in conversation, prolonging the visit. All characters work in 25-minute shifts, with breaks on the hour and half hour. Because characters in each category change frequently during the day, it's possible to see quite an assortment if you keep recirculating.

If the cast member can't tell you, walk over to the exit and ask departing guests which characters are on duty. Remember that there is some switching of characters on the hour and half hour.

A mother from Winchester, Virginia, reported her solution to seeing characters without waiting in lines:

> Some of the things that surprised us, both good and bad, were the crowding and lines to see the characters. We stopped to visit a few, especially when we got lucky with a shorter line, but mostly we couldn't justify stopping at many because we would have missed so many attractions. The best thing we did with regard to the characters was to have the Winnie the Pooh character dinner at The Crystal Palace. Tigger and Pooh are my kids' favorites, and the characters were VERY attentive; my just-turned three-year-old was in heaven and did not have to fight crowds.

A thirty-something mother of two comments:

> For parents with smaller children at the Magic Kingdom, take the train to Toontown as soon as the park opens—my six-year-old and eight-year-old rode Goofy's Barnstormer roller coaster seven times without getting off. After others wanted on, they moved on to the Toontown Hall of Fame for autographs—No lines!!

A Concord, Massachussets, mom suggests:

> *Mickey's Toontown was our longest line—should be done RIGHT AT OPENING!*

On many days, during the first half hour the park is open, characters are available for pics and autographs outside on the street in Mickey's Toontown Fair. It's just like the old days: spontaneous contact and no lines. After about 30 minutes, they retreat inside.

The Toontown Hall of Fame offers one of the largest and most dependably available collection of characters in Walt Disney World. If your children (or you) are character hounds, visit the Hall of Fame before 10 a.m. In early morning, you can meet all three categories in less than an hour.

The Barnstormer at Goofy's Wiseacres Farm

What It Is: Small roller coaster

Scope & Scale: Minor attraction

When to Go: Before 10:30 a.m., during parades and in the evening, and just before the park closes

Author's Rating: Great for little ones, but not worth the wait for adults; ★★

Appeal by Age Group:

Pre-school	Grade School	Teens	Young Adults	Over 30	Senior Citizens
★★★★	★★★	★★½	★★½	★★½	★★

Duration of Ride: About 53 seconds

Average Wait in Line per 100 People ahead of You: 7 minutes

Assumes: Normal staffing

Loading Speed: Slow

Description and Comments   The Barnstormer is a very small roller coaster. The ride is zippy but super short. In fact, of the 53 seconds the ride is in motion, 32 seconds are consumed in leaving the loading area, being racheted up the first hill, and braking into the off-loading area. The actual time you spend careering around the track is 21 seconds.

A 42-year-old woman from Westport, Connecticut, warns adults that the Barnstormer may not be as tame as it looks:

> *Goofy's Barnstormer was a nightmare that should have gone in your "Eats Adults" section. It looked so innocent—nothing hidden in the dark, over quickly. . . . It took hours to stop feeling nauseated and my eight-year-old son and I were terrified.*

Touring Tips   The cars of this dinky coaster are too small for most adults and whiplash taller people. This plus the limited capacity equal an engineering marvel along the lines of Dumbo. Parties without children should skip the Barnstormer. If you're touring with children, you have a problem. Like Dumbo, the ride is visually appealing. All kids want to ride, subjecting the whole family to slow-moving lines. If the Barnstormer is high on your children's hit parade, try to ride before 9:30 a.m.

Donald's Boat

What It Is: Interactive fountain and playground
Scope & Scale: Diversion
When to Go: Anytime
Special Comments: Children can get wet
Author's Rating: Spontaneous—yeah! ★★½
Appeal by Age Group:

Pre-school	Grade School	Teens	Young Adults	Over 30	Senior Citizens
★★★★	★★½	★	★½	★½	★½

Description and Comments Water spurts randomly from tiny holes in the side of Donald's Boat. The idea is that the boat is springing leaks. Children walk around plugging holes with their hands and trying to guess where the water will squirt next.

Touring Tips Young children love this attraction and will jump around in the spurting water until they're drenched. Our advice: "GET NAKED!" Even on cooler days, bare skin dries faster than wet clothes. Strip your munchkins to the legal limit and toss them into the fray. If you really want to plan ahead, bring extra underwear and a towel.

Tomorrowland

Tomorrowland is a mix of rides and experiences relating to the technological development of man and what life will be like in the future. If this sounds like Epcot's theme, it's because Tomorrowland was a breeding ground for ideas that spawned Epcot. Yet, Tomorrowland and Epcot are very different in more than scale. Epcot is mostly educational. Tomorrowland is more for fun, depicting the future as envisioned in science fiction.

Exhaustive renovation of Tomorrowland was completed in 1995. Before refurbishing, Tomorrowland's 24-year-old buildings resembled 1970s motels more than anyone's vision of the future. The new design is ageless, revealing the future as imagined by dreamers and scientists in the 1920s and '30s. Today's Tomorrowland conjures visions of Buck Rogers, fanciful mechanical rockets, and metallic cities spread beneath towering obelisks. Disney calls the renovated Tomorrowland the "Future That Never Was," while *Newsweek* dubbed it "retro-future."

In the new Tomorrowland, *Alien Encounter* replaced *Mission to Mars* (formerly *Spaceflight to the Moon*). Walt Disney's *Carousel of Progress* has been jazzed up and moved forward in time, and *Transportarium* has been recast as *The Timekeeper*. The StarJets ride, now sporting a campy Jules Verne look, is higher off the ground but still runs in circles. Its new name is Astro Orbiter. The WEDway PeopleMover has become the Tomorrowland Transit Authority. Venerable Space Mountain continues to hold its own, but the Tomorrowland Speedway and Skyway to Fantasyland seem incongruous.

Space Mountain

What It Is: Roller coaster in the dark

Scope & Scale: Super headliner

When to Go: First thing when the park opens, between 6 and 7 p.m., or during the hour before closing

Special Comments: Great fun and action; much wilder than Big Thunder Mountain Railroad. Children must be 44" tall to ride, and if younger than age 7, must be accompanied by an adult. Switching off option provided (pages 190–192).

Author's Rating: A great roller coaster with excellent special effects; not to be missed; ★★★★

Appeal by Age Group:

Pre-school	Grade School	Teens	Young Adults	Over 30	Senior Citizens
†	★★★★★	★★★★★	★★★★½	★★★★	†

† Some preschoolers loved Space Mountain; others were frightened. The sample size of senior citizens who experienced this ride was too small to develop an accurate rating.

Duration of Ride: Almost 3 minutes

Average Wait in Line per 100 People ahead of You: 3 minutes

Assumes: Two tracks dispatching at 21-second intervals

Loading Speed: Moderate to fast

A teen from Colchester, Connecticut, wrote us about her bad hair day:

> *WARN Space Mountain riders to take off hair scrunchies. I lost my best one on it and couldn't get it back. This ride was fast, curvy, and very hairdo messing.*

WARNING!

For Bouffants, Rug Wearers, and Elvis Impersonators

This Ride Will Muss Your 'Do

Description and Comments Totally enclosed in a mammoth futuristic structure, Space Mountain is a creative and engineering marvel. The theme is a space flight through dark recesses of the galaxy. Effects are superb, and the ride is the fastest and wildest in the Magic Kingdom. As a roller coaster, Space Mountain is much zippier than Big Thunder Mountain Railroad, but much tamer than the Rock 'n' Roller Coaster at the Studios.

Roller coaster aficionados will tell you (correctly) that Space Mountain is a designer version of The Wild Mouse, a carnival and state fair midway ride that's been around for at least 40 years. There are no long drops or swooping hills like on a traditional roller coaster, only quick, unexpected turns and small drops. Disney's contribution essentially was to add a space theme to The Wild Mouse and put it in the dark. And indeed, this does make the mouse seem wilder.

Touring Tips People who can handle a fairly wild roller coaster ride will take Space Mountain in stride. What sets Space Mountain apart is that cars plummet through darkness, with only occasional lighting. Half the fun of Space Mountain is not knowing where the car will go next.

Space Mountain is the favorite attraction of many Magic Kingdom visitors ages 7 to 50. Each morning before opening, particularly during summer and holiday periods, several hundred S.M. "junkies" crowd the rope barriers at the central hub, awaiting the signal to head to the ride's entrance. To get ahead of the competition, be one of the first in the park. Proceed to the end of Main Street and cut right past The Plaza Restaurant, stopping under an archway that says:

THE PLAZA PAVILION TERRACE DINING

where a Disney worker will be standing behind a rope barrier. From this point, you're about 100 yards closer to Space Mountain, on a route through The Plaza Pavilion, than your competition waiting to dash from the central hub. From here, middle-aged folks walking fast can beat most teens coming from the central hub. Another advantage of starting from The Plaza Pavilion entrance: you wait in the shade. Sometimes, Disney will drop the rope at the Plaza Pavilion a minute after the rope drop at the central hub. Even when this happens, you are in a better competitive position than all the central hubbers closest to the rope.

Couples touring with children too small to ride Space Mountain can both ride without waiting in line twice by taking advantage of "switching off." Here's how it works: When you enter the Space Mountain line, tell the first Disney attendant (Greeter One) that you want to switch off. The attendant will allow you, your spouse, and your small child (or children) to continue together, phoning ahead to tell Greeter Two to expect you. When you reach Greeter Two (at the turnstile near the boarding area), you'll be given specific directions. One of you will proceed to ride, while the other stays with the kids. Whoever rides will be admitted by the unloading attendant to stairs leading back up to the boarding area. Here you switch off. The second parent rides, and the first parent takes the kids down the stairs to the unloading area where everybody is reunited and exits together. Switching off is also available at Big Thunder Mountain Railroad, Splash Mountain, and *Alien Encounter.*

All riders have their own seat. Parents whose children meet the height and age requirements for Space Mountain can't sit next to their kids.

If you don't catch Space Mountain early in the morning, try again during the hour before closing. Often, would-be riders are held in line outside the entrance until all those previously in line have ridden, thus emptying the attraction. The appearance from the outside is that the line is enormous when, in fact, the only people waiting are those visible. This crowd-control technique, known as "stacking," discourages visitors from getting in line. Stacking is used in several Disney rides and attractions during the hour before closing to ensure that the ride will be able to close on schedule. It is also used to keep the number of people waiting inside from overwhelming the air conditioning. For those who aren't put off by the apparently long line, the wait is usually no longer than if you had been allowed to queue inside.

Splash Mountain siphons off some guests who would have made Space Mountain their first stop. Even so, a mob rushes to Space Mountain as soon as the park opens. If you especially like the thrill attractions and have only one day, see *Alien Encounter* first in the morning, followed by Space Mountain, Big Thunder Mountain Railroad, and Splash Mountain.

If you're a Disney resort guest eligible for early entry on designated days, you can ride Space Mountain to your heart's content for a half hour to an hour before the general public is admitted.

If you're an early entrant and Big Thunder Mountain Railroad and Splash Mountain also are high on your list, see *Alien Encounter* and ride Space Mountain (as well as Fantasyland attractions) until 10 to 15 minutes before the hour the general public is admitted. At this time, return to Fantasyland and continue to the boundary of Fantasyland and Liberty Square. Wait there for the rest of the park to open. When it does, enter Liberty Square and move quickly along the Liberty Square and Frontierland waterfronts to Big Thunder Mountain Railroad and Splash Mountain.

If you aren't eligible for early entry, visit the Magic Kingdom on a day when the program isn't in effect and make Space Mountain and *Alien Encounter* your first two attractions of the day. If you aren't eligible for early entry but your schedule requires that you visit on an early-entry day, ride Splash Mountain and Big Thunder Mountain Railroad first, then try to catch Space Mountain and *Alien Encounter* during a parade or just before the park closes.

Tomorrowland Speedway

What It Is: Drive-'em-yourself miniature cars

Scope & Scale: Major attraction

When to Go: Before 11 a.m. and after 5 p.m.

Special Comments: Must be 52" tall to drive

Author's Rating: Boring for adults (★); great for preschoolers

Appeal by Age Group:

Pre-school	Grade School	Teens	Young Adults	Over 30	Senior Citizens
★★★★	★★★	★	½	½	½

Duration of Ride: About 4¼ minutes

Average Wait in Line per 100 People ahead of You: 4½ minutes

Assumes: 285-car turnover every 20 minutes

Loading Speed: Slow

Description and Comments An elaborate miniature raceway with gasoline-powered cars that travel up to 7 miles per hour. The raceway, with sleek cars and racing noises, is quite alluring. Unfortunately, the cars poke along on a track, leaving the driver little to do. Pretty ho-hum for most adults and teenagers. The height requirement excludes small children who would enjoy the ride.

Touring Tips This ride is visually appealing but definitely one adults can skip. Preschoolers, however, love it. If your child is too short to drive, ride along and allow the child to steer the car on its guide rail while you work the foot pedal.

A mom from North Billerica, Massachusetts, writes:

> *I was truly amazed by the number of adults in the line. Please emphasize to your readers that these cars travel on a guided path and are not a whole lot of fun. The only reason I could think of for adults to be in the line would be an insane desire to go on absolutely every ride*

at Disney World. The other feature about the cars is that they tend to pile up at the end, so it takes almost as long to get off as it did to get on. Parents riding with their preschoolers should keep the car going as slow as [possible] without stalling. This prolongs the preschooler's joy and decreases the time you will have to wait at the end.

The line for the Tomorrowland Speedway snakes across a pedestrian bridge to the loading areas. For a shorter wait, turn right off the bridge to the first loading area (rather than continuing to the second).

Skyway to Fantasyland

What It Is: Scenic overhead transportation to Fantasyland
Scope & Scale: Minor attraction
When to Go: Before noon and during special events
Special Comments: If there's a line, it's probably quicker to walk
Author's Rating: Nice view; ★★½
Appeal by Age Group:

Pre-school	Grade School	Teens	Young Adults	Over 30	Senior Citizens
★★★★	★★★★	★★★	★★★	★★★	★★★

Duration of Ride: Approximately 5 minutes one way
Average Wait in Line per 100 People ahead of You: 10 minutes
Assumes: 45 or more cars operating
Loading Speed: Moderate

Description and Comments   Chair lift transports you from Tomorrowland to the far corner of Fantasyland near its border with Liberty Square. The view is one of the best in the Magic Kingdom, but walking is usually faster.

Touring Tips   Unless lines are short, Skyway transportation won't save you time. As a ride, however, it affords some incredible views. The Skyway sometimes opens later and closes earlier than other rides in Tomorrowland. Strollers aren't allowed on the ride.

Astro Orbiter

What It Is: Buck Rogers–style rockets revolving around a central axis
Scope & Scale: Minor attraction
When to Go: Before 11 a.m. or after 5 p.m.
Special Comments: This attraction, formerly StarJets, is not as innocuous as it appears

Motion Sickness

WARNING!

Author's Rating: Not worth the wait; ★★

Appeal by Age Group:

Pre-school	Grade School	Teens	Young Adults	Over 30	Senior Citizens
★★★★	★★★	★★½	★★½	★★	★

Duration of Ride: 1½ minutes

Average Wait in Line per 100 People ahead of You: 13½ minutes

Assumes: Normal staffing

Loading Speed: Slow

Description and Comments Though recently upgraded and visually appealing, the Astro Orbiter is still a slow-loading carnival ride. The far little rocketships simply fly in circles. The best thing about the Astro Orbiter is the nice view when you're aloft.

Touring Tips Expendable on any schedule. If you ride with preschoolers, seat them first, then board. The Astro Orbiter flies higher and faster than Dumbo and frightens some young children. It also apparently messes with some adults. A mother from Lev Hashomnon, Israel, attests:

> *I think your assessment of [Astro Orbiter] as "very mild" is way off. I was able to sit through all the "Mountains," the "Tours," and the "Wars" without my stomach reacting even a little, but after [Astro Orbiter] I thought I would be finished for the rest of the day. Very quickly I realized that my only chance for survival was to pick a point on the toe of my shoe and stare at it (and certainly not lift my eyes out of the "jet") until the ride was over. My four-year-old was my co-pilot, and she loved the ride (go figure) and she had us up high the whole time. It was a nightmare—people should be forewarned.*

Tomorrowland Transit Authority

What It Is: Scenic tour of Tomorrowland

Scope & Scale: Minor attraction

When to Go: During hot, crowded times of day (11:30 a.m.–4:30 p.m.)

Special Comments: A good way to check out the crowd at Space Mountain

Author's Rating: Scenic, relaxing, informative; ★★★

Appeal by Age Group:

Pre-school	Grade School	Teens	Young Adults	Over 30	Senior Citizens
★★★½	★★★	★★½	★★½	★★½	★★★

Duration of Ride: 10 minutes

Average Wait in Line per 100 People ahead of You: 1½ minutes

Assumes: 39 trains operating

Loading Speed: Fast

Description and Comments A once unique prototype of a linear induction–powered mass-transit system, the Authority's tramlike cars carry riders on a leisurely tour of Tomorrowland, including a peek inside Space Mountain. The attraction was formerly called the WEDway PeopleMover.

Touring Tips A relaxing ride, where lines move quickly and you seldom have to wait. It's good to take during busier times of day, and it can double as a nursery.

A Texas mom writes:

> *The [Transit Authority] is an excellent ride for getting a tired infant to fall asleep. You can stay on for several times around. It is also a moderately private and comfortable place for nursing an infant.*

A woman from upstate New York also found it relaxing:

> *Tomorrowland Transit Authority was a surprising treat; we rode it three times to see everything and to take a break from walking; it's especially nice when it goes through Space Mountain.*

Walt Disney's Carousel of Progress

What It Is: Audio-Animatronic theater production

Scope & Scale: Major attraction

When to Go: Anytime

Author's Rating: Nostalgic, warm, and happy; ★★★

Appeal by Age Group:

Pre-school	Grade School	Teens	Young Adults	Over 30	Senior Citizens
★★	★★½	★★½	★★★	★★★	★★★½

Duration of Presentation: 18 minutes

Preshow Entertainment: Documentary on the attraction's long history

Probable Waiting Time: Less than 10 minutes

Description and Comments Updated and improved during the Tomorrowland renovation, *Walt Disney's Carousel of Progress* offers a delightful look at how technology and electricity have changed the lives of an Audio-

Animatronic family over several generations. The family is easy to identify with, and a cheerful, sentimental tune bridges the generations.

Touring Tips This attraction is a great favorite among repeat visitors and is included on all of our one-day touring plans. The *Carousel* handles big crowds effectively and is a good choice during busier times of day.

Buzz Lightyear's Space Ranger Spin

What It Is: Whimsical space travel–themed indoor ride
Scope & Scale: Minor attraction
When to Go: Anytime
Author's Rating: A real winner! ★★★★
Appeal by Age Group:

Pre-school	Grade School	Teens	Young Adults	Over 30	Senior Citizens
★★★★	★★★★★	★★★★½	★★★★	★★★★	★★★★

Duration of Ride: About 4½ minutes
Average Wait in Line per 100 People ahead of You: 3 minutes
Assumes: Normal operation
Loading Speed: Fast

Description and Comments This attraction, based on the space-commando character of Buzz Lightyear from the film *Toy Story*, replaced the Take Flight attraction as the final installment of Tomorrowland's four-year makeover. The marginal story line has you and Buzz Lightyear trying to save the universe from the evil Emperor Zurg. The indoor ride is interactive to the extent that you can spin your car and shoot simulated "laser cannons" at Zurg and his minions.

Touring Tips Each car is equipped with two laser cannons and a scorekeeping display. Each scorekeeping display is independent, so you can compete with your riding partner. A joy stick allows you to spin the car to line up the various targets. Each time you pull the trigger you'll release a red laser beam that you can see hitting or missing the target. Most folks' first ride is occupied with learning how to use the equipment (fire off individual shots as opposed to keeping the trigger depressed) and figuring out how the targets work. The next ride (like certain potato chips, one is not enough) you'll surprise yourself by how much better you do. *Unofficial* readers are unanimous in their praise of Buzz Lightyear. Some, in fact, spend several hours on it, riding again and again. The following comments are representative:

From a Yorktown, Virginia, mom:

> *I am a 44-year-old woman who has never been fond of shoot-'em-up arcade games, but I decided I'd better check out Buzz Lightyear's Space Ranger Spin after the monorail driver told us that it along with Space Mountain were her favorite rides at the Magic Kingdom. What a blast! My husband and I enjoyed it every bit as much as our 10-year-old daughter. After riding it the first time, we couldn't wait to ride it again (and again) in an effort to improve our scores. Alas, I was never able to advance beyond Ranger 1st Class although my husband made it all the way to Space Ace. Warning—Buzz Lightyear is addictive!*

From a father of three from Cleveland, Ohio:

> *Without question, the favorite ride of my 11-year-old son was the Buzz Lightyear Ride. Come to think about it, it was my favorite too!*

And from an Austin, Texas, mom:

> *You undervalued Buzz Lightyear—our three- and five-year-old loved it!! As did we!! On E-Ticket night we must have ridden this ride ten times!!*

Because Buzz Lightyear is an exceedingly fast-loading attraction, the wait is always tolerable and sometimes short to nonexistent.

The Timekeeper

What It Is: Time-travel movie adventure
Scope & Scale: Major attraction
When to Go: Anytime
Special Comments: Audience must stand throughout presentation
Author's Rating: Outstanding; not to be missed; ★★★★
Appeal by Age Group:

Pre-school	Grade School	Teens	Young Adults	Over 30	Senior Citizens
★★	★★★½	★★★½	★★★½	★★★★	★★★★

Duration of Presentation: About 20 minutes
Preshow Entertainment: Robots, lasers, and movies
Probable Waiting Time: 8–15 minutes

Description and Comments   Developed as *Le Visionarium* for Disneyland Paris, *The Timekeeper* adds Audio-Animatronic characters and a story line to the long-successful Circle-Vision 360 technology. The preshow introduces Timekeeper (a humanoid) and 9-Eye (a time-traveling robot so named because she has nine cameras that serve as eyes). Afterward, the audience enters the main theater, where Timekeeper places 9-Eye into a time machine and dispatches her on a crazed journey into the past and future. What 9-Eye sees on her odyssey is projected onto huge screens that surround the audience with action. The robot travels to prehistoric Europe and then forward to meet French author and visionary Jules Verne, who hitches a ride into the future. Circle-Vision 360 technology, Disney Audio-Animatronics, and high-tech special effects combine to make *The Timekeeper* one of Tomorrowland's premier attractions.

The Timekeeper may be the most underrated attraction in the Magic Kingdom, but as this Westport, Connecticut, family attests, it's a "must-see":

> *We thought* The Timekeeper *was the best [Animatronics] in the whole of Disney World. Robin Williams was brilliant. We saw it twice—5 stars!!*

Touring Tips   *The Timekeeper* draws large crowds from midmorning on. Because the theater accommodates more than 1,000 guests per show, there never is much wait. Go during early afternoon when the park is hot and crowded.

Alien Encounter

What It Is: Theater-in-the-round sci-fi horror show
Scope & Scale: Headliner
When to Go: Before 10 a.m. or after 6 p.m.; try during parades
Special Comments: Frightens children of all ages
Author's Rating: ★★★
Appeal by Age Group:

Pre-school	Grade School	Teens	Young Adults	Over 30	Senior Citizens
—	★★★½	★★★★	★★★★	★★★★	★★★

Duration of Presentation: About 12 minutes
Preshow Entertainment: About 6 minutes
Probable Waiting Time: 12–40 minutes

Description and Comments   Heralded as the showpiece of the "new" Tomorrowland, *Alien Encounter* is staged in the building that previously housed *Mission to Mars*. Guests witness a demonstration of "interplanetary teleportation," a technique that converts travelers into electrons for transmission to distant locations. In this case, the demonstration goes awry (of course), and an unsavory alien arrives in the theater. Mayhem ensues.

Alien Encounter is the antithesis of most Disney attractions: there is no uplifting message and no happy ending. There is death in this attraction, and its tone is dark and foreboding. While *The Twilight Zone* Tower of Terror at Disney-MGM Studios is suspenseful and subtle, *Alien Encounter* is uncomfortable and gross. The discomfort begins at the preshow when, in a teleportation experiment, a cuddly Audio-Animatronic character is hideously fried, then vomited, screaming into outer space. Is this someone's idea of entertaiment?

Alien Encounter has its advocates, but we consider it mean and twisted. The *coup de grâce*, however, is the hawking of T-shirts (in the adjacent gift shop) decorated with the image of the tortured and maimed Audio-Animatronic creature. Enough already.

Because *Alien Encounter* is such a departure from typical Disney theme park entertainment, we consider it prudent to share the observations of readers.

A St. Louis father of three writes:

> Alien Encounter *in the new Tomorrowland—Outstanding and really scary! Not to be missed! The special effects may be too much for young kids, but ours (ages 10, 8, and 6) did okay.*

A mother of two from Botswana really let us have it:

> *We almost missed* Alien Encounter *due to your report and found it to be the best overall attraction, better than "Terminator" as the audience is smaller and closer to the action. It helped to know it was scary, but we felt your warnings were over the top. The adults laughed throughout.*

A Cape May, New Jersey, family agreed:

> *We also have to register in on the* Alien Encounter *saga. My ten-year-old and I liked it a lot. We would have gone again except I convinced him that since we already knew the surprises it wouldn't be nearly as scary the second time. When I later let my son read your comments (and others) about the ride, here's his logical reply. "Mom, how could anyone really think a monster was going to get them? It's a ride*

*that millions of people have been on and lived. It's not real after all."
How's that for logic? Nonetheless, he screamed with everyone else. Oh,
and I looked. I didn't see anyone crying or fainting. Nor was anyone
upset at the pre-game show when the little serpent got fried by Tim
Curry. It was cartoon violence of a kind reminiscent of the Roadrunner
and Wiley Coyote, for goodness sakes. Did it really upset you?*

A Rochester, New York, woman also comes to the defense of *Alien
Encounter*, writing:

> *I do disagree with you about* Alien Encounter. *Just because Disney
> is known for cute animals and happy endings, does that condemn them
> to a future of nothing but singing flowers and dancing hippos? I love
> A.E. and so did my whole family. And I really don't like scary movies or
> things like that. It's not really that bad. To say it's just water being
> spritzed on you, you're not really getting into it enough. But some
> people should know their own limits and the limits of their children.
> You say it is too dark and foreboding, but don't analyze it so much.*

A senior from North Charleston, South Carolina, disagrees:

> *Being put in the dark, with a lot of screaming and hollering and
> having water spritzed in your face, is not scary, nor is it entertaining.*

A woman from Milford, Michigan, has this to say:

> *Warning!!! And I can't stress this enough!* Alien Encounter *is the
> most intense attraction in any theme park. It is one of those rides I can
> say I've seen and that I have no intention of ever doing again. In fact,
> parents who take children under the age of six should be brought up on
> child abuse.*

A single mom from Phillipsburg, New Jersey, agrees:

> Alien Encounter *was the WORST experience for my 10-year-old
> (and almost every child in there). It starts out cute enough during the
> preshow, but the actual show is a disaster for children. My daughter
> screamed and cried in terror throughout it. I thought the Disney warn-
> ings were vague and inaccurate. When we left, there wasn't one child
> with dry eyes (even sturdy-looking 12-year-old boys were crying). I
> think an age requirement of 13 or 14 is more appropriate. I talked to a
> few adults, and we agreed that the special effects were extremely
> unpleasant even for us. This show isn't a Disney family experience—it's
> ATROCIOUS!!*

A parent from Laurel, Maryland, shares her experience:

> The preshow is very deceiving. It kind of lulls you into thinking "this isn't so bad." When the main part came up, I admit the experience gave me the absolute heebie-jeebies. It is INTENSE! I am grateful nothing touched me when we were plunged into the dark (my friend and I sat in the middle row of seats), because I swear I would have either passed out or screamed bloody murder. If someone is the least bit scared of the dark or is the least bit fearful, I do not recommend this attraction. (I am never doing that presentation again—it was way too intense for me, and I'm now 27 years of age!) All sorts of things go running through your mind when it happens. If you don't keep reminding yourself that it's just a theater, you really can get the stuffing scared out of you.

In the middle are a group of readers, including this mom from Providence, Rhode Island, who advocate Alien Encounter for adults but warn about taking children:

> Alien Encounter was scary in a different way than the other rides. The "theatre of the mind" element really worked. It wasn't just a jarring physical thing. Disney ought to develop more attractions like this one. Although parents of 6–9-year-olds should be forewarned that most of the kids that age were carried out at the end screaming and clinging to their parents. I was in the baby swap holding area (the exit lobby) and was glad I'd ridden before my husband. If I had seen all those kids shrieking before I'd queued, I would have chickened out.

A dad from Monona, Wisconsin, weighed in with this:

> Regarding Alien Encounter, I agree that it's pretty creepy and not for the faint of heart, but I think you missed a significant point. Disney is actually making fun of money-grubbing corporations! I was slightly appalled that some parents took very young children into that show. One little girl was just about in fetal position by the end.

Joining the chorus "in favor" is an Amarillo, Texas, mother who regrets subjecting her child to the attraction:

> My personal favorite was Alien Encounter, but it literally scared our daughter to pieces. She screamed and cried when ol' Mr. Alien busted loose. We didn't feel like parents of the year, needless to say. I will add that every other little girl I saw under the age of eight was crying also. I think they should have a warning like Terminator 2 does at Universal Studios—PG-13.

What do you get when you cross Alien Encounter with the Hall of Presidents?

A mother from Plum, Pennsylvania, adds this:

> *You were exactly right about* Alien Encounter—*it was far too scary for our nine-year-old—who ended up vomiting as a result of being so very frightened.*

A normally fearless New England teenager decided she was not quite "big enough" for *Alien Encounter*, writing:

> *Alien Encounter was very graphic, loud, and frightening. I am going to be 15 and to me it was too much. I love space and alien movies but that went too far. This place is supposed to be for kids and kids at heart. My feelings toward [Disney's] warnings are very negative. They say it may frighten small children but they don't tell you that it may frighten big "children."*

A dad from Greensboro, North Carolina, notes that there is no way possible to comfort your children while the show is in progress, writing:

> *Alien Encounter should not be seen by pre-adolescents. You are trapped, alone, isolated, with no way to comfort or explain. Our children could not (or would not) speak for an hour afterward.*

A mother of four from Winchester, Virginia, tells her family's story:

> *We mistakenly rode Alien Encounter first. Fortunately the four-year-old and I stayed out. My daughters came out petrified and in tears. Luckily, they recovered quickly. Warn any parents of children seven or younger to ride it first themselves before they subject their kids to it. It's great for adults, though. My vote for best new attraction in the Magic Kingdom.*

A mom from Glenview, Illinois, didn't enjoy it:

> *We saw Alien Encounter, and it was horrible! The seats were uncomfortable and we were strapped in with an overhead harness. This was done, no doubt, to keep all the truly terrified children from trying to escape during the show. An eight- or nine-year-old boy next to me was sobbing after the alien escaped. This attraction is pointless, incomprehensible, intense, and no fun at all. It lacked any Disney creativity and whimsy.*

Finally, from an Abbott Park, Illinois, dad:

> *After all the hype, I was a little disappointed. I thought it was a little mean-spirited in a very un-Disneylike way. And though the effects were good, I left with sort of a bad taste in my mouth.*

Touring Tips Disney's most disturbing and frightening attraction, *Alien Encounter* initially was rejected by Walt Disney Company chairman Michael Eisner for not being scary enough. Though reader reaction to *Alien Encounter* is mixed, almost everyone agrees this isn't an attraction for young children. *Alien Encounter* stays busy throughout the day. See it first thing in the morning.

Tomorrowland Eateries and Shops

Description and Comments Cosmic Ray's Starlight Cafe (formerly Tomorrowland Terrace) is the largest and most efficient Magic Kingdom fast-food restaurant. The Plaza Pavilion, however, serves better food, including a good Italian sub. Several shops provide yet more opportunities to buy souvenirs.

Touring Tips Unless shopping is your top priority, leave browsing until your second day.

Live Entertainment in the Magic Kingdom

Bands, Disney character appearances, parades, ceremonies, and singing and dancing further enliven the Magic Kingdom. For specific events the day you visit, check the live entertainment schedule in your Disney guidemap (free as you enter the park or at City Hall). Be aware: If you're short on time, it's impossible to see Magic Kingdom featured attractions *and* the live performances. Our one-day touring plans exclude live performances in favor of seeing as much of the park as time permits. This tactical decision is based on the fact that some parades and performances siphon crowds away from the more popular rides, thus shortening lines.

Nonetheless, the color and pageantry of live events are integral to the Magic Kingdom and a persuasive argument for a second day of touring. Here's a list and description of some performances and events presented with regularity that don't require reservations.

Fantasyland Pavilion   Site of various concerts in Fantasyland.

Steel Drum Bands and Luau Dancers   Perform daily at Caribbean Plaza in Adventureland.

Frontierland Stuntmen   Stuntmen stage shootouts in Frontierland; check the daily entertainment schedule.

Kids of the Kingdom   Youthful song-and-dance group performs popular music daily in the Castle Forecourt Stage (front of the castle). Disney characters usually join the fun.

Flag Retreat   At 5 p.m. daily at Town Square (railroad station end of Main Street). Sometimes performed with great fanfare and college marching bands, sometimes with a smaller Disney band.

Sword in the Stone Ceremony   A ceremony based on the Disney animated feature of the same name. Merlin the Magician selects youngsters from the audience to test their courage and strength by removing the sword, Excalibur, from the stone. Staged several times each day behind Cinderella Castle; check the daily entertainment schedule.

Bay Lake and Seven Seas Lagoon Floating Electrical Pageant   This is one of our favorites among the Disney extras, but it's necessary to leave the Magic Kingdom to view it. The pageant is a stunning electric light show afloat on small barges and set to nifty electronic music. It's performed at nightfall (about 9 p.m. most of the year) on Seven Seas Lagoon and Bay Lake. Leave the Magic Kingdom and take the monorail to the Polynesian Resort. Get yourself a drink and walk to the end of the pier to watch the show.

Fantasy in the Sky   A stellar fireworks display unleashed after dark on nights the park is open late. For an uncluttered view and lighter crowds, watch from the terrace of The Plaza Pavilion restaurant in Tomorrowland.

Cosmic Ray's Galaxy Palace Theater   These stages in Tomorrowland feature Top-40 rock music, rap, and jazz, as well as Disney characters and the Kids of the Kingdom.

Disney Character Shows & Appearances   Most days, a character is on duty for photos and autographs from 9 a.m. to 10 p.m. next to City Hall. Mickey and two or three assortments of other characters are available most of the day at Mickey's Toontown Fair. Shows at the Castle Forecourt Stage and Tomorrowland's Galaxy Palace Theater feature Disney characters several times daily (check the entertainment schedule). In Fantasyland, Ariel can be found in her Grotto daily, while a host of others can be seen at the Character Festival next to Dumbo. Characters also roam the park. For information on character whereabouts on the day you visit, check the *Disney Character Greeting Location Guide* printed on the inside of the handout park map.

Magic Kingdom Bands   Banjo, Dixieland, steel drum, marching, and fife-and-drum bands roam the park daily.

Tinker Bell's Flight   This nice special effect at 10 p.m. in the sky above Cinderella Castle heralds the beginning of Fantasy in the Sky fireworks (when the park is open late).

PARADES

Parades at the Magic Kingdom are full-fledged spectaculars with dozens of Disney characters and amazing special effects. We rate the afternoon parade as outstanding and the evening parade as "not to be missed."

In addition to providing great entertainment, parades lure guests away from the attractions. If getting on rides appeals to you more than watching a parade, you'll find substantially shorter lines just before and during parades. Because the parade route doesn't pass through Adventureland, Tomorrowland, or Fantasyland, attractions in these lands are particularly good bets. Be forewarned: Parades disrupt traffic in the Magic Kingdom. It's nearly impossible, for example, to get to Adventureland from Tomorrowland, or vice versa, during one.

Afternoon Parade

Usually staged at 3 p.m., the parade features bands, floats, and marching Disney characters. A new afternoon parade is introduced every year or two.

While some elements, such as Disney characters, remain constant, the theme, music, and float design change. Seasonal parades during major holidays round out the mix.

Evening Parade(s)

After trying myriad experiments employing electroluminescent and fiber-optic technologies, light-spreading thermoplastics, and clouds of underlit liquid-nitrogen smoke (I swear we're not making this up), Disney has caved in to popular sentiment and brought back the venerable and immensely popular Main Street Electrical Parade. With umpteen billion teeny, twinkling lights, jazzy fiber-optics, and a bouncy synthesizer musical score, the parade is still pretty high-tech, but at least you won't need a gas mask or an asbestos suit to watch. Depending on closing time, the evening parade is staged either once at 9 p.m. or twice when the park is open late: at 8 and 10 p.m., or at 9 and 11 p.m.

During less busy times of year, the evening parade is held only on weekends, and sometimes not even then. Call (407) 824-4321 before you go to be sure the parade is on.

Parade Route and Vantage Points

Magic Kingdom parades circle Town Square, head down Main Street, go around the central hub, and cross the bridge to Liberty Square. In Liberty Square, they follow the waterfront and end in Frontierland. Sometimes they begin in Frontierland and run the route in the opposite direction.

Most guests watch from the central hub, or from Main Street. One of the best and most popular vantage points is the upper platform of the Walt Disney World Railroad station at the Town Square end of Main Street. This is also a good place for watching the Fantasy in the Sky fireworks, as well as for ducking out of the park ahead of the crowd when the fireworks end. Problem is, you have to stake out your position 30–45 minutes before the events.

Because most spectators pack Main Street and the central hub, we recommend watching from Liberty Square or Frontierland. Great vantage points, frequently overlooked, are:

1. Sleepy Hollow snack and beverage shop, immediately to your right as you cross the bridge into Liberty Square. If you arrive early, buy refreshments and claim a table by the rail. You'll have a perfect view of the parade as it crosses the Liberty Square bridge, but only when the parade begins on Main Street.

2. The pathway on the Liberty Square side of the moat from Sleepy Hollow snack and beverage shop to Cinderella Castle. Any point along this path offers a clear and unobstructed view

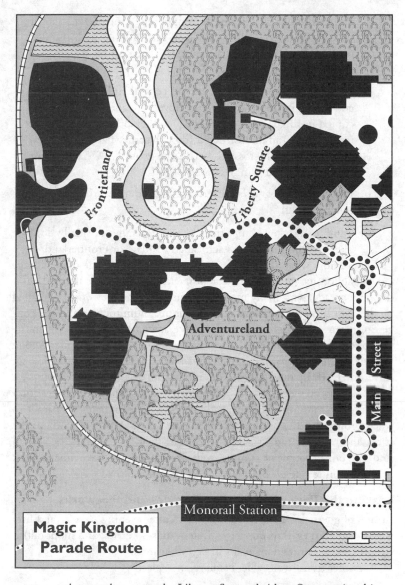

Frontierland

Liberty Square

Adventureland

Main Street

Monorail Station

**Magic Kingdom
Parade Route**

as the parade crosses the Liberty Square bridge. Once again, this spot works only for parades coming from Main Street.

3. The covered walkway between Liberty Tree Tavern and *The Diamond Horseshoe Saloon Revue*. This elevated vantage point is perfect (particularly on rainy days) and usually goes unnoticed until just before the parade starts.

4. Elevated wooden platforms in front of the Frontierland Shootin' Arcade, Frontier Trading Post, and the building with the sign reading FRONTIER MERCHANDISE. These spots usually get picked off 10–12 minutes before parade time.

5. Benches on the perimeter of the central hub, between the entrances to Liberty Square and Adventureland. Usually unoccupied until after the parade begins, they offer a comfortable resting place and unobstructed (though somewhat distant) view of the parade as it crosses Liberty Square bridge. What you lose in proximity, you gain in comfort.

6. Liberty Square and Frontierland dockside areas. These spots usually go early.

Assuming it starts on Main Street (evening parades normally do), the parade takes 16–20 minutes to reach Liberty Square or Frontierland.

On evenings when the parade runs twice, the first parade draws a huge crowd, siphoning guests from attractions. Many folks leave the park after the early parade, with many more departing after the fireworks (scheduled on the hour between the two parades). For optimum touring and less congestion, enjoy attractions during the early parade, then break to watch the fireworks. Continue to tour after the fireworks. This is a particularly good time to see *Alien Encounter*, ride Space Mountain, and enjoy attractions in Adventureland. If you're touring Adventureland and the parade begins on Main Street, you won't have to assume your viewing position in Frontierland until 15 minutes after the parade starts (the time it takes the parade to reach Frontierland). If you watch from the Splash Mountain side of the street and head for the attraction as the last float passes, you'll be able to ride with only a couple of minutes' wait. You might even have time to work in a last-minute ride on Big Thunder Mountain Railroad.

Leaving the Park after Evening Parades and Fireworks

Armies of guests leave the Magic Kingdom after evening parades and fireworks. The Disney Transportation System (buses, ferries, and monorail) is overwhelmed, causing long waits in boarding areas.

A mother from Kresgeville, Pennsylvania, pleads:

> *Please stress how terrifying these crowds can be. Our family of five made the mistake of going to the MK the Saturday night before Columbus Day to watch the parade and fireworks. Afterwards, we lingered at The Crystal Palace to wait for the crowds to lessen, but it was no use. We started walking toward the gates and soon became trapped by the throng, not able to go forward or back. There was no way to cross the hordes to get*

to the dock for our hotel's launch. Our group became separated, and it became a living nightmare. We left the park at 10:30 p.m. and didn't get back to the Polynesian (less than a mile away) until after midnight. How dare they expose children to that nightmare! Even if they were to raise Walt Disney himself from cryogenic sleep and parade him down Main Street, I would never go to the MK on a Saturday night again!

An Oklahoma City dad offers this advice:

Never, never leave the Magic Kingdom just after the 10 p.m. fireworks. I have never seen so many people in one spot before. Go for another ride—no lines because everyone else is trying to get out!

Congestion persists from the end of the early evening parade until closing time. Most folks watch the early parade and then the fireworks a few minutes later. If you're parked at the Transportation and Ticket Center and are intent on beating the crowd, view the early parade from the Town Square end of Main Street, leaving the park as soon as the parade ends. Walk (about 12 minutes) or ride the monorail to the Contemporary Resort. Note that the monorail loading platform for the hotels is different from the platform serving the TTC. At the Contemporary Resort, take the elevator to the top floor and go through the lounge (no problem for kids) to the outdoor promenade atop the hotel. There, watch the Magic Kingdom fireworks in a relaxed, uncrowded setting with a perfect, unobstructed view. After the fireworks, return to the TTC on the monorail.

If you're staying at a Disney hotel not served by the monorail and must depend on Disney transportation, watch the early parade and fireworks at the park and then enjoy the attractions until about 20–25 minutes before the late parade is scheduled to begin. At this time, leave the park and catch the Disney bus or boat back to your hotel. Don't cut it too close: Main Street will be so congested that you won't be able to reach the exit.

Here's what happened to a family from Cape Coral, Florida:

We tried to leave the park before the parade began. However, Main Street was already packed and we didn't see any way to get out of the park, so we were stuck. In addition, it was impossible to move across the street, and even the shops were so crowded that it was virtually impossible to maneuver a stroller through them to get close to the entrance.

If you don't have a stroller (or are willing to forgo the $1 return refund for rental strollers), catch the Walt Disney World Railroad in Frontierland or Mickey's Toontown Fair and ride to the park exit at Main Street. Be aware that the railroad shuts down during parades because the floats must cross the tracks when entering or exiting the parade route in Frontierland. If you plan to escape by train, don't cut it too close.

If you're on the Tomorrowland side of the park, it's actually possible for you to exit during a parade. Leaving Tomorrowland, cut through The Plaza Pavilion Restaurant to Main Street. Before you reach Main Street, bear left into the side door of the corner shop. Once inside, you'll see that Main Street shops have interior doors allowing you to pass from one shop to the next without having to get on Main Street. Work your way from shop to shop until you reach Town Square (easy, because people will be outside watching the parade). At Town Square, bear left and move to the train station and the park exit.

This strategy won't work if you're on the Adventureland side of the park. You can make your way through Casey's Corner restaurant to Main Street, then work your way through the interior of the Main Street shops, but when you pop out of the Emporium at Town Square, you'll be trapped by the parade. As soon the last float passes, however, you can bolt for the exit.

Another strategy for beating the masses out of the park (if your car is at the TTC lot) is to watch the early parade and then leave before the fireworks begin. Line up for the ferry. One will depart about every eight to ten minutes. Try to catch the ferry that will be crossing Seven Seas Lagoon while the fireworks are in progress. The best vantage point is on the top deck to the right of the pilot house as you face the Magic Kingdom, and the sight of fireworks silhouetting the castle and reflecting off Seven Seas Lagoon is unforgettable. While there's no guarantee that a ferry will load and depart within three or four minutes of the fireworks, your chances are about 50/50 of catching it just right. If you're in the front of the line for the ferry and don't want to board the boat that's loading, stop at the gate and let people pass you. You'll be the first to board the next boat.

Shopping in the Magic Kingdom

Shops add realism and atmosphere to Magic Kingdom settings and offer an extensive inventory including souvenirs, clothing, novelties, and decorator items. Much of the merchandise (except Disney trademark souvenir items) is available less expensively elsewhere, but there's also a lot of stuff we've never seen *anywhere* else. If shopping is your gig, you can have a field day at the Magic Kingdom, but don't say we didn't warn you when your family has you committed for hauling home coonskin caps, Goofy cufflinks, and a stuffed parrot. Also, as this Worthington, Ohio, dad recounts, the seemingly most innocuous souvenir can turn out to be a time bomb:

> *We allowed our 11-year-old daughter to buy a Disney music CD*
> *without looking to see what was on it. Two hours after we get home*

she's blasting "It's a Small World, after all" through the whole house. I felt like Sigourney Weaver when she discovered she had an alien on her spaceship. The next day the CD mysteriously disappeared.

We realize that Disney souvenirs and memorabilia are irresistible to many guests. If you have decided you would look good in a Goofy hat with shoulder-length floppy ears, you're in the right place. What's more, you have plenty of company. A reader observes:

> *I've discovered that people have a compelling need to buy Disney stuff when they are at WDW. When you get home you wonder why you ever got a cashmere sweater with Mickey Mouse embroidered on the breast, or a tie with tiny Goofys all over it. Maybe it's something they put in the food.*

Disney trademark merchandise tends to be more expensive at Disney shops than in independent stores outside the World. Quality, however, is better at Disney shops. The best place for quality and value is the Character Warehouse in Mall 2 of the Belz Factory Outlet World on International Drive off I-4. Unfortunately, selection is limited.

Bypass the shops if you're on a one-day visit. If you have two or more days in the Magic Kingdom, browse the shops in early afternoon when many of the attractions are crowded. Remember that Main Street and its shops open earlier and close later than the rest of the park. Store your purchases in lockers at the Main Street rail station while you tour. Or, have your packages forwarded from shops to Parcel Pick-up and retrieve them when you leave the park. Disney resort guests can have their purchases delivered to their hotel rooms.

If you remember on your flight home that you forgot to buy mouse ears for your nephew, call the Walt Disney Attractions Mail Order Department on weekdays at (407) 363-6200 or the catalog department at (800) 237-5751. Most trademark merchandise sold at Walt Disney World is available.

Behind the Scenes in the Magic Kingdom

Keys to the Kingdom takes guests behind the scenes at the Magic Kingdom. This fascinating guided tour provides an informative and detailed look at the park's logistical, technical, and operational sides. Included are the parade assembly area, the waste treatment plant, and tunnels under the theme park. For additional information, call (407) 939-8687. The program ($49 per person) runs about four to five hours. Advance reservations and payment by credit card are required. Park admission is not included. Discounts are usually available; ask when you call to book.

For those interested in the tour, a reader from Ludington, Michigan, offers the following advice:

> People thinking of taking the Keys to the Kingdom tour should know that it is not for the faint of heart. This is a four-hour walking tour with only one 15-minute break plus a few minutes to sit while on Pirates of the Caribbean, the Haunted Mansion, and the Tommorowland Transit Authority. It wore me out, and I am on my feet most of any given working day. If you do this, make it the last day of your visit—it took me three days to recover. Oh, by the way, it is worth every penny!

Backstage Magic, a seven-hour, $211 tour, goes behind the scenes at all of the parks except the Animal Kingdom.

Traffic Patterns in the Magic Kingdom

When we research the Magic Kingdom, we study its traffic patterns, asking:

1. Which sections of the park and what attractions do guests visit first? When visitors are admitted to the lands on non-early-entry days during summer and holiday periods, traffic to Tomorrowland and Frontierland is heaviest, followed by Fantasyland, Adventureland, Liberty Square, and Mickey's Toontown Fair. On early-entry days during busier times, Disney hotel and campground guests inundate Fantasyland and Tomorrowland before the general public is admitted. The early-morning crowds of Disney resort guests accelerate the filling of the park by about an hour.

During the school year, when fewer young people are in the park, early-morning traffic is more evenly distributed but remains heaviest in Tomorrowland, Frontierland, and Fantasyland. Our researchers tested the oft-repeated claim that most people turn right into Tomorrowland and tour the Magic Kingdom in a counterclockwise sequence. We found it to be baseless. As the park fills, visitors head for the top attractions they want to ride before lines get long. This, more than any other factor, determines morning traffic patterns.

2. How long does it take for the park to fill up? How are the visitors dispersed in the park? On non-early-entry days, a surge of "early birds" arrives before or around opening time but is quickly dispersed throughout the empty park. After the initial wave is absorbed, there's a lull lasting

Attractions That Are Crowded Early

Tomorrowland:	Space Mountain
	Alien Encounter
Frontierland:	Splash Mountain
	Big Thunder Mountain Railroad
Fantasyland:	Dumbo the Flying Elephant
	The Many Adventures of Winnie the Pooh
Adventureland:	Jungle Cruise

about an hour after opening. Then the park is inundated for about two hours, peaking between 10 a.m. and noon. Arrivals continue in a steady but diminishing stream until around 2 p.m. Lines we sampled were longest between 1 and 2 p.m., indicating more arrivals than departures into the early afternoon. For touring purposes, most attractions develop long lines between 10 and 11:30 a.m.

On early-entry days, Fantasyland and Tomorrowland fill with early entry guests who later spill over into Frontierland, Liberty Square, Adventureland, and Mickey's Toontown Fair. The presence of these resort guests slows the touring of day guests who are admitted later. During summer and holidays, the two successive waves of arrivals (first the early-entry resort guests, then the day guests) overwhelm many popular attractions by midmorning. On early-entry days, many rides develop long lines as early as 9:10 a.m. Guests continue to stream into the park throughout the morning and into the afternoon. Though many early-entry guests leave the park between noon and 2 p.m., early entry markedly increases daily attendance. Thus, on early-entry days during busier times, the Magic Kingdom is packed most of the day.

From late morning through early afternoon on both early-entry and non-early-entry days, guests are equally distributed through all of the lands. We found, however, that guests concentrate in Fantasyland, Liberty Square, and Frontierland in late afternoon, with a decrease of visitors in Adventureland and Tomorrowland. Adventureland's Jungle Cruise and Tomorrowland's *Alien Encounter* and Space Mountain continue to be crowded, but most other attractions in those lands are readily accessible.

3. How do most visitors tour the park? Do first-time visitors tour differently from repeat guests? Many first-time visitors are accompanied by friends or relatives familiar with the Magic Kingdom, who guide their tour.

These tours may or may not follow an orderly sequence. First-time visitors without personal guides tend to be more orderly in their touring. Many first-time visitors, however, are drawn to Cinderella Castle upon entering the park and thus begin their rotation from Fantasyland. Repeat visitors usually go directly to their favorite attractions.

Early-entry guests go directly to Fantasyland and Tomorrowland. Later, when the remainder of the Magic Kingdom opens, most continue touring Tomorrowland or head for Frontierland and Splash Mountain.

4. How do special events, such as parades and live shows, affect traffic patterns? Parades pull huge numbers of guests away from attractions and provide a window of opportunity for experiencing the more popular attractions with less of a wait. Castle Forecourt Stage shows also attract crowds but only slightly affect lines.

5. What are the traffic patterns near to and at closing time? On our sample days, in busy times and off-season at the park, departures outnumbered arrivals beginning in midafternoon. Many visitors left in late afternoon as the dinner hour approached. When the park closed early, guests departed steadily during the two hours before closing, with a huge exodus at closing time. When the park closed late, a huge exodus began immediately after the early-evening parade and fireworks, with a second mass departure after the late parade, continuing until closing. Because Main Street and the transportation services remain open after the other six lands close, crowds leaving at closing mainly affect conditions on Main Street and at the monorail, ferry, and bus boarding areas. In the hour before closing, the other six lands normally are uncrowded.

6. When there are two or more lines, is the shortest wait always in the left line? We don't recommend the "left-line strategy" because, with the occasional exception of food lines, it doesn't hold up. Disney has techniques for both internal and external crowd control that distribute traffic nearly equally. Placing researchers at the same time in each available line, we could discern no consistent pattern of who was served first. Further, researchers entering the same attraction by different lines almost always would exit the attraction within 30 to 90 seconds of each other.

Occasionally guests ignore a second line that has just opened and stay in the established line. As a rule, if you encounter a waiting area with two lines and no barrier to entry for either, and one line is empty or conspicuously shorter than the other, get in the short line.

Magic Kingdom Touring Plans

Our step-by-step touring plans are field-tested for seeing *as much as possible* in one day with a minimum of time wasted in lines. They're designed to help you avoid crowds and bottlenecks on days of moderate to heavy attendance. Understand, however, that there's more to see in the Magic Kingdom than can be experienced in one day. Since we began covering the Magic Kingdom, four headliner attractions and a new land have been added. Today, even if you could experience every attraction without any wait, you still wouldn't be able to see all of the park in a single day.

On days of lighter attendance (see "Selecting the Time of Year for Your Visit," page 41), our plans will save you time but won't be as critical to successful touring as on busier days. Don't worry that other people will be following the plans and render them useless. Fewer than 1 in every 500 people in the park will have been exposed to this information.

Choosing the Appropriate Touring Plan

We present five Magic Kingdom touring plans:

- Magic Kingdom One-Day Touring Plan for Adults
- Author's Selective Magic Kingdom One-Day Touring Plan for Adults
- Magic Kingdom One-Day Touring Plan for Parents with Young Children
- Magic Kingdom Dumbo-or-Die-in-a-Day Touring Plan for Parents with Young Children
- Magic Kingdom Two-Day Touring Plan

If you have two days (or two mornings) at the Magic Kingdom, the Two-Day Touring Plan is *by far* the most relaxed and efficient. The two-day plan takes advantage of early morning, when lines are short and the park hasn't filled with guests. This plan works well year-round and eliminates much of the extra walking required by the one-day plans. No matter when the park closes, our two-day plan guarantees the most efficient touring and the least time in lines. The plan is perfect for guests who wish to sample both the attractions and the atmosphere of the Magic Kingdom.

If you only have one day but wish to see as much as possible, use the One-Day Touring Plan for Adults. It's exhausting, but it packs in the maximum. If you prefer a more relaxed visit, use the Author's Selective One-Day Touring Plan. It includes the best the park has to offer (in the author's opinion), eliminating some less impressive attractions.

If you have children younger than age eight, adopt the One-Day Touring Plan for Parents with Young Children. It's a compromise, blending the preferences of younger children with those of older siblings and adults. The plan includes many children's rides in Fantasyland but omits roller coaster rides and other attractions that frighten young children or are off-limits because of height requirements. Or, use the One-Day Touring Plan for Adults or the Author's Selective One-Day Touring Plan and take advantage of switching off, a technique where children accompany adults to the loading area of a ride with age and height requirements but don't board (pages 190–192). Switching off allows adults to enjoy the more adventuresome attractions while keeping the group together.

The Dumbo-or-Die-in-a-Day Touring Plan for Parents with Young Children is designed for parents who will withhold no sacrifice for the children. On the Dumbo-or-Die plan, adults generally stand around, sweat, wipe noses, pay for stuff, and watch the children enjoy themselves. It's great.

Two-Day Touring Plans for Families with Young Children

If you have young children and are looking for a two-day itinerary, combine the Magic Kingdom One-Day Touring Plan for Parents with Young Children with the second day of the Magic Kingdom Two-Day Touring Plan.

Touring Plan Clip-out Pocket Outlines

Pocket versions of all touring plans presented in this guide begin on page 737. The outlines present the same itineraries as the detailed plans but with vastly abbreviated directions. Select the touring plan appropriate for your party and familiarize yourself with its detailed version. When you understand how the plan works, clip its pocket outline from the back of this guide and carry it as a quick reference when you visit the theme park.

The Single-Day Touring Conundrum

Touring the Magic Kingdom in a day is complicated by the fact that the premier attractions are at almost opposite ends of the park: Splash Mountain and Big Thunder Mountain Railroad in Frontierland and Space Mountain and *Alien Encounter* in Tomorrowland. It's virtually impossible to ride all four without encountering lines at one or another. If you ride Space Mountain and see *Alien Encounter* immediately after the park opens, you won't have much wait, if any. By the time you leave Tomorrowland and hurry to Frontierland, however, the line for Splash Mountain will be substantial. The same situation prevails if you ride the Frontierland duo first: Splash Mountain and Big Thunder Mountain Railroad, no problem; Space Mountain and *Alien Encounter*, fair-sized lines. From ten minutes after opening until just before closing, lines are long at these headliners.

The only effective way to ride all four without long waits is to tour the Magic Kingdom over two days: Ride Space Mountain and see *Alien Encounter* first thing one morning, and ride Splash Mountain and Big Thunder Mountain first thing on the other. If you have only one day and are unwilling to suffer waits of 45 minutes to 2 hours for these rides, experience one set when the park opens and the other just before closing. Many who attempt this fail because they become too worn out to stay until near closing.

Or, as we recommend in our one-day touring plans, arrive early and rush to *Alien Encounter*. After *Alien Encounter*, ride Space Mountain; then speed to Fronticrland and ride Splash Mountain. When you leave Splash Mountain, bear left to Big Thunder Mountain Railroad. If you're fast, your wait should be less than 5 minutes at *Alien Encounter*, about 10–20 minutes at Space Mountain, and about 25–35 minutes each at Splash Mountain and Big Thunder Mountain Railroad. This "bite-the-bullet" strategy requires a lot of hustle, but it probably works best. After riding Big Thunder Mountain Railroad, take comfort in the knowledge that you have the most popular attractions and the longest lines behind you.

This strategy takes advantage of the 30- to 45-minute morning lull, when guests on-hand at the park's opening have been absorbed and new arrivals are comparatively few. While you're riding Space Mountain and visiting *Alien Encounter*, Big Thunder Mountain Railroad and Splash Mountain are accommodating the early birds who rushed to Frontierland as soon as the park opened. By the time you finish Space Mountain and *Alien Encounter*, most of the first wave will have finished riding Big Thunder and Splash mountains. Because of the lull, crowds at Big Thunder and Splash mountains won't yet have built up again, and waits are tolerable.

Early entry at the Magic Kingdom eliminates any morning lull. If you plan to use the lull in your touring strategy, visit the park on a day when early entry isn't scheduled.

Magic Kingdom Early Entry for Walt Disney World Resort Guests

Walt Disney World hotel and campground guests are eligible to enter the Magic Kingdom one hour before the general public on selected days of the week. Early-entry guests can enjoy all attractions in Fantasyland except *Legend of the Lion King* and all attractions in Tomorrowland except *Walt Disney's Carousel of Progress* and *The Timekeeper*. Space Mountain, the Tomorrowland Transit Authority, and Astro Orbiter, however, sometimes open a half hour later than the other attractions.

Early entry is a mixed blessing during busier times of year. On one hand, the opportunity to get a jump on the general public lures so many Disney resort guests to the park that it fills much earlier than usual. After the general public is admitted, it's packed. If you remain in the Magic Kingdom, you'll have to fight incredible crowds. On the other hand, you have a great opportunity in the hour or so before the general public is admitted, particularly if you're among the first early-entry guests. You can experience the most popular attractions in Fantasyland and Tomorrowland and be poised to head for Splash Mountain and Big Thunder Mountain Railroad when the remainder of the park opens.

By our observation, the earlier the Magic Kingdom's official opening, the better early entry works. During major holiday periods, for example, the park opens to the general public at 8 a.m., with early entrants admitted at 6:30 a.m. Because comparatively few vacationers are willing to get out of bed and go to a theme park at 6 in the morning, those who do make the effort are substantially rewarded. On days when the official opening is 9 or 10 a.m., however, thousands of Disney resort guests are up and at 'em, waiting at the turnstiles to claim their early-entry privileges.

If you're eligible for early entry and visit the Magic Kingdom during the off-season, take advantage of your privileges. You'll get a jump on the general public and add an extra hour to what, in the off-season, is already a short touring day. If you participate in early entry during summer or holiday periods, arrive at the park 1 hour and 40 minutes before its official opening and see everything you can before it fills. At that point, leave the Magic Kingdom and spend the remainder of the day at one of the other parks.

How Early Entry Works

Nothing is simple at Walt Disney World, and everything is subject to tinkering. But here's how early entry usually works:

1. All times are based on the official opening time. If the official opening for day guests (those without early-entry privileges) is 9 a.m., early entry will commence an hour and a half earlier, at 7:30 a.m. If official opening is 8 a.m., the park will open for early entry at 6:30 a.m.

2. Disney transportation to the early-entry park begins about 2 hours and 15 minutes before official opening. If official opening is 8 a.m., Disney buses, monorails, and ferries will start running about 5:45–6 a.m.

3. Disney lodging guests who arrive for early entry can tour for one hour before day guests are admitted. If official opening is 9 a.m., for example, early-entry guests will be admitted at 7:30 a.m., and everybody else will enter at 8:30 a.m. So, you wonder, what happens at 9 a.m.? Who knows? This is Disney; maybe Goofy is in charge of the clocks.

If you're admitted for early entry, you'll encounter little or no congestion at the park's entrance. Be ready to show your Disney guest I.D. and a valid admission pass. Inside the park, you'll be directed down Main Street (everything on the street will be closed) to the central hub, and from there to Fantasyland or Tomorrowland. With early entry, you rarely will experience the crush associated with opening the park to the general public. Proceed leisurely to the attractions of your choice.

Combining Early Entry with the Touring Plans

Here's how to combine early entry with one of our touring plans:

1. Adults touring *without children* should enter when the park opens, experience *Alien Encounter* in Tomorrowland, then go directly to Space Mountain. Space Mountain sometimes opens a half hour later than *Alien Encounter*. If Space Mountain isn't open when you arrive, plant yourself in line and wait (10 minutes or less). After riding Space Mountain, go to Fantasyland and quiet your nerves on Peter Pan's Flight.

   Now, check your watch. Day-guests will usually be admitted 30 minutes before official opening time. When their numbers are added to the early-entry throng, the park suddenly becomes stuffed. If you want to continue touring at the Magic Kingdom, and most particularly if you want to ride Splash Mountain and Big Thunder Mountain Railroad without horrendous waits, position yourself on the border of Fantasyland and Liberty Square and hustle to the "mountains" the instant the rest of the park opens. Pick up the touring plan of your choice after you have ridden Big Thunder and Splash mountains, skipping any attractions you experienced during early entry.

2. Adults touring with children should arrive as early as possible and enjoy all attractions of interest in Fantasyland, as well as the Tomorrowland Speedway. About ten minutes before day-guests are admitted, position yourself to rush to either Frontierland or Adventureland. When the rest of the park opens, ride Splash Mountain in Frontierland (if your kids are at least 3'8" tall) or the Jungle Cruise in Adventureland. Afterward, return to Fantasyland and see *Legend of the Lion King*. Pick up the touring plan of your choice after *Legend of the Lion King*, bypassing attractions you experienced during early entry.

The E-Ticket Express

In 1999 Disney offered a program called the E-Ticket Express. As with early entry, only Disney resort guests with multiday passports (and annual and seasonal pass holders) are eligible. For $10 you can purchase a pass that allows you to remain in the Magic Kingdom for three hours after the official closing time and enjoy the following attractions:

Space Mountain   Splash Mountain   Big Thunder Mountain Railroad
Alien Encounter   Astro Orbiter   Pirates of the Caribbean
The Timekeeper   The Haunted Mansion *Country Bear Jamboree*

Disney limits the number of E-Ticket Express passes sold to 4–5,000 per night, ensuring short to nonexistent waits for most attractions. If you have fantasized about riding Space Mountain ten times in a row with practically no waiting, the E-Ticket Express makes it possible. The E-Ticket Express, however, is not good for admission to the park by itself. It must be used with a multiday admission used at any of the major theme parks on the day in question. In other words, you can spend the day at the Animal Kingdom (have your hand stamped upon exiting) and then head to the Magic Kingdom for after-hours fun. On arriving at the Magic Kingdom, enter the park before official closing time using your multiday pass. Once inside, take your E-Ticket Express voucher to either City Hall, the Tomorrowland Arcade, or Splashdown Photo and exchange it for a wristband that identifies you as eligible to stay in the park. After scheduled park closing, only guests with wristbands are allowed to remain in the park.

Now for the bad news. Thus far, Disney has operated this program only during the slower times of year when the Magic Kingdom closes relatively early (7 or 8 p.m.), and even then on just one day each week. It is unlikely, furthermore, that the E-Ticket Express will ever be operational during the summer or holiday periods when the park closes at 10 p.m. or later. As with all things Disney, this program is subject to change or cancellation at any time.

If You Are Not a Disney Resort Guest

If you aren't eligible for early entry, avoid the Magic Kingdom on early-entry days except as described below. Fantasyland and Tomorrowland will be mobbed even before you're allowed through the turnstiles, and the remainder of the park will be unusually crowded all day.

During major holiday periods Disney frequently opens all theme parks 90 minutes before official opening time, admitting everyone. If you're visiting at such a time, don't worry about early-entry privileges; just show up at the park of your choice, admission in hand, 1 hour and 40 minutes before official opening time.

Preliminary Instructions for All
Magic Kingdom Touring Plans

On days of moderate to heavy attendance, follow your chosen touring plan exactly, deviating only:

1. When you aren't interested in an attraction it lists. For example, the plan may tell you to go to Tomorrowland and ride Space Mountain, a roller coaster. If you don't enjoy roller coasters, skip this step and proceed to the next.

2. When you encounter a very long line at an attraction the touring plan calls for. Crowds ebb and flow at the park, and an unusually long line may have gathered at an attraction to which you're directed. For example, you arrive at The Haunted Mansion and find extremely long lines. It's possible that this is a temporary situation caused by several hundred people arriving en masse from a recently concluded performance of *The Hall of Presidents* nearby. If this is the case, skip The Haunted Mansion and go to the next step, returning later to retry The Haunted Mansion.

What to Do If You Get Off Track

If an unexpected interruption or problem throws the touring plan off, consult the "Magic Kingdom: Best Time to Visit Attractions" chart (page 737) for preferred times of day to visit attractions.

Park Opening Procedures

Your success during your first hour of touring will be affected somewhat by the opening procedure Disney uses that day:

A. All guests are held at the turnstiles until the entire park opens (which may or may not be at the official opening time). If this happens on the day you visit, blow past Main Street and head for the first attraction on the touring plan you're following.

B. Guests are admitted to Main Street a half hour to an hour before the remaining lands open. Access to other lands will be blocked by a rope barrier at the central hub end of Main Street. Once admitted, stake out a position at the rope barrier as follows:

   If you're going to Frontierland first (Splash Mountain and Big Thunder Mountain Railroad), stand in front of The Crystal Palace restaurant, on the left at the central hub end of Main Street. Wait next to the rope barrier blocking the walkway to

Adventureland. When the rope is dropped, move quickly to Frontierland by way of Adventureland. This is also the place to line up if your first stop is Adventureland.

If you're going to *Alien Encounter* and Space Mountain first, turn right at the end of Main Street and wait at the entrance of The Plaza Pavilion restaurant, or, alternatively, at the entrance bridge to Tomorrowland. When the rope drops, dash through The Plaza Pavilion into Tomorrowland.

If you're going to Fantasyland or Liberty Square first, go to the end of Main Street and line up left of center at the rope.

If you're going to Mickey's Toontown Fair first, go to the Main Street Station of the Walt Disney World Railroad and board the first train of the day. Disembark at the second stop. The train pulls out of the Main Street Station at the same time the rope is dropped at the central hub end of Main Street.

Before You Go

1. Call (407) 824-4321 the day before you go to check the official opening time. Also, ask whether early entry will be in effect the day you visit.

2. Purchase admission before you arrive. Order tickets from home by mail or buy them at the Disney Store in your local mall, the Ocala Disney AAA Travel Center off I-75 near Ocala (north of Orlando), the Disney Store in the Orlando airport, or Disney World lodging properties.

3. Familiarize yourself with park opening procedures (above) and reread the touring plan you've chosen so that you know what you're likely to encounter.

Magic Kingdom
One-Day Touring Plan for Adults

For: Adults without young children.
Assumes: Willingness to experience all major rides (including roller coasters) and shows.

This plan requires considerable walking and some backtracking; this is necessary to avoid long lines. Extra walking plus some morning hustle will spare you two to three hours of standing in line. You might not complete the tour. How far you get depends on how quickly you move from ride to ride, how many times you rest or eat, how quickly the park fills, and what time the park closes.

1. If you're a Disney hotel guest, use Disney transportation to commute to the park, arriving 90 minutes before official opening time on *early-entry days* and 40 minutes before official opening on *non-early-entry days.*

   If you're a day guest, arrive at the Magic Kingdom's parking lot 50 minutes before official opening time on a *non-early-entry day.* Arrive 90 minutes before official opening time if it's a holiday period. Add 15 minutes to the above if you have to buy your admission. These arrivals give you time to park and catch the tram to the Transportation and Ticket Center. At the TTC, transfer to the monorail or ferry to reach the park's entrance. If the line for the monorail is short, take the monorail; otherwise, catch the ferry.

2. At the park, proceed through the turnstiles and have one person go to City Hall for guidemaps containing the daily entertainment schedule.

3. Regroup and move quickly down Main Street to the central hub. Because the Magic Kingdom has two opening procedures, you probably will encounter one of the following:

   a. The entire park will be open. In this case, proceed quickly to *Alien Encounter* in Tomorrowland.

   b. Only Main Street will be open. In this case, turn right at the end of Main Street (before you reach the central hub), pass The Plaza Ice Cream Parlor and The Plaza Restaurant and position your group at the entrance to The Plaza Pavilion. When the rope barrier is dropped at opening time, walk through The Plaza Pavilion and on to *Alien Encounter.* Starting at The Plaza Pavilion entrance will give you a 50-yard advantage over anyone coming from the central hub. Experience *Alien Encounter.*

4. Exit *Alien Encounter,* turn left, and hurry to Space Mountain. Ride.

5. Leave Tomorrowland via the central hub and enter Liberty Square. Turn left and proceed along the waterfront to Splash Mountain. Ride.

6. Exit Splash Mountain to the left and go next door to Big Thunder Mountain Railroad. Ride.

7. Exit Big Thunder Mountain Railroad and bear right to experience the *Country Bear Jamboree,* also in Frontierland.

8. Exit the *Country Bear Jamboree* to your right and, keeping the waterfront on your left, proceed to The Haunted Mansion. Ride.

9. If you're hungry, eat. Fast-food eateries that generally are less crowded include Columbia Harbour House in Liberty Square, Aunt Polly's Dockside Inn on Tom Sawyer Island in Frontierland, El Pirata y el Perico in Adventureland, and The Crystal Palace at the central hub end of Main Street. As a lunchtime alternative, check your guidemap for the next performance of *The Diamond Horseshoe Saloon Revue.* If the timing is right, eat a sandwich while watching the show.

10. After lunch, enter Adventureland through the passage between the Frontierland Shootin' Arcade and the woodcarving shop. Ride Pirates of the Caribbean.

11. Exit Pirates to the left and proceed to the Frontierland railroad station. Ride the train to Mickey's Toontown Fair.

12. Quickly tour the Fair, exiting via the walkway to Tomorrowland.

13. In Tomorrowland, ride the Tomorrowland Transit Authority.

14. See *Walt Disney's Carousel of Progress.*

15. Ride Buzz Lightyear's Space Ranger Spin.

16. Proceed toward the central hub entrance to Tomorrowland and experience *The Timekeeper.*

17. Via the central hub, return to Liberty Square and check *The Hall of Presidents* and *Liberty Belle* Riverboat. Choose the one with the shorter wait. When you've experienced both, proceed to Step 18.

18. Return to Fantasyland. See *Legend of the Lion King.*

19. Check the line at The Many Adventures of Winnie the Pooh. If the wait is 25 minutes or less, ride. If the wait is longer, skip to Step 20.

20. Ride It's a Small World.

21. Check the line at Peter Pan's Flight. If the wait is 20 minutes or less, ride. If the wait is longer, skip to Step 22.

22. Exit Fantasyland into Liberty Square and return to Adventure-land via the shortcut next to the Frontierland Shootin' Arcade. In Adventureland, ride the Jungle Cruise.

23. After the Cruise, explore Swiss Family Treehouse next door on the right.

24. If you have time left before closing, backtrack to attractions you may have missed or bypassed because lines were too long. View any parades, fireworks, or live performances that interest you. Grab a bite. Save Main Street until last, because it remains open after the rest of the park closes.

25. End your day browsing along Main Street.

Author's Selective Magic Kingdom One-Day Touring Plan for Adults

For: Adults touring without young children.
Assumes: Willingness to experience all major rides (including roller coasters) and shows.

This plan includes only those attractions the author believes are the best in the Magic Kingdom. It requires a lot of walking and some backtracking to avoid long lines. Extra walking and morning hustle will spare you two to three hours of standing in line. You might not complete the tour. How far you get depends on how quickly you move from ride to ride, how many times you rest or eat, how quickly the park fills, and what time the park closes.

1. If you're a Disney hotel guest, use Disney transportation to commute to the park, arriving 90 minutes before official open-ing time on *early-entry days* and 40 minutes before official opening on *non-early-entry days.*

   If you're a day guest, arrive at the parking lot 50 minutes before the Magic Kingdom's official opening time on a *non-early-entry day.* Arrive 90 minutes earlier than official opening if it's a holiday period. Add 15 minutes to the above if you must buy your admission. These arrivals will give you time to park and catch the tram to the Transportation and Ticket Center. At the TTC, transfer to the monorail or ferry to reach the park's entrance. If the line for the monorail is short, take the monorail; otherwise, catch the ferry.

2. At the park, proceed through the turnstiles and have one person

go to City Hall for guidemaps containing the daily entertainment schedule.

3. Regroup and move quickly down Main Street to the central hub. Because the Magic Kingdom has two opening procedures, you probably will encounter one of the following:

   a. The entire park will be open. In this case, proceed quickly to *Alien Encounter* in Tomorrowland.

   b. Only Main Street will be open. In this case, turn right at the end of Main Street (before you reach the central hub), pass The Plaza Ice Cream Parlor and The Plaza Restaurant, and stand at the entrance to The Plaza Pavilion. When the rope barrier drops at opening time, walk through The Plaza Pavilion and on to *Alien Encounter*. Starting at the entrance to The Plaza Pavilion will give you a 50-yard advantage over anyone coming from the central hub. Experience *Alien Encounter*.

4. Exit *Alien Encounter*, turn left, and hurry to Space Mountain. Ride.

5. Leave Tomorrowland via the central hub and enter Liberty Square. Turn left and proceed along the waterfront to Splash Mountain. Ride.

6. Exit Splash Mountain to the left and go next door to Big Thunder Mountain Railroad. Ride.

7. Exit Big Thunder Mountain Railroad. Keeping the waterfront on your left, proceed to The Haunted Mansion. Ride.

8. Turn left upon leaving the Mansion and enter Fantasyland. Experience The Many Adventures of Winnie the Pooh.

9. Bear left after Winnie the Pooh and see *Legend of the Lion King*. The line will appear long, but don't worry. The theater holds 500 people.

10. Retrace your steps to Liberty Square. If you're hungry, eat. Fast-food eateries generally less crowded include the Columbia Harbour House in Liberty Square, Aunt Polly's Dockside Inn on Tom Sawyer Island in Frontierland, El Pirata y el Perico in Adventureland, and The Crystal Palace at the central hub end of Main Street. As a lunchtime alternative, check your guidemap for the next performance of *The Diamond Horseshoe Saloon Revue*. If the timing is right, eat a sandwich while watching the show.

11. After lunch, enter Adventureland through the passage between the Frontierland Shootin' Arcade and the woodcarving shop. Ride Pirates of the Caribbean.

12. Exit Pirates to the left and proceed to the Frontierland railroad station. Ride the train to Mickey's Toontown Fair.

13. Quickly tour the Fair, exiting via the walkway to Tomorrowland.

14. In Tomorrowland, ride the Tomorrowland Transit Authority.

15. See *Walt Disney's Carousel of Progress.*

16. Proceed toward the central hub entrance to Tomorrowland and experience *The Timekeeper.*

17. Return via the central hub to Liberty Square and see *The Hall of Presidents.*

18. Upon exiting *The Hall of Presidents,* turn right and return to Fantasyland. Ride It's a Small World.

19. Check the line at Peter Pan's Flight. If the wait is 20 minutes or less, ride. If the wait is longer, skip to Step 20.

20. Retrace your steps from Fantasyland to Liberty Square and Frontierland. See the *Country Bear Jamboree.*

21. Return to Adventureland via the shortcut next to the Frontierland Shootin' Arcade. Visit the Swiss Family Treehouse.

22. Take the Jungle Cruise, to the left of the Treehouse.

23. If you have time left before closing, backtrack to attractions you may have bypassed because lines were too long. See any parades, fireworks, or live performances that interest you. Grab a bite. Save Main Street until last, because it remains open after the rest of the park closes.

24. End your day browsing along Main Street.

Magic Kingdom One-Day Touring Plan for Parents with Young Children

For: Parents with children younger than age eight.
Assumes: Periodic stops for rest, rest rooms, and refreshments.

This plan represents a compromise between the observed tastes of adults and those of younger children. Included are many amusement park rides that children may have the opportunity to experience at fairs and amusement parks back home. Although these rides are included in the plan, omit them if possible. These cycle-loading rides often have long lines, consuming valuable touring time:

Mad Tea Party   Dumbo the Flying Elephant
Cinderella's Golden Carrousel   Astro Orbiter

This time could be better spent experiencing the many attractions that better demonstrate the Disney creative genius and are found only in the Magic Kingdom. Instead of this plan, try either of the one-day plans for adults and take advantage of "switching off." This allows parents and young children to enter the ride together. At the boarding area, one parent watches the children while the other rides.

Before entering the park, decide whether you will return to your hotel for a midday rest. We strongly recommend that you break from touring and return to your hotel for a swim and a nap (even if you aren't lodging in Walt Disney World). You won't see as much, but everyone will be more relaxed and happy.

This touring plan requires a lot of walking and some backtracking to avoid long lines. A little extra walking and some morning hustle will spare you two to three hours of standing in line. You probably won't complete the tour. How far you get depends on how quickly you move from ride to ride, how many times you rest or eat, how quickly the park fills, and what time the park closes.

1. If you're a Disney hotel guest, use Disney transportation to commute to the park, arriving 90 minutes before official opening time on *early-entry days* and 40 minutes before official opening on *non-early-entry days*.

   If you're a day guest, arrive at the parking lot 50 minutes before the Magic Kingdom's official opening time on a *non-early-entry day*. Arrive 90 minutes earlier than official opening if it's a holiday period. Add 15 minutes to the above if you must

---

To Convert This One-Day Touring Plan into a Two-Day Touring Plan

Skip steps 11 and 12 on the first day. On the second day, arrive 30 minutes prior to opening and take the Walt Disney World Railroad from Main Street to Mickey's Toontown Fair. See Mickey's Toontown Fair in its entirety.

purchase your admission. These arrivals will give you time to park and catch the tram to the Transportation and Ticket Center. At the TTC, transfer to the monorail or ferry to reach the park's entrance. If the line for the monorail is short, take the monorail; otherwise, catch the ferry.

2. At the Magic Kingdom, proceed through the turnstiles and have one person go to City Hall for guidemaps containing the daily entertainment schedule.

3. Rent strollers (if necessary).

4. Move briskly to the end of Main Street. If the entire park is open, go quickly to Fantasyland. Otherwise, position your group by the rope barrier at the central hub. When the park opens and the barrier drops, go through the main door of the castle and ride Dumbo the Flying Elephant in Fantasyland.

5. Enjoy The Many Adventures of Winnie the Pooh.

6. Ride Peter Pan's Flight.

7. See *Legend of the Lion King*.

8. Exit left from *Lion King* and go to Liberty Square. Turn right at the waterfront and go to The Haunted Mansion. Ride.

9. Enter Frontierland. See the *Country Bear Jamboree*.

10. Go to Adventureland via the passageway between the Frontierland Shootin' Arcade and the woodcarving shop. Ride Pirates of the Caribbean.

11. Turn left out of Pirates and return to Frontierland. At the Frontierland Station, catch the train to Mickey's Toontown Fair. Pick up a replacement stroller at Mickey's Toontown Fair.

12. At the Fair, visit the characters and enjoy Donald's Boat. Ride the roller coaster if the line isn't long.

13. Return to Main Street (walk or take the train) and leave the park for your hotel. Eat lunch and rest. (Have your hand stamped for re-entry as you leave, and keep your parking receipt to show when you return so you won't have to pay again for parking.) Return refreshed to the park between 3:30 and 5 p.m. Once inside, walk or take the train to Frontierland and proceed to Step 14.

14. Take the raft to Tom Sawyer Island. Children could play here all day; set time limits based on the park's closing, your energy, and

how many more attractions you wish to experience. If you stayed in the park instead of resting at your hotel, you may want to have lunch at Aunt Polly's Dockside Inn on Tom Sawyer Island. The food is good, and lunchtime crowds are usually lighter than elsewhere.

15. Return to Fantasyland. Ride It's a Small World.

16. Go to Tomorrowland via the castle and central hub. Ride Buzz Lightyear's Space Ranger Spin.

17. Ride the Tommorrowland Transit Authority.

18. Head back toward the central hub entrance to Tomorrowland and try *The Timekeeper*.

19. If you have time or energy left, check the entertainment schedule for parades, fireworks, or live events that interest you. Grab a bite or try any attractions on the plan that you might have missed.

20. End your day browsing Main Street. It stays open later than the rest of the park.

Magic Kingdom Dumbo-or-Die-in-a-Day Touring Plan for Parents with Young Children

For: Adults compelled to devote every waking moment to the pleasure and entertainment of their young children or rich people who are paying someone else to take their children to the theme park.

Prerequisite: This plan is designed for days when the Magic Kingdom doesn't close until 9 p.m. or later.

Assumes: Frequent stops for rest, rest rooms, and refreshment.

Note: Name aside, this touring plan is not a joke. Regardless of whether you're loving, guilty, masochistic, selfless, insane, or saintly, this itinerary will provide a young child with about as perfect a day as is possible at the Magic Kingdom.

This plan is a concession to adults determined to give their young children the ultimate Magic Kingdom experience. It addresses the preferences, needs, and desires of young children to the virtual exclusion of those of adults or older siblings. If you left the kids with a sitter yesterday or wouldn't let little Marvin eat barbecue for breakfast, this plan will expiate your

---

To Convert This One-Day Touring Plan into a Two-Day Touring Plan

Skip steps 20 and 21 on the first day. On the second day, arrive 30 minutes prior to opening and take the Walt Disney World Railroad from Main Street to Mickey's Toontown Fair. See Mickey's Toontown Fair in its entirety.

---

guilt. It is also a wonderful itinerary if you're paying a sitter, nanny, or chauffeur to take your children to the Magic Kingdom.

1. If you're a Disney hotel guest, use Disney transportation to commute to the park, arriving 90 minutes before official opening time on *early-entry days* and 40 minutes before official opening on *non-early-entry days.*

   If you're a day guest, arrive at the parking lot 50 minutes before the Magic Kingdom's official opening time on a *non-early-entry day.* Arrive 90 minutes earlier than official opening if it's a holiday period. Add 15 minutes to the above if you must purchase your admission. These arrivals will give you time to park and catch the tram to the Transportation and Ticket Center. At the TTC, transfer to the monorail or ferry to reach the park's entrance. If the line for the monorail is short, take the monorail; otherwise, catch the ferry.

2. At the Magic Kingdom, proceed through the turnstiles and have one person go to City Hall for guidemaps containing the daily entertainment schedule.

3. Rent a stroller (if needed).

4. Move briskly to the end of Main Street. If the entire park is open, go quickly to Fantasyland. Otherwise, position your group by the rope barrier at the central hub. When the park opens and the barrier is dropped, go through the main door of the castle to Cinderella's Royal Table, on your right as you enter Cinderella Castle.

5. Make a dinner priority seating at the Royal Table for 7 p.m. Eating there will let your kids see the inside of the castle and meet Cinderella. To make your priority seating before you leave home, call (407) 939-3463. If you're a Disney resort guest, dial 55 or 56 to make an advance priority seating.

6. Enter Fantasyland. Ride Dumbo the Flying Elephant.

7. Hey, you're on vacation! Ride again, using the Chuck Bubba Relay if there are two adults in your party (pages 192–193).

8. Experience The Many Adventures of Winnie the Pooh, near Dumbo.

9. Ride Peter Pan's Flight.

10. Ride Cinderella's Golden Carrousel.

11. See *Legend of the Lion King*.

12. Bearing left, go to the Skyway. Ride to Tomorrowland.

    Note: Strollers aren't allowed on the Skyway. If you have a stroller, walk to Tomorrowland.

13. In Tomorrowland, ride the Tomorrowland Speedway. Let your child steer (cars run on a guide rail) while you work the foot pedal.

14. Ride the Astro Orbiter.

    Safety note: Seat your children in the vehicle before you get in. Also, the Astro Orbiter goes higher and faster than Dumbo and may frighten some children.

15. Ride Buzz Lightyear's Space Ranger Spin (near the Astro Orbiter).

16. Return to Main Street via the central hub and leave the park for your hotel. Eat lunch and rest. (Have your hand stamped for re-entry when you leave the park. Keep your parking receipt to show when you return so you won't have to pay again for parking.) If you elect not to take a break out of the park, skip to Step 18.

17. Return to the Magic Kingdom refreshed about 4 or 4:30 p.m. Take the Walt Disney World Railroad to Frontierland.

18. Take the raft to Tom Sawyer Island. Stay as long as the kids want. If you're hungry, Aunt Polly's Dockside Inn on Tom Sawyer Island is a winner for both kids and adults.

19. After you return from the island, see the *Country Bear Jamboree*.

20. Return to the Frontierland Station. Ride the train to Mickey's Toontown Fair.

21. Walk through Mickey's Country House and Minnie's Country House and play on Donald's Boat (tips for the latter are on page 421). Meet Disney characters at the Toontown Hall of Fame and pose for photos.

22. You should be within an hour of your dinner priority seating at Cinderella's Royal Table. Take the direct path from Mickey's Toontown Fair to Fantasyland. In Fantasyland, if you have 20 minutes or more before your priority seating, ride It's a Small World. Don't forget to sing.

23. Eat; then leave Fantasyland and go to Liberty Square. If your children are up to it, see The Haunted Mansion. If not, skip to Step 24.

24. Evening parades are quite worthwhile. If you're interested, adjust the remainder of the touring plan to allow you to take a viewing position about 10 minutes before the early parade starts (usually 8 or 9 p.m.). See our recommendations for good vantage points (pages 440–442). If you aren't interested in the parade, enjoy attractions in Adventureland while the parade is in progress. Lines will be vastly diminished.

25. Go to Adventureland by way of Liberty Square, Frontierland, or the central hub. Take the Jungle Cruise if the lines aren't long. If they're prohibitive, try the *Tropical Serenade (Enchanted Tiki Birds)* and/or the Swiss Family Treehouse. If your children can stand a few skeletons, see Pirates of the Caribbean.

26. If you have time or energy left, repeat any attractions the kids especially liked, or try ones on the plan you might have bypassed because of long lines. Buy Goofy hats if that cranks your tractor.

27. If you're parked at the Transportation and Ticket Center, catch the ferry or express monorail. If the express monorail line is long, catch the resort monorail and disembark at the TTC.

Magic Kingdom Two-Day Touring Plan

For: Parties wishing to spread their Magic Kingdom visit over two days.

Assumes: Willingness to experience all major rides (including roller coasters) and shows.

Timing: This two-day touring plan takes advantage of early-morning touring. Each day, you should complete the structured part of the plan by about 4 p.m. This leaves plenty of time for live entertainment. If the park is open late (after 8 p.m.), consider returning to your hotel at midday for a swim and a nap. Eat an early dinner outside Walt Disney World and return refreshed to enjoy the park's nighttime festivities.

Day One

1. If you're a Disney hotel guest, use Disney transportation to commute to the park, arriving 90 minutes before official opening time on *early-entry days* and 40 minutes before official opening on *non-early-entry days*.

   If you're a day guest, arrive at the parking lot 50 minutes before the Magic Kingdom's official opening on a *non-early-entry day*. Arrive 90 minutes earlier than official opening if it's a holiday period. Add 15 minutes to the above if you must purchase your admission. These arrivals will give you time to park and catch the tram to the Transportation and Ticket Center. At the TTC, transfer to the monorail or ferry to reach the park's entrance. If the line for the monorail is short, take the monorail; otherwise, catch the ferry.

2. At the park, proceed through the turnstiles and have one person go to City Hall for guidemaps containing the daily entertainment schedule.

3. Move as fast as you can down Main Street to the central hub. Because the Magic Kingdom uses two procedures for opening, you probably will encounter one of the following:

   a. The entire park will be open. In this case, proceed quickly to *Alien Encounter* in Tomorrowland.

   b. Only Main Street will be open. In this case, turn right at the end of Main Street (before you reach the central hub), pass The Plaza Ice Cream Parlor and The Plaza Restaurant and position your group at the entrance to The Plaza Pavilion. When the park opens and the rope barrier drops, walk through The Plaza Pavilion and on to *Alien Encounter*. Starting at the entrance to The Plaza Pavilion will give you a 50-yard advantage over anyone coming from the central hub. Experience *Alien Encounter*.

4. Turn left after exiting *Alien Encounter* and move briskly to Space Mountain. Ride.

5. Exit Space Mountain, bear right past the Tomorrowland Speedway, and go to Fantasyland. Experience The Many Adventures of Winnie the Pooh.

6. Exit Pooh to the left and ride Peter Pan's Flight.

7. Exit Peter Pan to the right and turn the corner. See *Legend of the Lion King*.

8. Exit *Lion King* to the left, cross the courtyard, and ride It's a Small World.

9. Exit Small World to the right and go to Liberty Square. Experience The Haunted Mansion.

10. See *The Hall of Presidents*.

11. If you're hungry, eat. Fast-food eateries that generally are less crowded include the Columbia Harbour House in Liberty Square, Aunt Polly's Dockside Inn on Tom Sawyer Island in Frontierland, El Pirata y el Perico in Adventureland, and The Crystal Palace at the central hub end of Main Street. As a lunchtime alternative, check your guidemap for the next performance of *The Diamond Horseshoe Saloon Revue*. If the timing is right, eat a sandwich while watching the show.

12. After lunch, ride the *Liberty Belle* Riverboat.

   Note: At this point, check the entertainment schedule to see if any parades or live performances interest you. Note the times and alter the touring plan accordingly. Since you already have seen all the attractions that cause bottlenecks and have big lines, interrupting the touring plan here won't cause any problems. Simply pick up where you left off before the parade or show.

13. In Frontierland, take a raft to Tom Sawyer Island. Explore.

14. Return from the island and see the *Country Bear Jamboree*.

15. This concludes the touring plan for the day. Enjoy the shops, see some of the live entertainment, or revisit your favorite attractions until you're ready to leave.

Day Two

1. If you're a Disney hotel guest, use Disney transportation to commute to the park, arriving 60 minutes before official opening time on *early-entry days* and 40 minutes before official opening on *non-early-entry days*.

   If you're a day guest, arrive at the parking lot 50 minutes before the Magic Kingdom's official opening time on a *non-early-entry day*. Arrive 90 minutes earlier than official opening if it's a holiday period. Add 15 minutes to the above if you must purchase your admission. These arrivals will give you time to park and catch the tram to the Transportation and Ticket Center. At the TTC, transfer to the monorail or ferry to reach the park's entrance. If the line for the monorail is short, take the monorail; otherwise, catch the ferry.

2. At the park, proceed through the turnstiles. Stop at City Hall for guidemaps containing the day's entertainment schedule.

   Note: If you're a Disney resort guest and enter the park on an early-entry day, revisit your favorite Fantasyland and Tomorrowland attractions. As the time approaches for the park to open to the public, position yourself in Fantasyland at the boundary between Fantasyland and Liberty Square. When the other lands open, head for the Liberty Square waterfront and from there to Splash Mountain. After Splash Mountain, pick up the touring plan at Big Thunder Mountain Railroad (Step 4), skipping steps that direct you to attractions you experienced during your early-entry hour.

3. Proceed to the end of Main Street. If the entire park is open, go immediately to Splash Mountain in Frontierland. Otherwise, turn left past Casey's Corner and position yourself in front of The Crystal Palace, facing the walkway bridge to Adventureland. When the park opens and the rope barrier drops, cross the bridge and turn left into Adventureland. Cut through Adventureland into Frontierland. Go straight to Splash Mountain and ride.

4. Ride Big Thunder Mountain Railroad, next to Splash Mountain.

5. Return to Adventureland. Ride the Jungle Cruise.

6. Across the street, see the *Tropical Serenade (Enchanted Tiki Birds).*

7. Walk through the Swiss Family Treehouse.

8. Exit the Treehouse to the left. Enjoy Pirates of the Caribbean.

   Note: At this point, check the daily entertainment schedule to see if any parades or live performances interest you. Note the times, and alter the touring plan accordingly. Since you already have seen all the attractions that cause bottlenecks and have big lines, interrupting the touring plan here won't cause any problems. Simply pick up where you left off before the parade or show.

9. If you're hungry, eat. Fast-food eateries that generally are less crowded include the Columbia Harbour House in Liberty Square, Aunt Polly's Dockside Inn on Tom Sawyer Island in Frontierland, El Pirata y el Perico in Adventureland, and The Crystal Palace at the central hub end of Main Street.

10. Exit Adventureland and go to the Frontierland train station between Splash and Big Thunder mountains. Catch the Walt Disney World Railroad. Disembark at Mickey's Toontown Fair (first stop).

11. Tour the Fair and meet the Disney characters.

12. Exit the Fair via the path to Tomorrowland.

13. In Tomorrowland, if you haven't eaten, try Cosmic Ray's Starlight Cafe (okay) or The Plaza Pavilion (better).

14. Ride the Tomorrowland Transit Authority.

15. See *Walt Disney's Carousel of Progress.*

16. Ride Buzz Lightyear's Space Ranger Spin.

17. Proceed toward the central hub entrance of Tomorrowland and experience *The Timekeeper*

18. This concludes the touring plan. Enjoy the shops, see live entertainment, or revisit your favorite attractions until you are ready to leave.

Part Eleven

Epcot

Not to Be Missed at Epcot	
World Showcase	*The American Adventure*
	IllumiNations
Future World	Spaceship Earth
	Living with the Land
	Honey, I Shrunk the Audience
	Test Track
	Body Wars
	Cranium Command

OVERVIEW

Education, inspiration, and corporate imagery are the focus at Epcot, the most adult of the Disney theme parks. What it gains in taking a futuristic, visionary, and technological look at the world, it loses, just a bit, in warmth, happiness, and charm.

Some people find the attempts at education to be superficial; others want more entertainment and less education. Most visitors, however, are in between, finding plenty of entertainment *and* education.

Epcot is more than twice as big as the Magic Kingdom or Disney-MGM Studios and, though smaller than the Animal Kingdom, has more territory to be covered on foot. Epcot rarely sees the congestion so common to the Magic Kingdom, but it has lines every bit as long as those at the Jungle Cruise or Space Mountain. Visitors must come prepared to do considerable walking among attractions and a comparable amount of standing in line.

Epcot's size means you can't see it all in one day without skipping an attraction or two and giving others a cursory glance. A major difference between Epcot and the other parks, however, is that some Epcot attractions can be savored slowly or skimmed, depending on personal interests. For example, the first section of General Motors' Test Track is a thrill ride, the second a collection of walk-through exhibits. Nearly all visitors take the ride, but many people, lacking time or interest, bypass the exhibits.

We have identified several Epcot attractions as "not to be missed." But part of the enjoyment of the park is that there's something for everyone. Ask your group. They're sure to have a variety of opinions as to which attraction is "best."

OPERATING HOURS

Epcot has two theme areas: Future World and World Showcase. Each has its own operating hours. Though schedules change throughout the year, Future World always opens before World Showcase in the morning, and usually closes before World Showcase in the evening. Most of the year, World Showcase opens two hours later than Future World. For exact hours during your visit, call (407) 824-4321.

ARRIVING

Disney resort and campground guests are invited to enter Epcot one hour before official opening on specified days each week. If you have early-entry privileges and want to exercise them, arrive about an hour and a half before the official opening time. For example, if official opening is 9 a.m., arrive by 7:30 a.m.

Visitors lodging outside Walt Disney World (day-guests in Disney Speak) must balance the least crowded days of the week (page 51) with an estimation of early entry's impact. We recommend day guests avoid Epcot when it's designated for early entry. It's far better to arrive early and stay ahead of the crowd on non-early-entry days than to tour on an early-entry day when hordes of Disney lodging guests have been allowed into the park ahead of you. The key to efficient touring at any of the parks is to be among the first guests through the turnstiles. If you don't have early-entry privileges, arrive 40 to 50 minutes before official opening on a non-early-entry day and wait to be admitted.

Persons ineligible for early entry shouldn't try sneaking in with early-entry guests. All Disney lodging guests, including children, are issued dated identification cards when they check in at their hotel. These either serve as or must be presented with a valid admission pass in order to enter a park early.

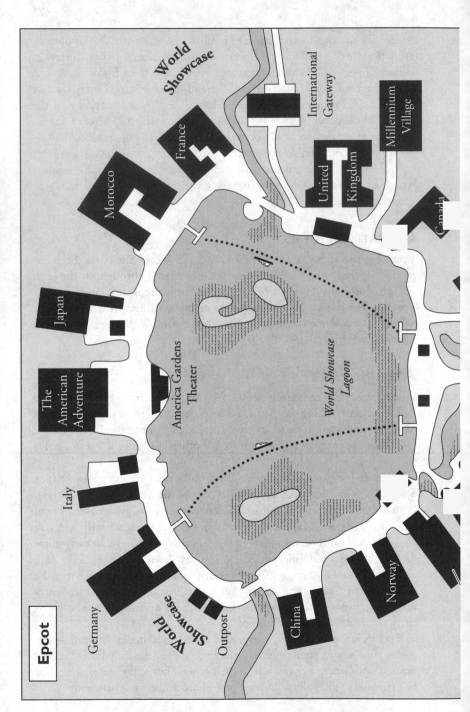

Epcot

World Showcase

France

Morocco

Japan

The American Adventure

Italy

Germany

World Showcase

Outpost

China

Norway

America Gardens Theater

World Showcase Lagoon

International Gateway

Millennium Village

United Kingdom

Canada

474

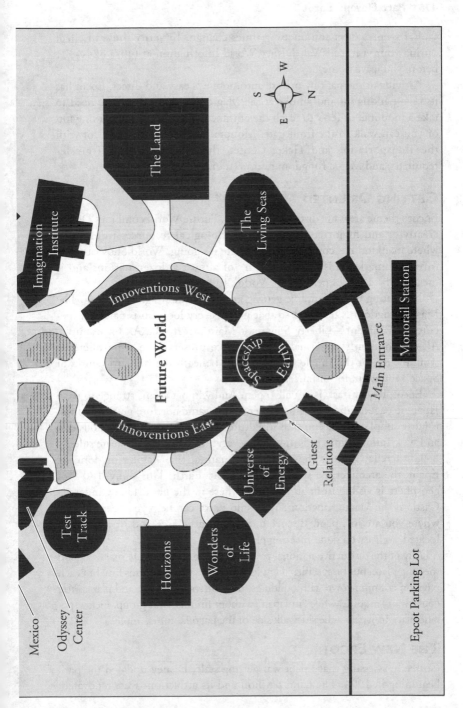

Early-entry days and opening times change. To verify those in effect during your visit, call Walt Disney World Information at (407) 824-4321 before you leave home.

Arriving at the park by private automobile is easy and direct. Epcot has its own parking lot and, unlike at the Magic Kingdom, there's no need to take a monorail or ferry to reach the entrance. Trams serve the parking lot, or you can walk to the front gate. Monorail service connects Epcot with the Transportation and Ticket Center, the Magic Kingdom (transfer required), and Magic Kingdom resorts (transfer required).

GETTING ORIENTED

Epcot's theme areas are distinctly different. Future World combines Disney creativity and major corporations' technological resources to examine where mankind has come from and where it's going. World Showcase features landmarks, cuisine, and culture of almost a dozen nations and is meant to be a sort of permanent World's Fair.

Navigating Epcot is unlike getting around at the Magic Kingdom. The Magic Kingdom is designed so that nearly every location is part of a specific environment—Liberty Square or Main Street, U.S.A., for example. All environments are visually separated to preserve the atmosphere. It wouldn't do for the Jungle Cruise to pass beneath the futuristic spires of Space Mountain, for instance.

Epcot, by contrast, is visually open. And while it seems strange to see a Japanese pagoda and the Eiffel Tower on the same horizon, getting around is fairly simple. An exception is in Future World, where the enormous east and west Innoventions buildings hide everything on their opposite sides.

Cinderella Castle is the central landmark at the Magic Kingdom. At Epcot, the architectural symbol is Spaceship Earth. This shiny, 180-foot geosphere is visible from almost everywhere in the park. Like Cinderella Castle at the Magic Kingdom, Spaceship Earth can help you keep track of where you are in Epcot. But it's in a high-traffic area and isn't centrally located, so it isn't a good meeting place.

Any of the distinctive national pavilions in World Showcase makes a good meeting place, but be specific. "Hey, let's meet in Japan!" sounds fun, but each pavilion is a mini-town with buildings, monuments, gardens, and plazas. You could wander quite awhile "in Japan" without finding your group. Pick a specific place in Japan—the sidewalk side of the pagoda, for example.

THE NEW EPCOT

Correctly assessing that Epcot was getting stale, Disney updated the park beginning in 1994. The Land pavilion and its attractions were renovated.

CommuniCore, at the heart of Future World, was replaced with Innoventions, an ongoing trade show featuring products and technologies of the near future. Spaceship Earth, the attraction inside the huge sphere, was partially redesigned and enhanced, and a new 3-D movie premiered at the Journey into Imagination pavilion. Additional street vendors and entertainers were introduced into World Showcase to make it more lively and give it a sense of community, and two new shows were integrated into the park's live entertainment. Upgrades continued into 1999, when a new ride opened at the Imagination pavilion and a number of temporary attractions were added for the Millennium celebration.

The EPCOT Acronym

"Epcot" originally was "EPCOT." When it was envisioned by Walt Disney as a utopian working city of the future until about 1995, EPCOT was the acronym for Experimental Prototype Community Of Tomorrow. Corporate Disney ultimately altered Walt's vision and the city became a theme park, but the name remained. Because EPCOT, however, was clearly nothing of the sort, the acronym "EPCOT" became the name "Epcot."

THE MILLENNIUM CELEBRATION AT EPCOT

Epcot is the Millennium headquarters for Walt Disney World, so you can expect larger than average crowds throughout the 15-month (October 1, 1999 through January 1, 2001) celebration.

As you enter Epcot (and before you get within rifle distance of an attraction) you'll have the opportunity for $35 to "Leave a Legacy." This little Disney money machine would have you buy a commemorative metallic tile with your photo etched on it to be placed on one of 30 granite monoliths near Spaceship Earth. The monoliths are very large and the tiles are very small, but not to worry, a handy computer will tell you where your tile is located.

Taking a page from the Walt Disney World anniversary celebration a couple of years back when Cinderella's Castle was disguised as a giant birthday cake, Epcot has appended a giant, magic-wand-wielding Mickey hand to Spaceship Earth (the 5-billion-pound golfball that serves as Epcot's architectural icon). The 116-foot-long, star-tipped wand reflects light on billboard size "2000" numerals perched on top of the geosphere. The overall effect, though suggestive of an exponentially bloated Mr. PotatoHead, is not nearly as dumb (or as garish) as the legendary birthday cake, and is actually pretty festive.

Behind Spaceship PotatoHead . . . er, Earth, is Millennium Central, an elaborate information kiosk with an electronic tip board that lists current park activities and events. In addition to checking out what's going on, you can make priority seatings for restaurants here.

Beyond Millennium Central to your right between the fountain and Innoventions West is a puffed-up igloo-looking thing that contains a Coca Cola exhibit. Inside (besides thousands of Coke souvenir gewgaws for sale) are machines dispensing free sample cups of Coke's international soft drink products. With apologies for sounding parochial, you'll be amazed at what passes for liquid refreshment in some parts of the world.

For the most part, the big deal Millennium attractions and events are found in the World Showcase section of the park. Between Great Britain and Canada is the Millennium Village, a new 65,000-square-foot building offering live entertainment, food, shopping, and exhibits sponsored by foreign countries and various corporations. Besides Millennium Village, World Showcase is also home to Tapestry of Nations, a parade of 120 giant puppets accompanied by 32 drummers (who thinks this stuff up?). The parade will be staged on the World Showcase Promenade (i.e., the walkway around the lake) twice each night when the park is open late. On tap to follow the parade is a special edition of *IllumiNations*, called *IllumiNations 2000: Reflections of Earth*. This modest little number traces the history of the universe from the big bang and winds up with a fireworks and laser crescendo heralding the dawn of a new age. A more detailed description of Millennium Village, the parade, and *IllumiNations* can be found later in this chapter.

Future World

Gleaming, futuristic structures of immense proportions define the first theme area you encounter at Epcot. Broad thoroughfares are punctuated with billowing fountains—all reflected in shining, space-age facades. Everything, including landscaping, is sparkling clean and seems bigger than life. Pavilions dedicated to mankind's past, present, and future technological accomplishments form the perimeter of Future World. Front and center is Spaceship Earth, flanked by Innoventions East and West.

Most Epcot services are concentrated in Future World's Entrance Plaza, near the main gate.

GUEST RELATIONS

Description and Comments   Guest Relations, left of the geodesic sphere, is Epcot's equivalent of the Magic Kingdom's City Hall. It serves as park

Future World Services	
Epcot's service facilities in Future World include:	
Wheelchair & Stroller Rental	Inside the main entrance and to the left, toward the rear of the Entrance Plaza
Banking Services	ATMs are outside the main entrance near the kennels, on the Future World bridge, and in World Showcase at the Germany pavilion.
Storage Lockers	Turn right at Spaceship Earth (lockers are cleaned out nightly).
Lost & Found	At the main entrance at the gift shop
Live Entertainment & Parade Information	At Guest Relations, left of Spaceship Earth
Lost Persons	At Guest Relations and the Baby Center on the World Showcase side of the Odyssey Center
Dining Priority Seating	At Guest Relations
Walt Disney World & Local Attraction Information	At Guest Relations
First Aid	Next to the Baby Center on the World Showcase side of the Odyssey Center
Baby Center / Baby-Care Needs	On the World Showcase side of the Odyssey Center

headquarters and as Epcot's primary information center. Attendants staff information booths and take same-day priority seating for Epcot restaurants.

Touring Tips If you wish to eat in one of Epcot's sit-down restaurants, you can make your priority seating at Guest Relations.

Spaceship Earth

What It Is: Educational dark ride through past, present, and future

Scope & Scale: Headliner

When to Go: Before 10 a.m. or after 4 p.m.

Special Comments: If lines are long when you arrive, try again after 4 p.m.

Author's Rating: One of Epcot's best; not to be missed; ★★★★

Appeal by Age Group:

Pre-school	Grade School	Teens	Young Adults	Over 30	Senior Citizens
★★★	★★★★	★★★½	★★★★	★★★★	★★★★

Duration of Ride: About 16 minutes

Average Wait in Line per 100 People ahead of You: 3 minutes

Assumes: Normal operation

Loading Speed: Fast

Description and Comments   This AT&T ride spirals through the 18-story interior of Epcot's premier landmark, taking visitors past Audio-Animatronic scenes depicting mankind's developments in communications, from cave painting to printing to television to space communications and computer networks. The ride, updated and improved in 1994, is compelling and well done.

Touring Tips   Because it's near Epcot's main entrance, Spaceship Earth is inundated with arriving guests throughout the morning. If you're interested in riding Test Track, postpone Spaceship Earth until, say, after 4 p.m. Spaceship Earth loads continuously and quickly. If the line runs only along the right side of the sphere, you'll board in less than 15 minutes.

Global Neighborhood

What It Is: Interactive communications playground

Scope & Scale: Diversion

When to Go: After riding Spaceship Earth

Special Comments: Spaceship Earth disembarks passengers directly into the Global Neighborhood

Author's Rating: High-tech fun; ★★½

Appeal by Age Group:

Pre-school	Grade School	Teens	Young Adults	Over 30	Senior Citizens
★★	★★★½	★★★½	★★★½	★★½	★★½

Duration of Attraction: Not limited

Average Wait in Line per 100 People ahead of You: No wait

Description and Comments Global Neighborhood is at the base of the geosphere. Presented by AT&T, it's a walk-through playground of futuristic, interactive communications devices. Platform simulator rides take two to six guests at a time on a tour of the AT&T Network. A *Storyteller* touch screen allows guests to embellish a story setting by accessing computer-programmed visual and sound effects. The best of the interactive devices is *Communications Breakthrough*, which combines word cues and teamwork with an electronic shooting gallery.

Touring Tips If Spaceship Earth is busy, the Global Neighborhood will be, too. If you want to spend some time there, go during late afternoon or evening. You don't have to ride Spaceship Earth to enter the Global Neighborhood. Walk directly in from the plaza on the far side of the geosphere.

INNOVENTIONS

What It Is: Static and "hands-on" exhibits relating to products and technologies of the near future

Scope & Scale: Major diversion

When to Go: On your second day at Epcot or after you have seen all major attractions

Special Comments: Most exhibits demand time and participation to be rewarding; not much gained here by a quick walk-through

Author's Rating: Vastly improved; ★★★½

Appeal by Age Group:

Pre-school	Grade School	Teens	Young Adults	Over 30	Senior Citizens
★½	★★★½	★★★★	★★★½	★★★	★★★

Description and Comments Innoventions consists of two huge, crescent-shaped, glass-walled structures separated by a central plaza. Formerly known as CommuniCore, the complex was designed to be the communications and community hub of Epcot, but something was lost in execution. During Epcot's first 12 years, CommuniCore was, at best, a staid museum of science and industry and, at worst, a huge obstacle to circumnavigate when you wanted to cross from one side of Future World to the other.

In 1994, Disney set out to return it to the original concept, this time with a marketplace rather than communications orientation. The result is a huge, busy collection of industry-sponsored, walk-through, hands-on exhibits. Dynamic, interactive, and forward-looking, Innoventions resembles a high-tech trade show. Products preview consumer and industrial goods of the near future. Electronics, communications, and entertainment technology play a prominent role. Exhibits, many of which are changed each year, demonstrate such products as virtual reality games, high-definition TV, voice-activated appliances, and CD-ROM applications. Each of the 15 or so major exhibit areas is sponsored by a different manufacturer or research lab. Each exhibit emphasizes the effect of its products or technology on daily living. The most popular Innoventions attraction is an arcade of video and simulator games. The buildings also house restaurants, gift shops, and the Epcot Discovery Center (described below).

Unofficial Guide reader response to Innoventions is mixed. A family from Port Chester, New York, writes:

> The more unstructured "interactive" parts were incredibly noisy and confusing—rather like a crowded video arcade with games that didn't work very well. Crowd control was poor. The setup leads to pushing and shoving to get to control boards. My kids, being small girls, didn't stand a chance of getting near anything. The display portions of the attraction "Home of the Future," etc., most clearly resembled a trade show at the Javits Center or the fixture displays at Home Depot. This whole pavilion seemed far more commercial than magical.

We receive a lot of complaints about how difficult it is for children (and even adults) to get a turn on Innoventions' more high-tech gadgets. This comment from a Michigan dad is typical:

> A warning about Innoventions. All those wonderful Sega games are there, if you can fight off all the pubescent Sega-geeks. And they're free . . . some of them. The ones that your kids will want to play are not free. They are, however, right next to the free games, close enough to tempt your children and result in temper tantrums.

A father of three from Tulsa, Oklahoma, however, liked Innoventions, writing:

> The best things at Epcot for my kids were the hands-on exhibits at Innoventions. We bumped into the computer games there as we were passing through en route to something else (I don't remember what, because we never got there).

A mom from Bartlesville, Oklahoma, adds:

> My 14-year-old son's favorite attraction was Innoventions. He spent

hours there and would have spent more if we'd let him. All those free Sega games were a teenage boy's idea of heaven.

Touring Tips Innoventions East and West provide visitors an opportunity to preview products of tomorrow in a fun, hands-on manner. Some exhibits are intriguing, while others are less compelling. We observed a wide range of reactions by visitors to the exhibits and can suggest only that you form your own opinion. Regarding touring strategy, spend time at Innoventions on your second day at Epcot. If you have only one day, visit during the evening if you have the time and endurance. Many exhibits, however, are technical and may not be compatible with your mood or energy toward the end of a long day. Also, you can't get much out of a walk-through; you have to invest time to understand what's going on.

THE LIVING SEAS

What It Is: Ride beneath a huge saltwater aquarium, plus exhibits on oceanography, ocean ecology, and sea life
Scope & Scale: Major attraction
When to Go: Before 10 a.m. or after 3 p.m.
Special Comments: The ride is only a small component of this attraction
Author's Rating: An excellent marine exhibit; ★★★½
Appeal by Age Group:

Pre-school	Grade School	Teens	Young Adults	Over 30	Senior Citizens
★★★	★★★	★★★	★★★★	★★★★	★★★★

Duration of Ride: 3 minutes
Average Wait in Line per 100 People ahead of You: 3½ minutes
Assumes: All elevators in operation
Loading Speed: Fast

Description and Comments The Living Seas is among Future World's most ambitious offerings. Scientists and divers conduct actual marine experiments in a 200-foot-diameter, 27-foot-deep main tank containing fish, mammals, and crustaceans in a simulation of an ocean ecosystem. Visitors can watch the activity through 8-inch-thick windows below the surface (including some in the Coral Reef restaurant) and aboard a three-part adventure ride consisting of a movie dramatizing the link between the ocean and man's survival, a simulated elevator descent to the bottom of the tank, and a three-minute gondola voyage through an underwater viewing tunnel.

The Living Seas' fish population has grown substantially, but the underwater ride is over almost before you're comfortably settled in the gondola. No matter, the strength of this attraction lies in the dozen or so exhibits offered afterward. Visitors can view fish-breeding experiments, watch short films about sea life, and more. The main aquarium, which the ride transits, can also be viewed through huge windows. Stay as long as you wish in the exhibit areas.

The Living Seas is a high-quality marine/aquarium exhibit, but it's no substitute for visiting Sea World, an outstanding marine theme park in Orlando. Sea World is on a par with the Disney theme parks in quality, appeal, educational value, and entertainment.

Touring Tips   Exhibits at the end of the ride are the best part of The Living Seas. In the morning, they're often bypassed by guests rushing to stay ahead of the crowd. The Living Seas needs to be lingered over when you aren't in a hurry. Go in late afternoon or evening, or on your second day at Epcot.

THE LAND PAVILION

Description and Comments   The Land is a huge pavilion containing three attractions and several restaurants. It was extensively renovated in 1994, and its three attractions were updated and improved. The original emphasis was on farming, but it now focuses on environmental concerns.

Touring Tips   This is a good place for a fast-food lunch. If you're there to see the attractions, however, don't go during mealtimes.

Living with the Land

What It Is: Indoor boat-ride adventure through the past, present, and future of U.S. farming and agriculture

Scope & Scale: Major attraction

When to Go: Before 10:30 a.m. or after 7:30 p.m.

Special Comments: Take the ride early in the morning, but save other Land attractions for later in the day. It's located on the pavilion's lower level.

Author's Rating: Interesting and fun; not to be missed; ★★★★

Appeal by Age Group:

Pre-school	Grade School	Teens	Young Adults	Over 30	Senior Citizens
★★½	★★★	★★★½	★★★★	★★★★	★★★★

Duration of Ride: About 12 minutes

Average Wait in Line per 100 People ahead of You: 3 minutes

Assumes: 15 boats operating

Loading Speed: Moderate

Description and Comments   Boat ride takes visitors through swamps, past inhospitable environments man has faced as a farmer, and through a futuristic, innovative greenhouse where real crops are grown using the latest agricultural technologies. Inspiring and educational, with excellent effects and good narrative.

Many Epcot guests who read about Living with the Land in guidebooks decide it sounds too dry and educational for their tastes. A woman from Houston, Texas, writes:

> *I had a bad attitude about Living with the Land, as I heard it was an agricultural exhibit. I just didn't think I was up for a movie about wheat farming. Wow, was I surprised. I really wished I had not had a preconceived idea about an exhibit. Living with the Land was truly wonderful.*

Touring Tips   See this attraction before the lunch crowd hits The Land restaurants or after 7:30 p.m.

If you really enjoy this ride or have a special interest in the agricultural techniques demonstrated, take the Behind the Seeds Greenhouse Tour. It's a one-hour guided walk behind the scenes for an in-depth examination of advanced and experimental growing methods. It costs $6 for adults and $4 for children ages three to nine. Reservations are made on a space-available basis at the guided tour waiting area (far right of the restaurants on the lower level).

Food Rocks

What It Is: Audio-Animatronic theater show about food and nutrition

Scope & Scale: Minor attraction

When to Go: Before 11 a.m. or after 2 p.m.

Special Comments: On the lower level of The Land pavilion

Author's Rating: Sugar-coated nutrition lesson; ★★½

Appeal by Age Group:

Pre-school	Grade School	Teens	Young Adults	Over 30	Senior Citizens
★★★	★★★	★★½	★★★	★★★	★★★

Duration of Presentation: About 13 minutes

Preshow Entertainment: None

Probable Waiting Time: Less than 10 minutes

Description and Comments   Audio-Animatronic foods and cooking utensils perform in a marginally educational rock concert. Featured artists include the Peach Boys, Chubby Cheddar, Neil Moussaka, and Pita Gabriel. Little Richard provides the voice of a pineapple singing "Tutti Frutti." Fast-paced and imaginative, *Food Rocks* is better entertainment than its predecessor, *Kitchen Kabaret,* and delivers the proper-diet-and-balanced-nutrition message about as well.

Touring Tips   One of the few light-entertainment offerings at Epcot. Slightly reminiscent of the *Country Bear Jamboree* in the Magic Kingdom (but not as humorous or endearing). The theater isn't large, but we never have encountered long waits, even during mealtimes.

Circle of Life Theater

What It Is: Film exploring man's relationship with his environment
Scope & Scale: Minor attraction
When to Go: Before 11 a.m. and after 2 p.m.
Author's Rating: Highly interesting and enlightening; ★★★½
Appeal by Age Group:

Pre-school	Grade School	Teens	Young Adults	Over 30	Senior Citizens
★★½	★★★	★★½	★★★	★★★	★★★

Duration of Presentation: About 12½ minutes
Preshow Entertainment: None
Probable Waiting Time: 10–15 minutes

Description and Comments   The featured attraction is *The Circle of Life*, starring Simba, Timon, and Pumbaa from Disney's animated feature *The Lion King.* This superb film spotlights the environmental interdependency of all creatures on earth, demonstrating how easily the ecological balance can be upset. It's sobering, but not too heavy-handed.

Touring Tips   Every visitor should see this highly worthwhile film. If you're trying to stay ahead of the crowd, see it in late afternoon. Long lines usually occur at mealtimes.

IMAGINATION INSTITUTE PAVILION

Description and Comments   Multiattraction pavilion on the west side of Innoventions West and down the walk from The Land. Outside is an "upside-down waterfall" and one of our favorite Future World landmarks, the "jumping water," a fountain that hops over the heads of unsuspecting passersby.

Touring Tips We recommend early-morning or late-evening touring. See the individual attractions for specifics.

Journey into Your Imagination

What It Is: Dark fantasy-adventure ride

Scope & Scale: Major attraction

When to Go: Before 10:30 a.m. or after 6 p.m.

Author's Rating: Not open at press time

Appeal by Age Group: Not open at press time

Duration of Ride: About 13 minutes

Average Wait in Line per 100 People ahead of You: 3 minutes

Assumes: 20 trains operating

Loading Speed: Moderate to fast

Description and Comments This attraction replaced its dull and vacuous predecessor in the fall of 1999. The name is nearly the same (Journey into *Your* Imagination vs. Journey into Imagination), but the attraction is totally different. Well, almost—the Figment dragon character has been retained. Drawing on the Imagination Institute theme from *Honey, I Shrunk the Audience* in the same pavilion, the new attraction takes you on a tour of the zany Institute. Sometimes you're a passive observer and sometimes you're a test subject as the ride provides a glimpse of the fictitious lab's inner workings. Stimulating all of your senses and then some, you are hit with optical illusions, an experiment where noise generates colors, a room that defies gravity, and other brain teasers. After the ride you can adjourn upstairs to the Image Works, an interactive exhibit area offering the latest in unique, hands-on imagery technology.

Touring Tips Because it's new, Journey into Your Imagination will draw large crowds. Try to ride before 10:30 a.m. You can enjoy the Image Works without taking the ride, so save it for later in the day.

Honey, I Shrunk the Audience

What It Is: 3-D film with special effects

Scope & Scale: Headliner

When to Go: Before 10 a.m. or just before Future World closes

Special Comments: Adults should not be put off by the sci-fi theme. The loud, intense show with tactile effects frightens some young children.

Author's Rating: An absolute hoot! Not to be missed; ★★★★½

Appeal by Age Group:

Pre-school	Grade School	Teens	Young Adults	Over 30	Senior Citizens
★★★	★★★★½	★★★★½	★★★★½	★★★★½	★★★★

Duration of Presentation: About 17 minutes

Preshow Entertainment: 8 minutes

Probable Waiting Time: 12 minutes (at suggested times)

Description and Comments   Honey, I Shrunk the Audience is a 3-D off-shoot of Disney's feature film, *Honey, I Shrunk the Kids. Honey, I Shrunk the Audience* features an array of special effects, including simulated explosions, smoke, fiber optics, lights, water spray, and moving seats. This attraction is played strictly for laughs, a commodity in short supply in Epcot entertainment.

Touring Tips   The sound level is earsplitting, frightening some young children. Many adults report that the loud soundtrack is distracting, even uncomfortable. While *Honey, I Shrunk the Audience* is a huge hit, it can be overwhelming for preschoolers. A dad from Lexington, South Carolina, writes:

> Honey, I Shrunk the Audience *is too intense for kids. Our four-year-old took off his [3-D] glasses five minutes into the movie. Because of this experience, he would not wear glasses in the Muppet movie at MGM.*

A Tucson, Arizona, mom tells of a similar reaction:

> *Our three- and four-year-olds loved all the rides. They giggled through Thunder Mountain three times, squealed with delight on Splash Mountain, thought Space Mountain was the coolest, and begged to ride Star Tours over and over. They even "fought ghosts" at the Haunted Mansion. But,* Honey, I Shrunk the Audience, *dissolved them into sobbing, sniveling, shaking, terrified preschoolers.*

Though launched with very little fanfare, *Honey, I Shrunk the Audience* has become one of Epcot's most popular attraction. Try to work the production into your touring before 10 a.m. The show is located to the left of the Journey into Imagination ride; it isn't necessary to ride in order to enter the theater. Avoid seats in the first several rows: if you're too close to the screen, the 3-D images don't focus properly.

TEST TRACK

Description and Comments   Test Track, presented by General Motors, contains the Test Track ride and TransCenter, a collection of transportation-themed stationary exhibits and mini theater productions. The pavilion is left of Spaceship Earth when you enter, down toward World Showcase from the Universe of Energy pavilion.

Many readers tell us that Test Track "is one big commercial" for General Motors. We agree that promotional hype is more heavy-handed here than in most other business-sponsored attractions. But Test Track is one of the most creatively conceived and executed attractions in Walt Disney World.

Test Track Ride

What It Is: Automobile test-track simulator ride

Scope & Scale: Super headliner

When to Go: Before 9:15 a.m. and just before closing

Author's Rating: Not to be missed; ★★★★

Appeal by Age Group:

Pre-school	Grade School	Teens	Young Adults	Over 30	Senior Citizens
★★★★	★★★★	★★★★	★★★★	★★★★	★★★★

Duration of Ride: About 4 minutes

Average Wait in Line per 100 People ahead of You: 4½ minutes

Assumes: Normal operation

Loading Speed: Moderate to fast

Description and Comments   Test Track combines roller coaster and simulator technologies. Visitors test a future-model car at high speeds through hairpin turns, up and down steep hills, and over rough terrain. The six-guest vehicle is a motion simulator that rocks and pitches. Unlike simulators at Star Tours, Body Wars, and *Back to the Future,* however, the Test Track model is affixed to a track and actually travels.

Though reader comments on Test Track have been mixed, most like it. A Shippensburg, Pennsylvania, couple, for example, gave Test Track two thumbs up:

> We did wait about 30 minutes for Test Track and it was worth it!
> At first we thought it was a bit of a bust, as the beginning of the ride is
> not very exciting (though it was interesting), but the last minute or so
> made up for it! It was wonderful!

But a Monona, Wisconsin, couple were somewhat underwhelmed:

In regard to Test Track, while it was a good ride, it was overrated; or perhaps it just wasn't what I expected. Based on the loud whoosh coming from the ride, the build-up in the preshow area, and your comments, I expected a much more intense experience. As it turned out, it just wasn't all that scary. Compared to the Tower of Terror, Test Track is a Sunday drive in the park.

Touring Tips Some great technology is at work here. The attraction is so complex, in fact, that Disney is still trying to work out the kinks. When it's running, it's one of the best attractions in any theme park and deserves its large crowds. As a Waban, Massachusetts, mother reports, however, it's not always running:

Test Track was the toughest ride to ride. Either it was broken or the lines were 1½–2 hours long.

There is only one way to experience this attraction without a long wait, and that's to head for Test Track as soon as you're admitted through the turnstiles. No stopping for Spaceship Earth or to make priority seatings. If you are admitted to the park before official opening time, you may be held up by a rope barrier before you reach Test Track. If this happens, don't worry—just stay put until you're allowed to proceed. When you finally arrive at the attraction you'll be among the first in line.

Because Test Track is so popular, Epcot tries to get it up and running early. Most mornings, when Epcot officially opens at 9 a.m. and permits guests to enter at 8:30 a.m., Test Track will be open by 8:45 or earlier. On days when we monitored crowd levels, the wait at 8:45 was about 5 minutes. By 9 a.m. it was 20–35 minutes and by 9:15 almost 90 minutes.

HORIZONS

Horizons, open only sporadically during the past few years, is now permanently closed. The word on the street is that Disney has been unsuccessful in landing a corporate partner to subsidize the attraction. If and when a sponsor materializes, we expect a completely new attraction and name.

WONDERS OF LIFE PAVILION

Description and Comments This multifaceted pavilion deals with the human body, health, and medicine. Housed in a 100,000-square-foot, gold-domed structure, Wonders of Life focuses on the capabilities of the human body and the importance of keeping fit.

Body Wars

What It Is: Flight-simulator ride through the human body

Scope & Scale: Headliner

When to Go: Before 10 a.m. or after 6 p.m.

Special Comments: Not recommended for pregnant women or people prone to motion sickness

Motion Sickness

WARNING!

Author's Rating: Anatomy made fun; not to be missed; ★★★★

Appeal by Age Group:

Pre-school	Grade School	Teens	Young Adults	Over 30	Senior Citizens
★★★	★★★★	★★★★	★★★★	★★★½	★★½

Duration of Ride: 5 minutes

Average Wait in Line per 100 People ahead of You: 4 minutes

Assumes: All simulators operating

Loading Speed: Moderate to fast

Description and Comments   This thrill ride through the human body was developed along the lines of Disney-MGM Studios' Star Tours space-simulation ride. The story is that you're a passenger in a miniature capsule injected into a human body to pick up a scientist who has been inspecting a splinter in the patient's finger. The scientist, however, is sucked into the circulatory system, and you rush throughout the body to rescue her. The simulator creates a visually graphic experience as it seems to hurtle at fantastic speeds through human organs. The story is more than a little silly, but we nevertheless rate Body Wars as "not to be missed."

Touring Tips   Epcot's first thrill ride, Body Wars remains popular with all ages. Ride early in the morning after Test Track and the attractions at the Imagination Institute, or during the hour before closing. Be aware that Body Wars makes a lot of people motion sick; it isn't unusual for a simulator to be taken off-line for attendants to clean up a previous rider's mess. If you're at all susceptible to motion sickness, reconsider riding. If you're on Body Wars and become nauseated, fix your gaze on something other than the screen and as far away as possible (the ceiling or side and back walls). Without the visual effects, the ride isn't rough enough to disturb most guests. If you get queasy, rest rooms are nearby as you get off the ride. Star Tours is just as wild but makes very few people sick. Successfully riding Star Tours doesn't necessarily mean you'll tolerate Body Wars. Conversely, if Body Wars makes you ill, you can't assume that Star Tours will, too.

Reader comments on Body Wars cover the spectrum. These are representative:

> *The only thing we won't do on this next trip is go on Body Wars in Epcot. The line is so deceptive. We waited almost two hours and then it was only to get motion sickness and feel awful!*

and:

> *I made the mistake of riding Body Wars first thing in the morning, on an empty stomach, and with a hangover. I thought I was going to throw up. It was very close. Strangely enough, I rode Body Wars again a week later, feeling fine. Guess what? I thought I was going to throw up. It was very close.*

and:

> *Body Wars did not measure up to all the hype and warnings. We expected Space Mountain with visual effects, and it wasn't even close. You weenies!*

and:

> *The ride felt more like the involuntary movements of a hammock.*

and finally:

> *Body Wars at Epcot was great fun. We rode it twice and loved it. A little scary, but exciting. Some of the other things seemed kind of boring after our ride here.*

Motion sickness aside, Body Wars is intense—too intense for some, especially preschoolers and seniors. One elderly gentleman confided, "Feeling sick at my stomach took my mind off being terrified."

Cranium Command

What It Is: Audio-Animatronic theater show about the brain

Scope & Scale: Major attraction

When to Go: Before 11 a.m. or after 3 p.m.

Author's Rating: Funny, outrageous, and educational; not to be missed; ★★★★½

Appeal by Age Group:

Pre-school	Grade School	Teens	Young Adults	Over 30	Senior Citizens
★★	★★★★	★★★★	★★★★½	★★★★½	★★★★½

Duration of Presentation: About 20 minutes

Preshow Entertainment: Explanatory lead-in to feature presentation

Probable Waiting Time: Less than 10 minutes at times suggested

Description and Comments *Cranium Command* is Epcot's great sleeper attraction. Stuck on the backside of the Wonders of Life pavilion and far less promoted than Body Wars, this most humorous Epcot offering is bypassed by many guests. Characters called "Brain Pilots" are trained to operate human brains. The show consists of a day in the life of one of these Cranium Commanders as he tries to pilot the brain of an adolescent boy. Epcot and Walt Disney World could use a lot more of this type of humor.

Touring Tips To understand the program, you need to see the preshow cartoon. If you arrive in the waiting area while it's in progress, be sure you see enough to get a sense of the story before you enter the theater. While most preschoolers enjoy *Cranium Command,* many don't really understand it.

The Making of Me

What It Is: Humorous movie about human conception and birth

Scope & Scale: Minor attraction

When to Go: Early in the morning or after 4:30 p.m.

Author's Rating: Sanitized sex education; ★★★

Appeal by Age Group:

Pre school	Grade School	Teens	Young Adults	Over 30	Senior Citizens
★½	★★★½	★★½	★★★	★★★	★★★

Duration of Presentation: 14 minutes

Preshow Entertainment: None

Probable Waiting Time: 25 minutes or more, unless you go at suggested times

Description and Comments This lighthearted and very sensitive movie about human conception, gestation, and birth was considered a controversial addition to Wonders of Life, but most viewers agree it's tasteful and creative. The plot's main character goes back in time to watch his parents date, fall in love, marry, and, yes, conceive and give birth to him. Look for the biological error in the film. If you spot it, write us.

Sexual material is well handled, with emphasis on loving relationships, not plumbing. Parents of children younger than age seven tell us the sexual information went over their children's heads for the most part. In older children, however, the film precipitates questions. You be the judge.

A gentleman from Cheshire, England, who believes (correctly, in our view) that Americans are sexually repressed, writes:

> *By the standards of sex education programmes shown to English*
> *children of ages eight to nine,* The Making of Me *seemed almost Mary*
> *Poppinsish in tone. Certainly other Brits found your warnings over*
> *content quite puzzling.*

This reader would have a great time in my hometown (Birmingham, Alabama), where some of the local clergy harangued the city council for months to have Bermuda shorts welded onto the bare buttocks of a large statue depicting Vulcan at his forge.

Touring Tips The Making of Me is excellent and should be moved from its tiny space to a larger theater. Until (and if) it is, expect long lines unless you go at recommended times.

Fitness Fairgrounds

Description and Comments Participatory exhibits allow guests to test their senses in a fun house, get computer-generated health analyses of their lifestyles, work out on electronically sophisticated exercise equipment, and watch a video called *Goofy about Health* (starring, who else?).

Touring Tips Save the Fitness Fair exhibits for your second day, or the end of your first day at Epcot.

UNIVERSE OF ENERGY: ELLEN'S ENERGY ADVENTURE

What It Is: Combination ride/theater presentation about energy

Scope & Scale: Major attraction

When to Go: Before 11:15 a.m. or after 4:30 p.m.

Special Comments: Don't be dismayed by long lines; 580 people enter the pavilion each time the theater turns over

Author's Rating: The most improved attraction at Walt Disney World; ★★★★

Appeal by Age Group:

Pre-school	Grade School	Teens	Young Adults	Over 30	Senior Citizens
★★★	★★★★	★★★½	★★★★	★★★★	★★★★

Duration of Presentation: About 26½ minutes

Preshow Entertainment: 8 minutes

Probable Waiting Time: 20–40 minutes

Description and Comments Audio-Animatronic dinosaurs and the unique traveling theater make this Exxon pavilion one of Future World's most popular. Because this is a theater with a ride component, the line doesn't move while the show is in progress. When the theater empties, however, a large chunk of the line will disappear as people are admitted for the next show. Visitors are seated in what appears to be an ordinary theater while they watch a film about energy sources. Then the theater seats divide into six 97-passenger traveling cars that glide among the swamps and reptiles of a prehistoric forest. Special effects include the feel of warm, moist air from the swamp, the smell of sulphur from an erupting volcano, and the sight of lava hissing and bubbling toward the passengers.

The original film on energy sources (which many guests characterized as boring) was scrapped in 1996 and replaced with a humorous and upbeat flick starring Ellen DeGeneres. The new film represents a huge improvement for adults, turning a major snoozer into a highly entertaining presentation. For kids, however, Universe of Energy remains a toss-up. The dinosaurs frighten some preschoolers, and kids of all ages lose the thread during the educational segments.

Touring Tips   This attraction draws large crowds beginning early in the morning. Because Universe of Energy can operate more than one show at a time, lines are generally tolerable. If you decide to skip the show, at least see the great dinosaur topiaries outside the pavilion.

THE "MOM, I CAN'T BELIEVE IT'S DISNEY!" FOUNTAIN

What It Is: Combination fountain and shower
When to Go: When it's hot
Scope & Scale: Diversion
Special Comments: Secretly installed by Martians during *IllumiNations*
Author's Rating: Yes!! ★★★★
Appeal by Age Group:

Pre-school	Grade School	Teens	Young Adults	Over 30	Senior Citizens
★★★★★	★★★★★	★★★★	★★★★	★★★★	★★★★★

Duration of Experience: Indefinite
Probable Waiting Time: None

Description and Comments   This simple fountain on the walkway linking Future World to World Showcase isn't much to look at, but it offers a truly spontaneous experience—rare in Walt Disney World, where everything is controlled, from the snow peas in your stir fry to how frequently the crocodile yawns in the Jungle Cruise.

Spouts of water erupt randomly from the sidewalk. You can frolic in the water or let it cascade down on you or blow up your britches. On a broiling Florida day, when you think you might suddenly combust, fling yourself into the fountain and do decidedly un-Disney things. Dance, skip, sing, jump, splash, cavort, roll around, stick your toes down the spouts, or catch the water in your mouth as it descends. You can do all of this with your clothes on or, depending on your age, with your clothes off. It's hard to imagine so much personal freedom at Disney World and almost unthinkable to contemplate soggy people slogging and squishing around the park, but there you have it. Hurrah!

Touring Tips   We don't know how long the fountain will last before its creator is hauled before the Disney Tribunal of People-Who-Sit-on-Sticks, but we hope it's around for a long time. We do know your kids will be right in the middle of this thing before your brain sounds the alert. Our advice: Pack a pair of dry shorts and turn the kids loose. You might even want to bring a spare pair for yourself. Or, maybe not . . . so much advance planning would stifle the spontaneity.

World Showcase

World Showcase, Epcot's second theme area, is an ongoing World's Fair encircling a picturesque, 40-acre lagoon. The cuisine, culture, history, and architecture of almost a dozen countries are permanently displayed in individual national pavilions spaced along a 1.2-mile promenade. Pavilions replicate familiar landmarks and present representative street scenes from the host countries.

World Showcase features some of the most lovely gardens in the United States. Located in Germany, France, England, Canada, and to a lesser extent, China, they are sometimes tucked away and out of sight of pedestrian traffic on the World Showcase promenade. They are best appreciated during daylight hours, as a Clio, Michigan, woman explains:

> *Make sure to visit the World Showcase in the daylight in order to view the beautiful gardens. We were sorry that we did not do this because we were following the guide and riding the rides that we could have done later in the dark.*

Most adults enjoy World Showcase, but many children find it boring. To make it more interesting to children, most Epcot retail shops sell Passport Kits for about $9. Each kit contains a blank passport and stamps for every World Showcase country. As kids accompany their folks to each country, they tear out the appropriate stamp and stick it in the passport. The kit also contains basic information on the nations and a Mickey Mouse button. Disney has built a lot of profit into this little product, but I guess that isn't the issue. More important, parents, including this dad from Birmingham, Alabama, tell us the Passport Kit helps get the kids through World Showcase with a minimum of impatience, whining, and tantrums.

Adding stamps from the Epcot countries was the only way I was able to see all the displays with cheerful children.

Incidentally, if you do not want to spring for the Passport Kit, the Disney folks will be happy to stamp an autograph book or just about anything else (we saw one four-year-old with a stamp from France right in the middle of his forehead).

Children also enjoy "Kidcot Fun Stops," a program Disney designed to make World Showcase more interesting for the 5-through-12 crowd. So simple and uncomplicated that you can't believe Disney people thought it up, the Fun Stops usually are nothing more than a large table on the sidewalk at each pavilion. Each table is staffed by a Disney cast member who stamps passports and supervises children in modest craft projects relating to the host country. While there's no telling how long the experiment will last, reports from parents about the Fun Stops have been uniformly positive.

Boats ferry the foot-sore and the weary across the lagoon, although it's almost always quicker to walk.

Moving clockwise around the promenade, here are the nations represented and their attractions.

MEXICO PAVILION

Description and Comments   Pre-Columbian pyramids dominate the architecture of this exhibit. One forms the pavilion's facade, and the other overlooks the restaurant and plaza alongside the boat ride, El Río del Tiempo, inside the pavilion.

Touring Tips   Romantic and exciting testimony to Mexico's charms, this installation probably contains more authentic and valuable artifacts and art objects than any other nation's pavilion. Many people zip past these treasures without stopping to look. The village scene inside the pavilion is beautiful and exquisitely detailed. We recommend visiting this pavilion before 11 a.m. or after 6 p.m.

El Río del Tiempo

What It Is: Indoor scenic boat ride
Scope & Scale: Minor attraction

When to Go: Before 11 a.m. or after 3 p.m.

Author's Rating: Light and relaxing; ★★

Appeal by Age Group:

Pre-school	Grade School	Teens	Young Adults	Over 30	Senior Citizens
★★	★★	★½	★★	★★	★★½

Duration of Ride: About 7 minutes (plus 1½-minute wait to disembark)

Average Wait in Line per 100 People ahead of You: 4½ minutes

Assumes: 16 boats in operation

Loading Speed: Moderate

Description and Comments   El Río del Tiempo (The River of Time) cruises among Audio-Animatronic and cinematic scenes depicting the history of Mexico from the ancient cultures of the Maya, Toltec, and Aztec civilizations to modern times. Special effects include fiber-optic projections that simulate fireworks near the ride's end.

The volcano at the entrance suggests great things to come, but the ride disappoints many guests.

A woman from Troy, New York, lambasts El Río del Tiempo:

> *My worst nightmare would be to get stuck in It's a Small World or El Río del Tiempo. They were both dreadful, boring, and need updating. I thought El Río was an insult to the Mexico Pavilion—it's a cheap tourist's version of Mexico and hardly a reflection on the culture, history, or people.*

We agree. Though tranquil and relaxing, El Río del Tiempo is neither particularly interesting nor compelling, and definitely is not worth a long wait.

Touring Tips   The ride tends to get crowded during early afternoon.

NORWAY PAVILION

Description and Comments   The Norway pavilion is complex, beautiful, and architecturally diverse. Surrounding a courtyard is an assortment of traditional Scandinavian buildings, including a replica of the 14th-century Akershus Castle, a wooden stave church, red-tiled cottages, and replicas of historic buildings representing the traditional designs of Bergen, Alesund, and Oslo. Attractions include an adventure boat ride in the mold of Pirates of the Caribbean, a movie about Norway, and a gallery of art and artifacts in the stave church. A Viking ship play area was added in 1999. The pavilion houses Restaurant Akershus, a sit-down eatery (priority seating required) that serves koldtboard (cold buffet), plus a variety of hot

Norwegian dishes. An open-air cafe and a bakery cater to those on the run. Shoppers find abundant native handicrafts.

Maelstrom

What It Is: Indoor adventure boat ride

Scope & Scale: Major attraction

When to Go: Before noon or after 4:30 p.m.

Author's Rating: Too short, but has its moments; ★★★

Appeal by Age Group:

Pre-school	Grade School	Teens	Young Adults	Over 30	Senior Citizens
★★★½	★★★½	★★★	★★★	★★★	★★★

Duration of Ride: 4½ minutes, followed by a 5-minute film with a short wait in between; about 14 minutes for the whole show

Average Wait in Line per 100 People ahead of You: 4 minutes

Assumes: 12 or 13 boats operating

Loading Speed: Fast

Description and Comments In one of Disney World's shorter water rides, guests board dragon-headed ships for a voyage through the fabled rivers and seas of Viking history and legend. They brave trolls, rocky gorges, waterfalls, and a storm at sea. A new generation Disney water ride, the Viking voyage assembles an impressive array of special effects, combining visual, tactile, and auditory stimuli in a fast-paced and often humorous odyssey. Afterward, guests see a five-minute film on Norway. We don't have any major problems with Maelstrom, but a vocal minority of our readers consider the ride too brief and resent having to sit through what they characterize as a travelogue.

Touring Tips Sometimes, several hundred guests from a recently concluded screening of *Wonders of China* arrive at Maelstrom en masse. Should you encounter this horde, postpone Maelstrom. If you don't want to see the Norway film, try to be one of the first to enter the theater. You can follow the preceding audience right through the exit doors on the far side.

CHINA PAVILION

Description and Comments A half-sized replica of the Temple of Heaven in Beijing identifies this pavilion. Gardens and reflecting ponds simulate those found in Suzhou, and an art gallery features a lotus blossom gate and formal saddle roof line.

Pass through the Hall of Prayer for Good Harvest to view the Circle-Vision 360 film *Wonders of China*. Warm and appealing, it's a brilliant introduction to the people and natural beauty of China. The China pavilion offers two restaurants: a fast-food eatery and a lovely, full-service establishment (priority seating required).

Touring Tips   The pavilion is truly beautiful, serene yet exciting. *Wonders of China* plays in a theater where guests must stand, but it can usually be enjoyed anytime without much waiting. If you're touring World Showcase in a counterclockwise rotation and plan next to go to Norway and ride Maelstrom, position yourself on the far left of the theater (as you face the attendant's podium). After the show, be one of the first to exit. Hurry to Maelstrom as fast as you can to arrive ahead of the several hundred other *Wonders of China* patrons who will be right behind you.

Wonders of China

What It Is: Film about the Chinese people and country

Scope & Scale: Major attraction

When to Go: Anytime

Special Comments: Audience stands throughout performance

Author's Rating: Well produced, though film glosses over political unrest and events in Tibet; ★★★

Appeal by Age Group:

Pre-school	Grade School	Teens	Young Adults	Over 30	Senior Citizens
★★	★★½	★★★	★★★½	★★★★	★★★★

Duration of Presentation: About 19 minutes

Preshow Entertainment: None

Probable Waiting Time: 10 minutes

GERMANY PAVILION

Description and Comments   A clock tower, adorned with boy and girl figures, rises above the platz (plaza) marking the Germany pavilion. Dominated by a fountain depicting St. George's victory over the dragon, the platz is encircled by buildings done in traditional German architecture. The main attraction is the Biergarten, a full-service (priority seating required) restaurant serving German food and beer. Yodeling, folk dancing, and oompah band music are included during mealtimes.

"Sorry, the countries aren't getting along today."

Also at Germany, be sure to check out the large and elaborate model railroad located just beyond the rest rooms as you walk from Germany toward Italy.

Touring Tips   The pavilion is pleasant and festive. Tour anytime.

ITALY PAVILION

Description and Comments   The entrance to Italy is marked by a 105-foot-tall campanile (bell tower) said to mirror the tower in St. Mark's Square in Venice. Left of the campanile is a replica of the 14th-century Doge's Palace, also in the famous square. Other buildings are composites of Italian architecture. For example, L'Originale Alfredo di Roma Ristorante is Florentine. Visitors can watch pasta being made in this popular restaurant, which specializes in fettucine Alfredo. The pavilion has a waterfront on the lagoon where gondolas are tied to striped moorings.

Touring Tips   Streets and courtyards in the Italy pavilion are among the most realistic in World Showcase. You really feel as if you're in Italy. Because there's no film or ride, tour at any hour.

THE AMERICAN ADVENTURE

What It Is: Patriotic mixed-media and Audio-Animatronic theater presentation on U.S. history

Scope & Scale: Headliner

When to Go: Anytime

Author's Rating: Disney's best historic/patriotic attraction; not to be missed; ★★★★

Appeal by Age Group:

Pre-school	Grade School	Teens	Young Adults	Over 30	Senior Citizens
★★	★★★	★★★	★★★★	★★★★½	★★★★★

Duration of Presentation: About 29 minutes

Preshow Entertainment: Voices of Liberty chorale singing

Probable Waiting Time: 16 minutes

Description and Comments   The United States pavilion, generally referred to as The American Adventure for the historical production performed there, consists (not surprisingly) of a fast-food restaurant and a patriotic show. A new, upscale, full-service American reastaurant is in the works stay tuned.

The American Adventure is a composite of everything Disney does best. Located in an imposing brick structure reminiscent of colonial Philadelphia, the production is a stirring, 29-minute sanitized rendition of American history narrated by Audio-Animatronic Mark Twain (who carries a smoking cigar) and Ben Franklin (who climbs a set of stairs to visit Thomas Jefferson). Behind a stage almost half the size of a football field is a 28 × 55–foot rear-projection screen (the largest ever used) on which motion picture images are interwoven with action on stage.

Though the production stimulates patriotic emotion in some viewers, others find it overstated and boring. A man from Fort Lauderdale, Florida, writes:

> *I've always disagreed with you about* The American Adventure. *I saw it about 10 years ago and snoozed through it. We tried it again since you said it was updated. It was still ponderous. Casey used the time for a nap, and I was checking my watch, waiting for it to be over. I'll try it again in 10 years.*

An Erie, Pennsylvania, couple resented Disney's squeaky-clean version of American history:

> *Our biggest gripe was with* The American Adventure. *What was that supposed to be? My husband and I were actually embarrassed by that show. They glossed over the dark points of American history and neatly cut out the audio about who bombed Pearl Harbor (after all, Japan is right next door and everyone is happy at WDW). Why do they not focus on the natural beauty of America, the ethnic diversity, immigration, contributions to the world society? No, it's a condensed and Disney-fied history lesson that made us want to pretend to be Canadians after seeing it.*

Touring Tips   Architecturally, The American Adventure isn't as interesting as most other pavilions. But the presentation, our researchers believe, is the very best patriotic attraction in the Disney repertoire. It usually plays to capacity audiences from around noon to 3:30 p.m., but it isn't hard to get into. Because of the theater's large capacity, the wait during busy times of day seldom approaches an hour, and averages 25–40 minutes. Because of its theme, the presentation is decidedly less compelling to non-Americans.

The adjacent Liberty Inn restaurant serves a quick, nonethnic, fast-food meal.

Japan Pavilion

Description and Comments   The five-story, blue-roofed pagoda, inspired by a seventh-century shrine in Nara, sets this pavilion apart. A hill garden behind it encompasses waterfalls, rocks, flowers, lanterns, paths, and rustic bridges. The building on the right (as one faces the entrance) was inspired by the ceremonial and coronation hall at the Imperial Palace at Kyoto. It contains restaurants and a large retail store.

Touring Tips   Tasteful and elaborate, the pavilion creatively blends simplicity, architectural grandeur, and natural beauty. Tour anytime.

Morocco Pavilion

Description and Comments   The bustling market, winding streets, lofty minarets, and stuccoed archways re-create the romance and intrigue of Marrakesh and Casablanca. Attention to detail makes Morocco one of the most exciting World Showcase pavilions. It also has a museum of Moorish art and the Restaurant Marrakesh, which serves some unusual and difficult-to-find North African specialties.

"I'm sorry, Mister. He thinks you're a Disney character."

Touring Tips Morocco has neither a ride nor theater; tour anytime.

FRANCE PAVILION

Description and Comments Naturally, a replica of the Eiffel Tower (a big one) is this pavilion's centerpiece. In the foreground, streets recall La Belle Epoque, France's "beautiful time" between 1870 and 1910. The sidewalk cafe and restaurant are very popular, as is the pastry shop. You won't be the first visitor to buy a croissant to tide you over until your next real meal.

A group from Chicago found the pavilion's realism exceeds what was intended:

> *There were no public rest rooms in the France part of Epcot—just like Paris. We had to go to Morocco to find facilities.*

Impressions de France is an 18-minute movie projected over 200° onto five screens. Unlike at China and Canada, the audience sits to view this well-made film introducing France's people, cities, and natural wonders.

Touring Tips Detail and the evocation of a bygone era enrich the atmosphere of this pavilion. Streets are small and become quite congested when visitors queue for the film.

Impressions de France

What It Is: Film essay on the French people and country
Scope & Scale: Major attraction
When to Go: Before noon and after 4 p.m.
Author's Rating: Exceedingly beautiful film; not to be missed; ★★★½
Appeal by Age Group:

Pre-school	Grade School	Teens	Young Adults	Over 30	Senior Citizens
★½	★★½	★★★	★★★★	★★★★	★★★★

Duration of Presentation: About 18 minutes
Preshow Entertainment: None
Probable Waiting Time: 12 minutes (at suggested times)

UNITED KINGDOM PAVILION

Description and Comments A variety of period architecture attempts to capture Britain's city, town, and rural atmospheres. One street alone has a thatched-roof cottage, a four-story timber-and-plaster building, a pre-Georgian plaster building, a formal Palladian exterior of dressed stone, and a city square with a Hyde Park bandstand (whew!).

The pavilion is mostly shops. The Rose & Crown Pub and Dining Room is the only World Showcase full-service restaurant with dining on the water side of the promenade.

Touring Tips   No attractions here create congestion; tour anytime. Priority seating isn't required to enjoy the pub section of the Rose & Crown, making it a nice place to stop for a midafternoon beer. In the category of dubious distinctions, the Rose & Crown Pub is the only place at Epcot where smoking is allowed indoors.

Millennium Village

What It Is: World's Fair–type exhibit hall
Scope & Scale: Major diversion
When to Go: On your second day at Epcot of after you've seen all the
    major attractions
Special Comments: Not open at press time

Description and Comments Located between and behind the Great
Britain and Canadian pavilions, Millennium Village is an eclectic mix of
entertainment, shopping, snacking opportunities, and exhibits sponsored
by various companies and corporations. At 65,000 square feet, it has the
size, look, and feel of an international trade show. Countries represented
include Brazil, Ethiopia, Indonesia, Israel, Kenya, Namibia, New Zealand,
Saudi Arabia, South Africa, and the United States, among others. The
theme, not unexpectedly, is world brotherhood and "a globe without
boundaries." Products for sale, food available, entertainment, and exhibits
are stupefyingly diverse. Performing artists, for example, include singers,
dancers, artisans, educators, and storytellers. Some of the exhibits are truly
dumbfounding. Sweden offers an "egg-shaped climate chamber where
guests can shiver in the chill of a Swedish winter," while at the Chilean
exhibit you can check out the work of scientists "who are harnessing fog
and converting it into drinking water." (Just imagine having a husband
who heads out to the barn every morning to harness the fog.) Less imaginative offerings include an authentic Tivoli Gardens puppet show
(Denmark), a presentation on boosting a village's economy (Kenya), and a
celebration of soccer (Brazil). The Israeli exhibit will feature live debates
about whether the exhibit should be open on Saturdays (alright, alright, I
confess making this one up).

Touring Tips There's a lot of stuff jammed into the Millennium Village.
We recommend spending some time there on your second day at Epcot or
during the late afternoon. Most of the offerings will not require the level of
cerebral energy required by Innoventions. Besides, if your brain overheats,
you can always stop by Sweden and cool off.

Canada Pavilion

Description and Comments Canada's cultural, natural, and architectural
diversity are reflected in this large and impressive pavilion. Thirty-foot-tall
totem poles embellish a Native American village at the foot of a magnificent
château-style hotel. Nearby is a rugged stone building said to be modeled after
a famous landmark near Niagara Falls and reflecting Britain's influence on

Canada. The pavilion also has a fine film extolling the nation's many virtues. *O Canada!* is very enlightening and demonstrates the immense pride Canadians have in their beautiful country. Visitors leave the theater through Victoria Gardens, inspired by the famed Butchart Gardens of British Columbia.

Touring Tips O Canada!, a large-capacity theater attraction (guests must stand), gets fairly heavy late-morning attendance because Canada is the first pavilion encountered as one travels counterclockwise around World Showcase Lagoon. Le Cellier, a steakhouse on the pavilion's lower level, accepts priority seating but also welcomes walk-ins.

O Canada!

What It Is: Film essay on the Canadian people and their country
Scope & Scale: Major attraction
When to Go: Anytime
Special Comments: Audience stands during performance
Author's Rating: Makes you want to catch the first plane to Canada!
   ★★★½
Appeal by Age Group:

Pre-school	Grade School	Teens	Young Adults	Over 30	Senior Citizens
★★	★★½	★★★	★★★½	★★★★	★★★★

Duration of Presentation: About 18 minutes
Preshow Entertainment: None
Probable Waiting Time: 10 minutes

Live Entertainment in Epcot

Live entertainment in Epcot is more diverse than it is in the Magic Kingdom. In World Showcase, it reflects the nations represented. Future World provides a perfect setting for new and experimental offerings. Information about live entertainment on the day you visit is contained in the Epcot guidemap you obtain upon entry or at Guest Relations.

Here are some performers and performances you're apt to encounter:

In Future World   A roving brass band, a musical crew of pseudo janitors, socializing robots (EpBOTS), and gymnasts in *Alien* attire striking statuesque poses work near the front entrance and at Innoventions Plaza (between the two Innoventions buildings and by the fountain) according to the daily entertainment schedule.

Innoventions Fountain Show   Numerous times each day, the fountain situated between the two Innoventions buildings comes alive with pulsating, arching plumes of water synchronized to a musical score. Because there is no posted schedule of performances, the fountain show comes as a surprise to many readers, such as this man from Berwickshire, England:

> *You don't mention one of the newer joys of Epcot, so the musical fountain came as a real surprise and treat. I sat down and listened to it from start to finish on two different occasions. The music is catchy, and played through the stereo speakers, the soaring effects of both music and water are really beautiful.*

A Frankenmuth, Michigan, man was likewise caught off guard:

> *And, finally, to show that things don't always work out as planned, our children were mesmerized and entertained by something that isn't in any tour plan. At Epcot, there is a fountain between the two Innoventions buildings. During the holidays, the fountain was wonderfully synchronized to Christmas carols. While we [adults] checked our watches to make sure we were on time, our children just wanted to sit and watch the dancing water. Eventually, Mom and Dad sat and watched too. It was better than many of the shows and rides that we encountered during our stay at Disney.*

Disney Characters   Once believed to be inconsistent with Epcot's educational image, Disney characters have now been imported in significant numbers. They appear for breakfast (from park opening to 11:10 or 11:40 a.m. daily) at The Garden Grill Restaurant at The Land pavilion. The menu is fixed, but seconds are available. Cost is $15 for adults (age 12 and older) and $9 for children ages 3 to 11. Characters include Mickey and Pluto (in farm attire) and Chip 'n' Dale. The Garden Grill also offers a character lunch ($17 for adults; $10 for children) and dinner ($18 and $10). The price is in addition to your theme park admission.

Characters now appear throughout the park and also join live shows at the American Gardens Theatre and at the Showcase Plaza between Mexico and Canada. Times are listed in the daily entertainment schedule in the Epcot guidemap available upon entry and at Guest Relations.

American Gardens Theatre   The site of Epcot's premier live performances is in a large amphitheater near The American Adventure, facing World Showcase Lagoon. International talent plays limited engagements there. Many shows spotlight the music, dance, and costumes of the performer's home country. Other programs feature Disney characters.

Tapestry of Nations Parade   This parade features 120 20-foot tall "puppets" and 32 drummers accompanied by a recorded musical score. The puppets are evocative of culture and costume around the world. Performed twice nightly according to the daily entertainment schedule, the parade route winds around the World Showcase Lagoon. The second performance is followed by *IllumiNations*. Because the parade route is fairly long, it takes the parade quite a while to complete the route. To avoid waiting for the parade to reach you, ask a Disney cast member where the parade begins and then select a viewing spot close by. If you watch the second parade, don't count on having much time after the parade to find a viewing spot for *IllumiNations*.

IllumiNations   An after-dark program of music, fireworks, erupting fountains, special lighting, and laser technology is performed on World Showcase Lagoon (see page 511).

Around World Showcase   Impromptu performances take place in and around the World Showcase pavilions. They include a strolling mariachi group in Mexico; street actors in Italy; a fife-and-drum corps or singing group (The Voices of Liberty) at The American Adventure; traditional songs, drums, and dances in Japan; street comedy in the United Kingdom; white-faced mimes in France; and bagpipes in Canada, among others. Street entertainment occurs about every half hour (though not necessarily *on* the hour or half hour).

Live entertainment in World Showcase exceeded the expectations of a mother from Rhode Island and led her son to develop a new talent:

> You should stress in the new edition that Epcot's World Showcase is really quite lively now. Street performances are scheduled throughout the day in the different pavilions. The schedules were printed on the daily map we picked up at the ticket booth.
>
> My two-year-old was taken with the Chinese acrobats and the Chinese variety performers. We must have watched their shows four times each! As I write this, he's balancing an empty trash can on his feet.

And an Ayden, North Carolina, woman offers this:

> I don't feel that you emphasize the street shows at Epcot enough. My husband and I loved the Japanese drumming, the Chinese and Moroccan acrobats, and the street theatre players in Great Britain. These activities were much more indicative of foreign cultures than the rides.

We think the reader's right on target. The quality of street entertainment throughout Epcot has improved exponentially over the last couple of years. Our personal favorite is the Living Statues at France—absolutely brilliant.

Dinner & Lunch Shows   Restaurants in World Showcase serve healthy portions of live entertainment to accompany the victuals. Find folk dancing and an oompah-pah band in Germany, singing waiters in Italy and Germany, and belly dancers in Morocco. Shows are performed only at dinner in Italy, but at both lunch and dinner in Germany and Morocco. Priority seating is required.

IllumiNations

IllumiNations is Epcot's great outdoor spectacle, integrating fireworks, laser lights, neon, and music in a stirring tribute to the nations of the world. It's the climax of every Epcot day when the park is open late. Don't miss it.

IllumiNations 2000 preempts the regular show during the 15-month Millennium Celebration. Unlike earlier *IllumiNations* renditions, this one has a plot as well as a theme and is loaded with symbolism. We'll provide the Cliff Notes version here because it all sort of runs together in the show itself. The show kicks off with colliding stars suggesting the big bang, following which "chaos reigns in the universe." This is soon replaced by twittering songbirds and various other manifestations signaling the nativity of the Earth. Next comes a brief history of time from the dinosaurs to ancient Rome, all projected in images on a huge, floating globe. Man's art and inspiration then flash across the globe "in a collage of creativity." All of this stimulates the globe to unfold "like a massive flower," bringing on the fireworks crescendo heralding the dawn of a new age. Although only the artistically sensitive will be able to differentiate all of this from, say, the last five minutes of any Bruce Willis movie, we thought you'd like to know what Disney says is happening.

One practical change affecting *IllumiNations* is that the Tapestry of Nations Parade directly precedes it. Thus, prior to *IllumiNations* you are facing away from the lagoon to watch the parade. Following the parade you must turn around to view *IllumiNations*. In practical terms, it's almost impossible to have a front-of-the-crowd viewing spot for both (an exception is to watch both events from the open veranda of the restaurant in Japan). We recommend, therefore, placing your priority on scoring a good *IllumiNations* viewing spot. The puppets in the parade are 20 feet tall, so you'll be able to see fairly well even if you're not in the front row. A second consideration is that the parade, as well as preparations for it, severely limit your mobility in the hour before *IllumiNations*. Expressed differently, you might be stuck for *IllumiNations* in exactly the same spot where you are when the parade ends.

Getting out of Epcot after *IllumiNations*
(Read This before Selecting a Viewing Spot)

Decide how quickly you want to leave the park after the show, then pick your vantage point. *IllumiNations* ends the day at Epcot. When it's over, only a couple of gift shops remain open. Because there's nothing to do, everyone leaves at once. This creates a great snarl at Package Pick-up, the Epcot monorail station, and the Disney bus stop. It also pushes to the limit the tram system hauling guests to their cars in the parking lot. Stroller return, however, is extraordinarily efficient and doesn't cause any delay.

If you're staying at an Epcot resort (Swan and Dolphin hotels, Yacht and Beach Club resorts, BoardWalk Inn and Villas), watch *IllumiNations* from somewhere on the southern (The American Adventure) half of World Showcase Lagoon and then leave through the International Gateway between France and the United Kingdom. You can walk or take a boat back to your hotel from the International Gateway. If you have a car and are visiting Epcot in the evening for dinner and *IllumiNations,* park at the Yacht or Beach Club. After the show, duck out the International Gateway and be on the road to your hotel in 15 minutes. If you're staying at any other Disney hotel and don't have a car, the fastest way home is to join the mass exodus through the main gate after *IllumiNations* and catch a bus or the monorail.

Those who have a car in the Epcot lot have a more problematic situation. If you want to beat the crowd, find a viewing spot at the end of World Showcase Lagoon nearest Future World (and the exits). Leave as soon as *IllumiNations* concludes, trying to exit ahead of the crowd. Be forewarned that thousands of people will be doing exactly the same thing. To get a good vantage point anywhere between Mexico and Canada on the northern end of the lagoon, you'll have to stake out your spot 45–90 minutes before the show. Conceivably, you may squander more time holding your spot before IllumiNations than you would if you watched from the less congested southern end of the lagoon and took your chances with the crowd upon departure.

More groups get separated, and more children lost, after *IllumiNations* than at any other time. In summer, you will be walking in a throng of up to 30,000 people. If you're heading for the parking lot, anticipate this congestion and preselect a point in the Epcot entrance area where you can meet in the event that someone gets separated from the group. We recommend the fountain just inside the main entrance. Everyone in your party should be told not to exit through the turnstiles until all noses have been counted. It can be a nightmare if the group gets split up and you don't know whether the others are inside or outside the park.

For those with a car, the main problem is reaching it. Once there, traffic leaves the parking lot pretty well. If you paid close attention to where you parked, consider skipping the tram and walking. If you walk, watch your children closely and hang on to them for all you're worth. The parking lot is pretty wild at this time of night, with hundreds of moving cars.

Good Locations for Viewing *IllumiNations* and Other World Showcase Lagoon Performances

The best place to be for any presentation on World Showcase Lagoon is in a seat on the lakeside veranda of the Cantina de San Angel in Mexico. Come early (*at least* 90 minutes before *IllumiNations*) and relax with a cold drink or snack while you wait for the show.

A woman from Pasadena, California, nailed down the seat but missed the relaxation. She writes:

> *Stake out a prime site for* IllumiNations *at least two hours ahead, and be prepared to defend it. We got a lakeside table at the Cantina de San Angel at 6:30 p.m. and had a great view of* IllumiNations. *Unfortunately, we had to put up with troops of people asking us to share our table and trying to wedge themselves between our table and the fence.*

The Rose & Crown Pub in the United Kingdom also has lagoonside seating. Because of a small wall, however, the view isn't quite as good as from the Cantina. If you want to combine dinner on the Rose & Crown's veranda with *IllumiNations*, make a dinner priority seating for about 1 hour and 15 minutes before show time. Report a few minutes early for your seating and tell the Rose & Crown host that you want a table outside where you can view *IllumiNations* during or after dinner. Our experience is that the Rose & Crown staff will bend over backward to accommodate you. If you aren't able to obtain a table outside, eat inside, then hang out until show time. When the lights dim, indicating the start of *IllumiNations*, you will be allowed to join the diners on the terrace to watch the show.

Because most guests run for the exits after a presentation, and because islands in the southern (The American Adventure) half of the lagoon block the view from some places, the most popular spectator positions are along the northern waterfront from Norway and Mexico on around to Canada and the United Kingdom. Although the northern end of the lagoon unquestionably offers excellent viewing, it's usually necessary to claim a spot 35–60 minutes before *IllumiNations* begins. For those who are late finishing dinner or don't want to spend 45 minutes standing by a rail, here are some good viewing spots along the southern perimeter (moving counterclockwise from the United Kingdom to Germany) that often go unnoticed until 10–20 minutes before show time:

1. *The Once-Secret Park.* There's a wonderful waterside park, accessible

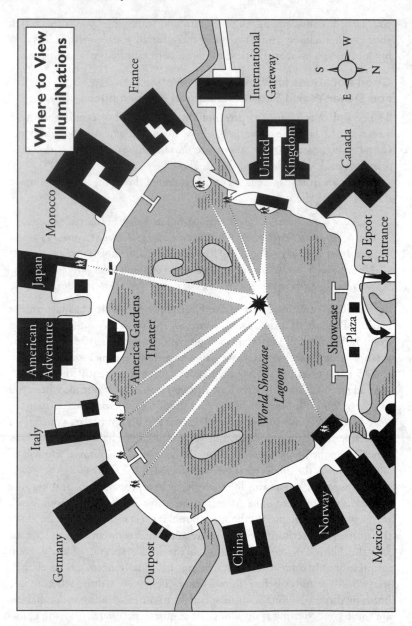

Where to View IllumiNations

International Gateway

France

Morocco

Japan

American Adventure

Italy

Germany

Outpost

China

America Gardens Theater

World Showcase Lagoon

Norway

Mexico

United Kingdom

Canada

To Epcot Entrance

Showcase Plaza

N W S E

from the United Kingdom, which is known to only a few. To reach it, walk toward France from the Rose & Crown Pub in the United Kingdom. As you near the end of the pub, stay on the sidewalk and bear left. You'll shortly find yourself in an almost private park, complete with benches and a perfect view of *IllumiNations*. En route to the park, you'll see a roped-off back entrance to the pub's terrace. This is another good viewing spot (don't be shy about ducking under the rope).

After earlier editions of the *Unofficial Guide*, the "secret park" became less secret. A reader from Demotte, Indiana, describes the scene:

> *We watched the* IllumiNations *show from the "Secret Park" behind the British pub. It was a very good location and allowed us an easy exit after the show. On a humorous note, about 10 minutes before the show was to begin, a lady came hiking down the path to the park with a copy of your guide in her hand. She became quite agitated when she saw that the area was full and exclaimed quite loudly, "I thought this place was a secret!" About half the people in place for the show held up copies of your book.*

A Texas man is more pointed:

> *Which brings us, finally, to the justly renowned* IllumiNations *at Epcot. Since we did not stake out our turf until 30 minutes before the*

The Smith family from East Wimple stakes out their viewing spot for *IllumiNations*.

show, we got the vantage point we deserved. Still, by now you should
probably concede to your readers that the cover has been thoroughly
blown from the so-called "Secret Park"—due, we suspect, to the wide
circulation of your guide.

In addition to the park's not being very secret, you should know that
Disney frequently closes it for private parties.

2. *International Gateway Island.* The pedestrian bridge across the
canal near International Gateway spans an island that offers great viewing.
This island is much more obvious to passersby than the secret park and
normally fills 30 minutes or more before show time.

3. *Second-Floor (Restaurant-Level) Deck of the Mitsukoshi Building in*
Japan. An Asian arch slightly blocks your sightline, but this covered deck
offers a great vantage point, especially if the weather is iffy. Only the
Cantina de San Angel in Mexico is more protected. Finally, the deck is the
only vantage point that works equally well for *IllumiNations* and the
Tapestry of Nations parade.

4. *Gondola Landing at Italy.* An elaborate waterfront promenade
offers excellent viewing positions. Claim your spot at least 30 minutes
before show time.

5. *The Boat Dock Opposite Germany.* Another good vantage point, the
dock generally fills 30 minutes before *IllumiNations.*

6. *Waterfront Promenade by Germany.* Views are good from the 90-
foot-long lagoonside walkway between Germany and China.

Do these suggestions work every time? No. A dad from San Ramon,
California, writes:

> *Your recommendations for* IllumiNations *didn't work out in the*
> *time frame you mentioned. People had the area staked out two hours*
> *ahead of time.*

None of the above viewing locations are reserved for *Unofficial Guide* readers, and on busier nights, good spots go early. But we still won't hold down a
slab of concrete for two hours before *IllumiNations* as some people do. Most
nights, you can find an acceptable vantage point 15–30 minutes before the
show. Because most of the action is significantly above ground level, you don't
need to be right on the rail or have an unobstructed view of the water. It's
important, however, not to position yourself under a tree, awning, or anything else that blocks your overhead view. If *IllumiNations* is a top priority for
you and you want to be absolutely certain of getting a good viewing position,
claim your place an hour or more before show time.

A New Yorker who staked out his turf well in advance made this suggestion for staying comfortable until show time:

> *Your excellent guidebook also served as [a] seat cushion while waiting seated on the ground. Make future editions thicker for greater comfort.*

Some American Express package vacations include a VIP viewing spot for *IllumiNations*. For details, call (800) 469-0430. Also, private pontoon boats, with driver, are available for rental at the Epcot resorts. Your driver will take you for a little boat ride followed by viewing *IllumiNations* from an unobstructed spot on the World Showcase Lagoon. Dinner cruises followed by *IllumiNations* are also available. For additional information, contact guest services at the Yacht Club, Beach Club, Boardwalk Inn, or Boardwalk Villas Resort.

Shopping in Epcot

Shops in Future World seem out of place. The atmosphere is too visionary and grand to accommodate the pettiness of the bargain table. Similarly, it obviously has been difficult to find merchandise consistent with the surroundings. What is available generally is sold elsewhere, except for Epcot and Disney trademark souvenirs.

The World Showcase shops add realism and atmosphere to the international street scenes, though much of the merchandise is overpriced and readily available elsewhere. Still, some shops really are special. In the United Kingdom, visit The Queen's Table (fine china); in China, Yong Feng Shangdian (crafts, rugs, carvings, furniture); and in Japan, Mitsukoshi Department Store (porcelain, bonsai trees, pearls straight from live oysters). Village Traders, a new shop between China and Germany, sells Kenyan woodcarvings for about the same price you would pay at the carving center in Mombasa where they're made.

Salespersons can forward your purchases to Package Pick-up, where you can retrieve them when you leave the park. Specify whether you'll depart through the main entrance or International Gateway. Allow three hours from the time of purchase for your goods to reach the pick-up facility. If you're a Disney resort guest, packages can be delivered directly to your room.

Behind-the-Scenes Tours in Epcot

Epcot's Gardens of the World offers adults a glimpse of Disney World's gardens, horticulture, and landscaping. The three-hour tour costs $49 plus Epcot admission. Adults (16 and older) can book Hidden Treasures East and West, a tour exploring the architecture of the international pavilions of all countries. The three-and-a-half-hour tour costs $49 plus Epcot admission. For $85, you can take the Hidden Treasures Plus tour, which includes everything in Hidden Treasures East and West, plus lunch and a backstage tour of Epcot.

Readers rave about guided walking tours at Epcot. A couple from Los Angeles writes:

> *The best-kept secret is the adult tour, Hidden Treasures of World Showcase in Epcot. The description is misleading and sounds like a real bore, but we got a behind-the-scenes tour with lots of information on everything we ever wanted to know or were curious about. Definitely the best part of our trip. (This is a walking tour and is mostly outside in the heat.)*

A gentleman in Houston, Texas, tells us:

> *Keep telling people about the Hidden Treasures of World Showcase tour; we finally got to take it, and it was a real highlight. The cast member who took us on the tour (there were only four of us) told us about a tour of the Magic Kingdom, called Keys to the Kingdom, which we took the very next day. It was similar, with backstage touring and a look at the utilidor system, although it also included going on several rides. Tell people about this one, too.*

Discounts for these tours are available if you charge them on an American Express card. For reservations, call (407) 939-8687.

The Behind the Seeds Tour is shorter and takes guests behind the scenes to vegetable gardens in The Land pavilion. It requires same-day reservations; make them on the lower level of The Land (far right of the fast-food windows). The cost of the hour-long tour is $6 for adults and $4 for children ages three to nine.

Dive Quest

The soggiest behind-the-scenes experience available anywhere is Epcot's Dive Quest, where open-water scuba-certified divers can swim around with the fish at The Living Seas. Each tour lasts about 3½ hours, including a 30-minute dive. The cost is about $140 per diver and includes all gear, a souvenir T-shirt, a dive log stamp, and refreshments. They will make a video recording of your dive, which you can buy for $30. Reservations are required and can be made with a credit card by calling (407) WDW-TOUR. For recorded information, call (407) 560-5590. The experience is for adults only: no junior certifications are accepted.

Traffic Patterns in Epcot

After long admiring traffic flow in the Magic Kingdom, we were amazed at Epcot's layout. In the Magic Kingdom, Main Street, U.S.A., with its shops and eateries, serves as a huge gathering place when the park opens and funnels visitors to the central hub, where entrances branch off to the lands. Thus, crowds are first welcomed and entertained (on Main Street), then distributed almost equally to the lands.

At Epcot, by contrast, Spaceship Earth, the park's premier landmark and one of its headliner attractions, is just inside the main entrance. When visitors enter the park, they almost irresistibly head for it. Hence, a bottleneck forms less than 75 yards from the turnstiles as soon as the park opens. Visitors aware of the congestion at Spaceship Earth can take advantage of the excellent opportunities it provides for escaping waits at other Future World attractions.

Early-morning crowds form in Future World because most of the park's rides and shows are there. Except at Test Track, Spaceship Earth, Body Wars (Wonders of Life pavilion), and *Honey, I Shrunk the Audience* (Imagination Institute pavilion), visitors are fairly equally distributed among Future World attractions.

Epcot's top draw is Test Track, and everybody in the know makes a fast break for this attraction as soon as they clear the park's entrance turnstiles. The word on the street, true in this case, is that unless you ride Test Track within the first 20 minutes Epcot is open, you're in for a 60–90 minute wait.

Between 9 and 11 a.m., crowds build in Future World. Even when World Showcase opens (usually 11 a.m.), more people are entering Future World than are leaving for the Showcase. Attendance continues building in Future World until between noon and 2 p.m. World Showcase attendance builds rapidly as lunch approaches. Exhibits at the far end of World Showcase Lagoon report capacity audiences from about noon through 6:30 or 7:30 p.m.

The Magic Kingdom's premier attractions are situated on the far perimeters of its lands to distribute crowds evenly. Epcot's cluster of attractions in Future World holds the greater part of the throng in the smaller part of the park. World Showcase has only two major draws (Maelstrom in Norway and *The American Adventure*). There is no compelling reason to rush to see them. The bottom line: Crowds build all morning and into early afternoon in Future World. Not until the evening meal approaches do crowds equalize in Future World and World Showcase. Evening crowds in World Showcase, however, don't compare in size to morning and midday crowds in Future World. Attendance throughout Epcot is normally lighter in the evening.

At the Magic Kingdom, repeat visitors make a mad dash for their favorite ride, and preferences are strong and well defined. At Epcot, by contrast, many returning guests say that with the possible exceptions of Test Track and *Honey, I Shrunk the Audience,* they enjoy the major attractions "about the same." The conclusion suggested is that touring at Epcot is more systematic and predictable (by the numbers, clockwise, or counter-clockwise) than at the Magic Kingdom.

Some guests leave Epcot in the early evening, but the vast majority exit en masse after *IllumiNations.* Upwards of 30,000 people head for the parking lot and monorail station at once.

Closing time at Epcot doesn't precipitate congestion as it does at the Magic Kingdom. One primary reason for the easier departure from Epcot is that its parking lot is adjacent to the park, not separated from it by a lake as at the Magic Kingdom. At the Magic Kingdom, departing visitors form bottlenecks at the monorail to the Transportation and Ticket Center and main parking lot. At Epcot, they proceed directly to their cars.

Epcot Touring Plans

Our Epcot touring plans are field-tested, step-by-step itineraries for seeing all major attractions at Epcot with a minimum of waiting in line. They're designed to keep you ahead of the crowds while the park is filling in the morning, and to place you at the less crowded attractions during Epcot's busier hours. They assume you would be happier doing a little extra walking rather than a lot of extra standing in line.

Touring Epcot is much more strenuous and demanding than touring the other theme parks. Epcot requires about twice as much walking. And, unlike the Magic Kingdom, Epcot has no effective in-park transportation; wherever you want to go, it's always quicker to walk. Our plans will help you avoid crowds and bottlenecks on days of moderate to heavy attendance, but they can't shorten the distance you have to walk. (Wear comfortable shoes.) On days of lighter attendance, when crowd conditions aren't a critical factor, the plans will help you organize your tour.

We offer four touring plans:

Epcot One-Day Touring Plan   This plan packs as much as possible into one long day and requires a lot of hustle and stamina. It can be used on early-entry or non-early-entry days.

Author's Selective Epcot One-Day Touring Plan   This plan eliminates some lesser attractions (in the author's opinion) and offers a somewhat more relaxed tour if you have only one day. It can be used on early-entry or non-early-entry days.

Epcot Two-Day Sunrise/Starlight Touring Plan   This plan combines the easy touring of early morning on one day with Epcot's festivity and live pageantry at night on the second day. The first day requires some back-tracking and hustle but is much more laid-back than either one-day plan. It can be used on early-entry or non-early-entry days.

Epcot Two-Day Early Riser Touring Plan   This is the most efficient Epcot touring plan, eliminating 90% of the backtracking and extra walking required by the others while still providing a comprehensive tour. It is designed to be used only on mornings when early entry isn't in effect.

Epcot One-Day Touring Plan

For: Adults and children eight or older.
Assumes: Willingness to experience all major rides and shows.

This plan requires a lot of walking and some backtracking in order to avoid long waits in line. A little extra walking and some early-morning hustle will spare you two to three hours of standing in line. You might not complete the tour. How far you get depends on how quickly you move from attraction to attraction, how many times you rest and eat, how quickly the park fills, and what time it closes.

This plan is not recommended for families with very young children. If you're touring with young children and have only one day, use the Author's Selective Epcot One-Day Touring Plan. Break after lunch and relax at your hotel, returning to the park in late afternoon. If you can allocate two days to Epcot, use one of the Epcot two-day touring plans.

1. If you're a Disney hotel guest, arrive 90 minutes before official opening time on *early-entry days* and 40 minutes before official opening on *non-early-entry days*. If you're a day guest, arrive at the parking lot 45 minutes before Epcot's official opening on a *non-early-entry day*.

   If you're a Disney resort guest taking advantage of early entry, expect Spaceship Earth, The Living Seas, The Land, and the Imagination Institute pavilions to be open. Our advice is to take in the ride and the 3-D movie at the Imagination Institute pavilion and then position yourself as close as possible to Test Track on the opposite side of Future World. If you want to ride

Test Track without a 60-to 100-minute wait, resist the temptation to cram more attractions into your early-entry period.
Limiting your early-entry sampling to the ride and the 3-D
movie will ensure that you'll have time to get in position for Test
Track. Pick up the Touring Plan at Test Track and thereafter
skip any steps directing you to attractions that you experienced
during the early-entry period.

2. When admitted, move quickly (jog if you can, but don't run)
   around the left side of Spaceship Earth. If so inclined, stop
   briefly at Guest Relations (to the left of Spaceship Earth) to
   make priority seatings for Epcot restaurants. Continue through
   the plaza with the crescent-shaped Innoventions East building
   on your left until you see an open passage through the building.
   Turn left through this passage. After emerging on the far side of
   Innoventions East, turn right and head to Test Track. If you are
   held up by a rope barrier anywhere along the route from the
   park entrance to Test Track, don't worry. Just stay put and proceed to Test Track when permitted. Similarly, if you get to Test
   Track and it's not operating yet, remain in place and be patient.
   If you do not want to experience Test Track, skip ahead to Step
   3.

3. After Test Track, bear right and head for the Wonders of Life
   pavilion located on the same side of Future World as Test Track
   but back toward the entrance. At the Wonders of Life pavilion,
   ride Body Wars. Be sure to read our motion sickness warning
   concerning Body Wars. If you don't want to ride, skip ahead to
   Step 4.

4. After Body Wars, skip the other attractions in the Wonders of
   Life pavilion for the time being. Heading back in the direction
   of Test Track, retrace your path through the Innoventions East
   passage back into the central plaza. Crossing the plaza, pass
   through the Innoventions West building on the opposite side.
   On the far side of Innoventions West, bear left to the Imagination
   Institute pavilion. The two main attractions at the Imagination
   Institute are a ride (on the right side) and a 3-D film, *Honey, I
   Shrunk the Audience,* on the left. Enjoy the ride first and then
   see the film.

5. After exiting the Imagination Institute, stay left and head to The Land pavilion next door. At The Land pavilion, ride Living with the Land, a boat ride. There are two other attractions in this pavilion. *Food Rocks* is an audio-animatronic show about nutrition, and *The Circle of Life* is a film about ecology and the interdependence of species. Check our profiles of both attractions. If they sound like something you'd enjoy, go ahead and see them now.

   Note: If you're hungry, feel free to stop for lunch or a snack at any time from here on.

6. Exiting The Land, turn left to The Living Seas. Experience the Living Seas.

7. After the Living Seas, bear left and pass back through the Innoventions West building. Ride Spaceship Earth, the attraction in the giant golf ball. Don't be too concerned if the line is long. Spaceship Earth is one of the fastest loading attractions in the Disney repertoire. At the exit of the ride is a communications electronics exhibit. Our advice is to bypass it for the time being.

8. Following Spaceship Earth, return to the Test Track/Wonders of Life side of Future World, passing once again through Innoventions East. Bear left to the Universe of Energy and see the show. Once again, the line might appear daunting, but because of the immense capacity of the attraction, your wait should be tolerable.

9. Exiting the Universe of Energy, turn left and return to the Wonders of Life Pavilion. See *Cranium Command.*

10. Departing the Wonders of Life pavilion, turn left. The pavilion next door is Horizons, closed when this guide went to press for lack of a sponsoring corporation. If Horizons (or something in its place) has reopened by the time of your visit, see it now.

11. Next, depart Future World and go to the World Showcase, initiating a counterclockwise circuit. If you are primarily interested in the attractions, try to limit your perusal of the dozens of shops.

12. At Canada, see the movie.

13. Exiting Canada to the right, you'll come to the entrance of the Millennium Village. Our advice is to skip it for the time being. If you're a World Showcase veteran and have previously experienced all of the permanent attractions, go ahead and tour the Millennium Village.

14. Next, tour the United Kingdom.

15. Proceed across the bridge to France. See the movie.

16. After France, visit Morocco next door.

    Note: Check your watch. Is your dinner priority seating soon? Suspend touring and go to the restaurant when it's time. Check the daily entertainment schedule for the time of the Tapestry of Nations parade and *IllumiNations*, both worthwhile. Give yourself at least 30 minutes after dinner to locate a good viewing spot.

17. Continue counterclockwise to Japan.

18. After Japan, see the *American Adventure.*

19. Continue to Italy.

20. Go next to Germany.

21. Proceed to China. See the movie.

22. After China, continue on to Norway. Ride Maelstrom if the wait is not prohibitive.

23. Next, tour Mexico and ride El Rio del Tiempo.

24. This concludes the touring plan. Unless an unusual holiday schedule is in effect, everything at Epcot closes after *IllumiNations* except for a few shops. Thirty or forty thousand people bolt for the exits at once. Suggestions for coping with this exodus are on pages 512–513.

Author's Selective Epcot One-Day Touring Plan

For: All parties.
Assumes: Willingness to experience major rides and shows.

This touring plan includes only what the author believes is the best Epcot has to offer. Exclusion of an attraction doesn't mean it isn't worthwhile.

Families with children younger than eight using this touring plan should review Epcot attractions in the Small-Child Fright-Potential Chart (pages 183–184). Rent a stroller for any child small enough to fit in one, and take your young children back to the hotel for a nap after lunch. If you can allocate two days to see Epcot, try one of the Epcot two-day touring plans.

1. If you're a Disney hotel guest, arrive 90 minutes before official opening time on *early-entry days* and 40 minutes before official opening on *non-early-entry days*. If you're a day guest, arrive at the parking lot 45 minutes before Epcot's official opening on *non-early-entry day*.

    If you're a Disney resort guest taking advantage of early entry, expect Spaceship Earth, The Living Seas, The Land, and the Imagination Institute pavilions to be open. Our advice is to take in the ride and the 3-D movie at the Imagination Institute pavilion and then position yourself as close as possible to Test Track on the opposite side of Future World. If you want to ride Test Track without a 60-to 100-minute wait, resist the temptation to cram more attractions into your early-entry period. Limiting your early-entry sampling to the ride and the 3-D movie will ensure that you'll have time to get in position for Test Track. Pick up the Touring Plan at Test Track and thereafter skip any steps directing you to attractions that you experienced during the early-entry period.

2. When admitted, move quickly (jog if you can, but don't run) around the left side of Spaceship Earth. If so inclined, stop briefly at Guest Relations (to the left of Spaceship Earth) to make priority seatings for Epcot restaurants. Continue through the plaza with the crescent-shaped Innoventions East building on your left until you see an open passage through the building. Turn left through this passage. After emerging on the far side of Innoventions East, turn right and head to Test Track. If you are held up by a rope barrier anywhere along the route from the

park entrance to Test Track, don't worry. Just stay put and proceed to Test Track when permitted. Similarly, if you get to Test Track and it's not operating yet, remain in place and be patient. If you do not want to experience Test Track, skip ahead to Step 3.

3. After Test Track, bear right and head for the Wonders of Life pavilion located on the same side of Future World as Test Track, but back toward the entrance. At the Wonders of Life pavilion, ride Body Wars. Be sure to read our motion sickness warning concerning Body Wars. If you don't want to ride, skip ahead to Step 4.

4. After Body Wars, skip the other attractions in the Wonders of Life pavilion for the time being. Heading back in the direction of Test Track, retrace your path through the Innoventions East passage back into the central plaza. Crossing the plaza, pass through the Innoventions West building on the opposite side. On the far side of Innoventions West, bear left to the Imagination Institute pavilion. The two main attractions at the Imagination Institute are a ride (on the right side) and a 3-D film, *Honey, I Shrunk the Audience,* on the left. Enjoy the ride first and then see the film.

5. After exiting the Imagination Institute, stay left and head to The Land pavilion next door. At The Land pavilion ride Living with the Land, a boat ride. Skip the two other attractions in this pavilion.

   Note: If you're hungry, feel free to stop for lunch or a snack at any time from here on.

6. Exiting The Land, turn left to The Living Seas. Experience the Living Seas.

7. After the Living Seas, bear left and pass back through the Innoventions West building. Ride Spaceship Earth, the attraction in the giant golf ball. Don't be too concerned if the line is long. Spaceship Earth is one of the fastest loading attractions in the Disney repertoire. At the exit of the ride is a communications electronics exhibit. Our advice is to bypass it for the time being.

8. Following Spaceship Earth, return to the Test Track/Wonders of Life side of Future World, passing once again through the Innoventions East. Bear left to the Universe of Energy and see the show. Once again, the line might appear daunting, but because of the immense capacity of the attraction, your wait should be tolerable.

9. Exiting the Universe of Energy, turn left and return to the Wonders of Life Pavilion. See *Cranium Command*.

10. Departing the Wonders of Life pavilion, turn left. The pavilion next door is Horizons, closed when this guide went to press for lack of a sponsoring corporation. If Horizons (or something in its place) has reopened by the time of your visit, see it now.

11. Next, depart Future World and go to the World Showcase, initiating a counterclockwise tour. If you are primarily interested in the attractions, try to limit your perusal of the dozens of shops. The street scenes at each World Showcase nation, however, are what make this section of Epcot special. Even when there is not a ride or a show, we recommend you spend some time enjoying the architecture, gardens, and street entertainment. The World Showcase is definitely a smell-the-roses kind of place, so try to relax and not hurry through.

12. There are three movies, two boat rides, and an Audio-Animatronic attraction (*The American Adventure*) in the World Showcase. As you complete your circuit we recommend experiencing *The American Adventure*, seeing the films at France and China, and taking the boat ride at Norway (if the wait is manageable). The film at Canada is very good, but not as interesting as the other two, in our opinion. The boat ride at Mexico is totally expendable.

13. To the right of Canada is the entrance of the Millennium Village. Our advice is to skip it for the time being. If you're a World Showcase veteran and have previously experienced all of the permanent attractions, go ahead and tour the Millennium Village.

    Note: Check your watch. Is your dinner priority seating soon? Suspend touring and go to the restaurant when it's time. Check the daily entertainment schedule for the time of the Tapestry of Nations parade and *IllumiNations*, both worthwhile. Give yourself at least 30 minutes after dinner to locate a good viewing spot.

14. This concludes the touring plan. Unless an unusual holiday schedule is in effect, everything at Epcot closes after *IllumiNations* except for a few shops. Thirty or forty thousand people bolt for the exits at once. Suggestions for coping with this exodus are on pages 512–513.

Epcot Two-Day Sunrise/Starlight Touring Plan

For: All parties.

This touring plan is for visitors who want to tour Epcot comprehensively over two days. Day One takes advantage of early-morning touring opportunities. Day Two begins in late afternoon and continues until the park closes.

Many readers spend part of their Disney World arrival day traveling, checking into their hotel, and unpacking. They aren't free to go to the theme parks until afternoon. The second day of the Epcot Two-Day Sunrise/Starlight Touring Plan is ideal for people who want to commence their Epcot visit later in the day.

Families with children younger than eight using this touring plan should review Epcot attractions in the Small-Child Fright-Potential Chart (pages 183–184). Rent a stroller for any child small enough to fit into one. Break off Day One no later than 2:30 p.m. and return to your hotel for rest. If you missed attractions called for in Day One, add them to your itinerary on Day Two.

Day One

1. If you're a Disney hotel guest, arrive 90 minutes before official opening time on *early-entry days* and 40 minutes before official opening on *non-early-entry days*. If you're a day guest, arrive at the parking lot 45 minutes before Epcot's official opening on a *non-early-entry day*.

If you're a Disney resort guest taking advantage of early entry, expect Spaceship Earth, The Living Seas, The Land, and the Imagination Institute pavilions to be open. Our advice is to take in the ride and the 3-D movie at the Imagination Institute pavilion and then position yourself as close as possible to Test Track on the opposite side of Future World. If you want to ride Test Track without a 60- to 100-minute wait, resist the temptation to cram more attractions into your early-entry period. Limiting your early-entry sampling to the ride and the 3-D movie will ensure that you'll have time to get in position for Test Track. Pick up the Touring Plan at Test Track, and thereafter skip any steps directing you to attractions that you experienced during the early-entry period.

2. When admitted, move quickly (jog if you can, but don't run) around the left side of Spaceship Earth. If so inclined, stop

briefly at Guest Relations (to the left of Spaceship Earth) to make priority seatings for Epcot restaurants. Continue through the plaza with the crescent-shaped Innoventions East building on your left until you see an open passage through the building. Turn left through this passage. After emerging on the far side of Innoventions East, turn right and head to Test Track. If you are held up by a rope barrier anywhere along the route from the park entrance to Test Track, don't worry. Just stay put and proceed to Test Track when permitted. Similarly, if you get to Test Track and it's not operating yet, remain in place and be patient. If you do not want to experience Test Track, skip ahead to Step 4.

3. Ride Test Track.

4. Exit Test Track and cross Future World to the Imagination Institute pavilion. Experience the ride and then see *Honey, I Shrunk the Audience*.

5. Skip other attractions at Imagination Institute and exit left to The Land pavilion. Take the Living with the Land boat ride.

6. Postpone other Land attractions. Go to the Wonders of Life pavilion. Ride Body Wars. *Warning:* This ride gives many people motion sickness (see pages 491–492).

7. While at Wonders of Life, see *Cranium Command*. Don't miss the cartoon preshow or you may not understand the main presentation.

8. Exit Wonders of Life. Turn right to Universe of Energy and see the show. Don't be dismayed if the line looks long. The large theater gobbles the whole crowd when the audience changes.

9. Turn left out of Universe of Energy. Head back toward Test Track. Go left past the Wonders of Life pavilion and see Horizons (or whatever may have taken its place).

10. Bear left after exiting Horizons, passing Test Track. Go left on the path leading to the Odyssey Center. Cut through the Odyssey Center to World Showcase.

11. Turn left and proceed clockwise around the World Showcase Lagoon. Experience El Río del Tiempo boat ride in Mexico. The ride is in the far-left corner of the interior courtyard and isn't very well marked. Consign any purchases to Package Pickup for collection when you leave the park.

12. Continue left to Norway. Ride Maelstrom.

Note: Check your watch. Is your lunch priority seating soon? Suspend touring and go to the restaurant when it's time. After lunch, resume the touring plan where you left off.

13. Continue left to China. See *Wonders of China.*

14. Visit Germany and Italy. Enjoy the settings; there are no rides or films. If you don't have a restaurant priority seating, Sommerfest (fast food) at Germany serves tasty bratwurst, soft pretzels, desserts, and Beck's beer on draft.

15. Continue clockwise to The American Adventure. See the show. If you don't have a restaurant priority seating, the Liberty Inn (left side of The American Adventure) serves hamburgers, hot dogs, and chicken breast sandwiches.

16. Visit Japan and Morocco. Consign any purchases to Package Pick-up for collection when you leave the park.

17. This concludes the touring plan for Day One. Attractions and pavilions not included today will be experienced tomorrow. If you're full of energy and wish to continue touring, follow the Epcot One-Day Touring Plan, starting at Step 18. If you've had enough, exit through the International Gateway or leave through the main entrance. To reach the main entrance without walking around the lagoon, catch a boat at the dock near Morocco.

Day Two

1. Enter Epcot about 2 p.m. Get a park guidemap containing the daily entertainment schedule at Guest Relations.

2. While at Guest Relations, make a dinner priority seating, if you haven't done so already. You can eat your evening meal in any Epcot restaurant without interrupting the sequence and efficiency of the touring plan. We recommend a 7 p.m. priority seating. The timing of the seating is important if you want to see *IllumiNations,* held over the lagoon at 9 p.m.

   If your preferred restaurants and seatings are filled, try for a priority seating at Morocco or Norway. Because these nations' delightful ethnic dishes are little known to most Americans, priority seatings may be available.

3. Ride Spaceship Earth.

4. Pass through Innoventions West and proceed to The Living Seas. For maximum efficiency, be one of the last people to enter the theater (where you sit) from the preshow area (where you

stand). Sit as close to the end of a middle row as possible. This will position you to be first on the ride that follows the theater presentation. Afterward, enjoy the exhibits of Sea Base Alpha.

5. Exit right from The Living Seas to The Land. See *Food Rocks* and *The Circle of Life,* featuring characters from *The Lion King.*

   Note: Check your watch. Is your dinner priority seating soon? Suspend touring and go to the restaurant when it's time. After dinner, check the daily entertainment schedule for the time of *IllumiNations.* Don't miss it. Give yourself at least a half hour after dinner to find a good viewing spot along the perimeter of World Showcase Lagoon. For details on the best spots, see pages 513–517.

6. Leave Future World and walk counterclockwise around World Showcase Lagoon to Canada. See *O Canada!*

7. Turn right and tour the Millennium Village.

8. Turn right and visit the United Kingdom.

9. Turn right and proceed to France. See the film.

10. This concludes the touring plan. Enjoy your dinner and *IllumiNations.* If you have time, shop or revisit your favorite attractions.

11. Unless a holiday schedule is in effect, everything at Epcot closes after *IllumiNations* except for a few shops. Thirty thousand or more people bolt for the exits at once. Suggestions for coping with this exodus are on pages 512–513.

Epcot Two-Day Early Riser Touring Plan

For: All parties.

The Two-Day Early Riser Touring Plan is the most efficient Epcot touring plan, eliminating much of the backtracking and crisscrossing required by the other plans. It takes advantage of easy touring made possible by morning's light crowds. Most folks will complete each day of the plan by midafternoon. While the plan doesn't include *IllumiNations* or other evening festivities, these activities plus dinner at an Epcot restaurant can be added to the itinerary at your discretion.

The Epcot Two-Day Early Riser Touring Plan is designed to be used on days when early entry isn't in effect.

Families with children younger than eight using this plan should review Epcot attractions in the Small-Child Fright-Potential Chart (pages 183–184). Rent a stroller for any child small enough to fit into one.

Day One

1. Arrive 45 minutes before official opening time on a day when early entry isn't scheduled.

2. When admitted, move quickly (jog if you can, but don't run) around the left side of Spaceship Earth to Guest Relations (across the walkway from the geosphere) and make lunch and dinner priority seatings. If you don't wish to do so or have already made them by phone, skip to Step 3.

3. Ride Spaceship Earth.

4. Crossing the Future World plaza, pass through the Innoventions West building and bear left to the Imagination Institute pavilion. The two main attractions at the Imagination Institute are a ride (on the right side) and a 3-D film, *Honey, I Shrunk the Audience,* on the left. Enjoy the ride first and then see the film.

5. Exit left and proceed to The Land. Take the Living with the Land boat ride.

6. In the same pavilion, see *Food Rocks* and *The Circle of Life.* Start with whichever is scheduled to begin first.

7. Exit The Land and bear left to The Living Seas. See the structured part of the presentation, then the exhibits at your leisure.

   Note: Check your watch. Is your priority seating soon? Suspend touring and go to the restaurant if it's time. Resume the plan after you eat.

8. Bear left from The Living Seas and pass through Innoventions West. Cross the plaza behind Spaceship Earth and proceed through Innoventions East to the Universe of Energy. Enjoy the show.

9. From the Universe of Energy, continue past the Wonders of Life pavilion to Horizons. This attraction might be closed or have a new name. If it's open, check it out.

10. Departing Horizons, explore attractions of Innoventions East and West.

11. This concludes Day One of the touring plan. If you linger over exhibits at The Living Seas and Innovations East and West, it may be late in the day when you finish, and you might consider staying for dinner and *IllumiNations*. If you toured more briskly, you probably will complete the plan by about 2:30 p.m., even with a full-service lunch.

Day Two

1. Arrive 45 minutes before official opening time on a day when early entry isn't scheduled.

2. When admitted, move quickly (jog if you can, but don't run) around the left side of Spaceship Earth to Guest Relations (across the walkway from the geosphere) and make lunch and dinner priority seatings. If you don't wish to do so or have already made them by phone, skip to Step 3.

3. After making priority seatings for Epcot restaurants, continue through the plaza with the crescent-shaped Innovations East building on your left until you see an open passage through the building. Turn left through this passage. After emerging on the far side of Innovations East, turn right and head to Test Track. If you are held up by a rope barrier anywhere along the route from the park entrance to Test Track, don't worry. Just stay put and proceed to Test Track when permitted. Similarly, if you get to Test Track and it's not operating yet, remain in place and be patient. If you do not want to experience Test Track, skip ahead to Step 5.

4. Ride Test Track.

5. Exit Test Track to the right and proceed to the Wonders of Life pavilion. Ride Body Wars. *Warning:* This ride gives many people motion sickness (see pages 491–492).

6. In the same pavilion, see *The Making of Me*.

7. In the same pavilion, see *Cranium Command*. Afterward, enjoy the exhibits and interactive displays.

8. Exit left from the Wonders of Life pavilion and, passing Horizons, return to Test Track. To the left of Test Track, bear left on the path that leads to the Odyssey Center. Cut through the Odyssey Center to World Showcase.

9. Turn left and proceed clockwise around World Showcase Lagoon. Experience El Río del Tiempo boat ride at Mexico. The

ride is in the far-left corner of the interior courtyard and isn't very well marked. Consign any purchases to Package Pick-up for collection when you leave the park.

10. Go left to Norway. Ride Maelstrom.

11. Go left to China. See *Wonders of China*.

12. Visit Germany and Italy. Enjoy the settings; there are no rides or films. If you don't have a restaurant priority seating, Sommerfest (fast food) at Germany serves tasty bratwurst, soft pretzels, desserts, and Beck's beer on draft.

13. Continue clockwise to The American Adventure. See the show. If you don't have a restaurant priority seating, the Liberty Inn (left side of The American Adventure) serves hamburgers, hot dogs, and chicken breast sandwiches.

14. Visit Japan and Morocco. Consign any purchases to Package Pick-up for collection when you leave the park.

15. Continue left to France. See *Impressions de France*.

16. Visit the United Kingdom.

17. Check out Millennium Village between the United Kingdom and Canada.

18. Go left to Canada. See *O Canada!*

19. This concludes Day Two of the touring plan. If you futzed around in World Showcase shops and it's late in the day, consider staying for dinner and *IllumiNations*. If you caught *IllumiNations* after Day One, consider exiting Epcot through the International Gateway (between the United Kingdom and France) and exploring the restaurants, shops, and clubs of Disney's BoardWalk. The BoardWalk is an easy five-minute walk from the International Gateway.

Part Twelve
Disney's Animal Kingdom

With its lush flora, winding streams, meandering paths, and exotic setting, the Animal Kingdom is a stunningly beautiful theme park. The landscaping alone conjurs images of rain forest, veldt, and even formal garden. Soothing, mysterious, and exciting all at once, every vista is a feast for the eye. Add to this loveliness a population of more than 1,000 animals, replicas of Africa's and Asia's most intriguing architecture, and a diverse array of singularly original attractions, and you have the most unique of all Disney theme parks. In the Animal Kingdom, Disney has created an environment to savor. And though you will encounter the typical long lines, pricey food, and shops full of Disney merchandise, you will also (with a little effort) experience a day of stimulating private discoveries.

Disney's Animal Kingdom opened in April 1998 amid a storm of controversy. Animal rights activists lambasted Disney, blaming Animal Kingdom zoologists and caretakers for the death of some three dozen various animals. What went largely unreported, however, was that many of these same detractors had for months castigated Disney for pirating away the best zoological talent in the country from America's zoos and research centers. The fact that investigations turned up no evidence of negligence, mistreatment, or neglect did little to satisfy the critics. The Animal Kingdom, for ill or good, is probably destined to be the lightning rod for the ongoing debate concerning the role of zoos and the moral rectitude of confining wild animals in cages (however elaborate) for the pleasure of humans.

At 500 acres, Disney's Animal Kingdom is five times the size of the Magic Kingdom and more than twice the size of Epcot. But like Disney-MGM Studios, most of the Animal Kingdom's vast geography is only accessible on guided tours or as part of attractions. When complete, the Animal Kingdom will feature seven sections or "lands": The Oasis, Safari Village, DinoLand U.S.A., Camp Minnie-Mickey, Africa, Asia, and an as-yet

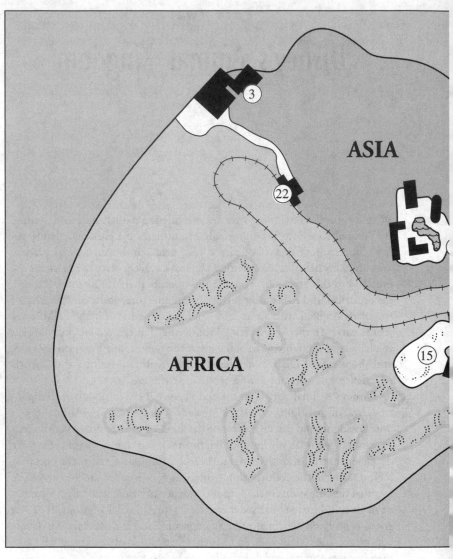

ASIA

AFRICA

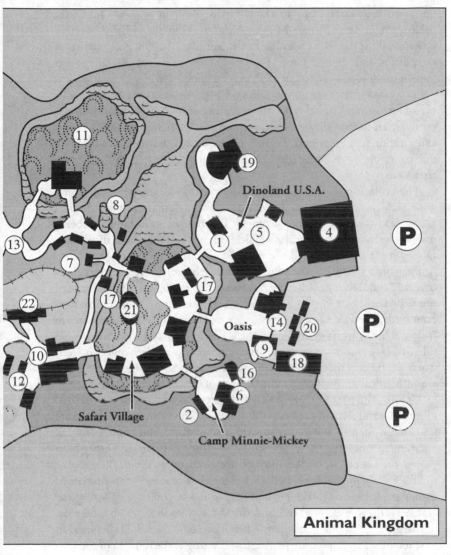

Animal Kingdom

13. Maharaja Jungle Trek
14. Main Entrance
15. Pangani Forest
    Exploration Trail
16. Pocahontas
17. Radio Disney River Cruise

18. Rainforest Cafe
19. Theater in the Wild
20. Ticket Booths
21. Tree of Life/*It's Tough to Be a Bug!*
22. Wildlife Express (Train)

unnamed land inspired by mythical beasts. Built in phases, The Oasis, Safari Village, Camp Minnie-Mickey, Africa, and DinoLand U.S.A. were all operational for the park's opening in the summer of 1998. Asia opened in early 1999, and "Beastie Land" (our suggestion) will come on-line sometime in the future, as subsequent phases are completed.

Its size notwithstanding, the Animal Kingdom features a limited number of attractions. To be exact, there are five rides, several walk-through exhibits, an indoor theater, four amphitheaters, a conservation exhibit, and a children's playground. Two of the attractions, however, Countdown to Extinction and Kilimanjaro Safaris, are among the best in the Disney repertoire.

The evolution of the Animal Kingdom has been interesting in several respects. First, with regard to the Florida theme park market, it is seen to be taking dead aim at the recently resurgent Busch Gardens in Tampa, a theme park known for its exceptional zoological exhibits and numerous thrill rides. Disney has always preferred the neatly controlled movements of Audio-Animatronic animals to the unpredictable behaviors of real critters. Discovery Island, Disney's only previous foray into zoological exhibits, landed the Walt Disney Company in court for exterminating a bunch of indigenous birds that tried to take up residence on the island. When it comes to "rides," Disney won't even dignify the term. In Disney parks there are no rides, you see—only adventures. Attractions such as modern roller coasters, where the thrill of motion dominates visual, audio, and story-line elements, are antithetical to the Imagineering notion of attraction design.

Unfortunately for Disney, however, the creative, natural-habitat zoological exhibits and state-of-the-art thrill rides developed by Busch Gardens are immensely popular, and as any student of the Walt Disney Company can attest, there is nothing like a successful competitor to make the Disney folks change their tune. So, smoke, mirrors, and press releases aside, here's what you'll get when the Animal Kingdom is complete a couple of years from now: natural-habitat zoological exhibits and state-of-the-art thrill rides. Big surprise!

Even if the recipe is tried and true, the Disney version serves up more than its share of innovations, particularly when it comes to the wildlife habitats. In fact, zoologists worldwide are practically salivating at the thought of the Disney Imagineers applying their talent to zoo design. Living up to expectations, the wildlife exhibits at the Animal Kingdom do break some new ground. For starters, there's lots of space, thus allowing for the sweeping vistas that Discovery Channel viewers would expect in, say, an African veldt setting. Then there are the enclosures, natural in appearance, with little or no apparent barriers between you and the animals. The operative word, of course, is "apparent." That flimsy stand of bamboo separating you from a gorilla is actually a neatly disguised set of steel rods imbedded in concrete. The Imagineers even take a crack at certain animals' stubborn unwillingness to be on display. A lion that would rather sleep out of sight under a bush, for example, is lured to center stage with nice, cool, climate-controlled artificial rocks.

A second anomaly in the development of the Animal Kingdom has been its erratic course from design to completion. Far from creating a master plan and sticking to it, the Animal Kingdom has been a continuously evolving project with more midstream about-faces than a kindergarten fire drill. Names of lands and attractions have changed (the land relating to mythical beasts has had no fewer than five names), as have the number of lands and their premier attractions. Some attraction concepts were half executed and then scrapped. The first attraction designed for the park's architectural icon, the Tree of Life, was discarded as the park entered its final stage of construction. Attractions and lands scheduled for Phase I of development were moved back to Phase II, and so on.

All of this, of course, is in the rearview mirror now—yet another example of Disney's penchant for doing things the hard way. What remains is a new star in Disney's growing galaxy of theme parks.

The Animal Kingdom has received mixed reviews in its first couple of years. Guests have complained loudly about the park layout and the necessity of backtracking through Safari Village in order to access the various theme areas. Congested walkways, lack of shade, poor signage, and insufficient air conditioning also rank high on the gripe list. However, most of the attractions (with one or two notable exceptions) have been well received. Also praised are the natural habitat animal exhibits as well as the park architecture and landscaping. At the *Unofficial Guide*, we marvel at how demographically similar readers come away with such vastly differing opinions. A 36-year-old mother of three, for example, exclaims that:

> *The Animal Kingdom is a monstrous disappointment! Disney should be ashamed to have their name on it!*

While a 34-year-old mom with two children reports:

> *The Animal Kingdom was our favorite theme park at Disney World. We spent four evenings out of our seven-day vacation there.*

ARRIVING

The Animal Kingdom is situated off Osceola Parkway in the southwest corner of Walt Disney World, and is not too far from Blizzard Beach, the Coronado Springs Resort, and the All-Star resorts. From I-4, take Exit 25B, US 192, to the so-called Walt Disney World main entrance (World Drive) and follow the signs to the Animal Kingdom. The Animal Kingdom has its own 6,000-car pay parking lot with close-in parking for the disabled. Once parked, you can walk to the entrance or catch a ride on one of Disney's trademark trams. Be sure to mark the location of your car on your parking receipt and tuck it in a safe place (preferably on your person as opposed to in your car).

Though there was some discussion about a monorail loop linking the Animal Kingdom with the Transportation and Ticket Center and Disney-MGM Studios, the new park will remain connected to other Walt Disney World destinations by the Disney bus system for the foreseeable future.

They don't have much experience with real animals, but I'm sure everything will be fine.

A WORD ABOUT ADMISSION

Be forewarned that unused days on multiday "hopper" passports issued prior to the opening of the Animal Kingdom are good only for admission to the Magic Kingdom, Epcot, and Disney-MGM Studios. Thus holders of these older passes must purchase a separate admission for the Animal Kingdom.

OPERATING HOURS AND EARLY ENTRY

The Animal Kingdom, not unexpectedly, hosted tremendous crowds during its first two years. Consequently, Disney management has done a fair amount of fiddling and experimenting with operating hours and opening procedures. Generally, the Animal Kingdom opens earlier than the other three parks. In the summer of 1999 it was common practice to advertise 7 or 8 a.m. as the official opening time, but to open certain sections of the park as early as 6 or 7 a.m. If you are wondering whether any guests are actually on hand at such an ungodly hour, the answer is yes. If you arrive at the Animal Kingdom between 6 and 7 a.m., you will have plenty of company.

The reasoning behind such an early opening is rooted in the basic circadian rhythms of the animals and how the zookeepers take care of them. Most of the Animal Kingdom's 1,000 or so specimens are lodged in buildings or large protected enclosures at night and released into the natural habitat viewing areas during the day. Simply put, almost all are early-to-rise, early-to-bed type critters. The ones that are not, such as lions, cheetahs, and hyenas, who might enjoy a little hunting at night, don't have anything to hunt. So, at the Animal Kingdom, everybody gets plenty of sleep. You, on the other hand, will require a day of recuperation from having stumbled out of bed in the dead of night to go to the theme park. In any event, opening early allows the Animal Kingdom to also close early (usually 8 p.m. or so) and still provide guests with approximately 12–13 hours of touring time.

Because the Animal Kingdom opens so early anyway, there are no designated early-entry days as at the other three parks. This means that everyone has the same opportunity to be among the first to enter the park.

Park opening procedures at the Animal Kingdom vary. Usually guests arriving prior to the official opening time are admitted to The Oasis and Safari Village. The remainder of the park will be roped off until official opening time. On holidays and other days of projected heavy attendance, Disney will open the entire park 30 or 60 minutes early. Our advice is to arrive, admission in hand, an hour before official opening during the summer and holiday periods, and 40 minutes before official opening the rest of the year.

WHEN TO GO

For the time being, expect to encounter large crowds at the Animal Kingdom. The best days of the week to go are Saturday and Sunday in the summer and Wednesday and Thursday year-round. Next best is Friday. Avoid Saturday and Sunday during the school year, and Monday regardless of season.

Because the park opens so early, many guests wrap up their tour and leave by 3:30 or 4 p.m. Lines for the major rides and the 3-D movie in the Tree of Life will usually thin appreciably between 4:30 p.m. and closing time. If you arrive at 3 p.m. and take in a couple of stage shows (described later), waits should be tolerable by the time you hit the Tree of Life and the rides. As an added bonus for late-afternoon touring, the animals tend to be more active.

GETTING ORIENTED

At the entrance plaza are ticket kiosks fronting the main entrance. To your right before the turnstiles are the kennel and an ATM. Passing through the turnstiles, wheelchair and stroller rentals are to your right. Guest Relations, the park headquarters for information, handout park maps, entertainment schedules, missing persons, and lost and found, is to the left. Nearby are rest rooms, public phones, and rental lockers. Beyond the entrance plaza you enter The Oasis, a lushly vegetated network of converging pathways winding through a landscape punctuated with streams, waterfalls, and misty glades, and inhabited by what Disney calls "colorful and unusual animals."

The park is arranged somewhat like the Magic Kingdom, in a hub-and-spoke configuration. The lush, tropical Oasis serves as Main Street, funneling visitors to Safari Village on an island at the center of the park. Dominated by the park's central icon, the 14-story-tall, handcarved Tree of Life, Safari Village is the park's retail and dining center. From Safari Village, guests can access the respective theme areas: Africa, Camp Minnie-Mickey, Asia, and DinoLand U.S.A. Safari Village additionally hosts two attractions: a boat ride and a theater in the Tree of Life.

To help you plan your day, we have profiled all of the Animal Kingdom's major attractions. We suggest, however, that you be open-minded and try everything. Disney rides and shows are rarely what you would anticipate. For the time being, even if you dawdle in the shops and linger over the wildlife exhibits, you should easily be able to take in the Animal Kingdom in one day.

The Oasis

Though the functional purpose of The Oasis is the same as that of Main Street in the Magic Kingdom (i.e., to funnel guests to the center of the park), it also serves as what Disney calls a "transitional experience." In plain English,

Not to Be Missed at the Animal Kingdom	
Safari Village	*It's Tough to Be a Bug!*
Camp Minnie-Mickey	*Festival of the Lion King*
Africa	Kilimanjaro Safaris
DinoLand U.S.A.	Countdown to Extinction
	Tarzan Rocks!

this means that it sets the stage and gets you into the right mood to enjoy the Animal Kingdom. You will know the minute you pass through the turnstiles that this is not just another Main Street. Where Main Street, Hollywood Boulevard, and the Epcot entrance plaza direct you like an arrow straight into the heart of the respective parks, The Oasis immediately envelops you in an environment that is replete with choices. There is not one broad thoroughfare, but rather multiple paths. Each will deliver you to Safari Village at the center of the park, but which path you choose and what you see along the way is up to you. There is nothing obvious about where you are going, no Cinderella Castle or giant golf ball to beckon you. There is instead a lush, green, canopied landscape with streams, grottos, and waterfalls, an environment that promises adventure without revealing its nature.

The natural-habitat zoological exhibits in The Oasis are representative of those throughout the park. Although extraordinarily lush and beautiful, the exhibits are primarily designed for the comfort and well-being of the animals. This means in essence that you must be patient and look closely if you want to see the animals. A sign will identify the animal(s) in each exhibit, but there's no guarantee the animals will be immediately visible. Because most habitats are large and provide ample terrain for the occupants to hide, you must linger and concentrate, looking for small movements in the vegetation. When you do spot the animal, you may only make out a shadowy figure, or perhaps only a leg or a tail will be visible. In any event, don't expect the animals to stand out like a lump of coal in the snow. Animal-watching Disney-style requires a sharp eye and a bit of effort.

Touring Tips The Oasis is a place to linger and appreciate, and although this is exactly what the designers intended, it will be largely lost on Disney-conditioned guests who blitz through at warp speed to queue up for the big attractions. If you are a blitzer in the morning, plan to spend some time in The Oasis on your way out of the park. The Oasis usually opens 30 minutes before and closes 30–60 minutes after the rest of the park.

Safari Village

Safari Village is an island of tropical greenery and whimsical equatorial African architecture, executed in vibrant hues of teal, yellow, red, and blue. Connected to the other lands by bridges, the island is the hub from which guests can access the park's various theme areas. The village is arrayed in a crescent around the base of the Animal Kingdom's signature landmark, the Tree of Life. Towering 14 stories above the village, the Tree of Life is this park's version of Cinderella Castle or Spaceship Earth. Flanked by pools, meadows, and exotic gardens populated by a diversity of birds and animals, the Tree of Life houses a theater attraction inspired by the Disney/Pixar film, *A Bug's Life*.

As you enter Safari Village via the bridge from The Oasis and the main entrance, you will see the Tree of Life directly ahead at the 12 o'clock position, with the village at its base in a rough semicircle. The bridge to Asia is to the left of the tree at the 2 o'clock position, with the bridge to DinoLand

---

Animal Kingdom Services

Most of the park's service facilities are located inside the main entrance and in Safari Village as follows:

Wheelchair & Stroller Rentals	Inside the main entrance to the right.
Banking Services	ATMs are located at the main entrance and at Safari Village.
Storage Lockers	Inside the main entrance to the left.
Lost & Found	Inside the main entrance to the left.
Guest Relations/Information	Inside the main entrance to the left.
Live Entertainment/ Parade Information	Included in the park guidemap available free at Guest Relations.
Lost Persons	Lost persons can be reported at Guest Relations and at Baby Services in Safari Village.
First Aid	In Safari Village, next to the Creature Comforts Shop.
Baby Center/ Baby-Care Needs	In Safari Village, next to the Creature Comforts Shop.
Film & Cameras	Just inside the main entrance at Garden Gate Gifts, in Safari Village at Disney Outfitters, and in Africa at Duka La Filimu.

U.S.A. at roughly 4 o'clock. The bridge connecting The Oasis to Safari Village is at the 6 o'clock position; the bridge to Camp Minnie-Mickey is at 8 o'clock; and the bridge to Africa is at 11 o'clock.

Safari Village is the park's central shopping, dining, and services headquarters. It is here that you will find the First Aid and Baby-Care Centers. For the best selection of Disney trademark merchandise, try the Island Mercantile or Disney Outfitters shops. Counter-service food and snacks are available, but there are no full-service restaurants at Safari Village (the only full-service restaurant in the park is the Rainforest Cafe located to the left of the main entrance).

The Tree of Life/It's Tough to Be a Bug!

What It Is: 3-D theater show

Scope & Scale: Major attraction

When to Go: Before 10 a.m. and after 4 p.m.

Special Comments: The theater is inside the tree

Author's Rating: Zany and frenetic; ★★★★

Appeal by Age Group:

Pre-school	Grade School	Teens	Young Adults	Over 30	Senior Citizens
★★½	★★★★★	★★★★★	★★★★	★★★★	★★★★

Duration of Presentation: Approximately 7½ minutes

Probable Waiting Time: 12–30 minutes

Description and Comments The Tree of Life, apart from its size, is quite a work of art. Although from afar it is certainly magnificent and imposing, it is not until you examine the tree at close range that you truly appreciate its rich detail. What appears to be ancient gnarled bark is in fact hundreds of carvings depicting all manner of wildlife, each integrated seamlessly into the trunk, roots, and limbs of the tree. A stunning symbol of the interdependence of all living things, the Tree of Life is the most visually compelling structure to be found in any Disney park.

In sharp contrast to the grandeur of the tree is the subject of the attraction housed within its trunk. Called *It's Tough to Be a Bug!*, this humorous 3-D film is about the difficulties of being a very small creature. *It's Tough to Be a Bug!* also contrasts with the relatively serious tone of the Animal Kingdom in general, standing virtually alone in providing some much needed levity and whimsy. *It's Tough To Be A Bug!* is similar to *Honey, I Shrunk the Audience* at Epcot in that it combines a 3-D film with an arsenal of tactile and visual special effects. In our view, the special effects are a bit overdone and the film somewhat anemic. Even so, we rate the bugs as not to be missed.

Another example of Disney's integrated marketing strategy, the 3-D presentation serves to stimulate demand for *A Bug's Life,* the Disney/Pixar collaboration employing the same computer-animation techniques used in *Toy Story*. In a departure from previous cross-marketing efforts, however, Disney premiered the attraction version first, with the release of the feature film later.

Touring Tips　Because it's situated in the most eye-popping structure in the park, and also because there aren't that many attractions anyway, you can expect *It's Tough to Be a Bug!* to be mobbed most of the day. We recommend going in the morning after Kilimanjaro Safaris, Kali River Rapids, and Countdown to Extinction. If you miss the bugs in the morning, try again in the late afternoon.

Be advised that *It's Tough to Be a Bug!* is very intense and that the special effects will do a number on young children as well as anyone who is squeamish about insects. A mother of two from Mobile shared this experience:

> It's Tough to Be a Bug! *was too intense for any kids. Our boys are five and seven and they were scared to death. They love bugs, and they hated this movie. All of the kids in the theater were screaming and*

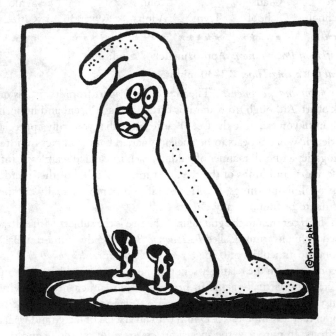

And now, from the people who brought you *A Bug's Life,* here's Larry the Liverfluke.

crying. I felt like a terrible mother for taking them into this movie. It is billed as a bug movie for kids, but nothing about it is for kids.

But a Williamsville, New York, woman had it even worse:

> *We went [to the Animal Kingdom] our very first day and almost lost the girls to any further Disney magic due to the 3-D movie* It's Tough to Be a Bug! *It was their first Disney experience, and almost their last. The story line was nebulous and difficult to follow—all they were aware of was the torture of sitting in a darkened theater being overrun with bugs. Total chaos, the likes of which I've never experienced, was breaking out around us. A constant stream of parents headed to the exits with terrorized children. Those that were left behind were screaming and crying as well. The 11-year-old refused to talk for 20 minutes after the fiasco, and the 3½-year-old wanted to go home—not back to the hotel, but home.*

Radio Disney River Cruise

What It Is: Boat ride around Safari Village

Scope & Scale: Minor attraction

When to Go: Before 10 a.m. or one hour before closing

Author's Rating: Not worth the wait; ★

Appeal by Age Group:

Pre-school	Grade School	Teens	Young Adults	Over 30	Senior Citizens
★★	★	½	½	★	★

Duration of Ride: 17 minutes

Average Wait in Line per 100 People ahead of You: 14 minutes

Assumes: All boats operating

Loading Speed: Slow

Description and Comments Every theme park has at least one really dumb and totally vacuous attraction (some parks have several). At the Animal Kingdom, it's the Radio Disney River Cruise. For an average wait in line of 45 minutes, the cruise treats you to . . . are you ready? . . . the same sights that you can see from the Safari Village bridges! Wow! Originally called Discovery River Boats, the attraction was reincarnated in 1999 as the Radio Disney River Cruise. Essentially, the same boats make the same trip around the Safari Village Island and (with one inconsequential exception) see the same lame sights. The only difference in the "new" attraction is the addition of hip-hop radio chatter and rock music. Whereas before you could at least rest and relax for a few moments, now you're persecuted with the incessant bleating of a pretend radio show. The Disney park map says that the cruise is "especially fun for the kids," but a New York woman begs to differ:

> After [It's Tough to Be a Bug!], we decided to go on something "soothing," the River Cruise. We went from complete chaos to complete boredom in a matter of minutes. This "attraction" needs a major revamping. It certainly wasn't what we've come to expect from Disney.

Touring Tips The best touring tip we can think of regarding the river cruise is to skip it. If you decide to go anyway, try to get on before 10 a.m. or after 6 p.m. Boats load from two docks, one near the Asia Bridge and one by the Oasis Bridge. You'll make the same round-trip circuit and see the same sights regardless of where you board.

Camp Minnie-Mickey

This land is designed to be the Disney characters' Animal Kingdom headquarters. A small land, Camp Minnie-Mickey is about the size of Mickey's Toontown Fair but has a rustic and woodsy theme like a summer camp. In addition to a character meeting and greeting area, Camp Minnie-Mickey is home to two live stage productions featuring Disney characters.

Situated in a cul-de-sac, Camp Minnie-Mickey is a pedestrian nightmare. Lines for the two stage shows and from the character greeting areas spill out into the congested walkways, making movement almost impossible. To compound the problem, hundreds of parked strollers clog the paths, squeezing the flow of traffic to a trickle. Meanwhile, hordes of guests trying to enter Camp Minnie-Mickey collide with guests trying to exit on the bridge connecting the camp to Safari Village. It's a planning error of the first order, one that seems totally avoidable in a theme park with as much usable acreage as the Animal Kingdom.

Character Trails

Description & Comments Characters can be found at the end of each of four "character trails" respectively named Jungle, Forest, Arbor, and Mickey. Each trail has its own private reception area and, of course, its own queue. Jungle Characters features characters from *The Lion King* and *The Jungle Book,* while Forest Characters generally offers characters from *Winnie the Pooh.* The Arbor trail leads to Minnie and the Mickey trail to Mickey. Usually two or three characters are present in the Forest and Jungle greeting areas, while Minnie and Mickey each work solo.

Touring Tips Waiting in line to see the characters can be very time-consuming. We recommend visiting early in the morning or late in the afternoon. Because there are fewer attractions at the Animal Kingdom than at the other parks, expect to find a disproportionate number of guests in Camp Minnie-Mickey. If the place is really mobbed, you may want to consider meeting the characters in one of the other parks. Ditto for the stage shows.

Festival of the Lion King

What It Is: Theater-in-the-round stage show

Scope & Scale: Major attraction

When to Go: Before 11 a.m. or after 4 p.m.

Special Comments: Performance times are listed in the handout park map

Author's Rating: Upbeat and spectacular; ★★★★

Appeal by Age Group:

Pre-school	Grade School	Teens	Young Adults	Over 30	Senior Citizens
★★★★	★★★★½	★★★★	★★★★	★★★★	★★★★

Duration of Presentation: 25 minutes

Preshow Entertainment: None

Probable Waiting Time: 20–35 minutes

Description and Comments This energetic production, inspired by Disney's *Lion King* feature, is part stage show, part parade, and part circus. Guests are seated in four sets of bleachers surrounding the stage and organized into separate cheering sections, which are called on to make elephant, warthog, giraffe, and lion noises. There is a great deal of parading around, some acrobatics, and a lot of singing and dancing. By our count, every tune from *The Lion King* (plus a couple of others) is belted out and reprised several times. No joke, if you don't know the words to all the songs by the end of the show, you must have been asleep.

Unofficial Guide readers have been almost unanimous in their praise of *Festival of the Lion King.* This letter from a Naples, Florida, mom is typical:

> Festival of the Lion King *is a spectacular show with singers, dancers, fire twirlers, acrobats, robotics, and great set design. My whole family agreed that this was the best thing we experienced at Animal Kingdom.*

Touring Tips This show is both popular and difficult to see. Your best bet is to go to the first show in the morning or to one of the last two performances in the evening. To see the show during the more crowded middle of the day, you'll need to queue up at least 35 minutes before show time. There are four separate lines, one for each set of bleachers. The queues fill from left to right and are seated in the same order. To minimize standing in the hot sun, refrain from hopping in line until the Disney people begin directing guests to the far-right queue. If you have small children or short adults in your party, sit higher up in the bleachers. The first five rows in particular have very little rise, making it difficult for those in rows 2–5 to see. Though the theater is covered and air is circulated by fans, there is no air conditioning.

Pocahontas and Her Forest Friends at Grandmother Willow's Grove

What It Is: Conservation-theme stage show

Scope & Scale: Major attraction

When to Go: Before 11 a.m. or after 4 p.m.

Special Comments: Performance times are listed in the handout park map

Author's Rating: A little sappy; ★★½

Appeal by Age Group:

Pre-school	Grade School	Teens	Young Adults	Over 30	Senior Citizens
★★★½	★★★½	★★★	★★★½	★★★	★★★

Duration of Presentation: 15 minutes

Preshow Entertainment: None

Probable Waiting Time: 20–30 minutes

Description and Comments   This show featuring Pocahontas addresses the role of man in protecting the natural world. Various live creatures of the forest, including a raccoon, a snake, and a turkey, as well as a couple of Animatronic trees (Grandmother Willow and Twig), assist Pocahontas in making the point. The presentation is gushy and overacted but has its moments nonetheless.

However, as a Michigan reader reports, *Pocahontas* is not in the same league as *Festival of the Lion King:*

> Festival of the Lion King *was a wonderful show. Unfortunately, we saw it just before seeing the Pocahontas show. It put Pocahontas to shame. Instead of being moved by the show's message, I wondered how much kindling Grandmother Willow would make.*

Touring Tips   Because the theater is relatively small, and because Camp Minnie-Mickey stays so mobbed, the Pocahontas show is hard to get into. Among other problems, its queuing area adjoins that of *Festival of the Lion King* next door. If you approach when a lot of guests are waiting, which is almost always, it's hard to figure out which show you're lining up for. To avoid the hassle, try to catch the show before 11 a.m. or after 4 p.m. Regardless of time of day, arrive at least 20 minutes before show time and ask a Disney cast member to steer you to the correct line.

Africa

The largest of the Animal Kingdom's lands, guests enter through Harambe, Disney's idealized and immensely sanitized version of a modern, rural African town. There is a market (with modern cash registers), and counter-service food is available. What distinguishes Harambe is its understatement. Far from the stereotypical great-white-hunter image of an African town,

Harambe is definitely (and realistically) not exotic. The buildings, while interesting, are quite plain and architecturally simple. Though certainly better maintained and more aseptic than the real McCoy, Disney's Harambe would be a lot more at home in Kenya than the Magic Kingdom's Main Street would be in Missouri.

Harambe serves as the gateway to the African veldt habitat, the Animal Kingdom's largest and most ambitious zoological exhibit. Access to the veldt is via the Kilimanjaro Safaris attraction, located at the end of Harambe's main drag near the fat-trunked baobab tree. Harambe is also the departure point for the train to Conservation Station, the park's veterinary headquarters.

Kilimanjaro Safaris

What It Is: Truck ride through an African wildlife reservation

Scope & Scale: Super headliner

When to Go: As soon as the park opens or in the two hours before closing

Author's Rating: Truly exceptional; ★★★★★

Appeal by Age Group:

Pre-school	Grade School	Teens	Young Adults	Over 30	Senior Citizens
★★★★	★★★★★	★★★★½	★★★★½	★★★★½	★★★★★

Duration of Ride: About 20 minutes

Average Wait in Line per 100 People ahead of You: 4 minutes

Assumes: Full-capacity operation with 18-second dispatch interval

Loading Speed: Fast

Description and Comments   The park's premier zoological attraction, Kilimanjaro Safaris offers an exceptionally realistic, albeit brief, imitation of an actual African photo safari. Thirty-two guests at a time board tall, open safari vehicles and are dispatched into a simulated African veldt habitat. Animals such as zebra, wildebeest, impala, Thomson's gazelle, giraffe, and even rhinos roam apparently free, while predators such as lions, as well as potentially dangerous large animals like hippos, are separated from both prey and guests by all-but-invisible, natural-appearing barriers. Although the animals have more than 100 acres of savanna, woodland, streams, and rocky hills to call home, careful placement of water holes, forage, and salt licks ensure that the critters are hanging out by the road when safari vehicles roll by.

A scripted narration provides a story line about finding Big Red and Little Red, a mother elephant and her baby, while an on-board guide points out and identifies the various animals encountered. Toward the end of the ride, the safari chases poachers who have just wounded Big Red. As the vehicle approaches the safari's terminating point, the poachers are seen being taken into custody.

Having traveled in Kenya and Tanzania, I will tell you that Disney has done an amazing job of replicating the sub-Saharan east African landscape. The main difference that an east African would notice is that Disney's version is greener and generally speaking less barren. And, like on a real African safari, what animals you see (and how many) is pretty much a matter of luck. We tried Disney's safari upwards of a dozen times and had a different experience on each trip.

If the attraction has a shortcoming, it is the rather strident story line about the poachers and Big Red, which while thought provoking, is somewhat distracting when you are trying to spot and enjoy the wildlife. Also, because the story is repeated on every trip, it really gets on your nerves after the first couple of times.

Touring Tips Kilimanjaro Safaris is the Animal Kingdom's top draw. In fact, we've not seen an attraction in any Disney park that so completely channels guest traffic. While Space Mountain, Test Track, and Tower of Terror attract throngs of early-morning guests, there remain a substantial number of additional guests who head for other attractions. At the Animal Kingdom, however, as many as 90% of those on hand at opening head straight for the safari, and later-arriving guests do exactly the same thing. Over the first couple of years, Disney tried any number of ploys to lure guests elsewhere, but to no avail. So, if you want to see Kilimanjaro Safaris without a long wait, be one of the first through the turnstiles and make a beeline for Africa. If you are held up en route by a rope barrier or by cast members, stay put until you are permitted to continue on to the attraction.

Unknown to most guests, there is a park entrance turnstile that can be accessed by passing through the retail area of the Rainforest Cafe. On a day when hundreds are lined up at the main entrance, less than ten guests will be waiting at the Rainforest Cafe entrance. The Rainforest Cafe retail shop usually opens about ten minutes before guests are admitted to the park. So to spell it out, if the official park opening time is 8 a.m., guests will usually be admitted at 7:30 a.m., and the Rainforest Cafe will open at about 7:20 a.m. If the park opens at 7 a.m., guests will usually be admitted at 6:30 and the cafe will open at 6:20. You get the idea. In any event, enter the Rainforest Cafe when they open the doors, turn right through the shop, and wait at the turnstile. Once through the turnstile, you'll pass down a walkway that connects the cafe with The Oasis. When you get to the Oasis turn left. Move quickly through The Oasis without stopping and cross the bridge into Safari Village. Turn left after the bridge and walk clockwise around the

Tree of Life until you reach the bridge to Africa. Cross the bridge and continue straight ahead to the entrance of Kilimanjaro Safaris.

Waits for the Kilimanjaro Safaris diminish in late afternoon, sometimes as early 3:30, but more commonly around 5 or 5:30 p.m. If you miss the safari in the morning, wait until late afternoon and try again.

If you want to take photos on your safari, be advised that the vehicle doesn't stop very often, so be prepared to snap while under way. Also, don't worry about the ride itself: it really isn't very rough. Finally, the only thing that a young child might find intimidating is crossing an "old bridge" that pretends to collapse under your truck.

Pangani Forest Exploration Trail

What It Is: Walk-through zoological exhibit
Scope & Scale: Major attraction
When to Go: Before 10 a.m. or after 3:30 p.m.
Author's Rating: ★★★
Appeal by Age Group:

Pre-school	Grade School	Teens	Young Adults	Over 30	Senior Citizens
★★½	★★★	★★½	★★★	★★★	★★★

Duration of Tour: About 20–25 minutes

Description and Comments Because guests disembark from the safari at the entrance to the Pangani Forest Exploration Trail, most guests try the trail immediately after the safari. Winding between the domain of two troops of lowland gorillas, it's hard to see what, if anything, separates you from the primates. Also on the trail are a hippo pool with an underwater viewing area, a naked mole rat exhibit (I promise I'm not making this up), and some hyenas. A highlight of the trail is an exotic bird aviary so craftily designed that you can barely tell you're in an enclosure.

Touring Tips The Pangani Forest Exploration Trail is lush, beautiful, and jammed to the gills with people most of the time. Guests exiting the safari can choose between returning to Harambe or walking the Pangani Forest Exploration Trail. Not unexpectedly, most opt for the trail. Thus, when the safari is operating at full tilt, it spews hundreds of guests every couple of minutes onto the Exploration Trail. The one-way trail in turn becomes so clogged that nobody can move or see much of anything. After a minute or two, however, you catch the feel of the mob moving forward in small lurches. From then on you shift, elbow, grunt, and wriggle your way along, every so often coming to an animal exhibit. Here you endeavor to work your way close to the rail but are opposed by people trapped against the rail who are trying to rejoin the forward-surging crowd. The animals, as well as their natural-habitat enclosures, are pretty nifty if you can fight close enough to see them.

Clearly this attraction is either badly designed, misplaced, or both. Your only real chance for enjoying it is to walk through before 10 a.m. (i.e., before the safari hits full stride) or after 3:30 p.m.

Wildlife Express

What It Is: Scenic railroad ride to Conservation Station
Scope & Scale: Major attraction
When to Go: Before 10:30 a.m. or after 3 p.m.

Special Comments: Most guests will take the train after returning to Harambe from the Kilimanjaro Safari

Author's Rating: Ho hum; ★★

Appeal by Age Group:

Pre-school	Grade School	Teens	Young Adults	Over 30	Senior Citizens
★★★	★★★	★½	★★½	★★½	★★½

Duration of Ride: About 5–7 minutes one way

Average Wait in Line per 100 People ahead of You: 9 minutes

Loading Speed: Moderate

Description and Comments A transportation ride that snakes behind the African wildlife reserve as it makes its loop connecting Harambe to Conservation Station. En route to Conservation Station, you see the nighttime enclosures for the animals that populate the Kilimanjaro Safaris. Similarly, returning from Conservation Station to Harambe, you see the backstage areas of Asia. Regardless which direction you're heading, the sights are not especially interesting.

Touring Tips Most guests will embark for Conservation Station after experiencing the Kilimanjaro Safaris and the Pangani Forest Exploration Trail. Thus the train begins to get crowded between 10 and 11 a.m. Though you may catch a glimpse of several species from the train, it can't compare to Kilimanjaro Safaris for seeing the animals.

Conservation Station

What It Is: Behind-the-scenes walk-through educational exhibit

Scope & Scale: Minor attraction

When to Go: Before 11 a.m. or after 3 p.m.

Author's Rating: Evolving; ★★★

Appeal by Age Group:

Pre-school	Grade School	Teens	Young Adults	Over 30	Senior Citizens
★★½	★★	★½	★★½	★★½	★★½

Probable Waiting Time: None

Description and Comments Conservation Station is the Animal Kingdom's veterinary and conservation headquarters. Located on the perimeter of the African section of the park, Conservation Station is, strictly speaking, a backstage, working facility. Here guests can meet wildlife experts, observe some of the Station's ongoing projects, and learn about the behind-the-scenes operations of the park. The Station includes, among other things, a rehabilitation area for injured animals and a nursery for recently born (or hatched) critters. Vets and other experts are on-hand to answer questions.

While there are several permanent exhibits, including an animal petting area, what you see at Conservation Station will largely depend on what's going on when you arrive. On the days we visited, there wasn't enough happening to warrant waiting in line twice (coming and going) for the train. Hopefully, Conservation Station will improve with age. Ditto for the train ride.

Most of our readers comment that Conservation Station is not worth the hassle of the train ride. A Tinley Park, Illinois, mom writes:

> Skip Conservation Station at the Animal Kingdom. Between the train ride to get to it and being there, we wasted a precious 1½ hours!

A mother of one from Austin, Texas, had a better experience:

> Best thing at Conservation Station was the wildlife experts presenting one animal at a time—live, with info—very interesting.

And a reader from Kent in the United Kingdom was amused by both the goings-on and the other guests:

> The most memorable part of the Animal Kingdom for me was watching a veterinary surgeon and his team [at Conservation Station] perform an operation on a rat snake that had inadvertently swallowed a golf ball! Presumably believing it to be an egg. This operation took about an hour and caused at least one onlooker to pass out.

You can access Conservation Station by taking the Wildlife Express train directly from Harambe. To return to the center of the park, continue the loop from Conservation Station back to Harambe.

Touring Tips   Conservation Station is interesting, but you have to invest a little effort and it helps to be inquisitive. Because it's on the far-flung border of the park, you'll never bump into Conservation Station unless you take the train.

Asia

Crossing the Asia Bridge from Safari Village, you enter Asia through the village of Anandapur, a veritable collage of Asian themes inspired by the architecture and ruins of India, Thailand, Indonesia, and Nepal. Situated near the bank of the Chakranadi River (translation: the river that runs in circles) and surrounded by lush vegetation, Anandapur provides access to a gibbon exhibit and to Asia's two feature attractions, the Kali River Rapids whitewater raft ride, and the Maharajah Jungle Trek. Also in Asia is the *Flights of Wonder* show, an educational production about birds.

Kali River Rapids

What It Is: Whitewater raft ride

Scope & Scale: Headliner

When to Go: Before 10 a.m. or after 4:30 p.m.

Special Comments: You are guaranteed to get wet

Author's Rating: Short but scenic; ★★★½

Appeal by Age Group:

Pre-school	Grade School	Teens	Young Adults	Over 30	Senior Citizens
★★★★	★★★★	★★★★	★★★½	★★★½	★★★

Duration of Ride: About 5 minutes

Average Wait in Line per 100 People ahead of You: 5 minutes

Loading Speed: Moderate

Description and Comments   Whitewater raft rides have been a hot-weather favorite of theme park patrons for almost 20 years. The ride itself consists of an unguided trip down a man-made river in a circular rubber raft with a platform seating 12 persons mounted on top. The raft essentially floats free in the current and is washed downstream through rapids and waves. Because the river is fairly wide with numerous currents, eddies, and obstacles, there is no telling exactly where the raft will go. Thus, each trip is different and exciting. At the end of the ride a conveyor belt hauls the raft up to be unloaded and prepared for the next group of guests.

What distinguishes Kali River Rapids from other theme park raft rides is Disney's trademark attention to visual detail. Where many raft rides essentially plunge down a concrete ditch, Kali River Rapids flows through a dense rain forest, past waterfalls, temple ruins, and bamboo thickets, emerging into a cleared area where greedy loggers have ravaged the forest, and finally drifting back under the tropical canopy as the river cycles back to Anandapur. Along the way your raft runs a gauntlet of raging cataracts, log jams, and other dangers.

Disney has done a great job with the visuals on this attraction. The queuing area, which winds through an ancient southeast Asian temple, is one of the most striking and visually interesting settings of any Disney attraction. And though the sights on the raft trip itself are also first class, the attraction is marginal in two important respects. First, it's only about 3½ minutes on the water, and second, well . . . it's a weenie ride. Sure, you get wet, but otherwise the drops and rapids are not all that exciting. And how wet do you get? A reader from Plymouth, Michigan, has the answer:

> *The new whitewater rafting ride is great fun but beware!! Rather than just getting a little wet, like Splash Mountain, we were soaked to the skin after this ride. It was beyond "fun getting wet," literally drenching you with buckets of water. Poncho sales were brisk the day we were there.*

Touring Tips This attraction is hugely popular, especially on hot summer days. Ride Kali River Rapids before 10 a.m. or after 4:30 p.m. You can expect to get wet and possibly drenched on this ride. Our recommendation is to wear shorts to the park and bring along a jumbo size trash bag as well as a smaller plastic bag. Before boarding the raft, take off your socks and punch holes in your jumbo bag for your head. Though you can also cut holes for your arms, you will probably stay dryer with your arms inside the bag. Use the smaller plastic bag to wrap around your shoes. If you are worried about mussing your hairdo, bring a third bag for your head.

A Shaker Heights, Ohio, family who adopted our garbage bag attire, however, discovered that staying dry on the Kali River Rapids is not without social consequences:

> *I must tell you that the Disney cast members and the other people in our raft looked at us like we had just beamed down from Mars. Plus, we didn't cut arm holes in our trash bags because we thought we'd stay drier. Only problem was once we sat down we couldn't fasten our seat belts. The Disney person was quite put out and asked sarcastically whether we needed wetsuits and snorkels. After a lot of wiggling and adjusting and helping each other we finally got belted in and off we went looking like sacks of fertilizer with little heads perched on top. It was very embarrassing, but I must admit that we stayed nice and dry.*

Maharaja Jungle Trek

What It Is: Walk-through zoological exhibit
Scope & Scale: Headliner
When to Go: Anytime
Author's Rating: A standard-setter for natural habitat design; ★★★★
Appeal by Age Group:

Pre-school	Grade School	Teens	Young Adults	Over 30	Senior Citizens
★★★	★★★½	★★★	★★★½	★★★★	★★★★

Duration of Tour: About 20–30 minutes

Description and Comments   The Maharaja Jungle Trek is a zoological nature walk similar to the Pangani Forest Exploration Trail, but with an Asian setting and Asian animals. You start with Komodo dragons and then work up to Malayan tapirs. Next is a cave with fruit bats. Ruins of the maharaja's palace provide the setting for Bengal tigers. From the top of a parapet in the palace you can view a herd of blackbuck antelope and Asian deer. The trek concludes with an aviary.

Labyrinthine, overgrown, and elaborately detailed, the temple ruin would be a compelling attraction even without the animals. Throw in a few bats, bucks, and Bengals and you're in for a treat.

Touring Tips   The Jungle Trek does not get as jammed up as the Pangani Forest Exploration Trail and is a good choice for midday touring when most other attractions are crowded. The downside, of course, is that the exhibit showcases tigers, tapirs, and other creatures that might not be as active in the heat of the day as the proverbial mad dogs and Englishmen.

Flights of Wonder at the Caravan Stage

What It Is: Stadium show about birds

Scope & Scale: Major attraction

When to Go: Anytime

Special Comments: Performance times are listed in the handout park map

Author's Rating: Unique; ★★★★

Appeal by Age Group:

Pre-school	Grade School	Teens	Young Adults	Over 30	Senior Citizens
★★★★	★★★★	★★★½	★★★★	★★★★	★★★★

Duration of Presentation: 30 minutes

Preshow Entertainment: None

Probable Waiting Time: 20 minutes

Description and Comments   This show is about a treasure hunter who bumps into the Disney version of the Birdman of Alcatraz. The Birdman helps the treasure hunter, through a sort of humorous, hard-knocks approach, to appreciate our feathery friends. Both interesting and fun, *Flights of Wonder* is well paced and showcases a surprising number of different bird species.

Touring Tips *Flights of Wonder* plays at the stadium located near the Asia Bridge on the walkway into Asia. Though the stadium is covered, it's not air-conditioned, thus, early-morning and late-afternoon performances are more comfortable. Though we did not have any problem getting a seat for *Flights of Wonder*, the show's attendance has picked up since the rest of Asia opened. To play it safe, arrive about 15–20 minutes before show time.

DinoLand U.S.A.

This most typically Disney of the Animal Kingdom's lands is a cross between an anthropological dig and a quirky roadside attraction. Accessible via the bridge from Safari Village, DinoLand U.S.A. is home to a children's play area, a nature trail, a 1500-seat amphitheater, a couple of natural history exhibits, and Countdown to Extinction, one of the Animal Kingdom's two thrill rides.

Countdown to Extinction

What It Is: Motion-simulator dark ride

Scope & Scale: Super headliner

When to Go: Before 10 a.m. or in the hour before closing

Special Comments: Children must be 46" tall to ride (See Switching off on pages 190–192)

Author's Rating: Really improved; ★★★★½

Appeal by Age Group:

Pre- school	Grade School	Teens	Young Adults	Over 30	Senior Citizens
†	★★★★½	★★★★½	★★★★½	★★★★½	★★★½

† Sample size too small for an accurate rating.

Duration of Ride: 3⅓ minutes

Average Wait in Line per 100 People ahead of You: 3 minutes

Assumes: Full-capacity operation with 18-second dispatch interval

Loading Speed: Fast

Description and Comments Countdown to Extinction is a combination track ride and motion simulator. In addition to moving along a cleverly hidden track, the ride vehicle also bucks and pitches (the simulator part) in sync with the visuals and special effects encountered. The plot has you traveling back in time on a mission of rescue and conservation. Your objective, believe it or not, is to haul back a living dinosaur before the species becomes extinct. Whoever is operating the clock, however, cuts it a little close, and you arrive on the prehistoric scene just as a giant asteroid is hurling toward

Earth. General mayhem ensues as you evade carnivorous predators, catch Barney, and make your escape before the asteroid hits.

Countdown to Extinction is a technological clone of the Indiana Jones ride at Disneyland. A good effort, though not as visually interesting as Indiana Jones, Countdown to Extinction serves up nonstop action from beginning to end with brilliant visual effects. Elaborate even by Disney standards, the attraction provides a tense, frenetic ride embellished by the entire Imagineering arsenal of high-tech gimmickry. Although the ride is jerky, it's not too rough for seniors. The menacing dinosaurs, however, along with the intensity of the experience, make Countdown to Extinction a no-go for younger children.

Countdown to Extinction, to our surprise and joy, had been refined and cranked up a couple of notches on the intensity scale after its first year of operation. The latest version is darker, more interesting, and much zippier. A mother from Kansasville, Wisconsin, liked it a lot, commenting:

> Countdown to Extinction is the best ride at WDW. Our group of ten, ranging in age from 65 (grandma) to 8 (grandson), immediately— and unanimously!—got back in line immediately after finishing.

A 20-something guy from Muncie, Indiana, however, wasn't so sure:

> The Countdown to Extinction attraction was the most scariest ride I have ever been on. I'm 24 and love thrill rides, but I didn't open my eyes for half of the ride. I can't believe younger children are permitted to ride.

And speaking of younger children, we got plenty of feedback about their reactions: First, from a Michigan family:

> Beware Countdown to Extinction. My seven-year-old son withstood every ride Disney threw at him, from Body Wars to Space Mountain to Tower of Terror. Countdown, however, did him in. By the end of the ride, he was riding with his head down, scared to look around. It is intense, combining scary visual dinosaur effects with some demanding, roller coaster–like simulation.

Next from a mother of two from Westford, Massachusetts:

> My six-year-old felt the ride Countdown to Extinction was far scarier than Alien Encounter or any other ride at Disney. It is very dark (like Alien), but the dinosaurs pop out at you very quickly—I witnessed several adults who were quite shaken by it as well.

Finally, from a Florida mom:

> *This is definitely not for the fainthearted, and small children should not go on it unless they have nerves of steel!*

Touring Tips   Disney situated Countdown to Extinction in such a remote corner of the park that it takes guests awhile to find it. This, in conjunction with the overwhelming popularity of Kilimanjaro Safaris, left Countdown to Extinction (C.T.E. in DisneySpeak) operating at less than capacity. To bump its numbers up, Disney even tried opening the attraction before the rest of the park, providing access to DinoLand through a backstage gate. By the time we went to press, Countdown was doing better but not attracting crowds comparable to Indiana Jones at Disneyland. Despite the slow start, we expect Countdown to turn into a big draw. Thus we continue to recommend that you ride early after experiencing Kilimanjaro Safaris and Kali River Rapids.

Be forewarned that the technology used in this attraction has been subject to frequent breakdowns at Disneyland. If the ride breaks while you are in line, our suggestion is to stick it out. Usually, it's just a matter of removing a defective ride vehicle, about 10–15 minutes' worth of work.

Theater in the Wild

What It Is: Open-air venue for live stage shows

Scope & Scale: Major attraction

When to Go: Anytime

Special Comments: Performance times are listed in the handout park map

Author's Rating: Not to be missed; ★★★★

Appeal by Age Group:

Pre-school	Grade School	Teens	Young Adults	Over 30	Senior Citizens
★★★★	★★★★	★★★★	★★★★	★★★★	★★★½

Duration of Presentation: 25–35 minutes

Preshow Entertainment: None

Probable Waiting Time: 20–30 minutes

Description and Comments   The Theater in the Wild is a 1500-seat, covered amphitheater. The largest stage production facility in the Animal Kingdom, the theater can host just about any type of stage show. In the summer of 1999, the Theater in the Wild unveiled a rock musical production based on Disney's animated *Tarzan* movie. Called *Tarzan Rocks!*, the show features aerial acts as well as acrobatic stunts, including extreme skating. The musical score is by Phil Collins and drawn from the soundtrack of the film. *Tarzan Rocks!* is fast-paced, funny, high energy, and (big surprise) high decibel. If it's still playing when you visit, try to catch a show. We rate it as not to be missed.

Touring Tips   To get a seat, show up 20–25 minutes in advance for morning and late-afternoon shows, and 25–30 minutes in advance for shows scheduled between noon and 4:30 p.m. Access to the theater is via a relatively narrow pedestrian path. If you arrive as the previous show is letting out, you will feel like a salmon swimming upstream.

The Boneyard

What It Is: Elaborate playground

Scope & Scale: Diversion

When to Go: Anytime

Author's Rating: Stimulating fun for children; ★★★½

Appeal by Age Group:

Pre-school	Grade School	Teens	Young Adults	Over 30	Senior Citizens
★★★★½	★★★★½	—	—	—	—

Duration of Visit: Varies

Waiting Time: None

Description and Comments   This attraction is an elaborate playground, particularly appealing to kids age ten and younger, but visually appealing to all ages. Arranged in the form of a rambling open-air dig site, The Boneyard offers plenty of opportunity for exploration and letting off steam. Playground equipment consists of the skeletons of Triceratops, Tyrannosaurus rex, Brachiosaurus, and the like, on which children can swing, slide, and climb. In addition, there are sand pits where little ones can scrounge around for bones and fossils.

Touring Tips   Not the cleanest Disney attraction, but certainly one where younger children will want to spend some time. Aside from getting dirty, or at least sandy, be aware that The Boneyard gets mighty hot in the Florida sun. Keep your kids well hydrated and drag them into the shade from time to time. If your children will let you, save the playground until after you have experienced the main attractions. Because The Boneyard is situated so close to the center of the park, it's easy to stop in whenever your kids get itchy. While the little ones clamber around on giant femurs and ribs, you can sip a tall cool one in the shade (still keeping an eye on them, of course).

As a Michigan family attests, kids love the Boneyard:

> *The highlight for our kids was the Boneyard, especially the dig site.*
> *They just kept digging and digging to uncover the bones of the wooly*
> *mammoth. It was also in the shade, and there were places for parents*
> *to sit, making it a wonderful resting place.*

A Woodridge, Illinois, dad thinks maybe children love it too much, warning:

> *Beware parents, my kid is eight years old, and in Dinoland all he*
> *wanted to do was dig up the dino bones in the huge sand box. I saw*
> *time and time again parents trying unsuccessfully to drag their kids*
> *away from here so they could visit another attraction. This sand box is*
> *best left toward the end of the day when you just want to sit and relax*
> *while the kids let off energy.*

Be aware that The Boneyard rambles over about a half-acre and is multi-storied. It's pretty easy to lose sight of a small child in the playground. Fortunately, there's only one entrance and exit. A mother of two from Stillwater, Minnesota, found the playground too large for her liking:

> *If you are a parent who likes to have your eyes on your kids at all*
> *times, The Boneyard is very scary for adults. Kids climb to the top [of*
> *the slides], and you can't see them at the top and you don't know what*
> *chute they will be exiting. It made me VERY nervous because I could*
> *not see them at all times. We left immediately!!*

Cretaceous Trail

What It Is: Walk-through floral exhibit

Scope & Scale: Diversion

When to Go: Anytime

Author's Rating: Stretches a point to be called an attraction; ★★

Appeal by Age Group:

Pre-school	Grade School	Teens	Young Adults	Over 30	Senior Citizens
★½	★★	★½	★★	★★	★★

Duration of Visit: Varies

Waiting Time: None

Description and Comments The Cretaceous Trail is a footpath through a replica of a primeval forest. Lush and haunting, the trail is enveloped by cycads, ferns, palms, and other flora that thrived in prehistoric forests and swamps. There are a few surprises as well, including a survivor or two from Countdown to Extinction. Most guests, however, just assume that the trail is part of the DinoLand landscaping and walk through without realizing that Disney calls it an attraction.

Touring Tips   Children will find the trail diverting for awhile but will be ready pretty quickly to move on to something else. Go whenever you are feeling green and shady.

Live Entertainment in the Animal Kingdom

Stage Shows   Stage shows are performed daily at the Theater in the Wild in DinoLand U.S.A., at Grandmother Willow's Grove and at the Lion King Theater in Camp Minnie-Mickey, and at the stadium in Asia. Presentations at Camp Minnie-Mickey and DinoLand U.S.A. feature the Disney characters.

Street Performers   Street performers can be found most of the time at Safari Village, at Harambe in Africa, at Anandapur in Asia, and in DinoLand U.S.A.

March of the ARTimals   The Animal Kingdom offers a modest parade called the *March of the ARTimals*. Though not as elaborate as parades at the Magic Kingdom or Disney-MGM Studios, the parade is pleasant enough. Parades in the Animal Kingdom start next to the Creature Comforts shop in Safari Village and cross the Africa Bridge. Turning right, the parade proceeds along the path connecting Africa and Asia before making a right turn over the Asia Bridge back into Safari Village. From here the parade completes the circuit through Safari Village back to the starting point.

There are either one or two parades each day, always in the afternoon. Check Guest Relations for starting times. If you are a big fan of Disney parades, check it out. Otherwise, for the moment, we don't think that the parade is worth a special effort to see.

Animal Encounters   Throughout the day, knowledgeable Disney staff conduct impromtu short lectures on specific animals at the park. Look for a cast member in safari garb holding a bird, reptile, or small mammal.

Goodwill Ambassadors   A number of Asian and African natives are on-hand throughout the park. Both gracious and knowledgeable, they are delighted to discuss their country and its wildlife. Look for them in Harambe and along the Pangani Forest Exploration Trail in Africa, and in Anandapur and along the Maharaja Jungle Trek in Asia. They can also be found near the main entrance and at The Oasis.

Shopping in the Animal Kingdom

While most of the shopping at the Animal Kingdom is concentrated in Safari Village, Harambe in Africa, Anandapur in Asia, and DinoLand U.S.A., any nook or hut large enough to house a cash register is likely to sell something. Typical items for sale include wildlife- and conservation-inspired merchandise a la The Nature Company, along with African wood-carving, crafts, and garb, as well as safari attire, dinosaur specialty items, and the inevitable assortment of Disney character goods. The two largest shops, both located in Safari Village, are Island Mercantile and Disney Outfitters.

Frankly, we are disappointed with the selection of merchandise at the Animal Kingdom. There is a surprising scarcity of imported wares from Africa and Asia, and a teeming overabundance of Disney trademark stuff and tacky souvenirs. If you are looking for something interesting and nice, you are much more likely to find it at World Showcase in Epcot or at Downtown Disney.

Traffic Patterns in the Animal Kingdom

For starters, because the Animal Kingdom is new, expect huge crowds for the foreseeable future, even during the off-season. The four crowd magnets are *It's Tough to Be a Bug!* in the Tree of Life, Kilimanjaro Safaris in Africa, Countdown to Extinction in DinoLand U.S.A., and Kali River Rapids in Asia.

Because the park hosts large crowds with only a relative handful of attractions, expect for all the attractions to be extremely busy, and for Kilimanjaro Safaris to be mobbed. Most guests arrive in the morning, with a sizable number on-hand prior to opening and a larger wave arriving between 8 and 9:30 a.m. Guests continue to stream in through the late morning and into the early afternoon, with the crowds peaking at around 2 p.m. From about 2:30 p.m. on, departing guests outnumber arriving guests by a wide margin, as guests who arrived early complete their tour and leave. Crowds thin appreciably by late afternoon and continue to decline into the early evening.

Because the number of attractions, including theater presentations, are limited, most guests complete a fairly comprehensive tour in two-thirds of a day if they arrive early. Thus, generally speaking, your best bet for easy touring is either to be on-hand when the park opens or to arrive at about 3 p.m., when the early birds are heading for the exits. If you decide to visit during the late afternoon, you might have to return on another afternoon to see everything.

How guests tour the Animal Kingdom depends on their prior knowledge of the park and its attractions. Guests arriving without much prior knowledge make their way to Safari Village and depend on their handout park map to decide what to do next. Most are drawn to Africa and Kilimanjaro Safaris. A smaller number visit DinoLand U.S.A. first. Those guests who have boned up on the Animal Kingdom make straight for Kilimanjaro Safaris in Africa and Countdown to Extinction in DinoLand U.S.A. Kali River Rapids in Asia and *It's Tough to Be a Bug!* in the Tree of Life are also early-morning favorites.

At the Magic Kingdom you can tour clockwise or counterclockwise without returning to the central hub. To go from land to land at the Animal Kingdom, however, you usually have to pass through Safari Village. Safari Village and its attractions thus draw crowds earlier than the other lands and remain inundated throughout the day. Africa, likewise, draws heavy attendance but is set up to move crowds through in a controlled sequence. Attractions in DinoLand U.S.A., with the exception of Countdown to Extinction, will be easily accessible most of the day. Camp Minnie-Mickey is congested from 9:30 a.m. until about 4 p.m., more because of poor traffic design than popularity.

Animal Kingdom One-Day Touring Plan for Visitors of All Ages

Touring the Animal Kingdom is not as complicated as touring the other parks because it offers a smaller number of attractions. Also, most Animal Kingdom rides, shows, and zoological exhibits are oriented to the entire family, thus eliminating differences of opinion regarding how to spend the day. At the Animal Kingdom the whole family can pretty much see and enjoy everything together.

Since there are fewer attractions than at the other parks, expect the crowds at the Animal Kingdom to be more concentrated. If a line seems unusually long, ask an Animal Kingdom cast member what the estimated wait is. If the wait exceeds your tolerance, try the same attraction again after 3 p.m., while a show is in progress at the Theater in the Wild in DinoLand U.S.A., or while some special event is going on.

The Animal Kingdom One-Day Touring Plan assumes a willingness to experience all major rides and shows. Be forewarned that Countdown to Extinction and Kali River Rapids are sometimes frightening to children under age eight. Similarly, the theater attraction at the Tree of Life might be too intense for some preschoolers. When following the touring plan, simply skip any attraction you do not wish to experience.

Before You Go

1. Call (407) 824-4321 before you go to learn the park's hours of operation.
2. Purchase your admission prior to arrival. You can either order tickets through the mail or buy them at a local Disney Store before you leave home. You can also buy them at the Ocala Disney AAA Travel Center off I-75, if you are driving. If you arrive by plane, purchase your admission at the Disney Store in the Orlando airport or at a Walt Disney World resort hotel.

At the Animal Kingdom

1. Arrive at the park *one hour* before the official opening time during the summer and holiday periods, and *40 minutes* before the official opening time the rest of the year. At the entrance plaza, pick up a park map. Wait at the entrance turnstiles or at the Rainforest Cafe turnstile to be admitted.
2. When admitted through the turnstiles move quickly through The Oasis without stopping and cross the bridge into Safari Village. Turn left after the bridge and walk clockwise around the Tree of Life until you reach the bridge to Africa. Cross the bridge and continue straight ahead to the entrance of Kilimanjaro Safaris. Experience Kilimanjaro Safaris.
3. After the safari, head back toward the Africa bridge to Safari Village, but turn left before crossing. Follow the walkway along the river to Asia. In Asia, ride Kali River Rapids. Be sure to check our suggestions for staying dry on page 559.
4. Following the raft trip, return to the entrance of Asia and turn left over the Asia bridge into Safari Village. Pass the Beastly Bazaar and Flame Tree Barbeque and then turn left and cross the bridge into DinoLand U.S.A. After passing beneath the brontosaurus skeleton angle right and follow the signs to Countdown to Extinction. Ride.
5. Next, retrace your steps to Safari Village, bearing left after you cross the DinoLand bridge. See *It's Tough to Be a Bug!* in the Tree of Life.

6. By now you will have most of the Animal Kingdom's potential bottlenecks behind you. Check your daily entertainment schedule for shows at the Theater in the Wild in DinoLand U.S.A., for *Flights of Wonder* in Asia, and for *Festival of the Lion King* and *Pocahontas* in Camp Minnie-Mickey. Plan the next part of your day around eating lunch and seeing these four shows. Before 11 a.m., arrive about 15 minutes prior to show time. During the middle of the day (11 a.m. to 4 p.m.), you will need to queue up as follows:

   For the Theater in the Wild: 20 minutes before show time

   For the Caravan Stage: 15 minutes before show time

   For Mother Willow's Grove   20–25 minutes before show time

   For the Lion King Theater: 25–35 minutes before show time

7. Between shows, check out Cretaceous Trail and The Boneyard in DinoLand U.S.A., and the zoological exhibits around the Tree of Life and in The Oasis. This is also a good tiem to meet the characters at Camp Minnie-Mickey.

8. Return to Asia and take the Maharajah Jungle Trek.

9. Return to Africa and take the Wildlife Express train to Conservation Station. Tour the exhibits.

10. Depart Conservation Station and catch the train back to Harambe.

11. In Harambe, walk the Pangani Forest Exploration Trail.

12. Shop, snack, or repeat any attractions you especially enjoyed.

13. This concludes the touring plan. Be sure to allocate some time to visit the zoological exhibits in The Oasis on your way out of the park.

Part Thirteen

Disney-MGM Studios, Universal Florida, and Sea World

Disney-MGM Studios vs. Universal Studios Florida

Disney-MGM Studios and Universal Studios Florida are direct competitors. Because both are large and expensive and require at least one day to see, some guests must choose one park over the other. To help you decide, we present a head-to-head comparison of the two parks, followed by a description of each in detail. In the summer of 1999, Universal launched its second major theme park, Universal's Islands of Adventure, which has no direct Disney competitor. The new park is previewed in detail later in this section. A summary profile of Sea World concludes Part 13.

Both Disney-MGM Studios and Universal Studios Florida draw their theme and inspiration from film and television. Both offer movie- and TV-themed rides and shows, some of which are just for fun, while others provide an educational, behind-the-scenes introduction to the cinematic arts. Both parks include working film and television production studios.

Nearly half of Disney-MGM Studios is off-limits to guests except by guided tour, while virtually all of Universal Studios Florida is open to exploration. Unlike Disney-MGM, Universal Florida's open area includes the entire backlot, where guests can walk at leisure among movie sets.

Universal hammers on the point that it's first a working motion-picture and television studio, and only incidentally a tourist attraction.

Whether this assertion is a point of pride with Universal or an apology to the tourist is unclear. It's true, however, that guests are more likely to see movie or television production in progress at Universal Florida than at Disney-MGM. On any day, production crews will be shooting on the Universal backlot in full view of guests who care to watch.

Universal Studios Florida is about twice as large as Disney-MGM, and because almost all of it is open to the public, most of the crowding and congestion so familiar in the streets and plazas of Disney-MGM is eliminated. Universal Studios Florida has plenty of elbow room.

Attractions are excellent at both parks, though Disney-MGM attractions are on average engineered to move people more efficiently. Each park offers a stellar attraction that breaks new ground, transcending in power, originality, and technology any prior standard for theme park entertainment. Universal offers *Terminator 2: 3-D,* which we consider the most extraordinary attraction in any American theme park. Disney-MGM Studios features *The Twilight Zone* Tower of Terror, our pick for the nation's second best attraction. The next best attractions in each park are also well matched: Back to the Future at Universal in a dead heat with Star Tours at Disney-MGM.

Though Universal Studios must be credited with pioneering a number of innovative and technologically advanced rides, it also must be pointed out that Universal's attractions break down more often than Disney-MGM's. Jaws and Kongfrontation, in particular, are notorious for frequent breakdowns.

A Detroit woman who visited Universal Studios on a particularly bad day writes:

> *Kongfrontation was broken, Earthquake was broken (with us in it for 30 minutes), and E.T. was broken (with us in line for 20 minutes). We got VIP passes for Earthquake, to come later without waiting. It was finally on-line at about 6:45, and when we were just about to get on, it broke again. The rides at this park are really stupendous—very different from WDW, but I think they've bit off more than they can chew.*

But a family from Baltimore, Ohio, reports a totally positive experience:

> *I won't categorize Universal [Studios] except to say that it was the best. We centered our trip around WDW, but Universal [Studios] puts Disney to shame. It was not very crowded, the shows are excellent, and the rides are the best we've ever been on as far as entertainment value.*

We all agreed we could spend two to three days at Universal [Studios] and not get bored.

Amazingly, and to the visitor's advantage, each park offers a completely different product mix, so there is little or no redundancy for a person who visits both. Disney-MGM and Universal Studios Florida each provide good exposure to the cinematic arts, though Universal's presentations are generally more informative and comprehensive. Disney-MGM had a distinct edge in educational content until recently, when it turned several of its better tours into infomercials for Disney films. At Universal, you can still learn about post-production, soundstages, set creation, special effects, directing, and cinematography without being bludgeoned by promotional hype.

Stunt shows are similar at both parks. Disney's *Indiana Jones Epic Stunt Spectacular* and Universal's *The Wild, Wild, Wild West Stunt Show* are both staged in 2,000-seat stadiums that allow a good view of the action. The *Dynamite Nights Stuntacular* at Universal is staged in the large lagoon, with patrons taking up viewing positions along the railing. The lagoon provides a realistic setting but is so large that the action sometimes is hard to see or follow. All three shows have their moments, and the two stadium shows are fairly informative. In the final analysis, Disney-MGM wins for drama and intensity, while Universal Studios gets the call for variety.

We recommend you try one of the studios. If you enjoy one, you probably will enjoy the other. If you have to choose between them, consider:

1. Touring Time If you tour efficiently, it takes about seven to eight hours to see Disney-MGM Studios (including a lunch break). Because Universal Studios Florida is larger and contains more (and often less efficiently engineered) rides and shows, touring, including one meal, takes about 9 to 11 hours.

One reader laments:

> *There is a lot more "standing" at Universal Studios, and it isn't as organized as [Disney-MGM]. Many of the attractions don't open until 10 a.m., and many shows seem to be going at the same time. We were not able to see nearly as many attractions at Universal as we were at [Disney-MGM] during the same amount of time. The one plus here is that there seems to be more property, and things are spaced out better so you have more elbow room.*

2. Convenience If you're lodging along International Drive, I-4's northeast corridor, the Orange Blossom Trail (US 441), or in Orlando, Universal

Studios Florida is closer. If you're lodging along US 27 or FL 192 or in Kissimmee or Walt Disney World, Disney-MGM Studios is more convenient.

3. Endurance   Universal Studios Florida is larger and requires more walking than Disney-MGM, but it is also much less congested, so the walking is easier. Both parks offer wheelchairs and disabled access.

4. Cost   Both parks cost about the same for one-day admission, food, and incidentals. All attractions are included in the admission price. If you go for two days, however, check to see if Universal Studios is running its Second-Day-Free promotion. This gives you two days at Universal Studios for the price of one.

5. Best Days to Go   In order, Tuesdays, Mondays, Thursdays, and Wednesdays are best to visit Universal Studios Florida. At Disney-MGM Studios, visit on a day when early entry isn't in effect.

6. When to Arrive   For Disney-MGM, arrive with your ticket in hand 40 minutes before official opening time. For Universal Studios, arrive with your admission already purchased about 50 minutes before official opening time.

7. Young Children   Both Disney-MGM Studios and Universal Studios Florida are relatively adult entertainment offerings. By our reckoning, half the rides and shows at Disney-MGM and about two-thirds at Universal Studios have a significant potential for frightening young children.

8. Food   Food is generally much better at Universal Studios.

Disney-MGM Studios

Disney-MGM Studios was hatched from a corporate rivalry and a wild, twisted plot. At a time when the Disney Company was weak and fighting off greenmail—hostile takeover bids—Universal's parent company, MCA announced they were going to build an Orlando clone of their wildly successful Universal Studios Hollywood theme park. Behind the scenes, MCA was courting the real-estate rich Bass brothers of Texas, hoping to secure the brothers' investment in the project. The Bass brothers, however, defected to the Disney camp, helped Disney squelch the hostile takeovers, and were front and center when Michael Eisner suddenly announced that Disney would also build a movie theme park in Florida. A construction race ensued, with Universal and Disney each intent on opening first. Universal, however, was midprocess in the development of a host of new attraction technologies and was no match for Disney, who could import proven concepts and attractions from their other parks. In the end,

Disney-MGM Studios opened almost two years before Universal Studios Florida.

THE MGM CONNECTION

To broaden the appeal and to lend additional historical impact, Disney obtained the rights to use the MGM (Metro-Goldwyn-Mayer) name, film library, motion-picture and television titles, excerpts, costumes, music, sets, and even Leo, the MGM lion. Probably the two most recognized names in motion pictures, Disney and MGM represent almost a century of movie history.

COMPARING DISNEY-MGM STUDIOS TO THE MAGIC KINGDOM AND EPCOT

The Magic Kingdom entertains, modeling its attractions on Disney movies and TV. Epcot educates, pioneering exhibits and rides that teach. Disney-MGM does both. All three parks rely heavily on Disney special effects and Audio-Animatronics (robotics) in their entertainment mix.

Disney-MGM Studios is about the size of the Magic Kingdom and about half as large as the sprawling Epcot. Unlike the parks, Disney-MGM is a working motion-picture and television production facility. This means, among other things, that about half of it has controlled access, with guests permitted only on guided tours or observation walkways.

When Epcot opened in 1982, Disney patrons expected a futuristic version of the Magic Kingdom. What they got was humanistic inspiration and a creative educational experience. Since then, Disney has tried to inject more magic, excitement, and surprise into Epcot. Remembering the occasional disappointment of those early Epcot guests, Disney fortified the Studios with megadoses of action, suspense, surprise, and, of course, special effects. The formula has proved so successful that it's being trotted out again at the new Animal Kingdom theme park. If you want to learn about the history and technology of movies and television, Disney-MGM Studios will teach you plenty. If you just want to be entertained, you won't leave disappointed.

Self-Promotion Run Amok

While it's true that Disney-MGM Studios educates and entertains, what it does best is promote. Self-promotion of Disney films and products was once subtle and in context. It is now blatant, inescapable, and detracting. The walking segment of the backstage tour, for example, at one time was an informative and masterfully scripted introduction to special effects, set

---

Not to Be Missed at Disney-MGM Studios

Star Tours
Disney-MGM Studios Backlot Tour
The Magic of Disney Animation
Indiana Jones Epic Stunt Spectacular
The Great Movie Ride
Jim Henson's MuppetVision 4D
Fantasmic!
Voyage of the Little Mermaid
The Twilight Zone Tower of Terror
Rock 'n' Roller Coaster

---

design, and the use of sound stages. The same tour today is no more than an infomercial for the latest Disney feature, with continuity, coherence, and educational content sacrificed for hype. Likewise, segments of The Magic of Disney Animation tour now advertise rather than enlighten. Although most visitors are willing to forgive Disney its excesses, Studios' veterans will lament the changes and remember how good it was when education was the goal instead of the medium.

HOW MUCH TIME TO ALLOCATE

It's impossible to see all of Epcot or the Magic Kingdom in one day. Disney-MGM Studios, however, is more manageable. There's much less ground to cover by foot. Trams carry guests through much of the backlot and working areas, and attractions in the open-access parts are concentrated in an area about the size of Main Street, Tomorrowland, and Frontierland combined. Someday, no doubt, as Disney-MGM develops and grows, you'll need more than a day to see everything. For now, the Studios is a nice one-day outing.

Because Disney-MGM is smaller, however, it's more affected by large crowds. Our touring plans will help you stay a step ahead of the mob and minimize waiting in line. Even when the park is crowded, however, you can see almost everything in a day.

DISNEY-MGM STUDIOS IN THE EVENING

Because Disney-MGM Studios can be seen in three-fourths of a day, many guests who arrive early in the morning run out of things to do by 3:30 or 4 p.m. and leave the park. Their departure greatly thins the crowd and makes the Studios ideal for evening touring. Lines for most attractions are manageable, and the park is cooler and more comfortable. The *Indiana Jones Epic*

Stunt Spectacular and productions at other outdoor theaters are infinitely more enjoyable during the evening than in the sweltering heat of the day.

One drawback to touring the Studios at night is that there won't be much activity on the production soundstages or in the Animation Building. Another is that you might get stuck eating dinner at the Studios. (If you must eat there, try Mama Melrose's or The Hollywood Brown Derby for full-service dining.)

In 1998, the Studios launched *Fantasmic!* (see pages 591–592), arguably the most spectacular nighttime entertainment event in the Disney repertoire. Staged nightly (weather permitting) in its own theater behind the Tower of Terror, *Fantasmic!* is rated as "not to be missed." Unfortunately, evening crowds have increased substantially at the studios because of *Fantasmic!* Some guests stay longer at Disney-MGM and others arrive after dinner from other parks expressly to see the show. Although crowds thin in the late afternoon, they build again as performance time approaches, making *Fantasmic!* a challenge to get into. Also adversely affected are the Tower of Terror and the Rock 'n' Roller Coaster, both situated near the entrance to *Fantasmic!* Crowd levels throughout the remainder of the park, however, are generally light.

ARRIVING

Disney-MGM Studios has its own pay parking lot and is served by the Disney transportation system. Most larger hotels outside the World shuttle guests to the Studios. If you drive, Disney's ubiquitous trams will transport you to the ticketing area and entrance gate.

GETTING ORIENTED

Guest Relations, on your left as you enter, serves as the park headquarters and information center, similar to City Hall in the Magic Kingdom and Guest Relations at Epcot and the Animal Kingdom. Go there for a schedule of live performances, lost persons, Package Pick-up, lost and found (on the right side of the entrance), general information, or in an emergency. If you haven't received a map of the Studios, get one here. To the right of the entrance are locker, stroller, and wheelchair rentals.

About one-half of the complex is set up as a theme park. As at the Magic Kingdom, you enter the park and pass down a main street. Only, this time it's Hollywood Boulevard of the 1920s and '30s. At the end of Hollywood Boulevard is a replica of Hollywood's famous Chinese Theater. While not as imposing as Cinderella Castle or Epcot's Spaceship Earth, the theater nevertheless is Disney-MGM Studios' most central landmark and a good meeting place if your group becomes separated.

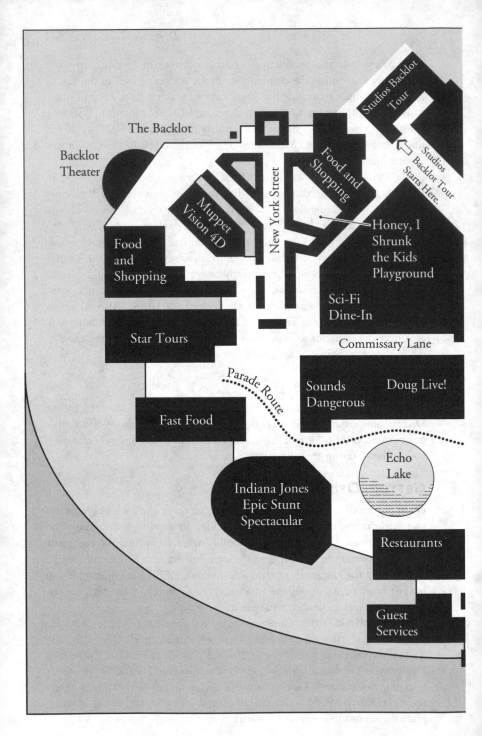

The Backlot

Backlot
Theater

Studios Backlot
Tour

Studios
Backlot Tour
Starts Here.

Food and
Shopping

Muppet
Vision 4D

New York Street

Honey, I
Shrunk
the Kids
Playground

Food
and
Shopping

Sci-Fi
Dine-In

Star Tours

Commissary Lane

Parade Route

Sounds
Dangerous

Doug Live!

Fast Food

Echo
Lake

Indiana Jones
Epic Stunt
Spectacular

Restaurants

Guest
Services

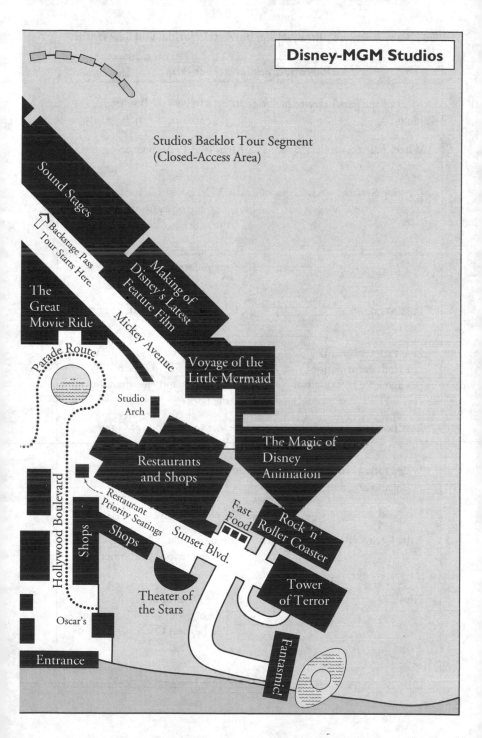

Disney-MGM Studios

Studios Backlot Tour Segment
(Closed-Access Area)

Sound Stages

Backstage Pass
Tour Starts Here.

The Great Movie Ride

Making of Disney's Latest Feature Film

Mickey Avenue

Parade Route

Voyage of the Little Mermaid

Studio Arch

The Magic of Disney Animation

Restaurants and Shops

Hollywood Boulevard

Restaurant Priority Seatings

Sunset Blvd.

Fast Food

Rock 'n' Roller Coaster

Shops

Shops

Theater of the Stars

Tower of Terror

Oscar's

Entrance

Fantasmic!

Hollywood Boulevard Services

Most of the park's service facilities are on Hollywood Boulevard, including:

Wheelchair & Stroller Rental Service	Right of the entrance at Oscar's
Banking Services	An ATM is outside the park to the right of the turnstiles.
Storage Lockers	Rental lockers are right of the main entrance, on the left of Oscar's.
Lost & Found	At Package Pick-up, right of the entrance
Live Entertainment/ Parade Information/ Character Information	Included in the park guidemap available free at Guest Relations and elsewhere in the park
Lost Persons	Report lost persons at Guest Relations.
Walt Disney World & Local Attraction Information	At Guest Relations
First Aid	At Guest Relations
Baby Center/Baby-Care Needs	At Guest Relations. Oscar's sells baby food and other necessities.
Film	At The Darkroom on the right side of Hollywood Boulevard, just beyond Oscar's

Though modest in size, the open-access areas of the Studios are confusingly arranged (a product of the park's hurried expansion in the early '90s). As you face the Chinese Theater, two guest areas, Sunset Boulevard and the Animation Courtyard, branch off Hollywood Boulevard to the right. Branching left off Hollywood Boulevard is the Echo Lake area. The open-access backlot wraps around the back of Echo Lake, the Chinese Theater, and the Animation Courtyard. You can experience all attractions here and in the other open-access sections of the park according to your tastes and time. Still farther to the rear is the limited access backlot, consisting of the working soundstages, technical facilities, wardrobe shops, administrative offices, animation studios, and backlot sets. These are accessible to visitors on a guided tour by tram and foot.

WHAT TO SEE

Try everything. As we have with the Magic Kingdom, Animal Kingdom, and Epcot, we identify attractions as "not to be missed." But Disney rides and shows usually exceed your expectations and always surprise.

CHALKBOARD WITH WAITING TIMES

At the corner of Hollywood and Sunset boulevards is a large chalkboard listing current waiting times for all Disney-MGM Studios attractions. It's updated continuously throughout the day. We've found the waiting times listed to be slightly conservative. If the chalkboard says the wait for Star Tours is 45 minutes, for example, you probably will have to wait about 35 to 40 minutes.

Disney-MGM Studios in Detail

Hollywood Boulevard

Hollywood Boulevard is a palm-lined re-creation of Hollywood's main drag during the city's golden age. Architecture is streamlined *moderne* with art deco embellishments. Most service facilities are here, interspersed with eateries and shops. Merchandise includes Disney trademark items, Hollywood and movie-related souvenirs, and one-of-a-kind collectibles obtained from studio auctions and estate sales.

Hollywood characters and roving performers entertain on the boulevard, and daily parades and other happenings pass this way.

Sunset Boulevard

Sunset Boulevard, evoking the 1940s, is a major new addition to Disney-MGM Studios. The first right off Hollywood Boulevard, Sunset Boulevard provides another venue for dining, shopping, and street entertainment.

The Twilight Zone Tower of Terror

What It Is: Sci-fi-theme indoor thrill ride

Scope & Scale: Super headliner

When to Go: Before 9:30 a.m. and after 6 p.m.

Author's Rating: Walt Disney World's best attraction; not to be missed;
★★★★★

Appeal by Age Group:

Pre-school	Grade School	Teens	Young Adults	Over 30	Senior Citizens
★★★	★★★★★	★★★★★	★★★★★	★★★★★	★★★★½

Duration of Ride: About 4 minutes plus preshow
Average Wait in Line per 100 People ahead of You: 4 minutes
Assumes: All elevators operating
Loading Speed: Moderate

Description and Comments　The Tower of Terror is a new species of Disney thrill ride, though it borrows elements of The Haunted Mansion at the Magic Kingdom. The story is that you're touring a once-famous Hollywood hotel gone to ruin. As at Star Tours, the queuing area integrates guests into the adventure as they pass through the hotel's once-opulent public rooms. From the lobby, guests are escorted into the hotel's library, where Rod Serling, speaking on an old black-and-white television, greets the guests and introduces the plot.

The Tower of Terror is a whopper, 13-plus-stories tall. Breaking tradition in terms of visually isolating themed areas, you can see the entire Studios from atop the tower, but you have to look quick.

The ride vehicle, one of the hotel's service elevators, takes guests to see the haunted hostelry. The tour begins innocuously, but about the fifth floor things get pretty weird. You have entered the Twilight Zone. Guests are subjected to a full range of special effects as they encounter unexpected horrors and optical illusions. The climax of the adventure occurs when the elevator reaches the top floor (the thirteenth, of course) and the cable snaps.

The Tower of Terror is an experience to savor. Though the final plunge is calculated to thrill, the meat of the attraction is its extraordinary visual and audio effects. There's richness and subtlety here, enough to keep the ride fresh and stimulating after many repetitions.

A senior from the United Kingdom tried the Tower of Terror and liked it very much, writing:

> *I was thankful I had read your review of the Tower of Terror, or I would certainly have avoided it. As you say, it is so full of magnificent detail that it is worth riding, even if you don't fancy the drops involved.*

The Tower has great potential for terrifying young children and rattling more mature visitors. If you have teenagers in your party, use them as experimental probes. If they report back that they really, really liked the Tower of Terror, run as fast as you can in the opposite direction.

Touring Tips　This one ride is worth your admission to Disney-MGM Studios. Because of its height, the Tower is a veritable beacon, visible from outside the park and luring curious guests as soon as they enter. Because of its popularity with school kids, teens, and young adults, you can count on a foot race to the attraction, as well as to the Rock 'n' Roller Coaster when the park opens. For the foreseeable future, expect the Tower to be mobbed most of the day. Experience it first thing in the morning or in the evening before the park closes.

To save time, when you enter the library waiting area, stand in the far back corner diagonally opposite from the door where you entered. When the doors to the loading area open, you'll be one of the first admitted.

If you have young children (or anyone) who are apprehensive about this attraction, ask the attendant about switching off (pages 190–192).

Rock 'n' Roller Coaster

What It Is: Rock music–themed roller coaster

Scope & Scale: Headliner

When to Go: Before 10 a.m. or in the hour before closing

Special Comments: Children must be 3'4" tall to ride. Those younger than age 7 must ride with an adult. Switching off option provided (pages 190–192).

Author's Rating: Disney's wildest American coaster; not to be missed; ★★★★

Appeal by Age Group:

Pre-school	Grade School	Teens	Young Adults	Over 30	Senior Citizens
★★★	★★★★	★★★★	★★★★	★★★★	★★★

Duration of Ride: Almost 3½ minutes

Average Wait in Line per 100 People ahead of You: 2½ minutes

Assumes: All trains operating

Loading Speed: Moderate to fast

Description and Comments This is Disney's answer to the roller coaster proliferation at Universal's Islands of Adventure and Busch Gardens theme parks. Exponentially wilder than Space Mountain or Big Thunder Mountain in the Magic Kingdom, the Rock 'n' Roller Coaster is an attraction for fans of cutting-edge thrill rides. Although the rock icons and synchronized music add measurably to the experience, the ride itself, as opposed to sights and sounds along the way, is the focus here. The Rock 'n' Roller Coaster offers loops, corkscrews, and drops that make Space Mountain seem like the Jungle Cruise. What really makes this metal coaster unusual, however, is that first, it's in the dark (like Space Mountain only with Southern California nighttime scenes instead of space), and second, you're launched up the first hill like a jet off a carrier deck. By the time you crest the hill you'll have gone from 0 to 57 miles per hour in less than three seconds. When you enter the first loop you'll be pulling five g's. By comparison, that's two more g's than astronauts experience at lift-off on a space shuttle.

Is the Rock 'n' Roller the baddest coaster in Florida? Hard to say. Rock 'n' Roller has the fastest launch acceleration by far, and, as we've discussed, it's a themed ride in the dark, but the Incredible Hulk Coaster at Universal's Islands of Adventure and Montu at Busch Gardens are both higher and offer more inversions (i.e., vertical loops, corkscrews, barrel rolls, etc.). Also, Montu is an inverted coaster (the track is overhead and your feet dangle). The Disney entry offers the best visuals, but the view from Hulk and Montu (for those with their eyes open) is pretty spectacular. Finally, Rock 'n' Roller is the only one of the three with a soundtrack synchronized throughout the entire ride.

Touring Tips This ride is not for everyone. If Space Mountain or Big Thunder push your limits, stay away from the Rock 'n' Roller Coaster.

It's new, it's eye-catching, and it's definitely a zippy, albeit deafening, ride. Expect long lines except in the first hour after opening and during the late-evening performance of *Fantasmic!* Ride first thing in the morning followed by the Tower of Terror.

The Great Movie Ride

What It Is: Movie-history indoor adventure ride

Scope & Scale: Headliner

When to Go: Before 10 a.m. and after 5 p.m.

Special Comments: Elaborate, with several surprises

Author's Rating: Unique; ★★★½

Appeal by Age Group:

Pre-school	Grade School	Teens	Young Adults	Over 30	Senior Citizens
★★½	★★★½	★★★½	★★★★	★★★★	★★★★

Duration of Ride: About 19 minutes

Average Wait in Line per 100 People ahead of You: 2 minutes

Assumes: All trains operating

Loading Speed: Fast

Description and Comments Entering through a re-creation of Hollywood's Chinese Theater, guests board vehicles for a fast-paced tour through sound-stage sets from classic films including *Casablanca, Tarzan, The Wizard of Oz, Aliens,* and *Raiders of the Lost Ark.* Each set is populated with new-generation

Disney Audio-Animatronic (robot) characters, as well as an occasional human, all augmented by sound and lighting effects. One of Disney's larger and more ambitious dark rides, The Great Movie Ride encompasses 95,000 square feet and showcases some of the most famous scenes in filmmaking. Life-sized Audio-Animatronic sculptures of stars including Gene Kelly, John Wayne, James Cagney, Julie Andrews, and Harrison Ford inhabit some of the largest sets ever constructed for a Disney ride.

Touring Tips   The Great Movie Ride draws large crowds (and lines) from the moment the park opens. As an interval-loading, high-capacity ride, lines disappear quickly. Even so, waits can exceed an hour after midmorning. (Actual waits usually run about one-third shorter than the time posted on the chalkboard. If the chalkboard indicates an hour's wait, your actual time will be around 40 minutes.)

Doug Live!

What It Is: Audience-participation television production based on Disney's *Doug* cartoon

Scope & Scale: Major attraction

When to Go: After 10 a.m.

Author's Rating: Pure smaltz; ★★★

Appeal by Age Group:

Pre-school	Grade School	Teens	Young Adults	Over 30	Senior Citizens
★★★½	★★★½	★★	★★★	★★½	★★½

Duration of Presentation: 30 minutes

Preshow Entertainment: Participants selected from guests waiting in the preshow area

Probable Waiting Time: 10–20 minutes

Description and Comments   This stage show is a live, musical adaptation of the Disney Channel's *Doug* cartoon show, and features Doug, his nemesis Roger, his friend Skeeter, his would-be girlfriend Patti, and his dog, Porkchop. The plot revolves around shy Doug as he tries to muster the courage to ask Patti to go to a rock concert. Unofficially speaking, if Disney has ever come up with anything sappier, we must have missed it. The Doug character is so fumbling, hesitant, insecure, and frightened that he's actually painful to watch. The characters and story line, however, are very true to the television show, so if you like the cartoon you'll probably enjoy the stage show. Guests are chosen (sometimes conscripted) prior to the show to play minor roles in the production.

Touring Tips   The theater seats 1,000 people, so it is not usually difficult to get in. If you want to be in the production, however, it is essential that you enter the preshow holding area at least 15 minutes before the next performance. Participants for the show are more or less drafted by a casting director from among guests of both genders and all age groups. Those who stand near the director and those who are distinctively (outlandishly?) attired seem to be selected most often. A woman from New York patted herself on the back, writing: "We were selected when we raised our hands and screamed 'Honeymooners!'" Finally, be aware that Disney sometimes uses this facility to tape game shows, temporarily preempting the usual presentation.

Star Tours

What It Is: Indoor space flight–simulation ride
Scope & Scale: Headliner
When to Go: First hour and a half the park is open
Special Comments: Expectant mothers or anyone prone to
   motion sickness are advised against riding. The ride is
   too intense for many children younger than 8.

Motion Sickness WARNING!

Author's Rating: Not to be missed; ★★★★
Appeal by Age Group:

Pre school	Grade School	Teens	Young Adults	Over 30	Senior Citizens
★★★★	★★★★	★★★★	★★★★	★★★★	★★★★

Duration of Ride: About 7 minutes
Average Wait in Line per 100 People ahead of You: 5 minutes
Assumes: All simulators operating
Loading Speed: Moderate to fast

Description and Comments   Based on the continuing *Star Wars* movie series, this attraction is so much fun that it just makes you grin and giggle. Guests ride in a flight simulator modeled after those used for training pilots and astronauts. You're supposedly on a vacation outing in space, piloted by a droid (android, a.k.a. humanoid, a.k.a. robot) on his first flight with real passengers. Mayhem ensues almost immediately. Scenery flashes by, and the simulator bucks and pitches. You could swear you were moving at the speed of light. After several minutes of this, the droid somehow lands the spacecraft, and you discover you're about ten times happier than you were when you boarded.

Touring Tips   Star Tours hasn't been as popular at Disney-MGM Studios as it has been at Disneyland in California. Except on unusually busy days, waits rarely exceed 35–45 minutes. For the first couple of hours the park is open, expect a wait of 25 minutes or less. Even so, see Star Tours before 11 a.m. If you have young children (or anyone) who are apprehensive about this attraction, ask the attendant about switching off (pages 190–192).

Star Tours is near the exit of the 2,000-seat stadium that houses *Indiana Jones*. When an *Indiana Jones* performance lets out, Star Tours is temporarily inundated. Ditto for *MuppetVision 4D* and Disney's *Doug Live!* nearby. If you arrive in the midst of this mayhem, come back later.

Sounds Dangerous

What It Is: Show demonstrating sound effects
Scope & Scale: Minor attraction
When to Go: Before 11 a.m. or after 5 p.m.
Author's Rating: Funny and informative; ★★★
Appeal by Age Group:

Pre-school	Grade School	Teens	Young Adults	Over 30	Senior Citizens
★★½	★★★½	★★★	★★★	★★★	★★★★

Duration of Presentation: 12 minutes
Preshow Entertainment: Video introduction to sound effects
Probable Waiting Time: 15–30 minutes

Description and Comments   *Sounds Dangerous*, a film presentation starring Drew Carey as a blundering detective, is the vehicle for a crash course on movie and TV sound effects. Funny, educational, well paced, and (for once) not hawking some Disney flick or product, *Sounds Dangerous* is both entertaining and worthwhile. Earphones worn throughout the show make the various sounds seem very real, indeed . . . perhaps too real for some younger children during a part of the show when the theater is plunged into darkness. Overall, *Sounds Dangerous* is a winner and a vast improvement over the production it replaced.

Touring Tips   Because the theater is relatively small, long waits (partially in the hot sun) are common here. Another thing: *Sounds Dangerous* is periodically inundated by guests coming from a just-concluded performance of *Doug Live!* or the *Indiana Jones Epic Stunt Spectacular*. This is not the time to get in line. Wait at least 30 minutes and try again.

A reader from Israel suggests that a good time to catch *Sounds Dangerous* is just before the afternoon parade. If the parade starts on Hollywood Boulevard, it takes about 15–18 minutes to wind over to the theater—just long enough to catch the show and pop out right in time for the parade.

Indiana Jones Epic Stunt Spectacular

What It Is: Movie-stunt demonstration and action show

Scope & Scale: Headliner

When to Go: First three morning shows or last evening show

Special Comments: Performance times posted on a sign at the entrance to the theater

Author's Rating: Done on a grand scale; ★★★★

Appeal by Age Group:

Pre-school	Grade School	Teens	Young Adults	Over 30	Senior Citizens
★★★	★★★★	★★★★	★★★★	★★★★	★★★★

Duration of Presentation: 30 minutes

Preshow Entertainment: Selection of "extras" from audience

Probable Waiting Time: None

Description and Comments Coherent and educational, though somewhat unevenly paced, the popular production showcases professional stunt men and women who demonstrate dangerous stunts with a behind-the-scenes look at how it's done. Sets, props, and special effects are very elaborate.

While most live shows at Walt Disney World are revised from time to time, the *Stunt Spectacular,* as a Hamden, Connecticut, man laments, has not changed for years:

> *Another bust was the Indy Jones show. The show is the same as it has been since it opened, but the acting grows tired. This is due for a restaging. Its counterpart at Universal,* The Wild [Wild, Wild] West Stunt Show, *was deemed superior by my group.*

Touring Tips The Stunt Theater holds 2,000 people; capacity audiences are common. The first performance is always the easiest to see. If the first show is at 9:30 a.m. or earlier, you usually can walk in, even if you arrive five minutes late. If the first show is scheduled for 9:45 a.m. or later, arrive 20 or so minutes early. For the second performance, show up about 20–35 minutes ahead of time. For the third and subsequent shows, arrive 30–45 minutes early. If you plan to tour during late afternoon and evening, attend the last scheduled performance. If you want to beat the crowd out of the stadium, sit on the far right (as you face the staging area) and near the top.

To be chosen from the audience to be an "extra" in the stunt show, arrive early, sit down front, and display unmitigated enthusiasm. A woman from Richmond, Virginia, explains:

> Indiana Jones *was far and away the best show—we saw it twice on two different days. After the first performance, I realized the best way to get picked was to stand up, wave my arms, and shout when the "casting director" called for volunteers—sheer enthusiasm wins every time, and sitting towards the front helps, too. We stayed afterwards for autographs of the performers in the obligatory Mickey Mouse autograph book.*

Theater of the Stars

What It Is: Live Hollywood-style musical, usually featuring Disney characters; performed in an open-air theater

Scope & Scale: Major attraction

When to Go: In the evening

Special Comments: Performances are listed in the daily entertainment schedule

Author's Rating: Excellent; ★★★★

Appeal by Age Group:

Pre-school	Grade School	Teens	Young Adults	Over 30	Senior Citizens
★★★★	★★★★	★★★	★★★★	★★★★	★★★★

Duration of Presentation: 25 minutes

Preshow Entertainment: None

Probable Waiting Time: 20–30 minutes

Description and Comments   The *Theater of the Stars* combines Disney characters with singers and dancers in upbeat and humorous Hollywood musicals. The *Beauty and the Beast* show, in particular, is outstanding. The theater, which has been in three locations in the park over the years, seems finally to have found a permanent home on Sunset Boulevard. Vastly improved, it now offers a clear field of vision from almost every seat. Best, a canopy protects the audience from the Florida sun (or rain). The theater still gets mighty hot in the summer, but you can make it through a performance now without succumbing to heatstroke.

Touring Tips   Unless you visit during the cooler months, see this show in the late afternoon or the evening. The production is so popular that you should show up 20–50 minutes early to get a seat.

Fantasmic!

What It Is: Mixed-media nighttime spectacular
Scope & Scale: Super headliner
When to Go: Only staged in the evening
Special Comments: Disney's best nighttime event
Author's Rating: Not to be missed; ★★★★★
Appeal by Age Group:

Pre-school	Grade School	Teens	Young Adults	Over 30	Senior Citizens
★★★★	★★★★★	★★★★½	★★★★½	★★★★½	★★★★½

Duration of Presentation: 25 minutes
Probable Waiting Time: 50–60 minutes if you want a seat; 30 minutes for standing room

Description and Comments   *Fantasmic!* is a mixed-media show presented one or more times each evening when the park is open late. Located off Sunset Boulevard behind the Tower of Terror, *Fantasmic!* is staged on a newly created lagoon and island opposite a 6,900-seat amphitheater. By far the largest theater facility ever created by Disney, the amphitheater can accommodate an additional 3,000 standing guests for a total audience of nearly 10,000.

Fantasmic! is far and away the most extraordinary and ambitious outdoor spectacle ever attempted in any theme park. Starring Mickey Mouse in his role as the Sorcerer's Apprentice from *Fantasia,* the production uses lasers, images projected on a shroud of mist, fireworks, lighting effects, and music in combinations so stunning you can scarcely believe what you have seen. The plot is simple: good versus evil. The story gets lost in all the special effects at times, but no matter, it is the spectacle, not the story line, that is so overpowering. While beautiful, stunning, and powerful are words that immediately come to mind, they fail to convey the uniqueness of this presentation. It could be argued, with some validity, that *Fantasmic!* alone is worth the price of the Disney-MGM Studios admission.

Readers, like this Amheart, Massachusetts, woman agree:

> Fantasmic! *was absolutely the best show any of us had ever seen. It is worth the 1½ hour wait to see it. Disney Magic at its best!*

Touring Tips   *Fantasmic!* provides a whole new dimension to nighttime at Disney-MGM Studios. As a day-capping event, it is to the Studios what *IllumiNations* is to Epcot. While it's hard to imagine running out of space in a 10,000-person stadium, it happens almost every day. On evenings when there are two performances, the second show will always be less crowded. If you attend the first (or only) scheduled performance, line up at least an hour in advance. If you opt for the second show, arrive 50 minutes early. Readers underscore the importance of queuing up early:

From a Yorktown, Virginia, mom:

> *I think you seriously underestimated the time when people should arrive to see* Fantasmic! *if they want to get a seat. The stadium was already full when we arrived 45 minutes before the show was scheduled to start, and the remaining seats filled up quickly. Keep in mind this was during the off-season on one of the slower days of the week at the Disney-MGM Studios.*
>
> *Another warning is to avoid sitting near the front. We were stuck in the fourth row and despite no detectable wind, we were constantly sprayed by the fountains during the show. That might feel good after a hot summer day, but it was very unpleasant on a cool fall evening.*

Rain and wind conditions sometimes cause *Fantasmic!* to be cancelled. Unfortunately, Disney officials usually do not make a final decision about whether to proceed or cancel until just before show time. We have seen guests wait stoically for over an hour with no assurance that their patience and sacrifice would be rewarded. We do not recommend arriving more than a few minutes before show time on rainy or especially windy nights. On nights like these, pursue your own agenda until ten minutes or so before show time and then head to the stadium to see what happens.

Finally, make sure to hang on to children after *Fantasmic!* and to give them explicit instructions for regrouping in the event you are separated.

Voyage of the Little Mermaid

What It Is: Musical stage show featuring characters from the Disney movie *The Little Mermaid*

Scope & Scale: Major attraction

When to Go: Before 9:45 a.m. or just before closing

Author's Rating: Romantic, lovable, and humorous in the best Disney tradition; not to be missed; ★★★★

Appeal by Age Group:

Pre-school	Grade School	Teens	Young Adults	Over 30	Senior Citizens
★★★★	★★★★	★★★½	★★★★	★★★★	★★★★

Duration of Presentation: 15 minutes

Preshow Entertainment: Taped ramblings about the decor in the preshow holding area

Probable Waiting Time: Before 9:30 a.m., 10–30 minutes; after 9:30 a.m., 35–70 minutes

Description and Comments *Voyage of the Little Mermaid* is a winner, appealing to every age. Cute without being silly or saccharine, and infinitely lovable, the *Little Mermaid* show is the most tender and romantic entertainment offered anywhere in Walt Disney World. The story is simple and engaging, the special effects impressive, and the Disney characters memorable.

We receive a lot of mail from Europeans who complain about the "soppy sentimentality" of Americans in general and of Disney attractions in particular. These comments of a man from Bristol, England, are typical:

> *Americans have an ability to think as a child and so enjoy the soppiness of the* Little Mermaid. *English cynicism made it hard for us at times to see Disney stories as anything other than gushing, namby-pamby, and full of stereotypes. Other Brits might also find the sentimentality cloying. Maybe you should prepare them for the need to rethink their wry outlook on life temporarily.*

Touring Tips Because it's well done and located at a busy pedestrian intersection, *Voyage of the Little Mermaid* plays to capacity crowds all day. Unless you make the first or second show, you probably will have to wait an hour or more.

When you enter the preshow lobby, stand near the doors to the theater. When they open, go inside, pick a row of seats, and let six to ten people enter the row ahead of you. The strategy is twofold: to obtain a good seat and be near the exit.

Finally, a Charlotte, North Carolina, mom took exception to our Fright Potential Rating for *Voyage of the Little Mermaid:*

> *The guide let me down on the Little Mermaid show at MGM—the huge sea witch portrayed in laser lights, cartoon, and live action TERRIFIED my three-year-old. The description of the show led me to believe it was all sweetness and romance with no scariness.*

The Making of (Disney's Latest Feature Film)

What It Is: Documentary about the making of Disney's latest feature film
Scope & Scale: Minor attraction
When to Go: Anytime
Author's Rating: Disney infomercial; ★★★

Appeal by Age Group:

Pre-school	Grade School	Teens	Young Adults	Over 30	Senior Citizens
★★	★★★	★★★½	★★★½	★★★½	★★★½

Duration of Presentation: 17 minutes

Preshow Entertainment: Tour of post-production facilities

Probable Waiting Time: 20 minutes

Description and Comments   A short documentary describing casting, art, music, and production of the latest Disney film follows a guided tour through the post-production studios, where combining sound with film animation is explained.

Touring Tips   Although this attraction offers an inside perspective on how movies are made, its primary purpose is to lure you to the box office. Transparent self-promotion aside, presentations contribute at least marginally to an enhanced understanding of filmmaking. The presentation usually isn't crowded; see it at your convenience.

Jim Henson's MuppetVision 4D

What It Is: 4-D movie starring the Muppets
Scope & Scale: Major attraction
When to Go: Before 11 a.m. and after 4 p.m.
Author's Rating: Uproarious; not to be missed; ★★★★½
Appeal by Age Group:

Pre-school	Grade School	Teens	Young Adults	Over 30	Senior Citizens
★★★★½	★★★★★	★★★★½	★★★★½	★★★★½	★★★★½

Duration of Presentation: 17 minutes
Preshow Entertainment: Muppets on television
Probable Waiting Time: 12 minutes

Description and Comments   *MuppetVision 4D* provides a total sensory experience, with wild 3-D action augmented by auditory, visual, and tactile special effects. If you're tired and hot, this zany presentation will make you feel brand new.

Touring Tips   This production is very popular. Before noon, waits are about 20 minutes. During the hot, busy midday, however, lines are long until about 4 p.m. Also, watch for throngs arriving from just-concluded performances of the *Indiana Jones Epic Stunt Spectacular*. If you encounter a long line, try again later.

Honey, I Shrunk the Kids Movie Set Adventure

What It Is: Small but elaborate playground
Scope & Scale: Diversion
When to Go: Before 10 a.m. or after dark
Author's Rating: Great for young children, optional for adults; ★★½
Appeal by Age Group:

Pre-school	Grade School	Teens	Young Adults	Over 30	Senior Citizens
★★★★½	★★★½	★★	★★½	★★★	★★½

Duration of Presentation: Varies
Average Wait in Line per 100 People ahead of You: 20 minutes

Description and Comments   This elaborate playground appeals particularly to kids age 11 and younger. The story is that you have been "miniaturized" and have to make your way through a yard full of 20-foot-tall blades of grass, giant ants, lawn sprinklers, and other oversized features.

Touring Tips   This imaginative playground has tunnels, slides, rope ladders, and a variety of oversized props. All surface areas are padded, and Disney personnel are on-hand to help keep children in some semblance of control.

While this Movie Set Adventure undoubtedly looked good on paper, the actual attraction has problems that are hard to "miniaturize." First, it isn't nearly large enough to accommodate the children who would like to play. Only 240 people are allowed "on the set" at a time, and many of these are supervising parents or curious adults who hopped in line without knowing what they were waiting for. Frequently by 10:30 or 11 a.m., the playground is full, with dozens waiting outside (some impatiently).

Also, there's no provision for getting people to leave. Kids play as long as parents allow. This creates uneven traffic flow and unpredictable waits. If it weren't for the third flaw, that the attraction is poorly ventilated (as hot and sticky as an Everglades swamp), there's no telling when anyone would leave.

A mom from Shawnee Mission, Kansas, however, disagrees with our assessment:

> *Some of the things your book said to skip were our favorites (at least for the kids). We all thought the playground from* Honey, I Shrunk the Kids *was great—definitely worth seeing.*

If you visit during warmer months and want your children to experience the playground, get them in and out before 11 a.m. (preferably before 10:30 a.m.). By late morning, this attraction is way too hot and crowded for anyone to enjoy. Reach the playground via the New York Backlot, or through the Studio Catering Company fast-food area.

To save time, a couple from Grand Rapids, Michigan, suggests:

> *We staked out a seat at the [fast-food] plaza near the exit of* [Honey, I Shrunk the Kids *playground] with our children. They then went in to play while I got their snacks and beverages. Meanwhile, we had an opportunity to rest and determine our next game plan. When they emerged, they were parched and tired, so the refreshment break was well timed.*

New York Street Backlot

What It Is: Walk-through backlot movie set
Scope & Scale: Diversion
When to Go: Anytime
Author's Rating: Interesting, with great detail; ★★★
Appeal by Age Group:

Pre-school	Grade School	Teens	Young Adults	Over 30	Senior Citizens
★½	★★★	★★★	★★★	★★★	★★★

Duration of Presentation: Varies

Average Wait in Line per 100 People ahead of You: No waiting

Description and Comments This part of the Studios' backlot was previously accessible only on the tram segment of the Backlot Tour. Now guests can stroll the elaborate New York Street set and appreciate its rich detail. Opening this area to pedestrians also relieves some of the congestion in the Hollywood Boulevard and Echo Lake areas.

Touring Tips There's never a wait to enjoy the New York Street Backlot; save it until you've seen those attractions that develop long lines. Mickey Mouse signs autographs and poses for photos on the steps of the hotel in the middle of the block. It has no sign or visible name, but it has flags above the entrance. Consult the daily entertainment schedule for sessions.

Backlot Theater

What It Is: Live Hollywood-style musical, usually based on a Disney film, and performed in an open-air theater

Scope & Scale: Major attraction

When to Go: First show in the morning or in the evening

Special Comments: Performance times are listed in the daily entertainment schedule

Author's Rating: Excellent; ★★★★

Appeal by Age Group:

Pre-school	Grade School	Teens	Young Adults	Over 30	Senior Citizens
★★★	★★★½	★★★	★★★★	★★★★	★★★★

Duration of Presentation: 25–35 minutes

Preshow Entertainment: None

Probable Waiting Time: 20–30 minutes

Description and Comments The *Backlot Theater,* like *Theater of the Stars,* is an open-air venue for musical theater and concerts. Most productions are based on Disney films or animated features. An excellent show inspired by *The Hunchback of Notre Dame* played through most of 1999. The theater, on the far back side of New York Street, is generally well designed but has several obtrusive support columns. Though protected from the weather, the theater gets terribly hot during warmer months.

A Pennsylvania mom who basically stumbled onto the *Backlot Theater* says:

> *The greatest suprise was* The Hunchback of Notre Dame *performance. I loved the staging, lighting, music, and costuming. It was excellent—a real highlight of our Disney experience.*

Touring Tips   Unless you visit during cooler times, see the first morning show or the last evening show. To get to the *Backlot Theater,* walk down New York Street toward the Washington Square monument. At the square, turn left for a short block. Even though the theater's location is obscure, enough guests find it to fill the seats. Arrive early by 25 minutes or more to avoid sitting behind the columns.

The Magic of Disney Animation

What It Is: Walking tour of the Disney Animation Studio

Scope & Scale: Major attraction

When to Go: Before 11 a.m. and after 5 p.m.

Author's Rating: A masterpiece; not to be missed; ★★★★

Appeal by Age Group:

Pre-school	Grade School	Teens	Young Adults	Over 30	Senior Citizens
★★★	★★★	★★★	★★★★	★★★★	★★★★

Duration of Presentation: 36 minutes

Preshow Entertainment: Gallery of animation art in waiting area

Average Wait in Line per 100 People ahead of You: 7 minutes

Description and Comments   The public, for the first time, sees Disney artists at work. Since Disneyland opened in 1955, fans have petitioned Walt Disney Productions to offer an animation studio tour. Finally, after an interminable wait, an admiring public may watch artists create Disney characters.

Revised in 1998, the animation tour exceeds expectations. It's dynamic, fast-paced, educational, and fun. After entering the Animation Building, you see an eight-and-a-half minute introductory film on animation. Starring Walter Cronkite and Robin Williams as your tour hosts, it's an absolute delight.

After the film, you enter the studio and watch artists and technicians through large windows. Starting with story and character development, artists work sequentially through animation (characters are brought to life in rough art); to clean up (rough art is refined to finished line drawings); to effects and backgrounds (backgrounds for the characters are developed); and to photocopying, where drawings are transferred from paper to plastic sheets, called cels, before being finished with ink and paint. The cels are then photographed, assembled, and edited. Finally, the group enters a comfortable theater for a film that melds all the elements of animation production. Clips from Disney animated classics are featured.

The Magic of Disney Animation tour depends on live video and film narration, and only secondarily on the work of animators in the studio. Though animation is well explained, you may be disappointed if you think you'll see a lot of animators working.

Touring Tips Some days, the animation tour doesn't open until 11 a.m., by which time the park is pretty full. Check the entertainment schedule for tour hours, and try to go before noon. The tour is a relatively small-volume attraction, and lines begin to build on busy days by mid- to late morning.

After the introductory film, stay in the studio to watch the artists and technicians as long as you like. You likely will catch up with your group. If you don't, conclude your tour with the next group.

Disney-MGM Studios Backlot Tour

What It Is: Combination tram and walking tour of modern film and video production

Scope & Scale: Headliner

When to Go: Anytime

Author's Rating: Educational and fun; not to be missed; ★★★★

Appeal by Age Group:

Pre-school	Grade School	Teens	Young Adults	Over 30	Senior Citizens
★★★	★★★★	★★★★	★★★★	★★★★	★★★★

Duration of Presentation: About 25 minutes

Special Comments: Can be combined with soundstage tour described below

Preshow Entertainment: A video before the special effects segment and another video in the tram boarding area

Average Wait in Line per 100 People ahead of You: 2 minutes

Assumes: 16 tour departures per hour

Loading Speed: Fast

Description and Comments   About two-thirds of Disney-MGM Studios is a working film and television facility, where actors, artists, and technicians work on productions year-round. Everything from TV commercials, specials, and game shows to feature motion pictures are produced. Visitors to Disney-MGM can take the backstage studio tour to learn production methods and technologies.

Disney periodically changes the name of this tour. At press time, it was called the Disney-MGM Studios Backlot Tour.

The tour begins on the edge of the backlot with the special effects walking segment, then continues with the tram segment. After the tram segment, you can bail out or continue to the soundstage tour. To reach the Disney-MGM Studios Backlot Tour, turn right off Hollywood Boulevard through the Studio Arch into the Animation Courtyard. Bear left at the corner where *Voyage of the Little Mermaid* is situated. Follow the street until you see a red brick warehouse on your right. Go through the door and up the ramp.

The first stop is a special effects water tank where technicians explain the mechanical and optical tricks that "turn the seemingly impossible into on-screen reality." Included are rain effects, a naval battle, and a storm at sea. The waiting area for this part of the tour displays miniature naval vessels used in filming famous war movies.

A prop room separates the special effects tank and the tram tour. Trams depart about once every four minutes on busy days, winding among production and shop buildings before stopping at the wardrobe and crafts shops. Here, costumes, sets, and props are designed, created, and stored. Still seated on the tram, you look through large windows to see craftsmen at work.

The tour continues through the backlot, where western desert canyons and New York City brownstones exist side by side with suburban residential streets. The tour's highlight is Catastrophe Canyon, an elaborate special-effects movie set where a thunderstorm, earthquake, oil-field fire, and flash flood are simulated. The tour's tram portion ends at Backstage Plaza, where you can avail yourself of rest rooms, food, and drink. To reach the start of the soundstage tour, most recently called Backstage Pass, head back past the entrance of the special effects/tram tour toward the *Little Mermaid*. The soundstage tour begins on the far-left end of the building next to the special effects and tram tour.

Touring Tips   Because the Backlot Tour is one of Disney's most efficient attractions, you will rarely wait more than 15–20 minutes (usually less than ten). Take the tour at your convenience, but preferably before 5 p.m., when the workday ends for the various workshops.

Backstage Pass

What It Is: Walking tour of modern film and video production sound-stages and special effects workshops

Scope & Scale: Minor attraction

When to Go: Anytime

Author's Rating: Latest version not the best, but improved; ★★★

Appeal by Age Group:

Pre-school	Grade School	Teens	Young Adults	Over 30	Senior Citizens
★½	★★	★★	★★★	★★★	★★★

Duration of Presentation: About 25 minutes

Special Comments: The preshow video starring Bette Midler is the best part of the tour

Probable Waiting Time: 10 minutes

Description and Comments The soundstage tour has had several names. Because it's a thinly disguised promo for a Disney film, the name is usually derived from the movie. Recently, for example, it was called Backstage Pass to "101 Dalmatians." Check your guidemap for the name in use when you visit.

You can take the soundstage tour before the Backlot Tour. In the Disney guidemap, the Backlot Tour and soundstage tours are listed separately. For continuity, start with the Backlot Tour, then tour the soundstages.

First, you enter the special effects workshop, where enlargement, miniaturization, stop-frame photographic animation, and other technical mysteries are demonstrated and explained. Moving to a second workshop, volunteers from the audience are integrated into an action scene using a blue-screen background.

Next, it's on to the soundstages where soundproofed observation platforms allow unobtrusive viewing of ongoing productions. At the next stop, you inspect sets and props used in a Disney film and watch a video explaining how the film was produced.

Touring Tips While the Backlot Tour is quite worthwhile, the educational value of the soundstage tour is marginal. Though revised and improved in 1999, what once was a compelling educational experience is now little more than a promo for Disney flicks. Waiting time for the tour is usually less than 20 minutes, even during busiest times. The soundstage tour is located roughly next door and to the right of the Backlot Tour on Mickey Avenue.

Live Entertainment at Disney-MGM Studios

When the Studios opened, live entertainment, parades, and special events weren't as fully developed or elaborate as those at the Magic Kingdom or Epcot. With the introduction of an afternoon parade and elaborate shows at *Theater of the Stars,* the Studios joined the big leagues. These outstanding performances, coupled with the Sorcery in the Sky fireworks spectacular, give Disney-MGM live entertainment every bit as compelling as that in the other parks. In the fall of 1998, Disney-MGM launched a new edition of *Fantasmic!,* a water, fireworks, and laser show that has drawn rave reviews. *Fantasmic!,* staged in its own specially designed 10,000-person amphitheater, makes the Studios the park of choice for spectacular nighttime entertainment. *Fantasmic!* is profiled in detail on pages 591–592.

Sorcery in the Sky Fireworks   An excellent fireworks show based on Mickey Mouse's exploits in his role as the Sorcerer's Apprentice in *Fantasia.* It is held daily at closing time, when the park stays open after dark. During the off-season, the show is staged only on weekends, and sometimes not even then. Watch the fireworks from anywhere along Hollywood Boulevard.

Afternoon Parade   Staged one or more times a day, the parade begins near the park's entrance, continues down Hollywood Boulevard, and circles in front of The Great Movie Ride. From there, it passes in front of *Doug Live!* and *Sounds Dangerous* and ends by Star Tours. An alternate route begins at the far end of Sunset Boulevard and turns right onto Hollywood Boulevard.

The parade features floats and characters from Disney's animated features. Excellent parades based on *Mulan, Aladdin, Toy Story,* and *Hercules,* among others, have been produced. Colorful, creative, and totally upbeat, the afternoon parade is great. It does, however, bring pedestrian traffic to a standstill along its route and hampers crossing the park. If you're anywhere on the parade route when the parade begins, your best bet is to stay put and enjoy it. Our favorite vantage point is the steps of *Doug Live!*

Theater of the Stars   This covered amphitheater on Sunset Boulevard is the stage for production reviews, usually featuring music from Disney movies and starring Disney characters. Performances are posted in front of the theater and are listed in the daily entertainment schedule in the handout guidemap.

Backlot Theater   This stage is home to musical productions featuring

Disney characters and/or based on Disney films. A stage adaptation of *Pocahontas* preceded a musical drawn from *The Hunchback of Notre Dame.* The Backlot Theater is roughly behind the Muppets theater. Walk down New York Street toward the back of the park. At the end of the street, turn left.

Many readers, including this woman from East Lansing, Michigan, are surprised by the quality of the Disney-MGM Studios stage shows:

> *What I loved most about MGM, though, were the shows, and especially the Hunchback of Notre Dame show. These shows were nearly Broadway caliber and had actors who were very talented singers and dancers. I think the shows are the best-kept secrets at Disney World. I expected some cute little show and was truly amazed by the quality of the performances, costumes, and sets.*

Disney Characters   Find characters at the *Theater of the Stars* and Backlot Theater, in parades, on New York Street, in the Animation Courtyard, in Backstage Plaza, and along the street running next to the soundstages. Mickey sometimes appears for autographs and photos on Sunset Boulevard. A breakfast or lunch with characters is offered most days at the Hollywood and Vine Cafeteria.

Street Entertainment   Jugglers and other roving performers appear on Hollywood and Sunset boulevards. The Studios' modest marching band and a brass quartet play Hollywood Boulevard, Sunset Boulevard, Studio Courtyard, and the Echo Lake area. Not exactly street entertainment, a piano player performs daily at The Hollywood Brown Derby.

Shopping at Disney-MGM Studios

Shops throughout the park carry movie-oriented merchandise and numerous Disney trademark souvenirs. Most shopping is concentrated on Sunset and Hollywood Boulevards and features movie nostalgia items ranging from black-and-white postcards of the stars to JuJubes (if you're over 45, you still probably have some stuck in your teeth).

Unusual shops include Animation Gallery in the Animation Building, which sells reproductions of cels from animated features and other animation art. Sid Cahuenga's near the park's entrance sells vintage movie posters and celebrity autographs. Disney collectibles are specialties at Celebrity 5 & 10 on Sunset Boulevard. Planet Hollywood Super Store on Hollywood Boulevard is the place for celebrity memorabilia and Planet Hollywood trademark apparel. Sunset Boulevard shop offers custom watches.

Disney-MGM Studios One-Day Touring Plan
for Visitors of All Ages

Because Disney-MGM offers fewer attractions, touring isn't as complicated as at the Magic Kingdom or Epcot. Most Disney-MGM rides and
shows are oriented to the entire family, eliminating disagreements on how
to spend the day. Whereas in the Magic Kingdom Mom and Dad want to
see *The Hall of Presidents,* Big Sis is revved to ride Space Mountain, and the
preschool twins are clamoring for Dumbo the Flying Elephant, at Disney-
MGM Studios the whole family can pretty much tour together.

Since there are fewer attractions, crowds are more concentrated at
Disney-MGM. If a line seems unusually long, ask an attendant what the
estimated wait is. If it exceeds your tolerance, retry the attraction while
Indiana Jones is in progress or during a parade or special event. These draw
people away from the lines.

Our touring plan assumes a willingness to experience all major rides
and shows. Be aware that the Rock 'n' Roller Coaster, Star Tours, The
Great Movie Ride, *The Twilight Zone* Tower of Terror, and the Catastrophe
Canyon segment of the tram tour sometimes frighten children younger
than eight. Further, Star Tours and the Rock 'n' Roller Coaster can upset
anyone prone to motion sickness. When following the plan, skip any
attraction you don't wish to experience.

Early Entry at Disney-MGM Studios

Two days each week, Disney resort and campground guests are invited to
enter Disney-MGM Studios 90 minutes before official opening time.
During the early-entry hour, guests usually can enjoy The Great Movie Ride,
the Rock 'n' Roller Coaster, *MuppetVision 4D,* Star Tours, and *The Twilight
Zone* Tower of Terror. (These attractions are subject to change, as are the days
early entry is scheduled.)

Early entry at Disney-MGM offers some real advantages. All of the
attractions that open early are top of the line and draw huge crowds when
the park fills. If you get them in the rearview mirror early, the remainder of
the day will run smoothly. If you participate in early entry, be ready to
enter the moment the park opens. If official opening is 9 a.m., arrive at the
park by 7:30 a.m. Once inside, hurry immediately to the Rock 'n' Roller
Coaster, then to the Tower of Terror, then to The Great Movie Ride, then
to Star Tours. If you use our touring plan, skip steps that call for seeing
attractions you already enjoyed.

If you aren't eligible for early entry, arrive at the Studios 40 minutes
before official opening time on a day when early entry is not in effect.

Before You Go

1. Call (407) 824-4321 to determine which days of the week early entry is in effect and to verify the park's hours.

2. Buy your admission before arriving. Order tickets by mail or purchase them at a local Disney Store before you leave home. They're also available at the Ocala Disney AAA Travel Center off I-75 if you're driving. If you arrive by plane, buy them at the Disney Store in the Orlando airport or at a Disney resort hotel.

3. Make lunch and dinner priority seatings (if desired) before you arrive by calling (407) 939-3463. Disney resort guests can dial 55 from their room to make advance lunch and dinner priority seatings.

4. The schedule of live entertainment changes from month to month and even from day to day. Review the examples in the touring plan to get a fairly clear picture of your options.

At Disney-MGM Studios

1. Arrive at the park 1 hour and 40 minutes before official opening time if you're a Disney resort guest taking advantage of early entry. On non-early-entry days, arrive 40 minutes before official opening. Day guests (those without early-entry privileges) should avoid early-entry days.

2. When you're admitted, go to Guest Relations for a guidemap containing the daily entertainment schedule. Then blow down Hollywood Boulevard and turn right at Sunset Boulevard. Proceed to the Rock 'n' Roller Coaster. If you are held up at a rope barrier en route, just stay put until you're allowed to proceed. Ride the Rock 'n' Roller Coaster. If young children or terrified adults are in your party, take advantage of switching off (pages 190–192).

3. After the coaster, return to Sunset Boulevard and bear left to the Tower of Terror. Ride. Once again, take advantage of switching off if you have young children or adults who are still woozy from the roller coaster ride.

4. After the Tower of Terror, cross the park to Star Tours as follows: Return via Sunset Boulevard to Hollywood Boulevard. Go right on Hollywood Boulevard until you see a lake to your left. Bear left around the top of the lake and then right to Star Tours.

Consult your park map if you get confused. Experience Star Tours.

5. Exit Star Tours to the right and return to Hollywood Boulevard. At the opposite end of Hollywood Boulevard from the park entrance is the Great Movie Ride. Ride.

6. After the Great Movie Ride, exit left and pass through the Studios Arch. To your immediate left as you pass through the arch is *Voyage of the Little Mermaid*. See the show.

7. When you exit *Little Mermaid*, you will see rest rooms on your left. If you continue straight across the Animation Courtyard you'll come to the Animation building, also on your left. Take the Magic of Disney Animation tour.

8. Head back through the Studios Arch, return to the Star Tours area, and pass Star Tours on your left. Proceed straight ahead and slightly left to *MuppetVision 4D*. Enjoy the show.

Note: Stops for meals, refreshments, or rest room breaks will not adversely affect the touring plan from this point on. If you have small children in your party, now is a good time to visit the "Honey, I Shrunk the Kids" playground.

9. After the Muppets, you will have experienced all of the rides and most of the attractions that cause major bottlenecks. There are four live shows that are worthwhile. Plan the next part of your day to work them in, checking respective show times listed on the daily entertainment schedule printed in your handout park map.

Show	When to Line Up
Indiana Jones Stunt Spectacular	30 minutes before show time
The stage show at Theater of the Stars	30 minutes before show time
The stage show at Backlot Theater	30 minutes before show time
Disney's *Doug Live!*	10 minutes before show time

How early to queue up for a show is a matter of judgement. If the park seems crowded and busy, give yourself more time than the above guidelines suggest. Conversely, if the crowd is thin, you can cut your arrival time a little closer. Generally speaking, shows scheduled between 11 a.m. and 3 p.m. will fill their seats faster than earlier or later shows. Although the waiting areas for all except the *Doug Live!* show are in the sun, you will usually be allowed into the theater to sit down about 10–15 minutes prior to the start of the show. Once seated, you'll be out of the sun. If you're trying to cram a lot into your day, locate the exits before taking your seats. If you sit near an exit you'll be one of the first out of the theater when the performance concludes.

10. Between or after the shows see *Sounds Dangerous,* located facing the lake next to *Doug Live!* If the line is long, it's probably because the audience from a recently concluded performance of *Indiana Jones* or *Doug Live!* descended en masse. Come back in 30 minutes and the line will have disappeared.

11. Between or after the shows, take the Backlot Tour.

12. Between or after the shows, take the Backstage Pass tour.

13. Between or after the shows, see *The Making of (Disney's Latest Feature Film),* next door to *Little Mermaid.*

14. At your leisure, check out the New York Street set.

15. Tour Hollywood and Sunset Boulevards. Consult the daily entertainment schedule for parades and special events. Remember that we rate *Fantasmic!,* the nighttime entertainment spectacular, as "not to be missed."

16. This concludes the touring plan. Eat, shop, enjoy live entertainment, or revisit your favorite Disney-MGM attractions. When you're ready to leave the park, walk (the Disney-MGM parking lot isn't that big) or take a tram to your car.

Universal Florida

Universal Florida is well along in the expansion project that will transform the facility into a destination resort with two theme parks; a shopping, dining, and entertainment complex; and two hotels. The second theme park, Islands of Adventure (described later in this section), opened in 1999 with five theme areas. Jurassic Park is the centerpiece, with a boat ride similar to one operating at Universal Studios Hollywood. Giving Disney some of its own medicine, other theme areas feature attractions designed to compete directly with Disney headliners. Superhero Island, inspired by Marvel Comic heroes, offers a free-fall thrill ride to rival Disney's Tower of Terror. Toon Lagoon is home to Popeye, Olive Oyl, and other cartoon characters. The main attraction is a flume ride (watch out, Splash Mountain!). Other theme areas include Seuss Landing, with children's attractions based on the Dr. Seuss books, and Lost Continent, inspired by legends of mythical explorers and places.

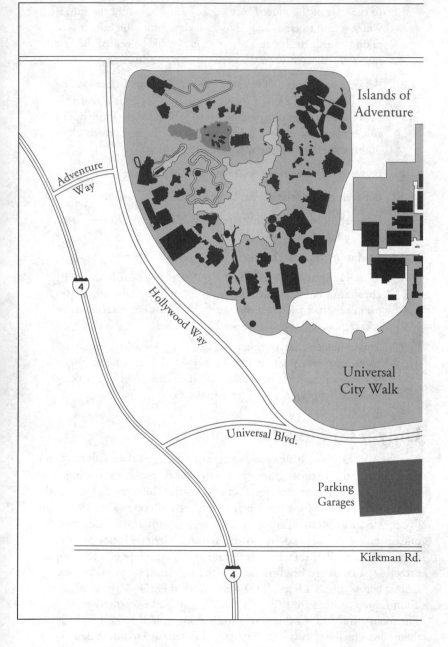

Islands of
Adventure

Adventure
Way

Hollywood Way

Universal
City Walk

Universal Blvd.

Parking
Garages

Kirkman Rd.

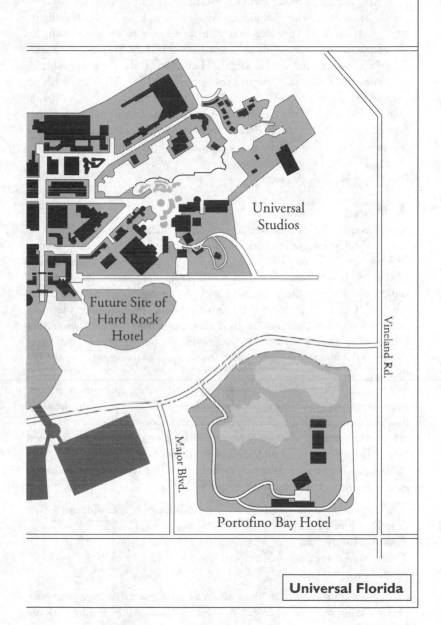

Universal Studios

Future Site of
Hard Rock
Hotel

Vineland Rd.

Major Blvd.

Portofino Bay Hotel

Universal Florida

A new system of roads and two multistory parking facilities are connected by moving sidewalks to CityWalk, a shopping, dining, and night-time entertainment complex that also serves as a gateway to both the Universal Studios Florida and the new Islands of Adventure theme parks. CityWalk includes the world's largest Hard Rock Cafe, complete with its own concert facility; an Emeril's restaurant; a NASCAR Cafe, with an auto-racing theme; a Pat O'Brien's New Orleans nightclub, with dueling pianos; a Motown Cafe; a Bob Marley restaurant and museum; a multi-faceted Jazz Center; an E! Entertainment production studio; Jimmy Buffett's Margaritaville Café; and a 16-screen cinema complex.

The Portofino Bay Resort, opened in 1999 with 750 rooms, will be followed by a Hard Rock Hotel.

ARRIVING

The Universal Florida complex can be accessed directly from I-4. Once on-site, you will be directed to park in one of two multitiered parking garages. Parking runs $6 for cars and $8 for RVs. Be sure to write down the location of your car before heading for the parks. From the garages, moving side-walks deliver you to the Universal CityWalk dining, shopping, and entertainment venue described above. From CityWalk you can access the main entrances of both Universal Studios Florida theme park and Universal's Islands of Adventure theme park. Even with the moving walkways it takes about 10–12 minutes to commute from the garages to the entrances of the theme parks.

Universal offers One-Day, Two-Day, Three-Day, and annual passes. Multiday passes allow you to visit both Universal theme parks on the same day, and unused days are good forever. Multiday passes also allow for early entry on select days. Discounts on the Three-Day passes can be obtained by purchasing in advance on the phone with your credit card at (800) 711-0080. All other prices are the same whether you buy your admission at the gate or in advance. Prices shown below include tax.

	Adults	Children (3–9)
One-Day, One Park Pass	$47	$37
Two-Day Escape Pass	$85	$69
Three-Day Escape Pass (sold at gate)	$122	$101
Annual Pass	$191	$165

If you want to visit more than one park on a given day, have your park pass and hand stamped when exiting your first park. At the second park use the readmission turnstile, showing your stamped pass and hand.

Combination passes are available: A four-park, seven-day pass allows unlimited entry to Universal Studios, Universal's Islands of Adventure, Sea

World, and Wet 'n Wild and costs about $170 for adults and $136 for children (ages three to nine). A five-park, ten-day pass provides unlimited entry to Universal Studios, Universal's Islands of Adventure, Sea World, Wet 'n Wild, and Busch Gardens and costs about $209 for adults, and $168 for children.

The main Universal Florida information number is (407) 363-8000. Reach Guest Services at (407) 224-6035, schedule a character breakfast at (407) 224-6339, and order tickets by mail at (800) 224-3838.

UNIVERSAL, KIDS, AND SCARY STUFF

Although there's plenty for younger children to enjoy at the Universal parks, the majority of the major attractions have the potential for wigging out kids under eight years of age. At Universal Studios Florida, forget Alfred Hitchcock, Twister, Kongfrontation, Earthquake, Jaws, Back to the Future, and *Terminator 2: 3-D*. The Funtastic World of Hanna-Barbera is a simulator ride with a cartoon theme. Most young children take it in stride. Ditto for the two stunt shows, though there are gunfire and explosions involved. E.T. is a toss-up. The first part of the ride is a little intense for a few preschoolers, but the end is all happiness and harmony. Interestingly, very few families report problems with *Beetlejuice's Rock 'n Roll Graveyard Revue* or *The Gory Gruesome & Grotesque Horror Make-up Show*. Anything not listed is pretty benign.

At Universal's Islands of Adventure, watch out for The Incredible Hulk Coaster, Dr. Doom's FearFall, The Adventures of Spider-Man, the Jurassic Park River Adventure, Dueling Dragons, and *Poseidon's Fury*. Popeye & Bluto's Bilge-Rat Barges is wet and wild, but most younger children handle it well. Dudley Do-Right's Ripsaw Falls is a toss-up, to be considered only if your kids liked Splash Mountain. The Sinbad stunt show includes some explosions and startling special effects, but once again, children tolerate it well. Nothing else should pose a problem.

Universal Studios Florida

Universal City Studios Inc. has run a studios tour and movie-theme tourist attraction for more than 29 years, predating all Disney parks except Disneyland. In the early 1980s, Universal announced plans to build a studios/theme park complex in Florida. While Universal labored over its new project, Disney jumped into high gear and rushed its own studios/theme park onto the market, beating Universal by a year and a half.

Universal Studios Florida opened in June 1990. At that time, it was almost four times the size of Disney-MGM Studios (Disney-MGM has since expanded somewhat), with much more of the facility accessible to visitors.

Like its sister facility in Hollywood, Universal Studios Florida is spacious, beautifully landscaped, meticulously clean, and delightfully varied in its entertainment. Rides are exciting and innovative and, as with many Disney rides, focus on familiar and/or beloved movie characters or situations.

On Universal Studios Florida's E.T. ride, you escape the authorities on a flying bike and leave Earth to visit E.T.'s home planet. In Kongfrontation, King Kong tears up a city with you in it. In Jaws, the persistent great white shark makes heart-stopping assaults on your small boat, and in Earthquake—The Big One, special effects create the most realistic earthquake simulation ever produced. The Funtastic World of Hanna-Barbera puts you in a bucking rocket simulator for a high-speed chase with Yogi Bear and the Flintstones. Guests also ride in a Delorean-cum-time machine in yet another chase, this one based on the film *Back to the Future*.

While many of these rides incorporate state-of-the-art technology and live up to their billing in terms of excitement, creativity, uniqueness, and special effects, they lack the capacity to handle the number of guests who frequent major Florida tourist destinations. If a ride has great appeal but can accommodate only a small number of guests per ride or per hour, long lines form. It isn't unusual for the wait to exceed an hour and a quarter for the E.T. ride and 50 minutes for the Hanna-Barbera ride.

Happily, most shows and theater performances at Universal Studios Florida are in theaters that accommodate large numbers of people. Since many shows run continuously, waits usually don't exceed twice the show's performance time (40–50 minutes). At several shows, the audience moves to three or more staging areas as the presentation unfolds.

Universal Studios Florida is laid out in an upside-down L configuration. Beyond the main entrance, a wide boulevard stretches past several shows and rides to a New York City backlot set. Branching off this pedestrian thoroughfare to the right are five streets that access other areas of the studios and intersect a promenade circling a large lake.

The park is divided into five sections: the Front Lot/Production Central, New York, Hollywood, San Francisco/Amity, and Expo Center. Where one section begins and another ends is blurry, but no matter. Guests orient themselves by the major rides, sets, and landmarks and refer, for instance, to "New York," "the waterfront," "over by E.T.," or "by Mel's Diner." The area of Universal Studios Florida open to visitors is about the size of Epcot.

The park offers all standard services and amenities, including stroller and wheelchair rental, lockers, diaper-changing and infant-nursing facilities, car assistance, and foreign-language assistance. Most of the park is accessible to disabled guests, and TDDs are available for the hearing impaired. Almost all services are in the Front Lot, just inside the main entrance.

Universal Studios offers a character breakfast on Tuesdays and Thursdays during slow season, and Monday through Friday during high season. Breakfast is hosted by at least four Hanna-Barbera characters at the International Food Bazaar, just inside the park on the right. The cost is $13.50 for adults and $8.75 for children ages three to nine for an all-you-can-eat cafeteria-style breakfast.

Not to Be Missed at Universal Studios Florida

Back to the Future	*Terminator 2: 3-D*
Earthquake—The Big One	*The Wild, Wild, Wild West*
Hercules and Xena	*Stunt Show*
Jaws	

UNIVERSAL STUDIOS FLORIDA ATTRACTIONS

Terminator 2: 3-D

What It Is: 3-D thriller mixed-media presentation

Scope & Scale: Super headliner

When to Go: After 3:30 p.m.

Special Comments: The nation's best theme park attraction; very intense for some preschoolers and grade-schoolers

Author's Rating: Furiously paced high-tech experience; not to be missed; ★★★★★

Appeal by Age Group:

Pre-school	Grade School	Teens	Young Adults	Over 30	Senior Citizens
★★★	★★★★★	★★★★★	★★★★★	★★★★★	★★★★

Duration of Presentation: 20 minutes, including an 8-minute preshow

Probable Waiting Time: 20–40 minutes

Description and Comments The Terminator "cop" from *Terminator 2* morphs to life and battles Arnold Schwarzenegger's T-800 cyborg character. If you missed the *Terminator* flicks, here's the plot: A bad robot arrives from the future to kill a nice boy. Another bad robot (who has been reprogrammed to be good) pops up at the same time to save the boy. The bad robot chases the boy and the rehabilitated robot, menacing the audience in the process.

Universal Studios Florida

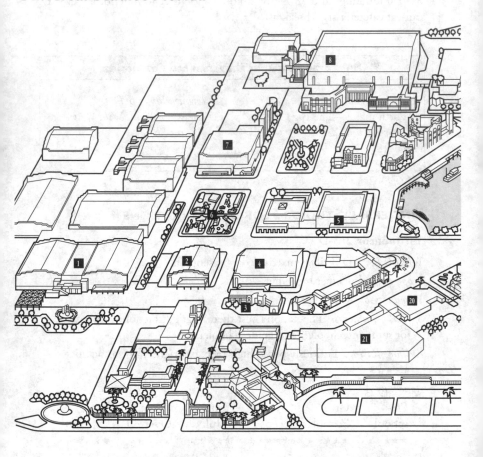

EXIT TO VINELAND RD. →

The attraction, like the films, is all action, and you really don't need to understand much. What's interesting is that it uses 3-D film and a theater full of sophisticated technology to integrate the real with the imaginary. Images seem to move in and out of the film, not only in the manner of traditional 3-D, but also in actuality. Remove your 3-D glasses momentarily and you'll see that the guy on the motorcycle is actually onstage.

We've watched this type of presentation evolve, pioneered by Disney's *Captain EO, Honey, I Shrunk the Audience,* and *MuppetVision 4D. Terminator 2: 3-D,* however, goes way beyond lasers, with moving theater seats, blasts of hot air, and spraying mist. It creates a multidimensional space that blurs the boundary between entertainment and reality. Is it seamless? Not quite, but it's close. We rank *Terminator 2: 3-D* as not to be missed and consider it the absolute best theme-park attraction in the United States. If *Terminator 2: 3-D* is the only attraction you see at Universal Studios Florida, you'll have received your money's worth.

Touring Tips   The 700-seat theater changes audiences about every 19 minutes. Even so, because the show is new and hot, expect to wait about 30–45 minutes. The attraction, on Hollywood Boulevard near the park's entrance, receives huge traffic during morning and early afternoon. By about 3 p.m., however, lines diminish somewhat. Though you'll still wait, we recommend holding off on *Terminator 2: 3-D* until then. If you can't stay until late afternoon, see the show first thing in the morning. Families with young children should know that the violence characteristic of the *Terminator* movies is largely absent from the attraction. There's suspense and action but not much blood and guts.

The Funtastic World of Hanna-Barbera

What It Is: Flight-simulation ride

Scope & Scale: Major attraction

When to Go: Before 11 a.m.

Special Comments: Very intense for some preschoolers

Author's Rating: A delight for all ages; ★★★½

Appeal by Age Group:

Pre-school	Grade School	Teens	Young Adults	Over 30	Senior Citizens
★★★★	★★★★	★★★½	★★★½	★★★½	★★★½

Duration of Ride: 4½ minutes with a 3½-minute preshow

Loading Speed: Moderate to slow

Description and Comments   A flight-simulation ride in the same family as Disney's Star Tours and Body Wars, except that all visuals are cartoons. Guests accompany Yogi Bear in a high-speed chase to rescue a kidnapped child.

Touring Tips   Unfortunately, this wild, funny, and thoroughly delightful attraction is a cycle ride. It must shut down completely during loading and unloading. Consequently, large lines build early and move very slowly. Ride during the first two hours the park is open.

"Alfred Hitchcock: The Art of Making Movies"

What It Is: Mini-course on filming action sequences and a testimonial to the talents of Alfred Hitchcock

Scope & Scale: Major attraction

When to Go: After 3:30 p.m.

Special Comments: May frighten young children

Author's Rating: A little slow-moving, but well done; ★★★½

Appeal by Age Group:

Pre-school	Grade School	Teens	Young Adults	Over 30	Senior Citizens
★★½	★★★	★★★½	★★★½	★★★½	★★★½

Duration of Presentation: 40 minutes

Probable Waiting Time: 22 minutes

Description and Comments   Guests view a film featuring famous scenes from Hitchcock movies (including some unreleased 3-D footage) and then go to an adjoining soundstage where the stabbing scene from *Psycho* is re-created using professional actors and audience volunteers. In a third area, the technology of filming action scenes is explained. The Hitchcock "greatest hits" film is disjointed and confusing unless you have a good recollection of the movies and scenes highlighted. Re-enactment of the scene from *Psycho* is both informative and entertaining, as are sets and techniques demonstrated in the third area.

Touring Tips   The attraction is just beyond the main entrance, and lines build. Usually, however, they disappear quickly. Let morning crowds clear; see the attraction just before you leave in the evening.

Nickelodeon Studios Walking Tour

What It Is: Behind-the-scenes guided tour

Scope & Scale: Minor attraction

When to Go: When Nickelodeon shows are in production (usually week-days)

Author's Rating: ★★★

Appeal by Age Group:

Pre-school	Grade School	Teens	Young Adults	Over 30	Senior Citizens
★★½	★★★★	★★★	★★★	★★★	★★★

Duration of Tour: 36 minutes

Probable Waiting Time: 30–45 minutes

Description and Comments   The tour examines set construction, soundstages, wardrobe, props, lighting, video production, and special effects. Much of this information is presented more creatively in the "Alfred Hitchcock," *Hercules and Xena,* and *Horror Make-Up Show* productions, but the Nickelodeon tour is tailored for kids. They're made to feel supremely important; their opinions are used to shape future Nickelodeon programming.

Adding some much-needed zip is the Game Lab, where guests preview strange games being tested for possible inclusion on Nickelodeon. Game Lab ends with a lucky child getting "slimed." If you don't understand, consult your children.

Touring Tips   While grade-schoolers, especially, enjoy this tour, it's expendable for everyone else. Go on a second day or second visit at Universal. If Nickelodeon isn't in production, forget it.

Twister

What It Is: Theater presentation featuring special effects from the movie *Twister*

Scope & Scale: Major attraction

When to Go: Should be your first show after experiencing all rides

Special Comments: High potential for frightening young children

Author's Rating: Gusty; ★★★½

Appeal by Age Group:

Pre-school	Grade School	Teens	Young Adults	Over 30	Senior Citizens
★★	★★★★	★★★★	★★★★	★★★★	★★★★

Duration of Presentation: 15 minutes

Probable Waiting Time: 26 minutes

Description and Comments   Replacing the *Ghostbusters* attraction in 1998, *Twister* combines an elaborate set and special effects, climaxing with a five-story-tall simulated tornado created by circulating more than 2 million cubic feet of air per minute.

Touring Tips The wind, pounding rain, and freight-train sound of the tornado are deafening, and the entire presentation is exceptionally intense. Schoolchildren are mightily impressed, while younger children are terrified and overwhelmed. Unless you want the kids hopping in your bed whenever they hear thunder, try this attraction yourself before taking your kids.

Kongfrontation

What It Is: Indoor adventure ride featuring King Kong
Scope & Scale: Major attraction
When to Go: Before 11 a.m.
Special Comments: May frighten young children
Author's Rating: ★★★★
Appeal by Age Group:

Pre-school	Grade School	Teens	Young Adults	Over 30	Senior Citizens
★★★½	★★★★	★★★½	★★★½	★★★	★★★

Duration of Ride: 4½ minutes
Loading Speed: Moderate

Description and Comments Guests board an aerial tram to ride from Manhattan to Roosevelt Island. En route, they hear the giant ape has escaped. The tram passes evidence of Kong's path of destruction and encounters the monster himself. In the course of the journey, King Kong demolishes buildings, uproots utility poles, swats helicopters, and hurls your tram car to the ground.

Touring Tips A lot of fun when it works. Ride in the morning after Back to the Future, E.T. Adventure, and Jaws.

The Gory Gruesome & Grotesque Horror Make-Up Show

What It Is: Theater presentation on the art of make-up
Scope & Scale: Major attraction
When to Go: After you have experienced all rides
Special Comments: May frighten young children
Author's Rating: A gory knee-slapper; ★★★½
Appeal by Age Group:

Pre-school	Grade School	Teens	Young Adults	Over 30	Senior Citizens
★★★	★★★½	★★★½	★★★½	★★★½	★★★½

Duration of Presentation: 25 minutes

Probable Waiting Time: 20 minutes

Description and Comments   Lively, well-paced look at how make-up artists create film monsters, realistic wounds, severed limbs, and other unmentionables. Funnier and more upbeat than many Universal Studios presentations, the show also presents a wealth of fascinating information. It's excellent and enlightening, if somewhat gory.

Touring Tips   Exceeding most guests' expectations, the *Horror Make-Up Show* is the sleeper attraction at Universal. Its humor and tongue-in-cheek style transcend the gruesome effects, and most folks (including preschoolers) take the blood and guts in stride. It usually isn't too hard to get into.

Hercules and Xena

What It Is: Course on special effects, mechanical and computer-generated creatures, blue-screen applications, and sound effects

Scope & Scale: Major attraction

When to Go: After you have experienced all the rides

Special Comments: A nice air-conditioned break during the hottest part of the day

Author's Rating: Sugar-coated education; ★★★★

Appeal by Age Group:

Pre-school	Grade School	Teens	Young Adults	Over 30	Senior Citizens
★★★½	★★★★	★★★★	★★★★	★★★★	★★★★

Duration of Presentation: 40 minutes

Probable Waiting Time: 20 minutes

Description and Comments   Guests move from theater to theater in this mini-course attraction. The presentation begins with a preshow that introduces the characters of Hercules and Xena. Next is the Creature Shop, a theater where members of the audience help to create a scene for a Hercules and Xena film by manipulating the limbs of mechanical critters. In the second theater, computer-created special effects are added to the mechanical critters scene and combined through blue-screen technology with backgrounds and footage of the characters Hercules and Xena. In the last theater, sound effects are added to complete the scene.

Touring Tips Informative, worthwhile, sometimes hilarious, and consistently high-tech, *Hercules and Xena* does a great job of making several complicated subjects understandable. The show borrows from the truly amazing technology developed for *Terminator 2: 3-D* and is a more lively presentation than "Murder, She Wrote," which covered much of the same territory. We recommend enjoying the show during the heat of the day.

Earthquake—The Big One

What It Is: Combination theater presentation and adventure ride

Scope & Scale: Major attraction

When to Go: In the morning, after Kongfrontation

Special Comments: May frighten young children

Author's Rating: Not to be missed; ★★★★

Appeal by Age Group:

Pre-school	Grade School	Teens	Young Adults	Over 30	Senior Citizens
★★★	★★★★	★★★★	★★★★	★★★★	★★★★

Duration of Presentation: 20 minutes

Loading Speed: Moderate

Description and Comments Film shows how miniatures are used to create special effects in earthquake movies, followed by a demonstration of how miniatures, blue screen, and matte painting are integrated with live-action stunt sequences (starring audience volunteers) to create a realistic final product. Afterward, guests board a subway from Oakland to San Francisco and experience an earthquake—the big one. Special effects range from fires and runaway trains to exploding tanker trucks and tidal waves. This is Universal's answer to Disney-MGM's Catastrophe Canyon. The special effects are comparable, but the field of vision is better at Catastrophe Canyon. Nonetheless, Earthquake is one of Universal's more compelling efforts.

Touring Tips Experience Earthquake in the morning, after you ride Back to the Future, E.T., Jaws, and Kongfrontation.

Jaws

What It Is: Adventure boat ride

Scope & Scale: Headliner

When to Go: Before 11 a.m.

Special Comments: Will frighten young children

Author's Rating: Not to be missed; ★★★★

Appeal by Age Group:

Pre-school	Grade School	Teens	Young Adults	Over 30	Senior Citizens
★★½	★★★★	★★★★	★★★★	★★★★	★★★★

Duration of Ride: 5 minutes

Loading Speed: Fast

Probable Waiting Time Per 100 People Ahead of You: 3 minutes

Assumes: All 8 boats are running

Description and Comments Jaws delivers five minutes of nonstop action, with the huge shark repeatedly attacking. A West Virginia woman, fresh from the Magic Kingdom, told us the shark is "about as pesky as that witch in Snow White." While the story is entirely predictable, the shark is realistic and as big as Rush Limbaugh.

What makes the ride unique is its sense of journey. Jaws builds an amazing degree of suspense. It isn't just a cruise into the middle of a pond where a rubber fish assaults the boat interminably. Add inventive sets and powerful special effects, and you have a first-rate attraction.

A variable at Jaws is the enthusiasm and acting ability of your boat guide. Throughout the ride, the guide must set the tone, elaborate the plot, drive the boat, and fight the shark. Most guides are quite good. They may overact a bit, but you can't fault them for lack of enthusiasm. Consider also that each guide repeats this wrenching ordeal every eight minutes.

Touring Tips Jaws is as well designed to handle crowds as any theme park attraction in Florida. People on the boat's left side tend to get splashed more. If you have young children, consider switching off (pages 190–192).

A mother of two from Williamsville, New York, who believes our warning about getting wet should be more strongly emphasized, has this to say:

> *Your warning about the "Jaws" attraction . . . is woefully understated. Please warn your readers—we were seated on the first row of the boat. My nine-year-old sat at the end of the boat (first person on the far left), and I was seated next to him. We were wary of these seats as I had read your warning, but I felt prepared. NOT!!!! At "that" moment the water came flooding over the left front side of the boat thoroughly drenching the two of us and filling our sneakers with water. Unfortunately for us, this was only our third attraction of the day (9:30 a.m.) and we still had a long day ahead of us. It was a rather chilly and windy 62° day. We went to the rest rooms, removed our shorts, and squeezed out as much water as*

we could, but we were very cold and uncomfortable all day. This will be our most vivid and lasting memory of our day at Universal Studios!!!

A dad from Seattle suggests that getting wet takes a backseat to being terrified:

Our 8-year-old was so frightened by Jaws that we scrapped the rest of the Universal tour and went back to E.T. An employee said she wouldn't recommend it to anyone under 10. Maybe you should change "may frighten small children" to "definitely will scare the pants off most children."

Back to the Future—The Ride

Motion Sickness WARNING!

What It Is: Flight-simulator thrill ride

Scope & Scale: Super headliner

When to Go: First thing in the morning

Special Comments: Very rough ride; may induce motion sickness. Must be 3'4" tall to ride. Switching off available (pages 190–192)

Author's Rating: Not to be missed, if you have a strong stomach; ★★★★★

Appeal by Age Group:

Pre-school	Grade School	Teens	Young Adults	Over 30	Senior Citizens
†	★★★★★	★★★★★	★★★★★	★★★★	★★½

† Sample size too small for an accurate rating

Duration of Ride: 4½ minutes

Loading Speed: Moderate

Description and Comments This attraction is to Universal Studios Florida what Space Mountain is to the Magic Kingdom: the most popular thrill ride in the park. Guests in Doc Brown's lab get caught up in a high-speed chase through time that spans a million years. An extremely intense simulator ride, Back to the Future is similar to Star Tours and Body Wars at Walt Disney World but is much rougher and more jerky. Though the story doesn't make much sense, the visual effects are wild and powerful. The vehicles (Delorean time machines) in Back to the Future are much smaller than those of Star Tours and Body Wars, so the ride feels more personal and less like a group experience.

In a survey of 84 tourists who had experienced simulator rides in both Universal Studios and Disney World, riders younger than 35 preferred

Back to the Future to the Disney attractions by a seven-to-four margin. Older riders, however, stated a two-to-one preference for Star Tours over Back to the Future or Body Wars. The remarks of a woman from Mount Holly, New Jersey, are typical:

> *Our favorite [overall] attraction was Back to the Future at Universal. Comparing it to Star Tours and Body Wars, it was more realistic because the screen surrounds you.*

An English woman from Fleet Hants, who was tired of being jerked around, finally got mad (go girl!):

> *The simulators were fun, but they do seem to go out of their way to jerk you about, and the Back to the Future one was SO jerky that it made me quite angry.*

A man from Evansville, Indiana, reminds us that Back to the Future can humble even the most intrepid:

> *The Back to the Future ride at Universal was very rough and we are members of a roller coaster club. We have seldom experienced such a rough ride and ridden over 300 coasters. If it was too strong for us, we shudder to think about mere mortals.*

Because the height requirement on Back to the Future has been lowered from 3'10" to 3'4", younger children are riding. Many of them require preparation. A Virginia mother suggests:

> *The five-year-old was apprehensive about the ride, but he liked it a lot. We assured him ahead of time that (1) it's only a movie, and (2) the car doesn't actually go anywhere, just shakes around. This seemed to increase his ability to enjoy that ride (rather than taking all the fun out of it).*

Touring Tips As soon the park opens, guests stampede to Back to the Future. Our recommendation: Be there when the park opens, and join the rush. If you don't ride before 10 a.m., your wait may be exceptionally long. *Note:* Sitting in the rear seat of the car makes the ride more realistic.

E.T. Adventure

What It Is: Indoor adventure ride based on the *E.T.* movie
Scope & Scale: Major attraction
When to Go: Before 10 a.m.
Author's Rating: ★★★★
Appeal by Age Group:

Pre-school	Grade School	Teens	Young Adults	Over 30	Senior Citizens
★★★★	★★★★	★★★½	★★★½	★★★½	★★★½

Duration of Ride: 4½ minutes
Load Speed: Moderate

Description and Comments Guests aboard a bicycle-like conveyance escape with E.T. from earthly law enforcement officials and then journey to E.T.'s home planet. The attraction is similar to Peter Pan's Flight at the Magic Kingdom but is longer and has more elaborate special effects and a wilder ride.

Touring Tips Most preschoolers and grade-school children love E.T. We think it worth a 20- to 30-minute wait, but nothing longer. Lines build quickly after 9:45 a.m., and waits can be more than two hours on busy days. Ride in the morning, right after Back to the Future. Guests who balk at sitting on the bicycle can ride in a comfortable gondola.

A mother from Columbus, Ohio, writes about horrendous lines at E.T.:

> *The line for E.T. took two hours! The rest of the family waiting outside thought that we had gone to E.T.'s planet for real.*

A woman from Richmond, Virginia, objects to how Universal represented the waiting time:

> *We got into E.T. without much wait, but the line is very deceptive. When you see a lot of people waiting outside and the sign says "10 minute wait from this point," it means 10 minutes until you are inside the building. But there's a very long wait inside [before] you get to the moving vehicles.*

Woody Woodpecker's KidZone

What It Is: Interactive playground and kid's roller coaster
Scope & Scale: Minor attraction
When to Go: Anytime
Author's Rating: A good place to let off steam; ★★★
Appeal by Age Group:

Pre-school	Grade School	Teens	Young Adults	Over 30	Senior Citizens
★★★★	★★★	—	—	—	

Description and Comments Rounding out the selection of other nearby kid-friendly attractions, the KidZone consists of Woody Woodpecker's Nuthouse Coaster and an interactive playground called Curious George Goes to Town. The child-sized roller coaster is small enough for kids to enjoy but sturdy enough for adults, though its moderate speed might unnerve some smaller children (the minimum age to ride is three years old). The Curious George playground exemplifies the Universal obsession with wet stuff: in addition to innumerable spigots, pipes, and spray guns, two giant roof-mounted buckets periodically dump a thousand gallons of water on unsuspecting visitors below. Kids who want to stay dry can mess around in the foam-ball playground, also equipped with chutes, tubes, and ball-blasters.

Touring Tips Universal employees have already dubbed this new children's area "Peckerland." Visit the playground after you've experienced all the major attractions.

Animal Actors Stage

What It Is: Trained-animals stadium performance
Scope & Scale: Major attraction
When to Go: After you have experienced all rides
Author's Rating: Warm and delightful; ★★★½
Appeal by Age Group:

Pre-school	Grade School	Teens	Young Adults	Over 30	Senior Citizens
★★★★½	★★★★	★★★½	★★★½	★★★½	★★★½

Duration of Presentation: 20 minutes
Probable Waiting Time: 25 minutes

Description and Comments Humorous demonstration of how animals are trained for films. Well-paced and informative, the show features cats, dogs, monkeys, birds, and other creatures. Sometimes animals don't behave as expected, but that's half the fun. Often the animal stars are quite famous. In 1998, for example, the pig from the acclaimed movie *Babe* was featured.

Touring Tips We would like this show better if guests could simply walk in and sit down. As it is, everyone must line up to be admitted. Presented six to ten times daily, the program's schedule is in the daily entertainment guide. Go when it's convenient for you; queue about 15 minutes before show time.

Dynamite Nights Stuntacular

What It Is: Simulated stunt-scene filming
Scope & Scale: Major attraction
When to Go: In the evening according to the daily entertainment schedule
Author's Rating: Well done; ★★★★
Appeal by Age Group:

Pre-school	Grade School	Teens	Young Adults	Over 30	Senior Citizens
★★★	★★★★	★★★★	★★★★	★★★½	★★★½

Duration of Presentation: 20 minutes
Probable Waiting Time: None

Description and Comments Each evening on the lagoon, stunt men demonstrate spectacular stunts and special effects. The plot involves lawmen trying to intercept and apprehend drug smugglers. Our main problem with this show is that the lagoon is so large that it's somewhat difficult to follow the action. The production was upgraded in 1994 and 1997.

Touring Tips This version is on a par with Disney-MGM's stunt show. Onlookers watch from the rail encircling the lagoon. There's no waiting in line, but if you want a really good vantage point, stake out your position about 25 minutes before show time. The best viewing spots are along the docks at Lombard's Landing and adjacent areas on the Embarcadero waterfront, across the street from Earthquake. Primary viewing spots are identified on the park map with a "PV" icon.

The Wild, Wild, Wild West Stunt Show

What It Is: Stunt show with a western theme
Scope & Scale: Major attraction
When to Go: After you've experienced all rides
Author's Rating: Solid and exciting; ★★★★
Appeal by Age Group:

Pre-school	Grade School	Teens	Young Adults	Over 30	Senior Citizens
★★★★½	★★★★	★★★★	★★★★	★★★★	★★★★

Duration of Presentation: 16 minutes
Probable Waiting Time: None

Description and Comments   The *Wild West* stunt show has shootouts, fist-fights, horse tricks, and high falls, all exciting and well executed. The fast-paced show is staged about ten times daily in a 2,000-seat, covered stadium. Unlike the stunt show on the lagoon, the action is easy to follow.

Touring Tips   Show times are listed in the daily entertainment guide; go at your convenience. In summer, the stadium is more comfortable after dusk.

Fievel's Playland

What It Is: Children's play area with water slide

Scope & Scale: Minor attraction

When to Go: Anytime

Author's Rating: A much-needed attraction for preschoolers; ★★★★

Appeal by Age Group:

Pre-school	Grade School	Teens	Young Adults	Over 30	Senior Citizens
★★★★	★★★★	★★★	★★★	★★★	★★★

Probable Waiting Time: 20–30 minutes for the water slide; otherwise, no waiting

Description and Comments   Imaginative playground features ordinary household items reproduced on a giant scale, as a mouse would experience them. Preschoolers and grade-schoolers can climb nets, walk through a huge boot, splash in a sardine-can fountain, seesaw on huge spoons, and climb onto a cow skull. Most of the playground is reserved for preschoolers, but a water slide/raft ride is open to all ages.

Touring Tips   Walk into Fievel's Playland without waiting, and stay as long as you want. Younger children love the oversized items, and there's enough to keep teens and adults busy while little ones let off steam. The water slide/raft ride is open to everyone but is extremely slow-loading and carries only 300 riders per hour. With the wait an average of 20–30 minutes, we don't think the 16-second ride is worth the trouble. Also, you're highly likely to get soaked.

Lack of shade is a major shortcoming of the entire attraction. Don't go during the heat of the day.

Beetlejuice's Rock 'n Roll Graveyard Revue

What It Is: Rock-and-roll stage show

Scope & Scale: Minor attraction

When to Go: At your convenience

Author's Rating: Outrageous; ★★★½
Appeal by Age Group:

Pre-school	Grade School	Teens	Young Adults	Over 30	Senior Citizens
★★★★	★★★★	★★★★	★★★½	★★★½	★★★½

Duration of Presentation: 16 minutes
Probable Waiting Time: None

Description and Comments High-powered rock-and-roll stage show stars Beetlejuice, Frankenstein, the Bride of Frankenstein, Wolfman, Dracula, and the Phantom of the Opera. In addition to fine vintage rock, the show features some of the most exuberant choreography found anywhere, plus impressive sets and special effects.

Touring Tips Mercifully, this attraction has been moved under cover.

A Day in the Park with Barney

What It Is: Live character stage show
Scope & Scale: Major children's attraction
When to Go: Anytime
Author's Rating: A great hit with preschoolers; ★★★★
Appeal by Age Group:

Pre-school	Grade School	Teens	Young Adults	Over 30	Senior Citizens
★★★★½	★★★	★★	★★½	★★★	★★★

Duration of Presentation: 12 minutes plus character greeting
Probable Waiting Time: 15 minutes

Description and Comments Barney, the purple dinosaur of Public Television fame, leads a sing-along with the help of the audience and side-kicks Baby Bop and BJ. A short preshow gets the kids lathered up before they enter the theater, Barney's Park. Interesting theatrical effects include wind, falling leaves, clouds and stars in the simulated sky, and snow. After the show, Barney exits momentarily to allow parents and children to gather along the stage. He then thunders back and moves from child to child, hugging each and posing for photos.

Touring Tips If your child likes Barney, this show is a must. It's happy and upbeat, and the character greeting that follows is the best organized we've seen in any theme park. There's no line and no fighting for Barney's attention. Just relax by the rail and await your hug.

Lucy, a Tribute

What It Is: Walk-through tribute to Lucille Ball

Scope & Scale: Diversion

When to Go: Anytime

Author's Rating: A touching remembrance; ★★★

Appeal by Age Group:

Pre-school	Grade School	Teens	Young Adults	Over 30	Senior Citizens
★	★	★★	★★★	★★★	★★★

Probable Waiting Time: None

Description and Comments   The life and career of comedienne Lucille Ball are spotlighted, with emphasis on her role as Lucy Ricardo in the long-running television series *I Love Lucy.* Well designed and informative, the exhibit succeeds admirably in recalling the talent and temperament of the beloved redhead.

Touring Tips   See Lucy during the hot, crowded midafternoon, or on your way out of the park. Adults could easily stay 15–30 minutes. Children, however, get restless after a couple of minutes.

Street Scenes

What It Is: Elaborate outdoor sets for making films

Scope & Scale: Diversion

When to Go: Anytime

Special Comments: You'll see most sets without special effort as you tour the park

Author's Rating: One of the park's great assets; ★★★★★

Appeal by Age Group:

Pre-school	Grade School	Teens	Young Adults	Over 30	Senior Citizens
★★★	★★★★½	★★★★½	★★★★½	★★★★★	★★★★★

Probable Waiting Time: No waiting

Description and Comments   Unlike at Disney-MGM Studios, all Universal Studios Florida's backlot sets are accessible for guest inspection. They include New York City streets, San Francisco's waterfront, a New England coastal town, the house from *Psycho,* Rodeo Drive and Hollywood Boulevard, and a Louisiana bayou.

Touring Tips   You'll see most as you walk through the park.

One-Day Touring Plan for Universal Studios Florida

This plan is for all visitors. If a ride or show is listed that you don't want to experience, skip that step and proceed to the next. Move quickly from attraction to attraction and, if possible, don't stop for lunch until after Step 10.

Buying Admission to Universal Studios Florida

One of our big gripes about Universal Studios is that there never are enough ticket windows open in the morning to accommodate the crowd. You can arrive 45 minutes before official opening time and still be in line to buy your admission when the park opens. Therefore, we strongly recommend you buy your admission in advance. Passes are available by mail from Universal Studios at (800) 224-3838. They are also sold at the concierge desk or attractions box office of many Orlando-area hotels. If your hotel doesn't offer tickets, try Guest Services at the Radisson Twin Towers (407) 351-1000, at the intersection of Major Boulevard and Kirkman Avenue.

Many hotels that sell Universal admissions don't issue actual passes. Instead, the purchaser gets a voucher that can be redeemed for a pass at the theme park. Fortunately, the voucher-redemption window is separate from the park's ticket sales operation. You can quickly exchange your voucher for a pass and be on your way with little or no wait.

Touring Plan

1. Call (407) 363-8000 the day before your visit for the official opening time.

2. On the day of your visit, eat breakfast and arrive at Universal Studios Florida 50 minutes before opening time with your admission pass or an admission voucher in hand. If you have a voucher, exchange it for a pass at the voucher-redemption window. Pick up a map and the daily entertainment schedule.

3. Line up at the turnstile. Ask any attendant whether any rides or shows are closed that day. Adjust the touring plan accordingly.

4. When the park opens, take a right on Hollywood Boulevard, pass Mel's Diner (on your left), and (keeping the lagoon on your left) go directly to Back to the Future. Ride.

5. Exit left and pass the International Food Bazaar. Continue bearing left past the *Animal Actors Stage* and go to the E.T. Adventure. Ride.

6. Retrace your steps toward Back to the Future. Keeping the lagoon on your left, cross the bridge to Amity. Ride Jaws.

7. Exit and turn left down The Embarcadero. Postpone Earthquake and head directly to Kongfrontation in the New York set. Go ape.

8. Return to San Francisco. Ride Earthquake—The Big One.

9. Work your way back toward the main entrance and ride The Funtastic World of Hanna-Barbera. Expect to wait 25–40 minutes. If you've had enough simulator rides for now, skip to Step 10.

10. If you're still intact after the Flintstones, a bike ride to another galaxy, a shark attack, an earthquake, and an encounter with King Kong, take on a tornado. Return to the New York set and see *Twister*. The line will appear long but should move quickly as guests are admitted inside.

11. If you haven't already eaten, do so now. Cafe La Bamba in the Hollywood area serves tacos and burgers, and Mel's Diner nearby has decent, machine-made milk shakes. The International Food Bazaar next to Back to the Future serves gyros, bratwurst, pizza, and other ethnic fare. In the New York area, we like Louie's Italian Restaurant for pizza, calzone, and salads. Outrageous sandwiches and pastries are the specialty of Beverly Hills Boulangerie near the park's main entrance. If you're in the mood for more relaxed, upscale dining, the park's nicest restaurant is Lombard's Landing on the waterfront (across from Earthquake). In addition to prime rib and creative seafood entrees, Lombard's serves an exceptional hamburger at a fair price.

12. At this point you have eight major attractions yet to see:

    Terminator 2: 3-D
    The Gory Gruesome & Grotesque Horror Make-Up Show
    Hercules and Xena
    Animal Actors Stage
    Dynamite Nights Stuntacular
    The Wild, Wild, Wild West Stunt Show
    "Alfred Hitchcock: The Art of Making Movies"
    Beetlejuice's Rock 'n Roll Graveyard Revue

    Animal Actors Stage, the *Beetlejuice* show, and the stunt shows are performed several times daily, as listed in the entertainment schedule. Plan the remainder of your itinerary according to the next listed shows for these presentations. The *Horror Make-Up*

Show and *Hercules and Xena* (on opposite sides of Mel's Diner) run pretty much continuously and can be worked in as time permits. Try to see *Terminator 2: 3-D* after 3:30 p.m., but whatever you do, don't miss it. Save "Alfred Hitchcock" for your last attraction as you leave the park.

13. Our touring plan doesn't include the Nickelodeon Studios Tour, Woody Woodpecker's Kidzone, or *A Day in the Park with Barney*. If you have school-age children in your party, consider taking the Nickelodeon tour in late afternoon or on a second day at the park. If you're touring with preschoolers, see Barney after you ride E.T., and then head for Kidzone.

14. This concludes the touring plan. Spend the remainder of your day revisiting your favorite attractions or inspecting sets and street scenes you may have missed. Also, check your daily entertainment schedule for live performances that interest you.

Universal's Islands of Adventure

When Universal's Islands of Adventure theme park opened in 1999, it provided Universal with enough critical mass to actually compete with Disney. For the first time, Universal has an on-site hotel, a shopping and entertainment complex, and two major theme parks. Doubly interesting is that the new Universal park is pretty much just for fun, in other words, a direct competitor to Disney's Magic Kingdom, the most visited theme park in the world.

How direct a competitor is it? Check this out:

Islands of Adventure	Magic Kingdom
Six Islands (includes Port of Entry)	Seven Lands (includes Main Street)
Two roller coaster attractions	Two roller coaster attractions
A Dumbo-type ride	Dumbo
One flume ride	One flume ride
Toon Lagoon character area	Mickey's Toontown Fair character area

And though it may take central Florida tourists awhile to make the connection, here's what will dawn on them when they finally do: Universal's Islands of Adventure is a brand-new, state-of-the-art park competing with

a Disney park that is more than 25 years old and has not added a major new attraction for four years.

Of course, that's only how it looks on paper. The reality, as they say, is still blowing in the wind. The Magic Kingdom, after all, is graceful in its maturity and much beloved. And then there was the question on everyone's mind: could Universal really pull it off? Recalling the disastrous first year that the Universal Studios Florida park experienced, we held our breath to see if Islands of Adventure's innovative, high-tech attractions would work. Well, not only did they work, they were up and running almost two months ahead of schedule. Thus, the clash of the titans is once again hot. Universal is coming on strong with the potential of sucking up three days of a tourist's week (more, if you include Universal's strategic relationship with Sea World and Busch Gardens). And that's more time than anyone has spent off the Disney campus for a long, long time.

Through it all, Disney and Universal spokesmen downplayed their fierce competition, pointing out that any new theme park makes central Florida a more marketable destination. Behind closed doors, however, it's a Pepsi/Coke–type rivalry that will undoubtedly keep both companies working hard to gain a competitive edge. The good news, of course, is that this competition translates into better and better attractions for you to enjoy.

BEWARE OF THE WET AND WILD

Although we have described Universal's Islands of Adventure as a direct competitor to the Magic Kingdom, there is one major qualification you should be aware of. Whereas most Magic Kingdom attractions are designed to be enjoyed by guests of any age, attractions at Islands of Adventure are largely created for an under-40 population. The roller coasters at Universal are serious with a capital "S," making Space Mountain and Big Thunder Mountain look about as tough as Dumbo. In fact, seven out of the nine top attractions at Islands of Adventure are thrill rides, and of these, there are three that not only scare the bejeezus out of you but also drench you with water.

In addition to thrill seekers, families with young children will find a lot to do at Islands of Adventure. There are three interactive playgrounds for little ones, as well as four rides that young children will enjoy. Of the thrill rides, only the two in Toon Lagoon (described later) are marginally appropriate for young children, and even on these rides your child needs to be fairly stalwart.

GETTING ORIENTED

Both Universal theme parks are accessed via the Universal CityWalk entertainment complex. Crossing CityWalk from the parking garages, you can bear right to Universal Studios Florida or left to Universal's Islands of Adventure.

Universal's Islands of Adventure is arranged much like the World Showcase section of Epcot, in a large circle surrounding a lake. Unlike Epcot, however, the Islands of Adventure theme areas evidence the sort of thematic continuity pioneered by Disneyland and the Magic Kingdom. Each land, or island in this case, is self-contained and visually consistent in its theme, though you can see parts of the other islands across the lake.

Passing through the turnstiles, you first encounter the Moroccan-style Port of Entry, where you will find Guest Services, lockers, stroller and wheelchair rentals, ATM banking, lost and found, and, of course, shopping. From the Port of Entry, moving clockwise around the lake, you can access Marvel Super Hero Island, Toon Lagoon, Jurassic Park, the Lost Continent, and Seuss Landing. You can crisscross the lake on small boats, but otherwise there is no in-park transportation.

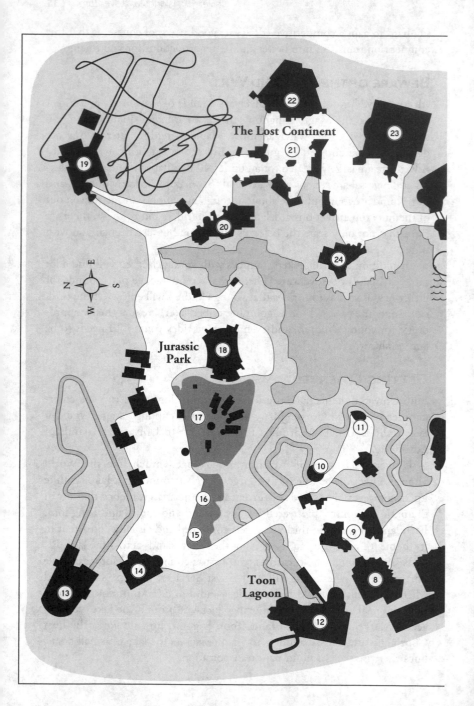

The Lost Continent

Jurassic Park

Toon Lagoon

Islands of Adventure

Port of Entry
1. Island Skipper Tours
2. Confisco's Grill

Marvel Super Hero Island
3. Incredible Hulk Coaster
4. Cafe 4
5. Dr. Doom's Fearfall
6. The Amazing Adventure of Spider-Man

Toon Lagoon
7. Pandemonium Cartoon Circus
8. Comic Strip Café
9. Comic Strip Lane
10. Popeye & Bluto's Bilge-Rat Barges
11. Me Ship, *The Olive*
12. Dudley Do-Right's Ripsaw Falls

Jurassic Park
13. Jurassic Park River Adventure
14. Thunder Falls Terrace
15. Camp Jurassic
16. Pteranodon Flyers
17. Triceratops Encounter
18. Jurassic Park Discovery Center

The Lost Continent
19. Dueling Dragons
20. The Enchanted Oak Tavern (and Alchemy Bar)
21. Sinbad's Village
22. *The Eighth Voyage of Sinbad*
23. *Poseidon's Fury!: Escape from the Lost City*
24. Mythos Restaurant

Seuss Landing
25. Sylvester McMonkey McBean
26. If I Ran the Zoo
27. Caro-Seuss-El
28. The Once-ler's House
29. Circus McGurkus Cafe Stoo-pendous
30. One Fish Two Fish Red Fish Blue Fish
31. The Cat in the Hat

Seuss Landing

Port of Entry

Pharos Lighthouse

Marvel Super Hero Island

Not to Be Missed at Islands of Adventure	
Incredible Hulk Coaster	Dueling Dragons
The Adventures of Spider-Man	*Poseidon's Fury!*
Jurassic Park River Adventure	

MARVEL SUPER HERO ISLAND

This island, with its futuristic and retro-future design, and comic book signage, offers shopping and attractions based on Marvel Comic characters.

The Adventures of Spider-Man

What It Is: Indoor adventure simulator ride based on Spider-Man

Scope & Scale: Super headliner

When to Go: Before 10 a.m.

Author's Rating: Our choice for the best attraction in the park; ★★★★★

Appeal by Age Group:

Pre-school	Grade School	Teens	Young Adults	Over 30	Senior Citizens
★★★	★★★★★	★★★★★	★★★★★	★★★★★	★★★★

Duration of Ride: 4½ minutes

Loading Speed: Fast

Description and Comments   Covering 1½ acres and combining moving ride vehicles, 3-D film, and live action, Spider-Man is frenetic, fluid, and astounding. The visuals are rich and the ride is wild, but not jerky. Although the attractions are not directly comparable, Spider-Man is technologically on a par with Disney-MGM's Tower of Terror, which is to say that it will leave you in awe. As a personal aside, we love both and would be hard-pressed to choose one over the other.

The story line is that you are a reporter for the *Daily Bugle* newspaper (where Peter Parker, a.k.a. Spider-Man, works as a mild-mannered photographer), when it's discovered that evil villains have stolen (I promise I'm not making this up) the Statue of Liberty. You are drafted on the spot by your cantankerous editor to go get the story. After speeding around and being thrust into "a battle between good and evil," you experience a "sensory drop" of 400 feet into darkness. Because the ride is so wild and the action so continuous, it's hard to understand the plot, but you're so thoroughly entertained that you don't really care. Plus, you'll want to ride again and again. Eventually, with repetition, the story line will begin to make sense.

Touring Tips Ride first thing in the morning after Dr. Doom's FearFall and The Incredible Hulk Coaster, or in the hour before closing.

The Incredible Hulk Coaster

What It Is: Roller coaster
Scope & Scale: Super Headliner
When to Go: Before 9:30 a.m.
Author's Rating: A coaster lover's coaster; ★★★★½
Appeal by Age Group:

Pre-school	Grade School	Teens	Young Adults	Over 30	Senior Citizens
½	★★★★★	★★★★★	★★★★★	★★★★	★★½

Duration of Ride: 1½ minutes
Loading Speed: Moderate

Description and Comments There is as always a story line, but for this attraction it's of no importance whatsoever. What you need to know about this attraction is simple. You will be launched like a cannonball shot from 0 to 40 miles per hour in two seconds, and then you will be flung upside down 100 feet off the ground, which will, of course, induce weightlessness. From there it's a mere seven rollovers punctuated by two plunges into holes in the ground before you're allowed to get out and throw up.

Seriously, the Hulk is a great roller coaster, perhaps the best in Florida, providing a ride comparable to Montu (Busch Gardens) with the added thrill of an accelerated launch (instead of the more typical uphill crank). Plus, like Montu, the ride is smooth. You won't be jarred and whiplashed on the Incredible Hulk.

Touring Tips The Hulk gives Spider-Man a run as the park's most popular attraction. Ride early in the morning immediately after Dr. Doom's FearFall. Universal provides electronic lockers near the entrance of the Hulk to deposit any items that might depart your person during the Hulk's seven inversions. Program the number of your locker into the terminal and follow the instructions. You'll receive a slip of paper with a code you can enter when you return to retrieve your stuff. The locker is free if you only use it for a short time. If you leave things in the locker for a couple of hours, however, you'll have to pay a modest rental charge.

Dr. Doom's FearFall

What It Is: Lunch liberator
Scope & Scale: Headliner
When to Go: Before 9:15 a.m.
Author's Rating: More bark than bite; ★★★
Appeal by Age Group:

Pre-school	Grade School	Teens	Young Adults	Over 30	Senior Citizens
—	★★★	★★★★	★★★½	★★★	—

Duration of Ride: 40 seconds
Loading Speed: Slow

Description and Comments   Here you are (again) strapped into a seat with your feet dangling and blasted 200 feet up in the air and then allowed to partially free-fall back down. If you are having trouble forming a mental image of this attraction, picture the midway game where a macho guy swings a sledgehammer, propelling a metal sphere up a vertical shaft. At the top of the shaft is a bell. If the macho man drives the sphere high enough to ring the bell, he wins a prize. Got the idea? OK, on this ride you are the metal sphere.

The good news is this ride looks much worse than it actually is. The scariest part by far is the apprehension that builds as you sit, strapped in, waiting for the thing to launch. The blasting up and free-falling down parts are really very pleasant.

Touring Tips   We've seen glaciers that move faster than the line to Dr. Doom. If you want to ride without investing half a day, be one of the first in the park to ride. Fortunately, if you're on hand at opening time, being among the first isn't too difficult (mainly because the nearby Hulk and Spider-Man attractions are bigger draws).

TOON LAGOON

Toon Lagoon is cartoon art translated into real buildings and settings. Whimsical and gaily colored, with rounded and exaggerated lines, Toon Lagoon is Universal's answer to Mickey's Toontown Fair in the Magic Kingdom. The main difference between the two toon lands is that (as you will see) you've about a 60% chance of going into hypothermia at Universal's version.

Dudley Do-Right's Ripsaw Falls

What It Is: Flume ride
Scope & Scale: Headliner
When to Go: Before 10:30 a.m.
Author's Rating: A minimalist Splash Mountain; ★★★½
Appeal by Age Group:

Pre-school	Grade School	Teens	Young Adults	Over 30	Senior Citizens
★★½	★★★★	★★★½	★★★	★★★½	★★½

Duration of Ride: 5 minutes
Loading Speed: Moderate

Description and Comments   Inspired by the *Rocky and Bullwinkle* cartoon series, this ride features Canadian Mountie Dudley Do-Right as he attempts to save Nell from evil Snidely Whiplash. Story line aside, it's a flume ride, with the inevitable big drop at the end. Universal claims this is the first flume ride to "send riders plummeting 15 feet below the surface of the water." We're not exactly sure how this works, but it sounds like you better bring your diving gear.

The only problem with this attraction is that everyone inevitably compares it to Splash Mountain at the Magic Kingdom. The flume is as good as Splash Mountain's, and the final drop is a whopper, but the theming and the visuals aren't even in the same league. The art, sets, audio, and jokes at Dudley Do-Right are minimalist at best; it's Dudley Do-Right's two-dimensional approach versus Splash Mountain's three-dimensional presentation. Taken on its own terms, however, Dudley Do-Right is a darn good flume ride.

Touring Tips   This ride will get you wet, but on average not as wet as you might expect (it looks worse than it is). If you want to stay dry, however, arrive prepared with a poncho or at least a big garbage bag with holes cut out for your head and arms. After riding, take a moment to gauge the timing of the water cannons that go off along the exit walk. This is where you can really get drenched. While younger children are often intimidated by the big drop, those who ride generally enjoy themselves. Ride first thing in the morning after experiencing the Marvel Super Hero rides.

Popeye & Bluto's Bilge-Rat Barges

What It Is: Whitewater raft ride
Scope & Scale: Headliner

When to Go: Before 10:30 a.m.

Author's Rating: Bring your own soap; ★★★★

Appeal by Age Group:

Pre-school	Grade School	Teens	Young Adults	Over 30	Senior Citizens
★★★	★★★★½	★★★★	★★★★	★★★½	★★½

Duration of Ride: 4½ minutes

Loading Speed: Moderate

Description and Comments   This sweetly named attraction is a whitewater raft ride that includes an encounter with an 18-foot-tall octopus. Engineered to ensure that everyone gets drenched, the ride even provides water cannons for highly intelligent nonparticipants ashore to fire at those aboard. The rapids are rougher and more interesting, and the ride longer, than the Animal Kingdom's Kali River Rapids. But nobody surpasses Disney for visuals and theming, though the settings of these two attractions (cartoon set and Asian jungle river, respectively) are hardly comparable.

Touring Tips   If you didn't drown on Dudley Do-Right, here's a second chance. You'll get a lot wetter from the knees down on this ride, so use your poncho or garbage bag and ride barefoot with your britches rolled up. In terms of beating the crowds, ride the barges in the morning after experiencing the Marvel Super Hero attractions and Dudley Do-Right. If you are lacking foul weather gear or forgot your trash bag, you might want to put off riding until last thing before leaving the park. Most preschoolers enjoy the raft ride. Those who are frightened react more to the way the rapids look as opposed to the roughness of the ride.

Me Ship, The Olive

What It Is: Interactive playground

Scope & Scale: Minor attraction

When to Go: Anytime

Author's Rating: Colorful and appealing for kids; ★★★

Appeal by Age Group:

Pre-school	Grade School	Teens	Young Adults	Over 30	Senior Citizens
★★★★	★★★½	½	½	½	—

Description and Comments   *The Olive* is Popeye's three-story boat come to life as an interactive playground. Younger children can scramble around in

Swee' Pea's Playpen, while older sibs shoot water cannons at riders trying to survive the adjacent Bilge-Rat raft ride.

Touring Tips If you are into the big rides, save the playground for later in the day.

Pandemonium Cartoon Circus

What It Is: Musical stage show featuring cartoon characters
Scope & Scale: Headliner
When to Go: After experiencing the rides
Author's Rating: ★★★½
Appeal by Age Group:

Pre-school	Grade School	Teens	Young Adults	Over 30	Senior Citizens
★★★★	★★★½	★★★	★★★	★★★	★★★

Duration of Presentation: 20 minutes
Probable Wait: 15 minutes

Description and Comments This stage show features seemingly any and every cartoon character whose rights aren't tied up by Disney or Warner Brothers. If you see it with your kids, you'll be busy helping each other identify characters that don't span the generation gap. The show itself is long on enthusiasm and energy. Though competently performed and certainly entertaining, you'll feel like you've been to cheerleading camp by the time it's over.

Touring Tips The show is staged in a large covered theater that is sometimes taken over by television shows taping on property. Character shows are scheduled about six times daily according to the show times listed in the handout park map. See the show at your convenience after experiencing the rides and seeing *Poseidon's Fury*.

Comic Strip Lane

What It Is: Walk-through exhibit and shopping/dining venue
Scope & Scale: Diversion
When to Go: Anytime

Description and Comments This is the main street of Toon Lagoon. Here you can visit the domains of Beetle Bailey, Hagar the Horrible, Krazy Kat, the Family Circus, and Blondie and Dagwood, among others. Shops and eateries tie into the cartoon strip theme.

Touring Tips   This is a great place for photo ops with cartoon characters in their own environment. It's also a great place to drop a few bucks in the diners and shops, but you probably already figured that out.

JURASSIC PARK

Jurassic Park (for anyone who's been asleep for 20 years) is a Steven Spielberg film about a fictitious theme park with real dinosaurs. Jurassic Park at Universal's Islands of Adventure is a real theme park (or at least a section of one) with fictitious dinosaurs.

Jurassic Park River Adventure

What It Is: Indoor/outdoor adventure ride based on the *Jurassic Park* movie
Scope & Scale: Super headliner
When to Go: Before 11 a.m.
Author's Rating: Better than it's Hollywood cousin; ★★★★
Appeal by Age Group:

Pre-school	Grade School	Teens	Young Adults	Over 30	Senior Citizens
★★★	★★★★½	★★★★	★★★★	★★★★	★★★½

Duration of Ride: 6½ minutes
Loading Speed: Fast

Description and Comments   Guests board boats for a water tour of Jurassic Park. Everything is tranquil as the tour begins, and the boat floats among large herbivorous dinosaurs such as brontosaurus and stegosaurus. Then, as word is received that some of the carnivores have escaped their enclosure, the tour boat is accidentally diverted into Jurassic Park's maintenance facilities. Here, the boat and its riders are menaced by an assortment of hungry meat eaters led by the ubiquitous T-Rex. At the climactic moment, the boat and its passengers escape by plummeting over an 85-foot drop billed as the "longest, fastest, steepest water descent ever built" (did anyone other than me notice the omission of the word wettest?).

Touring Tips   Though the boats make a huge splash at the bottom of the 85-foot drop, you don't get all that wet. Before the boat leaves the dock, however, you must sit in the puddles left by previous riders. Once underway there's a little splashing, but nothing major until the big drop at the end of the ride. When you hit the bottom, however, enough water will cascade into the air to extinguish a three-alarm fire. Fortunately, not all that much lands in the boat.

Young children must endure a double whammy on this ride. First, they are stalked by giant, salivating (sometimes spitting) reptiles, and then they're sent catapulting over the falls. Unless your children are fairly stalwart, wait a year or two before you spring the River Adventure on them.

Triceratops Encounter

What It Is: Prehistoric petting zoo

Scope & Scale: Minor attraction

When to Go: Before 11:30 a.m.

Author's Rating: Well executed; ★★★

Appeal by Age Group:

Pre-school	Grade School	Teens	Young Adults	Over 30	Senior Citizens
★★★★	★★★★	★★★½	★★★½	★★★½	★★★½

Duration of Show: 5 minutes

Probable Waiting Time: 15–25 minutes

Description and Comments   Guests are ushered in groups into a "feed and control station," where they can view and pet a 24-foot-long, animatronic triceratops dinosaur. While the trainer lectures about the creature's behaviors, habits, and lifestyle, the triceratops breathes, blinks, chews, and flinches at the touch of the guests.

Touring Tips   Nothing is for sure, but this may be the only attraction in the park where you won't get wet. Just to be sure, however, stand near the middle of the dinosaur. Though not a major attraction, Triceratops Encounter is popular and develops long lines. Make it your first show/exhibit after experiencing the rides.

Discovery Center

What It Is: Interactive natural history exhibit

Scope & Scale: Minor attraction

When to Go: Anytime

Author's Rating: ★★★

Appeal by Age Group: Not open at press time

Description and Comments   The Discovery Center is an interactive, educational exhibit that mixes fiction from the movie, such as using fossil DNA to bring dinosaurs to life, with various skeletal remains and other paleontological displays. One exhibit allows guests to watch an animatronic raptor being hatched. Another allows you to digitally "fuse" your DNA with a dinosaur to see what the resultant creature would look like. Other exhibits include dinosaur egg scanning and identification and a quiz call "You Bet Jurassic."

Touring Tips   Cycle back after experiencing all the rides or on a second day. Most folks can digest this exhibit in 10–15 minutes.

Pteranodon Flyers

What It Is: Dinosaur version of Dumbo, the Flying Elephant

Scope & Scale: Minor attraction

When to Go: When there's no line

Author's Rating: All sizzle, no steak; ½

Appeal by Age Group:

Pre-school	Grade School	Teens	Young Adults	Over 30	Senior Citizens
★★★	★★	★	★½	★	★½

Duration of Ride: 1¼ minutes

Loading Speed: Slower than anyone thought possible

Description and Comments   This attraction is Islands of Adventure's biggest blunder. Engineered to accommodate only 170 persons per hour (about half the hourly capacity of Dumbo!), the ride swings you along a track that passes over a small part of Jurassic Park. We recommend that you skip this one. Why? Because the Jurassic period will probably end before you reach the front of the line! And your reward for all that waiting? A one minute and fifteen second ride. Plus, the attraction has a name that nobody over 12 years old can pronounce.

Touring Tips   Photograph the pteranodon as it flies overhead. You're probably looking at something that will soon be extinct.

Camp Jurassic

What It Is: Interactive play area

Scope & Scale: Minor attraction

When to Go: Anytime

Author's Rating: Creative playground, confusing layout; ★★★

Appeal by Age Group:

Pre-school	Grade School	Teens	Young Adults	Over 30	Senior Citizens
★★★	★★★	—	—	—	—

Description and Comments Camp Jurassic is a great place for children to let off steam. Sort of a Jurassic version of Tom Sawyer Island, kids can explore lava pits, caves, mines, and a rain forest.

Touring Tips Camp Jurassic will fire the imaginations of the under-13 set. If you don't impose a time limit on the exploration, you could be here awhile. The layout of the play area is confusing and intersects the queuing area for the Pteranodon Flyers. If your child accidentally lines up for the Pteranodons, he'll be college age before you see him again.

LOST CONTINENT

This theme area is an exotic mix of Silk Road bazaar and ancient ruins, with Greco-Moroccan accents. And you thought your decorator was nuts. Anyway, this is the land of mythical gods, fabled beasts, and expensive souvenirs.

Poseidon's Fury! Escape from the Lost City

What It Is: High-tech theater attraction

Scope & Scale: Headliner

When to Go: After experiencing all the rides

Special Comments: Audience stands throughout

Author's Rating: Packs a punch; ★★★★

Appeal by Age Group:

Pre-school	Grade School	Teens	Young Adults	Over 30	Senior Citizens
★★	★★★★	★★★★	★★★★	★★★★	★★★★

Duration of Presentation: 17 minutes including preshow

Probable Waiting Time: 25 minutes

Description and Comments In this megatheater attraction, Poseidon, the Greek god of the sea, dukes it out with Zeus, the Greek gods' head honcho. All this happens, of course, with you in the middle, but with less subtlety than in the average dysfunctional family quarrel. The operative word in this brawl is special effects. Poseidon fights with water, 350,000 gallons to be specific, while Zeus uses fire.

The plot unravels in installments as you pass through a couple of preshow areas and finally into the main theater. Though the production is a little slow and plodding at first, it wraps up with quite an impressive flourish. The special effects are, well . . . special. There's some great technology at work here. Poseidon is by far and away the best of the Islands of

Adventure theater attractions and a close runner-up to *Terminator 2: 3-D* at the Studios.

Touring Tips   If you are still wet from Dudley Do-Right, the Bilge-Rat Barges, and the Jurassic Park River Adventure, you will probably be pulling for Zeus in hopes you might finally dry out. Our money, however, is on Poseidon. It's legal in Florida for theme parks to get you wet, but setting you on fire is somewhat frowned upon.

Frequent explosions and noise may frighten younger children, so exercise caution with preschoolers. Shows run continuously if the technology isn't on the blink. We recommend catching Poseidon after experiencing your fill of the rides.

Dueling Dragons

What It Is: Roller coaster

Scope & Scale: Headliner

When to Go: Before 10:30 a.m.

Author's Rating: Almost as good as the Hulk Coaster; ★★★★

Appeal by Age Group:

Pre-school	Grade School	Teens	Young Adults	Over 30	Senior Citizens
—	★★★★	★★★★	★★★★	★★★★	★★

Duration of Ride: A minute and 45 seconds

Loading Speed: Moderate

Description and Comments   This high-tech coaster launches two trains (Fire and Ice) at the same time on tracks that are closely intertwined. Each track, however, is differently configured so that you get a different experience on each. Several times, a collision with the other train seems imminent, a catastrophe that seems all the more real because the coasters are inverted (i.e., suspended from above so that you sit with your feet dangling). At times, the two trains and their passengers are separated by a mere 12 inches.

Because this is an inverted coaster, your view of the action is limited unless you are sitting in the front row. This means that most passengers miss seeing all these near collisions. But don't worry; regardless of where you sit, there's plenty to keep you busy. Dueling Dragons is the highest coaster in the park and also claims the longest drop at 115 feet, not to mention five inversions. And like the Hulk, it's a nice smooth ride all the way.

Coaster cadets are already arguing about which seat on which train provides the wildest ride. We prefer the front row on either train, but coaster loonies hype the front row of Fire and the last row of Ice.

Touring Tips The good news about this ride is that you won't get wet unless you wet yourself. The bad news is that wetting yourself comes pretty naturally. The other bad news is that the queuing area for Dueling Dragons is the longest, most convoluted affair we've ever seen, winding endlessly through a maze of subterranean passages. After what feels like a comprehensive tour of Mammoth Cave, you finally emerge at the loading area where you must choose between riding Fire or Ice. Of course, at this critical juncture, you're as blind as a mole rat from being in the dark for so long. Our advice is to follow the person in front of you until your eyes adjust to the light. Though the coasters are slightly different, it takes a lot of rides to apprehend the difference. Try to ride during the first 90 minutes the park is open. Finally, warn anyone waiting for you that you might be a while. Even if there is no line to speak of it takes 10–12 minutes just to navigate the caverns and not much less time to exit the attraction after riding.

The Eighth Voyage of Sinbad

What It Is: Theater stunt show
Scope & Scale: Major attraction
When to Go: Anytime as per the daily entertainment schedule
Author's Rating: Not inspiring; ★★
Appeal by Age Group:

Pre-school	Grade School	Teens	Young Adults	Over 30	Senior Citizens
★★★	★★★½	★★½	★★★	★★★	★★½

Duration of Presentation: 17 minutes
Probable Waiting Time: 15 minutes

Description and Comments A story about Sinbad the Sailor is the glue that (loosely) binds this stunt show featuring water explosions, ten-foot-tall circles of flame, and various other daunting eruptions. The show reminds us of those action genre movies that substitute a mind-numbing succession of explosions, crashes, and special effects for plot and character development. Concerning Sinbad, even if you bear in mind that it's billed as a stunt show, the production is so vacuous and redundant that it's hard to get into the action. Hercules and Xena fans might appreciate the humor more than the average showgoer.

Touring Tips   See Sinbad after you've experienced the rides and the better rated shows. The theater seats 1,700; performance times are listed in the daily entertainment schedule.

SEUSS LANDING

A ten-acre theme area based on Dr. Seuss's famous children's books. Like at Mickey's Toontown in the Magic Kingdom, all of the buildings and attractions replicate a whimsical, brightly colored cartoon style with exaggerated features and rounded lines.

The Cat in the Hat

What It Is: Indoor adventure ride
Scope & Scale: Major attraction
When to Go: Before 11:30 a.m.
Author's Rating: Seuss would be proud; ★★★½
Appeal by Age Group:

Pre-school	Grade School	Teens	Young Adults	Over 30	Senior Citizens
★★★★	★★★★	★★★	★★★½	★★★½	★★★½

Duration of Ride: 3½ minutes
Loading Speed: Moderate

Description and Comments   Guests ride on "couches" through 18 different sets inhabited by animatronic Seuss characters, including The Cat in the Hat, "Thing 1," "Thing 2," and the beleaguered goldfish who tries to maintain order in the midst of mayhem. Well done overall, with nothing that should frighten younger children.

Touring Tips   This should be fun for all ages. Try to ride early.

One Fish, Two Fish, Red Fish, Blue Fish

What It Is: Wet version of Dumbo, the Flying Elephant
Scope & Scale: Minor attraction
When to Go: Before 10 a.m.
Author's Rating: Who says you can't teach an old ride new tricks? ★★★½
Appeal by Age Group:

Pre-school	Grade School	Teens	Young Adults	Over 30	Senior Citizens
★★★★	★★★★	★★★	★★★	★★★	★★★

Duration of Ride: 2 minutes

Loading Speed: Slow

Description and Comments   Imagine Dumbo with Seuss-style fish instead of elephants and you've got half the story. The other half of the story involves yet another opportunity to drown. Guests steer their fish up or down 15 feet in the air while traveling in circles. At the same time, they try to avoid streams of water projected from "squirt posts." A catchy song provides clues for avoiding the squirting.

Though ostensibly a children's ride, the song and the challenge of steering your fish away from the water jets make this attraction fun for all ages.

Touring Tips   We don't know what it is about this theme park and water, but you'll get wetter than at a full-immersion baptism.

Caro-Seuss-El

What It Is: Merry-go-round
Scope & Scale: Minor attraction
When to Go: Before 10:30 a.m.
Author's Rating: Wonderfully unique; ★★★½
Appeal by Age Group:

Pre-school	Grade School	Teens	Young Adults	Over 30	Senior Citizens
★★★★	★★★★	—	—	—	—

Duration of Ride: 2 minutes
Loading Speed: Slow

Description and Comments   Totally outrageous, the Caro-Seuss-El is a full-scale, 56-mount merry-go-round made up exclusively of Dr. Seuss characters.

Touring Tips   Even if you are too old or don't want to ride, this attraction is worth an inspection. Whatever your age, chances are good you'll see some old friends. If you are touring with young children, try to get them on early in the morning.

Sylvester McMonkey McBean's Very Unusual Driving Machines

What It Is: Indoor/outdoor track ride
Scope & Scale: Major attraction
When to Go: Before 10:30 a.m.
Author's Rating: Not open at press time

Appeal by Age Group: Not open at press time

Duration of Ride: 5 minutes

Loading Speed: Slow

Description and Comments   This long-titled ride offers a tour of Seuss Landing on an elevated track, passing in and out of various attractions, shops, and restaurants. The inspiration, a Seuss book about discrimination, is sort of lost in the translation. Guests can, however (within limits), control the speed of their vehicle (conducive to bumping other cars), honk their horns, and shout expletives commonly associated with California freeway driving.

Touring Tips   Visually appealing. You can cover the same territory on foot.

If I Ran the Zoo

What It Is: Interactive playground

Scope & Scale: Minor attraction

When to Go: Anytime

Author's Rating: Eye-catching; ★★★

Appeal by Age Group:

Pre-school	Grade School	Teens	Young Adults	Over 30	Senior Citizens
★★★★	★★★	—	—	—	—

Description and Comments   Based on Dr. Seuss's *If I Ran the Zoo,* this playground is divided into three distinct areas—Hedges, Water, and the New Zoo. Each area features various interactive elements, including, of course, another opportunity for a good soaking.

Touring Tips   Visit this playground after you've experienced all the major attractions.

One-Day Touring Plan for Universal's Islands of Adventure

Be aware that there are an inordinate number of attractions in this park that will get you wet. If you want to experience them, come armed with ponchos, large plastic garbage bags, or some other protective covering. Failure to follow this prescription will make for a potentially squishy, sodden day.

This plan is for groups of all sizes and ages and includes thrill rides that may induce motion sickness or get you wet. If the plan calls for you to experience an attraction that does not interest you, simply skip that attraction and proceed to the next step. Be aware that the plan calls for some backtracking. If you have young children in your party, customize the plan to fit their needs and take advantage of switching off at thrill rides.

1. Call (407) 363-8000, the main information number, the day before your visit for the official opening time. Try to purchase your admission sometime prior to the day you intend to tour.

2. On the day of your visit, eat breakfast and arrive at Universal Florida 50 minutes before opening time. Park, buy your admission (if you did not purchase it in advance), and wait at the turnstiles to be admitted.

3. While at the turnstile, ask an attendant whether any rides or shows are closed that day. Adjust the touring plan accordingly.

4. When the park opens, go straight through the Port of Entry and take a left, crossing the bridge into Marvel Super Hero Island. At Super Hero Island, bear left to Dr. Doom's FearFall.

5. Ride Dr. Doom's FearFall.

6. Exit to the right and ride The Incredible Hulk Coaster.

7. Go back past Dr. Doom on Super Hero Island and experience The Adventures of Spider-Man.

   Note: Steps 8–10 involve attractions where you will get wet. If you're not up for a soaking this early in the morning, skip ahead to Step 11, but be advised that you may have a bit of a wait at the Toon Lagoon attractions later in the day.

8. Continuing clockwise around the lake, depart Super Hero Island and cross into Toon Lagoon.

9. In Toon Lagoon, ride Dudley Do-Right's Ripsaw Falls.

10. Also in Toon Lagoon, subject yourself to Popeye & Bluto's Bilge-Rat Barges.

11. After the barge ride, continue your clockwise circuit around the lake, passing through Jurassic Park without stopping. Continue to the Lost Continent.

12. At Lost Continent, ride both tracks of Dueling Dragons.

13. While at Lost Continent, experience *Poseidon's Fury! Escape from the Lost City.*

14. Depart Lost Continent, moving counterclockwise around the lake, and enter Jurassic Park.

15. In Jurassic Park, try the Jurassic Park River Adventure.

16. Also in Jurassic Park, check out Triceratops Encounter.

17. Return to Lost Continent. Check the daily entertainment schedule for the next performance of *The Eighth Voyage of Sinbad* stunt show. If a show is scheduled to begin within 30 minutes or so, go ahead and check it out. Otherwise, skip ahead to Step 18 and work *Sinbad* in later.

18. From Lost Continent, move clockwise around the lake to Seuss Landing. Ride The Cat in the Hat.

19. While in Seuss Landing, ride Sylvester McMonkey McBean if it's operating.

20. At this point, you will have done all the big stuff. Spend the rest of your day experiencing attractions you bypassed earlier or repeating ones you especially enjoyed.

About Sea World

Many dozens of readers have written to extol the virtues of Sea World. The following are representative.

An English family writes:

> The best organized park [is] Sea World. The computer printout we got on arrival had a very useful show schedule, told us which areas were temporarily closed due to construction, and had a readily understandable map. Best of all, there was almost no queuing. Overall, we rated this day so highly that it is the park we would most like to visit again.

A woman in Alberta, Canada, gives her opinion:

> We chose Sea World as our fifth day at "The World." What a pleasant surprise! It was every bit as good (and in some ways better) than WDW itself. Well worth the admission, an excellent entertainment value, educational, well run, and better value for the dollar in food services. Perhaps expand your coverage to give them their due!

A father of two from Winnipeg, Manitoba, gives Sea World's nighttime laser show top marks, commenting:

But the absolute topper is the closing laser show, which beats out IllumiNations *at Epcot for extravaganza. The Sea World show combines fireworks, lasers, and moving holographic images back-projected on a curtain of water. In the word of our older daughter: awesome! And you watch the whole thing seated in the lakeside arena, instead of jostling for a standing view around the Epcot lagoon.*

A reader from Sylvania, Georgia, believes Disney could learn a thing or two from Sea World:

Disney ought to take a look at how well this place is run. I know they don't have the same crowds or the exciting rides, but there is still a lot of entertainment here and never a wait. This allows you to set your pace without worrying about what you'll have to miss. You'll see it all no matter how you do it, you'll come away feeling you got better value for your dollars, you won't feel as tired as a Disney day, and you will probably learn more, too. Only downturn is you'll probably be hungry. Food is not one of the park's assets.

Okay here's what you need to know (for additional information, call (407) 363-2613):

Sea World is a world-class marine-life theme park near the intersection of I-4 and the Bee Line Expressway. Open daily from 9 a.m. to 10 p.m., Sea World charges about $44 admission (plus tax) for adults and $35 (plus tax) for children (ages three to nine). Combination passes, which include admission to Sea World, Universal Studios, Islands of Adventure, Wet 'n Wild, and Busch Gardens, are also available. Parking is $5 per car, $7 per RV or camper. Discount coupons for Sea World admission are available in the free visitor magazine found in most (but not Disney) hotel lobbies. Figure six to nine hours to see everything, but only five or so if you stick to the big deals.

Sea World is about the size of the Magic Kingdom and requires about the same amount of walking. Most attractions are accessible to nonambulatory disabled persons. In terms of size, quality, and creativity, Sea World is unequivocally on a par with Disney's major theme parks. Unlike Walt Disney World, however, Sea World primarily features stadium shows or walk-through exhibits. This means that you will spend about 90% less time waiting in line during eight hours at Sea World than you would for the same-length visit at a Disney park.

Because lines, with one or two exceptions, aren't much of a problem at Sea World, you can tour at almost any time of day. We recommend you start about 3:30 or 4 p.m. (when the park is open until 9 p.m. or later).

Star Ratings for Sea World Attractions	
★★★★½	Terrors of the Deep (shark and eel exhibit)
★★★★½	Penguin Encounter (penguin and puffin exhibit)
★★★★	Manatees: The Last Generation (manatee exhibit)
★★★★	Wild Arctic (simulation ride and Arctic wildlife polar bears)
★★★★	Shamu Killer Whale Show
★★★★	Sea Lion and Otter Show
★★★★	Atlantis Water Ski Show
★★★★	Journey to Atlantis
★★★★	Pacific Point Preserve (sea lion exhibit)
★★★★	Shamu's Happy Harbor (children's play area)
★★★★	Whale and Dolphin Discovery Show
★★★½	Tropical Reef (reef-fish aquarium exhibit)
★★★	Hawaiian Rhythms (Polynesian dance and music)
★★½	Mermaids, Myths, & Monsters (fireworks and lasers; nights only)
★★½	Sea World Theater (Sea World propaganda and dancing fountains)
★★	Nautilus Theatre (musical revue)

Many of the day's early guests will have left by this hour, and you'll be able to enjoy the outdoor attractions in the relative cool of late afternoon and evening. If you visit in the morning, arrive early or late. Midmorning arrivals tend to create long waits at the ticket windows.

A daily entertainment schedule is printed conveniently on a placemat-sized map of the park. The four featured shows are:

- Shamu Killer Whale Show
- Sea Lion and Otter Show
- Atlantis Water Ski Show
- Whale and Dolphin Discovery Show

When you arrive, build your itinerary around these shows. You'll notice immediately as you check the performance times that they're scheduled in a way that makes it almost impossible to see them back to back. The Shamu show, for example, might run from 5 to 5:25 p.m. Ideally, you'd like to bop over to the Sea Lion and Otter Show, which begins at 5:30 p.m. Unfortunately, five minutes isn't enough time to exit Shamu Stadium and cross the park to the Sea Lion & Otter Stadium. Sea World, of course, planned it this way so you would stay longer.

It is possible to catch the Shamu show and the Sea Lion and Otter Show in succession by sitting near an exit at Shamu Stadium and leaving a minute or two early (while the performers are taking their bows). Getting a couple of minutes' head start on the crowd and hurrying directly to the Sea Lion & Otter Stadium will get you seated just as the show is beginning. While this strategy allows you to see more in a short time, it makes for a somewhat frenetic and less relaxing tour.

If you're going to a show in Shamu Stadium or at the Atlantis Water Ski Stadium, don't worry about arriving late. Both stadiums are huge, so you almost certainly will get a seat. Plus, there isn't much in the first few minutes of either show that you can't afford to miss. The same goes for the Whale and Dolphin Discovery Show. The beginning of the Sea Lion and Otter Show, however, is really good; try to be on time.

Journey to Atlantis is Sea World's entry into the theme park super-attraction competition. Occupying the equivalent of six football fields, Journey to Atlantis is the world's first attraction to combine elements of a high-speed water ride and a roller coaster. Guests are invited to explore the lost city of Atlantis, recently risen from the depths. After boarding a rickety Greek fishing boat, however, they're sucked into the city and "plunged into a swirling vortex." While this obviously is press-release language, this is not a ride to trifle with. If you visit after Journey to Atlantis opens, catch it just after the park opens, or be prepared to wait. By the way, you'll get soaked.

Stand-alone exhibits feature dolphins, stingrays, pelicans, spoonbills, flamingos, and the Anheuser-Busch Clydesdale horses, plus a tidal pool and tropical rain forest.

Part Fourteen
The Water Theme Parks

Disney has three swimming theme parks, and two more independent water parks are in the area. At Disney World, River Country is the oldest and smallest park. Typhoon Lagoon, about five years old, is the most diverse Disney splash pad, while three-year-old Blizzard Beach takes the prize for the most slides and most bizarre theme. Outside the World, find Wet 'n Wild and Water Mania.

At all Disney water parks, the following rules and prices apply: one cooler per family or group is allowed, but no glass and no alcoholic beverages; towels $1, small locker $3, large locker $5 ($2 deposit required for lockers), life jacket $25 refundable deposit.

BLIZZARD BEACH

Blizzard Beach is Disney's most exotic water adventure park and, like Typhoon Lagoon, it arrived with its own legend. This time, the story goes, an entrepreneur tried to open a ski resort in Florida during a particularly savage winter. Alas, the snow melted; the palm trees grew back; and all that remained of the ski resort was its Alpine lodge, the ski lifts, and, of course, the mountain. Plunging off the mountain are ski slopes and bobsled runs transformed into water slides. Visitors to Blizzard Beach catch the thaw: icicles drip and patches of snow remain. The melting snow has formed a lagoon (the wave pool), fed by gushing mountain streams.

Like Typhoon Lagoon, Blizzard Beach is distinguished by its landscaping and the attention paid to executing its theme. As you enter Blizzard Beach, you face the mountain. Coming off the highest peak and bisecting the area at the mountain's base are two long slides. To the left of the slides is the wave pool. To the right are the children's swimming area and the ski lift. Surrounding the layout like a moat is a tranquil stream for floating in tubes. Picnic areas are scattered around the park, as are pleasant places for sunbathing.

On either side of the highest peak are tube, raft, and body slides. Including the two slides coming off the peak, Blizzard Beach has 17 slides.

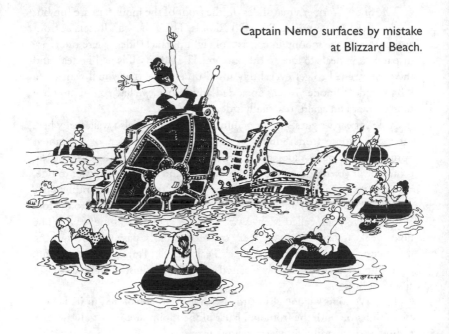

Captain Nemo surfaces by mistake
at Blizzard Beach.

Among them is Summit Plummet, Disney World's longest speed slide, which begins with a 120-foot free-fall, and the Teamboat Springs water bobsled run, 1,200 feet long.

For our money, the most exciting and interesting slides are the Slush Gusher and Teamboat Springs on the front right of the mountain, and Run-Off Rapids on the back side of the mountain. Slush Gusher is an undulating speed slide that we consider as exciting as the more vertical Summit Plummet without being as bone-jarring. On Teamboat Springs, you ride in a raft that looks like a round, children's blow-up wading pool. The more people you load into the raft, the faster it goes. If you have only a couple in it, the slide is kind of a snore.

Run-Off Rapids is accessible from a path that winds around the far left bottom of the mountain. The Rapids consists of three corkscrew tube slides, one of which is enclosed and dark. As at Teamboat Springs, you'll go much faster on a two- or three-person tube than on a one-person tube. If you lean so that you enter curves high and come out low, you'll really fly. Because we like to steer the tube and go fast, we much prefer the open slides (where we can see) to the dark, enclosed tube. We thought crashing through the pitch-dark tube felt disturbingly like being flushed down a toilet.

The Snow Stormer's mat slides on the front of the mountain are fun but not as fast or interesting as Run-Off Rapids. The Toboggan Racers at front and center on the mountain consists of eight parallel slides where riders are dispatched in heats to race to the bottom. The ride itself is no big deal, and the time needed to get everybody lined up ensures that you'll wait extra long to ride. On one visit, as an added annoyance, we had to line up once to get a mat and again to actually ride.

A ski lift carries guests to the mountaintop (you can also walk up) where they can choose from Summit Plummet, Slush Gusher, or Teamboat Springs. For all other slides at Blizzard Beach, the only way to reach the top is on foot. If you're among the first in the park and don't have to wait to ride, the ski lift is fun and provides a bird's-eye view of the park. After riding once to satisfy your curiosity, however, you're better off taking the stairs to the top.

The wave pool, called Melt-Away Bay, has gentle, bobbing waves. The float creek, Cross Country Creek, circles the park, passing through the mountain. The children's areas, Tike's Peak and Ski Patrol Training Camp, are creatively designed, nicely isolated, and, like the rest of the park, visually interesting.

Like Typhoon Lagoon, Blizzard Beach is a bit convoluted in its layout. With slides on both the front and back of the mountain, it isn't always easy to find a path leading to where you want to go.

At the ski resort's now-converted base area are shops; counter-service food; rest rooms; and tube, towel, and locker rentals. Blizzard Beach has its own parking lot but offers no lodging, though Disney's All-Star and Coronado Springs resorts are almost within walking distance. Disney resort and campground guests can commute to the park aboard Disney buses.

Because it's new and has popular slides, Blizzard Beach fills early during hotter months. To stake out a nice sunning spot and to enjoy the slides without long waits, arrive at least 35 minutes before the official opening time. Admission is about $29 per day for adults and $23 per day for children ages three to nine. Children younger than three are admitted free. If you're going primarily for the slides, you'll have about two hours in the early morning to enjoy them before the waiting becomes intolerable.

TYPHOON LAGOON

Typhoon Lagoon is comparable in size to Blizzard Beach and about four times larger than River Country. Ten water slides and streams, some as long as 400 feet, drop from the top of a 100-foot-tall, man-made mountain. Landscaping and an "aftermath-of-a-typhoon" theme add adventure to the wet rides.

Entry to Typhoon Lagoon is through a misty rain forest that emerges in a ramshackle tropical town, where concessions and services are situated. Special sets make every ride an odyssey as swimmers encounter bat caves, lagoons and pools, spinning rocks, formations of dinosaur bones, and many other imponderables.

Typhoon Lagoon has its own parking lot but no lodging. Disney resort and campground guests can commute to the park on Disney buses.

Like Blizzard Beach, Typhoon Lagoon is expensive: about $29 a day for adults and $23 a day for children ages three to nine. Children younger than three are admitted free. If you indulge in all features of Typhoon Lagoon, admission is a fair value. If you go primarily for the slides, you will have only two early-morning hours to enjoy them before the wait becomes prohibitive.

Typhoon Lagoon provides water adventure for all ages. Activity pools for young children and families feature geysers, tame slides, bubble jets, and fountains. For the older and more adventurous are two speed slides, four corkscrew body slides, and three tube rapids rides (plus one children's rapids ride) plopping off Mount Mayday. Slower metabolisms will like the scenic, meandering, 2,100-foot-long stream that floats tubers through a hidden grotto and rain forest. And, of course, the sedentary will usually find plenty of sun to sleep in. Typhoon Lagoon's surf pool and Shark Reef are unique, and the wave pool is the world's largest inland surf facility, with waves up to 6 feet in height (enough, so Disney says, to "encompass an oceanliner"). Shark Reef is a saltwater snorkeling pool where guests can swim among real fish.

Shark Reef

Fins, mask, snorkel, and wet-suit vest are provided free in the wooden building beside the diving pool. After you obtain the proper equipment (no forms or money involved), you shower and then report to a snorkeling instructor. After a brief lesson, you swim about 60 feet to the other side of the pool. You aren't allowed to paddle aimlessly, but must traverse the pool more or less directly.

The reef is fun in early morning. Equipment collection, shower, instruction, and the quick swim can be accomplished without much hassle. Also, because few guests are present, attendants are more flexible about your lingering in the pool or making minor departures from the charted course.

Later, as crowds build, it becomes increasingly difficult and time-consuming to provide the necessary instruction. The result is platoons of would-be frogmen restlessly awaiting their snorkeling lesson. Guests are grouped in impromptu classes with the entire class briefed and then launched together. What takes four or five minutes shortly after opening can take more than an hour by 11 a.m.

By far the most prevalent species in the pool are the dual-finned Homo sapiens. Other denizens include small, colorful tropical fish, some diminutive rays, and a few very small leopard and hammerhead sharks. In terms of numbers, it would be unusual to cross the pool and not see some fish. On the other hand, you aren't exactly bumping into them.

It's very important to fit your diving mask on your face so that it seals around the edges. Brush your hair from your forehead and sniff a couple of times once the mask is in place, to create a vacuum. Mustaches often prevent the mask from sealing properly. The first indication that your mask isn't correctly fitted will be saltwater in your nose.

If you don't want to swim with fish early in the morning or fight crowds later in the day, visit the underwater viewing chamber, accessible anytime without waiting, special equipment, showers, instruction, or water in your nose.

Typhoon Lagoon Surf Pool

While Blizzard Beach, Wet 'n Wild, and Water Mania have wave pools, Typhoon Lagoon has a *surf pool.* Most people will encounter larger waves here than they have in the ocean. The surf machine puts out a wave about every 90 seconds (just about how long it takes to get back in position if you caught the previous wave). Perfectly formed and ideal for riding, each wave is about five to six feet from trough to crest. Before you join the fray, watch two or three waves from shore. Since each wave breaks in almost the same spot, you can get a feel for position and timing. Observing other surfers is also helpful.

The best way to ride the waves is to swim about three-fourths of the way to the wall at the wave-machine end of the surf pool. When the wave comes (you will both feel and hear it), swim vigorously toward the beach, attempting to position yourself one-half to three-fourths of a body length below the breaking crest. The waves are so perfectly engineered that they will either carry you forward or bypass you. Unlike an ocean wave, they won't slam you down.

A teenage girl from Urbana, Illinois, notes that the primary hazard in the surf pool is colliding with other surfers and swimmers:

> *The surf pool was nice except that I kept landing on really hairy fat guys whenever the big waves came.*

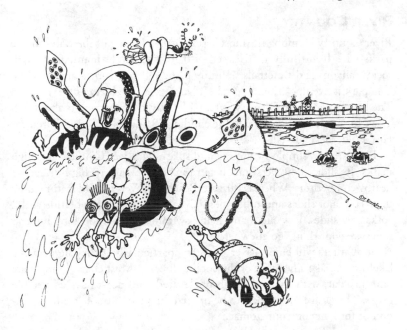

The best way to avoid collisions while surfing is to paddle out far enough that you will be at the top of the wave as it breaks. This tactic eliminates the possibility of anyone landing on you from above and assures maximum forward visibility. A corollary to this: The worst place to swim is where the wave actually breaks. You will look up to see a six-foot wall of water carrying eight dozen screaming surfers bearing down on you. This is the time to remember every submarine movie you've ever seen . . . Dive! Dive! Dive!

A final warning: The surf pool has a knack for loosening watchbands, stripping jewelry, and sucking stuff out of your pockets. Don't take anything out there except your swimsuit (and hold on to it).

Club Typhoon

On Friday nights from mid-June to mid-August, Typhoon Lagoon reopens from 7 p.m. until 11 p.m. as "Club Typhoon." Live music and organized activities augment the park's water attractions. Adult admission for the three-hour gig is about $15. Not only is the price right, but the park is less crowded than during the day and you don't have to worry about getting sunburned.

RIVER COUNTRY

River Country is among the most aesthetically pleasing of the water theme parks—it's beautifully landscaped and immaculately manicured, with rocky canyons and waterfalls skillfully blending with white-sand beaches. The park is even positioned to take advantage of the breeze off Bay Lake. The least expensive of Disney's water parks, River Country costs about $18 a day for adults and $14 a day for children ($14 adults, $11 children for Fort Wilderness guests).

For pure and simple swimming and splashing, River Country gets high marks. Its slides, however, don't begin to compete with its big brothers or nearby competitors. Whereas Blizzard Beach and Wet 'n Wild feature more than 16 major slides and tube rides, River Country has 1 tube ride and 2 corkscrew slides. Few slides and many swimmers add up to long lines. If slides are your thing, go elsewhere.

Sunbathers will enjoy River Country, particularly if they lie near the lakefront to take advantage of the cooling breezes. Most chaise lounges are basically flat, with the head slightly elevated, and don't have adjustable backs. They leave a great deal to be desired for a comfortable reading position or for lying on your stomach.

Reaching River Country by car is a hassle. You're directed to a parking lot, where you leave your car, gather your belongings, and wait for a Disney bus to take you to the park. The ride is rather lengthy, and pity the poor soul who left his bathing suit in the car (a round trip to retrieve it will take about 30 minutes). In the morning, the bus from the parking lot to River Country is very crowded. We suggest catching the bus to Pioneer Hall (which loads at the same place in the parking lot), then walking to River Country from there.

There's no lodging at River Country, but it's within walking distance of much of Fort Wilderness Campground. Food is available, or you can pack a lunch to eat in the park's picturesque, shaded, lakeside picnic area. Access is by bus from the Transportation and Ticket Center (junction and transfer point for the Epcot and Magic Kingdom monorails) or from the River Country parking lot at the entrance of Fort Wilderness Campground. River Country can also be reached by boat from the Magic Kingdom and from any hotel on Bay Lake or Seven Seas Lagoon.

DISNEY VS. WET 'N WILD AND
WATER MANIA THEME PARKS

Wet 'n Wild, on International Drive in Orlando, is on a par with Blizzard Beach and beats Typhoon Lagoon, River Country, and Water Mania for slides. The headliners at Wet 'n Wild are the Black Hole, the Surge, and the Fuji Flyer. At the Black Hole, guests descend on a two-person tube down a totally enclosed corkscrew slide, sort of a wet version of Space Mountain—only much darker. Our researchers think this is the most exciting slide at any Florida swimming theme park (Water Mania, Typhoon Lagoon, and Blizzard Beach have similar slides). The Surge launches groups of five down a 580-foot twisting, turning course. The Fuji Flyer is a 450-foot water-toboggan course. Another Wet 'n Wild thrill slide is Bomb Bay, which drops guests from a compartment resembling a bomb bay down a chute angled at 79°.

Water Mania, on US 192 south of I-4, edges out Typhoon Lagoon for slides and is less crowded than its competitors. In addition, it's the only water park to offer a stationary surfing wave.

What sets Disney water parks apart is not so much their slides and individual attractions but the Disney attention to detail in creating an integrated adventure environment. Both eye and body are deluged with the strange, the exotic, the humorous, and the beautiful. Wilder slides and rapids rides can be found elsewhere, but other water parks can't compete with Disney in diversity, variety, adventure, and total impact. Water Mania is nicely landscaped, but it doesn't have a theme. Wet 'n Wild, though attractive and clean, is cluttered and not especially appealing to the eye.

In the surf and wave pool department, Typhoon Lagoon wins hands down, with Wet 'n Wild taking second place. All of the parks have an outstanding water activity area for young children, and all except River Country feature unique attractions. Wet 'n Wild has a ride in which guests kneel on water skis, and Blizzard Beach has a 1,200-foot water bobsled. At Typhoon Lagoon, guests can snorkel among live fish, and Water Mania has a surfing wave.

Prices for one-day admission are about the same at Wet 'n Wild, Blizzard Beach, and Typhoon Lagoon, and slightly less at Water Mania. River Country is the least expensive of the water parks. Discount coupons are often available in local visitor magazines for Water Mania and Wet 'n Wild.

Wet 'n Wild is open until 11 p.m. during summer; the Disney swimming parks and Water Mania generally close between 5 and 8 p.m. The late closing is a huge plus for Wet 'n Wild. Warm Florida nights are great for enjoying a water theme park. There's less waiting for slides, and the pavement is cooler under your feet. To top it off, Wet 'n Wild features live music in the evening at its Wave Pool Stage and sells half-price tickets after 4 p.m. on days when the park is open late.

If your primary interest is sunning and swimming, you can't beat River Country. It's beautiful and usually has a nice breeze blowing off Bay Lake. If you're into slides, Blizzard Beach is tops among the Disney water parks, with Wet 'n Wild leading the independents. Typhoon Lagoon offers enough slides to keep most folks happy, has its signature surf pool, and provides the most variety. If you like slides but not crowds and are willing to sacrifice exotic surroundings for more elbow room, Water Mania is a good and cheaper choice. For evening and nighttime swimming fun, Wet 'n Wild is the only game in town, except on Friday nights from mid-June to mid August, when Typhoon Lagoon reopens as "Club Typhoon."

TYPHOON LAGOON VS. BLIZZARD BEACH

Many Walt Disney World guests aren't interested in leaving the World. For them, the question is which is better, Typhoon Lagoon or Blizzard Beach? Our readers answer.

A mother of four from Winchester, Virginia, gives her opinion:

> At Blizzard Beach the family raft ride is great, [but] the kids' area is poorly designed. As a parent, when you walk your child to the top of a slide or the tube ride, they are lost to your vision as they go down because of the fake snow drifts. There are no direct ways down to the end of the slides, so little ones are left standing unsupervised [while] parents scramble down from the top. The Typhoon Lagoon kids' area is far superior in design.

A couple from Woodridge, Illinois, writes:

> We liked Blizzard Beach much more. It seems like they took everything from Typhoon Lagoon and made it better and faster. Summit Plummet was awesome—a total rush. Worth the half-hour wait. Toboggan and bobsled rides were really exciting—bobsled really throws you around. Family tube ride was really good—much better and much longer than at Typhoon Lagoon. Tube rides were great, especially in enclosed tube. If you only have time to go to one water park, go to Blizzard Beach.

But a hungry reader from Aberdeen, New Jersey, complains:

> At Blizzard Beach, there is only one main place to get food (most of the other spots are more for snacks). At lunchtime, it took almost 45 minutes to get some sandwiches and drinks.

A couple from Bowie, Maryland, didn't enjoy Summit Plummet:

> The tallest and fastest slide at Blizzard Beach gave me a bunch of bruises. Even my husband hurt for a few days. It wasn't a fun ride, and we both agree that it wasn't worth waiting in line for. Basically, you drop until you hit the slide and that is why everyone comes off rubbing

their butts. They say you go 60 mph on a 120-foot drop. I'll never do it again.

A man from Lexington, Massachusetts, who felt like a "hen egg in a skillet" reports:

Blizzard Beach is not well thought out. No shade from the Florida sun and way too much hot concrete.

Typhoon Lagoon won over a Texas family:

The water parks were great! Our favorite for the whole family was Typhoon Lagoon. There was a lot of shade if you wanted, the river around was better [than at Blizzard Beach], and the surf pool was great.

WHEN TO GO

The best way to avoid standing in lines is to visit the water parks when they're less crowded. Because the parks are popular among locals, weekends can be tough. We recommend going on a Monday or Tuesday, when most other tourists will be visiting the Magic Kingdom, Epcot, the Animal Kingdom, or Disney-MGM Studios and locals will be at work or school. Fridays are good because people traveling by car commonly use this day to start home. Sunday morning also has lighter crowds. During summer and holiday periods, Typhoon Lagoon and Blizzard Beach fill to capacity and close their gates before 11 a.m.

A reader from Newbury Park, California, gives an idea of what "crowded" means:

The only disappointment we had at WDW was Typhoon Lagoon. While WDW was quite uncrowded, Typhoon Lagoon seemed choked with people. I'd hate to see it on a really crowded day. Even the small slides had lines greater than 30 minutes. They weren't worth half the wait. Castaway Creek might have been relaxing, but I found it to be a continuous traffic jam. I [also] would have enjoyed the snorkeling area except we were forced to go through at warp speed. After half a day we returned to the Yacht Club, where Stormalong Bay provided much more pleasant water recreation.

A mom from Manlius, New York, writes:

Because we had the 5-Day Park-Hopper, we also visited Typhoon Lagoon, arriving before opening so we could stake out a shady spot. The kids loved it until the lines got long (11 a.m. to noon), but I hated it. It made Coney Island seem like a deserted island in the Bahamas. Floating on Castaway Creek was really unpleasant. Whirling around in a chlorinated, concrete ditch with some stranger's feet in my face, periodically getting squirted by waterguns, passing under cascades of cold water, and getting hung up by the crowd is not at all relaxing for me. My husband and I then decided to "bob" in the surf pool. After about 10 minutes of being tossed around like corks in boiling water, he turned a little green around the gills and we sought the peace of our shady little territory which, in our absence, had become much, much smaller. We sat and read our books, elbow to elbow with other pleasure-seekers, until the kids had their fill. They, however, loved the body slides and the surf waves, commenting on how useful your "coach's tip" was.

A visitor from Middletown, New York, had a somewhat better experience:

On our second trip [to Typhoon Lagoon], we dispensed with the locker rental (having planned to stay for only the morning when it was least crowded), and at park's opening just took right off for the Storm Slides before the masses arrived—it was perfect! We must have ridden the slides at least five times before any kind of line built up, and then we were also able to ride the tube and raft rides (Keelhaul and Mayday Falls) in a similar uncrowded, quick fashion because everyone else was busy getting their lockers! We also experienced the Shark Reef snorkeling three times with minimal crowds that day, because, I think, most people overlook this attraction. Shark Reef is lots of fun and a great way to cool off since their water temp is well below the wave pool's.

If your schedule is flexible, a good time to visit the swimming parks is midafternoon to late in the day when the weather has cleared after a storm. The parks usually close during bad weather. If the storm is prolonged, most guests leave for their hotels. When Typhoon Lagoon, Blizzard Beach, or River Country reopen after inclement weather has passed, you almost have a whole park to yourself.

PLANNING YOUR DAY AT DISNEY WATER PARKS

Disney swimming theme parks are almost as large and elaborate as the major theme parks. You must be prepared for a lot of walking, exercise, sun, and jostling crowds. If your group really loves the water, schedule your visit early in your vacation. For many families, a visit to a water park is the highlight of their trip. If you go at the beginning of your stay, you'll have more flexibility if you want to return.

To have a great day and beat the crowd at any of the Disney water parks, consider:

1. *Getting Information.* Call (407) 824-4321 the night before you go to ask when your chosen park opens.

2. *To Picnic or Not to Picnic.* Decide whether you want to carry a picnic lunch. Guests are permitted to take lunches and beverage coolers into the parks. No alcoholic beverages are allowed. Glass containers of any kind (including mayonnaise, mustard, peanut butter, and pickle jars) are likewise forbidden.

3. *Getting Started.* If you are going to Blizzard Beach or Typhoon Lagoon, get up early, have breakfast, and arrive at the park 40 minutes before opening. If you have a car, drive instead of taking a Disney bus. If you're going to River Country, you don't have to get there so early.

4. *Attire.* Wear your bathing suit under shorts and a T-shirt so you don't need to use lockers or dressing rooms. Wear shoes. Paths are relatively easy on bare feet, but there's a lot of ground to cover. If you have tender feet, wear your shoes as you move around the park, removing them when you raft, slide, or go into the water. Shops in the parks sell sandals, "Reef Runners," and other protective footwear that can be worn in and out of the water.

5. *What to Bring.* You will need a towel, suntan lotion, and money. Since wallets and purses get in the way, lock them in your car's trunk or leave them at your hotel. Carry enough money for the day and your Disney resort I.D. (if you have one) in a plastic bag or Tupperware container. Though nowhere is completely safe, we felt very comfortable hiding our plastic money bags in our cooler. Nobody disturbed our stuff, and our cash was much easier to reach than if we'd stashed it in a locker across the park. If you're carrying a wad or you worry about money anyway, rent the locker.

6. *What Not to Bring.* Personal swim gear (fins, masks, rafts, etc.) aren't allowed. Everything you need is either provided or available to rent. If you forget your towel, you can rent one (cheap!). If you forget your swimsuit or lotion, they're for sale. Personal flotation devices (life jackets) are available free of charge, but you must leave a credit card number or a driver's license as a deposit (held until the equipment is returned).

7. *Admissions.* Purchase your admission in advance or about 45 minutes before official opening time. If you're staying at a Disney property, you may be entitled to an admission discount; bring your hotel or campground I.D. Guests staying five or more days should consider the Park-Hopper Plus or Unlimited Magic Passes, which include admission to all Disney swimming parks.

8. *Lockers.* Rental lockers come in small and large sizes for $5 or $7 per day, of which $2 is refunded when you return your key. Lockers are roomy enough for one person or a couple, but are a stretch for an entire family. Though you can access your locker freely all day, not all lockers are conveniently located.

   Getting a locker at Blizzard Beach or Typhoon Lagoon is truly competitive. When the gates open, guests race to the locker rental desk. Once there, the rental procedure is somewhat slow. If you aren't among the first in line, you can waste a lot of time waiting to be served. We recommend you skip the locker. Carry only as much cash as you will need for the day in a watertight container you can stash in your cooler. Ditto for personal items including watches and eyeglasses. With planning, you can manage nicely without the locker and save time and hassle in the bargain.

9. *Tubes.* Tubes for bobbing on the waves, floating in the creeks, and riding the tube slides are available for free.

10. *Getting Settled.* Establish your base for the day. There are many beautiful sunning and lounging spots scattered throughout all Disney swimming parks. Arrive early, and you can almost have your pick. The breeze is best along the beaches of the surf pools at Blizzard Bay and Typhoon Lagoon. At River Country, pick a spot that fronts Bay Lake. At Typhoon Lagoon, if there are children younger than six in your party, choose an area to the left of Mount Mayday (ship on top) near the children's swimming area.

    Available are flat lounges (unadjustable) and chairs (better for reading), shelters for guests who prefer shade, picnic tables, and a few hammocks.

    The best spectator sport at Typhoon Lagoon is the bodysurfing in the surf pool. It's second only to being out there yourself. With this in mind, position yourself to have an unobstructed view of the waves.

11. *A Word about the Slides.* Water slides come in many shapes and sizes. Some are steep and vertical, some long and undulating.

Some resemble corkscrews; others imitate the pool-and-drop nature of whitewater streams. Depending on which slide, swimmers ride mats, inner tubes, or rafts. On body slides, swimmers slosh to the bottom on the seat of their pants.

Modern traffic engineering bows to old-fashioned queuing. At water slides, it's one person, one raft (or tube) at a time, and the swimmer on deck can't go until the person preceding him is safely out of the way. Thus, the slide's hourly capacity is limited compared to the continuously loading rides in the major theme parks. Because a certain interval between swimmers is required for safety, the only way to increase capacity is to increase the number of slides and rapids rides.

Though Typhoon Lagoon and Blizzard Beach are huge parks with many slides, they're overwhelmed almost daily by armies of guests. If your main reason for going to Typhoon Lagoon or Blizzard Beach is the slides and you hate long lines, be among the first guests to enter the park. Go directly to the slides and ride as many times as you can before the park fills. When lines for the slides become intolerable, head for the surf or wave pool, or the tube-floating streams.

For maximum speed on a body slide, cross your legs at the ankles and cross your arms over your chest. When you take off, arch your back so that almost all of your weight is on your shoulder blades and heels (the less contact with the surface, the less resistance). Steer by shifting most of your upper-body weight onto one shoulder blade. For top speed on turns, weight the shoulder blade on the outside of each curve. If you want to go slow (what's the point?), distribute your weight equally as if you were lying on your back in bed. For all curving slides, maximize speed by hitting the entrance to each curve high and exiting the curve low.

Some slides and rapids have a minimum height requirement. Riders for Humunga Kowabunga at Typhoon Lagoon and for Slush Gusher and Summit Plummet at Blizzard Beach, for example, must be four feet tall. Pregnant women and persons with back problems or other health difficulties shouldn't ride.

12. *Floating Streams.* Disney's Blizzard Beach and Typhoon Lagoon and the independent Water Mania and Wet 'n Wild offer mellow floating streams. A great idea, the floating streams are long, tranquil, inner-tube rides that give you the illusion that you're doing something though you're being sedentary. For wimps,

wussies, and exhausted people of all ages, floating streams are an answered prayer.

Disney's streams flow ever so slowly around the entire park, through caves and beneath waterfalls, past gardens, and under bridges. They offer a relaxing alternative to touring a park on foot.

Floating streams can be reached from several put-in and take-out points. There never are lines; just wade into the creek and plop into one of the inner tubes floating by. Ride the gentle current all the way around or get out at any exit. If you lie back and go with the flow, it will take 30–35 minutes to float the full circuit.

Predictably, there will be guests on whom the subtlety of floating streams is lost. They will be racing, screaming, and splashing. Let them pass, stopping a few moments, if necessary, to distance yourself from them.

13. *Lunch.* If you didn't bring a picnic, you can buy food. Portions are adequate to generous; quality is comparable to fast-food chains; and prices (as you would expect) are a bit high.

14. *More Options.* If you really are a water puppy, consider returning to your hotel for a heat-of-the-day nap and coming back to the water park for some early-evening swimming. Special lighting after dusk makes Typhoon Lagoon and Blizzard Beach enchanting. Crowds tend to be lighter in the evening. If you leave the park and want to return, be sure to keep your admission ticket and have your hand stamped. If you're staying in a hotel served by Disney buses, older children can return on their own to the water parks, giving Mom and Dad a little private quiet time.

15. *Bad Weather.* Thunderstorms are common in Florida. During summer afternoons, such storms can be a daily occurrence. Swimming parks close during a storm. Most storms, however, are short lived, allowing the swimming park to resume normal operations. If a storm is severe and prolonged, it can cause a great deal of inconvenience. In addition to the park's closing, guests compete aggressively for shelter, and Disney resort guests may have to compete for seats on a bus back to the hotel.

We recommend you monitor the local weather forecast the day before you go, checking again in the morning before leaving for the swimming park. Scattered thundershowers are to be expected, but moving storm fronts are to be avoided. Because

Florida is so flat, approaching weather can be seen from atop the slide platforms at the swimming parks. Particularly if you're dependent on Disney buses, leave the park earlier, rather than later, when you see a storm moving in.

16. *Endurance.* The water parks are large and require almost as much walking as one of the theme parks. Add to this wave surfing, swimming, and all the climbing required to reach the slides, and you'll be pooped by day's end. Unless you spend your hours like a lizard on a rock, don't expect to return to the hotel with a lot of energy. Consider something low-key for the evening. You probably will want to hit the hay early.

17. *Lost Children & Lost Adults.* It's as easy to lose a child or become separated from your party at one of the water parks as it is at a major theme park. Upon arrival, pick a very specific place to meet in the event you are separated. If you split up on purpose, set times for checking in. Lost-children stations at the water parks are so out of the way that neither you nor your lost child will find them without help from a Disney employee. Explain to your children how to recognize a Disney employee (by their distinctive name tags) and how to ask for help.

Part Fifteen

Beyond the Parks

Downtown Disney

Downtown Disney is a shopping, dining, and entertainment development strung out along the banks of the Buena Vista Lagoon. On the far right is the Downtown Disney Marketplace (formerly known as the Disney Village Marketplace). In the middle is the gated (admission-required) Pleasure Island nighttime entertainment, and on the far left is Disney's West Side.

Marketplace   Although the Marketplace offers interactive fountains, a couple of playgrounds, a Lagoon-side amphitheater, and watercraft rentals, it is primarily a shopping and dining venue. The centerpiece of shopping is the World of Disney, the largest Disney trademark merchandise store in the world. If you can't find what you are looking for in this 38,000-square-foot Noah's Ark of Disney stuff, it probably doesn't exist. Another noteworthy retailer is the LEGO Imagination Center, showcasing a number of huge and unbelievable sculptures made entirely of LEGO "bricks." Almost worthy of a special trip, spaceships, sea serpents, sleeping tourists, and dinosaurs are just a few of the sculptures on display. Rounding out the selection are stores specializing in resort wear, athletic attire and gear, Christmas decorations, Barbie dolls, Disney art and collectibles, and handmade craft items. Also located in the Marketplace is Studio M, where guests can have a professional photograph taken with Mickey. Most retail establishments are open from 9:30 a.m. until 11:30 p.m.

Rainforest Cafe is the headliner restaurant at the Marketplace. There is also Cap'n Jack's Oyster Bar, Wolfgang Puck pizza kitchen, a soda fountain, a deli and bakery, and a McDonald's. Full-service restaurants are profiled in Part 9, "Dining in and around Walt Disney World."

Pleasure Island Pleasure Island is a nighttime entertainment complex. Though admission is charged after 7 p.m., shops and restaurants are open with no admission required during the day. Detailed coverage of the night-spots is provided in Part 16, "Nightlife in and out of Walt Disney World." Pleasure Island's shops offer more Disney art, casual fashions, Disney charac-ter merchandise, movie collectibles, and music memorabilia. Superstar Stu-dios is a recording studio where you can make your own music video. There are four full-service restaurants at Pleasure Island. Fulton's Crab House and the Portobello Yacht Club can be accessed at any time without paying admis-sion to Pleasure Island. The Wild Horse Saloon, a country music club and barbecue restaurant, and Pleasure Island Jazz Company are within the gated part of Pleasure Island.

Disney's West Side The West Side is the newest addition to Downtown Disney and offers a broad range of entertainment, dining, and shopping. Restaurants include the House of Blues, which serves Cajun specialties; Planet Hollywood, offering movie memorabilia and basic American fare; Bongo's Cuban Cafe, serving Cuban favorites; and Wolfgang Puck Cafe, fea-turing California cuisine. All four West Side restaurants are profiled in Part 9, "Dining in and around Walt Disney World."

West Side shopping is some of the most interesting in WDW. For starters, there's a Virgin (records and books) Megastore. Across the street is the Guitar Gallery by George's Music, specializing in custom, collector, rare, and unique guitars. Other specialty shops include a cigar shop, a rock-and-roll and movie memorabilia store, and a western apparel boutique.

In the entertainment department, there is DisneyQuest, an interactive theme park contained in a building; the House of Blues, a concert and din-ing venue; and a 24-screen AMC movie theater. The West Side is also home to *Cirque du Soleil*, a not-to-be-missed production show with a cast of almost 100 performers and musicians. The House of Blues concert hall and *Cirque du Soleil* are described in Part 16, "Nightlife in and out of Walt Disney World." DisneyQuest is described in detail below.

DISNEYQUEST

For more than a decade, major theme parks have experimented with attrac-tions based on motion-simulation and virtual reality technologies. Among other things, these technologies have allowed thrill rides with the punch of a roller coaster to be engineered and operated in spaces as small as a one-car garage. Analogous to the computer industry, where the power of a bulky main-frame is now available in a laptop, Disney is pioneering the concept of a theme park in a box, or in the case of DisneyQuest, a modest five-story building.

Opened in the summer of 1998 in the West Side area of Downtown Disney, DisneyQuest contains all the elements of the larger Disney theme parks. There is an entrance area that facilitates your transition into the park environment and leads to the gateways of four distinct themed lands, here referred to as zones. As at other Disney parks, almost everything is included in the price of your admission.

It takes about two to four hours to experience DisneyQuest, once you get it. Disney limits the number of guests admitted to ensure that queues are manageable and that guests have a positive experience. Once DisneyQuest hits capacity, newly arriving guests are lined up outside to wait until departing guests make some room. Weekday mornings are the least crowded times to visit.

DisneyQuest, in concept and attraction mix, is aimed at a youthful audience, say 8–35 years of age, though younger and older patrons will enjoy much of what it offers. The feel is dynamic, bustling, and noisy. Those who haunt the electronic games arcades at shopping malls will feel most at home at DisneyQuest. And like most malls, when late afternoon turns to evening, the median age at DisneyQuest rises toward adolescents and teens who have been released from parental supervision for awhile.

You begin your experience in the Departure Lobby, adjacent to admission sales. From the Departure Lobby you enter a "Cyberlator," a sort of "transitional attraction" (read elevator) hosted by the genie from *Aladdin,* that delivers you to an entrance plaza called Ventureport. From here you can enter the four zones. Like in the larger parks, each zone is distinctively themed. Some zones cover more than one floor, so, looking around, you can see things going on both above and below you. The four zones, in no particular order, are Explore Zone, Score Zone, Create Zone, and Replay Zone. In addition to the zones, DisneyQuest offers two restaurants and the inevitable gift shop.

Though most kids and adolescents aren't going to care, the zone layout at DisneyQuest may confuse adults trying to orient themselves. Don't count on trapping certain kids in certain zones either, or planning a rendezvous inside one without designating a specific location. Each zone spreads out over multiple levels, with stairways, elevators, slides, and walkways linking them in a variety of ways. Still, as we said, the labyrinthine design of the place won't bother most youngsters, who are usually happy just to wander (or dash madly) between games and rides.

Explore Zone   The gateway to Explore Zone is the tiger's-head cave from *Aladdin.* You can descend to the attractions area on a 150-foot corkscrew slide or use more traditional means like elevators or ramps. The headline attraction in Explore Zone is the Virtual Jungle Cruise, where you paddle a six-person raft. The raft is a motion simulator perched on top of blue air bags that replicate the motion of water. Responding to the film of the river projected before you, you can choose several routes through the rapids. The motion simulator responds to sensors on your paddle, so the ride you experience simulates the course you choose. As if navigating the river isn't enough, man-eating dinosaurs and a cataclysmic comet are tossed in for good measure. Another Explore Zone attraction, Aladdin's Magic Carpet Ride, has you seated on a motorcycle-shaped simulator. Here you are fitted with a head-mounted virtual reality display. Leaning left and right on your faux motorcycle allows you to navigate your magic carpet through the streets of Agraba.

Score Zone Here you pass through a slash in a giant comic book to enter a theme area based on comic book characters and competition. The big deal here are enlarged, high-tech versions of electronic and video games where you pit your skill and reflexes against other players. The headliner is Mighty Ducks Pinball Slam, where you stand atop a mammoth hockey puck. By manipulating a joystick, you control the motion of your puck as it bounces around a virtual reality pinball machine. In Ride the Comix, you once again don virtual reality headgear to ride off into comic book scenes and do battle with archvillains.

Create Zone A digital artist's palette serves as the entrance to Create Zone. Featured here is CyberSpace Mountain, an attraction where you can design your own roller coaster, including 360° loops, and then take a virtual reality–motion simulator ride on your creation. Also in the Create Zone is Sid's Create a Toy, where you can design a toy and receive the parts to actually construct it at home. Other creative attractions include virtual beauty salon makeovers and painting on an electronic canvas.

Replay Zone Replay Zone draws its theme from a 1950s view of the future. Basically, it's three levels of classic midway games with a few futuristic twists. The balls on the Skeeball games, for example, glow in the dark. Winners of the various games earn redemption tickets, which can be redeemed for midway-type prizes. The pièce de résistance of Replay Zone is Buzz Lightyear's Astro Blasters, a fancy version of bumper cars. Here guests pilot two-person bumper-bubbles that suck up grapefruit-sized balls from the floor and fire them from an air cannon at other vehicles. Direct hits cause the other vehicles to spin momentarily out of control.

The Disney Institute

In 1996 Disney launched the Disney Institute, an ambitious alternative to the typical Disney World vacation. The institute, situated on its own campus in the Villas of the Disney Institute, offers a variety of educational and life-enriching courses and programs.

Participants enroll by the day for a fixed tuition. They choose among four dozen programs in the areas of culinary arts, design arts, entertainment arts, environment, lifestyles, story arts, youth programs, and sports and fitness. Students typically take a class in the morning and another in the afternoon, filling any remaining time with sports and fitness offerings. In the evenings there are concerts, lectures, films, and storytelling.

The campus is self-contained with lodging, a restaurant, classrooms, studios, and recreational facilities that include a championship 18-hole golf course. The institute is also the site of Walt Disney World's most comprehensive spa and fitness facility.

For most of its first three years, the Disney Institute struggled to hit its stride. Travel agents didn't understand the concept, and neither did the traveling public. The notion of an educational vacation is not foreign to most, but the idea of spending four or five days at Walt Disney World without visiting the theme parks seemed like lunacy. Disney finally figured out that the institute was more likely to succeed as part of a guest's Disney World vacation than as the whole enchilada.

Most courses are without prerequisite. This means that the instructors can't make any assumptions about the student's knowledge of the topic. Our "Wine, Wonders, and Song" class, for example, included wine initiates and others who possessed extensive knowledge of wine. The course was too advanced for the former and too basic for the latter.

At present, you don't have to lodge at the Disney Institute or even at Walt Disney World to participate. What's more, if you take courses at the institute, you're eligible to use the extraordinary recreational facilities (except golf) as part of your tuition.

Before signing up, ask pointed questions about the courses that interest you. By our experience, most reservationists know their product and should be able to steer you to appropriate programs.

You can make reservations for courses with your credit card by calling (407) 827-4800 or (407) 827-1100, or by visiting the Institute Welcome Center in person. You will be required to arrive on the day of your course 45 minutes in advance to actually pay for and receive your course admission tickets, a process not appreciated by a dentist from Conyers, Georgia:

> *Our second surprise was associated with the Disney Institute. Since we were unable to obtain any specific program information from the Institute by phone before leaving home, we visited the Institute's Welcome Center for on-site registration. What we learned after two very frustrating hours was that the registration process is phenomenally inef-*

ficient! Once our courses were selected and reserved by credit card, we learned we still had to stand in line each day to "purchase our tickets" for that day's class! Although we were in line at 7:40 a.m. for 8:30 a.m. classes, we didn't make the classes on time! Five people in line ahead of us were registered for 8 a.m. classes. When they complained they were missing their program, the Disney employee snapped back that they "should have been here earlier!" WOW!

In defense of their registration process, the Disney Institute explains that the current system eliminates refunds and confusion when outdoor courses must be cancelled because of bad weather. Disney additionally claims that participants forget their course admission tickets when tickets are issued prior to the day of the course.

Disney's Wide World of Sports

Disney's Wide World of Sports complex is a 200-acre, state-of-the-art competition and training complex consisting of a 7,500-seat ballpark, a fieldhouse, and dedicated venues for baseball, softball, tennis, track and field, beach volleyball, and 27 other sports. From Little League Baseball to rugby to beach volleyball, the complex hosts a mind-boggling calendar of professional and amateur competitions, with one or more events scheduled nearly every day.

During late winter and early spring, the complex is the spring training home of the Atlanta Braves. Although Disney guests are welcome at the sports complex as paid spectators (prices vary according to event), none of the facilities are available for guests' use unless they are participants in a scheduled organized competition. To learn what events are scheduled during your visit, call (407) 828-3267.

In addition to scheduled competitive events, a program called the NFL Experience is operated daily from 11 a.m. until about 5 p.m. Appealing primarily to school-age boys, the NFL Experience is a supervised activity that allows kids to kick field goals, catch and throw passes, catch punts, and run through a small obstacle course, among other things. Though the NFL Experience is sometimes the only thing going on at the Wide World of Sports complex, Disney nevertheless charges full admission. Our advice is to pass on the Wide World of Sports unless there is a specific event you want to see. Call the sports complex directly to confirm event times and venues (as opposed to trusting Disney guest relations personnel at the theme parks or hotels).

Counter-service and full-service dining are available at the sports complex, but there's no on-site lodging. Disney's Wide World of Sports is off

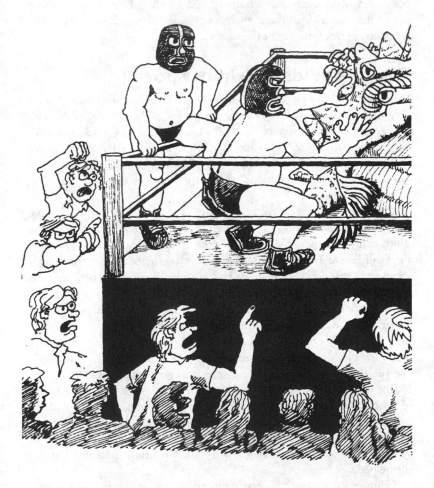

Conch Wrestling

Osceola Parkway, between World Drive and where the parkway crosses I-4 (no interstate access). The complex has its own parking lot and is accessible via the Disney Transportation System.

Walt Disney World Speedway

Adjacent to the Transportation and Ticket Center parking lot, the one-mile tri-oval course is host to several races each year. Between competitions, it's home to the Richard Petty Driving Experience, where you can ride in a two-seater stock car for $90 or learn to drive one. Courses are by reservation only and cost between $330 (8 laps) and $1,100 (30 laps). You must be age 18 or older, have a valid driver's license, and know how to drive a stick shift to take a course. For information, call (800) 237-3889.

Discovery Island

As anticipated, after the opening of the Animal Kingdom, Disney closed Discovery Island. At this time, it is used for private parties and special events.

Walt Disney World Recreation

Most Walt Disney World guests never make it beyond the theme parks, the water parks, and Downtown Disney. Those who do, however, discover an extraordinary selection of recreational opportunities ranging from guided fishing expeditions and water skiing outings to hay rides, horseback riding, fitness center workouts, and miniature golf. If it's something you can do at a resort, it's probably available at Walt Disney World.

Boat, bike, and fishing equipment rentals are handled on an hourly basis. Just show up at the rental office during operating hours and they'll fix you up. The same goes for various fitness centers in the resort hotels. Golf, tennis, fishing expeditions, water ski excursions, hayrides, trail rides, and most spa services must be scheduled in advance. Though every resort features an extensive selection of recreational options, those resorts located on a navigable body of water offer the greatest variety. Also, the more upscale a resort, the more likely it is to have such amenities as a fitness center and spa. In addition, you can rent boats and other recreational equipment at the Marketplace in Downtown Disney.

Walt Disney World Golf

Walt Disney World has six golf courses, all expertly designed and meticulously maintained. The Magnolia, the Palm, and the Oak Trail are across

Floridian Way from the Polynesian Resort. They envelop the Shades of Green recreational complex, and the pro shops and support facilities adjoin the Shades of Green hotel (for military personnel and retirees only). Lake Buena Vista Golf Course is at the Disney Institute, near Walt Disney World Village and across the lake from Pleasure Island. The Osprey Ridge and Eagle Pines courses are part of the Bonnet Creek Golf Club near the Fort Wilderness Campground. In addition to the golf courses, there are driving ranges and putting greens at each location.

Oak Trail is a nine-hole course for beginners. The other five courses are designed for the mid-handicap player and, while interesting, are quite forgiving. All courses are popular, with morning tee times at a premium, especially January through April. To avoid the crowds, play on a Monday, Tuesday, or Wednesday, and sign up for a late-afternoon tee time.

Peak season for all of the courses is September through April; off-season is May through August. Off season and afternoon twilight rates are available. Carts are required (except at Oak Trail) and are included in the greens fee. Tee times may be reserved 60 days in advance by Disney resort guests, 30 days in advance for day guests with a credit card, and 7 days in advance without guarantee. Proper golf attire is required: collared shirt and Bermuda-length shorts or slacks.

Lake Buena Vista Golf Course

Established: 1971

Designer: Joe Lee

Address: 2200 Club Lake Drive, Lake Buena Vista, FL 32830

Phone: (407) WDW-GOLF

Status: Resort

Tees:

> *Blue:* 6,819 yards, par 72, USGA 72.7, slope 128
> *White:* 6,268 yards, par 72, USGA 70.1, slope 123
> *Gold:* 5,919 yards, par 72, USGA 68.2, slope 120
> *Red:* 5,194 yards, par 73, USGA 69.4, slope 120

Fees: Seasonal. Call for current rates.

Facilities: Pro shop, driving range, practice green, locker rooms, snack bar, beverage cart, and club and shoe rentals

Comments   This Joe Lee design is styled in a classic country club setting, with narrow fairways meandering through dense forest and resort residential areas. Small, elevated, well-bunkered greens require accurate shotmaking. The course hosts the first three rounds of the Disney/Oldsmobile

Golf Classic PGA Tour Event and the Healthsouth Inaugural Classic LPGA Tour Event.

Osprey Ridge Golf Course

Established: 1992

Designer: Tom Fazio

Address: 3451 Golf View Drive, Lake Buena Vista, FL 32830

Phone: (407) WDW-GOLF

Status: Resort

Tees:

> *Black:* 7,101 yards, par 72, USGA 73.9, slope 135
> *Silver:* 6,680 yards, par 72, USGA 71.8, slope 128
> *Gold:* 6,103 yards, par 72, USGA 68.9, slope 121
> *Red:* 5,402 yards, par 72, USGA 70.5, slope 122

Fees: Seasonal. Call for current rates.

Facilities: Pro shop, driving range, practice green, locker rooms, Sand Trap Bar and Grill, beverage cart, and club and shoe rentals

Comments   Dramatically elevated tees and greens distinguish this Tom Fazio–designed course. Rolling fairways cut through tropical wilderness, while high mounds frame the medium-to-large greens.

Eagle Pines Golf Course

Established: 1992

Designer: Pete Dye

Address: 3451 Golf View Drive, Lake Buena Vista, FL 32830

Phone: (407) WDW-GOLF

Status: Resort

Tees:

> *Black:* 6,722 yards, par 72, USGA 72.3, slope 131
> *Silver:* 6,309 yards, par 72, USGA 69.9, slope 125
> *Gold:* 5,520 yards, par 72, USGA 66.3, slope 115
> *Red:* 4,838 yards, par 72, USGA 68, slope 111

Fees: Seasonal. Call for current rates.

Facilities: Pro shop, driving range, practice green, locker rooms, Sand Trap Bar and Grill, beverage cart, banquet facilities, and club and shoe rentals

Comments Low, dish-shaped fairways lend a unique look and challenge to the course. This design requires well-targeted shots to the appropriate transition areas and avoiding the water that dots 16 of the 18 holes. Medium-sized, undulating greens are guarded by St. Augustine grass bunkers.

Palm Golf Course

Established: 1970

Designer: Joe Lee

Address: 1950 West Magnolia/Palm Drive, Lake Buena Vista, FL 32830

Phone: (407) WDW-GOLF

Status: Resort

Tees:

> *Blue:* 6,957 yards, par 72, USGA 73.0, slope 133
> *White:* 6,461 yards, par 72, USGA 70.7, slope 129
> *Gold:* 6,029 yards, par 72, USGA 68.7, slope 124
> *Red:* 5,311 yards, par 72, USGA 70.4, slope 124

Fees: Seasonal. Call for current rates.

Facilities: Pro shop, driving range, practice green, locker rooms, snack bar, beverage cart, and club and shoe rentals

Comments This Joe Lee–designed course offers many tree-lined fairways and elevated greens, and boasts 9 water holes and 94 bunkers. Considered the most difficult tournament course, the Palm hosts the Disney/ Oldsmobile Classic PGA Tour Event.

Magnolia Golf Course

Established: 1970

Designer: Joe Lee

Address: 1950 West Magnolia/Palm Drive, Lake Buena Vista, FL 32830

Phone: (407) WDW-GOLF

Status: Resort

Tees:

> *Blue:* 7,190 yards, par 72, USGA 73.9, slope 133
> *White:* 6,642 yards, par 72, USGA 71.6, slope 128
> *Gold:* 6,091 yards, par 72, USGA 69.1, slope 123
> *Red:* 5,253 yards, par 72, USGA 70.5, slope 123

Fees: Seasonal. Call for current rates.

Facilities: Pro shop, driving range, practice green, locker rooms, sports bar, beverage cart, and club and shoe rentals

Comments   This is the longest of Disney's courses. Wide fairways invite you to hit the ball hard, but beware of the 97 bunkers, including the one shaped like Mickey Mouse that guards the sixth green. The championship round of the Disney/Oldsmobile Golf Classic is played here.

Oak Trail Golf Course

Designer: Ron Garl

Address: 1950 West Magnolia/Palm Drive, Lake Buena Vista, FL 32830

Phone: (407) WDW-GOLF

Status: Resort

Tees:

   White: 2,913 yards, par 36
   Red: 2,532 yards, par 36

Fees: Adult, $32; child, $20. Includes use of a pull cart (course is walking only). To replay the course costs an additional $16 for adults and $10 for children.

Facilities: Pro shop, driving range, practice green, locker rooms, sports bar, beverage cart, and club and shoe rentals

Comments   This nine-hole walking course is nestled within the back nine of the Magnolia Course.

Miniature Golf

A couple of years ago, the Disney Intelligence Patrol (DIP) noticed that as many as 113 guests a day were sneaking out of Walt Disney World to play Goofy Golf. Applying the logic of the boy who jammed his finger in the dike, Disney feared a hemorrhage of patrons from the theme parks. The thought of those truant guests making instant millionaires of miniature golf entrepreneurs on International Drive was enough to give a fat mouse ulcers.

The response to this assault on Disney's market share was Fantasia Gardens Miniature Golf, an 11-acre complex with two 18-hole dink-and-putt golf courses. One course is an "adventure" course, themed after Disney's animated film *Fantasia*. The other course, geared more toward older children and adults, is an innovative approach-and-putt course with sand traps and water hazards.

Fantasia Gardens is beautifully landscaped and creatively executed. There are fountains, animated statues, topiaries, flower beds, and a multitude of other imponderables that you're unlikely to find at most putt-putt courses.

Fantasia Gardens is on Epcot Resort Boulevard, across the street from the Walt Disney World Swan. To reach Fantasia Gardens via Disney transportation, take a bus or boat to the Swan resort.

The cost to putt at this course is $9 for adults and $8 for children. If you arrive hungry or naked, Fantasia Gardens has a snack bar and gift shop. For more information, call (407) 560-8760.

In 1999, Disney opened Winter Summerland, a second miniature golf facility located next to the Blizzard Beach water park. Winter Summerland offers two 18-hole courses—one has a blizzard in Florida theme, while the other sports a tropical holiday theme. The Winter Summerland courses are much easier than the Fantasia courses, making them a better choice for families with preteen children.

Part Sixteen

Nightlife in and out of Walt Disney World

Walt Disney World at Night

Disney so cleverly contrives to exhaust you during the day that the thought of night activity sends most visitors into shock. Walt Disney World, however, offers much for the hearty and the nocturnal to do in the evenings.

In the Parks

Epcot's major evening event is *IllumiNations,* a laser and fireworks show at World Showcase Lagoon. Show time is listed in the daily entertainment schedule.

In the Magic Kingdom are the popular evening parade(s) and *Fantasy in the Sky* fireworks. Consult the daily entertainment schedule for performances.

On nights when the park is open late, Disney-MGM Studios features a fireworks presentation called Sorcery in the Sky and *Fantasmic!*, a laser, special effects water spectacular. The daily entertainment schedule lists times. At present there is no nighttime entertainment at the Animal Kingdom.

At the Hotels

The Floating Electrical Pageant is a sort of Main Street Electrical Parade on barges. Starring King Neptune and creatures of the sea, the nightly pageant (backed by Handel played on a doozie of a synthesizer), is one of our favorite Disney productions. The first performance of the short but captivating show is at 9 p.m. off the Polynesian Resort docks. From there, it circles around and repeats at the Grand Floridian at 9:15 p.m., heading afterward to Fort Wilderness Campground, Wilderness Lodge, and the Contemporary Resort.

For something more elaborate, consider a dinner theater. If you want to go honky-tonkin', many lodgings at the Disney Village Hotel Plaza have lively bars.

At Fort Wilderness Campground

The nightly campfire program at Fort Wilderness Campground begins with a sing-along led by Disney characters Chip 'n' Dale and progresses to cartoons and a Disney movie. Only Disney lodging guests may attend. There's no charge.

At Disney's BoardWalk

Jellyrolls at the BoardWalk features dueling pianos and sing alongs in the image of New Orleans' Pat O' Brien's. The BoardWalk has Disney's first and only brew pub. A sports bar, an upscale dance club, and several restaurants complete the BoardWalk's entertainment mix. Access is by foot from Epcot, by launch from Disney-MGM Studios, and by bus from other Disney World locations.

At Downtown Disney

Pleasure Island   Pleasure Island, Walt Disney World's nighttime entertainment complex, offers eight nightclubs for one admission price. Dance to rock, soul, or country; take in a comedy show; or listen to some jazz. Pleasure Island is in Downtown Disney next to Downtown Disney Marketplace and is accessible from the theme parks and the Transportation and Ticket Center by shuttle bus. For details on Pleasure Island and a touring plan, see pages 696–703.

Downtown Disney Marketplace   It's flog your wallet each night at the Marketplace with shops open until 11:30 pm.

Disney's West Side   Disney's West Side is a 70-acre shopping, restaurant, and nightlife complex situated to the left of Pleasure Island. Not to be confused with the West End Stage at nearby Pleasure Island, this latest addition to Downtown Disney features a 24-screen AMC movie complex, the DisneyQuest pay-for-play indoor theme park (see pages 675–677), a permanent showplace for the extraordinary *Cirque du Soleil*, and a 2,000-capacity House of Blues concert hall. Dining options include Planet Hollywood, a 450-seat Cajun restaurant at House of Blues, Wolfgang Puck Cafe (serving gourmet pizza and California fare), and Bongo's (Cuban cuisine), owned by Gloria and Emilio Estefan. The complex can be accessed via Disney buses from most Disney World locations.

House of Blues

Type of Show: Live concerts with an emphasis on rock and blues
Tickets and Information: (407) 934-2222
Admission Cost with Taxes: $8–50, depending on who is performing
Nights of Lowest Attendance: Monday and Tuesday
Usual Show Times: Monday–Thursday, 8:30; Friday and Saturday, 9:30;
    Dark: Sunday

Description and Comments   The House of Blues, developed by original Blues Brother Dan Akroyd, features a restaurant and Blues Bar, as well as the concert hall. The restaurant serves from 11 a.m. until 2 a.m., making it one of the few late-night dining options in Walt Disney World. Live music cranks up nightly at 11 p.m. in the restaurant/Blues Bar, but even before then, the joint is way beyond ten decibels. The Music Hall next door features concerts by an eclectic array of musicians and groups. During our last visit, the showbill listed gospel, blues, funk, ska, dance, salsa, rap, zydeco, hard rock, groove rock, and reggae groups over a two-week period.

Touring Tips   Prices vary from night to night according to the fame and drawing power of the featured band. Tickets ranged from $7–30 during our visits but go higher when a really big name is scheduled.

    The Music Hall is set up like a nightclub, with tables and bar stools for only about 150 people and standing room for a whopping 1,850 people. Folks dance when there's room and sometimes when there isn't. The tables and stools are first-come, first-served, with doors opening an hour before show time on weekdays and 90 minutes before show time on weekends. Acoustics are good, and the showroom is small enough to provide a relatively intimate concert experience. All shows are all ages unless otherwise indicated.

Cirque du Soleil

Type of Show: Circus as theater
Tickets and Information: (407) 939-7600
Admission Cost with Taxes: $60; $47 ages 3–9
Cast Size: 72
Night of Lowest Attendance: Thursday
Usual Show Times: Wednesday–Saturday, 5:30 and 8:30 p.m.; Sunday, 2:30 and 5:30 p.m.; *Dark:* Monday and Tuesday
Smoking Allowed: No
Author's Rating: ★★★★★
Overall Appeal by Age Group:

Under 21	21–37	38–50	51 and older
★★★★	★★★★★	★★★★★	★★★★½

Duration of Presentation: An hour and a half (no intermission)

Description and Comments Cirque du Soleil is a far cry from a traditional circus but retains all the fun and excitement. It is whimsical, mystical, and sophisticated, yet pleasing to all ages. The action takes place on an elaborate stage that incorporates almost every part of the theater. The original musical score is exotic, like the show.

Note: In the following paragraph, I get into how the show *feels* and why it's special. If you don't care how it feels, or if you are not up to slogging through a boxcar of adjectives, the bottom line is simple: *Cirque du Soleil* is great. See it.

Cirque du Soleil is a most difficult show to describe. To categorize it as a circus does not begin to cover its depth, though its performers could perform with distinction in any circus on earth. *Cirque du Soleil* is more, much more, than a circus. It combines elements of Classical Greek theater, mime, the English morality play, Dali surrealism, Fellini characterization, and Chaplin comedy. *Cirque du Soleil* is at once an odyssey, a symphony, and an exploration of human emotions. The show pivots on its humor, which is sometimes black, and engages the audience with its unforgettable characters. Though light and uplifting, it is also poignant and dark. Simple in its presentation, it is at the same time extraordinarily intricate, always operating on multiple levels of meaning. As you laugh and watch the amazingly talented cast, you become aware that your mind has entered a dimension seldom encountered in a waking state. The presentation begins to register in your consciousness more as a seamless dream than as a stage production. You are moved, lulled, and soothed as well as excited and entertained. The sensitive, the imaginative, the literate, and those who love good theater and art will find nothing in all of Walt Disney World that compares with *Cirque du Soleil.*

Touring Tips   Be forewarned that the audience is an integral part of *Cirque du Soleil* and that at almost any time you might be plucked from your seat to participate. Our advice is to loosen up and roll with it. If you are too rigid, repressed, hungover, or whatever to get involved, politely but firmly decline to be conscripted. Then fix a death grip on the arms of your chair. Tickets for reserved seats can be purchased in advance at the *Cirque's* box office or over the phone using your credit card.

WALT DISNEY WORLD DINNER THEATERS

Several dinner theater shows play each night at Walt Disney World, and unlike other Disney dining venues, they make hard reservations instead of priority seatings. You must guarantee advance dinner-show reservations with a credit card. You will receive a confirmation number and be told to pick up your tickets at a Disney hotel Guest Services desk. Unless you cancel your tickets at least 48 hours before your reservation time, your credit card will still be charged the full amount. Dinner-show reservations can be made up to two years in advance; call (407) 939-3463. While getting reservations for the *Polynesian Luau* isn't too tough, booking the *Hoop-Dee-Doo Revue* is a trick of the first order. Call as soon as you're certain of the dates of your visit. The earlier you call, the better your seats will be.

A couple from Bismarck, North Dakota, explains:

> *I'm glad we made our reservations so early (a year in advance). I was able to reserve space for us at the* Luau *at the Polynesian and the* Hoop-Dee-Doo Revue. *At both of these, they seat you according to when you made your reservation. At the* Hoop-Dee-Doo Revue, *we had a front center table. We were so close to the stage, we could see how many cavities the performers had!*

If you can't get reservations and want to see one of the shows:

1. Call (407) 939-3463 at 9 a.m. each morning while you're at Disney World to make a same-day reservation. There are three performances each night, and for all three combined, only 3 to 24 people total will be admitted with same-day reservations.

2. Arrive at the show of your choice 45 minutes before show time (early and late shows are your best bets) and put your name on the standby list. If someone with reservations fails to show, you may be admitted.

Hoop-Dee-Doo Revue

Address: Pioneer Hall, Fort Wilderness Campground

Phone: (407) 939-3463

Show Times: 5, 7:15, and 9:30 p.m. nightly

Cost: $46; $24 ages 3–11.

Discounts: Seasonal; American Express discount at 9:30 show only

Type of Seating: Tables of various sizes to fit the number in each party, set in an Old West–style dance hall

Menu: All-you-can-eat barbecue ribs, fried chicken, corn-on-the-cob, and strawberry shortcake

Vegetarian Alternative: On request (at least 24 hours in advance)

Beverages: Unlimited beer, wine, sangria, and soft drinks

Description and Comments Six Wild West performers arrive by stagecoach (sound effects only) to entertain the crowd inside Pioneer Hall. There isn't much plot, just corny jokes interspersed with song or dance.

Given Disney's technical resources and its pool of talented entertainers, the *Hoop-Dee-Doo Revue* is rather amateurish, with decidedly low entertainment value. Jokes are lame and tend to dwell on puns. One marathon of puns using the word "bear" even prompted a six-year-old sitting nearby to shout in exasperation, "Stop saying 'bear.'" Audience participation includes sing-alongs, hand-clapping, and a finale that uses volunteers to play parts onstage. Performers are accompanied by a banjo player and pianist who provide quiet accompaniment while the food is being served.

The fried chicken and corn-on-the-cob are good, but the ribs are a bit tough. With the all-you-can-eat policy, at least you can get your money's worth by stuffing yourself silly. There isn't much value in the show.

While the *Hoop-Dee-Doo Revue* is far from being the best dinner show in the Disney World/Orlando area, traveling to Fort Wilderness and absorbing the rustic atmosphere of Pioneer Hall augments the adventure. For repeat Disney World visitors, an annual visit to the revue is a tradition of sorts. Plus, good or not, the revue is all Disney, and for some folks that's enough. The fact that performances sell out far in advance give the experience a special (if undeserved) aura.

Most of our readers enjoy the *Hoop-Dee-Doo Revue*, but not all. The thoughts of a Texas family are typical:

> *What is all the hoop-dee-doo with the* Hoop-Dee-Doo Revue? *The food was okay, if "gut-busting" fare is your idea of a fine night out, and the entertainment was pleasant. As a dinner theater, however, our family of three found it unexceptional in every respect but its cost. Had*

your review of the Revue *tempered its enthusiasm (much as you present its Polynesian counterpart), we probably would have canceled our reservation, pocketed the $100 and spent the evening joyously stunned by another glorious light-and-fireworks spectacle.*

An alternative to the *Hoop-Dee-Doo Revue* is the Fort Liberty show, a non-Disney attraction on FL 192.

If you go to the *Hoop-Dee-Doo Revue,* allow plenty of time to get there. The experience of a reader from Houston, Texas, makes the point:

> *We had 7:30 p.m. reservations for the* Hoop-Dee-Doo Revue, *so we left [Disney-]MGM just before 7 and drove directly to Fort Wilderness. Two important things to note: First, the road direction signs at WDW are terrible. I would recommend a daylight orientation drive upon arrival, except that there are so many ways to get confused that one might be lulled into a false sense of security. Second, when we got to Fort Wilderness, we had great difficulty determining where Pioneer Hall was and how to get there. I accosted several people and found a man who could tell us where we were on the map, and that a bus was the only way to get to Pioneer Hall. I would recommend leaving for Pioneer Hall one hour before your show reservations. Boredom is not nearly so painful as anxiety (reservations are held until 15 minutes after the stated time).*

A California dad suggests:

> *To go to the* Hoop-Dee-Doo Revue *at Fort Wilderness, take the boat from the Magic Kingdom rather than any bus. This [is] contrary to the "official" directions. The boat dock is a short walk from Pioneer Hall [in Fort Wilderness], while the bus goes to the [main] Fort Wilderness parking lot where one has to transfer to another bus to Pioneer Hall.*

Polynesian Luau

Address: Disney's Polynesian Resort

Phone: (407) 939-3463

Show Times: 6:45 and 9:30 p.m. nightly

Cost: $46; $24 ages 3–11

Discounts: Seasonal; American Express discount for all shows

Type of Seating: Long rows of tables, with some separation between individual parties. The show is performed on an outdoor stage, but all seating is covered. Ceiling fans provide some air movement, but it can get warm, especially at the early show.

Menu: Tropical fruit, roasted chicken, island pork, fresh catch, mixed
vegetables, rice, and pineapple cake; chicken tenders, mini–corn dogs,
and mac and cheese are also available for children
Vegetarian Alternative: On request
Beverages: Beer, wine, and soft drinks

Description and Comments South Sea–island native dancing follows a
"Polynesian-style," all-you-can-eat meal. The dancing is interesting and
largely authentic, and dancers are attractive though definitely PG in the
Disney tradition. We think the show has its moments and the meal is adequate, but neither is particularly special.

The *Polynesian Luau* suffers from excruciatingly slow pacing, with long
periods with nothing but recorded background music. The first part is little more than a fashion show. After a long intermission, there is a demonstration of island dances preceding a performance by a dancer twirling flam-
ing batons. All the dancers perform well, but this show becomes a snoozer
really early. The show has more value as a history lesson and is about as
interesting. Audience participation includes learning the hula and yelling
"a-LOHHH-ha" a lot.

A well-traveled, married couple from Fond du Lac, Wisconsin, comments:

> The Polynesian [Luau] *was a beautiful presentation, better than
> some shows we have seen in Hawaii! The food, however, lacked in
> all areas. Better food has come out of Disney kitchens. During our
> visit, the fruit platter was chintzy, the honey-roasted chicken was a
> bit fatty; and the pineapple cake was dry.*

Also at the Polynesian Resort's Luau Cove is *Mickey's Tropical Luau,* at
which Disney characters are added to the regular show. This performance
starts at 4:30 p.m., when it is too early to be hungry and too hot to be sitting outdoors. Cost is about $40 for adults and $20 for children ages 3–11.

OTHER AREA DINNER THEATERS

Central Florida probably has more dinner attractions than anywhere else on
earth. The name dinner attraction is something of a misnomer, because dinner is rarely the attraction. These are audience-participation shows or events
with food served along the way. They range from extravagant productions
where guests sit in arenas at long tables, to intimate settings at individual
tables. Don't expect terrific food, but if you're looking for something entertaining outside Walt Disney World, consider one of these.

If you decide to try a non-Disney dinner show, scavenge local tourist
magazines from brochure racks and hotel desks outside the World. These
free publications usually have discount coupons for area shows.

Pleasure Island

Pleasure Island is a six-acre nighttime entertainment complex on a man-made island in Downtown Disney. It consists of eight nightclubs, restaurants, and shops. A few of the restaurants and shops are open during the day, but the nightclubs don't start opening until 7 p.m. Some of the clubs may not open until 8 p.m. or later, and Pleasure Island doesn't fully come alive until after 9 or even 10 p.m.

Admission Options   One admission (about $20) entitles a guest to enjoy all eight nightclubs. Guests younger than 18 must be accompanied by a parent after 7 p.m. Unlimited eight-day admission to Pleasure Island is included in All-in-One passes.

Alcoholic Beverages   Guests not recognizably older than 21 must provide proof of their age if they wish to buy alcoholic beverages. To avoid repeated checking as the patron club-hops, a color-coded wristband indicates eligibility. All nightclubs serve alcohol. Those under 21, while allowed in all clubs except Mannequins and the BET Soundstage Club, aren't allowed to buy alcoholic beverages. Finally, and gratefully, you don't have to order drinks at all. You can enjoy the entertainment at any club and never buy that first beer. No server will hassle you.

Dress Code   Casual is in, but shirts and shoes are required.

New Variations on an Old Theme   The single-admission nightclub complex was originated in Florida at Orlando's Church Street Station, still very much alive in historic downtown Orlando. Starting fresh, Disney eliminated some problems that haunted Church Street Station and other nightspots over the years.

Good News for the Early-to-Bed Crowd   If you aren't nocturnal or you're tired from a long day in the theme parks, you don't have to wait until midnight for Pleasure Island to hit its stride. All bands, dancers, comedians, and showmen come on like gangbusters early in the evening. Later in the evening as the crowd builds and becomes more lubricated, Pleasure Island assumes the character of a real adult nightspot. During the transition (i.e., after dinner), however, it is not unusual to see a lot of kids in the clubs.

It's Possible to Visit All the Clubs in One Night   Whereas performances in nightclubs elsewhere might be an hour or more in duration, at Pleasure Island shows are shorter but more frequent. This allows guests to move among clubs without missing much. Since you can catch the essence of a club pretty quickly, there's no need to hang around for two or three drinks

to see what's going on. This format enables guests to have a complete and satisfying experience in a brief time, then move to another club if they want.

The music clubs (Rock n Roll Beach Club, 8TRAX, Wildhorse Saloon, BET Soundstage Club, Mannequins Dance Palace, and the Pleasure Island Jazz Company) go nonstop. Sometimes, there are special performances within the ongoing club entertainment. The Adventurers Club and the Comedy Warehouse offer scheduled shows.

We are very high on Pleasure Island. The cover is a little pricey and the drinks aren't cheap, but the entertainment is absolutely top-notch. And if you arrive before 9 p.m., you'll have time to sample all of the clubs, albeit briefly.

A reader reminds us that "sampling" the clubs, as we suggest, isn't the same as spending some time and really appreciating them:

> *Pleasure Island clubs take much more time to appreciate than you allow. We spent two evenings and only got to four places.*

We get considerable mail from couples in their 30s and 40s arguing Pleasure Island's merits (or lack thereof). These quotes are representative.

A reader from Bettendorf, Iowa, writes:

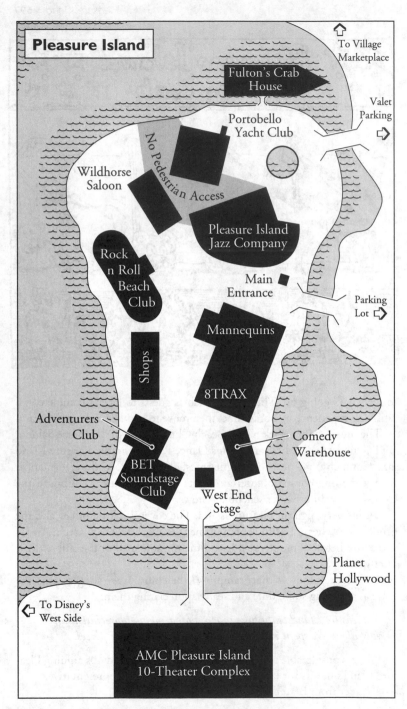

Pleasure Island

Fulton's Crab House

To Village Marketplace

Valet Parking

Portobello Yacht Club

No Pedestrian Access

Wildhorse Saloon

Pleasure Island Jazz Company

Rock n Roll Beach Club

Main Entrance

Parking Lot

Mannequins

Shops

8TRAX

Adventurers Club

Comedy Warehouse

BET Soundstage Club

West End Stage

Planet Hollywood

To Disney's West Side

AMC Pleasure Island 10-Theater Complex

I would not spend the money to go to Pleasure Island again. It is quite obvious that Disney is interested in the 21 to 30-year-old crowd here. There were many people our age (38) and older looking for something to do and not finding it. The Adventurers Club is the only real Disney creation on the island. Walt Disney World crosses all age brackets, and I expected the same from Pleasure Island. What a disappointment! I think you need to go back to the drawing board on your evaluation of Pleasure Island (and so does Disney).

A central Texas couple disagrees:

Your description, even with the statement that you are high on Pleasure Island, didn't prepare my wife and me for what a great place it is. Perhaps our expectations were moderate, but we thought it was an absolute blast, and we are neither under 40 nor club hounds.

Sorry, Invited Guests Only Occasionally, particularly before 9 p.m., certain Pleasure Island clubs are reserved for private parties and are declared temporarily off-limits to paying guests.

Parking Is a Hassle Pleasure Island's parking lot often fills up. On the bright side, the lot is now well marked. If you jot down the location of your space, you'll be able to find your car when it's time to leave. A good strategy is to park in the lot adjacent to the movie theaters and Disney's West Side and enter via the bridge connecting the West Side to Pleasure Island. Because there's an admission booth at the bridge, there's no need to enter through Pleasure Island's main gate.

Pleasure Island First-Timers' Touring Plan

This itinerary is for first-timers at Pleasure Island who want to visit all of the clubs in one night. It provides a taste of each venue. If you settle someplace that you really enjoy, you probably won't complete the circuit.

1. Arrive by 6 p.m. if you intend to eat at a Pleasure Island restaurant. If you eat before you go, arrive at about 7:30 or 8 p.m.

2. Buy your admission.

3. **Comedy Warehouse** Go left from the admission windows at the main entrance to the Comedy Warehouse. This is Pleasure Island's toughest ticket. There are normally five shows nightly, with the two earlier shows (usually 7:30 and 8:25 p.m.) easiest to

get into. If a show begins within 30 minutes, hop in line. If show time is more than 30 minutes away, check out the Rock n Roll Beach Club down the street. Use your judgment about whether you have time to buy a drink. Return to the Comedy Warehouse 30 minutes before show time. If you don't arrive at Pleasure Island in time to catch either of the first two shows, plan to queue at least 35 minutes before show time for subsequent performances.

4. **Wildhorse Saloon** Turning right from the Comedy Warehouse, mosey on down to the other end of Pleasure Island and the Wildhorse Saloon. This nightspot features country music ranging from Hank Williams to Shania Twain, and it sports a sizeable and usually crowded dance floor. Professional Disney dancers periodically strut their stuff in line dances or couples, and you're more than welcome to join in if you think you can keep up. Around and above the dance floor are tables for Wildhorse restaurant fare, consisting of barbecue and other country dinners.

5. **Pleasure Island Jazz Company** Turn left from Wildhorse and hit the Pleasure Island Jazz Company next door. The club features live jazz and blues and hosts jam sessions with local musicians. The crowd, more diverse in age and appearance than at other clubs, sits at tables flanking the stage on three sides.

6. **Adventurers Club** When you're done at the Jazz Company, walk left and back to the Comedy Warehouse side of the island, and enter the Adventurers Club. Patterned after a stuffy English gentlemen's club, the Adventurers Club is a two-story, turn-of-the-century affair with big armchairs, walls covered with animal heads (some of which talk), and other artifacts.

Many guests will stroll through the club, inspect the ridiculous decor, and leave, not realizing they missed the main attraction: a show in the club's library downstairs. About once every 30 or 40 minutes, all guests will be ushered into the library for a performance. Nobody tells guests a show is upcoming; they must either hang around long enough to be invited in or intuit that, with Disney, what you see isn't what you get.

When you arrive at the Adventurers Club, ask an attendant when the next show in the library will begin. If it's in 20 minutes or less, go in and have a drink. If it's a long while, the BET Soundstage Club is next door.

7. **BET Soundstage Club** Opened in partnership with Black Entertainment Television, this club features hip-hop, soul, and R&B. The dance floor is cool and showy, and the club gets packed as bands finish up at the West End Stage directly outside. The club is restricted to ages 21 and up, so there's a definite adult vibe.

8. **8TRAX** When Pleasure Island opened, this was an under-21 club called Videopolis East. For various reasons (fights and teenage gang conflicts), it was closed and reopened as Cage, which targeted older (over-21) rockers but never achieved much of an identity. Now it's 8TRAX, a '70s disco featuring the music of K. C. and the Sunshine Band, the Bee Gees, and Donna Summer. Though the decor during our last visit was the same steel beams, catwalks, and metal mesh that imbued the club's previous incarnations with such charm, it was clear that the '70s concept had taken root. The place was rocking.

9. **Mannequins Dance Palace** Backtrack toward Pleasure Island's front entrance to Mannequins, a ritzy, techno-pop, rock dance club with a revolving dance floor, incredible lighting, and wild special effects. The music is all DJ, but the sound system is superb (and very, very loud). There is often a line waiting to enter. This has less to do with the club's popularity than with the fact that Disney prefers guests to enter via an elevator to the second floor. The elevator helps distribute guests throughout the club, but there's a perfectly good entrance on the first floor. For some reason, cast members at the entrance will often invite 40-something (and older) guests to enter directly, without being subjected to the elevator. Patrons younger than 21 aren't allowed in Mannequins through either entrance.

10. **Rock n Roll Beach Club** Proceed to the Beach Club, featuring oldies and current rock. Bands here are always first-rate, and they raise the roof beginning early in the evening. Electronic games and pool are available for those who don't wish to dance.

11. **West End Stage** Continue to the West End Stage. It isn't a club, but it's the most happening place on Pleasure Island. Live rock bands perform under the stars in the plaza, with the BET Soundstage Club and Adventurers Club on one side and Comedy Warehouse on the other. Bands, without exception, are super, as are lighting and sound systems. The high stage provides excellent visibility. Performances usually occur four times each night, with a

grand finale at 11:45 p.m., accompanied by fireworks, showers of confetti, and blazing searchlights. Street vendors sell drinks.

12. **Pleasure Island Restaurants**   Though noisy, crowded, and expensive, restaurants here offer a variety of creative and well-prepared dishes. For detailed profiles of Pleasure Island restaurants, see Part 9: "Dining in and around Walt Disney World" (page 268).

The Island's newest restaurant is the Wildhorse Saloon, the barbecue capital of Walt Disney World. Other restaurants include Fulton's Crab House, on the *Empress Lilly* riverboat, specializing in shellfish and fresh Florida seafood, and the Portobello Yacht Club, serving seafood, pasta, and pizza. Casual yet stylish, the Portobello does a creditable job with its varied Italian fare.

Another big player on Pleasure Island is Planet Hollywood, at the entrance to Disney's West Side. While the food is pretty good and the servings large, the main draw is the Hollywood memorabilia decorating the restaurant. Unless you eat at strange times, expect long waits for a table.

Our researchers half-jokingly refer to Planet Hollywood as the restaurant with an attitude. A reader from Bartlesville, Oklahoma, agrees:

> *Planet Hollywood was NOT a pleasant experience. We arrived at 5 p.m. and still had to wait an hour [to be seated]. I had the feeling of being herded like cattle. I also felt the staff manipulated things so there was always a line (i.e., there were several tables that stayed empty during the time we were waiting). The hosts on duty were rude. By the time we were seated, our waiter was friendly and the food was good, but I was too stressed out to care . . . this was the only time at Disney World that we were treated rudely. I understand Planet Hollywood is not owned or operated by Disney, and the contrast in attitude was quite apparent.*

Priority seating is strongly recommended for all full-service restaurants. If you don't have one, arrive by 6 p.m. or eat after 10 p.m. An alternative is to eat sandwiches and snacks in the clubs. It isn't necessary to buy club admission to eat at the restaurants. Most are also open during the day.

If no Pleasure Island restaurant lights your candle, a number of themed and nonthemed restaurants are within easy walking distance at the Downtown Disney Marketplace and at Disney's West Side. Again, priority seating is advised for the full-service restaurants.

13. **Pleasure Island Shopping** Some shops on the Island are attractions in themselves. At Cover Story, guests dress up before being photographed for the mock cover of a major magazine. Want to see yourself on *Cosmo?* Here's the place. Similarly, Superstar Studio lets you star in your own music video. Props include keyboard, drums, and guitar. Video technicians record your lipsyncing (or you can actually sing); varying camera angles make you look good. Postproduction adds realism to your tape. Work alone or with a group of your friends. If you don't want your own magazine cover or rock video, watch others make them. It's a hoot!

It isn't necessary to pay admission to shop at Pleasure Island during the day. In the evening, all of the Island except the restaurants is gated.

The regular crowd settles in at Pleasure Island.

A Word about Universal CityWalk

CityWalk is Universal's version of Pleasure Island. In addition to a number of restaurants you'll find a jazz club, a Reggae club, a Pat O'Briens dueling-pianos club, a Hard Rock Cafe and concert venue, a Motown Cafe with live R&B, and a dance club called The Groove with high-tech lighting and visual effects. There's no admission charge to enjoy the shops, restaurants, and street entertainment. As concerns the clubs, you can buy a pass that admits you to all the clubs (like at Pleasure Island), or if you prefer, you can pay a cover charge (usually about $4) at each club you visit. In addition to the clubs, shops, and restaurants, there's a 20-screen Cineplex movie theater.

Appendix

Readers' Questions to the Author

Following are questions and comments from *Unofficial Guide* readers. Some frequently asked questions are addressed in every edition of the *Unofficial Guide*.

Q: When you do your research, are you admitted to the parks free? Do the Disney people know you are there?

A: We pay the regular admission and usually the Disney people do not know we are on-site. Similarly, both in and out of Walt Disney World, we pay for our own meals and lodging.

Q: How often is the Unofficial Guide *revised?*

A: We publish a new edition once a year, but we make corrections every time we go to press, usually about three times a year.

Q: Do you write each new edition from scratch?

A: We do not. With a destination the size of Walt Disney World it's hard enough keeping up with what's new. Moreover, we put great effort into communicating the most salient, useful information in the clearest possible language. If an attraction or hotel has not changed, we are very reluctant to tinker with its coverage for the sake of freshening up the writing.

Q. I have never read any other Unofficial Guides. *Are they all as negative and cynical as* The Unofficial Guide to Walt Disney World *or do you just resent Disney?*

A: What some readers perceive as negative and cynical, we see as objective and constructive. And no, we don't resent anyone. Our job is to prepare you for both the best and worst of Walt Disney World. As it happens, some folks are very passionate about what one reader called "the inherent goodness of Disney." These folks might be more comfortable with press releases or the *Official Guide* than with the strong consumer orientation found in the *Unofficial Guide*. That having been said, we would like to point out that while some readers take us to task for being overly negative about Walt Disney World, others complain that we are too positive.

Q: How are your age group ratings determined? I am 42 years old. During Star Tours, I was quite worried about hurting my back. If the senior citizens rating is determined only by those brave enough to ride, it will skew the results.
A: The reader makes a good point. Unfortunately, it's impossible to develop a rating unless the guest (of whatever age group) has actually experienced the attraction. So yes, all age group ratings are derived exclusively from members of that age group who have experienced the attraction. Health problems, such as a bad back, however, can affect guests of any age, and Disney provides more than ample warnings on attractions that warrant such admonitions. But if you're in good health, our ratings will give you a sense of how much others in your age group enjoyed the attraction. Our hope, of course, is twofold: first, that you will be stimulated to be adventurous, and second, that a positive experience will help you be more open-minded.

Q: I have an old edition of the Unofficial Guide. *How much of the information [in it] is still correct?*
A: Veteran travel writers will acknowledge that 5–8% of the information in a guidebook is out of date by the time it comes off the press! Walt Disney World is always changing. If you are using an old edition of the *Unofficial Guide,* descriptions of attractions still existing should be generally accurate. However, many other things change with every edition, particularly the touring plans and the hotel and restaurant reviews. Finally, and obviously, older editions of the *Unofficial Guide* do not include new attractions or developments.

Q: How many people have you surveyed for your "age group ratings" on the attractions?
A: Since the publication of the first edition of the *Unofficial Guide* in 1985, we have interviewed or surveyed just over 18,000 Walt Disney World patrons. Even with such a large survey population, however, we continue to have difficulty with certain age groups. Specifically, we love to hear from seniors about their experiences with Splash Mountain, Big Thunder Mountain Railroad, Space Mountain, *Alien Encounter,* Star Tours, Tower of Terror, Rock 'n' Roller Coaster, Body Wars, Test Track, Kali River Rapids, and Countdown to Extinction.

Q: Do you stay in Walt Disney World? If not, where do you stay?
A: We do stay at Walt Disney World lodging properties from time to time, usually when a new hotel opens. Since we began writing about Walt Disney World in 1982, we have stayed in over 52 different properties in various

locations around Orlando, Lake Buena Vista, and Kissimmee. During our last visit we stayed at the BoardWalk Resort and liked it very much.

Q: Why are there no photographs of the theme parks in the Unofficial Guide?
A: Disney has copyrighted many identifiable buildings and structures in Walt Disney World. Any recognizable photo of Walt Disney World that we publish without Disney's permission, even if we take the picture with our own camera, could constitute copyright infringement, according to Disney's legal representatives. Walt Disney World will not grant the *Unofficial Guide* permission to publish photographs because of its relationship with the *Official Guide to Walt Disney World.*

Q: What can we expect in terms of new developments over the next couple of years at Walt Disney World?
A: A new land at the Animal Kingdom based on mythical beasts has been a long time getting off the drawing board and may be postponed. An African-themed hotel adjacent to the Animal Kingdom had just broken ground at press time and is scheduled to open in 2001. The Horizons attraction at Epcot has been closed indefinitely, or at least until a new corporate sponsor comes aboard. Anxious about Universal's Islands of Adventure's strong appeal to the youth and young adults markets, Disney will most likely rush additional thrill rides into development.

Q: What is your favorite Florida attraction?
A: What attracts me (as opposed to my favorite attraction) is Juniper Springs, a stunningly beautiful stream about an hour north of Orlando in the Ocala National Forest. Originating as a limestone aquifer, crystal clear water erupts from the ground and begins a ten-mile journey to the creek's mouth at Lake George. Winding through palm, cypress, and live oak, the stream is more exotic than the Jungle Cruise, and alive with birds, animals, turtles, and alligators. Put in at the Juniper Springs Recreation Area on FL 40, 36 miles east of Ocala. The seven-mile trip to the FL 19 bridge takes about four and a half hours. Canoe rentals and shuttle service are available at the recreation area. Phone (352) 625-2808 for information.

Readers' Comments

On the topic of Disney marketing, a Philadelphia mom had this to say:

> *I had tried to avoid the Animal Kingdom because I knew it would be crowded. What I couldn't predict, however, was the effect of the marketing Disney put together about a month before we arrived. Good heavens, they can market anything to death, can't they? My children*

picked up on the commercials, the hour-long infomercial (disguised as an episode of Magic World of Disney on ABC), and even the slick brochures that arrived just before we left town. [We] had to go they insisted, so I tried to make the best of it.

A Perkiomenville, Pennsylvania, woman, however, can tolerate the sales pitch as long as the product is good, stating:

As for Disney being a money-hungry machine—if they make money by making people unbelievably happy, I'm for more companies going for that goal, and I'll gladly hand my money over again and again. I openly admit I have gone from a Disney skeptic to a complete Disneyholic.

A number of readers expressed a desire for a more tasteful Walt Disney World, remarking on various sights that offended their sensibilities. A Williamsville, New York, woman offered this:

My vote for the most absurd sight at any of the parks?? People gnawing huge turkey legs as they wandered around. Whose idea was that?! Must have been those Disney spies who, after sneaking into Medieval Times for dinner, decided to capitalize on the ingenious idea of having the public eat large pieces of roasted meat without utensils.

While a Portland, Oregon, couple balked at the crassness of it all:

Six days of "Disney magic" were all we could take. Being inundated with shops of merchandise at almost every turn became obscene after a while. It boggled my mind to think of how many [tractor-trailers] must be carrying everything from Dopey underwear to who knows what . . . Mickey-shaped suppositories (?) . . . into the place 24 hours a day. If this weren't enough, the endless, waddling parade of American men and women squeezed (respectively) into skin-tight Mickey shorts, Minnie leggings, and Tigger T-shirts, had me "wishing upon a star" for a cultural Alka-Seltzer.

And another Oregon couple grappled with the Catch-22 of the Animal Kingdom's conservation message, commenting:

It was difficult getting into the Animal Kingdom's "eco-friendly" theme when the first thing you see upon entering the park (or any of the parks, for that matter) are acres upon acres of parking lot where natural Florida habitat used to be. The lyrics "Pave paradise! Put up a parking lot!" came to mind, again and again.

Changing gears, a father from Longmeadow, Massachusetts, wilted during his visit to the World, writing:

> *You should prepare us Northerners (I am assuming you actually live in Alabama) for the incredible heat and humidity if you go to Disney World in the summer. It was at times overwhelming for us. Light-colored clothing, hats, and water bottles are an absolute must. [Speaking of water], you prepared us well for the expensive food, but $2.50 for 12 ounces of cold water is a hell of a lot to pay without a couple of shots of good scotch wrapped around it.*

How to stay calm, rested, and relaxed on a Walt Disney World vacation is a favorite topic of discussion. Here's what a Pittsburgh, Pennsylvania, mother of five had to say:

> *Our advice would be to slow down and enjoy the sights. It's impossible to relax and see it all. We let the children set the pace, see what they wanted to see, and we really enjoyed ourselves.*

In contrast, a woman from Baltimore, Ohio, elevated planning to new heights, reporting:

> *I made up little laminated pocket-size cards to take with me to help pinpoint items of interest and where to find them. (My co-workers thought I was nuts when they saw my cards-but they were very handy!) I also had day-to-day plans (that matched the laminated cards) typed out and taped to the wall of my hotel room to check every night for the next day, i.e., phone numbers to call for lunch/dinner reservations, questions to ask, etc. Am I too organized?*

A woman from Milford, Connecticut, learned something about letting the "tail wag the dog":

> *The plans we used for touring Epcot didn't work out perfectly mainly because I am one of those compulsive agenda followers and my husband was the complete opposite (wanted to do what he wanted to do, when he wanted to do it). Our second day at WDW was the make-it-or-break-it day for us. I learned to lighten up a bit with the plans, my husband decided to give the plans a chance, and we decided to do a vote as a family on certain attractions, whether to see them or not. Everything was great after that!*

From a Tinley Park, Illinois, family of four:

> *We found many parents of kids ages 2–11 just a tad stressed out. My husband and I laughed, empathetically of course, when we overheard a dad saying "This is WDW. It's supposed to be fun." to his son.*

We had said this just moments before. We highly recommend returning to the hotel for naps and even spreading visits per park across 2-3 days if possible. Last, pray for cool temps! The scorching heat just exacerbates young ones' impatience!

From a Portage, Indiana, couple who didn't want to get caught napping:

My husband is 28 and I'm 24, so when I read in your book about taking a midday nap—I laughed! We were young and could just keep going! Were we wrong! It was the best advice you gave!

A couple from Bloomington, Indiana, has this to say:

My wife and I are 42 years old. We took your advice on taking an afternoon break. That two-three hours' rest time back at the [hotel] kept us refreshed for our entire stay. I think without the afternoon breaks we would have missed more and enjoyed less.

Similarly, a Michigan woman states:

We were so glad we took the nap advice. At first we thought no way, but then thought about it and it was such good advice. I think the adults needed it more than the kids. We were all ready and willing for our afternoon naps, and had a great time when we returned [to the theme park].

A 12-year-old girl from Louisville, Kentucky, however, thought we had overstated the case, writing:

I do not understand why you are convinced that people cannot make it through the day without stopping to take a nap. I could probably make it through two days without stopping for a nap.

A Cape May, New Jersey, mom learned that a group is only as strong as its weakest member, writing:

I forgot one of your most important caveats. The plan you adopt must take into account the age and sophistication of your traveling companions. So that day at the Animal Kingdom I was reminded how, even forewarned, a parent can fall into the trap of turning a wonderful vacation day into the Bataan Death March for a small or even a medium-sized child.

And a mom from Wilmington, Delaware, reinforced the idea that pre-trip conditioning contributes to a better vacation:

One more thing!! Your advice about walking six miles per day before the trip really paid off!! We did not suffer blisters or sore feet, but we saw others with awful blisters and limps.

A dad from Kirkland, Washington, describes how he kept track of his teenage daughter:

We found WDW to be a relatively safe environment for all. My daughter, who is 14, got around just fine by herself with no problems. I would recommend giving your teenagers some space, and [allow them to] be by themselves. We rented pagers from the Port Orleans guest services, and if we needed to get in touch with each other we just called the other's pager. The cost is very minimal for the peace of mind [the pagers] give you.

On the subject of children's responses, a man from Plano, Texas, contributes this advice:

While on the subject, some parents might benefit from two other things that we learned. First, from our use in conversation of your terms "switching off" or "baby swapping," our daughter quickly caught on to the fact that she was standing in line for a ride that was potentially terrifying for her. As a result, her own imagination-driven panic sometimes led to messy scenes in the anterooms of rides (like Body Wars) that Mom and Dad took turns experiencing but had no intention of forcing on her. Second, and more happily, it occurred to us that Dumbo, the Mad Tea Party, and the delightful Cranium Command (all of which we experienced multiple times) were, in effect, "thrill rides" for our five-year-old. If a flying elephant can give a small child the same gleeful exhilaration that her parents enjoy on Star Tours, then the wait in line is justified in both cases.

A British husband complains that he didn't come all the way to Walt Disney World to be henpecked:

You may think the small, white wading birds with the hooked orange beaks are cute, but don't get caught by a bunch of them with food. They can be quite aggressive. (This happened at River Country).

Finally, a mother of three from Lisle, Illinois, added an item to that essential list of wisdom and knowledge a mother must pass along to a daughter before she becomes a woman:

*I have been to Disney World nine times (the first time in 1973!)
and have relied on your book for the past several visits. The main idea,
of course, is "go early." I said that to my 13-year-old daughter this trip:
"When you are grown up and come here without me, remember to get
up early."*

And so it goes.

Index

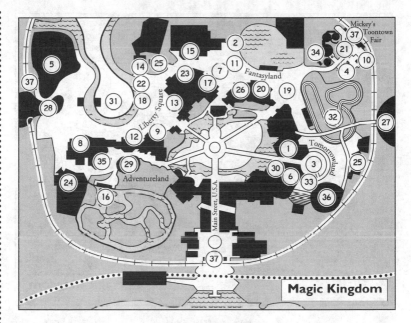

Magic Kingdom
Recommended Attraction Visitation Times

If you tour on an early entry day, move all recommended attraction visitation times up one hour. It is best to see attractions with visitation times listed as "anytime" during the more crowded middle part of the day (noon to 4 p.m.).

1. *Alien Encounter:* Before 10 a.m., during parades, or after 6 p.m.
2. *Ariel's Grotto:* Before 10 a.m./after 9 p.m.
3. Astro Orbiter: Before 11 a.m./after 5 p.m.
4. Barnstormer: Before 10:30 a.m., during events, or just before closing
5. Big Thunder Mountain Railroad: Before 10 a.m./hour before closing
6. Buzz Lightyear's Space Ranger Station: Anytime
7. Cinderella's Golden Carrousel: Before 11 a.m./after 8 p.m.
8. *Country Bear Jamboree:* Before 11:30 a.m., during parades, 2 hours before closing
9. *The Diamond Horseshoe Saloon Revue:* Per entertainment schedule
10. Donald's Boat: Anytime
11. Dumbo: Before 10 a.m./after 9 p.m.
12. Frontierland Shootin' Arcade: Anytime
13. *The Hall of Presidents:* Anytime
14. The Haunted Mansion: Before 11:30 a.m./after 8 p.m.
15. It's a Small World: Anytime
16. Jungle Cruise: Before 10 a.m./2 hours before closing
17. *Legend of the Lion King:* Before 11 a.m./during parades
18. *Liberty Belle* Riverboat: Anytime
19. Mad Tea Party: Before 11 a.m./after 5 p.m.

—continued on other side—

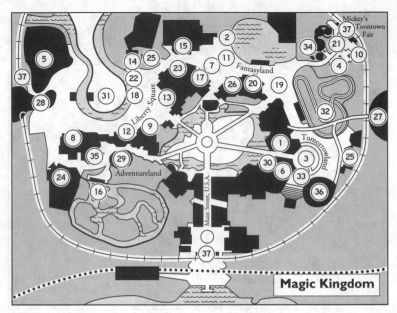

Magic Kingdom
Recommended Attraction Visitation Times

If you tour on an early-entry day, move all recommended attraction visitation times up one hour. It is best to see attractions with visitation times listed as "anytime" during the more crowded middle part of the day (noon to 4 p.m.).

—continued from other side—

20. The Many Adventures of Winnie the Pooh: Before 10 a.m./2 hours before closing
21. Mickey's and Minnie's Country Houses: Before 11:30 a.m./after 4:30 p.m.
22. Mike Fink Keelboats: Before 11:30 a.m./after 5 p.m. (closes at dusk)
23. Peter Pan's Flight: Before 10 a.m./after 6 p.m.
24. Pirates of the Caribbean: Before noon/after 5 p.m.
25. Skyway: Before noon/during special events
26. Snow White's Adventures: Before 11 a.m./after 6 p.m.
27. Space Mountain: Park opening, between 6 and 7 p.m., or hour before closing
28. Splash Mountain: Park opening, during parades, or just before closing
29. Swiss Family Treehouse: Before 11:30 a.m./after 5 p.m.
30. *The Timekeeper:* Anytime
31. Tom Sawyer Island: Midmorning thru late afternoon (closes at dusk)
32. Tomorrowland Speedway: Before 11 a.m./after 5 p.m.
33. Tomorrowland Transit Authority: Between 11:30 a.m. and 4:30 p.m.
34. Toontown Hall of Fame: Before 10:30 a.m./after 5:30 p.m.
35. *Tropical Serenade:* Before 11 a.m./after 3:30 p.m.
36. *Walt Disney's Carousel of Progress:* Anytime
37. Walt Disney World Railroad: Anytime

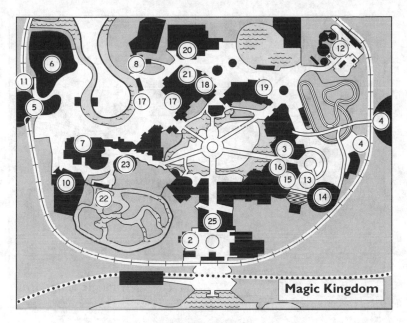

Magic Kingdom

Magic Kingdom
One-Day Touring Plan for Adults
Pocket Outline Version

For the detailed version of this touring plan, see page 456.

1. Arrive at TTC 50 min. prior to opening.
2. Go to City Hall for park maps containing the daily entertainment schedule.
3. As soon as Tomorrowland opens, experience *Alien Encounter.*
4. Ride Space Mountain.
5. Ride Splash Mountain.
6. Ride Big Thunder Mountain Railroad.
7. See the *Country Bear Jamboree.*
8. See The Haunted Mansion.
9. Eat lunch.
10. Ride Pirates of the Caribbean.
11. Take the train to Mickey's Toontown Fair.
12. Tour the Fair, then go to Tomorrowland.
13. Ride the Tomorrowland Transit Authority.
14. See *Walt Disney's Carousel of Progress.*
15. Ride Buzz Lightyear.
16. Experience *The Timekeeper.*
17. Experience *The Hall of Presidents* and the *Liberty Belle* Riverboat.
18. Return to Fantasyland and see *Legend of the Lion King.*
19. Ride The Many Adventures of Winnie the Pooh.
20. Ride It's a Small World.
21. Ride Peter Pan's Flight.
22. Back in Adventureland, ride the Jungle Cruise.
23. Explore the Swiss Family Treehouse.
24. Pick up any attractions you might have missed.
25. Browse Main Street.

Magic Kingdom

Magic Kingdom
Author's Selective One-Day Touring Plan for Adults
Pocket Outline Version
For the detailed version of this touring plan, see page 459.

1. Arrive at TTC 50 min. prior to opening.
2. Go to City Hall for park maps containing the daily entertainment schedule.
3. As soon as Tomorrowland opens, experience *Alien Encounter*.
4. Ride Space Mountain.
5. Ride Splash Mountain.
6. Ride Big Thunder Mountain Railroad.
7. See The Haunted Mansion.
8. Ride The Many Adventures of Winnie the Pooh.
9. See *Legend of the Lion King*.
10. Eat lunch.
11. Ride Pirates of the Caribbean.
12. Take the railroad from Frontierland to Mickey's Toontown Fair.

13. Tour the Fair, then go to Tomorrowland.
14. Ride the Tomorrowland Transit Authority.
15. See *Walt Disney's Carousel of Progress*.
16. Experience *The Timekeeper*.
17. See *The Hall of Presidents*.
18. Ride It's a Small World.
19. Ride Peter Pan's Flight.
20. See the *Country Bear Jamboree*.
21. Visit the Swiss Family Treehouse.
22. Take the Jungle Cruise.
23. Pick up any attractions you might have missed.
24. Browse Main Street.

Magic Kingdom

Magic Kingdom
One-Day Touring Plan for Parents with Young Children
Pocket Outline Version

For the detailed version of this touring plan, see page 461.
Review the Small Child Fright Potential Chart on pages 181–185.

1. Arrive at TTC 50 min. prior to opening.
2. Go to City Hall for park maps containing the daily entertainment schedule.
3. Rent strollers (if necessary).
4. Ride Dumbo the Flying Elephant.
5. Ride The Many Adventures of Winnie the Pooh.
6. Ride Peter Pan's Flight.
7. See *Legend of the Lion King*.
8. Go to The Haunted Mansion.
9. See the *Country Bear Jamboree*.
10. Ride Pirates of the Caribbean.
11. Take the train to Mickey's Toontown Fair.

12. Visit Mickey's Toontown Fair.
13. Return to the hotel for lunch and a nap.
14. Return to the Magic Kingdom and visit Tom Sawyer Island in Frontierland.
15. Ride It's a Small World.
16. Ride Buzz Lightyear.
17. Ride the Tomorrowland Transit Authority.
18. Try *The Timekeeper*.
19. Check the entertainment schedule for live performances, parades, fireworks, etc., or try any attractions you missed.
20. Tour Main Street.

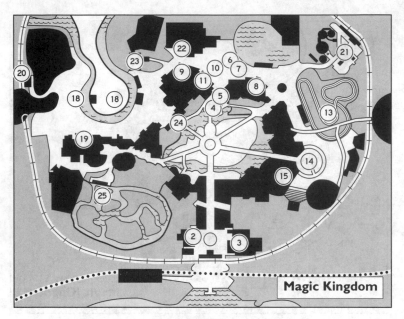

Magic Kingdom

Magic Kingdom
Dumbo-or-Die-in-a-Day Touring Plan
for Parents with Young Children
Pocket Outline Version

For the detailed version of this touring plan, see page 464.
Review the Small Child Fright Potential Chart on pages 181–185.
(Interrupt the touring plan for lunch, rest, and dinner.)

1. Arrive at TTC 50 min. prior to opening.
2. Go to City Hall for park maps containing the daily entertainment schedule.
3. Rent a stroller (if needed).
4. Go to Cinderella's Castle.
5. Make dinner reservation at the castle.
6. Ride Dumbo the Flying Elephant.
7. Ride Dumbo again.
8. Ride The Many Adventures of Winnie the Pooh.
9. Ride Peter Pan's Flight.
10. Ride Cinderella's Golden Carrousel.
11. See *Legend of the Lion King.*
12. Go to Tomorrowland.
13. Ride the Tomorrowland Speedway.
14. Ride the Astro Orbiter.
15. Ride Buzz Lightyear.
16. Return to the hotel for lunch and a nap.
17. Return to the Magic Kingdom. Go to Frontierland.
18. Go to Tom Sawyer Island.
19. See the *Country Bear Jamboree.*
20. Take the train to Mickey's Toontown Fair.
21. Walk through Mickey's and Minnie's Country Houses and play on Donald's Boat.
22. If you have time before dinner, ride It's a Small World.
23. Eat, then see The Haunted Mansion.
24. Watch the evening parade.
25. Ride the Jungle Cruise.
26. Repeat favorite attractions.
27. Depart Magic Kingdom.

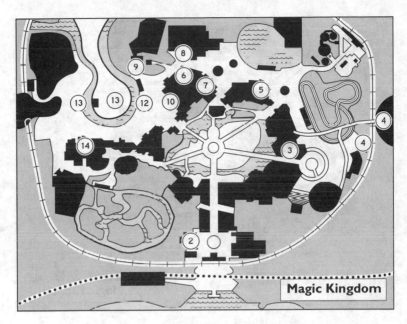

Magic Kingdom
Two-Day Touring Plan
Pocket Outline Version
For the detailed version of this touring plan, see page 467.

Day One

1. Arrive at TTC 50 min. prior to opening.
2. Go to City Hall for park maps containing the daily entertainment schedule.
3. As soon as Tomorrowland opens, experience *Alien Encounter*.
4. Ride Space Mountain.
5. Ride The Many Adventures of Winnie the Pooh.
6. Ride Peter Pan's Flight.
7. See *Legend of the Lion King*.
8. Ride It's a Small World.
9. Experience The Haunted Mansion.
10. See *The Hall of Presidents*.
11. Eat lunch.
12. Ride the *Liberty Belle* Riverboat.
13. In Frontierland, explore Tom Sawyer Island.
14. See the *Country Bear Jamboree*.
15. Enjoy the shops, see some live entertainment, or revisit favorite attractions.

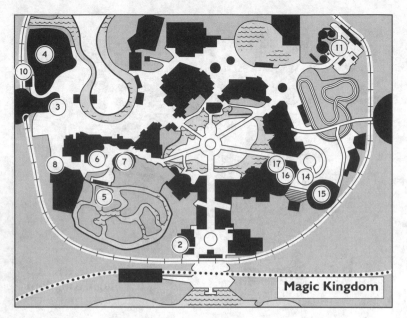

Magic Kingdom

Magic Kingdom
Two-Day Touring Plan
Pocket Outline Version

For the detailed version of this touring plan, see page 467.

Day Two

1. Arrive at TTC 50 min. prior to opening.
2. Go to City Hall for park maps containing the daily entertainment schedule.
3. In Frontierland, ride Splash Mountain.
4. Ride Big Thunder Mountain Railroad.
5. In Adventureland, ride the Jungle Cruise.
6. See the *Tropical Serenade (Enchanted Tiki Birds)*.
7. Walk through the Swiss Family Treehouse.
8. Enjoy Pirates of the Caribbean.
9. Eat lunch.
10. Take the Walt Disney World Railroad to Mickey's Toontown Fair.
11. Tour Mickey's Toontown Fair.
12. Go to Tomorrowland.
13. If you haven't eaten yet, try Cosmic Ray's Starlight Cafe or the Plaza Pavilion.
14. Ride the Tomorrowland Transit Authority.
15. See *Walt Disney's Carousel of Progress*.
16. Ride Buzz Lightyear.
17. Experience *The Timekeeper*.
18. Enjoy the shops, see some live entertainment, or revisit favorite attractions.

Epcot

Recommended Attraction Visitation Times

If you tour on an early-entry day, move all recommended attraction visitation times up one hour. It is best to see attractions with visitation times listed as "anytime" during the more crowded middle part of the day (noon to 4 p.m.).

1. *The American Adventure:* Anytime
2. *Body Wars* (Wonders of Life): Before 10 a.m./after 6 p.m.
3. *The Circle of Life* (The Land): Before 11 a.m./after 2 p.m.
4. *Cranium Command* (Wonders of Life): Before 11 a.m./after 3 p.m.
5. *El Río del Tiempo* (Mexico): Before 11 a.m./after 3 p.m.
6. *Food Rocks* (The Land): Before 11 a.m./after 2 p.m.
7. *Honey, I Shrunk the Audience:* Before 10 a.m./just before closing
8. *Impressions de France* (France): Before noon/after 4 p.m.
9. *Innoventions:* Second day or after major attractions
10. *Journey into Your Imagination* ride: Before 10:30 a.m./after 6 p.m.
11. *Living with the Land* (The Land): Before 10:30 a.m./after 7:30 p.m.
12. *The Living Seas:* Before 10 a.m./after 3 p.m.
13. *Maelstrom* (Norway): Before noon/after 4:30 p.m.
14. *The Making of Me* (Wonders of Life): Early morning/after 4:30 p.m.
15. *Millennium Village:* Second day or after major attractions
16. *O Canada!* (Canada): Anytime
17. *Spaceship Earth:* Before 10 a.m./after 4 p.m.
18. *Test Track:* Before 9:15 a.m./just before closing
19. *Universe of Energy:* Before 11:15 a.m./after 4:30 p.m.
20. *Wonders of China* (China): Anytime

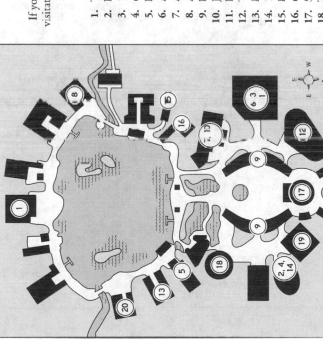

Epcot

Epcot
One-Day Touring Plan
Pocket Outline Version

For the detailed version of this touring plan, see page 521. (Interrupt the touring plan for lunch, dinner, and *IllumiNations*.)

1. Arrive 45 minutes before official opening time.
2. Go to Guest Relations and make restaurant priority seatings, then experience Test Track.
3. In the Wonders of Life pavilion, ride Body Wars.
4. Do the ride at Imagination Institute, then see *Honey, I Shrunk the Audience.*
5. Ride Living with the Land.
6. Experience The Living Seas.
7. Ride Spaceship Earth.
8. Visit the Universe of Energy.
9. See *Cranium Command.*
10. See Horizons.
11. Go to the World Showcase.
12. See *O Canada!*
13. Tour the Millennium Village.
14. Visit the United Kingdom.
15. See *Impressions de France.*
16. Visit Morocco.
17. Tour Japan.
18. See *The American Adventure.*
19. Visit Italy.
20. Tour Germany
21. See *Wonders of China.*
22. Ride Maelstrom in Norway.
23. Ride El Río del Tiempo in Mexico.
24. Depart Epcot.

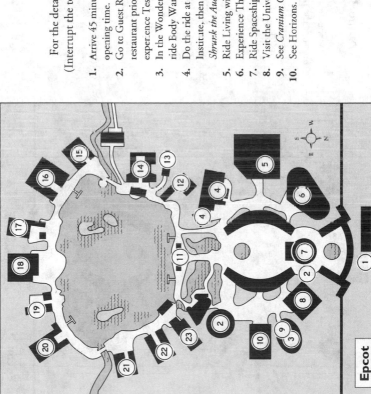

Epcot

Epcot
Author's Selective One-Day Touring Plan
Pocket Outline Version

For the detailed version of this touring plan, see page 525. (Interrupt the touring plan for lunch, dinner, and *IllumiNations*.)

1. Arrive 45 minutes before official opening time.
2. Go to Guest Relations and make restaurant priority seatings, then experience Test Track.
3. Ride Body Wars in the Wonders of Life pavilion.
4. Do the ride at Imagination Institute, then see *Honey, I Shrunk the Audience*.
5. Ride Living with the Land.
6. See The Living Seas.
7. Ride Spaceship Earth.
8. Visit the Universe of Energy.
9. See *Cranium Command*.
10. See Horizons.
11. Go to the World Showcase.
12. See the *American Adventure* and the films at France and China. Take the boat ride in Norway.
13. Tour the Millennium Village.
14. Enjoy *IllumiNations*, then depart Epcot.

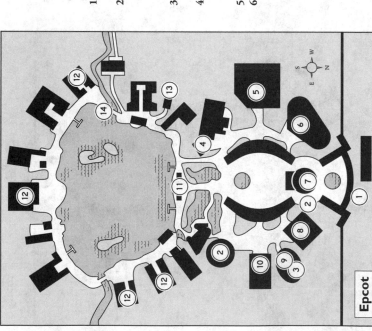

Epcot

Epcot
Two-Day Sunrise/Starlight Touring Plan
Pocket Outline Version

For the detailed version of this touring plan, see page 528.
(Interrupt the touring plan for lunch.)

Day One

1. Arrive 45 minutes before official opening time.
2. Go to Guest Relations and make priority seatings, then experience Test Track.
3. Ride Spaceship Earth.
4. Do the ride at Imagination Institute, then see *Honey, I Shrunk the Audience.*
5. Ride Living with the Land.
6. Ride Body Wars.
7. See *Cranium Command* at Wonders of Life.
8. Experience the Universe of Energy.
9. See Horizons.
10. Go to the World Showcase.
11. Ride El Río del Tiempo in Mexico.
12. Ride Maelstrom in Norway.
13. See *Wonders of China.*
14. Visit Germany and Italy.
15. See *The American Adventure.*
16. Visit Japan and Morocco.
17. Depart Epcot.

Epcot

Epcot
Two-Day Sunrise/Starlight Touring Plan
Pocket Outline Version

For the detailed version of this touring plan, see page 528. (Interrupt the touring plan for dinner and *IllumiNations*.)

Day Two

1. Arrive at Epcot at 2 p.m. Pick up a park map containing the daily entertainment schedule at Guest Relations.
2. Make dinner priority seatings.
3. Ride Spaceship Earth.
4. Go to The Living Seas.
5. See *Food Rocks* and *The Circle of Life* at The Land.
6. See *O Canada!*
7. Tour the Millennium Village.
8. Visit the United Kingdom.
9. See *Impressions de France*.
10. Enjoy dinner and *IllumiNations*.
11. Depart Epcot.

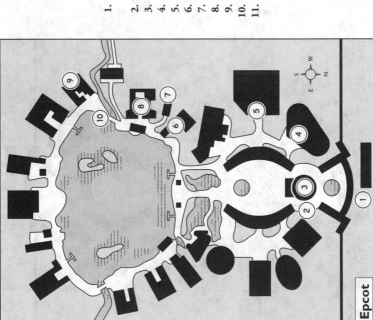

Epcot

Epcot
Two-Day Early Riser Touring Plan
Pocket Outline Version

For the detailed version of this touring plan, see page 531.
Parents with young children should review the Small Child Fright
Potential Chart on pages 181–185.

Day One

1. Arrive 45 minutes before official opening time.
2. Go to Guest Relations and make priority seatings.
3. Ride Spaceship Earth.
4. Do the ride at Imagination Institute, then see
   Honey, I Shrunk the Audience.
5. Ride Living with the Land.
6. See *Food Rocks* and *The Circle of Life* in The Land.
7. Visit the Living Seas.
8. Experience the Universe of Energy.
9. See Horizons.
10. Explore Innoventions East and West.

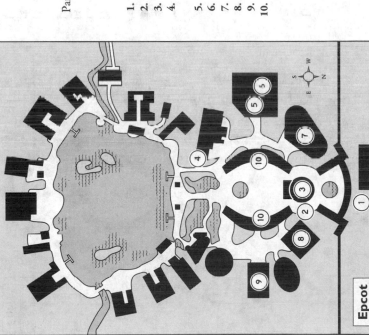

Epcot

Epcot
Two-Day Early Riser Touring Plan
Pocket Outline Version

For the detailed version of this touring plan, see page 531.
Parents with young children should review the Small Child Fright Potential Chart on pages 181–185.

Day Two

1. Arrive 45 minutes before official opening time.
2. Go to Guest Relations and make priority seatings.
3. Walk through Innoventions East and head to Test Track.
4. Ride Test Track.
5. Ride Body Wars at Wonders of Life.
6. See *The Making of Me* at Wonders of Life.
7. See *Cranium Command* at Wonders of Life.
8. Go to the World Showcase.
9. Ride El Río del Tiempo in Mexico.
10. Ride Maelstrom in Norway.
11. See *Wonders of China.*
12. Visit Germany and Italy.
13. See *The American Adventure.*
14. Visit Japan and Morocco.
15. See *Impressions de France.*
16. Visit the United Kingdom.
17. Tour the Millennium Village.
18. See *O Canada!*
19. Enjoy dinner and *IllumiNations.*

Epcot

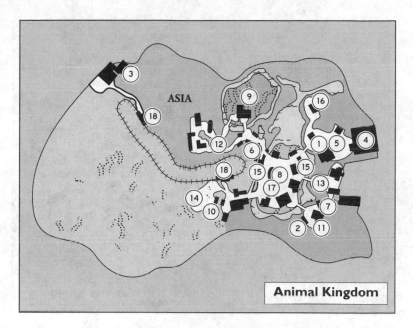

Animal Kingdom
Recommended Attraction Visitation Times

If you tour on an early-entry day, move all recommended attraction visitation times up one hour. It is best to see attractions with visitation times listed as "anytime" during the more crowded middle part of the day (11 a.m. to 3:30 p.m.).

1. The Boneyard: Anytime
2. Character Greeting Area: Early morning/late afternoon
3. Conservation Station: Before 11 a.m./after 3 p.m.
4. Countdown to Extinction: Before 10 a.m./just before closing
5. Cretaceous Trail: Anytime
6. *Flights of Wonder:* Anytime
7. Grandmother Willow's Grove Stage: Before 11 a.m./after 4 p.m.
8. *It's Tough to Be a Bug!:* Before 10 a.m./after 4:30 p.m.
9. Kali River Rapids: Before 10 a.m./after 4:30 p.m.
10. Kilimanjaro Safaris: Park opening/just before closing
11. Lion King Theater: Before 11 a.m./after 3:30 p.m.
12. Maharaja Jungle Trek: Anytime
13. Oasis: Anytime
14. Pangani Forest Exploration Trail: Before 10 a.m./after 3:30 p.m.
15. Radio Disney River Cruise: Before 10 a.m./1 hour before closing
16. Theater in the Wild: Anytime
17. Tree of Life Animal Exhibits: Anytime
18. Wildlife Express: Before 10:30 a.m./after 3 p.m.

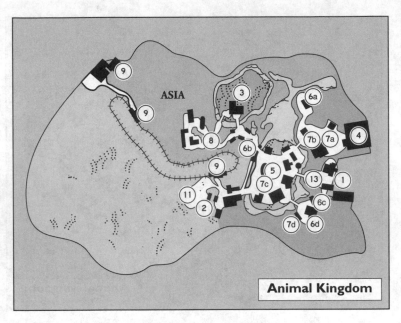

Animal Kingdom

Animal Kingdom
One-Day Touring Plan
Pocket Outline Version

For the detailed version of this touring plan, see page 568.

1. Arrive 40 minutes prior to opening.
2. Experience the Kilimanjaro Safaris.
3. Ride Kali River Rapids.
4. Ride Countdown to Extinction in DinoLand U.S.A.
5. See *It's Tough to Be a Bug!*
6. Eat lunch and work in the following shows: Theater in the Wild (a), *Flights of Wonder* (b), *Pocahontas* (c), and *Festival of the Lion King* (d).
7. Check out the Cretaceous Trail (a), The Boneyard (b), and exhibits at the Tree of Life (c). Also, meet the characters at Camp Minnie-Mickey (d).

8. Walk the Maharaja Jungle Trek.
9. Return to Africa and take the train to Conservation Station. Tour the exhibits.
10. Catch the train back to Harambe.
11. Walk the Pangani Forest Exploration Trail.
12. Shop, snack, or repeat any attractions you especially enjoyed.
13. Visit the zoological exhibits in The Oasis and exit the Animal Kingdom.

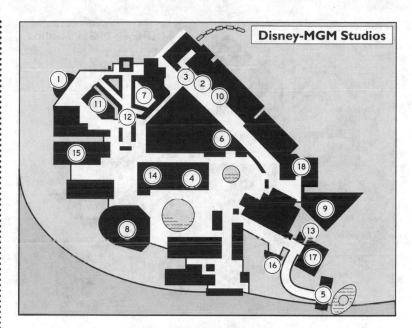

Disney-MGM Studios
Recommended Attraction Visitation Times

If you tour on an early-entry day, move all recommended attraction visitation times up one hour. It is best to see attractions with visitation times listed as "anytime" during the more crowded middle part of the day (noon to 4 p.m.).

1. *Backlot Theater:* First show/evening
2. Backstage Pass: Anytime
3. Disney-MGM Studios Backlot Tour: Anytime
4. *Doug Live!:* After 10 a.m.
5. *Fantasmic!:* Evening
6. The Great Movie Ride: Before 10 a.m./after 5 p.m.
7. Honey, I Shrunk the Kids playground: Before 10 a.m./after dark
8. *Indiana Jones Epic Stunt Spectacular:* First three morning or last evening show
9. The Magic of Disney Animation: Before 11 a.m./after 5 p.m.
10. *The Making of Disney's Latest Feature Film:* Anytime
11. *MuppetVision 4D:* Before 11 a.m./after 4 p.m.
12. New York Street Backlot: Anytime
13. Rock 'n' Roller Coaster: Before 10 a.m./just before closing
14. *Sounds Dangerous:* Before 11 a.m./after 5 p.m.
15. Star Tours: First hour and a half after opening
16. *Theater of the Stars:* Evening
17. Tower of Terror: Before 9:30 a.m./after 6 p.m.
18. *Voyage of the Little Mermaid:* Before 9:45 a.m./just before closing

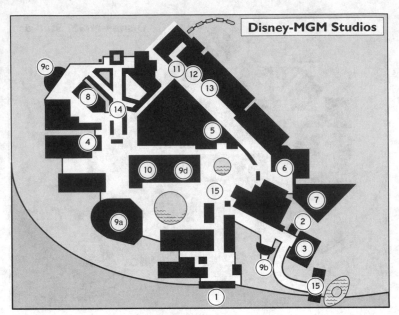

Disney-MGM Studios
One-Day Touring Plan
Pocket Outline Version

For the detailed version of this touring plan, see page 604.
(Before you go, check detailed itinerary for park opening procedures.)

1. Arrive 40 minutes before official opening time.
2. Pick up a handout guidemap containing the daily entertainment schedule. Ride the Rock 'n' Roller Coaster.
3. Ride the Tower of Terror.
4. Ride Star Tours.
5. Ride The Great Movie Ride.
6. See *Voyage of the Little Mermaid.*
7. Take the Magic of Disney Animation Tour.
8. See *MuppetVision 4D.*
9. Work in the following shows: *Indiana Jones Epic Stunt Spectacular* (9a), show at Theater of the Stars (9b), show at Backlot Theater (9c), and *Doug Live!* (9d).
10. See *Sounds Dangerous.*
11. Take the Disney-MGM Studios Backlot Tour.
12. Take Backstage Pass Tour.
13. See *The Making of Disney's Latest Feature Film.*
14. Explore the New York Street set.
15. Tour Hollywood and Sunset Boulevards. Enjoy *Fantasmic!*
16. Depart the Studios.

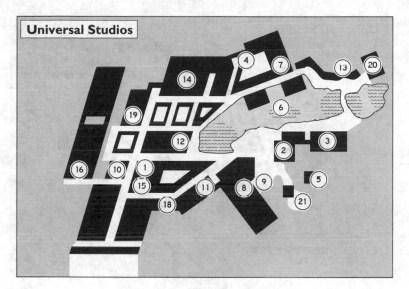

Universal Studios

Universal Studios Florida
Recommended Attraction Visitation Times

It is best to see attractions with visitation times listed as
"anytime" during the more crowded middle part of the day (noon to 4 p.m.).

1. "Alfred Hitchcock: The Art of Making Movies": After 3:30 p.m.
2. *Animal Actors Stage:* After experiencing all rides
3. Back to the Future—The Ride: First thing after park opens
4. *Beetlejuice's Rock 'n Roll Graveyard Revue:* At your convenience
5. *A Day in the Park with Barney:* Anytime
6. *Dynamite Nights Stuntacular:* Evening
7. Earthquake—The Big One: In morning, after Kongfrontation
8. E.T. Adventure: Before 10 a.m.
9. Fievel's Playland: Anytime
10. The Funtastic World of Hanna-Barbera: Before 11 a.m.
11. *The Gory Gruesome & Grotesque Horror Make-Up Show:* After experiencing all rides
12. *Hercules and Xena:* After experiencing all rides
13. Jaws: Before 11 a.m.
14. Kongfrontation: Before 11 a.m.
15. Lucy, a Tribute: Anytime
16. Nickelodeon Studios Walking Tour: When shows are in production
17. Street Scenes: Anytime
18. *Terminator 2: 3-D:* After 3:30 p.m.
19. *Twister:* First show after experiencing all rides
20. *The Wild, Wild, Wild West Stunt Show:* After experiencing all rides
21. Woody Woodpecker's Kid Zone: Anytime

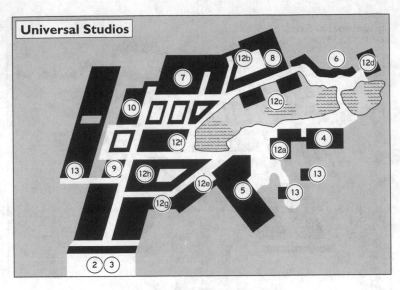

Universal Studios
One-Day Touring Plan
Pocket Outline Version

For the detailed version of this touring plan, see page 631.

For the detailed version of this touring plan, see page 631.

1. Call (407) 363-8000 the day before your visit for the official opening time.
2. Arrive 50 minutes before opening time and pick up a map and daily entertainment schedule.
3. Line up at the turnstile. Ask if any rides are closed and adjust touring plan accordingly.
4. Ride Back to the Future.
5. Ride E.T. Adventure.
6. Ride Jaws.
7. Ride Kongfrontation.
8. Ride Earthquake—The Big One.
9. Ride The Funtastic World of Hanna-Barbera.
10. See *Twister.*
11. This is a good time for lunch.
12. See the *Animal Actors Stage* (12a), *Beetlejuice's Rock 'n Roll Graveyard Revue* (12b), *Dynamite Nights Stuntacular* (12c), and *The Wild, Wild, Wild West Stunt Show* (12d) as convenient, according to the daily entertainment schedule. As time permits, work *The Gory Gruesome & Grotesque Horror Make-Up Show* (12e) and *Hercules and Xena* (12f), which run continuously, into your schedule. See *Terminator 2: 3-D* (12g) after 3:30 p.m. See "Alfred Hitchcock: The Art of Making Movies" (12h) last.
13. Take school-age children on the Nickelodeon tour in late afternoon and preschoolers to see Barney after riding E.T., and then head for Woody Woodpecker's Kid Zone.
14. Revisit favorite rides and shows. See any live performances you may have missed.

Universal's Islands of Adventure
Recommended Attraction Visitation Times

It is best to see attractions with visitation times listed as "anytime" during the more crowded middle part of the day (noon to 4 p.m.).

1. The Adventures of Spider-Man: Before 10 a.m.
2. Camp Jurassic: Anytime
3. Caro-Seuss-El: Before 10:30 a.m.
4. The Cat in the Hat: Before 11:30 a.m.
5. Comic Strip Lane: Anytime
6. Discovery Center: Anytime
7. Dr. Doom's FearFall: Before 9:15 a.m.
8. Dudley Do-Right's Ripsaw Falls: Before 10:30 a.m.
9. Dueling Dragons: Before 10:30 a.m.
10. *The Eighth Voyage of Sinbad:* Anytime per the entertainment schedule
11. If I Ran the Zoo: Anytime
12. The Incredible Hulk Coaster: Before 9:30 a.m.

—continued on other side—

Universal's Islands of Adventure
Recommended Attraction Visitation Times

It is best to see attractions with visitation times listed as "anytime" during the more crowded middle part of the day (noon to 4 p.m.).

—continued from other side—

13. Jurassic Park River Adventure: Before 11 a.m.
14. Me Ship, *The Olive:* Anytime
15. One Fish, Two Fish, Red Fish, Blue Fish: Before 10 a.m.
16. Pandemonium Cartoon Circus: After experiencing the rides
17. Popeye & Bluto's Blige-Rat Barges: Before 10:30 a.m.
18. *Posiedon's Fury! Escape from the Lost City:* After experiencing all the rides
19. Pteranodon Flyers: When there's no line
20. Sylvester McMonkey: Before 10:30 a.m.
21. Triceratops Encounter: Before 11:30 a.m.

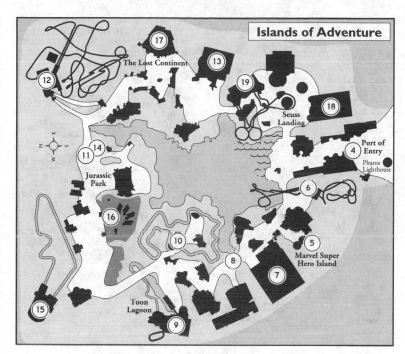

Universal's Islands of Adventure
One-Day Touring Plan

For the detailed version of this touring plan, see page 652.

1. Call (407) 363-8000 the day before your visit for the official opening time.
2. Arrive 50 minutes before opening time and pick up a map and daily entertainment schedule.
3. Line up at the turnstile. Ask if any rides are closed and adjust touring plan accordingly.
4. Go straight through the Port of Entry and cross into Marvel Super Hero Island. Head for Dr. Doom's FearFall.
5. Ride Dr. Doom's FearFall.
6. Ride The Incredible Hulk Coaster.
7. Experience The Adventures of Spider-Man.
8. Depart Super Hero Island and cross into Toon Lagoon.
9. Ride Dudley Do-Right's Ripsaw Falls.
10. Ride Popeye & Bluto's Bilge-Rat Barges.

—continued on other side—

Universal's Islands of Adventure
One-Day Touring Plan

For the detailed version of this touring plan, see page 652.

—continued from other side—

11. Continue around the lake and pass through Jurassic Park. Head to the Lost Continent.
12. Ride both tracks of Dueling Dragons.
13. Experience *Poseidon's Fury! Escape from the Lost City.*
14. Depart Lost Continent and go to Jurassic Park.
15. Ride the Jurassic Park River Adventure.
16. Experience the Triceratops Encounter.
17. See *The Eighth Voyage of Sinbad* stunt show in the Lost Continent.
18. Go to Seuss Landing and ride The Cat in the Hat.
19. Ride Sylvester McMonkey.
20. Revisit favorite rides and check out attractions you may have missed.

2000 *Unofficial Guide* Reader Survey

If you would like to express your opinion about Walt Disney World or this guidebook, complete the following survey and mail it to:

> *Unofficial Guide* Reader Survey
> P.O. Box 43673
> Birmingham, AL 35243

Inclusive dates of your visit _____

Members of your party:	Person 1	Person 2	Person 3	Person 4	Person 5
Gender (M or F)	____	____	____	____	____
Age	____	____	____	____	____

How many times have you been to Walt Disney World? _____

On your most recent trip, where did you stay? _____

Concerning accommodations, on a scale with 100 best and 0 worst, how would you rate:

    The quality of your room? ____   The value for the money? ____

    The quietness of your room? ____   Check-in/checkout efficiency? ____

    Shuttle service to the parks? ____   Swimming pool facilities? ____

Did you rent a car? _____   From whom? _____

Concerning your rental car, on a scale with 100 best and 0 worst, how would you rate:

    Pickup processing efficiency? ____   Return processing efficiency? ____

    Condition of the car? ____   Cleanliness of the car? ____

    Airport shuttle efficiency? ____

Concerning your touring:

    Who in your party was most responsible for planning the itinerary? ____

    What time did you normally get started in the morning? ____

    Did you usually arrive at the theme parks prior to opening? ____

    Did you return to your hotel for rest during the day? ____

    What time did you normally go to bed at night? ____

    If a Disney Resort guest, did you participate in early entry? ____

On a scale with 100 best and 0 worst, rate how the touring plans worked:

Park	*Name of Plan*	*Rating*
Magic Kingdom	_____	_____
Epcot	_____	_____
Animal Kingdom	_____	_____
Disney-MGM	_____	_____
Universal Studios	_____	_____
Islds. of Adventure	_____	_____

Concerning your dining experiences (also see WDW Restaurant Survey on following pages):

How many restaurant meals (including fast food) did you average per day? _____

How much (approximately) did your party spend on meals per day? _____

Favorite restaurant outside of Walt Disney World? _____

Did you buy this guide: Before leaving? _____ While on your trip? _____

How did you hear about this guide?

Loaned or recommended by a friend _____ Radio or TV _____

Newspaper or magazine _____ Bookstore salesperson _____

Just picked it out on my own _____ Library _____

Internet _____

What other guidebooks did you use on this trip? _____

_____

On the 100 best and 0 worst scale, how would you rate them? _____

_____

Using the same scale, how would you rate the *Unofficial Guide?* _____

Are *Unofficial Guides* readily available in bookstores in your area? _____

Have you used other *Unofficial Guides?* _____ Which one(s)? _____

Comments about your Walt Disney World vacation or about the *Unofficial Guide:* _____

_____

_____

_____

_____

_____

_____

_____

_____

_____

Walt Disney World Restaurant Survey

Tell us about your Walt Disney World dining experiences. Listed below are the full-service restaurants. Beside each restaurant is a thumbs-up and thumbs-down symbol. If you enjoyed the restaurant enough that you would like to eat there again, circle the thumbs-up symbol. If not, circle the thumbs-down symbol.

Walt Disney World Full-Service Restaurants (in alphabetical order):

Arthur's 27	Wyndham Palace	👍 👎
Artist Point	Wilderness Lodge Resort	👍 👎
Baskervilles	Grosvenor Resort	👍 👎
Benihana	Hilton	👍 👎
Biergarten	Germany: Epcot	👍 👎
Big River Grille & Brewing Works	Disney's BoardWalk	👍 👎
Bistro de Paris	France: Epcot	👍 👎
Boatwright's Dining Hall	Dixie Landings Resort	👍 👎
Bonfamille's Cafe	Port Orleans Resort	👍 👎
Bongos Cuban Cafe	Disney's West Side	👍 👎
California Grill	Contemporary Resort	👍 👎
Cape May Cafe	Beach Club Resort	👍 👎
Cap'n Jack's Oyster Bar	Downtown Disney	👍 👎
Captain's Tavern	Caribbean Beach Resort	👍 👎
Le Cellier Steakhouse	Canada: Epcot	👍 👎
Chef Mickey's	Contemporary Resort	👍 👎
Chefs de France	France: Epcot	👍 👎
Cinderella's Royal Table	Magic Kingdom	👍 👎
Citricos	Grand Floridian Resort	👍 👎
Concourse Steakhouse	Contemporary Resort	👍 👎
Coral Cafe	WDW Dolphin	👍 👎
Coral Reef	Living Seas: Epcot	👍 👎
Crystal Palace	Magic Kingdom	👍 👎
ESPN Club	Disney's BoardWalk	👍 👎
50's Prime Time Cafe	Disney-MGM Studios	👍 👎
Finn's Grill	Hilton	👍 👎
Flying Fish Cafe	Disney's BoardWalk	👍 👎
Fulton's Crab House	Pleasure Island	👍 👎
The Garden Grill	Land Pavilion: Epcot	👍 👎
Grand Floridian Cafe	Grand Floridian Resort	👍 👎
Gulliver's Grill at Garden Grove	WDW Swan	👍 👎
Harry's Safari Bar and Grill	WDW Dolphin	👍 👎

Walt Disney World Full-Service Restaurants

Hollywood & Vine ....Disney-MGM Studios .... 👍 👎
Hollywood Brown Derby ....Disney-MGM Studios .... 👍 👎
House of Blues ....Disney's West Side ....👍 👎
Juan & Only's Bar & Jail ....WDW Dolphin ....👍 👎
Kimonos ....WDW Swan ....👍 👎
Kona Cafe ....Polynesian Resort ....👍 👎
Liberty Tree Tavern ....Magic Kingdom ....👍 👎
Mama Melrose's Ristorante ....Disney-MGM Studios .... 👍 👎
Maya Grill ....Coronado Springs Resort .. 👍 👎
Narcoossee's ....Grand Floridian Resort ... 👍 👎
Nine Dragons Restaurant ....China: Epcot ....👍 👎
Official All-Star Cafe ....Disney's Wide World 👍 👎
of Sports
'Ohana ....Polynesian Resort ....👍 👎
Olivia's Cafe ....Old Key West Resort .....👍 👎
L'Originale Alfredo di Roma .....Italy: Epcot ....👍 👎
Ristorante
The Outback ....Buena Vista Palace ....👍 👎
Palio ....WDW Swan ....👍 👎
Planet Hollywood ....Pleasure Island ....👍 👎
Pleasure Island Jazz Company ....Pleasure Island ....👍 👎
Portobello Yacht Club ....Pleasure Island ....👍 👎
Rainforest Cafe ....Downtown Disney 👍 👎
and Animal Kingdom
Restaurant Akershus ....Norway: Epcot ....👍 👎
Restaurant Marrakesh ....Morocco: Epcot ....👍 👎
Rose & Crown Dining Room .....United Kingdom: Epcot ... 👍 👎
San Angel Inn ....Mexico: Epcot ....👍 👎
Sci-Fi Dine-In Theater Restaurant ..Disney-MGM Studios .... 👍 👎
Seasons Dining Room ....Disney Institute ....👍 👎
Spoodles ....Disney's BoardWalk ......👍 👎
Tempura Kiku ....Japan: Epcot ....👍 👎
Teppanyaki Dining Rooms ......Japan: Epcot ....👍 👎
Tony's Town Square Restaurant ....Magic Kingdom ....👍 👎
Victoria and Albert's ....Grand Floridian Resort ... 👍 👎
Whispering Canyon Cafe ....Wilderness Lodge Resort .. 👍 👎
Wild Horse Saloon ....Pleasure Island ....👍 👎
Wolfgang Puck Cafe ....Disney's West Side ....👍 👎
Yacht Club Galley ....Yacht Club Resort ....👍 👎
Yachtsman Steakhouse ....Yacht Club Resort ....👍 👎